W9-AMX-606

THE MODERN LIBRARY
of the World's Best Books

THE
PHILOSOPHY
OF
DAVID HUME

The publishers will be pleased to send, upon request, an illustrated folder setting forth the purpose and scope of THE MODERN LIBRARY, and listing each volume in the series. Every reader of books will find titles he has been looking for, handsomely printed, in definitive editions, and at an unusually low price.

THE
PHILOSOPHY
OF
DAVID HUME

Edited, and with an Introduction, by

V. C. CHAPPELL

ASSOCIATE PROFESSOR OF PHILOSOPHY,
UNIVERSITY OF CHICAGO

THE MODERN LIBRARY
NEW YORK

© Copyright, 1963, by Random House, Inc.

All rights reserved under International and Pan-American Copyright
Conventions. Published in New York by Random House, Inc., and
in Toronto, Canada, by Random House of Canada, Limited.

Library of Congress Catalog Card Number: 63–16158

THE MODERN LIBRARY
is published by
RANDOM HOUSE, INC.

BENNETT CERF   •   DONALD S. KLOPFER

Manufactured in the United States of America

Designed by Jeanette Young

B
1455
.C5
1963

CONTENTS

———•———

CONTENTS

INTRODUCTION

1. Hume's Life and Works

DAVID HUME is probably the greatest philosopher to write in English, and it is chiefly as a philosopher that he is read today. In his own time, however, he was more famous as an essayist, political theorist, historian, and man of letters than as a metaphysician and moralist. Of course philosophy was not so sharply separated from other disciplines in the eighteenth century as it is in our day. Also, the great philosophical figures of the seventeenth century had established a tradition of combining philosophical studies with other intellectual pursuits. There is this difference, however, between Hume and these earlier philosophers. Whereas Descartes and Leibniz, Malebranche and even Locke were primarily natural scientists, interested in mathematics, physics, and physiology when they were not philosophers, Hume's interest was in the social sciences, the studies of man as moral agent and social being. Hume was an indifferent mathematician and had no great knowledge of physics and anatomy, but in history, economics, politics, and literature his understanding was both broad and deep. This difference was in part, no doubt, a function of the age, for the majority of eighteenth century intellectuals, like Socrates before them, had turned to man, having been inspired by and yet dissatisfied with the great accomplishments of the preceding age in the sciences of nature. But the difference was also in part peculiarly Hume's; it found expression in the grand plan which he formed in his youth of constructing a complete and systematic "science of man." Others were pursuing human and social studies piecemeal and by various methods, but none, Hume thought, had undertaken to do the whole job and in the proper way, that is, on the basis of "experience and observation." Hume never carried out this grand plan, for a variety of reasons—among them the failure of his *Treatise* to make any impact on the learned world and also his own failure in the *Treatise* to achieve a single, coherent, intellectually satisfying account of even the foundations of his projected science of man. But the interest in man, as agent and as member of society, persisted, and found expression in all Hume's later writings. Not only is this interest the unifying theme of his various philosophical works, the common center about which they variously turn, it also serves to link them to Hume's nonphilosophical productions, most of which were written after he had abandoned his purely philosophical researches.

The main facts about Hume's life and personal character are recorded in his short autobiography, "My Own Life," which is included in this volume. Although his "ruling passion" was, as he says, a "love of literary fame," and he was before all a thinker and writer, he was no stranger to the world. He loved people, had many friends, and spent much time with them in conversation and in parlor games. He also made several incursions into the world of affairs, as the list of his various military, diplomatic, and government posts in his autobiography makes plain; as chargé d'affaires at the British Embassy in Paris he was a man of no small political importance. One thing Hume was not was a professor, though not by his own choice: he twice stood as a candidate for Scottish university professorships (in 1745 and 1751) and was rejected in favor of lesser men—in part owing to his reputation as an "infidel" or at least a skeptic in religious matters. (Hume, perhaps significantly, does not mention this fact in his autobiography.) For all his travels, however, Hume was essentially a homebody and a Scot; most of his life was spent in Edinburgh and at his family estate at Ninewells a few miles from the capital.

As far as can be judged from the testimony of his friends and from his own letters, the character that Hume sketches for himself at the end of "My Own Life" is just and accurate. Hume was a *good* man, kind, open, modest, even a bit simple. He was also a cheerful man, a jolly fat hedonist who loved to joke and banter, but who was sometimes criticized (by the earnest Boswell, for example) for jesting too much. Above all, Hume was his own man, independent, controlled, in command of himself. In his cool reasonableness, his opposition to superstition and cant on the one hand, and to "enthusiasm" and unwarranted emotional displays on the other, he epitomized the age of enlightenment which he helped to create. Even in his attitude toward religion he was moderate, and some of his best friends were clergymen, though, to be sure, of the "moderate" party.

Two episodes in Hume's life which he declines to mention in his autobiography are worth noting. The first concerns his relations with the Comtesse de Boufflers, one of the greatest ladies of eighteenth-century France, famous for her beauty and intelligence, friend and protector of Rousseau, and chief mistress of the Prince de Conti, third man in the kingdom. The Comtesse had written Hume a fan letter in 1761; she may have had something to do with his appointment as embassy secretary in 1763; and they saw a good deal of one another during Hume's first year in Paris. They may or may not have been lovers. Certainly they were more than friends, and Hume found himself more passionately involved with her than he had been with any other woman. His composure was shattered, his control wavered, and he was in danger of losing his cherished independence; he even thought of settling in France for the rest of his life. But the situation was impossible, and Hume knew it. The Comtesse had no intention of abandoning her position and her gay life, and the fast pace and loose morals of the French capital were too much for the simple Scot. In the end things took care of themselves: the Comte de Boufflers died, and the Comtesse immediately forgot about Hume and concentrated all her attention upon a single goal, to marry her official lover and become a princess —which goal, however, she did not achieve. Shocked and saddened as he was, Hume also was saved. But the incident shows that Hume, the epitome of prudence and temperance, was not incapable of passion and foolishness.

The second episode was the infamous quarrel with Jean-Jacques Rousseau. The Comtesse de Boufflers had put Hume in touch with Rousseau, who had been having a rather bad time of it in France. Hume, with typical generosity and dispatch, arranged for Rousseau to travel to England, and to receive a royal pension there. The two men became friends; Hume especially formed a deep attachment to "his pupil," as he sometimes called him—despite the warnings of various of Hume's French friends, who knew Rousseau better than he did. For Rousseau was everything that Hume was not: passionate, prejudiced, suspicious, and secretive. He was also, by that time, quite mad. After a few months in England he became convinced that Hume was part of a giant conspiracy to destroy him. He sent Hume a raving letter, full of wild charges. Hume, stung, wrote some rather nasty things in return, and also, unfortunately, sent angry letters to some of Rousseau's enemies in Paris. Eventually, Hume wrote (and d'Alembert published) a "succinct account" of the whole affair, containing transcripts of the various letters that had passed back and forth and a full record of the facts. This document was judicious and restrained, but a great deal of damage had already been done, both to the reputations of the principals and to philosophy herself, for the popular press made a great issue of the quarrel. The importance of this episode for an understanding of Hume is that, again, it shows him behaving out of character. Except for this occasion, Hume avoided public controversy and name-calling, though he had plenty of opportunity to defend himself against attack.

A list of Hume's works is given in the Bibliography which follows, but it will be useful to give some account of them here. They can be grouped, roughly, under three heads: philosophy, history, and essays. The essays are chiefly upon political, economic, literary, and religious subjects, and were the main basis of Hume's reputation as a writer in his own day. The historical works include the *History of England* and a long essay on "The Populousness of Ancient Nations"; *The Natural History of Religion* is also, in the main, an historical work. Although not at once successful, Hume's *History of*

England became a popular work, and was in any case the first important historical work in English and the first comprehensive history of Britian in any language. It has long since been superseded as history, although it remained a standard work for nearly a century, but is still well worth reading for its style.

Hume's main philosophical works are the *Treatise of Human Nature,* the two *Inquiries,* and the *Dialogues concerning Natural Religion.* The outline of Hume's philosophy in the next section of this Introduction is based, for the most part, on the *Treatise,* Hume's first and single most important philosophical work, so it is unnecessary to say anything about it here. The *Inquiries* are essentially revised versions of Books I and III of the *Treatise,* published nine and eleven years, respectively, after the latter had, in Hume's words, fallen "dead-born from the press." It was the style of the *Treatise,* Hume believed, that kept it from being read; he hoped that more elegant presentation would bring his philosophy the attention he thought it deserved. The *Inquiries* are better written than the *Treatise;* the style is purer, the organization better, the main points more clearly marked, and many inconsistencies removed. But these improvements were purchased at a cost, for the later works have not the richness and depth of the original. In the *Treatise* Hume reveals how he arrived at his various positions; the twistings and turnings of the exposition surely reflect those of Hume's thinking as he struggled with the problems he attacked. The reader is able to participate in those struggles and understands both Hume's problems and his solutions the better for doing so. But in the *Inquiries* Hume has covered his tracks; his final position is clearer but its basis is not. Further, some of the topics that are discussed in the *Treatise* are either not, or else just barely, mentioned in the *Inquiries.* Most of Parts II and IV of Book I of the *Treatise,* for example, are without counterpart in the first *Inquiry.* This is not altogether a bad thing: Hume's discussions of space and time and of *a priori* reasoning in these parts are radically confused. But the treatments of sense perception and of personal identity in Part IV are original and important, and their omission from the *Inquiry* impoverishes Hume's position. On the other hand, there are some new things in the first *Inquiry* and some improvements in doctrine as well as statement. The *Treatise* account of geometry, for example, is replaced with a more tenable view. And the two sections on religious topics—X on miracles and XI on "a particular providence and a future state"—have no counterparts in the *Treatise* (although a version of the former at least was originally intended by Hume to be included in the *Treatise;* Hume changed his mind at the last minute upon the urging of his friends, who thought his position too radical). There are fewer plain omissions of and additions to *Treatise* material in the second *Inquiry* than in the first—the differences here are mostly differences of order and emphasis and also, indeed, of doctrine—but it too is a thinner work than the original it was meant to replace.

It has been argued that Hume's *Inquiries* are nothing but bowdlerized versions of the *Treatise,* deliberately written down to appeal to vulgar taste in order to gain their author a literary reputation. The sections on religion were added to the first *Inquiry,* according to this view, for their sensational value. At the other extreme is the view which Hume himself seemed to hold at the end of his life, for he added an advertisement to the last revised edition of his *Essays and Treatises* disavowing the *Treatise* and expressing his wish that the *Inquiries* "alone be regarded as containing his philosophical sentiments and principles." The truth of the matter surely lies somewhere between these two extreme views. The *Treatise,* clearly, is Hume's major work, and cannot be ignored by anyone wishing to understand his philosophical position. But the *Inquiries* are important works in their own right. It is a mistake to treat them as mere popular abridgments, although neither is as profound a work as the *Treatise.* The *Inquiry concerning Human Understanding* does indeed contain simplified statements of *Treatise* positions and does leave out a number of difficult discussions, but even so has its own unity and aim. It is primarily a *critical* work whereas the *Treatise* was *constructive;* this change of direction and emphasis is made clear in the new introductory section (Section I) with which Hume replaced the *Treatise* Introduction, and is manifest throughout the succeeding sections. The *Inquiry concerning Morals,* moreover, is different enough from Book III of the *Treatise* to be considered an independent work. Hume's moral theory in this *Inquiry* is much more clearly utilitarian than it is in the *Treatise;* the notion of sympathy has been transformed and its role considerably reduced; the concepts of benevolence and self-love have been moved to the center of the stage; and the account of the place of reason in ethics has been expanded and clarified; besides which, the theory as a whole is much more tightly organized and perspicuously presented. It is not only on stylistic grounds that Hume's own judgment of the second *Inquiry*—that of all his writings it is "incomparably the best"—might be defended.

In the *Dialogues* Hume addresses himself to the basic question of so-called natural (as opposed to revealed) religion, the question whether the existence of God can be proved or even shown to be probable by argument. This question is basic because if the answer is "No" then there is nothing natural or rational in religion and no such subject as natural religion even exists. Hume had raised this question in Section XI of the *Inquiry concerning Human Understanding,* and there he does seem to answer it negatively, though his elaborate efforts to conceal his own sentiments make it a bit hard to be sure. The *Dialogues* were written sometime after the *Inquiry* was published in 1748, probably in the early '50's. In this work, too, Hume tried to hide his own position. Even so, his friends thought its publication dangerous, and prevailed upon him to withhold it; it was published only posthumously, by Hume's nephew, in 1779. The *Inquiry,* and especially the section on miracles, had already earned Hume a reputation as an infidel and enemy to religion; the *Dialogues,* Hume's friends felt, would only confirm this judgment in the public mind and might bring legal action against him as well. It is perhaps hard for us to understand such caution, at least in eighteenth-century Britain, and regarding a work so balanced, moderate, and fair as the *Dialogues* is, at any rate by our standards. It is not so hard, however, if we remember that a man was hanged in Edinburgh, as late as 1697, for speaking critically of the Old Testament.

What is Hume's position in the *Dialogues?* This is tantamount to asking which of the three parties to the discussion represents Hume's views. For this is not immediately obvious;

unlike Plato and Berkeley (the only successful writers of philosophical dialogues before Hume), Hume does not give all
the good lines to a single speaker, clearly identifying him as
his hero. Coming to the *Dialogues* from Hume's other works,
one might reasonably suppose that Philo, the skeptic, is the
one who speaks for Hume. Philo does, indeed, profess faith
in the Christian God in no uncertain terms, even while attack-
ing the efforts of Cleanthes and Demea to back this faith
with arguments; he also seems, at the end, to take back his
whole case against Cleanthes' favored argument from design;
and both things seem inconsistent with what we know of
Hume's views on other grounds. For as far as can be told,
apart from the *Dialogues*, Hume had no religion, no faith in
the Christian or in any other God, and he thought that no
argument of any sort could justify or tend to justify such faith.
But it is possible to write off these seeming inconsistencies
as prudential bows to convention, and a careful reading of
Part XII of the *Dialogues* may even justify the conclusion
that the inconsistencies are no more than apparent. The main
thing against identifying Hume with Philo is the number of
plain indications in the *Dialogues* that Cleanthes is the
favored speaker. The endorsement by Pamphilus, the narrator
of the whole conversation, of Cleanthes' views at the end of
Part XII might seem to be conclusive, and many interpreters
have taken it to be so. But this too can be seen as part of
Hume's camouflage, and also as an expression of his determination to give "the religious hypothesis" a full and careful
airing. Cleanthes is no mere straw man (though Demea perhaps is), but this means that in refuting his views (if he does
refute them), Philo (or Hume) is also refuting the views
actually held by many acute and able religious thinkers—
including, we may note, a number of Hume's closest griends,
such as Gilbert Elliot and the Reverends Hugh Blair and
William Robertson. Whatever their outcome and whatever
Hume's own position in them, however, the *Dialogues* remain
the most searching discussion of their subject in the whole
history of philosophy.

The principles of human nature are to be established from experience and observation; that is, empirically.

2. Hume's Philosophy in Outline

The most complete and systematic, if not the clearest, statement of Hume's philosophy is to be found in the *Treatise of Human Nature*. Hume's ultimate aim in this work was to provide a foundation for a "complete system of the sciences" (21).* The aim was hardly new—both Descartes and Locke had had it—but the foundation chosen was, or so Hume thought. For he proposed to ground all human knowledge in human nature itself: "There is no question of importance whose decision is not comprised in the science of man, and there is none which can be decided with any certainty before we become acquainted with that science" (ibid.). Nor did his innovation stop with this; he also proposed a new method for establishing this central science: "As the science of man is the only solid foundation for the other sciences, so the only solid foundation we can give to this science itself must be laid on experience and observation" (ibid.). Hume, in common with most eighteenth-century thinkers, had been tremendously impressed by the achievement of Newton in the natural sciences, and he recognized how much Newton's success depended on his employment of "the experimental method." Hume thought the time had come to apply this same method to "the moral subjects," and he believed a comparable success would thence be achieved. Earlier thinkers, he grants, had made a start in this direction; he mentions and has obviously been influenced by the work of Locke, Shaftesbury, Mandeville, Hutcheson, and Butler (*not* Berkeley, be it noted, for though Berkeley was an empiricist he did little work in moral philosophy). But he, Hume, was to be the first to put the whole science of man upon an empirical footing, and to appeal to experience exclusively and systematically in reaching his results.

It is clear that Hume was less original in these general aims than he himself supposed. Both Descartes and Locke,

* Unless otherwise noted, parenthetical references are to pages in the present volume.

to name no others, had made man the center and the
basis—if not quite the measure—of all things. And Locke at
least professed and practiced a systematic—if not a complete
—empiricism. Furthermore, Hume never did accomplish what
he set out to do. Not only did he fail to get clear even the
bottom stories of his projected science of man, as he himself
realized, but the results he did achieve did not by any means
rest solely on experience—and this he probably was not
aware of. One often reads in histories of philosophy that
Hume was the complete empiricist, that he practiced consistently and solely what Locke and Berkeley preached, and
that whereas Locke faltered in admitting both material substance and substantial minds and Berkeley in admitting minds
or spirits, Hume, showing the courage of his convictions, did
away with both; indeed this view is often coupled with the
philosophical claim that Hume's acknowledged failures in
Book I of the *Treatise* constitute a *reductio ad absurdum* of
a pure and strict empiricism. In fact, however, Hume's empiricism was neither strict nor pure, no more than Locke's
was. This is so in part because many of the questions that
Hume raises are logical or conceptual in nature and hence
do not admit of empirical answers, and also in part because
some of the questions to which empirical answers might be
appropriate Hume in fact answers *a priori*, without realizing
that he is doing so.

Despite these failures of practice and achievement, however,
it is in the light of Hume's stated aims in the *Treatise* that
that work—and indeed the whole body of Hume's work,
philosophical and otherwise—is to be understood. It is the
design of constructing an empirical science of human nature
that explains the plan of the *Treatise*, among other things.
The science is to rest upon experience, so we need to ask
what experience can teach and how results are to be established on its basis. This inquiry occupies Hume in Book I of
the *Treatise*. Since what experience does teach is considerably
less than many philosophers have claimed to know, an examination of their claims is in order, and this too is undertaken in Book I, with largely negative results: the metaphysical doctrines of previous philosophers, both ancient and
modern, are mostly found to be senseless. (The same holds

for the doctrines of theologians; Hume's philosophy of religion, which is almost entirely negative, belongs naturally
with the critical discussions of Part IV of Book I of the
Treatise.) In the course of this investigation of knowledge and
critical attack on past philosophies, a good many principles
of human nature are of course discovered, although it is
mainly the intellectual side of man that is thus brought to
light. But more than thought and knowledge are involved in
man's being as an agent and member of society; there is also
his emotional and active side to be considered. Hence in
Book II of the Treatise Hume investigates "the passions,"
seeking, still following experience, to make clear their nature
and operation. Finally, in Book III, he turns to moral and
political questions. Men make moral judgments and observe
(or violate) moral standards in their actions; they also in-
stitutionalize those standards in societies. So we must ask
what makes man a moral being, in an effort to lay bare the
source and ground of man's moral dimension and the factors
that lead him to form political associations. These questions
answered, it is then appropriate to investigate man's aesthetic
nature and to ask after his response to beauty and the arts.
But Hume broke off the Treatise before raising such questions
(which belong to the science of Criticism), no doubt because
of the failure of the three published volumes to attract
readers. Hence Hume's aesthetics must be reconstructed from
a few scattered passages in the Treatise and from such essays
as "Of the Standard of Taste."

This, then, is the plan of the Treatise. Hume begins his
execution of it by making a number of observations on "the
perceptions of the human mind," which he immediately
divides into two mutually exclusive classes, "impressions" and
"ideas." By beginning in this way Hume at once indicates his
acceptance of a certain philosophical theory, although the
contemporary currency of this theory made it natural for him
to begin in this way and he perhaps did not realize that his
beginning was dictated by this, or indeed any, theory. In
Hume's version of it, the theory can be stated in two propositions, (1) that all the operations of the human mind are instances of a single basic operation, which Hume terms "perception," and (2) that perception, and hence every mental act

of operation, consists in the consciousness or "presence to the mind" of perceptions, perceptions being momentary, private, mental objects. Descartes had made this theory prominent, and Locke and Berkeley both accepted it without question, as do many philosophers today. Hume himself hardly questions it, so much so that he offers almost no defense of it as such and indeed does not even state it explicitly until his work is well under way. It is not until Part II, Section VI, of Book I that he says—what has been implicit from the start—that "nothing is ever really present with the mind but its perceptions" and that "to hate, to love, to think, to feel, to see; all this is nothing but to perceive" (60); and such defense as Hume does offer of the theory does not come until Section II of Part IV, "Of Skepticism with Regard to the Senses." And yet the theory is there, from the outset, and powerfully determines the course and outcome of Hume's subsequent inquiries. Indeed if there is any single source for the difficulties in which Hume later finds himself, it is this "theory of ideas," as Reid called it, and not the (alleged) rigorous empiricism. Reid, indeed, tried to show that Hume's philosophy amounts to a final *reductio ad absurdum* of this theory, whose deficiencies lay hidden from earlier and lesser philosophers only because they saw less clearly and reasoned less consistently than Hume did.

Reid's view aside, it is clear that the "theory of ideas" was held by Hume and that it is presupposed by his very first statement in the *Treatise*. There are perceptions, or more particularly, impressions and ideas. These are the constituents of our experience, the objects of our thought and sense, the raw materials of all our knowledge. (They are this at least; Hume later argues that perceptions are the only real beings, the only things which, really and ultimately, exist.) Hume's first task, then, is to discover some truths about impressions and ideas, and, in keeping with his announced intentions, he proposes to do this by consulting experience. He professes to find, empirically, that impressions and ideas fall into various subclasses (simple and complex and original and secondary in the case of impressions), that an impression and an idea may be exactly similar in content and differ only in "force and vivacity," that all simple ideas resemble simple impres-

phenomena (Kant)
(appearances)

sions, and that no simple idea occurs in a mind until after its resembling simple impression has occurred there, from all of which Hume draws the conclusion that "all our simple ideas in their first appearance are *derived from* simple impressions which are correspondent to them and which they exactly represent" (28; whole sentence in italics in original). Resting as it does on empirical premises, this conclusion itself must have empirical force. Hume often uses it, however, as if it were a necessary truth, for he employs it to show the impossibility or unintelligibility of many of the favorite ideas, or alleged ideas, of other philosophers. The idea of substance, for example, is held to be no proper idea, since there is (and can be) no resembling impression which precedes it—as if ideas were not just in fact regularly preceded by resembling impressions but necessarily had to be. This, it seems clear, is one of the places at which Hume abandons empiricism.

In any case, Hume proceeds in Parts I and II of Book I to search out further truths about impressions and ideas, all allegedly from experience. He first considers the difference between remembered and imagined ideas. The difference cannot lie in the fact that the two sorts occur in different faculties or are the objects of different mental operations. For it is a consequence of the theory of ideas that differences of faculty or operation reduce, in the end, to differences in their respective objects; hence it is only by distinguishing the ideas of memory and imagination that we can distinguish memory and imagination. The only difference in the ideas that Hume can find is that, again, of force and vivacity; the ideas of memory are "more lively and strong" than those of the imagination. Hence different degrees of force and vivacity differentiate not only all ideas from all impressions but some ideas from others. And in fact memory stands for Hume as a kind of mean between original sensation or feeling, the objects of which are impressions, and imagination, whose objects are relatively faint ideas. It should be noted that imagination includes, for Hume, all that would normally be classified as thought and reason, so that the understanding is a part, and reasoning an operation or function of the imagination, and not a separate faculty.

Hume notes that ideas of the imagination, as opposed to

those of memory, occur in relative independence of one another and can be arranged and rearranged by us more or
less at will, whereas the ideas of memory must go together in
the order of the original sensed or felt impressions of which
they are the later copies. This is a feature of imagined ideas,
although it cannot be used to differentiate them from remembered ones (for how could we tell whether a given set of
ideas had the same order as some earlier set of impressions if
we didn't already know that the ideas were ideas of memory?).
But now Hume hastens to qualify this point, and the qualifi-
cation constitutes one of the most important items in his
whole philosophical position. It is true, Hume says, that the
ideas of imagination are relatively loose from one another,
but it is also true that they tend to group together, naturally,
and to form associations among themselves. One idea occur-
ring in a mind is apt to bring another with it; furthermore, the
associations that ideas form with one another tend to preserve
themselves over long periods of time and are of a small
number of kinds. In short, among the principles of human
nature, found out, Hume thinks, by experience and observation, is one regarding the *association of ideas*. This principle
had not quite the importance for Hume that it had for his
contemporary Hartley, who put the whole weight of his
philosophical system upon it (and who founded, thereby, the
"associationist" school of psychology, so prominent in the
nineteenth century). Hume regards and uses it as only one
among a number of fundamental principles. But it is fundamental for him, and it plays a crucial role in many of his
later analyses.

Hume distinguishes three particular principles of association,
or, as he calls them, "natural relations." Ideas tend to go
together in the imagination when they *resemble* one another,
when they are of things that have occurred *contiguously* in
time or space, and when they are of things which are related
as *cause and effect*. The first of these principles is appealed
to in Hume's account of general ideas, which comes at the
end of Part I of Book I. Such ideas constituted a problem for
Hume. Clearly, we can think about classes and kinds of
things, that is, of things in general as well as of particular
things, and to think of something is to have an idea of it. But

since all ideas are copies of impressions, and there is no such thing as a general impression, there can be no general ideas, no ideas which themselves stand for or comprehend whole classes of things. It will not do to say, as Locke did, that general ideas are constructed out of particular ones by abstracting from the differences among the latter, for the notion of such an abstract idea is unintelligible. Hume solves the problem as follows. When we think of a class of things, he says, we actually have the (particular) idea of one single member of that class before our minds. But this idea resembles the ideas of the other members of that class, and, by the principle of association whereby an idea tends to bring to mind all those ideas which resemble it, these other ideas are present too, in a certain sense. As Hume also puts it, we have a habit of thinking of all the members of the class together, and any one of the corresponding ideas would do as well to represent the others as the one we actually do think of; the general word which invokes the idea in question could have invoked any of these others without any loss or change of meaning. Hence it is that "some ideas are particular in their nature, but general in their representation" (45).

In Part II of Book I Hume considers the ideas of space and time, which evidently merit such special treatment because of their pervasiveness and also, perhaps, because they too present Hume with a problem. Space and time are not perceived as such, hence have no impressions, and this should mean that they have no ideas either. We might say that the ideas of space and time are general in the sense just explained, but this would imply that space and time are classes of things, which seems absurd. It is tempting then to regard space and time as aspects of (spatially and temporally extended) things, distinguishable in thought but not separate in fact. But this would mean that the ideas of such things were complex ideas, in which the ideas of space and time were simple elements, and space and time could then exist by themselves, as particular perceivable objects. For no other mode of composition of ideas is possible, according to Hume, and "whatever is distinguishable is separable, and can exist apart." In the end, Hume resorts to a notion for which his philosophy leaves no room, and in so doing fails to solve the problem that these

and yet, it is crucial to Hume's argument

ideas present. The ideas of space and time, he says, are "no separate or distinct ideas, but merely those of the manner or order in which objects exist" (58), or more accurately, in which impressions occur. The fact that all impressions are temporally extended and that all visual and tactual impressions are extended in space accounts for the pervasiveness of the ideas of space and time, and the fact that all impressions are distinct existences means that space and time must themselves consist of discrete atoms and hence are not divisible *in infinitum.* But the notion of a manner or order of appearance of objects or impressions, which is not itself an object or impression and yet is a source or original of ideas, is altogether illegitimate, on Hume's own grounds, and his whole account of space and time suffers in consequence. Indeed Part II of Book I has never been much read by students of Hume, and very little of it is included in this volume.

Part III is entitled "Of Knowledge and Probability," but is devoted almost entirely to Hume's analysis of causation, which is his best-known and most original contribution in the *Treatise.* The nature of ideas having been made clear, it is natural for Hume to turn his attention to knowledge, for ideas are the materials of knowledge and knowledge is what Hume is trying ultimately to understand in Book I. Hume's initial account of knowledge is reminiscent of Locke's. To know is to be aware of some relation holding between two or more ideas, and it is the relation and not the ideas which is the object of knowledge, as if to have an idea or ideas were not yet to have knowledge. The same holds for belief or opinion as first characterized, which differs from knowledge, *inter alia,* in being less certain; one's opinions are all and only probable in Hume's view. But this suggested distinction between knowing or believing, on the one hand, and merely having an idea or ideas, on the other, is finally impossible in Hume's philosophy. For on the theory of ideas there is only one basic type of mental act or operation, namely, perception. If, then, to have an idea is to perceive, so must to know and to believe, and whatever differences there are must lie in the ideas perceived, either in their content or in their force and vivacity. And Hume in fact does make the distinction in this way in the end. Actually there are two dis-

Knowledge is a complex idea containing an internal relation

tinctions to be made, that between having an idea or merely
conceiving, on the one hand, and assenting to the idea or
believing, on the other, and that between having an opinion
or merely believing and knowing. The first of these, Hume
says, is altogether a matter of force and vivacity; a belief
is simply a lively idea, and belief, far from being different
from conception, is in truth a species of it, "a strong and
steady conception . . . and such as approaches in some measure to an immediate impression" (87n.). It follows that belief
not only need not have a proposition as its object, as some
philosophers have held, but need not even be of a complex
idea, much less of one containing a relation. This means that
Hume's second distinction, that between opinion or belief
and knowledge, is not a distinction between knowledge and
belief in general but only between knowledge and a particular
sort of belief, that, namely, in which the object is a complex
idea with a relation as one of its components. Since whatever
is known is also a complex idea with a relational component,
the difference here must lie in the content of the ideas; it lies
in fact, Hume says, in the kind of relation which the respective
ideas contain. (This difference could not be one of force and
vivacity, for that would only serve to distinguish assent to an
idea from mere consideration of it, and knowledge involves
assent as much as belief does.) Hume claims to find, in all,
seven classes of relations (i.e., what he calls "philosophical
relations"; the "natural relations" are not relations at all but a
principle of association), but he then argues that these fall
into two general kinds, those which are internal to their
terms and hence cannot change unless the ideas related
change, and those which are not so internal. We have knowledge, Hume says, when we have a complex idea containing
an internal relation, and opinion or belief when the relation is
not internal.

It seems clear, however, that what Hume has thus distinguished is not knowledge and opinion in the ordinary sense, or
even knowledge and one sort of opinion, but rather two different kinds of knowledge. The basis of the distinction is a
distinction between two kinds of complex relational ideas, or
more accurately, two kinds of propositions; this is in fact the
distinction between what would now be called analytic and

which is that of modern science

synthetic propositions. Knowledge of an analytic proposition
is *a priori*. In Hume's terms, the relation between two ideas
is altogether determined, when the relation is internal, by the
ideas themselves; hence to know what the ideas are is to
know that the relation holds between them. This also accounts
for the certainty of this kind of knowledge, and the fact
that what is known is necessarily as it is. Knowledge of a
synthetic proposition, on the other hand, cannot be *a priori*
according to Hume. A noninternal relation may or may not
hold between two ideas, and we cannot tell whether it does
simply by examining the ideas. What we must do, Hume says,
is consult experience, and he also says (though he does not
justify this) that probability is all that we can claim for the
result. In any case, synthetic propositions, and our knowledge
of them, are always and only empirical in Hume's view, and
are never certain. Hence Hume's distinction here is really that
between *a priori* and empirical knowledge, made so as to
embody the two further views that all *a priori* knowledge
is of analytic propositions and that all synthetic (and hence
empirical) propositions are only probable. In Hume's own
terms, all "knowledge" is *a priori* and of necessary truths,
and all empirical facts are matters of mere "probable opinion."

Some analytic propositions can be known directly, according to Hume, by a mere *inspectio mentis* or, as he says, by
"intuition," employing this term in the Cartesian sense. We
have only to reflect upon the ideas concerned and we immediately "see" that they are related in the way they are. Some
analytic propositions, however, cannot be known in this direct
way; they can only be established by reasoning, i.e., by following through a chain of argument step by step. The difference here depends on the kind of (internal) relation that is
involved. Of the four internal relations, Hume says, only those
which fall under the head of "proportions of quantity or number" make reasoning necessary. Hence it is that algebra and
arithmetic are demonstrative sciences in Hume's view; indeed
they are the only *a priori* sciences which he recognizes in the
Treatise, though he also (correctly) includes geometry in this
category in the first *Inquiry*. Hume uses the term "demonstration" to mean "*a priori* reasoning," but demonstrative
reasoning is not merely deductive, in the sense that its con-

clusions follow logically from their premises. Since the conclusions must also be *a priori* (and hence for Hume analytic) the premises in demonstration must also be *a priori* (and hence analytic). But now in addition to such *a priori* reasoning, Hume also recognizes a kind of reasoning which is *a posteriori*, again in the double sense that its conclusions are only inductively connected to their premises and that these conclusions are themselves synthetic propositions. (Hume seems to have left no place for deductive reasoning with empirical conclusions.) This kind of reasoning he calls "probable" or "moral" or "experimental"; it is just this kind of reasoning that he is seeking, in the *Treatise,* to introduce into "moral subjects." But not all synthetic propositions need to be established by such reasoning. Here, as in the case of analytic propositions, there are some synthetic truths which can be known (or believed, in Hume's strict usage) directly, and again it is the kind of relation involved that makes the difference. When the objects of two ideas are identical or contiguous in time or space, that the ideas are (noninternally) related in these ways can simply be perceived. But if the relation holding between (the objects of) two ideas is that of causation, then that the relation holds can only be determined by reasoning, reasoning which is, in this case, "experimental."

Considering the importance of experimental reasoning to Hume's program in the *Treatise,* we might expect him to undertake a thorough investigation of it. In fact, however, his attention is diverted at this point to the idea of causation, with which, to be sure, empirical reasoning is always concerned in Hume's view but which becomes an almost independent subject of study in the rest of Part III. Hume does have more to say about probable reasoning, directly in some of the central sections of Part III and incidentally throughout his discussion of causation, but on the whole his treatment of this topic and indeed of knowledge and belief generally only serves to introduce—rather artificially, it must be said—the treatment of causation.

Hume begins his discussion of causation in his standard way, by asking for the origin of the idea of causation. Since all (legitimate) ideas are for Hume derived from impressions which they merely reproduce, the only thing that counts as understanding an idea, once it has been analyzed into its component parts (if it is a complex idea), is finding out what impression or impressions it arises from. <u>Causation, clearly, is a relation, one which holds between two terms, called, respectively, cause and effect.</u> So we have to look for some relational impression, some immediately perceivable relation between two objects. When we observe a situation in which one object (or event) is said to cause another we do indeed perceive certain relations between the two objects. We perceive that the one occurs next or near to the other in space and time and that the one said to be the cause precedes the effect. We have, in other words, a (complex) relational impression of contiguity and temporal priority whenever we perceive a cause and its effect. Is this impression, then, the source of the idea of causation, the original of the causal relation which we assume to hold between the two perceived objects? No, says Hume, for "an object may be contiguous and prior to another without being considered as its cause" (68). There is, he goes on, "a *necessary connection* to be taken into consideration," for when we say that something causes something else we imply not just that the effect does occur when the cause does but that it must occur. Insofar, therefore, as we have found no impression giving rise to this idea of necessary connection we have not found the whole of the (complex) impression which is the source of the idea of causation, though we do seem to have found part of it, since contiguity and priority do seem to be part of the notion of a causal relation. The trouble is that further examination of perceived cause and effect situations fails to reveal any such impression. There seems to be no impression of causation; causal relations seem not to be perceivable, at least as such, though certain of the elements that figure in them are perceivable. Unless we abandon the principle that all ideas derive, in their entirety, from impressions—and Hume is not ready to do that—we are up against a brick wall.

Hume then makes a new start. Past philosophers, he notes, have almost all regarded propositions about causation as necessary truths, capable of being known *a priori*. They claimed to know not only that everything must have a cause but also, in particular cases, that this was caused by, or will cause, that. We can at least establish something negative about causation, Hume thinks, by showing these philosophers to be mistaken. For if they were right, what this would mean in his terms is that propositions asserting causal connections, either in general or in particular cases, are analytic, their truth or falsity determinable by intuition or demonstration, and their denials contradictions. Causation would be an internal relation, and whether or not it held in a particular case would depend entirely on the nature or content of the related ideas. And this, Hume says, is clearly not the case. There is no contradiction in denying that all things have causes. "All effects have causes" is an analytic proposition but "All events have causes" clearly is not. Nor is there any contradiction in saying that this flame will freeze and this ice burn. The ideas here may stay the same while the relation varies—a sure sign that the relation is not internal. Negatively, then, causation is not an internal relation, and causal propositions are neither necessary truths nor knowable *a priori* (indeed in Hume's strict usage they are not matters of knowledge at all). Hume can then conclude, since this is the only other possibility for him, that causal propositions are empirical, their truth ascertainable only by experience and observation. But this does not take us very far toward understanding the idea of causation.

So Hume makes still another start. It is a fact, he says, that we do make judgments about causation, that we do have opinions which embody this idea. It has already been shown that we do not perceive causal relations, so it seems that these opinions must arise as the result of reasoning on our part: we *infer* effects from causes and causes from effects in particular cases. Hence the question Hume now raises is this: How do we proceed, why do we conclude as we do, when we make causal inferences? It is in answering this question that the truth about causation, at least as Hume sees it, finally emerges.

Let us consider a case in which we make a causal inference. If we see one billiard ball moving toward and about to strike another, we immediately conclude that the latter will soon be moving too, in consequence of being struck by the first, although we do not now see it moving. But would we so conclude, Hume asks, if we were not familiar with billiard balls and their behavior, or at least with moving objects like billiard balls? It seems clear that our making the inference here depends on our having had experience of similar situations in the past, on our having observed both one ball's motion and another's following it, upon impact. So past experience is somehow necessary to our being able to make a causal inference. But how? It would seem to be by providing premises from which we can then reason to our conclusion. But this cannot be, Hume argues. For reasoning is either demonstrative or probable. But no demonstrative reasoning could yield the conclusion we are considering, for the simple reason that that conclusion is, as we have just shown, an empirical and not an analytic proposition. And no piece of probable reasoning of the form: "This effect will (probably) ensue, because things of its sort have regularly been observed to follow things of the present cause's sort in the past," could possibly be valid. For we cannot, Hume says, draw any conclusion about something that we have not observed except on the basis of a causal relation known to hold between it and something that we have observed, and whether there is any such causal relation is precisely the point that the reasoning in question is supposed to establish. More generally, probable reasoning, to be sound, requires a knowledge of causal relations and cannot therefore be used to produce such knowledge. Hence the conclusion we draw in the case of our billiard balls cannot be the conclusion of any argument or (valid) piece of reasoning. We may continue, if we wish, to use the term "inference" in speaking of the drawing of such conclusions, but only if we realize that we must mean thereby, not any logical or rational procedure, but rather a mere mental transition from one thought to another.

This last point, it should be noted, has had a great effect on subsequent philosophical discussion. For it gives rise to the celebrated "problem of induction," which has been a major worry of philosophers since Hume. The problem is that of "justifying" inductive reasoning, i.e., of showing that, *inter alia*, arguments from observed causes to unobserved (but observable) effects really do provide a rational basis or warrant for their conclusions. A deductive justification is generally agreed to be out of the question, and any attempted induc-

PROBLEM OF INDUCTION

tive justification—this is Hume's point—would be question-begging and hence unsuccessful. We seem bound to conclude that inductive reasoning cannot be justified, or even that inductive reasoning, so called, is not reasoning at all. This, of course, is an unwelcome conclusion, and so philosophers have sought in various and often ingenious ways to avoid it, without being able to agree that any of their number has been successful. Recently doubts have been raised as to whether there really is any such problem to begin with, and whether Hume's point is really sound (see the works by Will and Flew listed in the Bibliography), but the fact remains that many philosophers have taken it to be.

To return to Hume's discussion of causation, we seem to have come to another dead end. We do make causal judgments, but we do so neither on the basis of perception (solely) nor by reasoning. How then do we make them? Hume meets this difficulty by embracing it. <u>Our causal judgments, he concludes, have no basis or (logical) ground whatsoever, and insofar as the question of how we make them presupposes that there is such a basis, the proper answer is that there is no "how" about it, that we just do make them, as a matter of fact.</u> The fact can be explained, in the sense that the psychological conditions under which people infer effects from causes and *vice versa* can be described. But no particular inference can in any way be *justified*, no set of logical conditions under which it would be reasonable or warranted to draw a particular conclusion can be given. Past experience, if it did provide premises from which conclusions about causal relations could be reasoned to, would justify at least some such conclusions. In truth, however, past experience only determines the mind to work in certain ways, so that certain transitions occur in it more readily than not when it is appropriately stimulated. Past experience functions, in short, not as a *reason* for but as a *cause* of our causal inferences. In more detail, what happens, Hume says, is this. We observe two sorts of things together, the one preceding the other, on a number of occasions. The ideas of these two sorts of things then tend to become associated in our minds, such that whenever one of them occurs to us the other tends to come to mind as well. We have already noted the mind's

general tendency to group its ideas in certain ways; the fact
that ideas of objects which have regularly succeeded one another in our experience tend to be so grouped constitutes a
particular principle of association for Hume, called, appropriately enough, the natural relation of causation. Hume does
not profess to know why the mind works in this way. It is just
a fact that it does, an (for us) ultimate principle of human
nature which cannot itself be explained. It is as if a habit
came to be established, as if we became conditioned by the
customary association of things often observed to expect the
one thing on observing the other, before the former is itself
observed. And not only does the idea of the customarily succeeding object, that which we call the effect, *come* to mind
when we observe the preceding object or cause; we also *believe* that the effect will occur. For when we observe the
cause we have an impression, a perception which is charged,
as it were, with a high degree of force and vivacity. And it
is a feature of the mind's associative mechanism, Hume says,
that such a charge is capable, on occasion, of being transferred to the other, less highly charged perceptions, i.e., ideas,
with which the charged perception happens to have become
associated. So some of the force and vivacity of the impression passes over to the associated idea, that of the as yet
unobserved effect, and makes that idea more "lively" than it
otherwise would have been. And a lively idea, we remember,
is a belief in Hume's view. Hence it is that we not only think
of the second billiard ball's motion in our example above, but
expect it to move, on seeing the first ball moving toward it.

Hume has, then, described and in a manner explained the
way in which we make causal inferences in particular cases.
But how does this bear upon the object of our original quest,
which was an understanding of the idea of causation? It does
so by providing a content for the idea, by locating something
familiar in terms of which the meaning of the notion of causation can be given. For Hume goes on to define causation as
the relation which holds between the pairs of things respect-
ing which we make causal inferences in the manner just explained. We know what it is to infer effects from causes and
causes from effects. To say that two things are causally re-

lated is then just to say that the one can or is apt to be inferred from the other in this familiar way. The causal relation is not so much discovered in as conferred upon things, and it is conferred by the fact that we make the inferences about them that we do. "A cause," Hume says, "is an object precedent and contiguous to another, and so united with it that the idea of the one determines the mind to form the idea of the other, and the impression of the one to form a more lively idea of the other" (116). Priority and contiguity are indeed observable relations and hence are discovered in objects, but the essential remaining factor which goes into the idea of causation, the necessary connection of cause and effect, is not. As Hume puts it, "the necessary connection depends on the inference, instead of the inference's depending on the necessary connection" (79); and again, "necessity is something that exists in the mind, not in objects" (112). Hume acknowledges the paradox of this result, but thinks we are nonetheless driven to it "by dint of solid proof and reasoning" (113).

One problem does remain, however. If we make the, albeit familiar, mental procedure of inferring causes from effects and *vice versa* the source or basis of our idea of causation, as we seem to have done, have we not violated the principle that ideas derive all and only from impressions? This problem appears, however, only because we have not told quite the full story about this mental procedure. When we make a causal inference, Hume says, we not only are determined to expect something that we have not observed, but we also *feel* determined to expect it. A feeling of constraint, a sensible inclination of the mind, accompanies the coming to mind of an idea which comes because associated with a present impression. And this feeling *is* an impression—not, to be sure, an impression of sensation, arising when the external senses are used, but an impression nonetheless, an "internal impression of the mind" (112). It is this internal impression then, which, properly speaking, is the source of the idea of necessary connection, and which, together with the "external" impressions which give rise to the ideas of contiguity and priority, constitutes the original basis of the idea of causation as a whole. This impression only occurs when we make causal inferences

and is an element in the process of making them, but it is this
and not the process as a whole from which the idea of causation derives.

This, in outline, is Hume's account of causation, the account which has been, especially on its negative and critical
side, so influential in the subsequent history of philosophy.
Hume next proceeds, in the *Treatise*, to his skeptical review of
the opinions of other philosophers; this takes up the bulk of
Part IV of Book I. But he should have first presented his doctrine of free will, as he did do at this point in the *Inquiry*. For
it is here that it naturally belongs, being little more than a
corollary of his doctrine of causation, and not where he does
put it, in Book II on the Passions. Hume's position on the
question of free will is simple, once indeed he has made clear
what the question is. For by "liberty of the will" may be
meant, he says, "a power of acting or not acting according to
the determinations of the will" (*Inquiry*, 351), i.e., the power
of doing what we choose. Alternatively, "liberty" may mean
freedom from causal determination; we would be free in this
sense only if our actions had no causes whatsoever and came
about wholly by chance. Now there is no doubt, Hume thinks,
that men, or their wills, are free in the former sense; he also
claims that the generality of mankind, saving only a few
philosophers, both use the term "liberty" in this sense and
agree that, in this sense, we are free. As for liberty in the second, philosophers', sense, the question here reduces, Hume
says, to whether there is any regular conjunction between
the voluntary actions of men, on the one hand, and their
"motives and circumstances and character," on the other. For
we have already seen that to say that anything is caused is
merely to say that it is constantly conjoined in our experience
with some other sort of thing, such that we are inclined to
infer its existence whenever we are presented with an instance
of this sort of thing. This applies as much to actions as to
physical objects and events. And it is obvious, as well as universally admitted, Hume says, that actions are regularly conjoined with certain specific motives and that we do make
inferences from men's actions to their motives and *vice versa*.
So in this sense it is plain that men are not free, and Hume is,
in this sense, a determinist. But he stresses that his determin-

ism in no way rules out freedom in the other and more proper sense, the only sort of freedom that is, in his view, worth bothering about.

In reviewing the opinions of other philosophers in Part IV, Hume not only illustrates and applies the philosophical doctrines arrived at in Parts I to III, he also makes explicit many of the so far hidden implications and presuppositions of those doctrines. He also wrestles, throughout Part IV, with his own incipient skepticism, trying to get clear in his mind just how far his principles are skeptical—and how much of a bad thing being skeptical is, if at all. For Hume realizes that the philosophical position he has been developing is not only destructive of the metaphysical views of a few philosophers, which is after all a mark in its favor. It also subverts, or threatens to subvert, common sense, the common beliefs that all of us hold and the common principles that all of us employ, and indeed cannot help employing, in our everyday dealings with one another. This consequence is hardly one that Hume can comfortably accept. For if a philosophical doctrine goes against common sense, then either that doctrine is wrong—and Hume seems on the whole to trust his reasonings and hence persists in thinking his doctrines right—or there is a fundamental disparity between philosophy and life, reason and nature, theory and practice—and that of course puts the value of philosophy and reasoning and theory in doubt. Hence Hume's struggles in Part IV, the vacillation and seeming inconsistency in his attitude toward skepticism which have both baffled and stimulated interpreters of his thought. Some students of Hume have stressed the negative force of his philosophy: Hume was a skeptic, and if he was not always easy about that fact, he nonetheless saw no alternative to divorcing philosophy and life: "Carelessness and inattention alone can afford us any remedy" (153). Others have claimed that Hume did not stop with skepticism and did not divorce philosophy and life, but developed a positive philosophical account of the actual workings of human nature, or of nature in us. On this view, Hume was a "naturalist," who took the part of nature against the cavils of the skeptics: "Nature, by an absolute and uncontrollable necessity, has determined us to judge as well as to breathe and feel" (122), and the thing for the philosopher to do is find out and make plain how it is that she does this. We cannot discuss the merits of these different interpretations here. But it is important to note that problems of interpretation, centering around Hume's worries about skepticism, do come to the fore in Part IV.

Hume divides the philosophical opinions to be examined in Part IV into two groups, those concerning the physical world and those concerning mind or soul. In the first group he considers views regarding the existence of physical objects as well as views regarding their nature or constitution; in the second group he examines philosophers' doctrines as to the nature of mind or soul and as to the identity of a mind or self or person through time. Hume confines his attention mainly to types of view or doctrine—he does not generally name names—and usually considers only (what he takes to be) the dominant or received philosophical opinion on each topic. Hs conclusions, furthermore, are almost wholly negative; the received doctrines are all to be rejected as false at best, or, more likely, as nonsense. In most cases, Hume sketches his own positive view, but there is usually not much to this—except that there are difficulties in the way of stating even modest truths on the questions of the existence of physical objects and the nature of the mind, as we shall see. In general, Hume's role in Part IV is that of the sworn enemy of traditional overblown metaphysics, a crusader on behalf of plain truth and unvarnished empirical fact.

It is easy enough for Hume to play this role regarding some of the metaphysical doctrines that he examines. He considers two traditional views concerning the nature of physical objects, that of the "ancient" philosophers (i.e., the Aristotelians) and that of the "moderns" (i.e., such philosophers as Descartes and Locke). According to the first, material bodies are composed of a "substance" or "original matter" on the one hand, and a collection of "accidents" on the other; sometimes "substantial forms" and "occult qualities" are added to the brew as well. The trouble with this doctrine, Hume says, is that its central notions, since they are derived from no impressions that do or could occur, are without sense. According to the second, "modern" view, material bodies are composed entirely of so-called "primary qualities" which are incapable of being sensed, and the "secondary qualities" which we do sense are nothing but perceptions in our minds, caused by the primary qualities in the objects but in no way resembling them. Hume's objection to this view is twofold. Not only does it violate the ideas-presuppose-impressions-principle, since we are supposed to have ideas of primary qualities and yet not be able to sense them, but the distinction on which it rests cannot be made, since the supposed primary qualities of motion and solidity are as much sensible as the supposed secondary qualities of color and heat—and hence are just as unreal as these are supposed to be, so that "we utterly annihilate" physical objects on this view. Hume's discussion of these two views occupies Sections III and IV of Part IV. In Section V he considers the traditional view regarding the nature of the mind or soul, that it too is a substance, only an immaterial substance and one in which not accidents but perceptions inhere. This view is no more intelligible in Hume's eyes than the corresponding view regarding bodies was found to be; here, as there, the very notion of substance is without sense, being derived from no antecedent impression. It follows that the traditional account of personal identity, whereby this was made to depend upon the numerical identity of a simple, immaterial soul or spiritual substance, is similarly unintelligible; Hume draws this conclusion in Section VI.

Hume also has little trouble in stating his own positive alternatives to these views, at least initially. "Our ideas of bodies," he says, "are nothing but collections formed by the mind of the ideas of the several distinct sensible qualities of which objects are composed, and which we find to have a constant union with each other" (154). The simplicity and identity which we ascribe to individual bodies, despite their diversity of qualities, are to be explained in part by the same associative tendencies of the mind that we noted earlier and in part by another feature of the mind's operation which we have not attended to so far but which can easily be discovered, Hume thinks, by experience and observation. This is a propensity to confuse a succession of similar but distinct objects with a single uninterruptedly persisting and unchanging

object. Only the latter is properly said to be identical, Hume
says, but we call the former identical if the similarity of the
successive objects is sufficient or our tendency to associate
their respective ideas is strong enough to prompt this confusion; and similarly in the case of simplicity. A physical object persisting through time is in reality a succession of similar
objects and not a single, self-same thing, Hume says, but we
all universally—and quite "naturally"—make the mistake of
supposing such things to be simple and single. Hume's doctrine of mind parallels this account of bodies almost exactly.
There is nothing to the mind but its qualities. Hence an individual mind is just "a bundle or collection of different perceptions, which succeed each other with an inconceivable
rapidity and are in a perpetual flux and movement" (174).
The identity which we ascribe to individual minds is also
"only a fictitious one," since "every distinct impression which
enters into the composition of the mind is a distinct existence,
and is different and distinguishable and separable from every
other perception, either contemporary or successive" (180).
That we do nonetheless ascribe identity to minds, and thence
to selves or persons, is a consequence of our associating their
constituent perceptions together, in accord with our mind's
natural tendencies, and then confusing the resulting related
chains of perceptions with single, continuously existing objects. The situation here is indeed a bit more complicated than
in the case of bodies. For the natural relation of contiguity
plays no part in our associating the different perceptions of a
mind with one another, and the natural relation of resemblance is of limited application, since resemblance among our
perceptions is almost entirely confined to memory ideas and
the impressions of which they are the copies. And yet we extend our own and others' identity beyond what we and they
are able to remember. So the natural relation of causation
must come into play here as well, that being the only remaining possibility for Hume. And recourse to this does indeed
enable us to explain our attributions of identity beyond the
reaches of our memories; we can, e.g., infer an unremembered
cause for some particular remembered impression; this cause
too must be a perception, and is related to that which we
remember; hence not only can this cause be thought of as an

element of some mind or self, it can be and naturally is thought of as an element of the same self with that of which the remembered impression is an element.

Hume's account of mind and of personal identity, despite this added complexity, seems straightforward enough, given his account of physical objects and the general principles which lie behind both these accounts. And so Hume does let the matter rest in Section VI, Part IV, Book I of the *Treatise*. In the Appendix, however, which was published a year after Book I had seen the light, Hume expresses dissatisfaction with his treatment of mind in the very strongest terms. He does not doubt that the mind is nothing but a bundle of perceptions, each distinct from every other. He is also sure that "the thought alone finds personal identity [i.e., no such thing exists in reality], when, reflecting on the train of past perceptions that compose a mind, the ideas of them are felt to be connected together, and naturally introduce each other" (310). But trouble arises when he comes "to explain the principles that unite our successive perceptions in our thought or consciousness" (ibid.). And the trouble is, evidently, that the explanation given in Section VI contradicts those very parts of his account of mind that Hume is sure of, or contradicts the principles on which they rest. Hume is less than explicit here, but perhaps what he has in mind is this. His theory of personal identity requires that our minds be capable of connecting ideas together in regular ways, or, more generally, that we be capable of forming mental habits; indeed Hume's positive accounts of causation, of general ideas, and of the existence of bodies require this as well. But how can minds which consist entirely of disjoined perceptions be so capable? Does not the mind's very capacity to associate ideas presuppose its being something more than just a collection of distinct ideas, or ideas and impressions? It certainly would seem so, and though it is not clear that this is the difficulty that Hume alludes to, it is certainly a difficulty to which his view of mind is subject. Indeed, since this view of mind is the view that Hume's general principles require—in stating it he is clearly only drawing out the implications of the assumptions with which he began in Part I—this is a difficulty which strikes to the heart of Hume's philosophy. In any case, Hume did feel himself to be in trouble on reflecting on his theory of mind, and had no confidence at all that the theory was correct.

Hume's doubts regarding his theory of mind, however, were as nothing compared to those he expressed in stating his views on the existence of physical objects. Here he does not formulate a clear doctrine which he then has second thoughts about. He is not even able to state a single view in a straightforward way, and it is no accident that Hume's worries about skepticism are most prominent in the section in which this question is discussed, and that this section, Section II of Part IV, is the most difficult to comprehend in the whole *Treatise*. Part of what Hume says is clear enough. He rejects the philosophical doctrine (of Descartes and Locke, among others) whereby physical objects are distinguished from perceptions, the former being held to exist, unperceived, independently of our minds, and to become known to us only by means of the perceptions which they cause. This doctrine, Hume says, "is the monstrous offspring of two philosophical principles which are contrary to each other" (150), and his rejection of it is in line with his treatment of the other metaphysical opinions that he examines in Part IV. But what are we to say positively regarding the existence of physical objects? First of all, Hume holds, everyone believes that such objects exist, independently of our perceiving them; this is, indeed, a natural belief that all of us, philosophers and plain men alike, can neither help having nor live without. Second, there is no justifying this belief; we cannot defend it rationally any more than we can defend our similarly natural belief that the things we observe have causes and will be succeeded by certain effects. Third, however, and unlike our belief in the causal connections of things, the belief that objects do exist independently of our perceiving them is demonstrably false. Hume is able to explain, though with considerable effort, the fact that we do hold this belief in spite of its falsity, by appealing once again to that battery of natural mental propensities which he claims to have discovered by experience and observation. But the fact remains that we do (as Hume thinks) naturally believe such a (to Hume) manifestly false doctrine, and this is ample cause for philosophical alarm. The philosophical doctrine already alluded to is regarded by

[Margin annotations, handwritten:] THINGS IN THEMSELVES — COMMON SENSE BELIEVES OBJECTS EXIST APART FROM US HAVE CAUSES ETC. BUT CANNOT PROVE IT.

Hume as a desperate attempt to meet or soften this difficulty, for he holds that its proponents seek, by postulating a double order of internal perceptions and external objects, to take account of both those considerations which show that objects don't exist outside our minds—these are made to apply to perceptions, which are acknowledged to be "internal and perishing"—and the universal conviction that bodies do exist—this conviction is made to hold for external objects only. Besides its own deficiencies, this philosophical doctrine also has, in Hume's view, all the faults of the vulgar opinion which it was designed to replace.

This is not the end of the matter, however. For it is not yet clear just what it is that the vulgar believe—and are mistaken about—when they believe that physical objects exist independently of our perceiving them. Hume has already maintained that "it is impossible for us so much as to conceive or form an idea of anything specifically different from ideas and impressions" (60)—and it is mainly for this reason that the philosophical doctrine just referred to must be given up. Now it may be possible for plain men to believe what is false, but they cannot believe what they cannot "so much as conceive." So it is clear, Hume says, that plain men accept, what philosophers also hold to be true, that "our perceptions are our only objects." And this means that the things that plain men believe to exist independently of our minds are in fact perceptions; it is thus to perceptions, "the very things we see and hear," that plain men ascribe "continued and distinct existence." And a very little philosophy is all that is needed, Hume says, to destroy this opinion. The philosophy in question is really an argument, or type of argument, which Hume states as follows: "When we press one eye with a finger, we immediately perceive all the objects to become double, and one half of them to be removed from their common and natural position. But as we do not attribute a continued existence to both these perceptions, and as they are both of the same nature, we clearly perceive that all our perceptions are dependent on our organs and the disposition of our nerves and animal spirits. This opinion is confirmed . . . by an infinite number of other experiments of the same kind, from all which we learn that our sensible perceptions are not possessed of

[handwritten marginal note: ARGUMENT]

[handwritten note at bottom: against the independent existence of external objects apart from our perceptions]

Since Hume rejects "necessary connections" i.e. causes, he must reject things-in-themselves

any distinct or independent existence" (146). But this argument, if sound, proves more than that the plain man's ascription of independent existence to perceptions is mistaken. For the argument is not framed in terms of *perceptions;* its first premise refers rather to *perceived objects,* the things we see. Hence the conclusion established, if the argument is sound, is that *perceived objects* have no existence apart from their being perceived. But this amounts to saying that perceived objects are *perceptions,* as Hume uses the term "perception," i.e., that perceived objects are momentarily existing, mind-dependent entities. The other conclusion, that *perceptions* are mind-dependent entities, only follows if perceived objects, the very things we see and hear, are assumed from the outset to be perceptions. That they are so assumed is clear; Hume says over and over that "perceptions are our only objects." But this means that the argument's proper conclusion, that perceived objects are perceptions, is really no more than the tautology that perceptions are perceptions! On the other hand, the assumption that "perceptions are our only objects" has nowhere been justified. This assumption forms, to be sure, one part of Hume's fundamental "theory of ideas," which is presupposed from the very beginning of his inquiry, as we have seen. But this theory has itself, so far, merely been assumed; no justification for it has been given or attempted. Hume says that the view in question is "pretty obvious of itself" (60) and is supposed by "the vulgar" to be true (145), and hence (presumably) needs no justification, but this is dubious at best. So we seem to have the following situation: on the one hand, an argument which proves something that has already been assumed, and on the other, an assumption for which proof is clearly necessary and yet for which no proof has been given. How are we to make sense of this?

The obvious way, it would seem, is this. The argument quoted above must constitute Hume's *basis* for the doctrine that perceptions are our only objects and thence for the whole theory of ideas, whether or not he consciously regarded it as such. It is to this argument that Hume would have appealed had he thought of justifying his theory of ideas or held such justification to be necessary. For there is no other argument stated or even suggested in Hume's writings to which he might have so appealed, and the alternative is to say that the theory of ideas had *no* basis for Hume. If then this argument is Hume's basis for the whole idea theory, not only should it have been stated earlier in the *Treatise* than Section II of Part IV of Book I; it should also have been stated earlier in Section II. For much of the obscurity of this section could then have been avoided. Hume could have started with the plain man's natural belief in the independent existence of the things he perceives; then introduced his argument and drawn the conclusion that the things we perceive are really perceptions, defined as discrete "internal and perishing" entities; drawn thence the conclusion that the plain man's natural belief is false; considered next, and rejected, the philosopher's attempt to avoid this result by his hypothesis of a double order of things; and ended with an account of the psychological process whereby people persist in believing that, not perceptions, but the objects they perceive exist independently of their perceiving them. Of course the question remains whether Hume's argument is sound and its conclusion true (and there is ample reason to think not, in both cases), and whether therefore the main paradoxes of Hume's position in this section might not have been avoided by some other way than by "carelessness and inattention." But the foregoing reordering of Hume's exposition at least enables us to remove two minor paradoxes of the section as it stands, that of attributing the view that perceptions are our only objects to the *vulgar* (for that is surely a sophisticated philosophical opinion) and that of supposing anyone to believe that *perceptions,* as opposed to perceived objects, have distinct existence independent of the mind (for that is too close to an explicit contradiction for even the vulgar to believe).

We are now able, having followed Hume through Part IV of Book I of the *Treatise,* to draw some conclusions regarding his general ontology, or theory of reality. One point stands out, though Hume himself seems disinclined to emphasize it. This is that perceptions are, in Hume's view, the only things that are fully and finally *real,* the only sort of thing, indeed, whose existence is even conceivable to us human beings. Neither bodies nor minds are ultimately real. The former reduce to qualities, but qualities, being things we perceive, are themselves only impressions. <u>Minds reduce directly to impressions and ideas.</u> Philosophers sometimes distinguish between mental objects and mental acts, between things perceived and acts of perceiving, but there is no room for any such distinction in Hume's philosophy. An individual perception must embody both act and object. Mental dispositions, habits, and propensities, must also reduce, for Hume, to collections of perceptions—however difficult it might be to carry the reduction out. <u>Abstract objects, relations, space and time, matter,</u> all either <u>have no existence in Hume's view or are to be regarded as collections of perceptions. <u>Even God is no real being,</u></u> so far as any human knows; the most we have to reckon with is people's ideas of God, and those of course are perceptions. <u>In short, perceptions are all and all is perceptions.</u> Now there are grave objections that must be met by any such ontology. Hume, however, not only does not meet them in the *Treatise,* he hardly considers them, as if he did not quite realize just what the position was to which his various principles committed him. He does not, for example, explain why it is that some perceptions form collections, or are formed by us into collections, that we call minds, and that others form bodies. Nor does he explain why we distinguish minds and bodies at all, as in fact we do. And yet there is no doubt that this is Hume's ontology, that this is the theory of reality to which his initial and underlying principles commit him; if nothing else, the inquiries of Part IV make that clear. The fact that Hume often speaks of bodies and minds and of objects generally, in contrast to perceptions or to impressions and ideas, might make us want to question this, or else charge him with inconsistency. But it is possible to avoid both these courses by treating Hume's reference to objects, bodies, and minds as mere *façons de parler,* adopted in order to facilitate his task of exposition. All terms for such objects could then, theoretically, be eliminated, and replaced by expressions in which only words for perceptions occur. The result would be a text more cumbersome than the existing one, but also more accurate and perspicuous in conveying Hume's essential meaning.

    Having now completed our survey of Hume's metaphysics and epistemology, we may turn to a consideration of his moral

[margin note: ULTIMATE REDUCTION]

philosophy, as it is presented in Books II and III of the *Treatise*. Book II, "Of the Passions," contains what are really only prolegomena to Hume's moral theory proper, but necessary prolegomena, since passions are for Hume the only motives to action and it is primarily motives to which moral qualities attach. "All virtuous actions," he says, "derive their merit only from virtuous motives" (254), and "the ultimate object of our praise and approbation" when we morally approve a given action "is the motive that produced" it (ibid.). These doctrines are not explicitly presented until the end of Book II and the beginning of Book III, but it is in their light that Hume's whole discussion of the passions must be understood. In one way, it is no surprise to find Hume holding that passions are the only motives to action, and that all human conduct, even the most conscious and deliberate, is prompted and directed by emotion. For one main conclusion of Book I was that many of man's supposedly intellectual activities are ultimately dependent on feeling and sentiment. "All probable reasoning," Hume says at one point, "is nothing but a species of sensation" (94). All thinking about matters of fact is guided and all factual judgments are determined by feeling, and belief in the truth of a factual proposition is itself nothing, in Hume's view, but a certain kind of forceful feeling. If such intellectual functions are only an expression, at bottom, of man's emotional nature, it is all the more to be expected that human conduct, man's overt actions as a member of society, will have the same ultimate source.

Although Hume's main purpose in treating the passions is to prepare the way for his moral theory, he proceeds systematically in discussing them and seeks to provide a complete account of man's emotional nature, even when its direct bearing on action and morality is slight—for not all passions are motives. A passion must, of course, be some sort of perception for Hume, and since all passions have a sensible force, they are obviously to be classified as impressions rather than as ideas. But they are impressions of a different sort from most of those we have considered. The impressions which occur in sense perception are "original impressions" or "impressions of sensation," as are also the bodily sensations such as pleasure and pain. These are "such as without any antecedent per-

PASSIONS DIVIDED — CALM VS VIOLENT
— DIRECT VS INDIRECT

ception arise in the soul, from the constitution of the body, from the animal spirits, or from the application of objects to the external organs" (194). Passions and emotions, however, are "secondary impressions" or "impressions of reflection." These are "such as proceed from some of [the] original [impressions], either immediately or by the interposition of its idea" (ibid.). Hume then introduces two main divisions within the class of passions as a whole. On the one hand he distinguishes the "calm" from the "violent" passions, and on the other the "direct" from the "indirect." The basis of these distinctions is never made very clear by Hume, nor is their relation to one another. It is plain, however, that they are distinctions of quite different kinds. Every species of human passion is either direct or indirect and none is both, either at once or successively, whereas the calm-violent distinction is neither exclusive nor fixed in this way: one and the same (specific) passion may be both calm and violent, even in the same person, though not at the same time, depending on factors other than the species of passion to which it belongs. Both direct and indirect passions may be violent, and it would seem that both sorts could be calm as well, though Hume is not quite explicit on this point.

Direct passions are "such as arise immediately from good or evil, from pain or pleasure"; the indirect "proceed from the same principles, but by the conjunction of other qualities" (195). Examples of the former are "desire, aversion, grief, joy, hope, fear, despair, and security"; of the latter, "pride, humility, ambition, vanity, love, hatred, envy, pity, malice, generosity" (196). Hume does not have much to say about the direct passions, beyond listing and distinguishing them; presumably, since a direct passion occurs naturally and at once upon the occurrence of a feeling or idea of pain or pleasure, or of an idea of good or evil, there is nothing much that can be said about them, at least by the descriptive philosopher. The indirect passions, however, Hume discusses in great detail; two of the three parts of Book II are devoted to them. Hume distinguishes two main pairs of indirect passions, pride and humility and love and hatred; the remaining indirect passions are then accounted for in terms of these. In general, what Hume does in discussing this class of passions is to describe the process by which he thinks (on the basis of "experience and observation") an individual instance of this class, an individual reflective impression, actually arises from some antecedent primary impression or idea. The process has the same form or structure in all cases; the resulting passions only differ according to the different primary perceptions from which they arise and the "other qualities" with which these primary perceptions are conjoined. The various stages in the process are all determined by "certain properties of human nature," prominent among which is the (by now familiar) tendency of the mind to associate certain of its ideas with one another. There is also, Hume says, a natural tendency of the mind to associate impressions, and the two kinds of association "very much assist and forward each other" (202). What Hume is really doing in all of this is describing an associative mechanism by which the various indirect passions might plausibly be supposed to occur in the mind, assuming that the mind is as Hume says it is. The details of this mechanism are often ingenious, and Hume tries hard to take note of actual facts about pride and humility, facts about their usual occurrence in human affairs and about the logical connections of their concepts with other concepts. But his account remains merely speculative; its content is determined more by *a priori* principles than by experience, and it is, on the whole, of little contemporary philosophical or psychological interest.

Hume's other division of the passions, into the calm and the violent, depends on the degree of emotion with which the passion is felt. Calm passions, Hume says, "produce little emotion in the mind, and are more known by their effects than by the immediate feeling or sensation" (229). Violent passions, on the other hand, produce a "sensible agitation," even a "disorder in the temper" (230). Certain species of passion, in particular "the sense of beauty and deformity in action, composition, and external objects," are predominantly calm, but the term "calm passion" does not, for Hume, mark off any settled class of specific passions. The same passion, resentment for example, may be successively calm and violent in the same man, or calm in one and violent in another. Also, since the felt force of an emotion is not something that admits

of precise measure, the line between calm and violent is far
from sharp. Indeed, the distinction itself is not very important, and would hardly be worth remarking apart from one
particular use to which Hume puts it. This occurs in his discussion of the will, which takes up most of Part III of Book
II and forms the connecting link between this book and the
next.

Def. of will

Hume defines the will as "the internal impression we feel
and are conscious of when we knowingly give rise to any new
motion of our body or new perception of our mind" (224); as
such it is an "immediate effect of pain and pleasure," although
it is not thereby "comprehended among the passions" (ibid.).
Hume does not, however, keep to this definition in his subsequent discussion. Instead he seems to conceive the will in the
traditional Augustinian way, as some sort of executive agency
subject to certain influences and which itself influences or
brings about our (voluntary) actions—for all that no such
thing is possible in his philosophy. But Hume is not in any
case much interested in what the will is, and once he has got-
ten the question of the will's freedom out of the way (which
he should have done just following his account of causation,
as we have seen), he turns at once to the topic of motivation,
of the "influencing motives of the will." Actually, he might
have treated this topic without mentioning the will at all. For
though Hume most often makes the will the thing that is influenced, caused, determined, directed, and operated upon
by our various motives, he sometimes departs from the traditional idiom and speaks of our motives as themselves giving
rise to, producing, and causing our actions—as if realizing
that the will as traditionally conceived can simply be
dropped out of account in any description of voluntary human action.

Be that as it may, Hume's chief thesis regarding motives is
that human motivation is exclusively emotional. It is here that
he presents and defends his doctrine that the passions are our
only motives to action. Negatively, this is equivalent to the
view that the will cannot be determined to any action by
reason, for reason, Hume thinks, is the only possible alternative to passion as a motive. Reason cannot be a motive, Hume
says, because it is "inert" and "impotent"; its role is that of

spectator rather than producer or doer. For reason—or a per- REASON
son using reason—discovers relations or acknowledges facts,
and that is all; reason alone can neither cause nor prevent
any action. The passions, on the other hand, do have motive
force; it is their very nature to impel, to urge, to prompt. It
follows that reason cannot, properly speaking, oppose any
passion. Hence, Hume observes in a famous passage, "we
speak not strictly and philosophically when we talk of the
combat of passion and of reason. Reason is and ought only
to be the slave of the passions" (227). How is it then that we
do so talk, and what is it that we should, "strictly and philosophically," say upon this subject? It is at this point that
Hume has recourse to his distinction between calm and violent passions. For calm passions, just because they "produce
little emotion in the mind," are "very readily taken for the
determinations of reason" (229). The calm passions are real
passions, and they often do "determine the will." When they
do, they often not only oppose but overcome the more violent
emotions; as Hume says, the strength of a passion as a motive,
its power in determining the will, is not always proportional
to its violence as a feeling. When a calm passion does overcome a violent one in this way, we often do say that reason
has prevailed over passion. But here as elsewhere we mistake
the true situation by misidentifying two things which are only
similar to one another. We do this quite "naturally," Hume
says, but it is still passion which determines the will, and not
reason at all. The notion of a calm passion provides Hume
with an explanation of the "mistake" in this case, an explanation that enables him to save the appearances while yet maintaining his own doctrine.

Hume's discussion of motivation, together with the misplaced treatment of freedom, is the most important thing in
Book II as a whole, both in itself and for Hume's later moral
theory. Most of the rest of the contents of Book II are of relatively minor importance, and it is noteworthy that Hume provided no counterpart for Book II when he recast the *Treatise*
into the two *Inquiries;* the separate and much reduced
"Dissertation of the Passions" was not published until some
years later. Nor is Book II very well organized as it stands—
in part, surely, because Hume's distinctions among the various

kinds of passions are so unclear. The first two parts are devoted entirely to the indirect passions, which indeed are treated systematically. But then not only are the direct passions and the whole division of calm and violent passions treated very cursorily and unsystematically in Part III, but the discussion of these topics is all mixed up with Hume's account of the will, or rather his accounts of freedom and motivation which both involve the will, though the will itself is not a passion and should have been separately treated. Hume did better in the "Dissertation." There he discusses the direct passions first, goes on to describe the indirect passions, proceeds to an account of motives, and ends by distinguishing the calm and violent passions and applying this distinction to his account of motivation. The treatment of liberty and necessity drops out altogether, having been moved to its proper position following the discussion of causation in the first *Inquiry*.

Hume's discussion of motivation in Book II carries him naturally into the subject of Book III, "Of Morals." Indeed the main contention of Part I of Book III is made to rest upon the conclusion of that discussion. Part I is devoted to morality in general, to the nature of moral qualities as objects of human consideration and judgment. Stated simply, Hume's doctrine in this part is that moral qualities are not recognized by reason, and that our apprehension of the moral features of an action or character is a function not of our intellectual but of our sensitive or affective nature. "Morality," he says, "is more properly felt than judged of" (248), and though this statement is misleading owing to the ambiguity of the word "judge"—and Hume himself speaks regularly of moral judgments, using "judgment" in the general sense of "opinion" or "pronouncement" and not as the name of something issuing specifically from reason—it does express the essence of Hume's view. Hume arrives at this position as follows. He first observes that morality has an active force in human affairs. "Morals excite passions and produce or prevent actions" (236); to take a moral view of something is to be moved to act regarding it, or at least to react emotionally in a way that might lead to action in the proper circumstances. Hume then combines this observation with the doctrine of motivation

worked out in Book II. If moral judgments affect our conduct, and if reason, by itself, has no influence on action, it
follows that "the rules of morality . . . are not conclusions of
our reason" (ibid.).

Hume's position has a number of implications which it is
important to sort out and distinguish. One such implication is
that moral questions cannot be decided by any rational procedure. Moral questions are of two sorts, those of the moral
agent—these concern what actions *ought* to be performed—
and those of the moral *judge* or *critic*—these concern the
value of actions already performed and of the motives and
characters from which all actions proceed. Hume confines his
attention mainly to questions of the latter sort in Book III of
the *Treatise;* his moral theory is primarily a theory of moral
value as opposed to moral obligation, although he does make
various incidental remarks about obligation. Concerning
moral value, then, Hume's position is that no process of reasoning will yield a decision as to whether an action or character is virtuous or vicious—"virtue" and "vice" being the terms
most frequently employed by Hume for positive and negative
moral value, respectively. We cannot so much as distinguish
virtue and vice by reason, according to Hume. This by itself
suffices to refute those philosophers—for example Samuel
Clarke and Wollaston—who claim that there are moral
truths discoverable by reasoning and that "virtuous" just
means "rational" or "rationally fitting," though Hume also
makes more particular objections against such claims later on.
For Hume, it is not reason but sense or some capacity for
feeling by which moral good and evil are discerned. The precise nature of this sense is not worked out by Hume at this
point, and indeed is never made very clear in the *Treatise.*
But he seems not to have regarded it as a special faculty of
moral perception with moral qualities as its peculiar objects;
hence his view is to be distinguished from that of such "moral
sense" philosophers as Hutcheson and Shaftesbury. For
Hume the moral sense is part of our general capacity for
feeling pleasure and pain. The pleasure attendant on virtue
has indeed a peculiar quality and only gives rise to moral
judgments in certain circumstances, as we shall see in a moment. But the sense employed in moral apprehensions has

nothing peculiar about it. Hume's point is only that it is some sense or disposition to respond emotionally—and not reason—by which moral qualities are recognized.

Hume's position regarding moral obligation parallels that concerning moral good and evil. No process of reasoning can decide the question whether I am obligated to perform a given action or the question what action is required of me as my duty. Judgments of obligation have motive force for Hume: "men are often . . . deterred from some actions by the opinion of injustice and impelled to others by that of obligation" (236). Reason can only inform us as to what is the case, not as to what ought to be, and the distinction between *is* and *ought*, Hume remarks in a famous passage, is fundamental. Moral philosophers commonly shift in their writings, he says, from propositions with "the usual copulations . . . , *is* and *is not*," to propositions connected with *ought* and *ought not*. "This change is imperceptible, but is, however, of the last consequence. For as this *ought* or *ought not* expresses some new relation or affirmation, it is necessary that it should be observed and explained, and at the same time that a reason should be given for what seems altogether inconceivable, how this new relation can be a deduction from others which are entirely different from it"(247-81). Recognition of this new relation, and hence of the obligatory character of actions, is again a matter of feeling or sense, as in the case of moral value. "All morality depends upon our sentiments, and when any action or quality of mind pleases us *after a certain manner* we say it is virtuous, and when the neglect or non-performance of it displeases us *after a like manner* we say that we lie under an obligation to perform it" (274). Hume says little, apart from this passage, about the feelings by which we determine obligations, though there is reason to think that his account of them would diverge in some measure from his treatment of our sense of virtue and vice. For the connection between the recognition of an obligation and action is direct in his view, whereas that between the recognition of virtue or vice and action is at best indirect.

Another implication of Hume's general doctrine of morality, that "moral distinctions are not derived from reason," concerns the nature of that virtue and vice which are the objects of our judgments of moral value. To bring this out it is necessary to look at the second line of argument which Hume adduces in favor of this doctrine in Part I of Book III (the first being that which rests upon his view of motivation). This argument runs as follows. If moral qualities were ascertainable by reasoning, they would have either to consist in certain relations between ideas or to exist as matters of fact. For these, as was shown in Book I of the *Treatise,* are the only possible objects of reasoning; the one is the object of demonstration, the other of probable reasoning, these being the only two kinds of reasoning there are. But the virtue of a thing cannot consist in any of those relations between it and something else, or rather between their ideas, which alone admit of demonstration, for the reason, among others, that we should then have to ascribe virtue to trees and colors and numbers as well as to human actions and characters. (This point provides Hume with another argument against the rationalistic view of Wollaston and Clarke.) Nor does the virtue of something exist in it as a matter of fact, for if it did we would be able to observe it, whereas experience reveals no such common quality of those objects we denominate as virtuous. Hence no judgment of moral value can be the conclusion of any process of reasoning. But if this argument proves this, it also proves much more than this, as Hume immediately realizes. For (if sound) it shows not only that moral qualities cannot be ascertained by reasoning but that they are not objects of thought or understanding in any form, or of sense perception either, or even of belief in the Book I sense in which belief is a lively *idea.* For moral judgments about things cannot, by Hume's argument, express true or false propositions about those things. If to say that something is virtuous is not to say that its idea is analytically related to some other idea, nor yet to state a matter of fact about it, then to ascribe virtue to an object is not to say anything about it at all. We have already noted the parallel claim in the case of obligation: a judgment of obligation does not, in Hume's view, express what is the case but rather what ought to be. Hume is here extending this view to the

case of moral value as well. It follows that virtue and vice are
not qualities of the things—actions and characters—to which
they are ascribed.

What then are they, and what is the nature of those judgments which we form of them; what does it *mean* to say that
something is virtuous or vicious? Hume's answers to these
questions are unfortunately less clear than they ought to be.
What he first *says* is straightforward enough. "Take any action
allowed to be vicious . . . The vice entirely escapes you as
long as you consider the object. You never can find it until
you turn your reflection into your own breast, and find a sentiment of disapprobation which arises in you towards this
action. . . . So that when you pronounce any action or character to be vicious, you mean nothing but that from the constitution of your nature you have a feeling or sentiment of blame
from the contemplation of it. Vice and virtue, therefore, . . .
are not qualities in objects but perceptions in the mind"
(247). Of what nature are these perceptions, Hume asks,
and answers that "the impression arising from virtue [is]
agreeable, and that proceeding from vice [is] uneasy" (248).
Furthermore, "the uneasiness and satisfaction are not only
inseparable from vice and virtue but constitute their very
nature and essence" (209). Hence "an action or sentiment or
character is virtuous or vicious . . . because its view causes
a pleasure or uneasiness of a particular kind. . . . To have
the sense of virtue is nothing but to *feel* a satisfaction of a
particular kind. . . . The very *feeling* constitutes our praise
or admiration. . . . We do not infer a character to be virtuous because it pleases, but in feeling that it pleases after such
a particular manner we in effect feel that it is virtuous"
(249). And again, "to approve of a character is to feel an
original delight upon its appearance. To disapprove of it is to
be sensible of an uneasiness." (209).

Now it is clear from these statements that Hume's position
is at bottom hedonistic; moral good and evil are tied ultimately to pleasure and pain. But if we had only these statements to go on we should have to conclude that good and
evil are the same with pleasant and unpleasant for Hume,
that we judge something good always and only when we feel

pleasure in regarding it, and that to judge something good is
simply to approve of it, which in turn is simply to be pleased
by it. And this sort of simple-minded hedonism is plainly un-
tenable. Enough qualifications and partial retractions of these
initial statements occur later on in Book III, however, to make
it unnecessary to ascribe any such position to Hume. In the
first place, Hume recognizes different kinds of pleasure and
pain. We feel a pleasure on the contemplation of something
beautiful, and our feeling pleasure constitutes its being beautiful; beauty, like virtue, is in the eye of the beholder for Hume.
But we do not thereby identify virtue and beauty. Hence the
pleasure must be different in the two cases—it must have a
different quality. Second, Hume notes that we distinguish
what is virtuous from what is in our interest, and says that "it
is only when a character is considered in general, without
reference to our particular interest, that it causes such a feeling or sentiment as denominates it morally good or evil"
(250). Hence it is that "the good qualities of an enemy are
hurtful to us, but may still command our esteem and respect"
(ibid.). Here the basis of the distinction seems not to lie in
the quality of the pleasure produced, as in the case of virtue
and beauty, but in the circumstances in which the judgment
of value is made, and in particular in the relation of the
judger to that which he is judging. Third, we often distinguish appearance from reality, Hume observes, in moral as in
aesthetic matters, or we distinguish what is temporary from
what is relatively permanent. And we rest our moral judgments, he says, on what is real and permanent. Then, despite
the fact that "all sentiments of praise or blame are variable,"
depending on our momentary situation, we "still apply the
terms expressive of our liking or dislike in the same manner
as if we remained in one point of view" (288). Hence, to
make a moral judgment is not so much to feel a pleasure or
pain, or even to approve or disapprove of something in abstraction from one's own interest, but to recognize qualities in
the thing judged that *would* give rise to the appropriate sentiments *if* the thing were properly regarded. "We blame
equally a bad action which we read of in history with one
performed in our neighborhood the other day, the meaning of

which is that we know from reflection that the former action would excite as strong sentiments of disapprobation as the latter, were it placed in the same position" (289-90).

These qualifications do make Hume's moral doctrine more tenable than it appears to be from his first statements of it. We can, on their basis, distinguish between "virtuous" and "pleasant," between "I approve of X" and "X pleases me," and between "I approve of X" and "X is morally good." And these are certainly distinctions that must be made, or at least allowed, by any adequate moral theory. But the last of the three qualifications mentioned threatens Hume's doctrine from another direction, and hence raises a problem of which Hume himself seemed unaware. If to make a moral judgment of something is to "know from reflection" what sentiments it "would excite" were certain conditions satisfied, is not the possibility opened up that moral judgments can be reached by reasoning and that they do express matters of fact about the things which they concern? If so, then of course the whole sentimental, noncognitive basis of Hume's moral theory is called into question.

Hume makes another point that serves to qualify his moral position as first stated in Part I of Book III of the *Treatise*. Throughout that part he speaks as if actions as well as characters and motives were subjects of moral qualities, that is, were objects to which virtue and vice may be ascribed. But at the beginning of Part II he disavows this view. It is only motives, he argues, that are virtuous and vicious. Actions are indeed signs of motives, but "the external performance has no merit. We must look within to find the moral quality. . . . The ultimate object of our praise and approbation is the motive" (254). We do ascribe virtue to actions, but this is strictly a mistake; "all virtuous actions derive their merit only from virtuous motives" (ibid.). If this is so, then we have another reason for denying the status of a moral judgment to any feeling of pleasure or pain arising from the contemplation of an action. For we cannot tell from one action what the motives of its agent are; this requires familiarity with him and his behavior over a period of time. But if we cannot properly determine the moral quality of an action without knowing the motive that produced it, we cannot rely upon our responses to particular actions in making moral judgments. This doctrine, however, makes a new problem for Hume. For if it is motives which are the locus of moral value it is also motives which are the subject of moral obligation. What are morally required of men, then, are not certain actions but certain traits of character, certain settled passions and dispositions to act in certain ways. And it is a real question whether passions and character traits can be so required. Hume appears to accept the Kantian dictum that ought implies can; I cannot be required or obligated to do or be what it is not possible for me to do or be. And in this he is surely right. Can I then have a duty to love my neighbor, for example? Kant says no; love cannot be commanded. My duty is to behave toward my neighbor in a certain way, and indeed it is only when I behave this way out of duty and not out of love that my action has moral value for Kant. Hume sees the consequence of his position; he sees that he must make passions the subject of obligations, and hence that he must regard passions as being, somehow, under our voluntary control. "We blame a father for neglecting his child. Why? Because it shows a want of natural affection, which is the duty of every parent. Were not natural affection a duty the care of children could not be a duty" (255). But it is hard to believe that such qualities as natural affection are under our voluntary control. And indeed Hume himself sometimes denies that they are. In writing on promises (Section V of Part II) he says that "a change of . . . obligation supposes a change of sentiment, and a creation of a new obligation supposes some new sentiment to arise. But it is certain we can naturally no more change our own sentiments than the motions of the heavens" (274). And again in the section on natural abilities (Section V of Part III), which Hume says there is no good reason to distinguish from the traditionally recognized moral virtues, he claims that all virtuous qualities are, in some degree, "involuntary and necessary, . . . it being almost impossible for the mind to change its character in any considerable article or cure itself of a passionate or splenetic temper when they are natural to it" (298-9). He does allow that moral qualities, if not natural abilities, "may be changed by the motives of rewards and punishments, praise and blame" (299). But these "motives" are ap-

plied by others, by "legislators and divines and moralists," and
not by the agent whose obligations are in question. And it is
surely absurd to hold a man responsible for having someone
else instill a certain motive in him, or blame him because this
has not been done. Hume seems here to have run into a real
difficulty.

In Parts II and III of Book III Hume considers particular
virtues and vices. These, he says, are of two main sorts, "artificial" and "natural"; the artificial virtues, of which justice is
the chief example, are discussed in Part II and the natural
virtues in Part III. Justice is an artificial virtue for Hume in
the sense that there is in human nature no natural motive to
the performance of just actions, no original disposition which
prompts us to be just or makes us feel pleasure when con-
fronted with instances of justice. No such thing as justice even
exists for man in an altogether "natural" condition. Yet justice
is an important element in our moral life. Hume sets himself
the task, therefore, of explaining how it is that justice first
came into being, and came to be an object of moral concern.
Part II is largely devoted to this task, and in the course of his
discussion Hume says a good deal about political societies,
laws, and institutions, which are the external trappings, so to
speak, of justice. Since most of this material has been omitted from the present edition, as having little connection with
Hume's philosophy, it need not concern us here. Nor need we
spend much time on the details of Hume's account of the
origin of justice. Justice comes into being, he says, when men
form societies, and they form societies in order to remedy
certain "inconveniences" which attend them in their "natural"
state. These inconveniences are due to their own selfishness
and limited generosity, in conjunction with the scarcity of
the objects they require for their sustenance and well-being.
The consequent avidity of acquiring goods, Hume says, "is
insatiable, perpetual, universal, and directly destructive of
society" (266). Men soon perceive, however, that this "passion is much better satisfied by its restraint than by its liberty,
and that in preserving society [they] make much greater advances in the acquiring possessions than in the solitary and
forlorn condition which must follow upon violence and a universal license" (267). Hence a system of rules for the re-

straint of each man's private interest is instituted; justice then consists in the observance of these rules. The rules are artifices, conventions only, although they are absolutely necessary for the preservation of society and society itself is an almost inevitable concomitant of human life, owing both to the natural passions which lead men to mate and form families and to the natural sagacity which enables them to see the advantages of social over solitary life. (Thus Hume does not regard the "state of nature" as something that actually existed, nor the institution of the rules of justice as any sort of "social contract"; his theory here is quite different from, e.g., Rousseau's.) The original motive to the establishment of the rules of justice, therefore, is the very passion which these rules are intended to control: self-interest, or the love of gain. And this is as it has to be, for there is, Hume says, no passion "capable of controlling the interested affection but the very affection itself, by an alteration of its direction" (ibid.). So much, then, for the manner in which justice came into being. But there is still the question as to how justice came to be counted as a virtue. For we now, in our social, cultivated state, observe the rules of justice not only because it is advantageous but because it is morally good to do so. There is a moral obligation to be just as well as the natural inclination to do what is in our interest, and we take the special sort of pleasure in the performance and contemplation of just acts that makes them morally commendable. How is this fact to be accounted for?

Hume's full answer to this question is not given until he treats of the natural virtues in Part III of Book III. A natural virtue differs from an artificial one in that men are naturally constituted so as to take pleasure in its contemplation—and also of course in that its existence is in no way dependent on human invention. Four sorts of natural virtue are distinguished by Hume, according to the source of the pleasure which each produces. Some qualities of mind are immediately agreeable to the person who possesses them; some are immediately agreeable to others; a third class are beneficial to the person who possesses them; and a fourth are beneficial to others, or to society at large. When a quality is immediately agreeable or beneficial to oneself, to account for the fact that it is a virtue is neither necessary nor possible. But when

some one of one's own qualities is either agreeable or beneficial to others, or some quality of someone else is agreeable or
beneficial to himself, some explanation is called for. For one
still continues, in such cases, to regard the quality as a virtue
and to take pleasure in its contemplation. Hume resorts here
to his doctrine of sympathy. That we "sympathize with the
passions and sentiments of others," not just by having ideas of
but by actually feeling what they feel—here there is, Hume
says, "an evident conversion of an idea into an impression"
(216)—is a fundamental fact of human nature, the workings of which can be described (and are described by
Hume in Book II) but which cannot otherwise be accounted
for. When we approve, therefore, of some quality of character
which is neither beneficial nor immediately agreeable to ourselves, it must be by a sympathetic entering into of the feelings of the person to whom the quality is agreeable or beneficial. The happiness of a stranger, Hume says, "concerns not
me further than the happiness of every human and indeed
of every sensible creature: that is, it affects me only by sympathy. From that principle, whenever I discover his happiness
and good, . . . I enter so deeply into it that it gives me a
sensible emotion. The appearance of qualities that have a
tendency to promote it have an agreeable effect upon my
imagination, and command my love and esteem" (294).

But not only are many of the natural virtues dependent in
this way upon sympathy, according to Hume; the moral approbation that we accord to the artificial virtues has the
same basis. Justice, he says, "is a moral virtue merely because
it has [a] tendency to the good of mankind." But since "the
means to an end can only be agreeable where the end is
agreeable, and as the good of society, where our own interest
is not concerned . . . , pleases only by sympathy, it follows
that sympathy is the source of the esteem which we pay" to
justice and indeed to all the artificial virtues (284). In short,
justice is approved because of its utility or social benefit,
which in turn is only an object of approval because of the
interest we take, by sympathy, in the good of society. And
that we take such an interest is simply a natural fact about
the human constitution. Hume ends the *Treatise* by stressing
the importance of this fact in man's moral life. Not only is

sympathy "a very powerful principle in human nature," but it may fairly be said to be "the chief source of moral distinctions" (600).

3. The Significance of Hume's Philosophy

Hume's philosophy, more than most, has been subject to varying interpretations. The reason is not far to seek. As Selby-Bigge puts it in the introduction to his edition of the *Inquiries*, Hume "says so many different things in so many different ways and different connections, and with so much indifference to what he has said before, that it is very hard to say positively that he taught, or did not teach, this or that particular doctrine. . . . He is ambitious rather than shy of saying the same thing in different ways, and at the same time he is often slovenly and indifferent about his words and formulae. This makes it easy to find all philosophies in Hume, or, by setting up one statement against another, none at all." Many commentators have tried nonetheless to find a single, self-consistent position in Hume's works. Hume is an empiricist, some have said, or a phenomenalist, or a sensationalist, or an atomist, or a realist, or a naturalist, or a positivist, or an emotivist, or something else again. The difficulty with all such attempts, apart from the fact that, in aggregate, they cancel each other out, is that they must ignore, or else vastly distort, various plain statements in Hume's writings. And yet there is a virtue in trying to make Hume's text yield a single doctrine. For Hume himself wanted very much to be a systematic thinker; he wanted to construct a coherent scheme of thought which would organize and unify the various separate sciences. He failed to do so, and he knew, at the end of the *Treatise*, that he had failed. But it is important, in reading him, to keep in mind his aspirations, and this the effort to interpret his thought systematically does help us to do. At the other extreme are those commentators for whom Hume's thought consists almost entirely of contradictions. They have delighted in searching out the inconsistencies with which Hume's text abounds. These are also the interpreters who have stressed the negative and skeptical force of his teaching. Such endeavors have their value too, for they encourage us to read attentively and with an eye to the detail which is too often overlooked by the more systematic commentators. But this approach is hardly fair to Hume. We must make some allowance for his youth when he composed the *Treatise* and for the excitement with which he wrote, believing as he did that he had discovered a whole "new scene of thought." Also, we must be grateful for Hume's honesty in refusing to suppress the implications of his results because they might conflict with things said before. One can learn from Hume, if not one true philosophy, at least how truly to philosophize.

Hand in hand with the variety of interpretations of Hume's thought has gone a similar variety of criticisms. No philosophy has been more criticized from so many different quarters than Hume's. It was only at first that the *Treatise* was unread; since 1760 or so few philosophical works have been so influential or so much discussed. And most of the discussion has been critical, beginning with the massive attacks of Reid and Kant in Hume's own century. Some of the criticism has been niggling; much of it has been unfair and uninformed and prejudiced; but the best of it has contributed materially to the progress of philosophy. Hume's works have been peculiarly successful in stimulating others to think further along the lines that he initiated. Hume himself may have landed in difficulties and his actual results perhaps deserve the treatment that the critics have given them, but he was able nonetheless to show the way to a remarkable degree to thinkers who succeeded him.

There is indeed much to criticize in Hume's philosophy. Several difficulties have been noted in the foregoing account of his teaching, and there are many others to be noted. And a good deal of Hume's doctrine has simply been forgotten, without anyone's having taken the trouble to refute it. His accounts of space and time and of the passions have suffered this fate, and deservedly so. His associationism, though it had a considerable vogue in the nineteenth century, is no longer credited by anyone. Large sections of his moral and political

philosophy attract little attention nowadays. On more particular points, concerning, e.g., memory, knowledge, belief, and
personal identity, there is wide dissatisfaction with Hume's
doctrines. The whole theory of ideas, with its attendant problem of "our knowledge of the external world," has been seriously questioned, as have Hume's views of motivation and
moral judgment: for many thinkers reason can be practical
and morality is not ultimately a matter of feeling. The account
of causation is the one thing that has survived criticism relatively unscathed; at least Hume's sort of view is still widely
accepted. But even here it is only the logical aspects of
Hume's theory that have persisted. Here as elsewhere, Hume's
elaborate psychological explanations have been rejected, not
because they are mistaken—the question of their correctness
has hardly, indeed, come up—but because they are inap-
propriate responses to the problems at hand.

The prominence of criticism in the philosophical reaction to
Hume and the extent to which his works invite criticism
make it hard to remember how much our present philosophical climate owes to Hume, at least in English-speaking countries. Some recent philosophers, notably Russell and the logical positivists, seem almost reincarnations of Hume, though
Hume divested of his peculiar psychology. But more generally, there is wide agreement on several fundamental doctrines which figure importantly in Hume's philosophy and
which are accepted nowadays in part because of Hume's
advocacy of them. In the first place, philosophers now are
almost all empiricists, in the sense that they regard experience
as the only source of significant knowledge, apart from mathematics. Their empiricism is both more rigorous and more
refined than Hume's, but the determination to follow experience no matter what, is the same. Second, there is a common
distrust of merely speculative, rationalistic, "metaphysical" answers to philosophical questions, as there is in Hume. Third,
the Humian distinction between analytic and empirical propositions—between those stating "relations of ideas" and those
which express "matters of fact"—and the exhaustiveness of
this distinction is almost universally accepted by contemporary philosophers. Many questions have been raised about the
distinction, and it is no longer made in quite the way that

Hume made it, but that there is some such distinction—and no third sort of proposition—is assumed almost as a matter of course. The corollary doctrine, that no existential propositions are demonstrable or necessary, is also widely held. Finally, the separation of "is" and "ought" as a fundamental principle of moral theory is taken for granted by almost all philosophers today. There is much disagreement as to what else ought to be accepted as truths of moral theory, and very few would be happy with the rest of Hume's position on meta-ethical questions, but this much is common property.

In sum, Hume would feel himself to be at home in the atmosphere of present-day philosophy, in part because he helped to make it what it is. He would, to be sure, have to give up many of the details of his doctrines and alter many of his ways of stating them. But the temper of his mind and the spirit with which he pursued his inquiries—analytic, skeptical, matter of fact, concrete—that he would not have to change at all.

V. C. CHAPPELL

SELECTED BIBLIOGRAPHY

———◆◆———

Entries are arranged chronologically, in order of publication. Only a few non-English works are listed, and only a few journal articles. More complete lists can be found in Jessop's *Bibliography* and Flew's *Hume's Philosophy of Belief* (see below).

Hume's Works

ORIGINAL EDITIONS

A Treatise of Human Nature. 3 vols. London, 1739-40.
An Abstract of . . . A Treatise of Human Nature. London, 1740.
Essays, Moral and Political [later title: *Essays, Moral, Political and Literary*]. 2 vols. Edinburgh, 1741-42.
Philosophical Essays concerning Human Understanding [later title: *An Enquiry concerning Human Understanding*]. London, 1748.
An Enquiry concerning the Principles of Morals. London, 1751.
Political Discourses. Edinburgh, 1752.
The History of Great Britain [later title: *The History of England*]. 6 vols. Edinburgh, London, 1754-62.
Four Dissertations ["The Natural History of Religion," "Of the Passions," "Of Tragedy," "Of the Standard of Taste"]. London, 1757.

Two Essays ["Of Suicide," "Of the Immortality of the Soul"]. London, 1777.

The Life of David Hume, Esq. Written by Himself ["My Own Life"]. London, 1777.

Dialogues concerning Natural Religion. [London], 1779.

COLLECTED EDITIONS

Essays and Treatises on Several Subjects. 4 vols. London, 1753-56. New edition (last revised by Hume), 2 vols. London, 1777.

The Philosophical Works of David Hume. 4 vols. Edinburgh, 1825.

The Philosophical Works of David Hume, ed. by T. H. Green and T. H. Grose. 4 vols. London, 1874-75.

CURRENT EDITIONS

A Treatise of Human Nature, ed. by L. A. Selby-Bigge. Oxford, 1888.

An Abstract of A Treatise of Human Nature, ed. by J. M. Keynes and P. Sraffa. Cambridge, 1938.

Enquiries concerning the Human Understanding and concerning the Principles of Morals, ed. by L. A. Selby-Bigge. 2nd ed., Oxford, 1902.

An Inquiry concerning Human Understanding, ed. by Charles W. Hendel. New York, 1955.

An Inquiry concerning the Principles of Morals, ed. by Charles W. Hendel. New York, 1957.

David Hume's Political Essays, ed. by Charles W. Hendel. New York, 1953.

The Natural History of Religion, ed. by H. E. Root. London, 1956.

Hume's Dialogues concerning Natural Religion, ed. by Norman Kemp Smith. 2nd ed., Edinburgh, 1947.

CORRESPONDENCE

The Letters of David Hume, ed. by J. Y. T. Grieg. 2 vols. Oxford, 1932.

New Letters of David Hume, ed. by Raymond Klibansky and Ernest C. Mossner. Oxford, 1954.

Works on Hume

BIBLIOGRAPHY

Grose, T. H. "History of the Editions," in *The Philosophical Works of David Hume*, ed. by T. H. Green and T. H. Grose, III (1875), 15-84.

Jessop, T. E. *A Bibliography of David Hume and of Scottish Philosophy from Francis Hutcheson to Lord Balfour.* London and Hull, 1938.

LIFE

Burton, J. H. *Life and Correspondence of David Hume.* 2 vols. Edinburgh, 1846.

Grieg, J. Y. T. *David Hume.* London, 1931.

Mossner, Ernest Campbell. *The Forgotten Hume: Le Bon David.* New York, 1943.

──────. *The Life of David Hume.* Edinburgh, 1954.

PHILOSOPHY: GENERAL

Green, T. H. "General Introductions," in *The Philosophical Works of David Hume*, ed. by T. H. Green and T. H. Grose, I (1874), 1-299; II (1874), 1-71.

Stephen, Sir Leslie. *History of English Thought in the Eighteenth Century.* 2 vols. London, 1876.

Huxley, T. H. *Hume.* London, 1879.

Adamson, Robert. "Hume," in *Encyclopedia Britannica*, 9th ed. (1881), XII, 346-55.

Knight, William. *Hume.* Edinburgh and London, 1886.

Calderwood, Henry. *David Hume.* Edinburgh and London, 1898.

Smith, Norman Kemp. "The Naturalism of Hume," *Mind*, XIV (1905), 149-73, 335-47.

Hendel, Charles William, Jr. *Studies in the Philosophy of David Hume.* Princeton, 1925.

Metz, Rudolf. *David Hume: Leben und Philosophie.* Stuttgart, 1929.

Kuypers, Mary S. *Studies in the Eighteenth Century Background of Hume's Empiricism*. Minneapolis, 1930.

Hobart, R. E. "Hume without Scepticism," *Mind*, XXXIX (1930), 273-301, 409-25.

Morris, C. R. *Locke, Berkeley, Hume*. Oxford, 1931.

Laing, B. M. *David Hume*. London, 1932.

Laird, John. *Hume's Philosophy of Human Nature*. London, 1932.

Smith, Norman Kemp. *The Philosophy of David Hume*. London, 1941.

Macnabb, D. G. C. *David Hume: His Theory of Knowledge and Morality*. London, 1951.

Passmore, J. A. *Hume's Intentions*. Cambridge, 1952.

Leroy, André. *David Hume*. Paris, 1953.

Basson, A. H. *David Hume*. London, 1958.

Aschenbrenner, Karl. "Psychologism in Hume," *Philosophical Quarterly*, XI (1961), 28-38.

PHILOSOPHY: PARTICULAR WORKS OR PROBLEMS

Leland, John. *A View of the Principal Deistical Writers that have Appeared in England in the Last and Present Centuries*. 3 vols. London, 1754-56.

Campbell, George. *A Dissertation on Miracles*. Edinburgh, 1762.

Brown, Thomas. *Observations on the Nature and Tendency of the Doctrine of Mr. Hume concerning the Relation of Cause and Effect* [later title: *Inquiry into the Relation of Cause and Effect*]. Edinburgh, [1805].

Taylor, A. E. *David Hume and the Miraculous*. Cambridge, 1927.

Mace, C. A. "Hume's Doctrine of Causation," *Proceedings of the Aristotelian Society*, XXXII (1931-32), 301-28.

Hedenius, Ingemar. *Studies in Hume's Ethics*. Upsala and Stockholm, 1937.

Price, H. H. *Hume's Theory of the External World*. Oxford, 1940.

Kydd, Rachael M. *Reason and Conduct in Hume's Treatise*. London, 1946.

Will, Frederick L. "Will the Future Be Like the Past?" *Mind*, LVI (1947), 332-47.

Price, Kingsley Blake. "Hume's Analysis of Generality," *Philosophical Review*, LIX (1950), 58-76.

Popkin, Richard H. "David Hume: His Pyrrhonism and his Critique of Pyrrhonism," *Philosophical Quarterly*, I (1950-51), 385-407.

Penelhum, Terence. "Hume on Personal Identity," *Philosophical Review*, LXIV (1955), 571-89.

Wand, Bernard. "Hume's Account of Obligation," *Philosophical Quarterly*, VI (1956), 155-68.

MacIntyre, A. C. "Hume on 'Is' and 'Ought'," *Philosophical Review*, LXVIII (1959), 451-68.

Atkinson, R. F. "Hume on Mathematics," *Philosophical Quarterly*, X (1960), 127-37.

Butler, Ronald J. "Natural Belief and the Enigma of Hume," *Archiv für Geschichte der Philosophie*, XLII (1960), 73-100.

Wolff, Robert Paul. "Hume's Theory of Mental Activity," *Philosophical Review*, LXIX (1960), 289-310.

Flew, Antony. *Hume's Philosophy of Belief*. London, 1961.

NOTE ON THE TEXT

THE TEXT of the works included in this volume is that of the
original editions published during Hume's lifetime or shortly
after his death. "My Own Life" is taken from the first edition, published (posthumously) in 1777. The *Treatise* also re-
produces the first (and only eighteenth-century) edition,
published in 1739-40. The text of the two *Inquiries* and the
essay "Of the Standard of Taste" is that of the 1777 edition
of the *Essays and Treatises on Several Subjects;* this is the
last edition that Hume revised before his death. The *Dialogues* were first published in 1779 in two separate but vir-
tually identical editions; the present text is that of the first of
these.

Every effort has been made to provide an accurate repro-
duction of these original editions. Several errors which appeared in later editions of Hume's works (and which have
been repeated in recent editions and volumes of selections)
have been corrected. Obvious errors in the original editions
have also been corrected; these include plain misprints and
mistakes, presumably Hume's, in quotations from and citations
of the works of other authors, chiefly classical. (The texts of
the Loeb Classical Library editions are the standard by which
Hume's quotations from classical authors have been corrected.) Spelling, punctuation, and capitalization have been
revised to accord with current American usage.

Three of the works included are given in their entirety; the
other three are printed with some omissions. Most of the
omitted material consists of whole sections, but in a few cases
paragraphs within sections and sentences within paragraphs

have been left out. Omitted sentences are marked in the text by three dots immediately following the last sentence printed. Omitted paragraphs are indicated by a row of dots on the next line following the end of the last paragraph printed. A few of Hume's merely illustrative notes have also been omitted; such omissions are indicated by editorial footnotes at the points at which they occur. A complete list of the contents, section by section, of the three abridged works—the *Treatise* and the two *Inquiries*—is printed at the beginning of each, with the omitted sections in brackets.

Most of Hume's notes to the *Inquiries* were printed in a separate section at the end of the volume containing them in the 1777 edition of the *Essays and Treatises*. In the present volume these notes have been placed on the appropriate pages. Most of the notes to the *Treatise* were printed with the text in the original edition, but Hume included a number of additional notes and passages for insertion in Book I in the Appendix following Book III, which was published by itself in a separate volume a year after Books I and II had appeared. In the present volume these notes and passages have been worked into the text of Book I at the proper places, with an editorial footnote indicating in each case that the material in question was first printed in the Appendix.

Editorial footnotes, which have been kept to a minimum, are enclosed in brackets. English translations of foreign-language quotations in Hume's text and notes have been provided, also in brackets; for these standard translations have been used and are identified in each case.

MY OWN
LIFE

IT IS DIFFICULT for a man to speak long of himself without vanity; therefore I shall be short. It may be thought an instance of vanity that I pretend at all to write my life, but this narrative shall contain little more than the history of my writings, as, indeed, almost all my life has been spent in literary pursuits and occupations. The first success of most of my writings was not such as to be an object of vanity.

I was born the 26th of April, 1711, old style, at Edinburgh. I was of a good family, both by father and mother. My father's family is a branch of the Earl of Home's, or Hume's; and my ancestors had been proprietors of the estate, which my brother possesses, for several generations. My mother was daughter of Sir David Falconer, President of the College of Justice; the title of Lord Halkerton came by succession to her brother.

My family, however, was not rich; and being myself a younger brother, my patrimony, according to the mode of my country, was of course very slender. My father, who passed for a man of parts, died when I was an infant, leaving me, with an elder brother and a sister, under the care of our mother, a woman of singular merit, who, though young and handsome, devoted herself entirely to the rearing and educating of her children. I passed through the ordinary course of education with success, and was seized very early with a passion for literature, which has been the ruling passion of my life and the great source of my enjoyments. My studious disposition, my sobriety, and my industry gave my family a notion that the law was a proper profession for me, but I found an unsurmountable aversion to everything but the pursuits of philosophy and general learning; and while they

fancied I was poring upon Voet and Vinnius, Cicero and
Vergil were the authors which I was secretly devouring.

My very slender fortune, however, being unsuitable to this
plan of life, and my health being a little broken by my ardent
application, I was tempted, or rather forced, to make a very
feeble trial for entering into a more active scene of life. In
1734, I went to Bristol with some recommendations to eminent merchants, but in a few months found that scene totally
unsuitable to me. I went over to France with a view of prosecuting my studies in a country retreat; and I there laid that
plan of life which I have steadily and successfully pursued.
I resolved to make a very rigid frugality supply my deficiency
of fortune, to maintain unimpaired my independence, and to
regard every object as contemptible except the improvement
of my talents in literature.

During my retreat in France, first at Reims, but chiefly at
La Flèche, in Anjou, I composed my *Treatise of Human Nature*. After passing three years very agreeably in that country, I came over to London in 1737. In the end of 1738, I
published my *Treatise*, and immediately went down to my
mother and my brother, who lived at his country house and
was employing himself very judiciously and successfully in
the improvement of his fortune.

Never literary attempt was more unfortunate than my
Treatise of Human Nature. It fell *deadborn from the press*,
without reaching such distinction as even to excite a murmur
among the zealots. But being naturally of a cheerful and sanguine temper, I very soon recovered from the blow and prosecuted with great ardor my studies in the country. In 1742, I
printed at Edinburgh the first part of my *Essays;* the work
was favorably received, and soon made me entirely forget my
former disappointment. I continued with my mother and
brother in the country, and in that time recovered the knowledge of the Greek language, which I had too much neglected
in my early youth.

In 1745, I received a letter from the Marquis of Annandale,
inviting me to come and live with him in England; I found
also that the friends and family of that young nobleman were
desirous of putting him under my care and direction, for the
state of his mind and health required it. I lived with him a

twelvemonth. My appointments during that time made a considerable accession to my small fortune. I then received an invitation from General St. Clair to attend him as a secretary to his expedition, which was at first meant against Canada, but ended in an incursion on the coast of France. Next year, to wit, 1747, I received an invitation from the General to attend him in the same station in his military embassy to the courts of Vienna and Turin. I then wore the uniform of an officer, and was introduced at these courts as aide-de-camp to the General, along with Sir Harry Erskine and Captain Grant, now General Grant. These two years were almost the only interruptions which my studies have received during the course of my life. I passed them agreeably and in good company; and my appointments, with my frugality, had made me reach a fortune which I called independent, though most of my friends were inclined to smile when I said so; in short, I was now master of near a thousand pounds.

I had always entertained a notion that my want of success in publishing the *Treatise of Human Nature* had proceeded more from the manner than the matter, and that I had been guilty of a very usual indiscretion in going to the press too early. I therefore cast the first part of that work anew in the *Inquiry concerning Human Understanding*, which was published while I was at Turin. But this piece was at first little more successful than the *Treatise of Human Nature*. On my return from Italy, I had the mortification to find all England in a ferment on account of Dr. Middleton's *Free Inquiry*, while my performance was entirely overlooked and neglected. A new edition, which had been published at London, of my *Essays, Moral and Political* met not with a much better reception.

Such is the force of natural temper that these disappointments made little or no impression on me. I went down in 1749 and lived two years with my brother at his country house, for my mother was now dead. I there composed the second part of my *Essays*, which I called *Political Discourses*, and also my *Inquiry concerning the Principles of Morals*, which is another part of my *Treatise* that I cast anew. Meanwhile, my bookseller, A. Millar, informed me that my former publications (all but the unfortunate *Treatise*) were beginning to be the subject of conversation, that the sale of them was gradually increasing, and that new editions were demanded. Answers by Reverends and Right Reverends came out two or three in a year, and I found, by Dr. Warburton's railing, that the books were beginning to be esteemed in good company. However, I had fixed a resolution which I inflexibly maintained, never to reply to anybody; and not being very irascible in my temper, I have easily kept myself clear of all literary squabbles. These symptoms of a rising reputation gave me encouragement, as I was ever more disposed to see the favorable than unfavorable side of things, a turn of mind which it is more happy to possess than to be born to an estate of ten thousand a year.

In 1751, I removed from the country to the town, the true scene for a man of letters. In 1752 were published at Edinburgh, where I then lived, my *Political Discourses*, the only work of mine that was successful on the first publication. It was well received abroad and at home. In the same year was published at London my *Inquiry concerning the Principles of Morals*, which in my own opinion (who ought not to judge on that subject) is of all my writings, historical, philosophical, or literary, incomparably the best. It came unnoticed and unobserved into the world.

In 1752, the Faculty of Advocates chose me their librarian, an office from which I received little or no emolument, but which gave me the command of a large library. I then formed the plan of writing the *History of England;* but being frightened with the notion of continuing a narrative through a period of 1700 years, I commenced with the accession of the House of Stuart, an epoch when, I thought, the misrepresentations of faction began chiefly to take place. I was, I own, sanguine in my expectations of the success of this work. I thought that I was the only historian that had at once neglected present power, interest, and authority, and the cry of popular prejudices; and as the subject was suited to every capacity, I expected proportional applause. But miserable was my disappointment: I was assailed by one cry of reproach, disapprobation, and even detestation; English, Scotch, and Irish, Whig and Tory, Churchman and Sectary,

Freethinker and Religionist, Patriot and Courtier united in their rage against the man who had presumed to shed a generous tear for the fate of Charles I and the Earl of Strafford; and after the first ebullitions of their fury were over, what was still more mortifying, the book seemed to sink into oblivion. Mr. Millar told me that in a twelvemonth he sold only forty-five copies of it. I scarcely, indeed, heard of one man in the three kingdoms, considerable for rank or letters, that could endure the book. I must only except the primate of England, Dr. Herring, and the primate of Ireland, Dr. Stone, which seem two odd exceptions. These dignified prelates separately sent me messages not to be discouraged.

I was however, I confess, discouraged; and had not the war been at that time breaking out between France and England, I had certainly retired to some provincial town of the former kingdom, have changed my name, and never more have returned to my native country. But as this scheme was not now practicable, and the subsequent volume was considerably advanced, I resolved to pick up courage and to persevere.

In this interval, I published at London my *Natural History of Religion*, along with some other small pieces. Its public entry was rather obscure, except only that Dr. Hurd wrote a pamphlet against it, with all the illiberal petulance, arrogance, and scurrility which distinguish the Warburtonian school. This pamphlet gave me some consolation for the otherwise indifferent reception of my performance.

In 1756, two years after the fall of the first volume, was published the second volume of my *History*, containing the period from the death of Charles I till the Revolution. This performance happened to give less displeasure to the Whigs, and was better received. It not only rose itself, but helped to buoy up its unfortunate brother.

But though I had been taught by experience that the Whig party were in possession of bestowing all places, both in the state and in literature, I was so little inclined to yield to their senseless clamor that in above a hundred alterations, which further study, reading, or reflection engaged me to make in the reigns of the two first Stuarts, I have made all of them invariably to the Tory side. It is ridiculous to consider the English constitution before that period as a regular plan of liberty.

In 1759, I published my *History of the House of Tudor.* The clamor against this performance was almost equal to that against the *History* of the two first Stuarts. The reign of Elizabeth was particularly obnoxious. But I was now callous against the impressions of public folly, and continued very peaceably and contentedly in my retreat at Edinburgh to finish, in two volumes, the more early part of the English *History,* which I gave to the public in 1761, with tolerable, and but tolerable, success.

But, notwithstanding this variety of winds and seasons to which my writings had been exposed, they had still been making such advances that the copy-money given me by the booksellers much exceeded anything formerly known in England; I was become not only independent but opulent. I retired to my native country of Scotland, determined never more to set my foot out of it, and retaining the satisfaction of never having preferred a request to one great man, or even making advances of friendship to any of them. As I was now turned to fifty, I thought of passing all the rest of my life in this philosophical manner, when I received, in 1763, an invitation from the Earl of Hertford, with whom I was not in the least acquainted, to attend him on his embassy to Paris, with a near prospect of being appointed secretary to the embassy, and, in the meanwhile, of performing the functions of that office. This offer, however inviting, I at first declined, both because I was reluctant to begin connections with the great and because I was afraid that the civilities and gay company of Paris would prove disagreeable to a person of my age and humor; but on his Lordship's repeating the invitation, I accepted of it. I have every reason, both of pleasure and interest, to think myself happy in my connections with that nobleman, as well as afterwards with his brother, General Conway.

Those who have not seen the strange effects of modes will never imagine the reception I met with at Paris from men and women of all ranks and stations. The more I resiled from their excessive civilities, the more I was loaded with them. There is, however, a real satisfaction in living at Paris, from the great number of sensible, knowing, and polite company with which that city abounds, above all places in the universe. I thought once of settling there for life.

I was appointed secretary to the embassy; and, in summer 1765, Lord Hertford left me, being appointed Lord Lieutenant of Ireland. I was *chargé d'affaires* till the arrival of the Duke of Richmond, toward the end of the year. In the beginning of 1766, I left Paris, and next summer went to Edinburgh, with the same view as formerly, of burying myself in a philosophical retreat. I returned to that place, not richer, but with much more money and a much larger income, by means of Lord Hertford's friendship, than I left it; and I was desirous of trying what superfluity could produce, as I had formerly made an experiment of a competency. But, in 1767, I received from Mr. Conway an invitation to be Undersecretary; and this invitation both the character of the person and my connections with Lord Hertford prevented me from declining. I returned to Edinburgh in 1769, very opulent (for I possessed a revenue of £1000 a year), healthy, and though somewhat stricken in years, with the prospect of enjoying long my ease and of seeing the increase of my reputation.

In spring 1775, I was struck with a disorder in my bowels, CANCER? which at first gave me no alarm, but has since, as I apprehend it, become mortal and incurable. I now reckon upon a speedy dissolution. I have suffered very little pain from my disorder, and what is more strange, have, notwithstanding the great decline of my person, never suffered a moment's abatement of my spirits, insomuch that were I to name the period of my life which I should most choose to pass over again, I might be tempted to point to this later period. I possess the same order as ever in study, and the same gaiety in company. I consider, besides, that a man of sixty-five, by dying, cuts off only a few years of infirmities; and though I see many symptoms of my literary reputation's breaking out at last with additional luster, I knew that I could have but few years to enjoy it. It is difficult to be more detached from life than I am at present.

To conclude historically with my own character, I am, or rather was (for that is the style I must now use in speaking

of myself, which emboldens me the more to speak my sentiments)—I was, I say, a man of mild dispositions, of command
of temper, of an open, social, and cheerful humor, capable of
attachment but little susceptible of enmity, and of great
moderation in all my passions. Even my love of literary fame,
my ruling passion, never soured my temper, notwithstanding
my frequent disappointments. My company was not unaccept-
able to the young and careless, as well as to the studious and
literary; and as I took a particular pleasure in the company
of modest women, I had no reason to be displeased with the
reception I met with from them. In a word, though most men
anywise eminent have found reason to complain of calumny, I
never was touched or even attacked by her baleful tooth; and
though I wantonly exposed myself to the rage of both civil
and religious factions, they seemed to be disarmed in my behalf of their wonted fury. My friends never had occasion to
vindicate any one circumstance of my character and conduct;
not but that the zealots, we may well suppose, would have
been glad to invent and propagate any story to my disadvantage, but they could never find any which they thought
would wear the face of probability. I cannot say there is no
vanity in making this funeral oration of myself, but I hope it
is not a misplaced one; and this is a matter of fact which is
easily cleared and ascertained.

April 18, 1776.

A TREATISE

OF

HUMAN

NATURE

A

TREATISE

O F

Human Nature:

B E I N G

An ATTEMPT to introduce the experimental Method of Reasoning

I N T O

MORAL SUBJECTS.

Rara temporum felicitas, ubi sentire, quæ velis; & quæ
sentias, dicere licet.   TACIT.

VOL. I.

OF THE
UNDERSTANDING.

L O N D O N:
Printed for JOHN NOON, at the *White-Hart,* near
Mercer's-Chapel in *Cheapside.*

MDCCXXXIX.

ADVERTISEMENT TO BOOKS I AND II

MY design in the present work is sufficiently explained in the Introduction. *The reader must only observe that all the subjects I have there planned out to myself are not treated of in these two volumes. The subjects of the* understanding *and* passions *make a complete chain of reasoning by themselves, and I was willing to take advantage of this natural division in order to try the taste of the public. If I have the good fortune to meet with success, I shall proceed to the examination of* morals, politics, *and* criticism, *which will complete this* Treatise of Human Nature. *The approbation of the public I consider as the greatest reward of my labors, but am determined to regard its judgment, whatever it be, as my best instruction.*

THE
CONTENTS.

Part IV.

OF THE SKEPTICAL AND OTHER SYSTEMS OF PHILOSOPHY.

BOOK II.

OF THE PASSIONS.

Part I.

OF PRIDE AND HUMILITY.

Part II.
OF LOVE AND HATRED.

Part III.
OF THE WILL AND DIRECT PASSIONS.

BOOK III.
OF MORALS.

Part I.
OF VIRTUE AND VICE IN GENERAL.

Part II.
OF JUSTICE AND INJUSTICE.

Part III.
OF THE OTHER VIRTUES AND VICES.

INTRODUCTION

NOTHING IS MORE usual and more natural for those who pretend to discover anything new to the world in philosophy and the sciences than to insinuate the praises of their own systems by decrying all those which have been advanced before them. And indeed were they content with lamenting that ignorance which we still lie under in the most important questions that can come before the tribunal of human reason, there are few who have an acquaintance with the sciences that would not readily agree with them. It is easy for one of judgment and learning to perceive the weak foundation even of those systems which have obtained the greatest credit, and have carried their pretensions highest to accurate and profound reasoning. Principles taken upon trust, consequences lamely deduced from them, want of coherence in the parts and of evidence in the whole, these are everywhere to be met with in the systems of the most eminent philosophers, and seem to have drawn disgrace upon philosophy itself.

Nor is there required such profound knowledge to discover the present imperfect condition of the sciences, but even the rabble without doors may judge from the noise and clamor which they hear that all goes not well within. There is nothing which is not the subject of debate, and in which men of learning are not of contrary opinions. The most trivial question escapes not our controversy, and in the most momentous we are not able to give any certain decision. Disputes are multiplied, as if everything was uncertain, and these disputes are managed with the greatest warmth, as if everything was certain. Amidst all this bustle it is not reason which carries the prize, but eloquence, and no man needs ever despair of gaining proselytes to the most extravagant hypothesis who has art enough to represent it in any favorable colors. The victory is not gained by the men at arms, who manage the pike and the sword, but by the trumpeters, drummers, and musicians of the army.

From hence in my opinion arises that common prejudice against metaphysical reasonings of all kinds, even among those who profess themselves scholars, and have a just value for every other part of literature. By metaphysical reasonings they do not understand those on any particular branch of science, but every kind of argument which is any way abstruse, and requires some attention to be comprehended. We have so often lost our labor in such researches that we commonly reject them without hesitation, and resolve, if we must forever be a prey to errors and delusions, that they shall at least be natural and entertaining. And indeed nothing but the most determined skepticism, along with a great degree of indolence, can justify this aversion to metaphysics. For if truth be at all within the reach of human capacity, it is certain it must lie very deep and abstruse, and to hope we shall arrive at it without pains, while the greatest geniuses have failed with the utmost pains, must certainly be esteemed sufficiently vain and presumptuous. I pretend to no such advantage in the philosophy I am going to unfold, and would esteem it a strong presumption against it, were it so very easy and obvious.

It is evident that all the sciences have a relation, greater or less, to human nature, and that however wide any of them may seem to run from it, they still return back by one passage or another. Even *mathematics, natural philosophy,* and *natural religon* are in some measure dependent on the science of MAN, since they lie under the cognizance of men and are judged of by their powers and faculties. It is impossible to tell what changes and improvements we might make in these sciences were we thoroughly acquainted with the extent and force of human understanding, and could we explain the nature of the ideas we employ and of the operations we perform in our reasonings. And these improvements are the more to be hoped for in natural religion, as it is not content with instructing us in the nature of superior powers but carries its views further, to their disposition towards us and our duties towards them, and consequently we ourselves are not only the beings that reason, but also one of the objects concerning which we reason.

If therefore the sciences of mathematics, natural philosophy, and natural religion have such a dependence on the knowledge of man, what may be expected in the other sciences, whose connection with human nature is more close and intimate? The sole end of logic is to explain the principles and operations of our reasoning faculty and the nature of our ideas; morals and criticism regard our tastes and sentiments; and politics consider men as united in society and dependent on each other. In these four sciences of *logic*, *morals*, *criticism*, and *politics* is comprehended almost everything which it can any way import us to be acquainted with, or which can tend either to the improvement or ornament of the human mind.

Here then is the only expedient from which we can hope for success in our philosophical reasearches, to leave the tedious lingering method which we have hitherto followed, and instead of taking now and then a castle or village on the frontier, to march up directly to the capital or center of these sciences, to human nature itself, which being once masters of, we may everywhere else hope for an easy victory. From this station we may extend our conquests over all those sciences which more intimately concern human life, and may afterwards proceed at leisure to discover more fully those which are the objects of pure curiosity. There is no question of importance whose decision is not comprised in the science of man, and there is none which can be decided with any certainty before we become acquainted with that science. In pretending therefore to explain the principles of human nature, we in effect propose a complete system of the sciences, built on a foundation almost entirely new, and the only one upon which they can stand with any security.

And as the science of man is the only solid foundation for the other sciences, so the only solid foundation we can give to this science itself must be laid on experience and observation. It is no astonishing reflection to consider that the application of experimental philosophy to moral subjects should come after that to natural at the distance of above a whole century, since we find in fact that there was about the same interval between the origins of these sciences, and that reckoning from THALES to SOCRATES the space of time is nearly equal to that between my Lord BACON[1] and some late philosophers in *England,* who have begun to put the science of man on a new footing, and have engaged the attention and excited the curiosity of the public. So true it is, that however other nations may rival us in poetry and excel us in some other agreeable arts, the improvements in reason and philosophy can only be owing to a land of toleration and of liberty.

Nor ought we to think that this latter improvement in the science of man will do less honor to our native country than the former in natural philosophy, but ought rather to esteem it a greater glory, upon account of the greater importance of that science, as well as the necessity it lay under of such a reformation. For to me it seems evident that the essence of the mind being equally unknown to us with that of external bodies, it must be equally impossible to form any notion of its power and qualities otherwise than from careful and exact experiments, and the observation of those particular effects which result from its different circumstances and situations. And though we must endeavor to render all our principles as universal as possible by tracing up our experiments to the utmost and explaining all effects from the simplest and fewest causes, it is still certain we cannot go beyond experience, and any hypothesis that pretends to discover the ultimate original qualities of human nature ought at first to be rejected as presumptuous and chimerical.

I do not think a philosopher who would apply himself so earnestly to the explaining the ultimate principles of the soul would show himself a great master in that very science of human nature which he pretends to explain, or very knowing in what is naturally satisfactory to the mind of man. For nothing is more certain than that despair has almost the same effect upon us with enjoyment, and that we are no sooner acquainted with the impossibility of satisfying any desire than the desire itself vanishes. When we see that we have

[1] Mr. *Locke,* by Lord *Shaftesbury,* Dr. *Mandeville,* Mr. *Hutcheson,* Dr. *Butler,* etc.

arrived at the utmost extent of human reason we sit down contented, though we be perfectly satisfied in the main of our ignorance, and perceive that we can give no reason for our most general and most refined principles beside our experience of their reality, which is the reason of the mere vulgar, and what it required no study at first to have discovered for the most particular and most extraordinary phenomenon. And as this impossibility of making any further progress is enough to satisfy the reader, so the writer may derive a more delicate satisfaction from the free confession of his ignorance, and from his prudence in avoiding that error, into which so many have fallen, of imposing their conjectures and hypotheses on the world for the most certain principles. When this mutual contentment and satisfaction can be obtained between the master and scholar, I know not what more we can require of our philosophy.

But if this impossibility of explaining ultimate principles should be esteemed a defect in the science of man, I will venture to affirm that it is a defect common to it with all the sciences and all the arts in which we can employ ourselves, whether they be such as are cultivated in the schools of the philosophers or practiced in the shops of the meanest artisans. None of them can go beyond experience, or establish any principles which are not founded on that authority. Moral philosophy has, indeed, this peculiar disadvantage, which is not found in natural, that in collecting its experiments it cannot make them purposely, with premeditation, and after such a manner as to satisfy itself concerning every particular difficulty which may arise. When I am at a loss to know the effects of one body upon another in any situation, I need only put them in that situation and observe what results from it. But should I endeavor to clear up after the same manner any doubt in moral philosophy by placing myself in the same case with that which I consider, it is evident this reflection and premeditation would so disturb the operation of my natural principles as must render it impossible to form any just conclusion from the phenomenon. We must therefore glean up our experiments in this science from a cautious observation of human life, and take them as they appear in the common course of the world, by men's behavior in company, in affairs, and in their pleasures. Where experiments of this kind are judiciously collected and compared, we may hope to establish on them a science which will not be inferior in certainty and will be much superior in utility to any other of human comprehension.

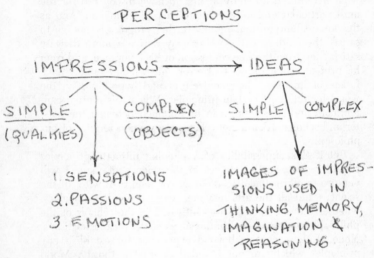

PERCEPTIONS

IMPRESSIONS ⟶ IDEAS

SIMPLE (QUALITIES) | COMPLEX (OBJECTS)

SIMPLE | COMPLEX

1. SENSATIONS
2. PASSIONS
3. EMOTIONS

IMAGES OF IMPRESSIONS USED IN THINKING, MEMORY, IMAGINATION & REASONING

PRINCIPLES:

(1) SIMPLE IMPRESSIONS ALWAYS PRECEED SIMPLE IDEAS & ARE IN 1 TO 1 CORRESPONDENCE.

(2) THEY DIFFER ONLY BY THEIR DEGREE OF FORCE & LIVILINESS.

(3) COMPLEX IMPRESSIONS & THEIR IDEAS ARE NOT ONE TO ONE

(4) IMPRESSIONS ALWAYS PRODUCE THEIR CORRESPONDING IDEAS, BUT IDEAS NEVE PRODUCE IMPRESSIONS.

A TREATISE OF HUMAN NATURE

BOOK I.
OF THE UNDERSTANDING

Part I.
OF IDEAS: THEIR ORIGIN,
COMPOSITION, CONNECTION,
ABSTRACTION, etc.

Section I.
OF THE ORIGIN OF OUR IDEAS

ALL THE PERCEPTIONS of the human mind resolve themselves into two distinct kinds, which I shall call IMPRESSIONS and IDEAS. The difference between these consists in the degrees of force and liveliness with which they strike upon the mind, and make their way into our thought or consciousness. Those perceptions which enter with most force and violence we may name *impressions*, and under this name I comprehend all our sensations, passions, and emotions, as they make their first appearance in the soul. By *ideas* I mean the faint images of these in thinking and reasoning, such as, for instance, are all the perceptions excited by the present discourse, excepting only those which arise from the sight and touch, and excepting the immediate pleasure or uneasiness it may occasion. I believe it will not be very necessary to employ many words in explaining this distinction. Everyone of himself will readily perceive the difference between feeling and thinking. The common degrees of these are easily distinguished, though it is not impossible but in particular instances they may very nearly approach to each other. Thus in sleep, in a fever, in madness, or in any very violent emotions of soul, our ideas may approach to our impressions, as on the other hand it sometimes happens that our impressions are so faint and low that we cannot distinguish them from our ideas. But notwithstanding this near resemblance in a few instances, they are in general so very different that no one can make a scruple to rank them under distinct heads, and assign to each a peculiar name to mark the difference.[1]

There is another division of our perceptions which it will be convenient to observe, and which extends itself both to our impressions and ideas. This division is into SIMPLE and COMPLEX. Simple perceptions or impressions and ideas are such as admit of no distinction nor separation. The complex are the contrary to these, and may be distinguished into parts. Though a particular color, taste, and smell are qualities all united together in this apple, it is easy to perceive they are not the same, but are at least distinguishable from each other.

Having by these divisions given an order and arrangement to our objects, we may now apply ourselves to consider with the more accuracy their qualities and relations. The first circumstance that strikes my eye is the great resemblance between our impressions and ideas in every other particular except their degree of force and vivacity. The one seem to be in a manner the reflection of the other, so that all the percep-

---

[1] I here make use of these terms, *impression* and *idea*, in a sense different from what is usual, and I hope this liberty will be allowed me. Perhaps I rather restore the word *idea* to its original sense, from which Mr. *Locke* had perverted it in making it stand for all our perceptions. By the term of *impression* I would not be understood to express the manner in which our lively perceptions are produced in the soul, but merely the perceptions themselves, for which there is no particular name either in the *English* or any other language that I know of.

tions of the mind are double, and appear both as impressions and ideas. When I shut my eyes and think of my chamber, the ideas I form are exact representations of the impressions I felt, nor is there any circumstance of the one which is not to be found in the other. In running over my other perceptions, I find still the same resemblance and representation. Ideas and impressions appear always to correspond to each other. This circumstance seems to me remarkable, and engages my attention for a moment.

Upon a more accurate survey I find I have been carried away too far by the first appearance, and that I must make use of the distinction of perceptions into *simple* and *complex* to limit this general decision, *that all our ideas and impressions are resembling.* I observe that many of our complex ideas never had impressions that corresponded to them, and that many of our complex impressions never are exactly copied in ideas. I can imagine to myself such a city as the *New Jerusalem,* whose pavement is gold and walls are rubies, though I never saw any such. I have seen *Paris,* but shall I affirm I can form such an idea of that city as will perfectly represent all its streets and houses in their real and just proportions?

I perceive, therefore, that though there is in general a great resemblance between our *complex* impressions and ideas, yet the rule is not universally true that they are exact copies of each other. We may next consider how the case stands with our *simple* perceptions. After the most accurate examination of which I am capable, I venture to affirm that the rule here holds without any exception, and that every simple idea has a simple impression which resembles it, and every simple impression a correspondent idea. That idea of red which we form in the dark, and that impression which strikes our eyes in sunshine, differ only in degree, not in nature. That the case is the same with all our simple impressions and ideas it is impossible to prove by a particular enumeration of them. Everyone may satisfy himself in this point by running over as many as he pleases. But if anyone should deny this universal resemblance, I know no way of convincing him but by desiring him to show a simple impression that has not a correspondent idea, or a simple idea that has not a correspondent impression. If he does not answer this challenge, as it is certain he cannot, we may from his silence and our own observation establish our conclusion.

Thus we find that all simple ideas and impressions resemble each other, and as the complex are formed from them, we may affirm in general that these two species of perception are exactly correspondent. Having discovered this relation, which requires no further examination, I am curious to find some other of their qualities. Let us consider how they stand with regard to their existence, and which of the impressions and ideas are causes and which effects.

The *full* examination of this question is the subject of the present treatise, and therefore we shall here content ourselves with establishing one general proposition, *that all our simple ideas in their first appearance are derived from simple impressions which are correspondent to them, and which they exactly represent.*

In seeking for phenomena to prove this proposition, I find only those of two kinds, but in each kind the phenomena are obvious, numerous, and conclusive. I first make myself certain, by a new review, of what I have already asserted, that every simple impression is attended with a correspondent idea, and every simple idea with a correspondent impression. From this constant conjunction of resembling perceptions I immediately conclude that there is a great connection between our correspondent impressions and ideas, and that the existence of the one has a considerable influence upon that of the other. Such a constant conjunction, in such an infinite number of instances, can never arise from chance, but clearly proves a dependence of the impressions on the ideas, or of the ideas on the impressions. That I may know on which side this dependence lies, I consider the order of their *first appearance,* and find by constant experience that the simple impressions always take the precedence of their correspondent ideas, but never appear in the contrary order. To give a child an idea of scarlet or orange, of sweet or bitter, I present the objects, or in other words, convey to him these impressions, but proceed not so absurdly as to endeavor to produce the impressions by exciting the ideas. Our ideas upon their appearance produce not their correspondent impressions, nor do we perceive any color or feel any sensation merely upon thinking of them. On the other hand, we find that any impression either of the mind or body is constantly followed by an idea which resembles it, and is only different in the degrees of force and liveliness. The constant conjunction of our resembling perceptions is a convincing proof that the one are the causes of the other, and this priority of the impressions is an equal proof that our impressions are the causes of our ideas, not our ideas of our impressions.

To confirm this I consider another plain and convincing phenomenon, which is that wherever by any accident the faculties which give rise to any impressions are obstructed in their operations, as when one is born blind or deaf, not only the impressions are lost, but also their correspondent ideas, so that there never appear in the mind the least traces of either of them. Nor is this only true where the organs of sensation are entirely destroyed, but likewise where they have never been put in action to produce a particular impression. We cannot form to ourselves a just idea of the taste of a pineapple without having actually tasted it.

There is however one contradictory phenomenon, which may prove that it is not absolutely impossible for ideas to go before their correspondent impressions. I believe it will readily be allowed that the several distinct ideas of colors, which enter by the eyes, or those of sounds, which are conveyed by the hearing, are really different from each other, though at the same time resembling. Now if this be true of different colors, it must be no less so of the different shades of the same color, that each of them produces a distinct idea, independent of the rest. For if this should be denied, it is possible, by the continual gradation of shades, to run a color insensibly into what is most remote from it, and if you will not allow any of the means to be different, you cannot without absurdity deny the extremes to be the same. Suppose therefore a person to have enjoyed his sight for thirty years, and to have become perfectly well acquainted with colors of all kinds, excepting one particular shade of blue, for instance, which it never has been his fortune to meet with. Let all the different shades of that color except that single one be placed before him, descending gradually from the deepest to the lightest; it is plain that he will perceive a blank where that shade is wanting, and will be sensible that there is a greater distance in that place between the contiguous colors than in any other. Now I ask whether it is possible for him, from his own imagination, to supply this deficiency, and raise up to himself the idea of that particular shade though it had never been conveyed to him by his senses? I believe there are few but will be of opinion that he can, and this may serve as a proof that the simple ideas are not always derived from the correspondent impressions, though the instance is so particular and singular that it is scarce worth our observing, and does not merit that for it alone we should alter our general maxim.

But besides this exception, it may not be amiss to remark on this head that the principle of the priority of impressions to ideas must be understood with another limitation, viz., that as our ideas are images of our impressions, so we can form secondary ideas which are images of the primary, as appears from this very reasoning concerning them. This is not, properly speaking, an exception to the rule so much as an explanation of it. Ideas produce the images of themselves in new ideas, but as the first ideas are supposed to be derived from impressions, it still remains true that all our simple ideas proceed either mediately or immediately from their correspondent impressions.

This then is the first principle I establish in the science of human nature, nor ought we to despise it because of the simplicity of its appearance. For it is remarkable that the present question concerning the precedency of our impressions or ideas is the same with what has made so much noise in other terms, when it has been disputed whether there be any *innate ideas,* or whether all ideas be derived from sensation and reflection. We may observe that in order to prove the ideas of extension and color not to be innate, philosophers do nothing but show that they are conveyed by our senses. To prove the ideas of passion and desire not to be innate they observe that we have a preceding experience of these emotions in ourselves. Now if we carefully examine these arguments, we shall find that they prove nothing but that ideas are preceded by other more lively perceptions, from which they are derived and which they represent. I hope this clear stating of the question will remove all disputes concerning it, and will render this principle of more use in our reasonings than it seems hitherto to have been.

Section II.

DIVISION OF THE SUBJECT

Since it appears that our simple impressions are prior to their correspondent ideas, and that the exceptions are very rare, method seems to require we should examine our impressions before we consider our ideas. Impressions may be divided into two kinds, those of SENSATION and those of REFLECTION. The first kind arises in the soul originally, from unknown causes. The second is derived in a great measure from our ideas, and that in the following order. An impression first strikes upon the senses and makes us perceive heat or cold, thirst or hunger, pleasure or pain of some kind or other. Of this impression there is a copy taken by the mind, which remains after the impression ceases, and this we call an idea. This idea of pleasure or pain, when it returns upon the soul, produces the new impressions of desire and aversion, hope and fear, which may properly be called impressions of reflection, because derived from it. These again are copied by the memory and imagination and become ideas, which perhaps in their turn give rise to other impressions and ideas. So that the impressions of reflection are only antecedent to their correspondent ideas, but posterior to those of sensation, and derived from them. The examination of our sensations belongs more to anatomists and natural philosophers than to moralists, and therefore shall not at present be entered upon. And as the impressions of reflection, viz., passions, desires, and emotions, which principally deserve our attention, arise mostly from ideas, it will be necessary to reverse that method which at first sight seems most natural, and in order to explain the nature and principles of the human mind, give a particular account of ideas before we proceed to impressions. For this reason I have here chosen to begin with ideas.

Passions, desires & emotion are, taken as a whole, impressions of reflection

Section III.

OF THE IDEAS OF THE MEMORY AND IMAGINATION

We find by experience that when any impression has been present with the mind, it again makes its appearance there as an idea, and this it may do after two different ways: either when in its new appearance it retains a considerable degree of its first vivacity and is somewhat intermediate between an impression and an idea, or when it entirely loses that vivacity and is a perfect idea. The faculty by which we repeat our impressions in the first manner is called the MEMORY, and the other the IMAGINATION. It is evident at first sight that the ideas of the memory are much more lively and strong than those of the imagination, and that the former faculty paints its objects in more distinct colors than any which are employed by the latter. When we remember any past event, the idea of it flows in upon the mind in a forcible manner, whereas in the imagination the perception is faint and languid, and cannot without difficulty be preserved by the mind steady and uniform for any considerable time. Here then is a sensible difference between one species of ideas and another. But of this more fully hereafter.[1]

There is another difference between these two kinds of ideas which is no less evident, namely that though neither the ideas of the memory nor imagination, neither the lively nor faint ideas, can make their appearance in the mind unless their correspondent impressions have gone before to prepare the way for them; yet the imagination is not restrained to the same order and form with the original impressions, while the memory is in a manner tied down in that respect, without any power of variation.

It is evident that the memory preserves the original form in which its objects were presented, and that wherever we depart from it in recollecting anything, it proceeds from some

[1] Part III, Section V.

defect or imperfection in that faculty. An historian may, perhaps, for the more convenient carrying on of his narration, relate an event before another, to which it was in fact posterior; but then he takes notice of this disorder, if he be exact, and by that means replaces the idea in its due position. It is the same case in our recollection of those places and persons with which we were formerly acquainted. The chief exercise of the memory is not to preserve the simple ideas, but their order and position. In short, this principle is supported by such a number of common and vulgar phenomena that we may spare ourselves the trouble of insisting on it any further.

The same evidence follows us in our second principle, *of the liberty of the imagination to transpose and change its ideas*. The fables we meet with in poems and romances put this entirely out of question. Nature there is totally confounded, and nothing mentioned but winged horses, fiery dragons, and monstrous giants. Nor will this liberty of the fancy appear strange when we consider that all our ideas are copied from our impressions, and that there are not any two impressions which are perfectly inseparable. Not to mention that this is an evident consequence of the division of ideas into simple and complex. Wherever the imagination perceives a difference among ideas, it can easily produce a separation.

Section IV.

OF THE CONNECTION OR ASSOCIATION
OF IDEAS

As all simple ideas may be separated by the imagination and may be united again in what form it pleases, nothing would be more unaccountable than the operations of that faculty were it not guided by some universal principles, which render it, in some measure, uniform with itself in all times and places. Were ideas entirely loose and unconnected, chance alone would join them, and it is impossible the same simple ideas should fall regularly into complex ones (as they commonly do) without some bond of union among them, some associating quality by which one idea naturally introduces another. This uniting principle among ideas is not to be considered as an inseparable connection, for that has been already excluded from the imagination; nor yet are we to conclude that without it the mind cannot join two ideas, for nothing is more free than that faculty; but we are only to regard it as a gentle force which commonly prevails, and as the cause why, among other things, languages so nearly correspond to each other, nature in a manner pointing out to every one those simple ideas which are most proper to be united into a complex one. The qualities from which this association arises, and by which the mind is after this manner conveyed from one idea to another, are three, viz., RESEMBLANCE, CONTIGUITY in time or place, and CAUSE and EFFECT.

I believe it will not be very necessary to prove that these qualities produce an association among ideas, and upon the appearance of one idea naturally introduce another. It is plain that in the course of our thinking and in the constant revolution of our ideas, our imagination runs easily from one idea to any other that *resembles* it, and that this quality alone is to the fancy a sufficient bond and association. It is likewise evident that as the senses, in changing their objects, are necessitated to change them regularly, and take them as they lie *contiguous* to each other, the imagination must by long custom acquire the same method of thinking, and run along the parts of space and time in conceiving its objects. As to the connection that is made by the relation of *cause and effect*, we shall have occasion afterwards to examine it to the bottom, and therefore shall not at present insist upon it. It is sufficient to observe that there is no relation which produces a stronger connection in the fancy and makes one idea more readily recall another than the relation of cause and effect between their objects.

That we may understand the full extent of these relations, we must consider that two objects are connected together in the imagination, not only when the one is immediately resembling, contiguous to, or the cause of the other, but also when there is interposed between them a third object which bears to both of them any of these relations. This may be carried on to a great length, though at the same time we may observe that each remove considerably weakens the relation. Cousins in the fourth degree are connected by *causation,* if I may be allowed to use that term, but not so closely as brothers, much less as child and parent. In general we may observe that all the relations of blood depend upon cause and effect, and are esteemed near or remote according to the number of connecting causes interposed between the persons.

Of the three relations above-mentioned this of causation is the most extensive. Two objects may be considered as placed in this relation, as well when one is the cause of any of the actions or motions of the other, as when the former is the cause of the existence of the latter. For as that action or motion is nothing but the object itself, considered in a certain light, and as the object continues the same in all its different situations, it is easy to imagine how such an influence of objects upon one another may connect them in the imagination.

We may carry this further and remark, not only that two objects are connected by the relation of cause and effect when the one produces a motion or any action in the other, but also when it has a power of producing it. And this we may observe to be the source of all the relations of interest and duty, by which men influence each other in society and are placed in the ties of government and subordination. A master is such-a-one as by his situation, arising either from force or agreement, has a power of directing in certain particulars the actions of another, whom we call servant. A judge is one who in all disputed cases can fix by his opinion the possession or property of anything between any members of the society. When a person is possessed of any power, there is no more required to convert it into action but the exertion of the will, and *that* in every case is considered as possible and in many as probable, especially in the case of authority, where the obedience of the subject is a pleasure and advantage to the superior.

These are therefore the principles of union or cohesion among our simple ideas, and in the imagination supply the place of that inseparable connection by which they are united in our memory. Here is a kind of ATTRACTION, which in the mental world will be found to have as extraordinary effects as in the natural, and to show itself in as many and as various forms. Its effects are everywhere conspicuous; but as to its causes, they are mostly unknown, and must be resolved into *original* qualities of human nature, which I pretend not to explain. Nothing is more requisite for a true philosopher than to restrain the intemperate desire of searching into causes, and having established any doctrine upon a sufficient number of experiments, rest contented with that, when he sees a further examination would lead him into obscure and uncertain speculations. In that case his inquiry would be much better employed in examining the effects than the causes of his principle.

Among the effects of this union or association of ideas, there are none more remarkable than those complex ideas which are the common subjects of our thoughts and reasoning, and generally arise from some principle of union among our simple ideas. These complex ideas may be divided into *relations, modes,* and *substances.* We shall briefly examine each of these in order, and shall subjoin some considerations concerning our *general* and *particular* ideas, before we leave the present subject, which may be considered as the elements of this philosophy.

Section V.

OF RELATIONS

The word RELATION is commonly used in two senses considerably different from each other. Either for that quality by which two ideas are connected together in the imagination and the one naturally introduces the other, after the manner above-explained, or for that particular circumstance in which, even upon the arbitrary union of two ideas in the fancy, we may think proper to compare them. In common language the former is always the sense in which we use the word relation, and it is only in philosophy that we extend it to mean any particular subject of comparison, without a connecting principle. Thus distance will be allowed by philosophers to be a true relation, because we acquire an idea of it by the comparing of objects. But in a common way we say *that nothing can be more distant than such or such things from each other, nothing can have less relation,* as if distance and relation were incompatible.

It may perhaps be esteemed an endless task to enumerate all those qualities which make objects admit of comparison, and by which the ideas of *philosophical* relation are produced. But if we diligently consider them, we shall find that without difficulty they may be comprised under seven general heads, which may be considered as the sources of all *philosophical* relation.

1. The first is *resemblance*, and this is a relation without which no philosophical relation can exist, since no objects will admit of comparison but what have some degree of resemblance. But though resemblance be necessary to all philosophical relation, it does not follow that it always produces a connection or association of ideas. When a quality becomes very general and is common to a great many individuals, it leads not the mind directly to any one of them, but by presenting at once too great a choice, does thereby prevent the imagination from fixing on any single object.

2. *Identity* may be esteemed a second species of relation. This relation I here consider as applied in its strictest sense to constant and unchangeable objects, without examining the nature and foundation of personal identity, which shall find its place afterwards. Of all relations the most universal is that of identity, being common to every being whose existence has any duration.

3. After identity the most universal and comprehensive relations are those of *space* and *time*, which are the sources of an infinite number of comparisons, such as *distant, contiguous, above, below, before, after,* etc.

4. All those objects which admit of *quantity* or *number* may be compared in that particular, which is another very fertile source of relation.

5. When any two objects possess the same *quality* in common, the *degrees* in which they possess it form a fifth species of relation. Thus of two objects which are both heavy, the one

may be either of greater or less weight than the other. Two
colors that are of the same kind may yet be of different
shades, and in that respect admit of comparison.

6. The relation of *contrariety* may at first sight be regarded
as an exception to the rule *that no relation of any kind can
subsist without some degree of resemblance.* But let us consider that no two ideas are in themselves contrary except
those of existence and non-existence, which are plainly resembling, as implying both of them an idea of the object,
though the latter excludes the object from all times and
places, in which it is supposed not to exist.

7. All other objects, such as fire and water, heat and cold,
are only found to be contrary from experience, and from the
contrariety of their *causes* or *effects,* which relation of cause
and effect is a seventh philosophical relation, as well as a natural one. The resemblance implied in this relation shall be
explained afterwards.

It might naturally be expected that I should join *difference* to the other relations. But that I consider rather as a
negation of relation than as anything real or positive. Difference is of two kinds, as opposed either to identity or resemblance. The first is called a difference of *number,* the other of
kind.

Section VI.

OF MODES AND SUBSTANCES

I would fain ask those philosophers who found so much
of their reasonings on the distinction of substance and accident and imagine we have clear ideas of each, whether the
idea of *substance* be derived from the impressions of sensation or reflection? If it be conveyed to us by our senses, I ask
which of them, and after what manner? If it be perceived by
the eyes, it must be a color, if by the ears, a sound, if by the
palate, a taste, and so of the other senses. But I believe none
will assert that substance is either a color or a sound, or a taste.
The idea of substance must therefore be derived from an

impression of reflection, if it really exist. But the impressions of reflection resolve themselves into our passions and emotions, none of which can possibly represent a substance. We have therefore no idea of substance, distinct from that of a collection of particular qualities, nor have we any other meaning when we either talk or reason concerning it.

The idea of a substance as well as that of a mode is nothing but a collection of simple ideas that are united by the imagination and have a particular name assigned them, by which we are able to recall, either to ourselves or others, that collection. But the difference between these ideas consists in this, that the particular qualities which form a substance are commonly referred to an unknown *something* in which they are supposed to inhere, or granting this fiction should not take place, are at least supposed to be closely and inseparably connected by the relations of contiguity and causation. The effect of this is that whatever new simple quality we discover to have the same connection with the rest, we immediately comprehend it among them, even though it did not enter into the first conception of the substance. Thus our idea of gold may at first be a yellow color, weight, malleableness, fusibility, but upon the discovery of its dissolubility in *aqua regia*, we join that to the other qualities, and suppose it to belong to the substance as much as if its idea had from the beginning made a part of the compound one. The principle of union, being regarded as the chief part of the complex idea, gives entrance to whatever quality afterwards occurs and is equally comprehended by it, as are the others which first presented themselves.

That this cannot take place in modes is evident from considering their nature. The simple ideas of which modes are formed either represent qualities which are not united by contiguity and causation but are dispersed in different subjects, or if they be all united together, the uniting principle is not regarded as the foundation of the complex idea. The idea of a dance is an instance of the first kind of modes, that of beauty of the second. The reason is obvious why such complex ideas cannot receive any new idea without changing the name which distinguishes the mode.

Section VII.

OF ABSTRACT IDEAS

A very material question has been started concerning *abstract* or *general* ideas, *whether they be general or particular in the mind's conception of them.* A great philosopher[1] has disputed the received opinion in this particular, and has asserted that all general ideas are nothing but particular ones annexed to a certain term, which gives them a more extensive signification and makes them recall upon occasion other individuals which are similar to them. As I look upon this to be one of the greatest and most valuable discoveries that has been made of late years in the republic of letters, I shall here endeavor to confirm it by some arguments which I hope will put it beyond all doubt and controversy.

It is evident that in forming most of our general ideas, if not all of them, we abstract from every particular degree of quantity and quality, and that an object ceases not to be of any particular species on account of every small alteration in its extension, duration, and other properties. It may therefore be thought that here is a plain dilemma, that decides concerning the nature of those abstract ideas which have afforded so much speculation to philosophers. The abstract idea of a man represents men of all sizes and all qualities, which it is concluded it cannot do but either by representing at once all possible sizes and all possible qualities, or by representing no particular one at all. Now it having been esteemed absurd to defend the former proposition, as implying an infinite capacity in the mind, it has been commonly inferred in favor of the latter, and our abstract ideas have been supposed to represent no particular degree either of quantity or quality. But that this inference is erroneous, I shall endeavor to make appear, *first,* by proving that it is utterly impossible to conceive any quantity or quality without forming a precise notion of its degrees; and *secondly* by showing that though the

[1] Dr. *Berkeley.*

capacity of the mind be not infinite, yet we can at once form a notion of all possible degrees of quantity and quality, in such a manner at least as, however imperfect, may serve all the purposes of reflection and conversation.

To begin with the first proposition, *that the mind cannot form any notion of quantity or quality without forming a precise notion of degrees of each,* we may prove this by the three following arguments. First, we have observed that whatever objects are different are distinguishable, and that whatever objects are distinguishable are separable by the thought and imagination. And we may here add that these propositions are equally true in the *inverse,* and that whatever objects are separable are also distinguishable, and that whatever objects are distinguishable are also different. For how is it possible we can separate what is not distinguishable, or distinguish what is not different? In order therefore to know whether abstraction implies a separation, we need only consider it in this view, and examine whether all the circumstances which we abstract from in our general ideas be such as are distinguishable and different from those which we retain as essential parts of them. But it is evident at first sight that the precise length of a line is not different nor distinguishable from the line itself, nor the precise degree of any quality from the quality. These ideas, therefore, admit no more of separation than they do of distinction and difference. They are consequently conjoined with each other in the conception, and the general idea of a line, notwithstanding all our abstractions and refinements, has in its appearance in the mind a precise degree of quantity and quality, however it may be made to represent others which have different degrees of both.

Secondly, it is confessed that no object can appear to the senses, or in other words that no impression can become present to the mind, without being determined in its degrees both of quantity and quality. The confusion in which impressions are sometimes involved proceeds only from their faintness and unsteadiness, not from any capacity in the mind to receive any impression which in its real existence has no particular degree nor proportion. That is a contradiction in terms, and even implies the flattest of all contradictions, *viz.,* that it is possible for the same thing both to be and not to be.

Now since all ideas are derived from impressions and are nothing but copies and representations of them, whatever is true of the one must be acknowledged concerning the other. Impressions and ideas differ only in their strength and vivacity. The foregoing conclusion is not founded on any particular degree of vivacity. It cannot therefore be affected by any variation in that particular. An idea is a weaker impression, and as a strong impression must necessarily have a determinate quantity and quality, the case must be the same with its copy or representative.

Thirdly, it is a principle generally received in philosophy that everything in nature is individual, and that it is utterly absurd to suppose a triangle really existent which has no precise proportion of sides and angles. If this therefore be absurd in *fact and reality*, it must also be absurd in *idea*, since nothing of which we can form a clear and distinct idea is absurd and impossible. But to form the idea of an object and to form an idea simply is the same thing, the reference of the idea to an object being an extraneous denomination of which in itself it bears no mark or character. Now as it is impossible to form an idea of an object that is possessed of quantity and quality, and yet is possessed of no precise degree of either, it follows that there is an equal impossibility of forming an idea that is not limited and confined in both these particulars. Abstract ideas are therefore in themselves individual, however they may become general in their representation. The image in the mind is only that of a particular object, though the application of it in our reasoning be the same as if it were universal.

This application of ideas beyond their nature proceeds from our collecting all their possible degrees of quantity and quality in such an imperfect manner as may serve the purposes of life, which is the second proposition I proposed to explain. When we have found a resemblance[1] among several

---

[1] It is evident that even different simple ideas may have a similarity or resemblance to each other; nor is it necessary that the point or circumstance of resemblance should be distinct or separable from that in which they differ. *Blue* and *green* are different simple ideas, but are more resembling than *blue* and *scarlet*, though their perfect simplicity excludes all possibility of separation or distinction. It

objects that often occur to us, we apply the same name to all of them, whatever differences we may observe in the degrees of their quantity and quality, and whatever other differences may appear among them. After we have acquired a custom of this kind, the hearing of that name revives the idea of one of these objects, and makes the imagination conceive it with all its particular circumstances and proportions. But as the same word is supposed to have been frequently applied to other individuals that are different in many respects from that idea which is immediately present to the mind, the word, not being able to revive the idea of all these individuals, only touches the soul, if I may be allowed so to speak, and revives that custom which we have acquired by surveying them. They are not really and in fact present to the mind, but only in power; nor do we draw them all out distinctly in the imagination, but keep ourselves in a readiness to survey any of them, as we may be prompted by a present design or necessity. The word raises up an individual idea, along with a certain custom, and that custom produces any other individual one for which we may have occasion. But as the production of all the ideas to which the name may be applied is in most cases impossible, we abridge that work by a more partial consideration, and find but few inconveniences to arise in our reasoning from that abridgment.

For this is one of the most extraordinary circumstances in the present affair, that after the mind has produced an individual idea upon which we reason, the attendant custom, revived by the general or abstract term, readily suggests any other individual, if by chance we form any reasoning that agrees not with it. Thus should we mention the word

---

is the same case with particular sounds and tastes and smells. These admit of infinite resemblances upon the general appearance and comparison, without having any common circumstance the same. And of this we may be certain, even from the very abstract terms *simple idea*. They comprehend all simple ideas under them. These resemble each other in their simplicity. And yet from their very nature, which excludes all composition, this circumstance in which they resemble, is not distinguishable nor separable from the rest. It is the same case with all the degrees in any quality. They are all resembling, and yet the quality, in any individual, is not distinct from the degree. [This note was first printed in the Appendix.—Ed.]

triangle, and form the idea of a particular equilateral one to correspond to it, and should we afterwards assert *that the three angles of a triangle are equal to each other,* the other individuals of a scalenum and isoceles, which we overlooked at first, immediately crowd in upon us, and make us perceive the falsehood of this proposition, though it be true with relation to that idea which we had formed. If the mind suggests not always these ideas upon occasion, it proceeds from some imperfection in its faculties, and such a one as is often the source of false reasoning and sophistry. But this is principally the case with those ideas which are abstruse and compounded. On other occasions the custom is more entire, and it is seldom we run into such errors.

Nay so entire is the custom, that the very same idea may be annexed to several different words, and may be employed in different reasonings without any danger of mistake. Thus the idea of an equilateral triangle of an inch perpendicular may serve us in talking of a figure, of a rectilineal figure, of a regular figure, of a triangle, and of an equilateral triangle. All these terms, therefore, are in this case attended with the same idea, but as they are wont to be applied in a greater or lesser compass, they excite their particular habits, and thereby keep the mind in a readiness to observe that no conclusion be formed contrary to any ideas which are usually comprised under them.

Before those habits have become entirely perfect, perhaps the mind may not be content with forming the idea of only one individual, but may run over several in order to make itself comprehend its own meaning, and the compass of that collection which it intends to express by the general term. That we may fix the meaning of the word figure, we may revolve in our mind the ideas of circles, squares, parallelograms, triangles of different sizes and proportions, and may not rest on one image or idea. However this may be, it is certain *that* we form the idea of individuals whenever we use any general term, *that* we seldom or never can exhaust these individuals, and *that* those which remain are only represented by means of that habit by which we recall them whenever any present occasion requires it. This then is the nature of our abstract ideas and general terms, and it is after this manner we account for the foregoing paradox, *that some ideas are particular in their nature, but general in their representation*. A particular idea becomes general by being annexed to a general term, that is, to a term which from a customary conjunction has a relation to many other particular ideas, and readily recalls them in the imagination.

The only difficulty that can remain on this subject must be with regard to that custom which so readily recalls every particular idea for which we may have occasion, and is excited by any word or sound to which we commonly annex it. The most proper method, in my opinion, of giving a satisfactory explication of this act of the mind is by producing other instances which are analogous to it, and other principles which facilitate its operation. To explain the ultimate causes of our mental actions is impossible. It is sufficient if we can give any satisfactory account of them from experience and analogy.

First then I observe that when we mention any great number, such as a thousand, the mind has generally no adequate idea of it, but only a power of producing such an idea by its adequate idea of the decimals under which the number is comprehended. This imperfection, however, in our ideas is never felt in our reasonings, which seems to be an instance parallel to the present one of universal ideas.

Secondly, we have several instances of habits which may be revived by one single word, as when a person who has by rote any periods of a discourse, or any number of verses, will be put in remembrance of the whole, which he is at a loss to recollect, by that single word or expression with which they begin.

Thirdly, I believe everyone who examines the situation of his mind in reasoning will agree with me, that we do not annex distinct and complete ideas to every term we make use of, and that in talking of *government, church, negotiation, conquest*, we seldom spread out in our minds all the simple ideas of which these complex ones are composed. It is however observable that notwithstanding this imperfection we may avoid talking nonsense on these subjects, and may perceive any repugnance among the ideas, as well as if we had a full comprehension of them. Thus if instead of saying *that in war the weaker have always recourse to negotiation,* we should say *that they have always recourse to conquest,* the custom which we have acquired of attributing certain relations to ideas still follows the words, and makes us immediately perceive the absurdity of that proposition, in the same manner as one particular idea may serve us in reasoning concerning other ideas, however different from it in several circumstances.

Fourthly, as the individuals are collected together and placed under a general term with a view to that resemblance which they bear to each other, this relation must facilitate their entrance in the imagination, and make them be suggested more readily upon occasion. And indeed if we consider the common progress of the thought, either in reflection or conversation, we shall find great reason to be satisfied in this particular. Nothing is more admirable than the readiness with which the imagination suggests its ideas, and presents them at the very instant in which they become necessary or useful. The fancy runs from one end of the universe to the other in collecting those ideas which belong to any subject. One would think the whole intellectual world of ideas was at once subjected to our view, and that we did nothing but pick out such as were most proper for our purpose. There may not, however, be any present beside those very ideas that are thus collected by a kind of magical faculty in the soul, which, though it be always most perfect in the greatest geniuses and is properly what we call a genius, is however inexplicable by the utmost efforts of human understanding.

Perhaps these four reflections may help to remove all difficulties to the hypothesis I have proposed concerning abstract ideas, so contrary to that which has hitherto prevailed in philosophy. But to tell the truth I place my chief confidence in what I have already proved concerning the impossibility of general ideas, according to the common method of explaining them. We must certainly seek some new system on this head, and there plainly is none beside what I have proposed. If ideas be particular in their nature and at the same time finite in their number, it is only by custom they can become general in their representation, and contain an infinite number of other ideas under them.

Before I leave this subject I shall employ the same principles to explain that *distinction of reason* which is so much talked of, and is so little understood, in the schools. Of this kind is the distinction between figure and the body figured, motion and the body moved. The difficulty of explaining this distinction arises from the principle above explained, *that all ideas which are different are separable.* For it follows from thence that if the figure be different from the body, their ideas must be separable as well as distinguishable; if they be not different, their ideas can neither be separable nor distinguishable. What then is meant by a distinction of reason, since it implies neither a difference nor separation?

To remove this difficulty we must have recourse to the foregoing explication of abstract ideas. It is certain that the mind would never have dreamed of distinguishing a figure from the body figured, as being in reality neither distinguishable nor different nor separable, did it not observe that even in this simplicity there might be contained many different resemblances and relations. Thus when a globe of white marble is presented, we receive only the impression of a white color disposed in a certain form, nor are we able to separate and distinguish the color from the form. But observing afterwards a globe of black marble and a cube of white, and comparing them with our former object, we find two separate resemblances in what formerly seemed, and really is, perfectly inseparable. After a little more practice of this kind, we begin to distinguish the figure from the color by a *distinction of reason;* that is, we consider the figure and color together, since they are in effect the same and undistinguishable, but still view them in different aspects according to the resemblances of which they are susceptible. When we would consider only the figure of the globe of white marble, we form in reality an idea both of the figure and color, but tacitly carry our eye to its resemblance with the globe of black marble. And in the same manner, when we would consider its color only, we turn our view to its resemblance with the cube of white marble. By this means we accompany our ideas with a kind of reflection, of which custom renders us, in a great measure, insensible. A person who desires us to consider the figure of a globe of white marble without thinking on its color desires an impossibility, but his meaning is that we should consider the color and figure together, but still keep in our eye the resemblance to the globe of black marble, or that to any other globe of whatever color or substance.

Part II.

OF THE IDEAS OF SPACE AND TIME

Section I.

OF THE INFINITE DIVISIBILITY OF OUR IDEAS OF SPACE AND TIME

WHATEVER HAS the air of a paradox and is contrary to the first and most unprejudiced notions of mankind is often greedily embraced by philosophers, as showing the superiority of their science, which could discover opinions so remote from vulgar conception. On the other hand, anything proposed to us which causes surprise and admiration gives such a satisfaction to the mind that it indulges itself in those agreeable emotions, and will never be persuaded that its pleasure is entirely without foundation. From these dispositions in philosophers and their disciples arises that mutual complaisance between them, while the former furnish such plenty of strange and unaccountable opinions, and the latter so readily believe them. Of this mutual complaisance I cannot give a more evident instance than in the doctrine of infinite divisibility, with the examination of which I shall begin this subject of the ideas of space and time.

It is universally allowed that the capacity of the mind is limited and can never attain a full and adequate conception of infinity, and though it were not allowed, it would be sufficiently evident from the plainest observation and experience. It is also obvious that whatever is capable of being divided *in infinitum* must consist of an infinite number of parts, and that it is impossible to set any bounds to the number of parts without setting bounds at the same time to the division. It requires scarce any induction to conclude from hence that the *idea* which we form of any finite quality is not infinitely divisible, but that by proper distinctions and separations we may run up this idea to inferior ones which will be perfectly simple and indivisible. In rejecting the infinite capacity of the mind, we suppose it may arrive at an end in the division of its ideas, nor are there any possible means of evading the evidence of this conclusion.

It is therefore certain that the imagination reaches a *minimum,* and may raise up to itself an idea of which it cannot conceive any subdivision, and which cannot be diminished without a total annihilation. When you tell me of the thousandth and ten thousandth part of a grain of sand, I have a distinct idea of these numbers and of their different proportions, but the images which I form in my mind to represent the things themselves are nothing different from each other, nor inferior to that image by which I represent the grain of sand itself, which is supposed so vastly to exceed them. What consists of parts is distinguishable into them, and what is distinguishable is separable. But whatever we may imagine of the thing, the idea of a grain of sand is not distinguishable, nor separable into twenty, much less into a thousand, ten thousand, or an infinite number of different ideas.

It is the same case with the impressions of the senses as with the ideas of the imagination. Put a spot of ink upon paper, fix your eye upon that spot, and retire to such a distance that at last you lose sight of it; it is plain that the moment before it vanished the image or impression was perfectly indivisible. It is not for want of rays of light striking on our eyes that the minute parts of distant bodies convey not any sensible impression, but because they are removed beyond that distance at which their impressions were reduced to a *minimum,* and were incapable of any further diminution. A microscope or telescope which renders them visible produces not any new rays of light, but only spreads those which always flowed from them, and by that means both

gives parts to impressions which to the naked eye appear
simple and uncompounded, and advances to a *minimum* what
was formerly imperceptible.

. . . . . .

Section II.

OF THE INFINITE DIVISIBILITY OF
SPACE AND TIME

Wherever ideas are adequate representations of objects,
the relations, contradictions, and agreements of the ideas are
all applicable to the objects, and this we may in general observe to be the foundation of all human knowledge. But our
ideas are adequate representations of the most minute parts
of extension, and through whatever divisions and subdivisions
we may suppose these parts to be arrived at, they can never
become inferior to some ideas which we form. The plain consequence is that whatever *appears* impossible and contradictory upon the comparison of these ideas must be *really* impossible and contradictory, without any further excuse or
evasion.

Everything capable of being infinitely divided contains an
infinite number of parts; otherwise the division would be
stopped short by the indivisible parts, which we should
immediately arrive at. If therefore any finite extension be infinitely divisible, it can be no contradiction to suppose that a
finite extension contains an infinite number of parts. And *vice
versa*, if it be a contradiction to suppose that a finite extension contains an infinite number of parts, no finite extension
can be infinitely divisible. But that this latter supposition is
absurd, I easily convince myself by the consideration of
my clear ideas. I first take the least idea I can form of a part
of extension, and being certain that there is nothing more
minute than this idea, I conclude that whatever I discover by
its means must be a real quality of extension. I then repeat
this idea once, twice, thrice, etc. and find the compound idea
of extension arising from its repetition always to augment,

and become double, triple, quadruple, etc., till at last it swells up to a considerable bulk, greater or smaller, in proportion as I repeat more or less the same idea. When I stop in the addition of parts, the idea of extension ceases to augment, and were I to carry on the addition *in infinitum,* I clearly perceive that the idea of extension must also become infinite. Upon the whole, I conclude that the idea of an infinite number of parts is individually the same idea with that of an infinite extension, that no finite extension is capable of containing an infinite number of parts, and consequently that no finite extension is infinitely divisible.[1]

· · · · ·

It is true mathematicians are wont to say that there are here equally strong arguments on the other side of the question, and that the doctrine of indivisible points is also liable to unanswerable objections. Before I examine these arguments and objections in detail, I will here take them in a body, and endeavor by a short and decisive reason to prove at once that it is utterly impossible they can have any just foundation.

It is an established maxim in metaphysics *that whatever the mind clearly conceives includes the idea of possible existence,* or in other words, *that nothing we imagine is absolutely impossible.* We can form the idea of a golden mountain, and from thence conclude that such a mountain may actually exist. We can form no idea of a mountain without a valley, and therefore regard it as impossible.

Now it is certain we have an idea of extension, for otherwise why do we talk and reason concerning it? It is likewise certain that this idea, as conceived by the imagination, though divisible into parts or inferior ideas, is not infinitely divisible, nor consists of an infinite number of parts; for that exceeds the comprehension of our limited capacities. Here then is an idea of extension which consists of parts or inferior

---

[1] It has been objected to me that infinite divisibility supposes only an infinite number of *proportional* not of *aliquot* parts, and that an infinite number of proportional parts does not form an infinite extension. But this distinction is entirely frivolous. Whether these parts be called *aliquot* or *proportional,* they cannot be inferior to those minute parts we conceive, and therefore cannot form a less extension by their conjunction.

ideas that are perfectly indivisible; consequently this idea
implies no contradiction; consequently it is possible for extension really to exist conformable to it; and consequently all
the arguments employed against the possibility of mathematical points are mere scholastic quibbles, and unworthy of
our attention.

These consequences we may carry one step further, and
conclude that all the pretended demonstrations for the infinite divisibility of extension are equally sophistical, since it
is certain these demonstrations cannot be just without proving
the impossibility of mathematical points, which it is an evident
absurdity to pretend to.

Section III.

OF THE OTHER QUALITIES OF OUR IDEAS
OF SPACE AND TIME

No discovery could have been made more happily for deciding all controversies concerning ideas than that above-
mentioned, that impressions always take the precedency of
them, and that every idea with which the imagination is fur-
nished first makes its appearance in a correspondent impression. These latter perceptions are all so clear and evident that
they admit of no controversy, though many of our ideas are
so obscure that it is almost impossible even for the mind
which forms them to tell exactly their nature and composition.
Let us apply this principle in order to discover further the nature of our ideas of space and time.

Upon opening my eyes and turning them to the surrounding objects, I perceive many visible bodies, and upon shutting them again and considering the distance between these
bodies, I acquire the idea of extension. As every idea is derived from some impression which is exactly similar to it, the
impressions similar to this idea of extension must either be
some sensations derived from the sight, or some internal impressions arising from these sensations.

Our internal impressions are our passions, emotions, desires,
and aversions, none of which, I believe, will ever be asserted

to be the model from which the idea of space is derived. There remains therefore nothing but the senses which can convey to us this original impression. Now what impression do our senses here convey to us? This is the principal question, and decides without appeal concerning the nature of the idea.

The table before me is alone sufficient by its view to give me the idea of extension. This idea, then, is borrowed from and represents some impression which this moment appears to the senses. But my senses convey to me only the impressions of colored points, disposed in a certain manner. If the eye is sensible of anything further, I desire it may be pointed out to me. But if it be impossible to show anything further, we may conclude with certainty that the idea of extension is nothing but a copy of these colored points, and of the manner of their appearance.

Suppose that in the extended object, or composition of colored points, from which we first received the idea of extension, the points were of a purple color; it follows that in every repetition of that idea we would not only place the points in the same order with respect to each other, but also bestow on them that precise color with which alone we are acquainted. But afterwards having experience of the other colors of violet, green, red, white, black, and of all the different compositions of these, and finding a resemblance in the disposition of colored points of which they are composed, we omit the peculiarities of color, as far as possible, and found an abstract idea merely on that disposition of points, or manner of appearance, in which they agree. Nay even when the resemblance is carried beyond the objects of one sense, and the impressions of touch are found to be similar to those of sight in the disposition of their parts, this does not hinder the abstract idea from representing both, upon account of their resemblance. All abstract ideas are really nothing but particular ones considered in a certain light, but being annexed to general terms, they are able to represent a vast variety, and to comprehend objects which, as they are alike in some particulars, are in others vastly wide of each other.

The idea of time, being derived from the succession of our perceptions of every kind, ideas as well as impressions and impressions of reflection as well as of sensation, will afford us an instance of an abstract idea which comprehends a still greater variety than that of space, and yet is represented in the fancy by some particular individual idea of a determinate quantity and quality.

As it is from the disposition of visible and tangible objects we receive the idea of space, so from the succession of ideas and impressions we form the idea of time, nor is it possible for time alone ever to make its appearance, or be taken notice of by the mind. A man in a sound sleep, or strongly occupied with one thought, is insensible of time, and according as his perceptions succeed each other with greater or less rapidity, the same duration appears longer or shorter to his imagination. It has been remarked by a great philosopher[1] that our perceptions have certain bounds in this particular, which are fixed by the original nature and constitution of the mind, and beyond which no influence of external objects on the senses is ever able to hasten or retard our thought. If you wheel about a burning coal with rapidity, it will present to the senses an image of a circle of fire, nor will there seem to be any interval of time between its revolutions, merely because it is impossible for our perceptions to succeed each other with the same rapidity that motion may be communicated to external objects. Wherever we have no successive perceptions, we have no notion of time, even though there be a real succession in the objects. From these phenomena, as well as from many others, we may conclude that time cannot make its appearance to the mind either alone or attended with a steady unchangeable object, but is always discovered by some *perceivable* succession of changeable objects.

To confirm this we may add the following argument, which to me seems perfectly decisive and convincing. It is evident that time or duration consists of different parts, for otherwise we could not conceive a longer or shorter duration. It is also evident that these parts are not coexistent, for that quality of the coexistence of parts belongs to extension, and is what distinguishes it from duration. Now as time is composed of parts that are not coexistent, an unchangeable object, since it produces none but coexistent impressions, produces none that can give us the idea of time, and consequently that idea

[1] Mr. *Locke*.

must be derived from a succession of changeable objects, and time in its first appearance can never be severed from such a succession.

Having therefore found that time in its first appearance to the mind is always conjoined with a succession of changeable objects, and that otherwise it can never fall under our notice, we must now examine whether it can be *conceived* without our conceiving any succession of objects, and whether it can alone form a distinct idea in the imagination.

In order to know whether any objects which are joined in impression be separable in idea, we need only consider if they be different from each other, in which case it is plain they may be conceived apart. Everything that is different is distinguishable, and everything that is distinguishable may be separated, according to the maxims above-explained. If on the contrary they be not different they are not distinguishable, and if they be not distinguishable they cannot be separated. But this is precisely the case with respect to time, compared with our successive perceptions. The idea of time is not derived from a particular impression mixed up with others and plainly distinguishable from them, but arises altogether from the manner in which impressions appear to the mind, without making one of the number. Five notes played on a flute give us the impression and idea of time, though time be not a sixth impression which presents itself to the hearing or any other of the senses. Nor is it a sixth impression which the mind by reflection finds in itself. These five sounds making their appearance in this particular manner excite no emotion in the mind, nor produce an affection of any kind, which being observed by it can give rise to a new idea. For *that* is necessary to produce a new idea of reflection, nor can the mind, by revolving over a thousand times all its ideas of sensation, ever extract from them any new original idea, unless nature has so framed its faculties that it feels some new original impression arise from such a contemplation. But here it only takes notice of the *manner* in which the different sounds make their appearance, and that it may afterwards consider without considering these particular sounds, but may conjoin it with any other objects. The ideas of some objects it certainly must have, nor is it possible for it without these ideas ever to arrive at any conception of time, which, since it appears not as any primary distinct impression, can plainly be nothing but different ideas or impressions or objects disposed in a certain manner, that is, succeeding each other.

I know there are some who pretend that the idea of duration is applicable in a proper sense to objects which are perfectly unchangeable, and this I take to be the common opinion of philosophers as well as of the vulgar. But to be convinced of its falsehood we need but reflect on the foregoing conclusion, that the idea of duration is always derived from a succession of changeable objects, and can never be conveyed to the mind by anything steadfast and unchangeable. For it inevitably follows from thence that since the idea of duration cannot be derived from such an object, it can never in any propriety or exactness be applied to it, nor can anything unchangeable be ever said to have duration. Ideas always represent the objects or impressions from which they are derived, and can never without a fiction represent or be applied to any other. By what fiction we apply the idea of time, even to what is unchangeable, and suppose, as is common, that duration is a measure of rest as well as of motion, we shall consider afterwards.[1]

There is another very decisive argument which establishes the present doctrine concerning our ideas of space and time, and is founded only on that simple principle, *that our ideas of them are compounded of parts which are indivisible*. This argument may be worth the examining.

Every idea that is distinguishable being also separable, let us take one of those simple indivisible ideas of which the compound one of *extension* is formed, and separating it from all others and considering it apart, let us form a judgment of its nature and qualities.

It is plain it is not the idea of extension. For the idea of extension consists of parts, and this idea, according to the supposition, is perfectly simple and indivisible. Is it therefore nothing? That is absolutely impossible. For as the compound idea of extension, which is real, is composed of such ideas, were these so many non entities there would be a real existence composed of non entities, which is absurd. Here there-

[1] Section V.

fore I must ask, *What is our idea of a simple and indivisible point?* No wonder if my answer appear somewhat new, since the question itself has scarce ever yet been thought of. We are wont to dispute concerning the nature of mathematical points, but seldom concerning the nature of their ideas.

The idea of space is conveyed to the mind by two senses, the sight and touch, nor does anything ever appear extended that is not either visible or tangible. That compound impression which represents extension consists of several lesser impressions that are indivisible to the eye or feeling, and may be called impressions of atoms or corpuscles endowed with color and solidity. But this is not all. It is not only requisite that these atoms should be colored or tangible in order to discover themselves to our senses, it is also necessary we should preserve the idea of their color or tangibility in order to comprehend them by our imagination. There is nothing but the idea of their color or tangibility which can render them conceivable by the mind. Upon the removal of the ideas of these sensible qualities, they are utterly annihilated to the thought or imagination.

Now such as the parts are, such is the whole. If a point be not considered as colored or tangible, it can convey to us no idea, and consequently the idea of extension, which is composed of the ideas of these points, can never possibly exist. But if the idea of extension really can exist, as we are conscious it does, its parts must also exist, and in order to that must be considered as colored or tangible. We have therefore no idea of space or extension but when we regard it as an object either of our sight or feeling.

The same reasoning will prove that the indivisible moments of time must be filled with some real object or existence, whose succession forms the duration and makes it be conceivable by the mind.

Section IV.

OBJECTIONS ANSWERED

Our system concerning space and time consists of two parts, which are intimately connected together. The first depends on this chain of reasoning. The capacity of the mind is not infinite; consequently no idea of extension or duration consists of an infinite number of parts or inferior ideas, but of a finite number, and these simple and indivisible. It is therefore possible for space and time to exist conformable to this idea. And if it be possible, it is certain they actually do exist conformable to it, since their infinite divisibility is utterly impossible and contradictory.

The other part of our system is a consequence of this. The parts into which the ideas of space and time resolve themselves become at last indivisible, and these indivisible parts, being nothing in themselves, are inconceivable when not filled with something real and existent. The ideas of space and time are therefore no separate or distinct ideas, but merely those of the manner or order in which objects exist. Or in other words, it is impossible to conceive either a vacuum and extension without matter, or a time when there was no succession or change in any real existence. . . .

. . . . . .

Section VI.

OF THE IDEA OF EXISTENCE AND
OF EXTERNAL EXISTENCE

It may not be amiss, before we leave this subject, to explain the ideas of *existence* and of *external existence*, which have their difficulties as well as the ideas of space and time. By this means we shall be the better prepared for the examination of knowledge and probability, when we understand perfectly all those particular ideas which may enter into our reasoning.

There is no impression nor idea of any kind, of which we have any consciousness or memory, that is not conceived as existent, and it is evident that from this consciousness the most perfect idea and assurance of *being* is derived. From hence we may form a dilemma, the most clear and conclusive that can be imagined, *viz.*, that since we never remember any idea or impression without attributing existence to it, the idea of existence must either be derived from a distinct impression, conjoined with every perception or object of our thought, or must be the very same with the idea of the perception or object.

As this dilemma is an evident consequence of the principle that every idea arises from a similar impression, so our decision between the propositions of the dilemma is no more doubtful. So, far from there being any distinct impression attending every impression and every idea, I do not think there are any two distinct impressions which are inseparably conjoined. Though certain sensations may at one time be united, we quickly find they admit of a separation, and may be presented apart. And thus though every impression and idea we remember be considered as existent, the idea of existence is not derived from any particular impression.

The idea of existence, then, is the very same with the idea of what we conceive to be existent. To reflect on anything simply, and to reflect on it as existent, are nothing different from each other. That idea, when conjoined with the idea of any object, makes no addition to it. Whatever we conceive, we conceive to be existent. Any idea we please to form is the idea of a being, and the idea of a being is any idea we please to form.

Whoever opposes this must necessarily point out that distinct impression from which the idea of entity is derived, and must prove that this impression is inseparable from every perception we believe to be existent. This we may without hesitation conclude to be impossible.

Our foregoing[1] reasoning concerning the *distinction* of ideas

[1] Part I, Section VII.

without any real *difference* will not here serve us in any stead. That kind of distinction is founded on the different resemblances which the same simple idea may have to several different ideas. But no object can be presented resembling some object with respect to its existence, and different from others in the same particular, since every object that is presented must necessarily be existent.

A like reasoning will account for the idea of *external existence*. We may observe that it is universally allowed by philosophers, and is besides pretty obvious of itself, that nothing is ever really present with the mind but its perceptions or impressions and ideas, and that external objects become known to us only by those perceptions they occasion. To hate, to love, to think, to feel, to see; all this is nothing but to perceive.

Now since nothing is ever present to the mind but perceptions, and since all ideas are derived from something antecedently present to the mind, it follows that it is impossible for us so much as to conceive or form an idea of anything specifically different from ideas and impressions. Let us fix our attention out of ourselves as much as possible; let us chase our imagination to the heavens, or to the utmost limits of the universe; we never really advance a step beyond ourselves, nor can conceive any kind of existence but those perceptions which have appeared in that narrow compass. This is the universe of the imagination, nor have we any idea but what is there produced.

The farthest we can go towards a conception of external objects, when supposed *specifically* different from our perceptions, is to form a relative idea of them, without pretending to comprehend the related objects. Generally speaking we do not suppose them specifically different, but only attribute to them different relations, connections, and durations. But of this more fully hereafter.[1]

[1] Part IV, Section II.

Part III.
OF KNOWLEDGE AND PROBABILITY

―――――・◆・―――――

Section I.

OF KNOWLEDGE

THERE ARE seven[1] different kinds of philosophical relation, *viz., resemblance, identity, relations of time and place, proportion in quantity or number, degrees in any quality, contrariety, and causation.* These relations may be divided into two classes, into such as depend entirely on the ideas which we compare together, and such as may be changed without any change in the ideas. It is from the idea of a triangle that we discover the relation of equality which its three angles bear to two right ones, and this relation is invariable as long as our idea remains the same. On the contrary, the relations of *contiguity* and *distance* between two objects may be changed merely by an alteration of their place, without any change on the objects themselves or on their ideas, and the place depends on a hundred different accidents which cannot be foreseen by the mind. It is the same case with *identity* and *causation.* Two objects, though perfectly resembling each other, and even appearing in the same place at different times, may be numerically different. And as the power by which one object produces another is never discoverable merely from their idea, it is evident *cause and effect* are relations of which we receive information from experience, and not from any abstract reasoning or reflection. There is no single phenomenon, even the most simple, which can be accounted for from the qualities of the objects as they appear to us, or which we could foresee without the help of our memory and experience.

It appears, therefore, that of these seven philosophical rela-

[1] Part I, Section V.

tions, there remain only four which, depending solely upon ideas, can be the objects of knowledge and certainty. These four are *resemblance, contrariety, degrees in quality,* and *proportions in quantity or number*. Three of these relations are discoverable at first sight, and fall more properly under the province of intuition than demonstration. When any objects *resemble* each other, the resemblance will at first strike the eye, or rather the mind, and seldom requires a second examination. The case is the same with *contrariety*, and with the *degrees of any quality*. No one can once doubt but existence and nonexistence destroy each other, and are perfectly incompatible and contrary. And though it be impossible to judge exactly of the degrees of any quality, such as color, taste, heat, cold, when the difference between them is very small, yet it is easy to decide that any of them is superior or inferior to another when their difference is considerable. And this decision we always pronounce at first sight, without any inquiry or reasoning.

We might proceed after the same manner in fixing the *proportions of quantity or number,* and might at one view observe a superiority or inferiority between any numbers or figures, especially where the difference is very great and remarkable. As to equality or any exact proportion, we can only guess at it from a single consideration, except in very short numbers or very limited portions of extension, which are comprehended in an instant, and where we perceive an impossibility of falling into any considerable error. In all other cases we must settle the proportions with some liberty, or proceed in a more *artificial* manner.

I have already observed that geometry, or the *art* by which we fix the proportions of figures, though it much excels, both in universality and exactness, the loose judgments of the senses and imagination, yet never attains a perfect precision and exactness. Its first principles are still drawn from the general appearance of the objects, and that appearance can never afford us any security when we examine the prodigious minuteness of which nature is susceptible. Our ideas seem to give a perfect assurance that no two right lines can have a common segment, but if we consider these ideas we shall find that they always suppose a sensible inclination of the two lines, and that where the angle they form is extremely small, we have no standard of a right line so precise as to assure us of the truth of this proposition. It is the same case with most of the primary decisions of the mathematics.

There remain, therefore, algebra and arithmetic as the only sciences in which we can carry on a chain of reasoning to any degree of intricacy, and yet preserve a perfect exactness and certainty. We are possessed of a precise standard by which we can judge of the equality and proportion of numbers, and according as they correspond or not to that standard, we determine their relations, without any possibility of error. When two numbers are so combined as that the one has always a unit answering to every unit of the other, we pronounce them equal, and it is for want of such a standard of equality in extension that geometry can scarce be esteemed a perfect and infallible science.

But here it may not be amiss to obviate a difficulty which may arise from my asserting that though geometry falls short of that perfect precision and certainty which are peculiar to arithmetic and algebra, yet it excels the imperfect judgments of our senses and imagination. The reason why I impute any defect to geometry is because its original and fundamental principles are derived merely from appearances, and it may perhaps be imagined that this defect must always attend it, and keep it from ever reaching a greater exactness in the comparison of objects or ideas than what our eye or imagination alone is able to attain. I own that this defect so far attends it as to keep it from ever aspiring to a full certainty. But since these fundamental principles depend on the easiest and least deceitful appearances, they bestow on their consequences a degree of exactness of which these consequences are singly incapable. It is impossible for the eye to determine the angles of a chiliagon to be equal to 1996 right angles, or make any conjecture that approaches this proportion; but when it determines that right lines cannot concur, that we cannot draw more than one right line between two given points, its mistakes can never be of any consequence. And this is the nature and use of geometry, to run us up to such appearances as, by reason of their simplicity, cannot lead us into any considerable error.

I shall here take occasion to propose a second observation concerning our demonstrative reasonings, which is suggested by the same subject of the mathematics. It is usual with mathematicians to pretend that those ideas which are their objects are of so refined and spiritual a nature that they fall not under the conception of the fancy, but must be comprehended by a pure and intellectual view, of which the superior faculties of the soul are alone capable. The same notion runs through most parts of philosophy, and is principally made use of to explain our abstract ideas, and to show how we can form an idea of a triangle, for instance, which shall neither be an isosceles nor scalenum, nor be confined to any particular length and proportion of sides. It is easy to see why philosophers are so fond of this notion of some spiritual and refined perceptions, since by that means they cover many of their absurdities, and may refuse to submit to the decisions of clear ideas by appealing to such as are obscure and uncertain. But to destroy this artifice, we need but reflect on that principle so oft insisted on, *that all our ideas are copied from our impressions.* For from thence we may immediately conclude that since all impressions are clear and precise, the ideas which are copied from them must be of the same nature, and can never, but from our fault, contain anything so dark and intricate. An idea is by its very nature weaker and fainter than an impression, but being in every other respect the same, cannot imply any very great mystery. If its weakness render it obscure, it is our business to remedy that defect as much as possible by keeping the idea steady and precise, and till we have done so, it is in vain to pretend to reasoning and philosophy.

Section II.

OF PROBABILITY, AND OF THE IDEA
OF CAUSE AND EFFECT

This is all I think necessary to observe concerning those four relations which are the foundation of science, but as to the other three, which depend not upon the idea and may be absent or present even while *that* remains the same, it will be proper to explain them more particularly. These three relations are *identity, the situations in time and place,* and *causation.*

All kinds of reasoning consist in nothing but a *comparison,* and a discovery of those relations, either constant or inconstant, which two or more objects bear to each other. This comparison we may make either when both the objects are present to the senses, or when neither of them is present, or when only one. When both the objects are present to the senses along with the relation, we call *this* perception rather than reasoning; nor is there in this case any exercise of the thought, or any action, properly speaking, but a mere passive admission of the impressions through the organs of sensation. According to this way of thinking, we ought not to receive as reasoning any of the observations we may make concerning *identity* and the *relations of time and place,* since in none of them the mind can go beyond what is immediately present to the senses, either to discover the real existence or the relations of objects. It is only *causation* which produces such a connection as to give us assurance from the existence or action of one object that it was followed or preceded by any other existence or action, nor can the other two relations be ever made use of in reasoning, except so far as they either affect or are affected by it. There is nothing in any objects to persuade us that they are either always *remote* or always *contiguous,* and when from experience and observation we discover that their relation in this particular is invariable, we always conclude there is some secret *cause* which separates or unites them. The same reasoning extends to *identity*. We readily suppose an object may continue individually the same though several times absent from and present to the senses, and ascribe to it an identity, notwithstanding the interruption of the perception, whenever we conclude that if we had kept our eye or hand constantly upon it, it would have conveyed an invariable and uninterrupted perception. But this conclusion beyond the impressions of our senses can be founded only on the connection of *cause and effect,* nor can we otherwise have any security that the object is not changed upon us, however much the new object may resemble that which was formerly present to the senses. Whenever we discover such a perfect resemblance, we consider whether it be common in that species of objects, whether possibly or probably any cause could operate in producing the change and resemblance; and according as we determine concerning these causes and effects, we form our judgment concerning the identity of the object.

Here then it appears that of those three relations which depend not upon the mere ideas, the only one that can be traced beyond our senses and informs us of existences and objects which we do not see or feel is *causation.* This relation, therefore, we shall endeavor to explain fully before we leave the subject of the understanding.

To begin regularly, we must consider the idea of *causation,* and see from what origin it is derived. It is impossible to reason justly without understanding perfectly the idea concerning which we reason, and it is impossible perfectly to understand any idea without tracing it up to its origin, and examining that primary impression from which it arises. The examination of the impression bestows a clearness on the idea, and the examination of the idea bestows a like clearness on all our reasoning.

Let us therefore cast our eye on any two objects which we call cause and effect, and turn them on all sides in order to find that impression which produces an idea of such prodigious consequence. At first sight I perceive that I must not search for it in any of the particular *qualities* of the objects, since whichever of these qualities I pitch on, I find some object that is not possessed of it, and yet falls under the denomination of cause or effect. And indeed there is nothing existent, either externally or internally, which is not to be considered either as a cause or an effect, though it is plain there is no one quality which universally belongs to all beings, and gives them a title to that denomination.

The idea, then, of causation must be derived from some *relation* among objects, and that relation we must now endeavor to discover. I find in the first place that whatever objects are considered as causes or effects are *contiguous,* and that nothing can operate in a time or place which is ever so little removed from those of its existence. Though distant objects may sometimes seem productive of each other, they are commonly found upon examination to be linked by a chain of causes, which are contiguous among themselves and to the distant objects, and when in any particular instance we cannot discover this connection, we still presume it to exist. We may therefore consider the relation of CONTIGUITY as essential to that of causation, at least may suppose it such, according to the general opinion, till we can find a more proper occasion[1] to clear up this matter, by examining what objects are or are not susceptible of juxtaposition and conjunction.

The second relation I shall observe as essential to causes and effects is not so universally acknowledged, but is liable to some controversy. It is that of PRIORITY of time in the cause before the effect. Some pretend that it is not absolutely necessary a cause should precede its effect, but that any object or action, in the very first moment of its existence, may exert its productive quality, and give rise to another object or action perfectly co-temporary with itself. But beside that experience in most instances seems to contradict this opinion, we may establish the relation of priority by a kind of inference or reasoning. It is an established maxim both in natural and moral philosophy that an object which exists for any time in its full perfection without producing another is not its sole cause, but is assisted by some other principle, which pushes it from its state of inactivity, and makes it exert that energy of which it was secretly possessed. Now if any cause may be perfectly co-temporary with its effect, it is certain, according to this

[1] Part IV, Section V.

maxim, that they must all of them be so, since any one of them which retards its operation for a single moment exerts not itself at that very individual time in which it might have operated, and therefore is no proper cause. The consequence of this would be no less than the destruction of that succession of causes which we observe in the world, and indeed, the utter annihilation of time. For if one cause were co-temporary with its effect, and this effect with *its* effect, and so on, it is plain there would be no such thing as succession, and all objects must be coexistent.

If this argument appear satisfactory, it is well. If not, I beg the reader to allow me the same liberty, which I have used in the preceding case, of supposing it such. For he shall find that the affair is of no great importance.

Having thus discovered or supposed the two relations of *contiguity* and *succession* to be essential to causes and effects, I find I am stopped short, and can proceed no further in considering any single instance of cause and effect. Motion in one body is regarded upon impulse as the cause of motion in another. When we consider these objects with the utmost attention, we find only that the one body approaches the other, and that the motion of it precedes that of the other, but without any sensible interval. It is in vain to rack ourselves with *further* thought and reflection upon this subject. We can go no *further* in considering this particular instance.

Should anyone leave this instance, and pretend to define a cause by saying it is something productive of another, it is evident he would say nothing. For what does he mean by *production?* Can he give any definition of it that will not be the same with that of causation? If he can, I desire it may be produced. If he cannot, he here runs in a circle, and gives a synonymous term instead of a definition.

Shall we then rest contented with these two relations of contiguity and succession, as affording a complete idea of causation? By no means. An object may be contiguous and prior to another without being considered as its cause. There is a NECESSARY CONNECTION to be taken into consideration, and that relation is of much greater importance than any of the other two above-mentioned.

Here again I turn the object on all sides in order to discover the nature of this necessary connection, and find the impression, or impressions, from which its idea may be derived. When I cast my eye on the *known qualities* of objects, I immediately discover that the relation of cause and effect depends not in the least on *them*. When I consider their *relations*, I can find none but those of contiguity and succession, which I have already regarded as imperfect and unsatisfactory. Shall the despair of success make me assert that I am here possessed of an idea which is not preceded by any similar impression? This would be too strong a proof of levity and inconstancy, since the contrary principle has been already so firmly established as to admit of no further doubt, at least till we have more fully examined the present difficulty.

We must, therefore, proceed like those who, being in search of anything that lies concealed from them and not finding it in the place they expected, beat about all the neighboring fields, without any certain view or design, in hopes their good fortune will at last guide them to what they search for. It is necessary for us to leave the direct survey of this question concerning the nature of that *necessary connection* which enters into our idea of cause and effect, and endeavor to find some other questions, the examination of which will perhaps afford a hint that may serve to clear up the present difficulty. Of these questions there occur two, which I shall proceed to examine.

First, for what reason we pronounce it *necessary* that everything whose existence has a beginning should also have a cause.

Secondly, why we conclude that such particular causes must *necessarily* have such particular effects, and what is the nature of that *inference* we draw from the one to the other, and of the *belief* we repose in it.

I shall only observe before I proceed any further that though the ideas of cause and effect be derived from the impressions of reflection as well as from those of sensation, yet for brevity's sake I commonly mention only the latter as the origin of these ideas, though I desire that whatever I say of them may also extend to the former. Passions are connected with their objects and with one another no less than external bodies are connected together. The same relation, then, of

cause and effect which belongs to one must be common to all
of them.

Section III.

WHY A CAUSE IS ALWAYS NECESSARY

To begin with the first question concerning the necessity of
a cause, it is a general maxim in philosophy that *whatever
begins to exist must have a cause of existence*. This is commonly taken for granted in all reasonings, without any proof
given or demanded. It is supposed to be founded on intuition,
and to be one of those maxims which, though they may be
denied with the lips, it is impossible for men in their hearts
really to doubt of. But if we examine this maxim by the idea
of knowledge above-explained, we shall discover in it no
mark of any such intuitive certainty, but on the contrary shall
find that it is of a nature quite foreign to that species of conviction.

All certainty arises from the comparison of ideas, and from
the discovery of such relations as are unalterable, so long as
the ideas continue the same. These relations are *resemblance,
proportions in quantity and number, degrees of any quality,*
and *contrariety,* none of which are implied in this proposition, *whatever has a beginning has also a cause of existence.*
That proposition therefore is not intuitively certain. At least
anyone who would assert it to be intuitively certain must
deny these to be the only infallible relations, and must find
some other relation of that kind to be implied in it, which it
will then be time enough to examine.

But here is an argument which proves at once that the foregoing proposition is neither intuitively nor demonstrably certain. We can never demonstrate the necessity of a cause to
every new existence, or new modification of existence, without showing at the same time the impossibility there is that
anything can ever begin to exist without some productive
principle, and where the latter proposition cannot be proved,

we must despair of ever being able to prove the former. Now that the latter proposition is utterly incapable of a demonstrative proof, we may satisfy ourselves by considering that as all distinct ideas are separable from each other, and as the ideas of cause and effect are evidently distinct, it will be easy for us to conceive any object to be nonexistent this moment, and existent the next, without conjoining to it the distinct idea of a cause or productive principle. The separation, therefore, of the idea of a cause from that of a beginning of existence is plainly possible for the imagination, and consequently the actual separation of these objects is so far possible that it implies no contradiction nor absurdity, and is therefore incapable of being refuted by any reasoning from mere ideas, without which it is impossible to demonstrate the necessity of a cause.

Accordingly we shall find upon examination that every demonstration which has been produced for the necessity of a cause is fallacious and sophistical. All the points of time and place, say some philosophers,[1] in which we can suppose any object to begin to exist are in themselves equal, and unless there be some cause which is peculiar to one time and to one place, and which by that means determines and fixes the existence, it must remain in eternal suspense, and the object can never begin to be for want of something to fix its beginning. But I ask, is there any more difficulty in supposing the time and place to be fixed without a cause, than to suppose the existence to be determined in that manner? The first question that occurs on this subject is always, *whether* the object shall exist or not; the next, *when* and *where* it shall begin to exist. If the removal of a cause be intuitively absurd in the one case, it must be so in the other; and if that absurdity be not clear without a proof in the one case, it will equally require one in the other. The absurdity, then, of the one supposition can never be a proof of that of the other, since they are both upon the same footing, and must stand or fall by the same reasoning.

The second argument [2]which I find used on this head labors under an equal difficulty. Everything, it is said, must

[1] Mr. *Hobbes*.
[2] Dr. *Clarke* and others.

have a cause, for if anything wanted a cause *it* would produce *itself*, that is, exist before it existed, which is impossible. But this reasoning is plainly inconclusive, because it supposes that in our denial of a cause we still grant what we expressly deny, *viz.*, that there must be a cause, which therefore is taken to be the object itself; and *that*, no doubt, is an evident contradiction. But to say that anything is produced, or to express myself more properly, comes into existence, without a cause, is not to affirm that it is itself its own cause, but on the contrary in excluding all external causes excludes *a fortiori* the thing itself which is created. An object that exists absolutely without any cause certainly is not its own cause, and when you assert that the one follows from the other, you suppose the very point in question, and take it for granted that it is utterly impossible anything can ever begin to exist without a cause, but that upon the exclusion of one productive principle we must still have recourse to another.

It is exactly the same case with the third argument[1] which has been employed to demonstrate the necessity of a cause. Whatever is produced without any cause is produced by *nothing*, or in other words has nothing for its cause. But nothing can never be a cause, no more than it can be something, or equal to two right angles. By the same intuition that we perceive nothing not to be equal to two right angles, or not to be something, we perceive that it can never be a cause, and consequently must perceive that every object has a real cause of its existence.

I believe it will not be necessary to employ many words in showing the weakness of this argument, after what I have said of the foregoing. They are all of them founded on the same fallacy, and are derived from the same turn of thought. It is sufficient only to observe that when we exclude all causes we really do exclude them, and neither suppose nothing nor the object itself to be the causes of the existence, and consequently can draw no argument from the absurdity of these suppositions to prove the absurdity of that exclusion. If everything must have a cause, it follows that upon the exclusion of other causes we must accept of the object itself or of nothing as causes. But it is the very point in question, whether every-

[1] Mr. *Locke*.

thing must have a cause or not, and therefore, according to all just reasoning, it ought never to be taken for granted.

They are still more frivolous who say that every effect must have a cause because it is implied in the very idea of effect. Every effect necessarily presupposes a cause, effect being a relative term of which cause is the correlative. But this does not prove that every being must be preceded by a cause, no more than it follows, because every husband must have a wife, that therefore every man must be married. The true state of the question is whether every object which begins to exist must owe its existence to a cause, and this I assert neither to be intuitively nor demonstratively certain, and hope to have proved it sufficiently by the foregoing arguments.

Since it is not from knowledge or any scientific reasoning that we derive the opinion of the necessity of a cause to every new production, that opinion must necessarily arise from observation and experience. The next question, then, should naturally be, *how experience gives rise to such a principle.* But as I find it will be more convenient to sink this question in the following, *why we conclude that such particular causes must necessarily have such particular effects, and why we form an inference from one to another,* we shall make that the subject of our future inquiry. It will, perhaps, be found in the end that the same answer will serve for both questions.

Section IV.

OF THE COMPONENT PARTS OF OUR REASONINGS CONCERNING CAUSES AND EFFECTS

Though the mind in its reasonings from causes or effects carries its view beyond those objects which it sees or remembers, it must never lose sight of them entirely, nor reason merely upon its own ideas, without some mixture of impressions, or at least of ideas of the memory, which are equivalent to impressions. When we infer effects from causes, we must establish the existence of these causes, which we have only two ways of doing, either by an immediate perception of our memory or senses, or by an inference from other causes, which causes again we must ascertain in the same manner, either by a present impression, or by an inference from *their* causes, and so on, till we arrive at some object which we see or remember. It is impossible for us to carry on our inferences *in infinitum,* and the only thing that can stop them is an impression of the memory or senses, beyond which there is no room for doubt or inquiry.

To give an instance of this, we may choose any point of history, and consider for what reason we either believe or reject it. Thus we believe that CAESAR was killed in the senate-house on the *ides* of *March,* and that because this fact is established on the unanimous testimony of historians, who agree to assign this precise time and place to that event. Here are certain characters and letters present either to our memory or senses, which characters we likewise remember to have been used as the signs of certain ideas, and these ideas were either in the minds of such as were immediately present at that action and received the ideas directly from its existence, or they were derived from the testimony of others, and that again from another testimony, by a visible gradation, till we arrive at those who were eye-witnesses and spectators of the event. It is obvious all this chain of argument or connection of causes and effects is at first founded on those characters or letters which are seen or remembered, and that without the authority either of the memory or senses our whole reasoning would be chimerical and without foundation. Every link of the chain would in that case hang upon another, but there would not be anything fixed to one end of it, capable of sustaining the whole, and consequently there would be no belief nor evidence. And this actually is the case with all *hypothetical* arguments, or reasonings upon a supposition, there being in them neither any present impression nor belief of a real existence.

I need not observe that it is no just objection to the present doctrine that we can reason upon our past conclusions or principles without having recourse to those impressions from which they first arose. For even supposing these impressions should be entirely effaced from the memory, the conviction they produced may still remain, and it is equally true that all reasonings concerning causes and effects are originally derived from some impression in the same manner as the assurance of a demonstration proceeds always from a comparison of ideas, though it may continue after the comparison is forgotten.

Section V.

OF THE IMPRESSIONS OF THE SENSES AND MEMORY

In this kind of reasoning, then, from causation, we employ materials which are of a mixed and heterogeneous nature, and which, however connected, are yet essentially different from each other. All our arguments concerning causes and effects consist both of an impression of the memory or senses and of the idea of that existence which produces the object of the impression, or is produced by it. Here therefore we have three things to explain, *viz., first*, the original impression, *secondly*, the transition to the idea of the connected cause or effect, *thirdly*, the nature and qualities of that idea.

As to those *impressions* which arise from the *senses*, their ultimate cause is, in my opinion, perfectly inexplicable by human reason, and it will always be impossible to decide with certainty whether they arise immediately from the object, or are produced by the creative power of the mind, or are derived from the author of our being. Nor is such a question any way material to our present purpose. We may draw inferences from the coherence of our perceptions, whether they be true or false, whether they represent nature justly, or be mere illusions of the senses.

When we search for the characteristic which distinguishes the *memory* from the imagination, we must immediately perceive that it cannot lie in the simple ideas it presents to us, since both these faculties borrow their simple ideas from the impressions, and can never go beyond these original perceptions. These faculties are as little distinguished from each other by the arrangement of their complex ideas. For though it be a peculiar property of the memory to preserve the original order and position of its ideas, while the imagination transposes and changes them as it pleases, yet this difference is not sufficient to distinguish them in their operation, or make us know the one from the other, it being impossible to recall the past impressions in order to compare them with our present ideas, and see whether their arrangement be exactly similar. Since therefore the memory is known neither by the order of its *complex* ideas nor the nature of its *simple* ones, it follows that the difference between it and the imagination lies in its superior force and vivacity. A man may indulge his fancy in feigning any past scene of adventures, nor would there be any possibility of distinguishing this from a remembrance of a like kind, were not the ideas of the imagination fainter and more obscure.

[1]It frequently happens that when two men have been engaged in any scene of action, the one shall remember it much better than the other, and shall have all the difficulty in the world to make his companion recollect it. He runs over several circumstances in vain, mentions the time, the place, the company, what was said, what was done on all sides, till at last he hits on some lucky circumstance that revives the whole, and gives his friend a perfect memory of everything. Here the person that forgets receives at first all the ideas from the discourse of the other, with the same circumstances of time and place, though he considers them as mere fictions of the imagination. But as soon as the circumstance is mentioned that touches the memory, the very same ideas now appear in a new light, and have, in a manner, a different feeling from what they had before. Without any other alteration beside that of the feeling, they become immediately ideas of the memory, and are assented to.

Since, therefore, the imagination can represent all the same objects that the memory can offer to us, and since those faculties are only distinguished by the different *feeling* of the ideas they present, it may be proper to consider what is the nature of that feeling. And here I believe everyone will read-

1 [This paragraph and the first two sentences of the following paragraph were first printed in the Appendix.—Ed.]

ily agree with me that the ideas of the memory are more *strong* and *lively* than those of the fancy. A painter who intended to represent a passion or emotion of any kind would endeavor to get a sight of a person actuated by a like emotion, in order to enliven his ideas, and give them a force and vivacity superior to what is found in those which are mere fictions of the imagination. The more recent this memory is, the clearer is the idea, and when after a long interval he would return to the contemplation of his object, he always finds its idea to be much decayed, if not wholly obliterated. We are frequently in doubt concerning the ideas of the memory as they become very weak and feeble, and are at a loss to determine whether any image proceeds from the fancy or the memory, when it is not drawn in such lively colors as distinguish that latter faculty. I think I remember such an event, says one, but am not sure. A long tract of time has almost worn it out of my memory, and leaves me uncertain whether or not it be the pure offspring of my fancy.

And as an idea of the memory, by losing its force and vivacity, may degenerate to such a degree as to be taken for an idea of the imagination, so on the other hand an idea of the imagination may acquire such a force and vivacity as to pass for an idea of the memory, and counterfeit its effects on the belief and judgment. This is noted in the case of liars, who by the frequent repetition of their lies come at last to believe and remember them as realities, custom and habit having in this case, as in many others, the same influence on the mind as nature, and infixing the idea with equal force and vigor.

Thus it appears that the *belief* or *assent* which always attends the memory and senses is nothing but the vivacity of those perceptions they present, and that this alone distinguishes them from the imagination. To believe is in this case to feel an immediate impression of the senses, or a repetition of that impression in the memory. It is merely the force and liveliness of the perception which constitutes the first act of the judgment, and lays the foundation of that reasoning which we build upon it when we trace the relation of cause and effect.

Section VI.

OF THE INFERENCE FROM THE
IMPRESSION TO THE IDEA

It is easy to observe that in tracing this relation, the inference we draw from cause to effect is not derived merely from a survey of these particular objects, and from such a penetration into their essences as may discover the dependence of the one upon the other. There is no object which implies the existence of any other if we consider these objects in themselves, and never look beyond the ideas which we form of them. Such an inference would amount to knowledge, and would imply the absolute contradiction and impossibility of conceiving anything different. But as all distinct ideas are separable, it is evident there can be no impossibility of that kind. When we pass from a present impression to the idea of any object, we might possibly have separated the idea from the impression, and have substituted any other idea in its room.

It is therefore by EXPERIENCE only that we can infer the existence of one object from that of another. The nature of experience is this. We remember to have had frequent instances of the existence of one species of objects, and also remember that the individuals of another species of objects have always attended them, and have existed in a regular order of contiguity and succession with regard to them. Thus we remember to have seen that species of object we call *flame*, and to have felt that species of sensation we call *heat*. We likewise call to mind their constant conjunction in all past instances. Without any further ceremony, we call the one *cause* and the other *effect*, and infer the existence of the one from that of the other. In all those instances from which we learn the conjunction of particular causes and effects, both the causes and effects have been perceived by the senses, and are remembered. But in all cases wherein we reason concerning them, there is only one perceived or remembered, and the other is supplied in conformity to our past experience.

Thus in advancing we have insensibly discovered a new relation between cause and effect, when we least expected it, and were entirely employed upon another subject. This relation is their CONSTANT CONJUNCTION. Contiguity and succession are not sufficient to make us pronounce any two objects to be cause and effect, unless we perceive that these two relations are preserved in several instances. We may now see the advantage of quitting the direct survey of this relation, in order to discover the nature of that *necessary connection* which makes so essential a part of it. There are hopes that by this means we may at last arrive at our proposed end, though to tell the truth this new-discovered relation of a constant conjunction seems to advance us but very little in our way. For it implies no more than this, that like objects have always been placed in like relations of contiguity and succession; and it seems evident, at least at first sight, that by this means we can never discover any new idea, and can only multiply but not enlarge the objects of our mind. It may be thought that what we learn not from one object, we can never learn from a hundred which are all of the same kind, and are perfectly resembling in every circumstance. As our senses show us in one instance two bodies or motions or qualities in certain relations of succession and contiguity, so our memory presents us only with a multitude of instances wherein we always find like bodies, motions, or qualities in like relations. From the mere repetition of any past impression, even to infinity, there never will arise any new original idea, such as that of a necessary connection, and the number of impressions has in this case no more effect than if we confined ourselves to one only. But though this reasoning seems just and obvious, yet as it would be folly to despair too soon, we shall continue the thread of our discourse, and having found that after the discovery of the constant conjunction of any objects we always draw an inference from one object to another, we shall now examine the nature of that inference, and of the transition from the impression to the idea. Perhaps it will appear in the end that the necessary connection depends on the inference, instead of the inference's depending on the necessary connection.

Since it appears that the transition from an impression present to the memory or senses to the idea of an object which we call cause or effect is founded on past *experience* and on our remembrance of their *constant conjunction*, the next question is whether experience produces the idea by means of the understanding or of the imagination, whether we are determined by reason to make the transition or by a certain association and relation of perceptions. If reason determined us, it would proceed upon that principle, *that instances of which we have had no experience must resemble those of which we have had experience, and that the course of nature continues always uniformly the same.* In order therefore to clear up this matter, let us consider all the arguments upon which such a proposition may be supposed to be founded, and as these must be derived either from *knowledge* or *probability,* let us cast our eye on each of these degrees of evidence, and see whether they afford any just conclusion of this nature.

Our foregoing method of reasoning will easily convince us that there can be no *demonstrative* arguments to prove *that those instances of which we have had no experience resemble those of which we have had experience.* We can at least conceive a change in the course of nature, which sufficiently proves that such a change is not absolutely impossible. To form a clear idea of anything is an undeniable argument for its possibility, and is alone a refutation of any pretended demonstration against it.

Probability, as it discovers not the relations of ideas considered as such, but only those of objects, must in some respects be founded on the impressions of our memory and senses, and in some respects on our ideas. Were there no mixture of any impression in our probable reasonings, the conclusion would be entirely chimerical, and were there no mixture of ideas the action of the mind, in observing the relation, would, properly speaking, be sensation, not reasoning. It is therefore necessary that in all probable reasonings there be something present to the mind, either seen or remembered, and that from this we infer something connected with it, which is not seen nor remembered.

The only connection or relation of objects which can lead

us beyond the immediate impressions of our memory and senses is that of cause and effect, and that because it is the only one on which we can found a just inference from one object to another. The idea of cause and effect is derived from *experience*, which informs us that such particular objects, in all past instances, have been constantly conjoined with each other; and as an object similar to one of these is supposed to be immediately present in its impression, we thence presume on the existence of one similar to its usual attendant. According to this account of things, which is, I think, in every point unquestionable, probability is founded on the presumption of a resemblance between those objects of which we have had experience, and those of which we have had none; and therefore it is impossible this presumption can arise from probability. The same principle cannot be both the cause and effect of another, and this is, perhaps, the only proposition concerning that relation which is either intuitively or demonstratively certain.

Should anyone think to elude this argument, and without determining whether our reasoning on this subject be derived from demonstration or probability, pretend that all conclusions from causes and effects are built on solid reasoning, I can only desire that this reasoning may be produced, in order to be exposed to our examination. It may, perhaps, be said that after experience of the constant conjunction of certain objects we reason in the following manner. Such an object is always found to produce another. It is impossible it could have this effect if it was not endowed with a power of production. The power necessarily implies the effect, and therefore there is a just foundation for drawing a conclusion from the existence of one object to that of its usual attendant. The past production implies a power, the power implies a new production, and the new production is what we infer from the power and the past production.

It were easy for me to show the weakness of this reasoning were I willing to make use of those observations I have already made, that the idea of *production* is the same with that of *causation* and that no existence certainly and demonstratively implies a power in any other object, or were it proper to anticipate what I shall have occasion to remark afterwards concerning the idea we form of *power* and *efficacy*. But as such a method of proceeding may seem either to weaken my system by resting one part of it on another, or to breed a confusion in my reasoning, I shall endeavor to maintain my present assertion without any such assistance.

It shall therefore be allowed for a moment that the production of one object by another in any one instance implies a power, and that this power is connected with its effect. But it having been already proved that the power lies not in the sensible qualities of the cause, and there being nothing but the sensible qualities present to us, I ask why in other instances you presume that the same power still exists, merely upon the appearance of these qualities? Your appeal to past experience decides nothing in the present case, and at the utmost can only prove that that very object which produced any other was at that very instant endowed with such a power, but can never prove that the same power must continue in the same object or collection of sensible qualities, much less that a like power is always conjoined with like sensible qualities. Should it be said that we have experience that the same power continues united with the same object, and that like objects are endowed with like powers, I would renew my question, *why from this experience we form any conclusion beyond those past instances of which we have had experience.* If you answer this question in the same manner as the preceding, your answer gives still occasion to a new question of the same kind, even *in infinitum*, which clearly proves that the foregoing reasoning had no just foundation.

Thus not only our reason fails us in the discovery of the *ultimate connection* of causes and effects, but even after experience has informed us of their *constant conjunction*, it is impossible for us to satisfy ourselves by our reason why we should extend that experience beyond those particular instances which have fallen under our observation. We suppose, but are never able to prove, that there must be a resemblance between those objects of which we have had experience and those which lie beyond the reach of our discovery.

We have already taken notice of certain relations which make us pass from one object to another, even though there be no reason to determine us to that transition; and this we may establish for a general rule, that wherever the mind constantly and uniformly makes a transition without any reason, it is influenced by these relations. Now this is exactly the present case. Reason can never show us the connection of one object with another, though aided by experience and the observation of their constant conjunction in all past instances. When the mind, therefore, passes from the idea or impression of one object to the idea or belief of another, it is not determined by reason, but by certain principles which associate together the ideas of these objects, and unite them in the imagination. Had ideas no more union in the fancy than objects seem to have to the understanding, we could never draw any inference from causes to effects, nor repose belief in any matter of fact. The inference, therefore, depends solely on the union of ideas.

The principles of union among ideas I have reduced to three general ones, and have asserted that the idea or impression of any object naturally introduces the idea of any other object that is resembling, contiguous to, or connected with it. These principles I allow to be neither the *infallible* nor the *sole* causes of a union among ideas. They are not the infallible causes. For one may fix his attention during some time on any one object without looking further. They are not the sole causes. For the thought has evidently a very irregular motion in running along its objects, and may leap from the heavens to the earth, from one end of the creation to the other, without any certain method or order. But though I allow this weakness in these three relations and this irregularity in the imagination, yet I assert that the only *general* principles which associate ideas are resemblance, contiguity, and causation.

There is indeed a principle of union among ideas which at first sight may be esteemed different from any of these, but will be found at the bottom to depend on the same origin. When every individual of any species of objects is found by experience to be constantly united with an individual of another species, the appearance of any new individual of either species naturally conveys the thought to its usual attendant. Thus because such a particular idea is commonly annexed to such a particular word, nothing is required but the hearing of that word to produce the correspondent idea, and it will scarce be possible for the mind, by its utmost efforts, to prevent that transition. In this case it is not absolutely necessary that upon hearing such a particular sound we should reflect on any past experience, and consider what idea has been usually connected with the sound. The imagination of itself supplies the place of this reflection, and is so accustomed to pass from the word to the idea that it interposes not a moment's delay between the hearing of the one and the conception of the other.

But though I acknowledge this to be a true principle of association among ideas, I assert it to be the very same with that between the ideas of cause and effect, and to be an essential part in all our reasonings from that relation. We have no other notion of cause and effect but that of certain objects which have been *always conjoined* together, and which in all past instances have been found inseparable. We cannot penetrate into the reason of the conjunction. We only observe the thing itself, and always find that from the constant conjunction the objects acquire a union in the imagination. When the impression of one becomes present to us, we immediately form an idea of its usual attendant, and consequently we may establish this as one part of the definition of an opinion or belief, that it is *an idea related to or associated with a present impression.*

Thus though causation be a *philosophical* relation, as implying contiguity, succession, and constant conjunction, yet it is only so far as it is a *natural* relation, and produces a union among our ideas, that we are able to reason upon it, or draw any inference from it.

Section VII.

OF THE NATURE OF THE IDEA OR BELIEF

The idea of an object is an essential part of the belief of it, but not the whole. We conceive many things which we do not believe. In order then to discover more fully the nature of belief, or the qualities of those ideas we assent to, let us weigh the following considerations.

It is evident that all reasonings from causes or effects terminate in conclusions concerning matter of fact, that is, concerning the existence of objects or of their qualities. It is also evident that the idea of existence is nothing different from the idea of any object, and that when after the simple conception of anything we would conceive it as existent, we in reality make no addition to or alteration on our first idea. Thus when we affirm that God is existent, we simply form the idea of such a being as he is represented to us; nor is the existence which we attribute to him conceived by a particular idea which we join to the idea of his other qualities, and can again separate and distinguish from them. But I go further, and not content with asserting that the conception of the existence of any object is no addition to the simple conception of it, I likewise maintain that the belief of the existence joins no new ideas to those which compose the idea of the object. When I think of God, when I think of him as existent, and when I believe him to be existent, my idea of him neither increases nor diminishes. But as it is certain there is a great difference between the simple conception of the existence of an object and the belief of it, and as this difference lies not in the parts or composition of the idea which we conceive, it follows that it must lie in the *manner* in which we conceive it.

Suppose a person present with me who advances propositions to which I do not assent, *that* Caesar *died in his bed, that silver is more fusible than lead, or mercury heavier than gold;* it is evident that notwithstanding my incredulity I clearly understand his meaning, and form all the same ideas which he forms. My imagination is endowed with the same powers as his, nor is it possible for him to conceive any idea which I cannot conceive, or conjoin any which I cannot conjoin. I therefore ask, Wherein consists the difference between believing and disbelieving any proposition? The answer is easy with regard to propositions that are proved by intuition or demonstration. In that case, the person who assents not only conceives the ideas according to the proposition, but is necessarily determined to conceive them in that particular manner, either immediately or by the interposition of other ideas. Whatever is absurd is unintelligible, nor is it possible for the imagination to conceive anything contrary to a demonstration.

But as in reasonings from causation and concerning matters of fact this absolute necessity cannot take place, and the imagination is free to conceive both sides of the question, I still ask, *Wherein consists the difference between incredulity and belief?* since in both cases the conception of the idea is equally possible and requisite.

It will not be a satisfactory answer to say that a person who does not assent to a proposition you advance, after having conceived the object in the same manner with you, immediately conceives it in a different manner, and has different ideas of it. This answer is unsatisfactory, not because it contains any falsehood, but because it discovers not all the truth. It is confessed that in all cases wherein we dissent from any person we conceive both sides of the question, but as we can believe only one, it evidently follows that the belief must make some difference between that conception to which we assent and that from which we dissent. We may mingle and unite and separate and confound and vary our ideas in a hundred different ways, but till there appears some principle which fixes one of these different situations, we have in reality no opinion, and this principle, as it plainly makes no addition to our precedent ideas, can only change the *manner* of our conceiving them.

All the perceptions of the mind are of two kinds, *viz.*, impressions and ideas, which differ from each other only in their different degrees of force and vivacity. Our ideas are copied from our impressions and represent them in all their parts. When you would any way vary the idea of a particular object, you can only increase or diminish its force and vivacity.[1] If you make any other change on it, it represents a different object or impression. The case is the same as in colors. A particular shade of any color may acquire a new degree of liveliness or brightness without any other variation. But when you produce any other variation, it is no longer the same shade or

[1] [In the Appendix Hume confesses an "error" at this point "which more mature reflection has discovered to me in my reasoning." The error occurs "where I say that two ideas of the same object can only be different by their different degrees of force and vivacity. I believe there are other differences among ideas which cannot properly be comprehended under these terms. Had I said that two ideas of the same object can only be different by their different *feeling*, I should have been nearer the truth."—Ed.]

color. So that as belief does nothing but vary the manner in which we conceive any object, it can only bestow on our ideas an additional force and vivacity. An opinion, therefore, or belief may be most accurately defined, A LIVELY IDEA RELATED TO OR ASSOCIATED WITH A PRESENT IMPRESSION.[1]

Here are the heads of those arguments which lead us to this conclusion. When we infer the existence of an object from that of others, some object must always be present either to the memory or senses in order to be the foundation of our reason-

---

[1] We may here take occasion to observe a very remarkable error, which, being frequently inculcated in the schools, has become a kind of established maxim, and is universally received by all logicians. This error consists in the vulgar division of the acts of the understanding into *conception, judgment,* and *reasoning,* and in the definitions we give of them. Conception is defined to be the simple survey of one or more ideas, judgment to be the separating or uniting of different ideas, reasoning to be the separating or uniting of different ideas by the interposition of others which show the relation they bear to each other. But these distinctions and definitions are faulty in very considerable articles. For *first,* it is far from being true that in every judgment which we form we unite two different ideas, since in that proposition, *God is,* or indeed any other which regards existence, the idea of existence is no distinct idea which we unite with that of the object, and which is capable of forming a compound idea by the union. *Secondly,* as we can thus form a proposition which contains only one idea, so we may exert our reason without employing more than two ideas, and without having recourse to a third to serve as a medium between them. We infer a cause immediately from its effect, and this inference is not only a true species of reasoning, but the strongest of all others, and more convincing than when we interpose another idea to connect the two extremes. What we may in general affirm concerning these three acts of the understanding is that, taking them in a proper light, they all resolve themselves into the first, and are nothing but particular ways of conceiving our objects. Whether we consider a single object or several, whether we dwell on these objects or run from them to others, and in whatever form or order we survey them, the act of the mind exceeds not a simple conception; and the only remarkable difference which occurs on this occasion is when we join belief to the conception, and are persuaded of the truth of what we conceive. This act of the mind has never yet been explained by any philosopher, and therefore I am at liberty to propose my hypothesis concerning it, which is that it is only a strong and steady conception of any idea, and such as approaches in some measure to an immediate impression.

ing, since the mind cannot run up with its inferences *in infinitum*. Reason can never satisfy us that the existence of any one object does ever imply that of another, so that when we pass from the impression of one to the idea or belief of another, we are not determined by reason, but by custom or a principle of association. But belief is somewhat more than a simple idea. It is a particular manner of forming an idea, and as the same idea can only be varied by a variation of its degrees of force and vivacity, it follows upon the whole that belief is a lively idea produced by a relation to a present impression, according to the foregoing definition.

[1]This operation of the mind, which forms the belief of any matter of fact, seems hitherto to have been one of the greatest mysteries of philosophy, though no one has so much as suspected that there was any difficulty in explaining it. For my part I must own that I find a considerable difficulty in the case, and that even when I think I understand the subject perfectly, I am at a loss for terms to express my meaning. I conclude, by an induction which seems to me very evident, that an opinion or belief is nothing but an idea that is different from a fiction, not in the nature or the order of its parts, but in the *manner* of its being conceived. But when I would explain this *manner*, I scarce find any word that fully answers the case, but am obliged to have recourse to everyone's feeling, in order to give him a perfect notion of this operation of the mind. An idea assented to *feels* different from a fictitious idea that the fancy alone presents to us, and this different feeling I endeavor to explain by calling it a superior *force* or *vivacity* or *solidity* or *firmness* or *steadiness*. This variety of terms, which may seem so unphilosophical, is intended only to express that act of the mind which renders realities more present to us than fictions, causes them to weigh more in the thought, and gives them a superior influence on the passions and imagination. Provided we agree about the thing, it is needless to dispute about the terms. The imagination has the command over all its ideas, and can join and mix and vary them in all the ways possible. It may conceive objects with all the circumstances of place and time. It may set them, in a manner, before our eyes in their true colors, just as they might have

1 [This paragraph was first printed in the Appendix.—Ed.]

existed. But as it is impossible that that faculty can ever, of it-self, reach belief, it is evident that belief consists not in the nature and order of our ideas, but in the manner of their conception, and in their feeling to the mind. I confess that it is impossible to explain perfectly this feeling or manner of conception. We may make use of words that express something near it. But its true and proper name is *belief*, which is a term that everyone sufficiently understands in common life. And in philosophy we can go no further than assert that it is something *felt* by the mind which distinguishes the ideas of the judgment from the fictions of the imagination. It gives them more force and influence, makes them appear of greater importance, infixes them in the mind, and renders them the governing principles of all our actions.

This definition will also be found to be entirely conformable to everyone's feeling and experience. Nothing is more evident than that those ideas to which we assent are more strong, firm, and vivid than the loose reveries of a castle-builder. If one person sits down to read a book as a romance, and another as a true history, they plainly receive the same ideas, and in the same order; nor does the incredulity of the one and the belief of the other hinder them from putting the very same sense upon their author. His words produce the same ideas in both, though his testimony has not the same influence on them. The latter has a more lively conception of all the incidents. He enters deeper into the concerns of the persons, represents to himself their actions and characters and friendships and enmities. He even goes so far as to form a notion of their features and air and person. While the former, who gives no credit to the testimony of the author, has a more faint and languid conception of all these particulars, and except on account of the style and ingenuity of the composition, can receive little entertainment from it.

Section VIII.

OF THE CAUSES OF BELIEF

Having thus explained the nature of belief, and shown that it consists in a lively idea related to a present impression, let us now proceed to examine from what principles it is derived, and what bestows the vivacity on the idea.

I would willingly establish it as a general maxim in the science of human nature, *that when any impression becomes present to us, it not only transports the mind to such ideas as are related to it, but likewise communicates to them a share of its force and vivacity*. All the operations of the mind depend in a great measure on its disposition when it performs them, and according as the spirits are more or less elevated and the attention more or less fixed, the action will always have more or less vigor and vivacity. When therefore any object is presented which elevates and enlivens the thought, every action to which the mind applies itself will be more strong and vivid, as long as that disposition continues. Now it is evident the continuance of the disposition depends entirely on the objects about which the mind is employed, and that any new object naturally gives a new direction to the spirits and changes the disposition; as on the contrary, when the mind fixes constantly on the same object, or passes easily and insensibly along related objects, the disposition has a much longer duration. Hence it happens that when the mind is once enlivened by a present impression, it proceeds to form a more lively idea of the related objects, by a natural transition of the disposition from the one to the other. The change of the objects is so easy that the mind is scarce sensible of it, but applies itself to the conception of the related idea with all the force and vivacity it acquired from the present impression.

If in considering the nature of relation and that facility of transition which is essential to it, we can satisfy ourselves concerning the reality of this phenomenon, it is well; but I must confess I place my chief confidence in experience to prove so material a principle. We may, therefore, observe, as the first experiment to our present purpose, that upon the appearance of the picture of an absent friend, our idea of him is evidently enlived by the *resemblance*, and that every passion which that idea occasions, whether of joy or sorrow, acquires new force and vigor. In producing this effect there concur both a relation and a present impression. Where the picture bears him no resemblance, or at least was not intended for him, it never so much as conveys our thought to him; and where it is absent, as well as the person, though the mind may pass from the thought of the one to that of the other, it feels its idea to be rather weakened than enlivened by that transition. We take a pleasure in viewing the picture of a friend when it is set before us, but when it is removed, rather choose to consider him directly than by reflection in an image which is equally distant and obscure.

The ceremonies of the *Roman Catholic* religion may be considered as experiments of the same nature. The devotees of that strange superstition usually plead in excuse of the mummeries with which they are upbraided that they feel the good effect of those external motions and postures and actions in enlivening their devotion and quickening their fervor, which otherwise would decay away, if directed entirely to distant and immaterial objects. We shadow out the objects of our faith, say they, in sensible types and images, and render them more present to us by the immediate presence of these types than it is possible for us to do merely by an intellectual view and contemplation. Sensible objects have always a greater influence on the fancy than any other, and this influence they readily convey to those ideas to which they are related, and which they resemble. I shall only infer from these practices and this reasoning that the effect of resemblance in enlivening the idea is very common; and as in every case a resemblance and a present impression must concur, we are abundantly supplied with experiments to prove the reality of the foregoing principle.

We may add force to these experiments by others of a different kind, in considering the effects of *contiguity* as well as of *resemblance*. It is certain that distance diminishes the force of every idea, and that upon our approach to any object, though it does not discover itself to our senses, it operates upon the mind with an influence that imitates an immediate impression. The thinking on any object readily transports the mind to what is contiguous, but it is only the actual presence of an object that transports it with a superior vivacity. When I am a few miles from home, whatever relates to it touches me more nearly than when I am two hundred leagues distant, though even at that distance the reflecting on anything in the neighborhood of my friends and family naturally produces an idea of them. But as in this latter case both the objects of the mind are ideas, notwithstanding there is an easy transition between them, that transition alone is not able to give a superior vivacity to any of the ideas, for want of some immediate impression.[1]

No one can doubt but causation has the same influence as the other two relations of resemblance and contiguity. Superstitious people are fond of the relics of saints and holy men for the same reason that they seek after types and images, in order to enliven their devotion, and give them a more intimate and strong conception of those exemplary lives which they desire to imitate. Now it is evident one of the best relics a devotee could procure would be the handiwork of a saint, and if his clothes and furniture are ever to be considered in this light it is because they were once at his disposal, and were moved and affected by him, in which respect they are to be considered as imperfect effects, and as connected with him by a shorter chain of consequences than any of those from which we learn the reality of his existence. This phenomenon clearly proves that a present impression with a relation of causation may enliven any idea, and consequently produce belief or assent, according to the precedent definition of it.

But why need we seek for other arguments to prove that a present impression with a relation or transition of the fancy may enliven any idea, when this very instance of our reasonings from cause and effect will alone suffice to that purpose? It is certain we must have an idea of every matter of fact which we believe. It is certain that this idea arises only from a relation to a present impression. It is certain that the belief super-

[1] [In the Appendix Hume added, as a note to this passage, a long quotation from Cicero's *de Finibus,* Bk. v; this has been omitted in this edition.—Ed.]

adds nothing to the idea, but only changes our manner of conceiving it, and renders it more strong and lively. The present conclusion concerning the influence of relation is the immediate consequence of all these steps, and every step appears to me sure and infallible. There enters nothing into this operation of the mind but a present impression, a lively idea, and a relation or association in the fancy between the impression and idea, so that there can be no suspicion of mistake.

In order to put this whole affair in a fuller light, let us consider it as a question in natural philosophy, which we must determine by experience and observation. I suppose there is an object presented, from which I draw a certain conclusion, and form to myself ideas which I am said to believe or assent to. Here it is evident that however that object which is present to my senses, and that other, whose existence I infer by reasoning, may be thought to influence each other by their particular powers or qualities, yet as the phenomenon of belief which we at present examine is merely internal, these powers and qualities, being entirely unknown, can have no hand in producing it. It is the present impression which is to be considered as the true and real cause of the idea, and of the belief which attends it. We must therefore endeavor to discover by experiments the particular qualities by which it is enabled to produce so extraordinary an effect.

First then I observe that the present impression has not this effect by its own proper power and efficacy and when considered alone, as a single perception, limited to the present moment. I find that an impression from which, on its first appearance, I can draw no conclusion may afterwards become the foundation of belief, when I have had experience of its usual consequences. We must in every case have observed the same impression in past instances, and have found it to be constantly conjoined with some other impression. This is confirmed by such a multitude of experiments that it admits not of the smallest doubt.

From a second observation I conclude that the belief which attends the present impression and is produced by a number of past impressions and conjunctions, that this belief, I say, arises immediately, without any new operation of the reason or imagination. Of this I can be certain, because I never am conscious of any such operation, and find nothing in the subject on which it can be founded. Now as we call everything CUSTOM which proceeds from a past repetition without any new reasoning or conclusion, we may establish it as a certain truth that all the belief which follows upon any present impression is derived solely from that origin. When we are accustomed to see two impressions conjoined together, the appearance or idea of the one immediately carries us to the idea of the other.

Being fully satisfied on this head, I make a third set of experiments, in order to know whether anything be requisite, beside the customary transition, towards the production of this phenomenon of belief. I therefore change the first impression into an idea, and observe that though the customary transition to the correlative idea still remains, yet there is in reality no belief nor persuasion. A present impression, then, is absolutely requisite to this whole operation; and when after this I compare an impression with an idea, and find that their only difference consists in their different degrees of force and vivacity, I conclude upon the whole that belief is a more vivid and intense conception of an idea, proceeding from its relation to a present impression.

Thus all probable reasoning is nothing but a species of sensation. It is not solely in poetry and music we must follow our taste and sentiment, but likewise in philosophy. When I am convinced of any principle, it is only an idea which strikes more strongly upon me. When I give the preference to one set of arguments above another, I do nothing but decide from my feeling concerning the superiority of their influence. Objects have no discoverable connection together, nor is it from any other principle but custom operating upon the imagination that we can draw any inference from the appearance of one to the existence of another.

It will here be worth our observation that the past experience, on which all our judgments concerning cause and effect depend, may operate on our mind in such an insensible manner as never to be taken notice of, and may even in some measure be unknown to us. A person who stops short in his journey upon meeting a river in his way forsees the consequences of his proceeding forward, and his knowledge of these consequences is conveyed to him by past experience, which informs him of such certain conjunctions of causes and effects. But can we think that on this occasion he reflects on any past experience, and calls to remembrance instances that he has seen or heard of, in order to discover the effects of water on animal bodies? No surely; this is not the method in which he proceeds in his reasoning. The idea of sinking is so closely connected with that of water, and the idea of suffocating with that of sinking, that the mind makes the transition without the assistance of the memory. The custom operates before we have time for reflection. The objects seem so inseparable that we interpose not a moment's delay in passing from the one to the other. But as this transition proceeds from experience and not from any primary connection between the ideas, we must necessarily acknowledge that experience may produce a belief and a judgment of causes and effects by a secret operation, and without being once thought of. This removes all pretext, if there yet remains any, for asserting that the mind is convinced by reasoning of that principle, *that instances of which we have no experience must necessarily resemble those of which we have.* For we here find that the understanding or imagination can draw inferences from past experience without reflecting on it, much more without forming any principle concerning it, or reasoning upon that principle.

In general we may observe that in all the most established and uniform conjunctions of causes and effects, such as those of gravity, impulse, solidity, etc., the mind never carries its view expressly to consider any past experience, though in other associations of objects, which are more rare and unusual, it may assist the custom and transition of ideas by this reflection. Nay we find in some cases that the reflection produces the belief without the custom, or more properly speaking, that the reflection produces the custom in an *oblique* and *artificial* manner. I explain myself. It is certain that not only in philosophy but even in common life we may attain the knowledge of a particular cause merely by one experiment, provided it be made with judgment, and after a careful removal of all foreign and superfluous circumstances. Now as after one experiment of this kind the mind, upon the appearance either of the cause or the effect, can draw an inference concerning the existence of its correlative, and as a habit can never be acquired merely by one instance, it may be thought that belief cannot in this case be esteemed the effect of custom. But this difficulty will vanish if we consider that though we are here supposed to have had only one experiment of a particular effect, yet we have many millions to convince us of this principle, *that like objects, placed in like circumstances, will always produce like effects;* and as this principle has established itself by a sufficient custom, it bestows an evidence and firmness on any opinion to which it can be applied. The connection of the ideas is not habitual after one experiment, but this connection is comprehended under another principle that is habitual, which brings us back to our hypothesis. In all cases we transfer our experience to instances of which we have no experience, either *expressly* or *tacitly,* either *directly* or *indirectly.*

I must not conclude this subject without observing that it is very difficult to talk of the operations of the mind with perfect propriety and exactness, because common language has seldom made any very nice distinctions among them, but has generally called by the same term all such as nearly resemble each other. And as this is a source almost inevitable of obscurity and confusion in the author, so it may frequently give rise to doubts and objections in the reader, which otherwise he would never have dreamed of. Thus my general position, that an opinion or belief is *nothing but a strong and lively idea derived from a present impression related to it,* may be liable to the following objection, by reason of a little ambiguity in those words *strong and lively.* It may be said that not only an impression may give rise to reasoning, but that an idea may also have the same influence, especially upon my principle *that all our ideas are derived from correspondent impressions.* For suppose I form at present an idea of which I have forgotten the correspondent impression; I am able to conclude from this idea that such an impression did once exist, and as this conclusion is attended with belief, it may be asked from whence are the qualities of force and vivacity derived which constitute this belief? And to this I answer very readily, *from the present idea.* For as this idea is not here considered as the representation of any absent object, but as a real perception in the mind of which we are intimately conscious, it must be able to bestow on whatever is related to it the same quality, call it *firmness or solidity or force or vivacity,* with which the mind reflects upon it and is assured of its present existence. The idea here supplies the place of an impression, and is entirely the same, so far as regards our present purpose.

Upon the same principles we need not be surprised to hear of the remembrance of an idea, that is, of the idea of an idea, and of its force and vivacity superior to the loose conceptions of the imagination. In thinking of our past thoughts we not only delineate out the object of which we were thinking, but also conceive the action of the mind in the meditation, that certain *je-ne-sais-quoi,* of which it is impossible to give any definition or description, but which everyone sufficiently understands. When the memory offers an idea of this and represents it as past, it is easily conceived how that idea may have more vigor and firmness than when we think of a past thought of which we have no remembrance.

After this anyone will understand how we may form the idea of an impression and of an idea, and how we may believe the existence of an impression and of an idea.

Section XI.

OF THE PROBABILITY OF CHANCES

But in order to bestow on this system its full force and evidence, we must carry our eye from it a moment to consider its consequences, and explain from the same principles some other species of reasoning which are derived from the same origin.

Those philosophers who have divided human reason into *knowledge and probability,* and have defined the first to be *that evidence which arises from the comparison of ideas,* are obliged to comprehend all our arguments from causes or effects under the general term of probability. But though everyone be free to use his terms in what sense he pleases, and accordingly in the precedent part of this discourse I have followed this method of expression, it is however certain that in common discourse we readily affirm that many arguments from causation exceed probability, and may be received as a superior kind of evidence. One would appear ridiculous who would say that it is only probable the sun will rise tomorrow or that all men must die, though it is plain we have no further assurance of these facts than what experience affords us. For this reason, it would perhaps be more convenient, in order at once to preserve the common signification of words and mark the several degrees of evidence, to distinguish human reason into three kinds, *viz.*, *that from knowledge, from proofs, and from probabilities*. By knowledge, I mean the assurance arising from the comparison of ideas. By proofs, those arguments which are derived from the relation of cause and effect and which are entirely free from doubt and uncertainty. By probability, that evidence which is still attended with uncertainty. It is this last species of reasoning I proceed to examine.

Probability or reasoning from conjecture may be divided into two kinds, *viz.*, that which is founded on *chance,* and that which arises from *causes.* . . .

. . . . .

Section XII.

OF THE PROBABILITY OF CAUSES

What I have said concerning the probability of chances can serve to no other purpose than to assist us in explaining the probability of causes, since it is commonly allowed by philosophers that what the vulgar call chance is nothing but a secret and concealed cause. That species of probability, therefore, is what we must chiefly examine.

The probabilities of causes are of several kinds, but are all derived from the same origin, *viz.*, *the association of ideas to a present impression.* As the habit which produces the association arises from the frequent conjunction of objects, it must arrive at its perfection by degrees, and must acquire new force from each instance that falls under our observation. The first instance has little or no force; the second makes some addition to it; the third becomes still more sensible; and it is by these slow steps that our judgment arrives at a full assurance. But before it attains this pitch of perfection, it passes through several inferior degrees, and in all of them is only to be esteemed a presumption or probability. The gradation, therefore, from probabilities to proofs is in many cases insensible, and the difference between these kinds of evidence is more easily perceived in the remote degrees than in the near and contiguous.

It is worthy of remark on this occasion that though the species of probability here explained be the first in order, and naturally takes place before any entire proof can exist, yet no one who is arrived at the age of maturity can any longer be acquainted with it. It is true, nothing is more common than for people of the most advanced knowledge to have attained only an imperfect experience of many particular events, which naturally produces only an imperfect habit and transition. But then we must consider that the mind, having formed another observation concerning the connection of causes and effects, gives new force to its reasoning from that observation, and by means of it can build an argument on one single experiment, when duly prepared and examined. What we have found once to follow from any object, we conclude will forever follow from it; and if this maxim be not always built upon as certain, it is not for want of a sufficient number of experiments, but because we frequently meet with instances to the contrary; which leads us to the second species of probability, where there is a *contrariety* in our experience and observation.

. . . . .

. . . contrary experiments produce an imperfect belief, either by weakening the habit, or by dividing and afterwards joining in different parts that *perfect* habit which makes us conclude in general that instances of which we have no exerience must necessarily resemble those of which we have.

. . . . .

But beside these two species of probability, which are derived from an *imperfect* experience and from *contrary* causes, there is a third arising from ANALOGY, which differs from them in some material circumstances. According to the hypothesis above explained all kinds of reasoning from causes or effects are founded on two particulars, *viz.*, the constant conjunction of any two objects in all past experience, and the resemblance of a present object to any one of them. The effect of these two particulars is that the present object invigorates and enlivens the imagination, and the resemblance, along with the constant union, conveys this force and vivacity to the related idea, which we are therefore said to believe, or assent to. If you weaken either the union or resemblance, you weaken the principle of transition, and of consequence that belief which arises from it. The vivacity of the first impression cannot be fully conveyed to the related idea, either where the conjunction of their objects is not constant, or where the present impression does not perfectly resemble any of those whose union we are accustomed to observe. In those probabilities of chance and causes above-explained, it is the constancy of the union which is diminished; and in the probability derived from analogy, it is the resemblance only which is affected. Without some degree of resemblance, as well as union, it is impossible there can be any reasoning, but as this resemblance admits of many different degrees, the reasoning becomes proportionably more or less firm and certain. An experiment loses of its force when transferred to instances which are not exactly resembling, though it is evident it may still retain as much as may be the foundation of probability as long as there is any resemblance remaining.

Section XIII.

OF UNPHILOSOPHICAL PROBABILITY

. . . . .

Thus it appears upon the whole that every kind of opinion or judgment which amounts not to knowledge is derived entirely from the force and vivacity of the perception, and that these qualities constitute in the mind what we call the BELIEF of the existence of any object. This force and this vivacity are most conspicuous in the memory, and therefore our confidence in the veracity of that faculty is the greatest imaginable, and equals in many respects the assurance of a demonstration. The

next degree of these qualities is that derived from the relation of cause and effect, and this too is very great, especially when the conjunction is found by experience to be perfectly constant, and when the object which is present to us exactly resembles those of which we have had experience. But below this degree of evidence there are many others which have an influence on the passions and imagination, proportioned to that degree of force and vivacity which they communicate to the ideas. It is by habit we make the transition from cause to effect, and it is from some present impression we borrow that vivacity which we diffuse over the correlative idea. But when we have not observed a sufficient number of instances to produce a strong habit, or when these instances are contrary to each other, or when the resemblance is not exact, or the present impression is faint and obscure, or the experience in some measure obliterated from the memory, or the connection dependent on a long chain of objects, or the inference derived from general rules and yet not conformable to them; in all these cases the evidence diminishes by the diminution of the force and intenseness of the idea. This therefore is the nature of the judgment and probability.

What principally gives authority to this system is, beside the undoubted arguments upon which each part is founded, the agreement of these parts, and the necessity of one to explain another. The belief which attends our memory is of the same nature with that which is derived from our judgments; nor is there any difference between that judgment which is derived from a constant and uniform connection of causes and effects and that which depends upon an interrupted and uncertain. It is indeed evident that in all determinations where the mind decides from contrary experiments, it is first divided within itself, and has an inclination to either side in proportion to the number of experiments we have seen and remember. This contest is at last determined to the advantage of that side where we observe a superior number of these experiments, but still with a diminution of force in the evidence correspondent to the number of the opposite experiments. Each possibility of which the probability is composed operates separately upon the imagination, and it is the larger collection of possibilities which at last prevails, and that with a force proportionable to its superiority. All these phenomena lead directly to the precedent system, nor will it ever be possible upon any other principles to give a satisfactory and consistent explication of them. Without considering these judgments as the effects of custom on the imagination, we shall lose ourselves in perpetual contradiction and absurdity.

Section XIV.

OF THE IDEA OF NECESSARY CONNECTION

Having thus explained the manner *in which we reason beyond our immediate impressions and conclude that such particular causes must have such particular effects,* we must now return upon our footsteps to examine that question which first occurred to us,[1] and which we dropped in our way, *viz., What is our idea of necessity, when we say that two objects are necessarily connected together?* Upon this head I repeat what I have often had occasion to observe, that as we have no idea that is not derived from an impression, we must find some impression that gives rise to this idea of necessity, if we assert we have really such an idea. In order to this I consider in what objects necessity is commonly supposed to lie, and finding that it is always ascribed to causes and effects, I turn my eye to two objects supposed to be placed in that relation, and examine them in all the situations of which they are susceptible. I immediately perceive that they are *contiguous* in time and place, and that the object we call cause *precedes* the other we call effect. In no one instance can I go any further, nor is it possible for me to discover any third relation between these objects. I therefore enlarge my view to comprehend several instances, where I find like objects always existing in like relations of contiguity and succession. At first sight this seems to serve but little to my purpose. The reflection on several instances only repeats the same object, and therefore can never give rise to a new idea. But upon further inquiry I find that the repetition is not in every particular the same, but produces
[1] Section II.

a new impression, and by that means the idea which I at present examine. For after a frequent repetition I find that upon the appearance of one of the objects, the mind is *determined* by custom to consider its usual attendant, and to consider it in a stronger light upon account of its relation to the first object. It is this impression, then, or *determination*, which affords me the idea of necessity.

I doubt not but these consequences will at first sight be received without difficulty, as being evident deductions from principles which we have already established, and which we have often employed in our reasonings. This evidence both in the first principles and in the deductions may seduce us unwarily into the conclusion, and make us imagine it contains nothing extraordinary, nor worthy of our curiosity. But though such an inadvertence may facilitate the reception of this reasoning, it will make it be the more easily forgotten, for which reason I think it proper to give warning that I have just now examined one of the most sublime questions in philosophy, *viz., that concerning the power and efficacy of causes,* where all the sciences seem so much interested. Such a warning will naturally rouse up the attention of the reader, and make him desire a more full account of my doctrine, as well as of the arguments on which it is founded. This request is so reasonable that I cannot refuse complying with it, especially as I am hopeful that these principles, the more they are examined, will acquire the more force and evidence.

There is no question which on account of its importance, as well as difficulty, has caused more disputes both among ancient and modern philosophers than this concerning the efficacy of causes, or that quality which makes them be followed by their effects. But before they entered upon these disputes, methinks it would not have been improper to have examined what idea we have of that efficacy which is the subject of the controversy. This is what I find principally wanting in their reasonings, and what I shall here endeavor to supply.

I begin with observing that the terms of *efficacy, agency, power, force, energy, necessity, connection,* and *productive quality* are all nearly synonymous, and therefore it is an absurdity to employ any of them in defining the rest. By this observation we reject at once all the vulgar definitions which philosophers have given of power and efficacy, and instead of searching for the idea in these definitions, must look for it in the impressions from which it is originally derived. If it be a compound idea, it must arise from compound impressions. If simple, from simple impressions.

I believe the most general and most popular explication of this matter is to say[1] that finding from experience that there are several new productions in matter, such as the motions and variations of body, and concluding that there must somewhere be a power capable of producing them, we arrive at last by this reasoning at the idea of power and efficacy. But to be convinced that this explication is more popular than philosophical, we need but reflect on two very obvious principles. *First,* that reason alone can never give rise to any original idea, and *secondly,* that reason, as distinguished from experience, can never make us conclude that a cause or productive quality is absolutely requisite to every beginning of existence. Both these considerations have been sufficiently explained, and therefore shall not at present be any further insisted on.

I shall only infer from them that since reason can never give rise to the idea of efficacy, that idea must be derived from experience, and from some particular instances of this efficacy which make their passage into the mind by the common channels of sensation or reflection. Ideas always represent their objects or impressions; and *vice versa,* there are some objects necessary to give rise to every idea. If we pretend, therefore, to have any just idea of this efficacy, we must produce some instance wherein the efficacy is plainly discoverable to the mind, and its operations obvious to our consciousness or sensation. By the refusal of this, we acknowledge that the idea is impossible and imaginary, since the principle of innate ideas, which alone can save us from this dilemma, has been already refuted, and is now almost universally rejected in the learned world. Our present business, then, must be to find some natural production where the operation and efficacy of a cause can be clearly conceived and comprehended by the mind, without any danger of obscurity or mistake.

[1] See Mr. *Locke,* chapter on power.

In this research we meet with very little encouragement from that prodigious diversity which is found in the opinions of those philosophers who have pretended to explain the secret force and energy of causes.[1] There are some who maintain that bodies operate by their substantial form; others, by their accidents or qualities; several, by their matter and form; some, by their form and accidents; others, by certain virtues and faculties distinct from all this. All these sentiments again are mixed and varied in a thousand different ways and form a strong presumption that none of them have any solidity or evidence and that the supposition of an efficacy in any of the known qualities of matter is entirely without foundation. This presumption must increase upon us when we consider that these principles of substantial forms and accidents and faculties are not in reality any of the known properties of bodies, but are perfectly unintelligible and inexplicable. For it is evident philosophers would never have had recourse to such obscure and uncertain principles had they met with any satisfaction in such as are clear and intelligible, especially in such an affair as this, which must be an object of the simplest understanding, if not of the senses. Upon the whole, we may conclude that it is impossible in any one instance to show the principle in which the force and agency of a cause is placed, and that the most refined and most vulgar understandings are equally at a loss in this particular. If anyone think proper to refute this assertion, he need not put himself to the trouble of inventing any long reasonings, but may at once show us an instance of a cause where we discover the power or operating principle. This defiance we are obliged frequently to make use of, as being almost the only means of proving a negative in philosophy.

The small success which has been met with in all the attempts to fix this power has at last obliged philosophers to conclude that the ultimate force and efficacy of nature is perfectly unknown to us, and that it is in vain we search for it in all the known qualities of matter. In this opinion they are almost unanimous, and it is only in the inference they draw from it that they discover any difference in their sentiments.

[1] See Father *Malebranche*, Bk. vi. Pt. ii. chap. 3, and the illustrations upon it.

For some of them, as the *Cartesians* in particular, having established it as a principle that we are perfectly acquainted with the essence of matter, have very naturally inferred that it is endowed with no efficacy, and that it is impossible for it of itself to communicate motion, or produce any of those effects which we ascribe to it. As the essence of matter consists in extension, and as extension implies not actual motion but only mobility, they conclude that the energy which produces the motion cannot lie in the extension.

This conclusion leads them into another, which they regard as perfectly unavoidable. Matter, say they, is in itself entirely inactive, and deprived of any power by which it may produce or continue or communicate motion. But since these effects are evident to our senses, and since the power that produces them must be placed somewhere, it must lie in the DEITY, or that divine being who contains in his nature all excellence and perfection. It is the deity, therefore, who is the prime mover of the universe, and who not only first created matter and gave it its original impulse, but likewise by a continued exertion of omnipotence supports its existence, and successively bestows on it all those motions and configurations and qualities with which it is endowed.

This opinion is certainly very curious, and well worth our attention, but it will appear superfluous to examine it in this place if we reflect a moment on our present purpose in taking notice of it. We have established it as a principle, that as all ideas are derived from impressions or some precedent *perceptions,* it is impossible we can have any idea of power and efficacy unless some instances can be produced wherein this power *is perceived* to exert itself. Now as these instances can never be discovered in body, the *Cartesians,* proceeding upon their principle of innate ideas, have had recourse to a supreme spirit or deity, whom they consider as the only active being in the universe, and as the immediate cause of every alteration in matter. But the principle of innate ideas being allowed to be false, it follows that the supposition of a deity can serve us in no stead in accounting for that idea of agency which we search for in vain in all the objects which are presented to our senses, or which we are internally conscious of in our own minds. For if every idea be derived from an impression, the idea of a deity proceeds from the same origin; and if no impression, either of sensation or reflection, implies any force or efficacy, it is equally impossible to discover or even imagine any such active principle in the deity. Since these philosophers, therefore, have concluded that matter cannot be endowed with any efficacious principle, because it is impossible to discover in it such a principle, the same course of reasoning should determine them to exclude it from the supreme being. Or if they esteem that opinion absurd and impious, as it really is, I shall tell them how they may avoid it, and that is by concluding from the very first that they have no adequate idea of power or efficacy in any object, since neither in body nor spirit, neither in superior nor inferior natures, are they able to discover one single instance of it.

The same conclusion is unavoidable upon the hypothesis of those who maintain the efficacy of second causes, and attribute a derivative but a real power and energy to matter. For as they confess that this energy lies not in any of the known qualities of matter, the difficulty still remains concerning the origin of its idea. If we have really an idea of power, we may attribute power to an unknown quality. But as it is impossible that that idea can be derived from such a quality, and as there is nothing in known qualities which can produce it, it follows that we deceive ourselves when we imagine we are possessed of any idea of this kind, after the manner we commonly understand it. All ideas are derived from and represent impressions. We never have any impression that contains any power or efficacy. We never therefore have any idea of power.

[1]Some have asserted that we feel an energy or power in our own mind, and that having in this manner acquired the idea of power, we transfer that quality to matter, where we are not able immediately to discover it. The motions of our body and the thoughts and sentiments of our mind (say they) obey the will, nor do we seek any further to acquire a just notion of force or power. But to convince us how fallacious this reasoning is, we need only consider that the will being here considered as a cause has no more a discoverable connection with its effects than any material cause has with

1 [This paragraph was first printed in the Appendix.—Ed.]

its proper effect. So far from perceiving the connection between an act of volition and a motion of the body, it is allowed that no effect is more inexplicable from the powers and
essence of thought and matter. Nor is the empire of the will
over our mind more intelligible. The effect is there distinguishable and separable from the cause, and could not be foreseen
without the experience of their constant conjunction. We have
command over our mind to a certain degree, but beyond *that*
lose all empire over it; and it is evidently impossible to fix any
precise bounds to our authority, where we consult not experience. In short, the actions of the mind are, in this respect,
the same with those of matter. We perceive only their constant conjunction, nor can we ever reason beyond it. No internal impression has an apparent energy, more than external
objects have. Since, therefore, matter is confessed by philosophers to operate by an unknown force, we should in vain
hope to attain an idea of force by consulting our own minds.[1]

It has been established as a certain principle that general or
abstract ideas are nothing but individual ones taken in a certain light, and that, in reflecting on any object, it is as impossible to exclude from our thought all particular degrees of
quantity and quality as from the real nature of things. If we
be possessed, therefore, of any idea of power in general, we
must also be able to conceive some particular species of it;
and as power cannot subsist alone, but is always regarded
as an attribute of some being or existence, we must be able to
place this power in some particular being, and conceive that
being as endowed with a real force and energy, by which
such a particular effect necessarily results from its operation.
We must distinctly and particularly conceive the connection
between the cause and effect, and be able to pronounce, from
a simple view of the one, that it must be followed or preceded by the other. This is the true manner of conceiving a
particular power in a particular body, and a general idea be-

[1] The same imperfection attends our ideas of the deity; but this
can have no effect either on religion or morals. The order of the
universe proves an omnipotent mind, that is, a mind whose will is
constantly attended with the obedience of every creature and being.
Nothing more is requisite to give a foundation to all the articles of
religion, nor is it necessary we should form a distinct idea of the
force and energy of the supreme being.

ing impossible without an individual; where the latter is impossible, it is certain the former can never exist. Now nothing is more evident than that the human mind cannot form such an idea of two objects as to conceive any connection between them, or comprehend distinctly that power or efficacy by which they are united. Such a connection would amount to a demonstration, and would imply the absolute impossibility for the one object not to follow, or to be conceived not to follow upon the other, which kind of connection has already been rejected in all cases. If anyone is of a contrary opinion, and thinks he has attained a notion of power in any particular object, I desire he may point out to me that object. But till I meet with such-a-one, which I despair of, I cannot forbear concluding that since we can never distinctly conceive how any particular power can possibly reside in any particular object, we deceive ourselves in imagining we can form any such general idea.

Thus upon the whole we may infer that when we talk of any being, whether of a superior or inferior nature, as endowed with a power or force proportioned to any effect, when we speak of a necessary connection between objects and suppose that this connection depends upon an efficacy or energy with which any of these objects are endowed, in all these expressions, *so applied,* we have really no distinct meaning, and make use only of common words without any clear and determinate ideas. But as it is more probable that these expressions do here lose their true meaning by being *wrongly applied* than that they never have any meaning, it will be proper to bestow another consideration on this subject, to see if possibly we can discover the nature and origin of those ideas we annex to them.

Suppose two objects to be presented to us, of which the one is the cause and the other the effect; it is plain that from the simple consideration of one or both these objects we never shall perceive the tie by which they are united, or be able certainly to pronounce that there is a connection between them. It is not, therefore, from any one instance that we arrive at the idea of cause and effect, of a necessary connection, of power, of force, of energy, and of efficacy. Did we never see any but particular conjunctions of objects, entirely different from each other, we should never be able to form any such ideas.

But again, suppose we observe several instances in which the same objects are always conjoined together, we immediately conceive a connection between them, and begin to draw an inference from one to another. This multiplicity of resembling instances, therefore, constitutes the very essence of power or connection, and is the source from which the idea arises. In order, then, to understand the idea of power, we must consider that multiplicity; nor do I ask more to give a solution of that difficulty which has so long perplexed us. For thus I reason. The repetition of perfectly similar instances can never *alone* give rise to an original idea different from what is to be found in any particular instance, as has been observed and as evidently follows from our fundamental principle, *that all ideas are copied from impressions.* Since therefore the idea of power is a new original idea, not to be found in any one instance, and which yet arises from the repetition of several instances, it follows that the repetition *alone* has not that effect, but must either *discover* or *produce* something new, which is the source of that idea. Did the repetition neither discover nor produce anything new, our ideas might be multiplied by it, but would not be enlarged above what they are upon the observation of one single instance. Every enlargement, therefore (such as the idea of power or connection), which arises from the multiplicity of similar instances, is copied from some effects of the multiplicity, and will be perfectly understood by understanding these effects. Wherever we find anything new to be discovered or produced by the repetition, there we must place the power, and must never look for it in any other object.

But it is evident, in the first place, that the repetition of like objects in like relations of succession and contiguity *discovers* nothing new in any one of them, since we can draw no inference from it nor make it a subject either of our demonstrative or probable reasonings, [1]as has been already proved. Nay suppose we could draw an inference, it would be of no consequence in the present case, since no kind of reasoning can give rise to a new idea such as this of power is, but wherever

[1] Section VI.

we reason, we must antecedently be possessed of clear ideas which may be the objects of our reasoning. The conception always precedes the understanding, and where the one is obscure, the other is uncertain; where the one fails, the other must fail also.

Secondly, it is certain that this repetition of similar objects in similar situations *produces* nothing new either in these objects or in any external body. For it will readily be allowed that the several instances we have of the conjunction of resembling causes and effects are in themselves entirely independent, and that the communication of motion which I see result at present from the shock of two billiard balls is totally distinct from that which I saw result from such an impulse a twelve-month ago. These impulses have no influence on each other. They are entirely divided by time and place, and the one might have existed and communicated motion though the other never had been in being.

There is, then, nothing new either discovered or produced in any objects by their constant conjunction, and by the uninterrupted resemblance of their relations of succession and contiguity. But it is from this resemblance that the ideas of necessity, of power, and of efficacy are derived. These ideas, therefore, represent not anything that does or can belong to the objects which are constantly conjoined. This is an argument which, in every view we can examine it, will be found perfectly unanswerable. Similar instances are still the first source of our idea of power or necessity, at the same time that they have no influence by their similarity either on each other or on any external object. We must therefore turn ourselves to some other quarter to seek the origin of that idea.

Though the several resembling instances which give rise to the idea of power have no influence on each other, and can never produce any new quality *in the object* which can be the model of that idea, yet the *observation* of this resemblance produces a new impression *in the mind*, which is its real model. For after we have observed the resemblance in a sufficient number of instances, we immediately feel a determination of the mind to pass from one object to its usual attendant, and to conceive it in a stronger light upon account of that relation. This determination is the only effect of the resemblance, and therefore must be the same with power or efficacy, whose idea is derived from the resemblance. The several instances of resembling conjunctions leads us into the notion of power and necessity. These instances are in themselves totally distinct from each other and have no union but in the mind, which observes them and collects their ideas. Necessity, then, is the effect of this observation, and is nothing but an internal impression of the mind, or a determination to carry our thoughts from one object to another. Without considering it in this view, we can never arrive at the most distant notion of it, or be able to attribute it either to external or internal objects, to spirit or body, to causes or effects.

The necessary connection between causes and effects is the foundation of our inference from one to the other. The foundation of our inference is the transition arising from the accustomed union. These are, therefore, the same.

The idea of necessity arises from some impression. There is no impression conveyed by our senses which can give rise to that idea. It must, therefore, be derived from some internal impression or impression of reflection. There is no internal impression which has any relation to the present business but that propensity which custom produces to pass from an object to the idea of its usual attendant. This therefore is the essence of necessity. Upon the whole, necessity is something that exists in the mind, not in objects; nor is it possible for us ever to form the most distant idea of it, considered as a quality in bodies. Either we have no idea of necessity, or necessity is nothing but that determination of the thought to pass from causes to effects and from effects to causes, according to their experienced union.

Thus as the necessity which makes two times two equal to four, or three angles of a triangle equal to two right ones, lies only in the act of the understanding by which we consider and compare these ideas, in like manner the necessity or power which unites causes and effects lies in the determination of the mind to pass from the one to the other. The efficacy or energy of causes is neither placed in the causes themselves, nor in the deity, nor in the concurrence of these two principles, but belongs entirely to the soul, which considers the union of two or more objects in all past instances. It is here

that the real power of causes is placed, along with their connection and necessity.

I am sensible that of all the paradoxes which I have had
or shall hereafter have occasion to advance in the course of
this treatise, the present one is the most violent, and that it
is merely by dint of solid proof and reasoning I can ever hope
it will have admission, and overcome the inveterate prejudices of mankind. Before we are reconciled to this doctrine,
how often must we repeat to ourselves *that* the simple view
of any two objects or actions, however related, can never
give us any idea of power, or of a connection between
them; *that* this idea arises from the repetition of their union;
that the repetition neither discovers nor causes anything in
the objects, but has an influence only on the mind, by that
customary transition it produces; *that* this customary transition is, therefore, the same with the power and necessity,
which are consequently qualities of perceptions, not of objects, and are internally felt by the soul and not perceived
externally in bodies? There is commonly an astonishment attending everything extraordinary, and this astonishment
changes immediately into the highest degree of esteem or contempt, according as we approve or disapprove of the subject. I am much afraid that though the foregoing reasoning
appears to me the shortest and most decisive imaginable, yet
with the generality of readers the bias of the mind will prevail, and give them a prejudice against the present doctrine.

This contrary bias is easily accounted for. It is a common
observation that the mind has a great propensity to spread
itself on external objects, and to conjoin with them any internal impressions which they occasion and which always make
their appearance at the same time that these objects discover themselves to the senses. Thus as certain sounds and
smells are always found to attend certain visible objects, we
naturally imagine a conjunction, even in place, between the
objects and qualities, though the qualities be of such a nature
as to admit of no such conjunction, and really exist nowhere.
But of this more fully hereafter.[1] Meanwhile it is sufficient to
observe that the same propensity is the reason why we suppose necessity and power to lie in the objects we consider, not

[1] Part IV, Section V.

in our mind that considers them, notwithstanding it is not possible for us to form the most distant idea of that quality, when it is not taken for the determination of the mind to pass from the idea of an object to that of its usual attendant.

But though this be the only reasonable account we can give of necessity, the contrary notion is so riveted in the mind from the principles above-mentioned that I doubt not but my sentiments will be treated by many as extravagant and ridiculous. What! the efficacy of causes lie in the determination of the mind! As if causes did not operate entirely independent of the mind, and would not continue their operation even though there was no mind existent to contemplate them or reason concerning them. Thought may well depend on causes for its operation, but not causes on thought. This is to reverse the order of nature, and make that secondary which is really primary. To every operation there is a power proportioned, and this power must be placed on the body that operates. If we remove the power from one cause we must ascribe it to another, but to remove it from all causes and bestow it on a being that is no way related to the cause or effect but by perceiving them is a gross absurdity, and contrary to the most certain principles of human reason.

I can only reply to all these arguments that the case is here much the same as if a blind man should pretend to find a great many absurdities in the supposition that the color of scarlet is not the same with the sound of a trumpet, nor light the same with solidity. If we have really no idea of a power or efficacy in any object, or of any real connection between causes and effects, it will be to little purpose to prove that an efficacy is necessary in all operations. We do not understand our own meaning in talking so, but ignorantly confound ideas which are entirely distinct from each other. I am, indeed, ready to allow that there may be several qualities both in material and immaterial objects with which we are utterly unacquainted, and if we please to call these *power* or *efficacy*, it will be of little consequence to the world. But when, instead of meaning these unknown qualities, we make the terms of power and efficacy signify something of which we have a clear idea, and which is incompatible with those objects to which we apply it, obscurity and error begin then to take place, and we are led astray by a false philosophy. This is the case when we transfer the determination of the thought to external objects, and suppose any real intelligible connection between them, that being a quality which can only belong to the mind that considers them.

As to what may be said, that the operations of nature are independent of our thought and reasoning, I allow it, and accordingly have observed that objects bear to each other the relations of contiguity and succession; that like objects may be observed in several instances to have like relations; and that all this is independent of and antecedent to the operations of the understanding. But if we go any further and ascribe a power or necessary connection to these objects, this is what we can never observe in them, but must draw the idea of it from what we feel internally in contemplating them. And this I carry so far that I am ready to convert my present reasoning into an instance of it by a subtlety which it will not be difficult to comprehend.

When any object is presented to us, it immediately conveys to the mind a lively idea of that object which is usually found to attend it, and this determination of the mind forms the necessary connection of these objects. But when we change the point of view from the objects to the perceptions, in that case the impression is to be considered as the cause and the lively idea as the effect, and their necessary connection is that new determination which we feel to pass from the idea of the one to that of the other. The uniting principle among our internal perceptions is as unintelligible as that among external objects, and is not known to us any other way than by experience. Now the nature and effects of experience have been already sufficiently examined and explained. It never gives us any insight into the internal structure or operating principle of objects, but only accustoms the mind to pass from one to another.

It is now time to collect all the different parts of this reasoning, and by joining them together form an exact definition of the relation of cause and effect, which makes the subject of the present inquiry. This order would not have been excusable, of first examining our inference from the relation before we had explained the relation itself, had it been possible to proceed in a different method. But as the nature of the relation depends so much on that of the inference, we have been obliged to advance in this seemingly preposterous manner, and make use of terms before we were able exactly to define them, or fix their meaning. We shall now correct this fault by giving a precise definition of cause and effect.

There may two definitions be given of this relation, which are only different by their presenting a different view of the same object, and making us consider it either as a *philosophical* or as a *natural* relation, either as a comparison of two ideas or as an association between them. We may define a CAUSE to be 'An object precedent and contiguous to another, and where all the objects resembling the former are placed in like relations of precedency and contiguity to those objects that resemble the latter.' If this definition be esteemed defective, because drawn from objects foreign to the cause, we may substitute this other definition in its place, *viz.*, "A CAUSE is an object precedent and contiguous to another, and so united with it that the idea of the one determines the mind to form the idea of the other, and the impression of the one to form a more lively idea of the other." Should this definition also be rejected for the same reason, I know no other remedy than that the persons who express this delicacy should substitute a juster definition in its place. But for my part I must own my incapacity for such an undertaking. When I examine with the utmost accuracy those objects which are commonly denominated causes and effects, I find, in considering a single instance, that the one object is precedent and contiguous to the other, and in enlarging my view to consider several instances, I find only that like objects are constantly placed in like relations of succession and contiguity. Again, when I consider the influence of this constant conjunction, I perceive that such a relation can never be an object of reasoning, and can never operate upon the mind but by means of custom, which determines the imagination to make a transition from the idea of one object to that of its usual attendant, and from the impression of one to a more lively idea of the other. However extraordinary these sentiments may appear, I think it fruitless to trouble myself with any further inquiry or reasoning upon the subject, but shall repose myself on them as on established maxims.

It will only be proper, before we leave this subject, to draw some corollaries from it, by which we may remove several prejudices and popular errors that have very much prevailed in philosophy. First we may learn from the foregoing doctrine that all causes are of the same kind, and that in particular there is no foundation for that distinction which we sometimes make between efficient causes and causes *sine qua non,* or between efficient causes and formal and material and exemplary and final causes. For as our idea of efficiency is derived from the constant conjunction of two objects, wherever this is observed the cause is efficient, and where it is not, there can never be a cause of any kind. For the same reason we must reject the distinction between *cause* and *occasion,* when supposed to signify anything essentially different from each other. If constant conjunction be implied in what we call occasion, it is a real cause. If not, it is no relation at all, and cannot give rise to any argument or reasoning.

Secondly, the same course of reasoning will make us conclude that there is but one kind of *necessity,* as there is but one kind of cause, and that the common distinction between *moral* and *physical* necessity is without any foundation in nature. This clearly appears from the precedent explication of necessity. It is the constant conjunction of objects, along with the determination of the mind, which constitutes a physical necessity, and the removal of these is the same thing with *chance.* As objects must either be conjoined or not, and as the mind must either be determined or not to pass from one object to another, it is impossible to admit of any medium between chance and an absolute necessity. In weakening this conjunction and determination you do not change the nature of the necessity, since even in the operation of bodies these have different degrees of constancy and force, without producing a different species of that relation.

The distinction which we often make between *power* and the *exercise* of it is equally without foundation.

Thirdly, we may now be able fully to overcome all that

repugnance which it is so natural for us to entertain against the foregoing reasoning by which we endeavored to prove that the necessity of a cause to every beginning of existence is not founded on any arguments either demonstrative or intuitive. Such an opinion will not appear strange after the foregoing definitions. If we define a cause to be *an object precedent and contiguous to another, and where all the objects resembling the former are placed in a like relation of priority and contiguity to those objects that resemble the latter,* we may easily conceive that there is no absolute nor metaphysical necessity that every beginning of existence should be attended with such an object. If we define a cause to be *an object precedent and contiguous to another, and so united with it in the imagination that the idea of the one determines the mind to form the idea of the other, and the impression of the one to form a more lively idea of the other,* we shall make still less difficulty of assenting to this opinion. Such an influence on the mind is in itself perfectly extraordinary and incomprehensible, nor can we be certain of its reality but from experience and observation.

I shall add as a fourth corollary that we can never have reason to believe that any object exists of which we cannot form an idea. For as all our reasonings concerning existence are derived from causation, and as all our reasonings concerning causation are derived from the experienced conjunction of objects, not from any reasoning or reflection, the same experience must give us a notion of these objects, and must remove all mystery from our conclusions. This is so evident that it would scarce have merited our attention were it not to obviate certain objections of this kind which might arise against the following reasonings concerning *matter* and *substance.* I need not observe that a full knowledge of the object is not requisite, but only of those qualities of it which we believe to exist.

Part IV.

OF THE SKEPTICAL AND OTHER SYSTEMS OF PHILOSOPHY

Section I.

OF SKEPTICISM WITH REGARD TO REASON

IN ALL DEMONSTRATIVE sciences the rules are certain and infallible, but when we apply them our fallible and uncertain faculties are very apt to depart from them and fall into error. We must, therefore, in every reasoning form a new judgment, as a check or control on our first judgment or belief, and must enlarge our view to comprehend a kind of history of all the instances wherein our understanding has deceived us, compared with those wherein its testimony was just and true. Our reason must be considered as a kind of cause of which truth is the natural effect, but such-a-one as by the irruption of other causes, and by the inconstancy of our mental powers, may frequently be prevented. By this means all knowledge degenerates into probability, and this probability is greater or less, according to our experience of the veracity or deceitfulness of our understanding, and according to the simplicity or intricacy of the question.

There is no algebraist nor mathematician so expert in his science as to place entire confidence in any truth immediately upon his discovery of it, or regard it as anything but a mere probability. Every time he runs over his proofs his confidence increases, but still more by the approbation of his friends, and is raised to its utmost perfection by the universal assent and applauses of the learned world. Now it is evident that this gradual increase of assurance is nothing but the addition of new probabilities, and is derived from the constant union of causes and effects, according to past experience and observation.

In accounts of any length or importance, merchants seldom trust to the infallible certainty of numbers for their security, but by the artificial structure of the accounts produce a probability beyond what is derived from the skill and experience of the accountant. For that is plainly of itself some degree of probability, though uncertain and variable, according to the degrees of his experience and length of the account. Now as none will maintain that our assurance in a long numeration exceeds probability, I may safely affirm that there scarce is any proposition concerning numbers of which we can have a fuller security. For it is easily possible, by gradually diminishing the numbers, to reduce the longest series of addition to the most simple question which can be formed, to an addition of two single numbers; and upon this supposition we shall find it impracticable to show the precise limits of knowledge and of probability, or discover that particular number at which the one ends and the other begins. But knowledge and probability are of such contrary and disagreeing natures that they cannot well run insensibly into each other, and that because they will not divide, but must be either entirely present or entirely absent. Besides, if any single addition were certain every one would be so, and consequently the whole or total sum, unless the whole can be different from all its parts. I had almost said that this was certain, but I reflect that it must reduce *itself*, as well as every other reasoning, and from knowledge degenerate into probability.

Since therefore all knowledge resolves itself into probability and becomes at last of the same nature with that evidence which we employ in common life, we must now examine this latter species of reasoning, and see on what foundation it stands.

In every judgment which we can form concerning probability, as well as concerning knowledge, we ought always to correct the first judgment, derived from the nature of the object, by another judgment, derived from the nature of the understanding. It is certain a man of solid sense and long experience ought to have, and usually has, a greater assurance in his opinions than one that is foolish and ignorant, and that

our sentiments have different degrees of authority, even with
ourselves, in proportion to the degrees of our reason and experience. In the man of the best sense and longest experience,
this authority is never entire, since even such-a-one must be
conscious of many errors in the past, and must still dread
the like for the future. Here then arises a new species of probability to correct and regulate the first, and fix its just standard and proportion. As demonstration is subject to the control
of probability, so is probability liable to a new correction by a
reflex act of the mind, wherein the nature of our understanding and our reasoning from the first probability become our
objects.

Having thus found in every probability, beside the original
uncertainty inherent in the subject, a new uncertainty derived
from the weakness of that faculty which judges, and having
adjusted these two together, we are obliged by our reason to
add a new doubt derived from the possibility of error in the
estimation we make of the truth and fidelity of our faculties.
This is a doubt which immediately occurs to us and of which,
if we would closely pursue our reason, we cannot avoid giving
a decision. But this decision, though it should be favorable to
our preceding judgment, being founded only on probability,
must weaken still further our first evidence, and must itself be
weakened by a fourth doubt of the same kind, and so on *in
infinitum*, till at last there remain nothing of the original probability, however great we may suppose it to have been and
however small the diminution by every new uncertainty. No
finite object can subsist under a decrease repeated *in infinitum*, and even the vastest quantity which can enter into
human imagination must in this manner be reduced to nothing. Let our first belief be ever so strong, it must infallibly
perish by passing through so many new examinations, of
which each diminishes somewhat of its force and vigor.
When I reflect on the natural fallibility of my judgment, I
have less confidence in my opinions than when I only consider
the objects concerning which I reason; and when I proceed
still further, to turn the scrutiny against every successive estimation I make of my faculties, all the rules of logic require
a continual diminution, and at last a total extinction of belief
and evidence.

Should it here be asked me whether I sincerely assent to this argument, which I seem to take such pains to inculcate, and whether I be really one of those skeptics who hold that all is uncertain and that our judgment is not in *anything* possessed of *any* measures of truth and falsehood, I should reply that this question is entirely superfluous, and that neither I nor any other person was ever sincerely and constantly of that opinion. Nature, by an absolute and uncontrollable necessity, has determined us to judge as well as to breathe and feel, nor can we any more forbear viewing certain objects in a stronger and fuller light, upon account of their customary connection with a present impression, than we can hinder ourselves from thinking as long as we are awake, or seeing the surrounding bodies when we turn our eyes towards them in broad sunshine. Whoever has taken the pains to refute the cavils of this *total* skepticism has really disputed without an antagonist, and endeavored by arguments to establish a faculty which nature has antecedently implanted in the mind and rendered unavoidable.

My intention then in displaying so carefully the arguments of that fantastic sect is only to make the reader sensible of the truth of my hypothesis, *that all our reasonings concerning causes and effects are derived from nothing but custom, and that belief is more properly an act of the sensitive than of the cogitative part of our natures.* I have here proved that the very same principles which make us form a decision upon any subject, and correct that decision by the consideration of our genius and capacity and of the situation of our mind when we examined that subject; I say, I have proved that these same principles, when carried further and applied to every new reflex judgment, must, by continually diminishing the original evidence, at last reduce it to nothing, and utterly subvert all belief and opinion. If belief, therefore, were a simple act of the thought, without any peculiar manner of conception or the addition of a force and vivacity, it must infallibly destroy itself, and in every case terminate in a total suspense of judgment. But as experience will sufficiently convince anyone who thinks it worthwhile to try, that though he can find no error in the foregoing arguments, yet he still continues to believe and think and reason as usual, he may safely conclude that his reasoning and belief is some sensation or peculiar manner of conception, which it is impossible for mere ideas and reflections to destroy.

But here, perhaps, it may be demanded how it happens, even upon my hypothesis, that these arguments above explained produce not a total suspense of judgment, and after what manner the mind ever retains a degree of assurance in any subject? For as these new probabilities, which by their repetition perpetually diminish the original evidence, are founded on the very same principles, whether of thought or sensation, as the primary judgment, it may seem unavoidable that in either case they must equally subvert it, and by the opposition, either of contrary thoughts or sensations, reduce the mind to a total uncertainty. I suppose there is some question proposed to me, and that after revolving over the impressions of my memory and senses and carrying my thoughts from them to such objects as are commonly conjoined with them, I feel a stronger and more forcible conception on the one side than on the other. This strong conception forms my first decision. I suppose that afterwards I examine my judgment itself, and observing from experience that it is sometimes just and sometimes erroneous, I consider it as regulated by contrary principles or causes, of which some lead to truth and some to error; and in balancing these contrary causes I diminish by a new probability the assurance of my first decision. This new probability is liable to the same diminution as the foregoing, and so on, *in infinitum*. It is therefore demanded, *how it happens that even after all we retain a degree of belief which is sufficient for our purpose, either in philosophy or common life.*

I answer that after the first and second decision, as the action of the mind becomes forced and unnatural and the ideas faint and obscure, though the principles of judgment and the balancing of opposite causes be the same as at the very beginning, yet their influence on the imagination and the vigor they add to or diminish from the thought is by no means equal. Where the mind reaches not its objects with easiness and facility, the same principles have not the same effect as in a more natural conception of the ideas, nor does the imagination feel a sensation which holds any proportion with that which arises from its common judgments and opinions. The attention is on the stretch; the posture of the mind is uneasy; and the spirits, being diverted from their natural course, are not governed in their movements by the same laws, at least not to the same degree, as when they flow in their usual channel.

If we desire similar instances, it will not be very difficult to find them. The present subject of metaphysics will supply us abundantly. The same argument which would have been esteemed convincing in a reasoning concerning history or politics has little or no influence in these abstruser subjects, even though it be perfectly comprehended, and that because there is required a study and an effort of thought in order to its being comprehended, and this effort of thought disturbs the operation of our sentiments on which the belief depends. The case is the same in other subjects. The straining of the imagination always hinders the regular flowing of the passions and sentiments. A tragic poet that would represent his heroes as very ingenious and witty in their misfortunes would never touch the passions. As the emotions of the soul prevent any subtle reasoning and reflection, so these latter actions of the mind are equally prejudicial to the former. The mind, as well as the body, seems to be endowed with a certain precise degree of force and activity, which it never employs in one action but at the expense of all the rest. This is more evidently true where the actions are of quite different natures, since in that case the force of the mind is not only diverted, but even the disposition changed, so as to render us incapable of a sudden transition from one action to the other, and still more of performing both at once. No wonder, then, the conviction which arises from a subtle reasoning diminishes in proportion to the efforts which the imagination makes to enter into the reasoning, and to conceive it in all its parts. Belief, being a lively conception, can never be entire where it is not founded on something natural and easy.

This I take to be the true state of the question, and cannot approve of that expeditious way which some take with the skeptics, to reject at once all their arguments without inquiry or examination. If the skeptical reasonings be strong, say they, it is a proof that reason may have some force and authority;

if weak, they can never be sufficient to invalidate all the conclusions of our understanding. This argument is not just, because the skeptical reasonings, were it possible for them to exist and were they not destroyed by their subtlety, would be successively both strong and weak, according to the successive dispositions of the mind. Reason first appears in possession of the throne, prescribing laws and imposing maxims, with an absolute sway and authority. Her enemy, therefore, is obliged to take shelter under her protection, and by making use of rational arguments to prove the fallaciousness and imbecility of reason, produces, in a manner, a patent under her hand and seal. This patent has at first an authority proportioned to the present and immediate authority of reason, from which it is derived. But as it is supposed to be contradictory to reason, it gradually diminishes the force of that governing power, and its own at the same time, till at last they both vanish away into nothing, by a regular and just diminution. The skeptical and dogmatical reasons are of the same kind, though contrary in their operation and tendency, so that where the latter is strong, it has an enemy of equal force in the former to encounter, and as their forces were at first equal, they still continue so as long as either of them subsists, nor does one of them lose any force in the contest without taking as much from its antagonist. It is happy, therefore, that nature breaks the force of all skeptical arguments in time, and keeps them from having any considerable influence on the understanding. Were we to trust entirely to their self-destruction, that can never take place till they have first subverted all conviction, and have totally destroyed human reason.

Section II.

OF SKEPTICISM WITH REGARD TO THE SENSES

Thus the skeptic still continues to reason and believe, even though he asserts that he cannot defend his reason by reason; and by the same rule he must assent to the principle concerning the existence of body, though he cannot pretend by any arguments of philosophy to maintain its veracity. Nature has not left this to his choice, and has doubtless esteemed it an affair of too great importance to be trusted to our uncertain reasonings and speculations. We may well ask *what causes induce us to believe in the existence of body*, but it is in vain to ask *whether there be body or not*. That is a point which we must take for granted in all our reasonings.

The subject, then, of our present inquiry is concerning the *causes* which induce us to believe in the existence of body, and my reasonings on this head I shall begin with a distinction which at first sight may seem superfluous but which will contribute very much to the perfect understanding of what follows. We ought to examine apart those two questions which are commonly confounded together, *viz.*, why we attribute a CONTINUED existence to objects even when they are not present to the senses, and why we suppose them to have an existence DISTINCT from the mind and perception. Under this last head I comprehend their situation as well as relations, their *external* position as well as the *independence* of their existence and operation. These two questions concerning the continued and distinct existence of body are intimately connected together. For if the objects of our senses continue to exist, even when they are not perceived, their existence is of course independent of and distinct from the perception; and *vice versa*, if their existence be independent of the perception and distinct from it, they must continue to exist, even though they be not perceived. But though the decision of the one question decides the other, yet that we may the more easily discover the principles of human nature from whence the decision arises, we shall carry along with us this distinction, and shall consider whether it be the *senses, reason,* or the *imagination* that produces the opinion of a *continued* or of a *distinct* existence. These are the only questions that are intelligible on the present subject. For as to the notion of external existence, when taken for something specifically different from our perceptions, [1]we have already shown its absurdity.

To begin with the SENSES, it is evident these faculties are incapable of giving rise to the notion of the *continued* existence of their objects after they no longer appear to the senses.

[1] Part II, Section VI.

For that is a contradiction in terms, and supposes that the senses continue to operate even after they have ceased all manner of operation. These faculties, therefore, if they have any influence in the present case, must produce the opinion of a distinct, not of a continued, existence, and in order to that, must present their impressions either as images and representations, or as these very distinct and external existences.

That our senses offer not their impressions as the images of something *distinct*, or *independent*, and *external* is evident, because they convey to us nothing but a single perception, and never give us the least intimation of anything beyond. A single perception can never produce the idea of a double existence but by some inference either of the reason or imagination. When the mind looks further than what immediately appears to it, its conclusions can never be put to the account of the senses, and it certainly looks further when from a single perception it infers a double existence, and supposes the relations of resemblance and causation between them.

If our senses, therefore, suggest any idea of distinct existences, they must convey the impressions as those very existences, by a kind of fallacy and illusion. Upon this head we may observe that all sensations are felt by the mind such as they really are, and that when we doubt whether they present themselves as distinct objects or as mere impressions, the difficulty is not concerning their nature, but concerning their relations and situation. Now if the senses presented our impressions as external to and independent of ourselves, both the objects and ourselves must be obvious to our senses; otherwise they could not be compared by these faculties. The difficulty, then, is how far we are *ourselves* the objects of our senses.

It is certain there is no question in philosophy more abstruse than that concerning identity, and the nature of the uniting principle which constitutes a person. So far from being able by our senses merely to determine this question, we must have recourse to the most profound metaphysics to give a satisfactory answer to it, and in common life it is evident these ideas of self and person are never very fixed nor determinate. It is absurd, therefore, to imagine the senses can ever distinguish between ourselves and external objects.

Add to this that every impression, external and internal, passions, affections, sensations, pains, and pleasures, are originally on the same footing, and that whatever other differences we may observe among them they appear, all of them, in their true colors as impressions or perceptions. And indeed, if we consider the matter aright, it is scarce possible it should be otherwise, nor is it conceivable that our senses should be more capable of deceiving us in the situation and relations than in the nature of our impressions. For since all actions and sensations of the mind are known to us by consciousness, they must necessarily appear in every particular what they are, and be what they appear. Everything that enters the mind being in *reality* a perception, it is impossible anything should to *feeling* appear different. This were to suppose that even where we are most intimately conscious we might be mistaken.

But not to lose time in examining whether it is possible for our senses to deceive us and represent our perceptions as distinct from ourselves, that is as *external* to and *independent* of us, let us consider whether they really do so, and whether this error proceeds from an immediate sensation or from some other causes.

To begin with the question concerning *external* existence, it may perhaps be said that, setting aside the metaphysical question of the identity of a thinking substance, our own body evidently belongs to us, and as several impressions appear exterior to the body, we suppose them also exterior to ourselves. The paper on which I write at present is beyond my hand. The table is beyond the paper. The walls of the chamber beyond the table. And in casting my eye towards the window, I perceive a great extent of fields and buildings beyond my chamber. From all this it may be inferred that no other faculty is required, beside the senses, to convince us of the external existence of body. But to prevent this inference, we need only weigh the three following considerations. *First,* that, properly speaking, it is not our body we perceive when we regard our limbs and members, but certain impressions which enter by the senses; so that the ascribing a real and corporeal existence to these impressions, or to their objects, is an act of the mind as difficult to explain as that which we examine at present. *Secondly*, sounds and tastes and smells, though commonly regarded by the mind as continued independent qualities, appear not to have any existence in extension, and consequently cannot appear to the senses as situated externally to the body. The reason why we ascribe a place to them shall be considered afterwards.[1] *Thirdly*, even our sight informs us not of distance or outness (so to speak) immediately and without a certain reasoning and experience, as is acknowledged by the most rational philosophers.

As to the *independence* of our perceptions on ourselves, this can never be an object of the senses, but any opinion we form concerning it must be derived from experience and observation; and we shall see afterwards that our conclusions from experience are far from being favorable to the doctrine of the independence of our perceptions. Meanwhile we may observe that when we talk of real distinct existences, we have commonly more in our eye their independence than external situation in place, and think an object has a sufficient reality when its being is uninterrupted, and independent of the incessant revolutions which we are conscious of in ourselves.

Thus to resume what I have said concerning the senses, they give us no notion of continued existence, because they cannot operate beyond the extent in which they really operate. They as little produce the opinion of a distinct existence, because they neither can offer it to the mind as represented nor as original. To offer it as represented, they must present both an object and an image. To make it appear as original, they must convey a falsehood, and this falsehood must lie in the relations and situation, in order to which they must be able to compare the object with ourselves; and even in that case they do not, nor is it possible they should, deceive us. We may, therefore, conclude with certainty that the opinion of a continued and of a distinct existence never arises from the senses.

To confirm this we may observe that there are three different kinds of impressions conveyed by the senses. The first are those of the figure, bulk, motion, and solidity of bodies. The second those of colors, tastes, smells, sounds, heat, and cold. The third are the pains and pleasures that arise from the ap-

[1] Section V.

plication of objects to our bodies, as by the cutting of our flesh with steel, and such like. Both philosophers and the vulgar suppose the first of these to have a distinct continued existence. The vulgar only regard the second as on the same footing. Both philosophers and the vulgar, again, esteem the third to be merely perceptions, and consequently interrupted and dependent beings.

Now it is evident that, whatever may be our philosophical opinion, colors, sounds, heat, and cold, as far as appears to the senses, exist after the same manner with motion and solidity, and that the difference we make between them in this respect arises not from the mere perception. So strong is the prejudice for the distinct continued existence of the former qualities that when the contrary opinion is advanced by modern philosophers, people imagine they can almost refute it from their feeling and experience, and that their very senses contradict this philosophy. It is also evident that colors, sounds, etc., are originally on the same footing with the pain that arises from steel and pleasure that proceeds from a fire, and that the difference between them is founded neither on perception nor reason, but on the imagination. For as they are confessed to be, both of them, nothing but perceptions arising from the particular configurations and motions of the parts of body, wherein possibly can their difference consist? Upon the whole, then, we may conclude that, as far as the senses are judges, all perceptions are the same in the manner of their existence.

We may also observe in this instance of sounds and colors that we can attribute a distinct continued existence to objects without ever consulting REASON, or weighing our opinions by any philosophical principles. And indeed, whatever convincing arguments philosophers may fancy they can produce to establish the belief of objects independent of the mind, it is obvious these arguments are known but to very few, and that it is not by them that children, peasants, and the greatest part of mankind are induced to attribute objects to some impressions and deny them to others. Accordingly we find that all the conclusions which the vulgar form on this head are directly contrary to those which are confirmed by philosophy.

For philosophy informs us that everything which appears to the mind is nothing but a perception, and is interrupted and dependent on the mind; whereas the vulgar confound perceptions and objects, and attribute a distinct continued existence to the very things they feel or see. This sentiment, then, as it is entirely unreasonable, must proceed from some other faculty than the understanding. To which we may add that as long as we take our perceptions and objects to be the same, we can never infer the existence of the one from that of the other, nor form an argument from the relation of cause and effect, which is the only one that can assure us of matter of fact. Even after we distinguish our perceptions from our objects, it will appear presently that we are still incapable of reasoning from the existence of one to that of the other. So that upon the whole our reason neither does, nor is it possible it ever should, upon any supposition, give us an assurance of the continued and distinct existence of body. That opinion must be entirely owing to the IMAGINATION, which must now be the subject of our inquiry.

Since all impressions are internal and perishing existences, and appear as such, the notion of their distinct and continued existence must arise from a concurrence of some of their qualities with the qualities of the imagination; and since this notion does not extend to all of them, it must arise from certain qualities peculiar to some impressions. It will therefore be easy for us to discover these qualities by a comparison of the impressions to which we attribute a distinct and continued existence with those which we regard as internal and perishing.

We may observe, then, that it is neither upon account of the involuntariness of certain impressions, as is commonly supposed, nor of their superior force and violence, that we attribute to them a reality and continued existence which we refuse to others that are voluntary or feeble. For it is evident our pains and pleasures, our passions and affections, which we never suppose to have any existence beyond our perception, operate with greater violence, and are equally involuntary, as the impressions of figure and extension, color and sound, which we suppose to be permanent beings. The heat of a fire, when moderate, is supposed to exist in the fire, but the pain which it causes upon a near approach is not taken to have any being except in the perception.

These vulgar opinions, then, being rejected, we must search for some other hypothesis, by which we may discover those peculiar qualities in our impressions which makes us attribute to them a distinct and continued existence.

After a little examination, we shall find that all those objects to which we attribute a continued existence have a peculiar *constancy* which distinguishes them from the impressions whose existence depends upon our perception. Those mountains and houses and trees which lie at present under my eye have always appeared to me in the same order, and when I lose sight of them by shutting my eyes or turning my head, I soon after find them return upon me without the least alteration. My bed and table, my books and papers, present themselves in the same uniform manner, and change not upon account of any interruption in my seeing or perceiving them. This is the case with all the impressions whose objects are supposed to have an external existence, and is the case with no other impressions, whether gentle or violent, voluntary or involuntary.

This constancy, however, is not so perfect as not to admit of very considerable exceptions. Bodies often change their position and qualities, and after a little absence or interruption may become hardly knowable. But here it is observable that even in these changes they preserve a *coherence* and have a regular dependence on each other, which is the foundation of a kind of reasoning from causation, and produces the opinion of their continued existence. When I return to my chamber after an hour's absence, I find not my fire in the same situation in which I left it. But then I am accustomed in other instances to see a like alteration produced in a like time, whether I am present or absent, near or remote. This coherence, therefore, in their changes is one of the characteristics of external objects, as well as their constancy.

Having found that the opinion of the continued existence of body depends on the COHERENCE and CONSTANCY of certain impressions, I now proceed to examine after what manner these qualities give rise to so extraordinary an opinion. To begin with the coherence, we may observe that though those internal impressions which we regard as fleeting and perishing have also a certain coherence or regularity in their appearances, yet it is of somewhat a different nature from that which we discover in bodies. Our passions are found by experience to have a mutual connection with and dependence on each other, but on no occasion is it necessary to suppose that they have existed and operated when they were not perceived in order to preserve the same dependence and connection of which we have had experience. The case is not the same with relation to external objects. Those require a continued existence, or otherwise lose, in a great measure, the regularity of their operation. I am here seated in my chamber with my face to the fire, and all the objects that strike my senses are contained in a few yards around me. My memory, indeed, informs me of the existence of many objects, but then this information extends not beyond their past existence, nor do either my senses or memory give any testimony to the continuance of their being. When therefore I am thus seated, and revolve over these thoughts, I hear on a sudden a noise as of a door turning upon its hinges, and a little after see a porter, who advances towards me. This gives occasion to many new reflections and reasonings. First, I never have observed that this noise could proceed from anything but the motion of a door, and therefore conclude that the present phenomenon is a contradiction to all past experience unless the door which I remember on the other side [of] the chamber be still in being. Again, I have always found that a human body was possessed of a quality which I call gravity, and which hinders it from mounting in the air, as this porter must have done to arrive at my chamber unless the stairs I remember be not annihilated by my absence. But this is not all. I receive a letter, which upon opening it I perceive by the handwriting and subscription to have come from a friend, who says he is two hundred leagues distant. It is evident I can never account for this phenomenon, conformable to my experience in other instances, without spreading out in my mind the whole sea and continent between us, and supposing the effects and continued existence of posts and ferries, according to my memory and observation. To consider these phenomena of the porter and letter in a certain light, they are contradictions to common experience, and may be regarded as objections to those maxims which we form concerning the connections of causes and effects. I am accustomed to hear such a sound and see such an object in motion at the same time. I have not received in this particular instance both these perceptions. These observations are contrary, unless I suppose that the door still remains, and that it was opened without my perceiving it. And this supposition, which was at first entirely arbitrary and hypothetical, acquires a force and evidence by its being the only one upon which I can reconcile these contradictions. There is scarce a moment of my life wherein there is not a similar instance presented to me and I have not occasion to suppose the continued existence of objects, in order to connect their past and present appearances and give them such a union with each other as I have found by experience to be suitable to their particular natures and circumstances. Here then I am naturally led to regard the world as something real and durable, and as preserving its existence even when it is no longer present to my perception.

But though this conclusion from the coherence of appearances may seem to be of the same nature with our reasonings concerning causes and effects, as being derived from custom and regulated by past experience, we shall find upon examination that they are at the bottom considerably different from each other, and that this inference arises from the understanding and from custom in an indirect and oblique manner. For it will readily be allowed that since nothing is ever really present to the mind besides its own perceptions, it is not only impossible that any habit should ever be acquired otherwise than by the regular succession of these perceptions, but also that any habit should ever exceed that degree of regularity. Any degree, therefore, of regularity in our perceptions can never be a foundation for us to infer a greater degree of regularity in some objects which are not perceived, since this supposes a contradiction, *viz.*, a habit acquired by what was never present to the mind. But it is evident that whenever we infer the continued existence of the objects of sense from their coherence and the frequency of their union, it is in order to bestow on the objects a greater regularity than what is observed in our mere perceptions. We remark a connection between two kinds of objects in their past appearance to the senses, but are not able to observe this connection to be perfectly constant, since the turning about of our head or the shutting of our eyes is able to break it. What then do we suppose in this case but that these objects still continue their usual connection, notwithstanding their apparent interruption, and that the irregular appearances are joined by something of which we are insensible? But as all reasoning concerning matters of fact arises only from custom, and custom can only be the effect of repeated perceptions, the extending of custom and reasoning beyond the perceptions can never be the direct and natural effect of the constant repetition and connection, but must arise from the cooperation of some other principles.

I have already observed,[1] in examining the foundation of mathematics, that the imagination, when set into any train of thinking, is apt to continue even when its object fails it, and like a galley put in motion by the oars, carries on its course without any new impulse. This I have assigned for the reason why, after considering several loose standards of equality and correcting them by each other, we proceed to imagine so correct and exact a standard of that relation as is not liable to the least error or variation. The same principle makes us easily entertain this opinion of the continued existence of body. Objects have a certain coherence even as they appear to our senses, but this coherence is much greater and more uniform if we suppose the objects to have a continued existence; and as the mind is once in the train of observing a uniformity among objects, it naturally continues, till it renders the uniformity as complete as possible. The simple supposition of their continued existence suffices for this purpose, and gives us a notion of a much greater regularity among objects than what they have when we look no further than our senses.

But whatever force we may ascribe to this principle, I am afraid it is too weak to support alone so vast an edifice as is that of the continued existence of all external bodies, and that we must join the *constancy* of their appearance to the

[1] Part II, Section IV.

coherence in order to give a satisfactory account of that opinion. As the explication of this will lead me into a considerable compass of very profound reasoning, I think it proper, in order to avoid confusion, to give a short sketch or abridgment of my system, and afterwards draw out all its parts in their full compass. This inference from the constancy of our perceptions, like the precedent from their coherence, gives rise to the opinion of the *continued* existence of body, which is prior to that of its *distinct* existence, and produces that latter principle.

When we have been accustomed to observe a constancy in certain impressions, and have found that the perception of the sun or ocean, for instance, returns upon us after an absence or annihilation with like parts and in a like order as at its first appearance, we are not apt to regard these interrupted perceptions as different (which they really are) but on the contrary consider them as individually the same, upon account of their resemblance. But as this interruption of their existence is contrary to their perfect identity, and makes us regard the first impression as annihilated and the second as newly created, we find ourselves somewhat at a loss, and are involved in a kind of contradiction. In order to free ourselves from this difficulty, we disguise, as much as possible, the interruption, or rather remove it entirely, by supposing that these interrupted perceptions are connected by a real existence of which we are insensible. This supposition or idea of continued existence acquires a force and vivacity from the memory of these broken impressions, and from that propensity which they give us to suppose them the same; and according to the precedent reasoning, the very essence of belief consists in the force and vivacity of the conception.

In order to justify this system, there are four things requisite. *First,* to explain the *principium individuationis,* or principle of identity. *Secondly,* give a reason why the resemblance of our broken and interrupted perceptions induces us to attribute an identity to them. *Thirdly,* account for that propensity which this illusion gives to unite these broken appearances by a continued existence. *Fourthly* and lastly, explain that force and vivacity of conception which arises from the propensity.

First, as to the principle of individuation, we may observe that the view of any one object is not sufficient to convey the idea of identity. For in that proposition, *an object is the same with itself,* if the idea expressed by the word *object* were no ways distinguished from that meant by *itself,* we really should mean nothing, nor would the proposition contain a predicate and a subject, which however are implied in this affirmation. One single object conveys the idea of unity, not that of identity.

On the other hand, a multiplicity of objects can never convey this idea, however resembling they may be supposed. The mind always pronounces the one not to be the other, and considers them as forming two, three, or any determinate number of objects, whose existences are entirely distinct and independent.

Since then both number and unity are incompatible with the relation of identity, it must lie in something that is neither of them. But to tell the truth, at first sight this seems utterly impossible. Between unity and number there can be no medium, no more than between existence and nonexistence. After one object is supposed to exist, we must either suppose another also to exist, in which case we have the idea of number, or we must suppose it not to exist, in which case the first object remains at unity.

To remove this difficulty, let us have recourse to the idea of time or duration. I have already observed[1] that time, in a strict sense, implies succession, and that when we apply its idea to any unchangeable object, it is only by a fiction of the imagination, by which the unchangeable object is supposed to participate of the changes of the coexistent objects, and in particular of that of our perceptions. This fiction of the imagination almost universally takes place, and it is by means of it that a single object, placed before us and surveyed for any time without our discovering in it any interruption or variation, is able to give us a notion of identity. For when we consider any two points of this time, we may place them in different lights. We may either survey them at the very same instant, in which case they give us the idea of number, both by themselves and by the object, which must be mul-

[1] Part II, Section V.

tiplied in order to be conceived at once, as existent in these two different points of time. Or on the other hand, we may trace the succession of time by a like succession of ideas, and conceiving first one moment, along with the object then existent, imagine afterwards a change in the time without any *variation* or *interruption* in the object, in which case it gives us the idea of unity. Here then is an idea which is a medium between unity and number, or more properly speaking, is either of them according to the view in which we take it, and this idea we call that of identity. We cannot, in any propriety of speech, say that an object is the same with itself unless we mean that the object existent at one time is the same with itself existent at another. By this means we make a difference between the idea meant by the word *object* and that meant by *itself*, without going the length of number, and at the same time without restraining ourselves to a strict and absolute unity.

Thus the principle of individuation is nothing but the *invariableness* and *uninterruptedness* of any object through a supposed variation of time, by which the mind can trace it in the different periods of its existence without any break of the view, and without being obliged to form the idea of multiplicity or number.

I now proceed to explain the *second* part of my system, and show why the constancy of our perceptions makes us ascribe to them a perfect numerical identity, though there be very long intervals between their appearance and they have only one of the essential qualities of identity, *viz.*, *invariableness*. That I may avoid all ambiguity and confusion on this head, I shall observe that I here account for the opinions and belief of the vulgar with regard to the existence of body, and therefore must entirely conform myself to their manner of thinking and of expressing themselves. Now we have already observed that however philosophers may distinguish between the objects and perceptions of the senses, which they suppose coexistent and resembling, yet this is a distinction which is not comprehended by the generality of mankind, who, as they perceive only one being, can never assent to the opinion of a double existence and representation. Those very sensations which enter by the eye or ear are with them the true objects, nor can they readily conceive that this pen or paper which is immediately perceived represents another which is different from but resembling it. In order, therefore, to accommodate myself to their notions, I shall at first suppose that there is only a single existence, which I shall call indifferently *object* or *perception,* according as it shall seem best to suit my purpose, understanding by both of them what any common man means by a hat, or shoe, or stone, or any other impression conveyed to him by his senses. I shall be sure to give warning when I return to a more philosophical way of speaking and thinking.

To enter, therefore, upon the question concerning the source of the error and deception with regard to identity, when we attribute it to our resembling perceptions, notwithstanding their interruption, I must here recall an observation which I have already proved and explained.[1] Nothing is more apt to make us mistake one idea for another than any relation between them which associates them together in the imagination and makes it pass with facility from one to the other. Of all relations, that of resemblance is in this respect the most efficacious, and that because it not only causes an association of ideas but also of dispositions, and makes us conceive the one idea by an act or operation of the mind similar to that by which we conceive the other. This circumstance I have observed to be of great moment, and we may establish it for a general rule that whatever ideas place the mind in the same disposition or in similar ones are very apt to be confounded. The mind readily passes from one to the other, and perceives not the change without a strict attention, of which, generally speaking, it is wholly incapable.

In order to apply this general maxim, we must first examine the disposition of the mind in viewing any object which preserves a perfect identity, and then find some other object that is confounded with it by causing a similar disposition. When we fix our thought on any object and suppose it to continue the same for some time, it is evident we suppose the change to lie only in the time, and never exert ourselves to produce any new image or idea of the object. The faculties of the mind repose themselves in a manner, and take no more

[1] Part II, Section V.

exercise than what is necessary to continue that idea of which we were formerly possessed, and which subsists without variation or interruption. The passage from one moment to another is scarce felt, and distinguishes not itself by a different perception or idea, which may require a different direction of the spirits in order to its conception.

Now what other objects, beside identical ones, are capable of placing the mind in the same disposition when it considers them, and of causing the same uninterrupted passage of the imagination from one idea to another? This question is of the last importance. For if we can find any such objects, we may certainly conclude, from the foregoing principle, that they are very naturally confounded with identical ones, and are taken for them in most of our reasonings. But though this question be very important, it is not very difficult nor doubtful. For I immediately reply that a succession of related objects places the mind in this disposition, and is considered with the same smooth and uninterrupted progress of the imagination as attends the view of the same invariable object. The very nature and essence of relation is to connect our ideas with each other, and upon the appearance of one to facilitate the transition to its correlative. The passage between related ideas is, therefore, so smooth and easy that it produces little alteration on the mind, and seems like the continuation of the same action; and as the continuation of the same action is an effect of the continued view of the same object, it is for this reason we attribute sameness to every succession of related objects. The thought slides along the succession with equal facility as if it considered only one object, and therefore confounds the succession with the identity.

We shall afterwards see many instances of this tendency of relation to make us ascribe an *identity* to *different* objects, but shall here confine ourselves to the present subject. We find by experience that there is such a *constancy* in almost all the impressions of the senses that their interruption produces no alteration on them, and hinders them not from returning the same in appearance and in situation as at their first existence. I survey the furniture of my chamber, I shut my eyes and afterwards open them, and find the new percep-

A TREATISE OF HUMAN NATURE

tions to resemble perfectly those which formerly struck my
senses. This resemblance is observed in a thousand instances,
and naturally connects together our ideas of these interrupted
perceptions by the strongest relation, and conveys the mind
with an easy transition from one to another. An easy transition or passage of the imagination along the ideas of these
different and interrupted perceptions is almost the same disposition of mind with that in which we consider one constant
and uninterrupted perception. It is therefore very natural for
us to mistake the one for the other.[1]

The persons who entertain this opinion concerning the identity of our resembling perceptions are in general all the un-
thinking and unphilosophical part of mankind (that is, all of
us at one time or other), and consequently such as suppose
their perceptions to be their only objects, and never think of
a double existence internal and external, representing and represented. The very image which is present to the senses is
with us the real body, and it is to these interrupted images
we ascribe a perfect identity. But as the interruption of the
appearance seems contrary to the identity, and naturally
leads us to regard these resembling perceptions as different
from each other, we here find ourselves at a loss how to
reconcile such opposite opinions. The smooth passage of the
imagination along the ideas of the resembling perceptions
makes us ascribe to them a perfect identity. The interrupted
manner of their appearance makes us consider them as so
many resembling but still distinct beings, which appear after
certain intervals. The perplexity arising from this contradic-

---

[1] This reasoning, it must be confessed, is somewhat abstruse and
difficult to be comprehended, but it is remarkable that this very
difficulty may be converted into a proof of the reasoning. We may
observe that there are two relations, and both of them resemblances,
which contribute to our mistaking the succession of our interrupted
perceptions for an identical object. The first is the resemblance of
the perceptions; the second is the resemblance which the act of the
mind in surveying a succession of resembling objects bears to that
in surveying an identical object. Now these resemblances we are
apt to confound with each other, and it is natural we should, according to this very reasoning. But let us keep them distinct, and
we shall find no difficulty in conceiving the precedent argument.

tion produces a propension to unite these broken appearances by the fiction of a continued existence, which is the *third* part of that hypothesis I proposed to explain.

Nothing is more certain from experience than that any contradiction either to the sentiments or passions gives a sensible uneasiness, whether it proceeds from without or from within, from the opposition of external objects or from the combat of internal principles. On the contrary, whatever strikes in with the natural propensities, and either externally forwards their satisfaction, or internally concurs with their movements, is sure to give a sensible pleasure. Now there being here an opposition between the notion of the identity of resembling perceptions and the interruption of their appearance, the mind must be uneasy in that situation, and will naturally seek relief from the uneasiness. Since the uneasiness arises from the opposition of two contrary principles, it must look for relief by sacrificing the one to the other. But as the smooth passage of our thought along our resembling perceptions makes us ascribe to them an identity, we can never without reluctance yield up that opinion. We must, therefore, turn to the other side, and suppose that our perceptions are no longer interrupted, but preserve a continued as well as an invariable existence, and are by that means entirely the same. But here the interruptions in the appearance of these perceptions are so long and frequent that it is impossible to overlook them, and as the *appearance* of a perception in the mind and its *existence* seem at first sight entirely the same, it may be doubted whether we can ever assent to so palpable a contradiction, and suppose a perception to exist without being present to the mind. In order to clear up this matter and learn how the interruption in the appearance of a perception implies not necessarily an interruption in its existence, it will be proper to touch upon some principles which we shall have occasion to explain more fully afterwards.[1]

We may begin with observing that the difficulty in the present case is not concerning the matter of fact, or whether the mind forms such a conclusion concerning the continued existence of its perceptions, but only concerning the manner in which the conclusion is formed, and principles from which

[1] Section VI.

it is derived. It is certain that almost all mankind and even philosophers themselves, for the greatest part of their lives, take their perceptions to be their only objects, and suppose that the very being which is intimately present to the mind is the real body or material existence. It is also certain that this very perception or object is supposed to have a continued uninterrupted being, and neither to be annihilated by our absence nor to be brought into existence by our presence. When we are absent from it, we say it still exists but that we do not feel, we do not see it. When we are present, we say we feel or see it. Here then may arise two questions, *first*, how we can satisfy ourselves in supposing a perception to be absent from the mind without being annihilated; *secondly*, after what manner we conceive an object to become present to the mind without some new creation of a perception or image, and what we mean by this *seeing* and *feeling* and *perceiving*.

As to the first question, we may observe that what we call a *mind* is nothing but a heap or collection of different perceptions, united together by certain relations and supposed, though falsely, to be endowed with a perfect simplicity and identity. Now as every perception is distinguishable from another and may be considered as separately existent, it evidently follows that there is no absurdity in separating any particular perception from the mind, that is, in breaking off all its relations with that connected mass of perceptions which constitute a thinking being.

The same reasoning affords us an answer to the second question. If the name of *perception* renders not this separation from a mind absurd and contradictory, the name of *object*, standing for the very same thing, can never render their conjunction impossible. External objects are seen and felt and become present to the mind, that is, they acquire such a relation to a connected heap of perceptions as to influence them very considerably in augmenting their number by present reflections and passions, and in storing the memory with ideas. The same continued and uninterrupted being may, therefore, be sometimes present to the mind and sometimes absent from it without any real or essential change in the being itself. An interrupted appearance to the senses implies not necessarily an interruption in the existence. The supposition of the continued existence of sensible objects or perceptions involves no contradiction. We may easily indulge our inclination to that supposition. When the exact resemblance of our perceptions makes us ascribe to them an identity, we may remove the seeming interruption by feigning a continued being which may fill those intervals and preserve a perfect and entire identity to our perceptions.

But as we here not only *feign* but *believe* this continued existence, the question is, *from whence arises such a belief;* and this question leads us to the *fourth* member of this system. It has been proved already that belief in general consists in nothing but the vivacity of an idea, and that an idea may acquire this vivacity by its relation to some present impression. Impressions are naturally the most vivid perceptions of the mind, and this quality is in part conveyed by the relation to every connected idea. The relation causes a smooth passage from the impression to the idea, and even gives a propensity to that passage. The mind falls so easily from the one perception to the other that it scarce perceives the change, but retains in the second a considerable share of the vivacity of the first. It is excited by the lively impression, and this vivacity is conveyed to the related idea without any great diminution in the passage, by reason of the smooth transition and the propensity of the imagination.

But suppose that this propensity arises from some other principle besides that of relation; it is evident it must still have the same effect, and convey the vivacity from the impression to the idea. Now this is exactly the present case. Our memory presents us with a vast number of instances of perceptions perfectly resembling each other that return at different distances of time and after considerable interruptions. This resemblance gives us a propension to consider these interrupted perceptions as the same, and also a propension to connect them by a continued existence in order to justify this identity and avoid the contradiction in which the interrupted appearance of these perceptions seems necessarily to involve us. Here then we have a propensity to feign the continued existence of all sensible objects, and as this propensity arises from some lively impressions of the memory, it bestows a vivacity on that fiction, or in other words, makes us believe the continued existence of body. If sometimes we ascribe a continued existence to objects which are perfectly new to us, and of whose constancy and coherence we have no experience, it is because the manner in which they present themselves to our senses resembles that of constant and coherent objects, and this resemblance is a source of reasoning and analogy, and leads us to attribute the same qualities to the similar objects.

I believe an intelligent reader will find less difficulty to assent to this system than to comprehend it fully and distinctly, and will allow, after a little reflection, that every part carries its own proof along with it. It is indeed evident that as the vulgar *suppose* their perceptions to be their only objects, and at the same time *believe* the continued existence of matter, we must account for the origin of the belief upon that supposition. Now upon that supposition, it is a false opinion that any of our objects, or perceptions, are identically the same after an interruption, and consequently the opinion of their identity can never arise from reason, but must arise from the imagination. The imagination is seduced into such an opinion only by means of the resemblance of certain perceptions, since we find they are only our resembling perceptions which we have a propension to suppose the same. This propension to bestow an identity on our resembling perceptions produces the fiction of a continued existence, since that fiction, as well as the identity, is really false, as is acknowledged by all philosophers, and has no other effect than to remedy the interruption of our perceptions, which is the only circumstance that is contrary to their identity. In the last place this propension causes belief by means of the present impressions of the memory, since without the remembrance of former sensations, it is plain we never should have any belief of the continued existence of body. Thus in examining all these parts, we find that each of them is supported by the strongest proofs, and that all of them together form a consistent system which is perfectly convincing. A strong propensity or inclination alone, without any present impression, will sometimes cause a belief or opinion. How much more when aided by that circumstance?

But though we are led after this manner, by the natural propensity of the imagination, to ascribe a continued existence to those sensible objects or perceptions which we find to resemble each other in their interrupted appearance, yet a very little reflection and philosophy is sufficient to make us perceive the fallacy of that opinion. I have already observed that there is an intimate connection between those two principles, of a *continued* and of a *distinct* or *independent* existence, and that we no sooner establish the one than the other follows as a necessary consequence. It is the opinion of a continued existence which first takes place, and without much study or reflection draws the other along with it, wherever the mind follows its first and most natural tendency. But when we compare experiments and reason a little upon them, we quickly perceive that the doctrine of the independent existence of our sensible perceptions is contrary to the plainest experience. This leads us backward upon our footsteps to perceive our error in attributing a continued existence to our perceptions, and is the origin of many very curious opinions, which we shall here endeavor to account for.

It will first be proper to observe a few of those experiments which convince us that our perceptions are not possessed of any independent existence. When we press one eye with a finger, we immediately perceive all the objects to become double, and one half of them to be removed from their common and natural position. But as we do not attribute a continued existence to both these perceptions, and as they are both of the same nature, we clearly perceive that all our perceptions are dependent on our organs and the disposition of our nerves and animal spirits. This opinion is confirmed by the seeming increase and diminution of objects according to their distance, by the apparent alterations in their figure, by the changes in their color and other qualities from our sickness and distempers, and by an infinite number of other experiments of the same kind, from all which we learn that our sensible perceptions are not possessed of any distinct or independent existence.

The natural consequence of this reasoning should be that our perceptions have no more a continued than an independent existence; and indeed philosophers have so far run into this opinion that they change their system and distinguish (as we shall do for the future) between perceptions and objects, of which the former are supposed to be interrupted and perishing and different at every different return, the latter to be uninterrupted and to preserve a continued existence and identity. But however philosophical this new system may be esteemed, I assert that it is only a palliative remedy, and that it contains all the difficulties of the vulgar system, with some others that are peculiar to itself. There are no principles either of the understanding or fancy which lead us directly to embrace this opinion of the double existence of perceptions and objects, nor can we arrive at it but by passing through the common hypothesis of the identity and continuance of our interrupted perceptions. Were we not first persuaded that our perceptions are our only objects and continue to exist even when they no longer make their appearance to the senses, we should never be led to think that our perceptions and objects are different, and that our objects alone preserve a continued existence. "The latter hypothesis has no primary recommendation either to reason or the imagination, but acquires all its influence on the imagination from the former." This proposition contains two parts, which we shall endeavor to prove as distinctly and clearly as such abstruse subjects will permit.

As to the first part of the proposition, *that this philosophical hypothesis has no primary recommendation either to reason or the imagination,* we may soon satisfy ourselves with regard to *reason* by the following reflections. The only existences of which we are certain are perceptions, which, being immediately present to us by consciousness, command our strongest assent and are the first foundation of all our conclusions. The only conclusion we can draw from the existence of one thing to that of another is by means of the relation of cause and effect, which shows that there is a connection between them, and that the existence of one is dependent on that of the other. The idea of this relation is derived from past experience, by which we find that two beings are constantly conjoined together, and are always present at once to the mind. But as no beings are ever present to the mind but perceptions, it follows that we may observe a conjunction or a relation of cause and effect between different perceptions, but can never observe it between perceptions and objects. It is impossible, therefore, that from the existence or any of the qualities of the former, we can ever form any conclusion concerning the existence of the latter, or ever satisfy our reason in this particular.

It is no less certain that this philosophical system has no primary recommendation to the *imagination,* and that that faculty would never, of itself and by its original tendency, have fallen upon such a principle. I confess it will be somewhat difficult to prove this to the full satisfaction of the reader, because it implies a negative, which in many cases will not admit of any positive proof. If anyone would take the pains to examine this question, and would invent a system to account for the direct origin of this opinion from the imagination, we should be able, by the examination of that system, to pronounce a certain judgment in the present subject. Let it be taken for granted that our perceptions are broken and interrupted, and, however like, are still different from each other; and let anyone upon this supposition show why the fancy, directly and immediately, proceeds to the belief of another existence, resembling these perceptions in their nature, but yet continued and uninterrupted and identical; and after he has done this to my satisfaction I promise to renounce my present opinion. Meanwhile I cannot forbear concluding, from the very abstractedness and difficulty of the first supposition, that it is an improper subject for the fancy to work upon. Whoever would explain the origin of the *common* opinion concerning the continued and distinct existence of body must take the mind in its *common* situation, and must proceed upon the supposition that our perceptions are our only objects, and continue to exist even when they are not perceived. Though this opinion be false, it is the most natural of any, and has alone any primary recommendation to the fancy.

As to the second part of the proposition, *that the philosophical system acquires all its influence on the imagination from the vulgar one,* we may observe that this is a natural and unavoidable consequence of the foregoing conclusion, *that it has no primary recommendation to reason or the im-*

agination. For as the philosophical system is found by experience to take hold of many minds, and in particular of all those who reflect ever so little on this subject, it must derive all its authority from the vulgar system, since it has no original authority of its own. The manner in which these two systems, though directly contrary, are connected together may be explained as follows.

The imagination naturally runs on in this train of thinking. Our perceptions are our only objects; resembling perceptions are the same, however broken or uninterrupted in their appearance; this appearing interruption is contrary to the identity; the interruption consequently extends not beyond the appearance, and the perception or object really continues to exist, even when absent from us; our sensible perceptions have, therefore, a continued and uninterrupted existence. But as a little reflection destroys this conclusion, that our perceptions have a continued existence, by showing that they have a dependent one, it would naturally be expected that we must altogether reject the opinion that there is such a thing in nature as a continued existence, which is preserved even when it no longer appears to the senses. The case, however, is otherwise. Philosophers are so far from rejecting the opinion of a continued existence upon rejecting that of the independence and continuance of our sensible perceptions that, though all sects agree in the latter sentiment, the former, which is, in a manner, its necessary consequence, has been peculiar to a few extravagant skeptics, who after all maintained that opinion in words only, and were never able to bring themselves sincerely to believe it.

There is a great difference between such opinions as we form after a calm and profound reflection and such as we embrace by a kind of instinct or natural impulse, on account of their suitableness and conformity to the mind. If these opinions become contrary, it is not difficult to foresee which of them will have the advantage. As long as our attention is bent upon the subject, the philosophical and studied principle may prevail; but the moment we relax our thoughts, nature will display herself, and draw us back to our former opinion. Nay she has sometimes such an influence that she can stop our progress, even in the midst of our most profound

reflections, and keep us from running on with all the consequences of any philosophical opinion. Thus though we clearly
perceive the dependence and interruption of our perceptions,
we stop short in our career, and never upon that account reject the notion of an independent and continued existence.
That opinion has taken such deep root in the imagination
that it is impossible ever to eradicate it, nor will any strained
metaphysical conviction of the dependence of our perceptions be sufficient for that purpose.

But though our natural and obvious principles here prevail
above our studied reflections, it is certain there must be some
struggle and opposition in the case, at least so long as these
reflections retain any force or vivacity. In order to set ourselves at ease in this particular, we contrive a new hypothesis,
which seems to comprehend both these principles of reason
and imagination. This hypothesis is the philosophical one of
the double existence of perceptions and objects, which
pleases our reason in allowing that our dependent perceptions
are interrupted and different, and at the same time is agreeable to the imagination in attributing a continued existence to
something else, which we call *objects*. This philosophical
system, therefore, is the monstrous offspring of two principles
which are contrary to each other, which are both at once
embraced by the mind, and which are unable mutually to
destroy each other. The imagination tells us that our resembling perceptions have a continued and uninterrupted existence, and are not annihilated by their absence. Reflection
tells us that even our resembling perceptions are interrupted
in their existence, and different from each other. The contradiction between these opinions we elude by a new fiction,
which is conformable to the hypotheses both of reflection
and fancy, by ascribing these contrary qualities to different
existences, the *interruption* to perceptions and the *continuance* to objects. Nature is obstinate and will not quit the
field, however strongly attacked by reason, and at the same
time reason is so clear in the point that there is no possibility
of disguising her. Not being able to reconcile these two enemies, we endeavor to set ourselves at ease as much as possible by successively granting to each whatever it demands,
and by feigning a double existence, where each may find

something that has all the conditions it desires. Were we fully convinced that our resembling perceptions are continued and identical and independent, we should never run into this opinion of a double existence, since we should find satisfaction in our first supposition and would not look beyond. Again, were we fully convinced that our perceptions are dependent and interrupted and different, we should be as little inclined to embrace the opinion of a double existence, since in that case we should clearly perceive the error of our first supposition of a continued existence, and would never regard it any further. It is therefore from the intermediate situation of the mind that this opinion arises, and from such an adherence to these two contrary principles as makes us seek some pretext to justify our receiving both, which happily at last is found in the system of a double existence.

Another advantage of this philosophical system is its similarity to the vulgar one, by which means we can humor our reason for a moment when it becomes troublesome and solicitous, and yet upon its least negligence or inattention can easily return to our vulgar and natural notions. Accordingly we find that philosophers neglect not this advantage, but immediately upon leaving their closets mingle with the rest of mankind in those exploded opinions, that our perceptions are our only objects, and continue identically and uninterruptedly the same in all their interrupted appearances.

There are other particulars of this system wherein we may remark its dependence on the fancy in a very conspicuous manner. Of these, I shall observe the two following. *First*, we suppose external objects to resemble internal perceptions. I have already shown that the relation of cause and effect can never afford us any just conclusion from the existence or qualities of our perceptions to the existence of external continued objects, and I shall further add that even though they could afford such a conclusion, we should never have any reason to infer that our objects resemble our perceptions. That opinion, therefore, is derived from nothing but the quality of the fancy above-explained, *that it borrows all its ideas from some precedent perception.* We never can conceive anything but perceptions, and therefore must make everything resemble them.

Secondly, as we suppose our objects in general to resemble our perceptions, so we take it for granted that every particular object resembles that perception which it causes. The relation of cause and effect determines us to join the other of resemblance, and the ideas of these existences being already united together in the fancy by the former relation, we naturally add the latter to complete the union. We have a strong propensity to complete every union by joining new relations to those which we have before observed between any ideas, as we shall have occasion to observe presently.[1]

Having thus given an account of all the systems, both popular and philosophical, with regard to external existences, I cannot forbear giving vent to a certain sentiment which arises upon reviewing those systems. I began this subject with premising that we ought to have an implicit faith in our senses, and that this would be the conclusion I should draw from the whole of my reasoning. But to be ingenuous, I feel myself *at present* of a quite contrary sentiment, and am more inclined to repose no faith at all in my senses, or rather imagination, than to place in it such an implicit confidence. I cannot conceive how such trivial qualities of the fancy, conducted by such false suppositions, can ever lead to any solid and rational system. They are the coherence and constancy of our perceptions which produce the opinion of their continued existence, though these qualities of perceptions have no perceivable connection with such an existence. The constancy of our perceptions has the most considerable effect, and yet is attended with the greatest difficulties. It is a gross illusion to suppose that our resembling perceptions are numerically the same; and it is this illusion which leads us into the opinion that these perceptions are uninterrupted, and are still existent even when they are not present to the senses. This is the case with our popular system. And as to our philosophical one, it is liable to the same difficulties, and is over and above loaded with this absurdity, that it at once denies and establishes the vulgar supposition. Philosophers deny our resembling perceptions to be identically the same and uninterrupted, and yet have so great a propensity to believe them such that they arbitrarily invent a new set of perceptions to

[1] Section V.

which they attribute these qualities. I say a new set of perceptions, for we may well suppose in general, but it is impossible for us distinctly to conceive, objects to be in their nature anything but exactly the same with perceptions. What then can we look for from this confusion of groundless and extraordinary opinions but error and falsehood? And how can we justify to ourselves any belief we repose in them?

This skeptical doubt, both with respect to reason and the senses, is a malady which can never be radically cured, but must return upon us every moment, however we may chase it away and sometimes may seem entirely free from it. It is impossible upon any system to defend either our understanding or senses, and we but expose them further when we endeavor to justify them in that manner. As the skeptical doubt arises naturally from a profound and intense reflection on those subjects, it always increases the further we carry our reflections, whether in opposition or conformity to it. Carelessness and inattention alone can afford us any remedy. For this reason I rely entirely upon them, and take it for granted, whatever may be the reader's opinion at this present moment, that an hour hence he will be persuaded there is both an external and internal world; and going upon that supposition, I intend to examine some general systems, both ancient and modern, which have been proposed of both, before I proceed to a more particular inquiry concerning our impressions. This will not, perhaps, in the end be found foreign to our present purpose.

Section III.

OF THE ANCIENT PHILOSOPHY

Several moralists have recommended it as an excellent method of becoming acquainted with our own hearts and knowing our progress in virtue to recollect our dreams in a morning, and examine them with the same rigor that we would our most serious and most deliberate actions. Our character is the same throughout, say they, and appears best where artifice, fear, and policy have no place, and men can neither be hypocrites with themselves nor others. The generosity or baseness of our temper, our meekness or cruelty, our courage or pusillanimity, influence the fictions of the imagination with the most unbounded liberty, and discover themselves in the most glaring colors. In like manner, I am persuaded, there might be several useful discoveries made from a criticism of the fictions of the ancient philosophy concerning *substances* and *substantial forms* and *accidents* and *occult qualities*, which, however unreasonable and capricious, have a very intimate connection with the principles of human nature.

It is confessed by the most judicious philosophers that our ideas of bodies are nothing but collections formed by the mind of the ideas of the several distinct sensible qualities of which objects are composed, and which we find to have a constant union with each other. But however these qualities may in themselves be entirely distinct, it is certain we commonly regard the compound which they form as ONE thing, and as continuing the SAME under very considerable alterations. The acknowledged composition is evidently contrary to this supposed *simplicity*, and the variation to the *identity*. It may, therefore, be worthwhile to consider the *causes* which make us almost universally fall into such evident contradictions, as well as the *means* by which we endeavor to conceal them.

It is evident that as the ideas of the several distinct *successive* qualities of objects are united together by a very close relation, the mind, in looking along the succession, must be carried from one part of it to another by an easy transition, and will no more perceive the change than if it contemplated the same unchangeable object. This easy transition is the effect or rather essence of relation, and as the imagination readily takes one idea for another, where their influence on the mind is similar, hence it proceeds that any such succession of related qualities is readily considered as one continued object, existing without any variation. The smooth and uninterrupted progress of the thought, being alike in both cases, readily deceives the mind, and makes us ascribe an identity to the changeable succession of connected qualities.

But when we alter our method of considering the succession, and instead of tracing it gradually through the successive points of time, survey at once any two distinct periods of its duration and compare the different conditions of the successive qualities, in that case the variations which were insensible when they arose gradually do now appear of consequence, and seem entirely to destroy the identity. By this means there arises a kind of contrariety in our method of thinking from the different points of view in which we survey the object, and from the nearness or remoteness of those instants of time which we compare together. When we gradually follow an object in its successive changes, the smooth progress of the thought makes us ascribe an identity to the succession, because it is by a similar act of the mind we consider an unchangeable object. When we compare its situation after a considerable change the progress of the thought is broken, and consequently we are presented with the idea of diversity, in order to reconcile which contradictions the imagination is apt to feign something unknown and invisible, which it supposes to continue the same under all these variations, and this unintelligible something it calls a *substance, or original and first matter*.

We entertain a like notion with regard to the *simplicity* of substances, and from like causes. Suppose an object perfectly simple and indivisible to be presented, along with another object, whose *coexistent* parts are connected together by a strong relation, it is evident the actions of the mind in considering these two objects are not very different. The imagination conceives the simple object at once, with facility, by a single effort of thought, without change or variation. The connection of parts in the compound object has almost the same effect, and so unites the object within itself that the fancy feels not the transition in passing from one part to another. Hence the color, taste, figure, solidity, and other qualities combined in a peach or melon are conceived to form *one thing*, and that on account of their close relation, which makes them affect the thought in the same manner as if perfectly uncompounded. But the mind rests not here. Whenever it views the object in another light, it finds that all these qualities are different and distinguishable and separable from each other, which view of things being destructive of its primary and more natural notions, obliges the imagination to feign an unknown something, or *original* substance and matter, as a principle of union or cohesion among these qualities, and as what may give the compound object a title to be called one thing, notwithstanding its diversity and composition.

The peripatetic philosophy asserts the *original* matter to be perfectly homogeneous in all bodies and considers fire, water, earth, and air as of the very same substance, on account of their gradual revolutions and changes into each other. At the same time it assigns to each of these species of objects a distinct *substantial form,* which it supposes to be the source of all those different qualities they possess and to be a new foundation of simplicity and identity to each particular species. All depends on our manner of viewing the objects. When we look along the insensible changes of bodies, we suppose all of them to be of the same substance or essence. When we consider their sensible differences, we attribute to each of them a substantial and essential difference. And in order to indulge ourselves in both these ways of considering our objects, we suppose all bodies to have at once a substance and a substantial form.

The notion of *accidents* is an unavoidable consequence of this method of thinking with regard to substances and substantial forms, nor can we forbear looking upon colors, sounds, tastes, figures, and other properties of bodies, as existences which cannot subsist apart, but require a subject of inhesion to sustain and support them. For having never discovered any of these sensible qualities where, for the reasons above-mentioned, we did not likewise fancy a substance to exist, the same habit which makes us infer a connection between cause and effect makes us here infer a dependence of every quality on the unknown substance. The custom of imagining a dependence has the same effect as the custom of observing it would have. This conceit, however, is no more reasonable than any of the foregoing. Every quality, being a distinct thing from another, may be conceived to exist apart, and may exist apart, not only from every other quality, but from that unintelligible chimera of a substance.

A TREATISE OF HUMAN NATURE

But these philosophers carry their fictions still further in their sentiments concerning *occult qualities,* and both suppose a substance supporting, which they do not understand, and an accident supported, of which they have as imperfect an idea. The whole system, therefore, is entirely incomprehensible, and yet is derived from principles as natural as any of these above-explained.

In considering this subject we may observe a gradation of three opinions that rise above each other according as the persons who form them acquire new degrees of reason and knowledge. These opinions are that of the vulgar, that of a false philosophy, and that of the true, where we shall find upon inquiry that the true philosophy approaches nearer to the sentiments of the vulgar than to those of a mistaken knowledge. It is natural for men, in their common and careless way of thinking, to imagine they perceive a connection between such objects as they have constantly found united together; and because custom has rendered it difficult to separate the ideas, they are apt to fancy such a separation to be in itself impossible and absurd. But philosophers, who abstract from the effects of custom and compare the ideas of objects, immediately perceive the falsehood of these vulgar sentiments, and discover that there is no known connection among objects. Every different object appears to them entirely distinct and separate, and they perceive that it is not from a view of the nature and qualities of objects we infer one from another, but only when in several instances we observe them to have been constantly conjoined. But these philosophers, instead of drawing a just inference from this observation and concluding that we have no idea of power or agency separate from the mind and belonging to causes; I say, instead of drawing this conclusion, they frequently search for the qualities in which this agency consists, and are displeased with every system which their reason suggests to them in order to explain it. They have sufficient force of genius to free them from the vulgar error that there is a natural and perceivable connection between the several sensible qualities and actions of matter, but not sufficient to keep them from ever seeking for this connection in matter or causes. Had they fallen upon the just conclusion, they would have returned back to the situation of the vulgar, and would have regarded all these disquisitions with indolence and indifference. At present they seem to be in a very lamentable condition, and such as the poets have given us but a faint notion of in their descriptions of the punishment of *Sisyphus* and *Tantalus*. For what can be imagined more tormenting than to seek with eagerness what forever flees us, and seek for it in a place where it is impossible it can ever exist?

But as nature seems to have observed a kind of justice and compensation in everything, she has not neglected philosophers more than the rest of the creation, but has reserved them a consolation amid all their disappointments and afflictions. This consolation principally consists in their invention of the words *faculty* and *occult quality*. For it being usual, after the frequent use of terms which are really significant and intelligible, to omit the idea which we would express by them, and to preserve only the custom by which we recall the idea at pleasure, so it naturally happens that after the frequent use of terms which are wholly insignificant and unintelligible, we fancy them to be on the same footing with the precedent, and to have a secret meaning which we might discover by reflection. The resemblance of their appearance deceives the mind, as is usual, and makes us imagine a thorough resemblance and conformity. By this means these philosophers set themselves at ease, and arrive at last, by an illusion, at the same indifference which the people attain by their stupidity, and true philosophers by their moderate skepticism. They need only say that any phenomenon which puzzles them arises from a faculty or an occult quality, and there is an end of all dispute and inquiry upon the matter.

But among all the instances wherein the peripatetics have shown they were guided by every trivial propensity of the imagination, no one is more remarkable than their *sympathies, antipathies, and horrors of a vacuum*. There is a very remarkable inclination in human nature to bestow on external objects the same emotions which it observes in itself, and to find everywhere those ideas which are most present to it. This inclination, it is true, is suppressed by a little reflection, and only takes place in children, poets, and the ancient philosophers. It appears in children by their desire of beating the

stones which hurt them, in poets by their readiness to person-
ify everything, and in the ancient philosophers by these
fictions of sympathy and antipathy. We must pardon children because of their age, poets because they profess to follow implicitly the suggestions of their fancy, but what excuse shall we find to justify our philosophers in so signal a
weakness?

Section IV.

OF THE MODERN PHILOSOPHY

But here it may be objected that the imagination, according to my own confession, being the ultimate judge of all
systems of philosophy, I am unjust in blaming the ancient
philosophers for making use of that faculty and allowing
themselves to be entirely guided by it in their reasonings. In
order to justify myself, I must distinguish in the imagination
between the principles which are permanent, irresistible, and
universal, such as the customary transition from causes to
effects and from effects to causes, and the principles which
are changeable, weak, and irregular, such as those I have
just now taken notice of. The former are the foundation of all
our thoughts and actions, so that upon their removal human
nature must immediately perish and go to ruin. The latter
are neither unavoidable to mankind nor necessary, or so much
as useful in the conduct of life, but on the contrary are observed only to take place in weak minds, and being opposite
to the other principles of custom and reasoning, may easily
be subverted by a due contrast and opposition. For this reason the former are received by philosophy, and the latter rejected. One who concludes somebody to be near him when he
hears an articulate voice in the dark reasons justly and naturally, though that conclusion be derived from nothing but
custom, which infixes and enlivens the idea of a human creature on account of his usual conjunction with the present impression. But one who is tormented he knows not why with
the apprehension of specters in the dark may, perhaps, be

said to reason, and to reason naturally too. But then it must be in the same sense that a malady is said to be natural, as arising from natural causes, though it be contrary to health, the most agreeable and most natural situation of man.

The opinions of the ancient philosophers, their fictions of substance and accident, and their reasonings concerning substantial forms and occult qualities, are like the specters in the dark, and are derived from principles which, however common, are neither universal nor unavoidable in human nature. The *modern philosophy* pretends to be entirely free from this defect, and to arise only from the solid, permanent, and consistent principles of the imagination. Upon what grounds this pretension is founded must now be the subject of our inquiry.

The fundamental principle of that philosophy is the opinion concerning colors, sounds, tastes, smells, heat, and cold, which it asserts to be nothing but impressions in the mind, derived from the operation of external objects and without any resemblance to the qualities of the objects. Upon examination, I find only one of the reasons commonly produced for this opinion to be satisfactory, *viz.*, that derived from the variations of those impressions, even while the external object, to all appearance, continues the same. These variations depend upon several circumstances. Upon the different situations of our health: a man in a malady feels a disagreeable taste in meats which before pleased him the most. Upon the different complexions and constitutions of men: that seems bitter to one which is sweet to another. Upon the difference of their external situation and position: colors reflected from the clouds change according to the distance of the clouds, and according to the angle they make with the eye and luminous body. Fire also communicates the sensation of pleasure at one distance and that of pain at another. Instances of this kind are very numerous and frequent.

The conclusion drawn from them is likewise as satisfactory as can possibly be imagined. It is certain that when different impressions of the same sense arise from any object, every one of these impressions has not a resembling quality existent in the object. For as the same object cannot, at the same time, be endowed with different qualities of the same sense, and as the same quality cannot resemble impressions entirely different, it evidently follows that many of our impressions have no external model or archetype. Now from like effects we presume like causes. Many of the impressions of color, sound, etc. are confessed to be nothing but internal existences, and to arise from causes which no ways resemble them. These impressions are in appearance nothing different from the other impressions of color, sound, etc. We conclude, therefore, that they are, all of them, derived from a like origin.

This principle being once admitted, all the other doctrines of that philosophy seem to follow by an easy consequence. For upon the removal of sounds, colors, heat, cold, and other sensible qualities from the rank of continued independent existences, we are reduced merely to what are called primary qualities as the only *real* ones of which we have any adequate notion. These primary qualities are extension and solidity with their different mixtures and modifications, figure, motion, gravity, and cohesion. The generation, increase, decay, and corruption of animals and vegetables are nothing but changes of figure and motion, as also the operations of all bodies on each other, of fire, of light, water, air, earth, and of all the elements and powers of nature. One figure and motion produces another figure and motion, nor does there remain in the material universe any other principle, either active or passive, of which we can form the most distant idea.

I believe many objections might be made to this system, but at present I shall confine myself to one which is in my opinion very decisive. I assert that instead of explaining the operations of external objects by its means, we utterly annihilate all these objects, and reduce ourselves to the opinions of the most extravagant skepticism concerning them. If colors, sounds, tastes, and smells be merely perceptions, nothing we can conceive is possessed of a real, continued, and independent existence, not even motion, extension, and solidity, which are the primary qualities chiefly insisted on.

To begin with the examination of motion, it is evident this is a quality altogether inconceivable alone, and without a reference to some other object. The idea of motion necessarily supposes that of a body moving. Now what is our idea of the moving body, without which motion is incomprehensible? It must resolve itself into the idea of extension or of solidity, and consequently the reality of motion depends upon that of these other qualities.

This opinion, which is universally acknowledged concerning motion, I have proved to be true with regard to extension, and have shown that it is impossible to conceive extension but as composed of parts endowed with color or solidity. The idea of extension is a compound idea, but as it is not compounded of an infinite number of parts or inferior ideas, it must at last resolve itself into such as are perfectly simple and indivisible. These simple and indivisible parts, not being ideas of extension, must be nonentities unless conceived as colored or solid. Color is excluded from any real existence. The reality, therefore, of our idea of extension depends upon the reality of that of solidity, nor can the former be just while the latter is chimerical. Let us, then, lend our attention to the examination of the idea of solidity.

The idea of solidity is that of two objects which, being impelled by the utmost force, cannot penetrate each other, but still maintain a separate and distinct existence. Solidity, therefore, is perfectly incomprehensible alone, and without the conception of some bodies which are solid and maintain this separate and distinct existence. Now what idea have we of these bodies? The ideas of colors, sounds, and other secondary qualities are excluded. The idea of motion depends on that of extension, and the idea of extension on that of solidity. It is impossible, therefore, that the idea of solidity can depend on either of them. For that would be to run in a circle, and make one idea depend on another, while at the same time the latter depends on the former. Our modern philosophy, therefore, leaves us no just nor satisfactory idea of solidity, nor consequently of matter.

This argument will appear entirely conclusive to everyone that comprehends it, but because it may seem abstruse and intricate to the generality of readers, I hope to be excused if I endeavor to render it more obvious by some variation of the expression. In order to form an idea of solidity, we must conceive two bodies pressing on each other without any penetration, and it is impossible to arrive at this idea when we confine ourselves to one object, much more without conceiving any. Two nonentities cannot exclude each other from their places, because they never possess any place, nor can be endowed with any quality. Now I ask, what idea do we form of these bodies or objects to which we suppose solidity to belong? To say that we conceive them merely as solid is to run on *in infinitum*. To affirm that we paint them out to ourselves as extended either resolves all into a false idea or returns in a circle. Extension must necessarily be considered either as colored, which is a false idea, or as solid, which brings us back to the first question. We may make the same observation concerning mobility and figure, and upon the whole must conclude that after the exclusion of colors, sounds, heat, and cold from the rank of external existences, there remains nothing which can afford us a just and consistent idea of body.

Add to this that, properly speaking, solidity or impenetrability is nothing but an impossibility of annihilation, as has been already observed,[1] for which reason it is the more necessary for us to form some distinct idea of that object whose annihilation we suppose impossible. An impossibility of being annihilated cannot exist, and can never be conceived to exist, by itself, but necessarily requires some object or real existence to which it may belong. Now the difficulty still remains, how to form an idea of this object or existence without having recourse to the secondary and sensible qualities.

Nor must we omit on this occasion our accustomed method of examining ideas by considering those impressions from which they are derived. The impressions which enter by the sight and hearing, the smell and taste, are affirmed by modern philosophy to be without any resembling objects, and consequently the idea of solidity, which is supposed to be real, can never be derived from any of these senses. There remains, therefore, the feeling as the only sense that can convey the impression which is original to the idea of solidity, and indeed we naturally imagine that we feel the solidity of bodies, and need but touch any object in order to perceive this quality. But this method of thinking is more

[1] Part II, Section IV.

popular than philosophical, as will appear from the following reflections.

First it is easy to observe that though bodies are felt by means of their solidity, yet the feeling is a quite different thing from the solidity, and that they have not the least resemblance to each other. A man who has the palsy in one hand has as perfect an idea of impenetrability when he observes that hand to be supported by the table as when he feels the same table with the other hand. An object that presses upon any of our members meets with resistance, and that resistance, by the motion it gives to the nerves and animal spirits, conveys a certain sensation to the mind; but it does not follow that the sensation, motion, and resistance are any ways resembling.

Secondly, the impressions of touch are simple impressions, except when considered with regard to their extension, which makes nothing to the present purpose; and from this simplicity I infer that they neither represent solidity nor any real object. For let us put two cases, *viz.*, that of a man who presses a stone or any solid body with his hand, and that of two stones which press each other; it will readily be allowed that these two cases are not in every respect alike, but that in the former there is conjoined with the solidity a feeling or sensation of which there is no appearance in the latter. In order, therefore, to make these two cases alike, it is necessary to remove some part of the impression which the man feels by his hand or organ of sensation, and that being impossible in a simple impression, obliges us to remove the whole, and proves that this whole impression has no archetype or model in external objects. To which we may add that solidity necessarily supposes two bodies, along with contiguity and impulse, which, being a compound object, can never be represented by a simple impression. Not to mention that though solidity continues always invariably the same, the impressions of touch change every moment upon us, which is a clear proof that the latter are not representations of the former.

Thus there is a direct and total opposition between our reason and our senses, or more properly speaking, between those conclusions we form from cause and effect and those

that persuade us of the continued and independent existence of body. When we reason from cause and effect, we
conclude that neither color, sound, taste, nor smell has a
continued and independent existence. When we exclude these
sensible qualities there remains nothing in the universe which
has such an existence.

Section V.

OF THE IMMATERIALITY OF THE SOUL

Having found such contradictions and difficulties in every
system concerning external objects and in the idea of matter,
which we fancy so clear and determinate, we shall naturally
expect still greater difficulties and contradictions in every
hypothesis concerning our internal perceptions and the nature
of the mind, which we are apt to imagine so much more
obscure and uncertain. But in this we should deceive ourselves. The intellectual world, though involved in infinite
obscurities, is not perplexed with any such contradictions as
those we have discovered in the natural. What is known concerning it agrees with itself, and what is unknown we must
be contented to leave so.

It is true, would we hearken to certain philosophers, they
promise to diminish our ignorance, but I am afraid it is at
the hazard of running us into contradictions from which
the subject is of itself exempted. These philosophers are the
curious reasoners concerning the material or immaterial substances in which they suppose our perceptions to inhere. In
order to put a stop to these endless cavils on both sides, I
know no better method than to ask these philosophers in a
few words *what they mean by substance and inhesion.* And
after they have answered this question, it will then be
reasonable, and not till then, to enter seriously into the
dispute.

This question we have found impossible to be answered
with regard to matter and body. But besides that in the
case of the mind it labors under all the same difficulties, it is
burdened with some additional ones which are peculiar to

the subject. As every idea is derived from a precedent impression, had we any idea of the substance of our minds, we must also have an impression of it, which is very difficult, if not impossible, to be conceived. For how can an impression represent a substance otherwise than by resembling it? And how can an impression resemble a substance, since, according to this philosophy, it is not a substance and has none of the peculiar qualities or characteristics of a substance?

But leaving the question *of what may or may not be* for that other, *what actually is,* I desire those philosophers who pretend that we have an idea of the substance of our minds to point out the impression that produces it, and tell distinctly after what manner that impression operates, and from what object it is derived. Is it an impression of sensation or of reflection? Is it pleasant or painful or indifferent? Does it attend us at all times, or does it only return at intervals? If at intervals, at what times principally does it return, and by what causes is it produced?

If instead of answering these questions, anyone should evade the difficulty by saying that the definition of a substance is *something which may exist by itself,* and that this definition ought to satisfy us; should this be said, I should observe that this definition agrees to everything that can possibly be conceived, and never will serve to distinguish substance from accident, or the soul from its perceptions. For thus I reason. Whatever is clearly conceived may exist, and whatever is clearly conceived after any manner may exist after the same manner. This is one principle which has been already acknowledged. Again, everything which is different is distinguishable, and everything which is distinguishable is separable by the imagination. This is another principle. My conclusion from both is that since all our perceptions are different from each other and from everything else in the universe, they are also distinct and separable, and may be considered as separately existent, and may exist separately, and have no need of anything else to support their existence. They are, therefore, substances, as far as this definition explains a substance.

Thus neither by considering the first origin of ideas nor by means of a definition are we able to arrive at any satisfactory notion of substance, which seems to me a sufficient reason for abandoning utterly that dispute concerning the materiality and immateriality of the soul, and makes me absolutely condemn even the question itself. We have no perfect idea of anything but of a perception. A substance is entirely different from a perception. We have, therefore, no idea of a substance. Inhesion in something is supposed to be requisite to support the existence of our perceptions. Nothing appears requisite to support the existence of a perception. We have, therefore, no idea of inhesion. What possibility then of answering that question, *whether perceptions inhere in a material or immaterial substance,* when we do not so much as understand the meaning of the question?

There is one argument commonly employed for the immateriality of the soul which seems to me remarkable. Whatever is extended consists of parts, and whatever consists of parts is divisible, if not in reality, at least in the imagination. But it is impossible anything divisible can be *conjoined* to a thought or perception, which is a being altogether inseparable and indivisible. For supposing such a conjunction, would the indivisible thought exist on the left or on the right hand of this extended divisible body? On the surface or in the middle? On the back- or fore-side of it? If it be conjoined with the extension, it must exist somewhere within its dimensions. If it exist within its dimensions, it must either exist in one particular part, and then that particular part is indivisible and the perception is conjoined only with it, not with the extension; or if the thought exists in every part, it must also be extended and separable and divisible, as well as the body, which is utterly absurd and contradictory. For can anyone conceive a passion of a yard in length, a foot in breadth, and an inch in thickness? Thought, therefore, and extension are qualities wholly incompatible, and never can incorporate together into one subject.

This argument affects not the question concerning the *substance* of the soul but only that concerning its *local conjunction* with matter, and therefore it may not be improper to consider in general what objects are or are not susceptible of a local conjunction. This is a curious question and may lead us to some discoveries of considerable moment.

The first notion of space and extension is derived solely from the senses of sight and feeling, nor is there anything but what is colored or tangible that has parts disposed after such a manner as to convey that idea. When we diminish or increase a relish, it is not after the same manner that we diminish or increase any visible object, and when several sounds strike our hearing at once, custom and reflection alone make us form an idea of the degrees of the distance and contiguity of those bodies from which they are derived. Whatever marks the place of its existence either must be extended or must be a mathematical point, without parts or composition. What is extended must have a particular figure, as square, round, triangular, none of which will agree to a desire, or indeed to any impression or idea except of these two senses above-mentioned. Neither ought a desire, though indivisible, to be considered as a mathematical point. For in that case it would be possible, by the addition of others, to make two, three, four desires, and these disposed and situated in such a manner as to have a determinate length, breadth, and thickness, which is evidently absurd.

It will not be surprising after this if I deliver a maxim which is condemned by several metaphysicians, and is esteemed contrary to the most certain principles of human reason. This maxim is *that an object may exist and yet be nowhere,* and I assert that this is not only possible but that the greatest part of beings do and must exist after this manner. An object may be said to be nowhere when its parts are not so situated with respect to each other as to form any figure or quantity, nor the whole with respect to other bodies so as to answer to our notions of contiguity or distance. Now this is evidently the case with all our perceptions and objects except those of the sight and feeling. A moral reflection cannot be placed on the right or on the left hand of a passion, nor can a smell or sound be either of a circular or a square figure. These objects and perceptions, so far from requiring any particular place, are absolutely incompatible with it, and even the imagination cannot attribute it to them. And as to the absurdity of supposing them to be nowhere, we may consider that if the passions and sentiments appear to the perception to have any particular place, the idea of extension might be derived from them as well as from the sight and touch, contrary to what we have already established. If they *appear* not to have any particular place, they may possibly *exist* in the same manner, since whatever we conceive is possible.

It will not now be necessary to prove that those perceptions which are simple and exist nowhere are incapable of any conjunction in place with matter or body, which is extended and divisible, since it is impossible to found a relation[1] but on some common quality. . . .

. . . . .

But though in this view of things we cannot refuse to condemn the materialists, who conjoin all thought with extension, yet a little reflection will show us equal reason for blaming their antagonists, who conjoin all thought with a simple and indivisible substance. The most vulgar philosophy informs us that no external object can make itself known to the mind immediately and without the interposition of an image or perception. That table which just now appears to me is only a perception, and all its qualities are qualities of a perception. Now the most obvious of all its qualities is extension. The perception consists of parts. These parts are so situated as to afford us the notion of distance and contiguity, of length, breadth, and thickness. The termination of these three dimensions is what we call figure. This figure is movable, separable, and divisible. Mobility and separability are the distinguishing properties of extended objects. And to cut short all disputes, the very idea of extension is copied from nothing but an impression, and consequently must perfectly agree to it. To say the idea of extension agrees to anything is to say it is extended.

The free-thinker may now triumph in his turn, and having found there are impressions and ideas really extended, may ask his antagonists how they can incorporate a simple and indivisible subject with an extended perception? All the arguments of theologians may here be retorted upon them. Is the indivisible subject, or immaterial substance, if you will, on the left or on the right hand of the perception? Is it in this particular part or in that other? Is it in every part without

[1] Part I, Section V.

being extended? Or is it entire in any one part without deserting the rest? It is impossible to give any answer to these questions but what will both be absurd in itself and will account for the union of our indivisible perceptions with an extended substance.

. . . . .

From these hypotheses concerning the *substance* and *local conjunction* of our perceptions, we may pass to another which is more intelligible than the former and more important than the latter, *viz.*, concerning the *cause* of our perceptions. Matter and motion, it is commonly said in the schools, however varied, are still matter and motion, and produce only a difference in the position and situation of objects. Divide a body as often as you please, it is still body. Place it in any figure, nothing ever results but figure, or the relation of parts. Move it in any manner, you still find motion or a change of relation. It is absurd to imagine that motion in a circle, for instance, should be nothing but merely motion in a circle, while motion in another direction, as in an ellipse, should also be a passion or moral reflection; that the shocking of two globular particles should become a sensation of pain, and that the meeting of two triangular ones should afford a pleasure. Now as these different shocks and variations and mixtures are the only changes of which matter is susceptible, and as these never afford us any idea of thought or perception, it is concluded to be impossible that thought can ever be caused by matter.

Few have been able to withstand the seeming evidence of this argument, and yet nothing in the world is more easy than to refute it. We need only reflect on what has been proved at large, that we are never sensible of any connection between causes and effects, and that it is only by our experience of their constant conjunction we can arrive at any knowledge of this relation. Now as all objects which are not contrary are susceptible of a constant conjunction, and as no real objects are contrary,[1] I have inferred from these principles that, to consider the matter *a priori,* anything may produce anything, and that we shall never discover a reason why any object may or may not be the cause of any other, however

[1] Part III, Section XV.

great or however little the resemblance may be between them. This evidently destroys the precedent reasoning concerning the cause of thought or perception. For though there appear no manner of connection between motion or thought, the case is the same with all other causes and effects. Place one body of a pound weight on one end of a lever, and another body of the same weight on another end; you will never find in these bodies any principle of motion dependent on their distances from the center, more than of thought and perception. If you pretend, therefore, to prove *a priori* that such a position of bodies can never cause thought, because turn it which way you will it is nothing but a position of bodies, you must by the same course of reasoning conclude that it can never produce motion, since there is no more apparent connection in the one case than in the other. But as this latter conclusion is contrary to evident experience, and as it is possible we may have a like experience in the operations of the mind and may perceive a constant conjunction of thought and motion, you reason too hastily when from the mere consideration of the ideas you conclude that it is impossible motion can ever produce thought, or a different position of parts give rise to a different passion or reflection. Nay it is not only possible we may have such an experience, but it is certain we have it, since everyone may perceive that the different dispositions of his body change his thoughts and sentiments. And should it be said that this depends on the union of soul and body, I would answer that we must separate the question concerning the substance of the mind from that concerning the cause of its thought, and that confining ourselves to the latter question we find by the comparing their ideas that thought and motion are different from each other, and by experience that they are constantly united, which being all the circumstances that enter into the idea of cause and effect when applied to the operations of matter, we may certainly conclude that motion may be, and actually is, the cause of thought and perception.

. . . . . .

To pronounce, then, the final decision upon the whole, the question concerning the substance of the soul is absolutely unintelligible. All our perceptions are not susceptible of a local union, either with what is extended or unextended, there being some of them of the one kind and some of the other. And as the constant conjunction of objects constitutes the very essence of cause and effect, matter and motion may often be regarded as the causes of thought, as far as we have any notion of that relation.

It is certainly a kind of indignity to philosophy, whose sovereign authority ought everywhere to be acknowledged, to oblige her on every occasion to make apologies for her conclusions, and justify herself to every particular art and science which may be offended at her. This puts one in mind of a king arraigned for high treason against his subjects. There is only one occasion when philosophy will think it necessary and even honorable to justify herself, and that is when religion may seem to be in the least offended, whose rights are as dear to her as her own, and are indeed the same. If anyone, therefore, should imagine that the foregoing arguments are any ways dangerous to religion, I hope the following apology will remove his apprehensions.

There is no foundation for any conclusion *a priori,* either concerning the operations or duration of any object, of which it is possible for the human mind to form a conception. Any object may be imagined to become entirely inactive or to be annihilated in a moment, and it is an evident principle *that whatever we can imagine is possible.* Now this is no more true of matter than of spirit, of an extended compounded substance than of a simple and unextended. In both cases the metaphysical arguments for the immortality of the soul are equally inconclusive, and in both cases the moral arguments and those derived from the analogy of nature are equally strong and convincing. If my philosophy, therefore, makes no addition to the arguments for religion, I have at least the satisfaction to think it takes nothing from them, but that everything remains precisely as before.

Section VI.

OF PERSONAL IDENTITY

There are some philosophers who imagine we are every moment intimately conscious of what we call our SELF, that we feel its existence and its continuance in existence, and are certain, beyond the evidence of a demonstration, both of its perfect identity and simplicity. The strongest sensation, the most violent passion, say they, instead of distracting us from this view, only fix it the more intensely, and make us consider their influence on *self* either by their pain or pleasure. To attempt a further proof of this were to weaken its evidence, since no proof can be derived from any fact of which we are so intimately conscious, nor is there anything of which we can be certain if we doubt of this.

Unluckily all these positive assertions are contrary to that very experience which is pleaded for them, nor have we any idea of *self* after the manner it is here explained. For from what impression could this idea be derived? This question it is impossible to answer without a manifest contradiction and absurdity, and yet it is a question which must necessarily be answered if we would have the idea of self pass for clear and intelligible. It must be some one impression that gives rise to every real idea. But self or person is not any one impression, but that to which our several impressions and ideas are supposed to have a reference. If any impression gives rise to the idea of self, that impression must continue invariably the same through the whole course of our lives, since self is supposed to exist after that manner. But there is no impression constant and invariable. Pain and pleasure, grief and joy, passions and sensations succeed each other, and never all exist at the same time. It cannot, therefore, be from any of these impressions, or from any other, that the idea of self is derived, and consequently there is no such idea.

But further, what must become of all our particular perceptions upon this hypothesis? All these are different and distinguishable and separable from each other, and may be separately considered and may exist separately, and have no need of anything to support their existence. After what manner, therefore, do they belong to self, and how are they connected with it? For my part, when I enter most intimately into what I call *myself*, I always stumble on some particular perception or other, of heat or cold, light or shade, love or hatred, pain or pleasure. I never can catch *myself* at any time without a perception, and never can observe anything but the perception. When my perceptions are removed for any time, as by sound sleep, so long am I insensible of *myself*, and may truly be said not to exist. And were all my perceptions removed by death, and could I neither think nor feel nor see nor love nor hate after the dissolution of my body, I should be entirely annihilated, nor do I conceive what is further requisite to make me a perfect nonentity. If anyone upon serious and unprejudiced reflection thinks he has a different notion of *himself*, I must confess I can reason no longer with him. All I can allow him is that he may be in the right as well as I, and that we are essentially different in this particular. He may, perhaps, perceive something simple and continued which he calls *himself*, though I am certain there is no such principle in me.

But setting aside some metaphysicians of this kind, I may venture to affirm of the rest of mankind that they are nothing but a bundle or collection of different perceptions, which succeed each other with an inconceivable rapidity and are in a perpetual flux and movement. Our eyes cannot turn in their sockets without varying our perceptions. Our thought is still more variable than our sight, and all our other senses and faculties contribute to this change; nor is there any single power of the soul which remains unalterably the same perhaps for one moment. The mind is a kind of theater, where several perceptions successively make their appearance, pass, re-pass, glide away, and mingle in an infinite variety of postures and situations. There is properly no *simplicity* in it at one time nor *identity* in different, whatever natural propension we may have to imagine that simplicity and identity. The comparison of the theater must not mislead us. They are the successive perceptions only that constitute the mind, nor have we the most distant notion of the place where these scenes are represented, or of the materials of which it is composed.

What then gives us so great a propension to ascribe an identity to these successive perceptions, and to suppose ourselves possessed of an invariable and uninterrupted existence through the whole course of our lives? In order to answer this question, we must distinguish between personal identity as it regards our thought or imagination and as it regards our passions or the concern we take in ourselves. The first is our present subject, and to explain it perfectly we must take the matter pretty deep, and account for that identity which we attribute to plants and animals, there being a great analogy between it and the identity of a self or person.

We have a distinct idea of an object that remains invariable and uninterrupted through a supposed variation of time, and this idea we call that of *identity* or *sameness*. We have also a distinct idea of several different objects existing in succession and connected together by a close relation, and this to an accurate view affords as perfect a notion of *diversity* as if there was no manner of relation among the objects. But though these two ideas of identity and a succession of related objects be in themselves perfectly distinct, and even contrary, yet it is certain that in our common way of thinking they are generally confounded with each other. That action of the imagination by which we consider the uninterrupted and invariable object, and that by which we reflect on the succession of related objects, are almost the same to the feeling, nor is there much more effort of thought required in the latter case than in the former. The relation facilitates the transition of the mind from one object to another, and renders its passage as smooth as if it contemplated one continued object. This resemblance is the cause of the confusion and mistake, and makes us substitute the notion of identity instead of that of related objects. However at one instant we may consider the related succession as variable or interrupted, we are sure the next to ascribe to it a perfect identity, and regard it as invariable and uninterrupted. Our propensity to this mistake is so great from the resemblance above-mentioned that we fall into it before we are aware, and though we incessantly correct ourselves by reflection and return to a more accurate method of thinking, yet we cannot long sustain our philosophy, or take off this bias from the imagination. Our last resource is to yield to it, and boldly assert that these different related objects are in effect the same, however interrupted and variable. In order to justify to ourselves this absurdity, we often feign some new and unintelligible principle that connects the objects together and prevents their interruption or variation. Thus we feign the continued existence of the perceptions of our senses to remove the interruption, and run into the notion of a *soul* and *self* and *substance* to disguise the variation. But we may further observe that where we do not give rise to such a fiction, our propension to confound identity with relation is so great that we are apt to imagine[1] something unknown and mysterious connecting the parts beside their relation; and this I take to be the case with regard to the identity we ascribe to plants and vegetables. And even when this does not take place, we still feel a propensity to confound these ideas, though we are not able fully to satisfy ourselves in that particular, nor find anything invariable and uninterrupted to justify our notion of identity.

Thus the controversy concerning identity is not merely a dispute of words. For when we attribute identity, in an improper sense, to variable or interrupted objects, our mistake is not confined to the expression, but is commonly attended with a fiction, either of something invariable and uninterrupted, or of something mysterious and inexplicable, or at least with a propensity to such fictions. What will suffice to prove this hypothesis to the satisfaction of every fair inquirer is to show from daily experience and observation that the objects which are variable or interrupted and yet are supposed to continue the same are such only as consist of a succession of parts, connected together by resemblance,

---

[1] If the reader is desirous to see how a great genius may be influenced by these seemingly trivial principles of the imagination, as well as the mere vulgar, let him read my Lord *Shaftesbury's* reasonings concerning the uniting principle of the universe, and the identity of plants and animals. See his *Moralists: A Philosophical Rhapsody.*

contiguity, or causation. For as such a succession answers evidently to our notion of diversity, it can only be by mistake we ascribe to it an identity; and as the relation of parts which leads us into this mistake is really nothing but a quality which produces an association of ideas and an easy transition of the imagination from one to another, it can only be from the resemblance which this act of the mind bears to that by which we contemplate one continued object that the error arises. Our chief business, then, must be to prove that all objects to which we ascribe identity, without observing their invariableness and uninterruptedness, are such as consist of a succession of related objects.

In order to this, suppose any mass of matter, of which the parts are contiguous and connected, to be placed before us; it is plain we must attribute a perfect identity to this mass, provided all the parts continue uninterruptedly and invariably the same, whatever motion or change of place we may observe either in the whole or in any of the parts. But supposing some very *small* or *inconsiderable* part to be added to the mass or subtracted from it, though this absolutely destroys the identity of the whole, strictly speaking, yet as we seldom think so accurately, we scruple not to pronounce a mass of matter the same where we find so trivial an alteration. The passage of the thought from the object before the change to the object after it is so smooth and easy that we scarce perceive the transition, and are apt to imagine that it is nothing but a continued survey of the same object.

There is a very remarkable circumstance that attends this experiment, which is that though the change of any considerable part in a mass of matter destroys the identity of the whole, yet we must measure the greatness of the part, not absolutely, but by its *proportion* to the whole. The addition or diminution of a mountain would not be sufficient to produce a diversity in a planet, though the change of a very few inches would be able to destroy the identity of some bodies. It will be impossible to account for this but by reflecting that objects operate upon the mind and break or interrupt the continuity of its actions not according to their real greatness, but according to their proportion to each other. And therefore, since this interruption makes an object cease to appear the same, it must be the uninterrupted progress of the thought which constitutes the imperfect identity.

This may be confirmed by another phenomenon. A change in any considerable part of a body destroys its identity, but it is remarkable that where the change is produced *gradually* and *insensibly* we are less apt to ascribe to it the same effect. The reason can plainly be no other than that the mind, in following the successive changes of the body, feels an easy passage from the surveying of its condition in one moment to the viewing of it in another, and at no particular time perceives any interruption in its actions. From which continued perception it ascribes a continued existence and identity to the object.

But whatever precaution we may use in introducing the changes gradually, and making them proportionable to the whole, it is certain that where the changes are at last observed to become considerable, we make a scruple of ascribing identity to such different objects. There is, however, another artifice by which we may induce the imagination to advance a step farther, and that is by producing a reference of the parts to each other and a combination to some *common end* or purpose. A ship, of which a considerable part has been changed by frequent reparations, is still considered as the same, nor does the difference of the materials hinder us from ascribing an identity to it. The common end in which the parts conspire is the same under all their variations, and affords an easy transition of the imagination from one situation of the body to another.

But this is still more remarkable when we add a *sympathy* of parts to their *common end,* and suppose that they bear to each other the reciprocal relation of cause and effect in all their actions and operations. This is the case with all animals and vegetables, where not only the several parts have a reference to some general purpose, but also a mutual dependence on and connection with each other. The effect of so strong a relation is that though everyone must allow that in a very few years both vegetables and animals endure a *total* change, yet we still attribute identity to them while their form, size, and substance are entirely altered. An oak that grows from a small plant to a large tree is still the same oak, though there be not one particle of matter or figure of its parts the same. An infant becomes a man, and is sometimes fat, sometimes lean, without any change in his identity.

We may also consider the two following phenomena, which are remarkable in their kind. The first is that though we commonly be able to distinguish pretty exactly between numerical and specific identity, yet it sometimes happens that we confound them, and in our thinking and reasoning employ the one for the other. Thus a man who hears a noise that is frequently interrupted and renewed says it is still the same noise, though it is evident the sounds have only a specific identity or resemblance, and there is nothing numerically the same but the cause which produced them. In like manner it may be said without breach of the propriety of language that such a church, which was formerly of brick, fell to ruin, and that the parish rebuilt the same church of free-stone and according to modern architecture. Here neither the form nor materials are the same, nor is there anything common to the two objects but their relation to the inhabitants of the parish, and yet this alone is sufficient to make us denominate them the same. But we must observe that in these cases the first object is in a manner annihilated before the second comes into existence, by which means we are never presented in any one point of time with the idea of difference and multiplicity, and for that reason are less scrupulous in calling them the same.

Secondly, we may remark that though in a succession of related objects it be in a manner requisite that the change of parts be not sudden nor entire in order to preserve the identity, yet where the objects are in their nature changeable and inconstant, we admit of a more sudden transition than would otherwise be consistent with that relation. Thus as the nature of a river consists in the motion and change of parts, though in less than four and twenty hours these be totally altered, this hinders not the river from continuing the same during several ages. What is natural and essential to anything is, in a manner, expected, and what is expected makes less impression, and appears of less moment, than what is unusual and extraordinary. A considerable change of the former kind seems really less to the imagination than the most trivial alteration of the latter, and by breaking less the continuity of the thought has less influence in destroying the identity.

We now proceed to explain the nature of *personal identity*, which has become so great a question in philosophy, especially of late years in *England*, where all the abstruser sciences are studied with a peculiar ardor and application. And here it is evident the same method of reasoning must be continued which has so successfully explained the identity of plants and animals and ships and houses, and of all the compounded and changeable productions either of art or nature. The identity which we ascribe to the mind of man is only a fictitious one, and of a like kind with that which we ascribe to vegetables and animal bodies. It cannot, therefore, have a different origin, but must proceed from a like operation of the imagination upon like objects.

But lest this argument should not convince the reader, though in my opinion perfectly decisive, let him weigh the following reasoning, which is still closer and more immediate. It is evident that the identity which we attribute to the human mind, however perfect we may imagine it to be, is not able to run the several different perceptions into one, and make them lose their characters of distinction and difference which are essential to them. It is still true that every distinct perception which enters into the composition of the mind is a distinct existence, and is different and distinguishable and separable from every other perception, either contemporary or successive. But as, notwithstanding this distinction and separability, we suppose the whole train of perceptions to be united by identity, a question naturally arises concerning this relation of identity, whether it be something that really binds our several perceptions together or only associates their ideas in the imagination. That is, in other words, whether in pronouncing concerning the identity of a person, we observe some real bond among his perceptions, or only feel one among the ideas we form of them. This question we might easily decide if we would recollect what has been already proved at large, that the understanding never observes any real connection among objects, and that even the union of cause and effect, when strictly examined, resolves itself into a customary association of ideas. For from thence it evidently follows that identity is nothing really belonging to these different perceptions and uniting them together, but is merely a quality which we attribute to them because of the union of their ideas in the imagination when we reflect upon them. Now the only qualities which can give ideas a union in the imagination are these three relations above-mentioned. These are the uniting principles in the ideal world, and without them every distinct object is separable by the mind, and may be separately considered, and appears not to have any more connection with any other object than if disjoined by the greatest difference and remoteness. It is, therefore, on some of these three relations of resemblance, contiguity, and causation that identity depends; and as the very essence of these relations consists in their producing an easy transition of ideas, it follows that our notions of personal identity proceed entirely from the smooth and uninterrupted progress of the thought along a train of connected ideas, according to the principles above-explained.

The only question, therefore, which remains is by what relations this uninterrupted progress of our thought is produced, when we consider the successive existence of a mind or thinking person. And here it is evident we must confine ourselves to resemblance and causation, and must drop contiguity, which has little or no influence in the present case.

To begin with *resemblance,* suppose we could see clearly into the breast of another, and observe that succession of perceptions which constitutes his mind or thinking principle, and suppose that he always preserves the memory of a considerable part of past perceptions; it is evident that nothing could more contribute to the bestowing a relation on this succession amidst all its variations. For what is the memory but a faculty by which we raise up the images of past perceptions? And as an image necessarily resembles its object, must not the frequent placing of these resembling perceptions in the chain of thought convey the imagination more easily from one link to another, and make the whole seem like the continuance of one object? In this particular, then, the memory not only discovers the identity, but also contributes to its production by producing the relation of resemblance among the perceptions. The case is the same whether we consider ourselves or others.

As to *causation*, we may observe that the true idea of the human mind is to consider it as a system of different perceptions or different existences which are linked together by the relation of cause and effect, and mutually produce, destroy, influence, and modify each other. Our impressions give rise to their correspondent ideas, and these ideas in their turn produce other impressions. One thought chases another, and draws after it a third, by which it is expelled in its turn. In this respect, I cannot compare the soul more properly to anything than to a republic or commonwealth, in which the several members are united by the reciprocal ties of government and subordination, and give rise to other persons who propagate the same republic in the incessant changes of its parts. And as the same individual republic may not only change its members, but also its laws and constitutions, in like manner the same person may vary his character and disposition, as well as his impressions and ideas, without losing his identity. Whatever changes he endures, his several parts are still connected by the relation of causation. And in this view our identity with regard to the passions serves to corroborate that with regard to the imagination, by the making our distant perceptions influence each other, and by giving us a present concern for our past or future pains or pleasures.

As memory alone acquaints us with the continuance and extent of this succession of perceptions, it is to be considered, upon that account chiefly, as the source of personal identity. Had we no memory, we never should have any notion of causation, nor consequently of that chain of causes and effects which constitute our self or person. But having once acquired this notion of causation from the memory, we can extend the same chain of causes and consequently the identity of our persons beyond our memory, and can comprehend times and circumstances and actions which we have entirely forgotten but suppose in general to have existed. For how few of our past actions are there of which we have any memory? Who can tell me, for instance, what were his thoughts and actions on the first of January 1715, the 11th of March 1719, and the 3d of August 1733? Or will he affirm, because he has entirely forgotten the incidents of these days, that the present self is not the same person with the self of that time, and by that means overturn all the most established notions of personal identity? In this view, therefore, memory does not so much *produce* as *discover* personal identity, by showing us the relation of cause and effect among our different perceptions. It will be incumbent on those who affirm that memory produces entirely our personal identity to give a reason why we can thus extend our identity beyond our memory.

The whole of this doctrine leads us to a conclusion which is of great importance in the present affair, *viz.*, that all the nice and subtle questions concerning personal identity can never possibly be decided, and are to be regarded rather as grammatical than as philosophical difficulties. Identity depends on the relations of ideas, and these relations produce identity by means of that easy transition they occasion. But as the relations and the easiness of the transition may diminish by insensible degrees, we have no just standard by which we can decide any dispute concerning the time when they acquire or lose a title to the name of identity. All the disputes concerning the identity of connected objects are merely verbal, except so far as the relation of parts gives rise to some fiction or imaginary principle of union, as we have already observed.

What I have said concerning the first origin and uncertainty of our notion of identity, as applied to the human mind, may be extended with little or no variation to that of *simplicity*. An object whose different coexistent parts are bound together by a close relation operates upon the imagination after much the same manner as one perfectly simple and indivisible, and requires not a much greater stretch of thought in order to its conception. From this similarity of operation we attribute a simplicity to it, and feign a principle of union as the support of this simplicity and the center of all the different parts and qualities of the object.

Thus we have finished our examination of the several systems of philosophy, both of the intellectual and natural world, and in our miscellaneous way of reasoning have been led into several topics which will either illustrate and confirm some preceding part of this discourse or prepare the way for our following opinions. It is now time to return to a more close examination of our subject, and to proceed in the accurate anatomy of human nature, having fully explained the nature of our judgment and understanding.

Section VII.

CONCLUSION OF THIS BOOK

But before I launch out into those immense depths of philosophy which lie before me, I find myself inclined to stop a moment in my present station, and to ponder that voyage which I have undertaken and which undoubtedly requires the utmost art and industry to be brought to a happy conclusion. Methinks I am like a man who, having struck on many shoals and having narrowly escaped shipwreck in passing a small frith, has yet the temerity to put out to sea in the same leaky weather-beaten vessel, and even carries his ambition so far as to think of compassing the globe under these disadvantageous circumstances. My memory of past errors and perplexities makes me diffident for the future. The wretched condition, weakness, and disorder of the faculties I must employ in my inquiries increase my apprehensions. And the impossibility of amending or correcting these faculties reduces me almost to despair, and makes me resolve to perish on the barren rock on which I am at present, rather than venture myself upon that boundless ocean which runs out into immensity. This sudden view of my danger strikes me with melancholy, and as it is usual for that passion, above all others, to indulge itself, I cannot forbear feeding my despair with all those desponding reflections which the present subject furnishes me with in such abundance.

I am first affrighted and confounded with that forlorn solitude in which I am placed in my philosophy, and fancy myself some strange uncouth monster, who not being able to mingle and unite in society, has been expelled [from] all human commerce, and left utterly abandoned and disconsolate. Fain would I run into the crowd for shelter and warmth, but cannot prevail with myself to mix with such deformity. I call upon others to join me, in order to make a company apart, but no one will hearken to me. Everyone keeps at a distance, and dreads that storm which beats upon me from every side. I have exposed myself to the enmity of all metaphysicians, logicians, mathematicians, and even theologians, and can I wonder at the insults I must suffer? I have declared my disapprobation of their systems, and can I be surprised if they should express a hatred of mine and of my person? When I look abroad, I foresee on every side dispute, contradiction, anger, calumny, and detraction. When I turn my eye inward, I find nothing but doubt and ignorance. All the world conspires to oppose and contradict me, though such is my weakness that I feel all my opinions loosen and fall of themselves when unsupported by the approbation of others. Every step I take is with hesitation, and every new reflection makes me dread an error and absurdity in my reasoning.

For with what confidence can I venture upon such bold enterprises when beside those numberless infirmities peculiar to myself I find so many which are common to human nature? Can I be sure that in leaving all established opinions I am following truth, and by what criterion shall I distinguish her, even if fortune should at last guide me on her footsteps? After the most accurate and exact of my reasonings, I can give no reason why I should assent to it, and feel nothing but a *strong* propensity to consider objects *strongly* in that view under which they appear to me. Experience is a principle which instructs me in the several conjunctions of objects for the past; habit is another principle, which determines me to expect the same for the future; and both of them conspiring to operate upon the imagination, make me form certain ideas in a more intense and lively manner than others, which are not attended with the same advantages. Without this quality, by which the mind enlivens some ideas beyond others (which seemingly is so trivial, and so little founded on reason), we could never assent to any argument, nor carry our view beyond those few objects which are present to our senses. Nay, even to these objects we could never attribute any existence but what was dependent on the senses, and must comprehend them entirely in that succession of perceptions which constitutes our self or person. Nay further, even with relation to that succession, we could only admit of those perceptions which are immediately present to our consciousness, nor could those lively images with which the memory presents us be ever received as true pictures of past perceptions. The memory, senses, and understanding are, therefore, all of them founded on the imagination, or the vivacity of our ideas.

No wonder a principle so inconstant and fallacious should lead us into errors when implicitly followed (as it must be) in all its variations. It is this principle which makes us reason from causes and effects, and it is the same principle which convinces us of the continued existence of external objects when absent from the senses. But though these two operations be equally natural and necessary in the human mind, yet in some circumstances[1] they are directly contrary, nor is it possible for us to reason justly and regularly from causes and effects and at the same time believe the continued existence of matter. How then shall we adjust those principles together? Which of them shall we prefer? Or in case we prefer neither of them but successively assent to both, as is usual among philosophers, with what confidence can we afterwards usurp that glorious title, when we thus knowingly embrace a manifest contradiction?

This contradiction[2] would be more excusable were it compensated by any degree of solidity and satisfaction in the other parts of our reasoning. But the case is quite contrary. When we trace up the human understanding to its first principles, we find it to lead us into such sentiments as seem to turn into ridicule all our past pains and industry, and to discourage us from future inquiries. Nothing is more curiously inquired after by the mind of man than the causes of every phenomenon, nor are we content with knowing the immediate causes, but push on our inquiries till we arrive at the original and ultimate principle. We would not willingly stop before we are acquainted with that energy in the cause by which it operates on its effect, that tie which connects them together,

[1] Section IV.
[2] Part III, Section XIV.

and that efficacious quality on which the tie depends. This is our aim in all our studies and reflections, and how must we be disappointed when we learn that this connection, tie, or energy lies merely in ourselves, and is nothing but that determination of the mind which is acquired by custom and causes us to make a transition from an object to its usual attendant, and from the impression of one to the lively idea of the other? Such a discovery not only cuts off all hope of ever attaining satisfaction, but even prevents our very wishes, since it appears that when we say we desire to know the ultimate and operating principle, as something which resides in the external object, we either contradict ourselves or talk without a meaning.

This deficiency in our ideas is not, indeed, perceived in common life, nor are we sensible that in the most usual conjunctions of cause and effect we are as ignorant of the ultimate principle which binds them together as in the most unusual and extraordinary. But this proceeds merely from an illusion of the imagination, and the question is how far we ought to yield to these illusions. This question is very difficult, and reduces us to a very dangerous dilemma, whichever way we answer it. For if we assent to every trivial suggestion of the fancy, beside that these suggestions are often contrary to each other, they lead us into such errors, absurdities, and obscurities that we must at last become ashamed of our credulity. Nothing is more dangerous to reason than the flights of the imagination, and nothing has been the occasion of more mistakes among philosophers. Men of bright fancies may in this respect be compared to those angels whom the scripture represents as covering their eyes with their wings. This has already appeared in so many instances that we may spare ourselves the trouble of enlarging upon it any further.

But on the other hand if the consideration of these instances makes us take a resolution to reject all the trivial suggestions of the fancy and adhere to the understanding, that is, to the general and more established properties of the imagination, even this resolution, if steadily executed, would be dangerous, and attended with the most fatal consequences. For I have already shown [1] that the understanding, when it

[1] Section I.

acts alone and according to its most general principles, entirely subverts itself, and leaves not the lowest degree of evidence in any proposition, either in philosophy or common life. We save ourselves from this total skepticism only by means of that singular and seemingly trivial property of the fancy by which we enter with difficulty into remote views of things, and are not able to accompany them with so sensible an impression as we do those which are more easy and natural. Shall we, then, establish it for a general maxim that no refined or elaborate reasoning is ever to be received? Consider well the consequences of such a principle. By this means you cut off entirely all science and philosophy; you proceed upon one singular quality of the imagination, and by a parity of reason must embrace all of them; and you expressly contradict yourself, since this maxim must be built on the preceding reasoning, which will be allowed to be sufficiently refined and metaphysical. What party, then, shall we choose among these difficulties? If we embrace this principle and condemn all refined reasoning, we run into the most manifest absurdities. If we reject it in favor of these reasonings, we subvert entirely the human understanding. We have, therefore, no choice left but between a false reason and none at all. For my part, I know not what ought to be done in the present case. I can only observe what is commonly done, which is that this difficulty is seldom or never thought of, and even where it has once been present to the mind, is quickly forgotten, and leaves but a small impression behind it. Very refined reflections have little or no influence upon us, and yet we do not and cannot establish it for a rule that they ought not to have any influence, which implies a manifest contradiction.

But what have I here said, that reflections very refined and metaphysical have little or no influence upon us? This opinion I can scarce forbear retracting, and condemning from my present feeling and experience. The *intense* view of these manifold contradictions and imperfections in human reason has so wrought upon me and heated my brain that I am ready to reject all belief and reasoning, and can look upon no opinion even as more probable or likely than another. Where am I, or what? From what causes do I derive my existence, and to what condition shall I return? Whose favor shall I court, and whose anger must I dread? What beings surround me, and on whom have I any influence, or who has any influence on me? I am confounded with all these questions, and begin to fancy myself in the most deplorable condition imaginable, environed with the deepest darkness, and utterly deprived of the use of every member and faculty.

Most fortunately it happens that since reason is incapable of dispelling these clouds, nature herself suffices to that purpose, and cures me of this philosophical melancholy and delirium, either by relaxing this bent of mind, or by some avocation and lively impression of my senses, which obliterate all these chimeras. I dine, I play a game of backgammon, I converse and am merry with my friends, and when after three or four hours' amusement I would return to these speculations, they appear so cold and strained and ridiculous that I cannot find in my heart to enter into them any further.

Here then I find myself absolutely and necessarily determined to live and talk and act like other people in the common affairs of life. But notwithstanding that my natural propensity and the course of my animal spirits and passions reduce me to this indolent belief in the general maxims of the world, I still feel such remains of my former disposition that I am ready to throw all my books and papers into the fire, and resolve never more to renounce the pleasures of life for the sake of reasoning and philosophy. For those are my sentiments in that splenetic humor which governs me at present. I may, nay I must yield to the current of nature, in submitting to my senses and understanding, and in this blind submission I show most perfectly my skeptical disposition and principles. But does it follow that I must strive against the current of nature which leads me to indolence and pleasure, that I must seclude myself, in some measure, from the commerce and society of men which is so agreeable, and that I must torture my brain with subtleties and sophistries, at the very time that I cannot satisfy myself concerning the reasonableness of so painful an application, nor have any tolerable prospect of arriving by its means at truth and certainty? Under what obligation do I lie of making such an abuse of time? And to what end can it serve either for the service of mankind or for my own private interest? No, if I must be a fool, as all those who reason or believe anything *certainly* are, my follies shall at least be natural and agreeable. Where I strive against my inclination I shall have a good reason for my resistance, and will no more be led a-wandering into such dreary solitudes and rough passages as I have hitherto met with.

These are the sentiments of my spleen and indolence, and indeed I must confess that philosophy has nothing to oppose to them, and expects a victory more from the returns of a serious good-humored disposition than from the force of reason and conviction. In all the incidents of life we ought still to preserve our skepticism. If we believe that fire warms or water refreshes, it is only because it costs us too much pain to think otherwise. Nay if we are philosophers, it ought only to be upon skeptical principles, and from an inclination which we feel to the employing ourselves after that manner. Where reason is lively and mixes itself with some propensity, it ought to be assented to. Where it does not, it never can have any title to operate upon us.

At the time, therefore, that I am tired with amusement and company, and have indulged in a *reverie* in my chamber or in a solitary walk by a riverside, I feel my mind all collected within itself, and am naturally *inclined* to carry my view into all those subjects about which I have met with so many disputes in the course of my reading and conversation. I cannot forbear having a curiosity to be acquainted with the principles of moral good and evil, the nature and foundation of government, and the cause of those several passions and inclinations which actuate and govern me. I am uneasy to think I approve of one object and disapprove of another, call one thing beautiful and another deformed, decide concerning truth and falsehood, reason and folly, without knowing upon what principles I proceed. I am concerned for the condition of the learned world, which lies under such a deplorable ignorance in all these particulars. I feel an ambition to arise in me of contributing to the instruction of mankind, and of acquiring a name by my inventions and discoveries. These sentiments spring up naturally in my present disposition, and should I endeavor to banish them by attaching myself to any other business or diversion, I *feel* I should be a loser in point of pleasure; and this is the origin of my philosophy.

But even suppose this curiosity and ambition should not transport me into speculations without the sphere of common life, it would necessarily happen that from my very weakness I must be led into such inquiries. It is certain that superstition is much more bold in its systems and hypotheses than philosophy, and while the latter contents itself with assigning new causes and principles to the phenomena which appear in the visible world, the former opens a world of its own, and presents us with scenes and beings and objects which are altogether new. Since therefore it is almost impossible for the mind of man to rest, like those of beasts, in that narrow circle of objects which are the subject of daily conversation and action, we ought only to deliberate concerning the choice of our guide, and ought to prefer that which is safest and most agreeable. And in this respect I make bold to recommend philosophy, and shall not scruple to give it the preference to superstition of every kind or denomination. For as superstition arises naturally and easily from the popular opinions of mankind, it seizes more strongly on the mind, and is often able to disturb us in the conduct of our lives and actions. Philosophy on the contrary, if just, can present us only with mild and moderate sentiments, and if false and extravagant, its opinions are merely the objects of a cold and general speculation, and seldom go so far as to interrupt the course of our natural propensities. The CYNICS are an extraordinary instance of philosophers who from reasonings purely philosophical ran into as great extravagancies of conduct as any *Monk* or *Dervish* that ever was in the world. Generally speaking, the errors in religion are dangerous, those in philosophy only ridiculous.

I am sensible that these two cases of the strength and weakness of the mind will not comprehend all mankind, and that there are in *England*, in particular, many honest gentlemen who being always employed in their domestic affairs or amusing themselves in common recreations, have carried their thoughts very little beyond those objects which are every day exposed to their senses. And indeed, of such as these I pretend not to make philosophers, nor do I expect them either to be associates in these researches or auditors of these discoveries. They do well to keep themselves in their present situation, and instead of refining them into philosophers, I wish we could communicate to our founders of systems a share of this gross earthy mixture, as an ingredient which they commonly stand much in need of, and which would serve to temper those fiery particles of which they are composed. While a warm imagination is allowed to enter into philosophy, and hypotheses embraced merely for being specious and agreeable, we can never have any steady principles, nor any sentiments which will suit with common practice and experience. But were these hypotheses once removed, we might hope to establish a system or set of opinions which if not true (for that, perhaps, is too much to be hoped for) might at least be satisfactory to the human mind, and might stand the test of the most critical examination. Nor should we despair of attaining this end because of the many chimerical systems which have successively arisen and decayed away among men, would we consider the shortness of that period wherein these questions have been the subjects of inquiry and reasoning. Two thousand years with such long interruptions and under such mighty discouragements are a small space of time to give any tolerable perfection to the sciences, and perhaps we are still in too early an age of the world to discover any principles which will bear the examination of the latest posterity. For my part, my only hope is that I may contribute a little to the advancement of knowledge by giving in some particulars a different turn to the speculations of philosophers, and pointing out to them more distinctly those subjects where alone they can expect assurance and conviction. Human nature is the only science of man, and yet has been hitherto the most neglected. It will be sufficient for me if I can bring it a little more into fashion, and the hope of this serves to compose my temper from that spleen, and invigorate it from that indolence, which sometimes prevail upon me. If the reader finds himself in the same easy disposition, let him follow me in my future speculations. If not, let him follow his inclination, and wait the returns of application and good humor. The conduct of a man who studies philosophy in this careless manner is more truly skeptical than that of one who, feeling in himself an inclination to it, is yet so overwhelmed with doubts and scruples as totally to reject it. A true skeptic will be diffident of his philosophical doubts as well as of his philosophical conviction, and will never refuse any innocent satisfaction which offers itself upon account of either of them.

Nor is it only proper we should in general indulge our inclination in the most elaborate philosophical researches, notwithstanding our skeptical principles, but also that we should yield to that propensity which inclines us to be positive and certain in *particular points,* according to the light in which we survey them in any *particular instant.* It is easier to forbear all examination and inquiry than to check ourselves in so natural a propensity, and guard against that assurance which always arises from an exact and full survey of an object. On such an occasion we are apt not only to forget our skepticism but even our modesty too, and make use of such terms as these, *it is evident, it is certain, it is undeniable,* which a due deference to the public ought, perhaps, to prevent. I may have fallen into this fault after the example of others, but I here enter a *caveat* against any objections which may be offered on that head, and declare that such expressions were extorted from me by the present view of the object, and imply no dogmatical spirit nor conceited idea of my own judgment, which are sentiments that I am sensible can become nobody, and a skeptic still less than any other.

BOOK II.

OF THE PASSIONS

Part I.

OF PRIDE AND HUMILITY

Section I.

DIVISION OF THE SUBJECT

AS ALL THE PERCEPTIONS of the mind may be divided into *impressions* and *ideas,* so the impressions admit of another division into *original* and *secondary*. This division of the impressions is the same with that which [1] I formerly made use of when I distinguished them into impressions of *sensation* and *reflection*. Original impressions or impressions of sensation are such as without any antecedent perception arise in the soul, from the constitution of the body, from the animal spirits, or from the application of objects to the external organs. Secondary or reflective impressions are such as proceed from some of these original ones, either immediately or by the interposition of its idea. Of the first kind are all the impres-

[1] Book I, Part I, Section II.

sions of the senses and all bodily pains and pleasures; of the second are the passions and other emotions resembling them.

It is certain that the mind, in its perceptions, must begin somewhere, and that since the impressions precede their correspondent ideas, there must be some impressions which without any introduction make their appearance in the soul. As these depend upon natural and physical causes, the examination of them would lead me too far from my present subject into the sciences of anatomy and natural philosophy. For this reason I shall here confine myself to those other impressions which I have called secondary and reflective, as arising either from the original impressions or from their ideas. Bodily pains and pleasures are the source of many passions both when felt and considered by the mind, but arise originally in the soul, or in the body, whichever you please to call it, without any preceding thought or perception. A fit of the gout produces a long train of passions, as grief, hope, fear, but is not derived immediately from any affection or idea.

The reflective impressions may be divided into two kinds, *viz.*, the *calm* and the *violent*. Of the first kind is the sense of beauty and deformity in action, composition, and external objects. Of the second are the passions of love and hatred, grief and joy, pride and humility. This division is far from being exact. The raptures of poetry and music frequently rise to the greatest height, while those other impressions, properly called *passions*, may decay into so soft an emotion as to become, in a manner, imperceptible. But as in general the passions are more violent than the emotions arising from beauty and deformity, these impressions have been commonly distinguished from each other. The subject of the human mind being so copious and various, I shall here take advantage of this vulgar and specious division, that I may proceed with the greater order; and having said all I thought necessary concerning our ideas, shall now explain these violent emotions or passions, their nature, origin, causes, and effects.

When we take a survey of the passions, there occurs a division of them into *direct* and *indirect*. By direct passions I understand such as arise immediately from good or evil, from pain or pleasure. By indirect such as proceed from the same principles, but by the conjunction of other qualities. This distinction I cannot at present justify or explain any further. I can only observe in general that under the indirect passions I comprehend pride, humility, ambition, vanity, love, hatred, envy, pity, malice, generosity, with their dependents. And under the direct passions, desire, aversion, grief, joy, hope, fear, despair, and security. I shall begin with the former.

Section II.

OF PRIDE AND HUMILITY: THEIR OBJECTS AND CAUSES

The passions of PRIDE and HUMILITY being simple and uniform impressions, it is impossible we can ever, by a multitude of words, give a just definition of them, or indeed of any of the passions. The utmost we can pretend to is a description of them by an enumeration of such circumstances as attend them. But as these words, *pride* and *humility,* are of general use, and the impressions they represent the most common of any, everyone of himself will be able to form a just idea of them without any danger of mistake. For which reason, not to lose time upon preliminaries, I shall immediately enter upon the examination of these passions.

It is evident that pride and humility, though directly contrary, have yet the same OBJECT. This object is self, or that succession of related ideas and impressions of which we have an intimate memory and consciousness. Here the view always fixes when we are actuated by either of these passions. According as our idea of ourself is more or less advantageous, we feel either of those opposite affections, and are elated by pride or dejected with humility. Whatever other objects may be comprehended by the mind, they are always considered with a view to ourselves; otherwise they would never be able either to excite these passions or produce the smallest increase or diminution of them. When self enters not into the consideration, there is no room either for pride or humility.

But though that connected succession of perceptions which we call *self* be always the object of these two passions, it is impossible it can be their CAUSE, or be sufficient alone to excite them. For as these passions are directly contrary and have the same object in common, were their object also their cause it could never produce any degree of the one passion but at the same time it must excite an equal degree of the other, which opposition and contrariety must destroy both. It is impossible a man can at the same time be both proud and humble; and where he has different reasons for these passions, as frequently happens, the passions either take place alternately or, if they encounter, the one annihilates the other as far as its strength goes, and the remainder only of that which is superior continues to operate upon the mind. But in the present case neither of the passions could ever become superior, because supposing it to be the view only of ourself which excited them, that being perfectly indifferent to either, must produce both in the very same proportion, or in other words, can produce neither. To excite any passion and at the same time raise an equal share of its antagonist is immediately to undo what was done, and must leave the mind at last perfectly calm and indifferent.

We must, therefore, make a distinction between the cause and the object of these passions, between that idea which excites them and that to which they direct their view when excited. Pride and humility, being once raised, immediately turn our attention to ourself and regard that as their ultimate and final object; but there is something further requisite in order to raise them, something which is peculiar to one of the passions and produces not both in the very same degree. The first idea that is presented to the mind is that of the cause or productive principle. This excites the passion connected with it, and that passion, when excited, turns our view to another idea, which is that of self. Here then is a passion placed between two ideas, of which the one produces it and the other is produced by it. The first idea, therefore, represents the *cause,* the second the *object* of the passion.

To begin with the causes of pride and humility, we may observe that their most obvious and remarkable property is the vast variety of *subjects* on which they may be placed. Every valuable quality of the mind, whether of the imagination, judgment, memory, or disposition, wit, good sense, learning, courage, justice, integrity: all these are the causes of pride, and their opposites of humility. Nor are these passions confined to the mind, but extend their view to the body likewise. A man may be proud of his beauty, strength, agility, good mein, address in dancing, riding, fencing, and of his dexterity in any manual business or manufacture. But this is not all. The passion looking further comprehends whatever objects are in the least allied or related to us. Our country, family, children, relations, riches, houses, gardens, horses, dogs, clothes, any of these may become a cause either of pride or of humility.

From the consideration of these causes, it appears necessary we should make a new distinction in the causes of the passion between that *quality* which operates and the *subject* on which it is placed. A man, for instance, is vain of a beautiful house which belongs to him or which he has himself built and contrived. Here the object of the passion is himself and the cause is the beautiful house, which cause again is subdivided into two parts, *viz.*, the quality which operates upon the passion and the subject in which the quality inheres. The quality is the beauty and the subject is the house, considered as his property or contrivance. Both these parts are essential, nor is the distinction vain and chimerical. Beauty considered merely as such, unless placed upon something related to us, never produces any pride or vanity, and the strongest relation alone, without beauty or something else in its place, has as little influence on that passion. Since, therefore, these two particulars are easily separated, and there is a necessity for their conjunction in order to produce the passion, we ought to consider them as component parts of the cause, and infix in our minds an exact idea of this distinction.

Section III.

WHENCE THESE OBJECTS AND CAUSES ARE DERIVED

Being so far advanced as to observe a difference between the *object* of the passions and their *cause,* and to distinguish in the cause the *quality* which operates on the passions from the *subject* in which it inheres, we now proceed to examine what determines each of them to be what it is, and assigns such a particular object and quality and subject to these affections. By this means we shall fully understand the origin of pride and humility.

It is evident in the first place that these passions are determined to have self for their *object* not only by a natural but also by an original property. No one can doubt but this property is *natural* from the constancy and steadiness of its operations. It is always self which is the object of pride and humility, and whenever the passions look beyond, it is still with a view to ourselves, nor can any person or object otherwise have any influence upon us.

That this proceeds from an *original* quality or primary impulse will likewise appear evident if we consider that it is the distinguishing characteristic of these passions. Unless nature had given some original qualities to the mind it could never have any secondary ones, because in that case it would have no foundation for action, nor could ever begin to exert itself. Now these qualities which we must consider as original are such as are most inseparable from the soul and can be resolved into no other, and such is the quality which determines the object of pride and humility.

We may, perhaps, make it a greater question whether the *causes* that produce the passion be as *natural* as the object of which it is directed, and whether all that vast variety proceeds from caprice or from the constitution of the mind. This doubt we shall soon remove if we cast our eye upon human nature, and consider that in all nations and ages the same objects still give rise to pride and humility, and that upon the view even of a stranger we can know pretty nearly what will either increase or diminish his passions of this kind. If there be any variation in this particular, it proceeds from nothing but a difference in the tempers and complexions of men, and is besides very inconsiderable. Can we imagine it possible that while human nature remains the same, men will ever become entirely indifferent to their power, riches, beauty, or personal merit, and that their pride and vanity will not be affected by these advantages?

But though the causes of pride and humility be plainly *natural,* we shall find upon examination that they are not *original,* and that it is utterly impossible they should each of them be adapted to these passions by a particular provision and primary constitution of nature. Beside their prodigious number, many of them are the effects of art and arise partly from the industry, partly from the caprice, and partly from the good fortune of men. Industry produces houses, furniture, clothes. Caprice determines their particular kinds and qualities. And good fortune frequently contributes to all this by discovering the effects that result from the different mixtures and combinations of bodies. It is absurd, therefore, to imagine that each of these was foreseen and provided for by nature, and that every new production of art which causes pride or humility, instead of adapting itself to the passion by partaking of some general quality that naturally operates on the mind, is itself the object of an original principle which till then lay concealed in the soul and is only by accident at last brought to light. Thus the first mechanic that invented a fine escritoire produced pride in him who became possessed of it by principles different from those which made him proud of handsome chairs and tables. As this appears evidently ridiculous, we must conclude that each cause of pride and humility is not adapted to the passions by a distinct original quality, but that there are some one or more circumstances common to all of them on which their efficacy depends.

Besides, we find in the course of nature that though the effects be many, the principles from which they arise are commonly but few and simple, and that it is the sign of an unskillful naturalist to have recourse to a different quality in order to explain every different operation. How much more must this be true with regard to the human mind, which being so confined a subject may justly be thought incapable of containing such a monstrous heap of principles as would be necessary to excite the passions of pride and humility, were each distinct cause adapted to the passion by a distinct set of principles?

Here, therefore, moral philosophy is in the same condition as natural with regard to astronomy before the time of *Copernicus*. The ancients, though sensible of that maxim *that nature does nothing in vain*, contrived such intricate systems of the heavens as seemed inconsistent with true philosophy, and gave place at last to something more simple and natural. To invent without scruple a new principle to every new phenomenon instead of adapting it to the old, to overload our hypotheses with a variety of this kind, are certain proofs that none of these principles is the just one, and that we only desire by a number of falsehoods to cover our ignorance of the truth.

Section IV.

OF THE RELATIONS OF IMPRESSIONS AND IDEAS

Thus we have established two truths without any obstacle or difficulty, *that it is from natural principles this variety of causes excite pride and humility,* and *that it is not by a different principle each different cause is adapted to its passion.* We shall now proceed to inquire how we may reduce these principles to a lesser number, and find among the causes something common on which their influence depends.

In order to this we must reflect on certain properties of human nature which, though they have a mighty influence on every operation both of the understanding and passions, are not commonly much insisted on by philosophers. The *first* of these is the association of ideas, which I have so often observed and explained. It is impossible for the mind to fix itself steadily upon one idea for any considerable time, nor can it by its utmost efforts ever arrive at such a constancy. But however changeable our thoughts may be, they are not entirely without rule and method in their changes. The rule by which they proceed is to pass from one object to what is resembling, contiguous to, or produced by it. When one idea is present to the imagination, any other, united by these relations, naturally follows it, and enters with more facility by means of that introduction.

The *second* property I shall observe in the human mind is a like association of impressions. All resembling impressions are connected together, and no sooner one arises than the rest immediately follow. Grief and disappointment give rise to anger, anger to envy, envy to malice, and malice to grief again, till the whole circle be completed. In like manner our temper, when elevated with joy, naturally throws itself into love, generosity, pity, courage, pride, and the other resembling affections. It is difficult for the mind, when actuated by any passion, to confine itself to that passion alone without any change or variation. Human nature is too inconstant to admit of any such regularity. Changeableness is essential to it. And to what can it so naturally change as to affections or emotions which are suitable to the temper and agree with that set of passions which then prevail? It is evident, then, there is an attraction or association among impressions as well as among ideas, though with this remarkable difference, that ideas are associated by resemblance, contiguity, and causation, and impressions only by resemblance.

In the *third* place, it is observable of these two kinds of association that they very much assist and forward each other, and that the transition is more easily made where they both concur in the same object. Thus a man who, by any injury from another, is very much discomposed and ruffled in his temper is apt to find a hundred subjects of discontent, impatience, fear, and other uneasy passions, especially if he can discover these subjects in or near the person who was the cause of his first passion. Those principles which forward the transition of ideas here concur with those which operate on the passions, and both uniting in one action, bestow on the mind a double impulse. The new passion, therefore, must arise with so much greater violence, and the transition to it must be rendered so much more easy and natural.

Upon this occasion I may cite the authority of an elegant writer, who expresses himself in the following manner. "As the fancy delights in everything that is great, strange, or beautiful, and is still more pleased the more it finds of these perfections in the *same* object, so it is capable of receiving a new satisfaction by the assistance of another sense. Thus any continued sound, as the music of birds or a fall of waters, awakens every moment the mind of the beholder, and makes him more attentive to the several beauties of the place that lie before him. Thus if there arises a fragrancy of smells or perfumes, they heighten the pleasure of the imagination and make even the colors and verdure of the landscape appear more agreeable; for the ideas of both senses recommend each other, and are pleasanter together than when they enter the mind separately, as the different colors of a picture, when they are well disposed, set off one another and receive an additional beauty from the advantage of the situation." In this phenomenon we may remark the association both of impressions and ideas, as well as the mutual assistance they lend each other.

Section V.

OF THE INFLUENCE OF THESE RELATIONS ON PRIDE AND HUMILITY

These principles being established on unquestionable experience, I begin to consider how we shall apply them by revolving over all the causes of pride and humility, whether these causes be regarded as the qualities that operate or as the subjects on which the qualities are placed. In examining these *qualities* I immediately find many of them to concur in producing the sensation of pain and pleasure independent of those affections which I here endeavor to explain. Thus the beauty of our person, of itself and by its very appearance, gives pleasure as well as pride, and its deformity, pain as well as humility. A magnificent feast delights us and a sordid one displeases. What I discover to be true in some instances, I *suppose* to be so in all, and take it for granted at present without any further proof that every cause of pride, by its peculiar qualities, produces a separate pleasure, and of humility a separate uneasiness.

Again, in considering the *subjects* to which these qualities adhere, I make a new *supposition* which also appears probable from many obvious instances, *viz.*, that these subjects are either parts of ourselves or something nearly related to us. Thus the good and bad qualities of our actions and manners constitute virtue and vice and determine our personal character, than which nothing operates more strongly on these passions. In like manner, it is the beauty or deformity of our person, houses, equipage, or furniture by which we are rendered either vain or humble. The same qualities when transferred to subjects which bear us no relation influence not in the smallest degree either of these affections.

Having thus in a manner supposed two properties of the causes of these affections, *viz.*, that the *qualities* produce a separate pain or pleasure and that the *subjects* on which the qualities are placed are related to self, I proceed to examine the passions themselves, in order to find something in them correspondent to the supposed properties of their causes. *First,* I find that the peculiar object of pride and humility is determined by an original and natural instinct, and that it is absolutely impossible, from the primary constitution of the mind, that these passions should ever look beyond self, or that individual person of whose actions and sentiments each of us is intimately conscious. Here at last the view always rests when we are actuated by either of these passions, nor can we, in that situation of mind, ever lose sight of this object. For this I pretend not to give any reason, but consider such a peculiar direction of the thought as an original quality.

The *second* quality which I discover in these passions and which I likewise consider as an original quality is their sensations, or the peculiar emotions they excite in the soul, and which constitute their very being and essence. Thus pride is a pleasant sensation and humility a painful, and upon the removal of the pleasure and pain there is in reality no pride nor humility. Of this our very feeling convinces us, and beyond our feeling it is here in vain to reason or dispute.

If I compare, therefore, these two *established* properties of the passions, *viz.*, their object, which is self, and their sensation, which is either pleasant or painful, to the two *supposed* properties of the causes, *viz.*, their relation to self and their tendency to produce a pain or pleasure independent of the passion, I immediately find that taking these suppositions to be just the true system breaks in upon me with an irresistible evidence. That cause which excites the passion is related to the object which nature has attributed to the passion; the sensation which the cause separately produces is related to the sensation of the passion; from this double relation of ideas and impressions the passion is derived. The one idea is easily converted into its correlative, and the one impression into that which resembles and corresponds to it. With how much greater facility must this transition be made where these movements mutually assist each other and the mind receives a double impulse from the relations both of its impressions and ideas?

That we may comprehend this the better, we must suppose that nature has given to the organs of the human mind a certain disposition fitted to produce a peculiar impression or emotion which we call *pride*. To this emotion she has assigned a certain idea, *viz.*, that of *self*, which it never fails to produce. This contrivance of nature is easily conceived. We have many instances of such a situation of affairs. The nerves of the nose and palate are so disposed as in certain circumstances to convey such peculiar sensations to the mind. The sensations of lust and hunger always produce in us the idea of those peculiar objects which are suitable to each appetite. These two circumstances are united in pride. The organs are so disposed as to produce the passion, and the passion, after its production, naturally produces a certain idea. All this needs no proof. It is evident we never should be possessed of that passion were there not a disposition of mind proper for it, and it is as evident that the passion always turns our view to ourselves and makes us think of our own qualities and circumstances.

This being fully comprehended, it may now be asked

whether nature produces the passion immediately of herself, or whether she must be assisted by the cooperation of other causes. For it is observable that in this particular her conduct is different in the different passions and sensations. The palate must be excited by an external object in order to produce any relish, but hunger arises internally, without the concurrence of any external object. But however the case may stand with other passions and impressions, it is certain that pride requires the assistance of some foreign object, and that the organs which produce it exert not themselves like the heart and arteries, by an original internal movement. For *first,* daily experience convinces us that pride requires certain causes to excite it, and languishes when unsupported by some excellence in the character, in bodily accomplishments, in clothes, equipage, or fortune. *Secondly,* it is evident pride would be perpetual if it arose immediately from nature, since the object is always the same and there is no disposition of body peculiar to pride, as there is to thirst and hunger. *Thirdly,* humility is in the very same situation with pride, and therefore either must, upon this supposition, be perpetual likewise, or must destroy the contrary passion from the very first moment, so that none of them could ever make its appearance. Upon the whole, we may rest satisfied with the foregoing conclusion, that pride must have a cause as well as an object, and that the one has no influence without the other.

The difficulty, then, is only to discover this cause, and find what it is that gives the first motion to pride and sets those organs in action which are naturally fitted to produce that emotion. Upon my consulting experience in order to resolve this difficulty, I immediately find a hundred different causes that produce pride; and upon examining these causes I suppose, what at first I perceive to be probable, that all of them concur in two circumstances, which are that of themselves they produce an impression allied to the passion, and are placed on a subject allied to the object of the passion. When I consider after this the nature of *relation* and its effects both on the passions and ideas, I can no longer doubt, upon these suppositions, that it is the very principle which gives rise to pride and bestows motion on those organs which, being naturally disposed to produce that affection, require only a first impulse or beginning to their action. Anything that gives a pleasant sensation and is related to self excites the passion of pride, which is also agreeable and has self for its object.

What I have said of pride is equally true of humility. The sensation of humility is uneasy, as that of pride is agreeable, for which reason the separate sensation arising from the causes must be reversed, while the relation to self continues the same. Though pride and humility are directly contrary in their effects and in their sensations, they have notwithstanding the same object, so that it is requisite only to change the relation of impressions without making any change upon that of ideas. Accordingly we find that a beautiful house belonging to ourselves produces pride, and that the same house, still belonging to ourselves, produces humility when by any accident its beauty is changed into deformity, and thereby the sensation of pleasure which corresponded to pride is transformed into pain, which is related to humility. The double relation between the ideas and impressions subsists in both cases, and produces an easy transition from the one emotion to the other.

In a word, nature has bestowed a kind of attraction on certain impressions and ideas, by which one of them, upon its appearance, naturally introduces its correlative. If these two attractions or associations of impressions and ideas concur on the same object, they mutually assist each other, and the transition of the affections and of the imagination is made with the greatest ease and facility. When an idea produces an impression related to an impression which is connected with an idea related to the first idea, these two impressions must be in a manner inseparable, nor will the one in any case be unattended with the other. It is after this manner that the particular causes of pride and humility are determined. The quality which operates on the passion produces separately an impression resembling it; the subject to which the quality adheres is related to self, the object of the passion. No wonder the whole cause, consisting of a quality and of a subject, does so unavoidably give rise to the passion.

To illustrate this hypothesis, we may compare it to that by which I have already explained the belief attending the judgments which we form from causation. I have observed that in all judgments of this kind there is always a present impression and a related idea, and that the present impression gives a vivacity to the fancy, and the relation conveys this vivacity by an easy transition to the related idea. Without the present impression, the attention is not fixed, nor the spirits excited. Without the relation, this attention rests on its first object, and has no further consequence. There is evidently a great analogy between that hypothesis and our present one of an impression and idea that transfuse themselves into another impression and idea by means of their double relation, which analogy must be allowed to be no despicable proof of both hypotheses.

Section VII.

OF VICE AND VIRTUE

. . . let us proceed to examine the causes of pride and humility, and see whether in every case we can discover the double relations by which they operate on the passions. If we find that all these causes are related to self, and produce a pleasure or uneasiness separate from the passion, there will remain no further scruple with regard to the present system. We shall principally endeavor to prove the latter point, the former being in a manner self-evident.

To begin with VICE and VIRTUE, which are the most obvious causes of these passions, it would be entirely foreign to my present purpose to enter upon the controversy which of late years has so much excited the curiosity of the public, *whether these moral distinctions be founded on natural and original principles or arise from interest and education.* The examination of this I reserve for the following book, and in the meantime shall endeavor to show that my system maintains its ground upon either of these hypotheses, which will be a strong proof of its solidity.

For granting that morality had no foundation in nature, it must still be allowed that vice and virtue, either from self-interest or the prejudices of education, produce in us a real pain and pleasure, and this we may observe to be strenuously asserted by the defenders of that hypothesis. Every passion, habit, or turn of character (say they) which has a tendency to our advantage or prejudice gives a delight or uneasiness, and it is from thence the approbation or disapprobation arises. We easily gain from the liberality of others, but are always in danger of losing by their avarice; courage defends us, but cowardice lays us open to every attack; justice is the support of society, but injustice, unless checked, would quickly prove its ruin; humility exalts, but pride mortifies us. For these reasons the former qualities are esteemed virtues and the latter regarded as vices. Now since it is granted there is a delight or uneasiness still attending merit or demerit of every kind, this is all that is requisite for my purpose.

But I go further and observe that this moral hypothesis and my present system not only agree together, but also that, allowing the former to be just, it is an absolute and invincible proof of the latter. For if all morality be founded on the pain or pleasure which arises from the prospect of any loss or advantage that may result from our own characters or from those of others, all the effects of morality must be derived from the same pain or pleasure, and among the rest, the passions of pride and humility. The very essence of virtue, according to this hypothesis, is to produce pleasure, and that of vice to give pain. The virtue and vice must be part of our character in order to excite pride or humility. What further proof can we desire for the double relation of impressions and ideas?

The same unquestionable argument may be derived from the opinion of those who maintain that morality is something real, essential, and founded on nature. The most probable hypothesis which has been advanced to explain the distinction between vice and virtue and the origin of moral rights and obligations is that from a primary constitution of nature certain characters and passions, by the very view and contemplation, produce a pain, and others in like manner excite a pleasure. The uneasiness and satisfaction are not only inseparable from vice and virtue but constitute their very nature and essence. To approve of a character is to feel an original delight upon its appearance. To disapprove of it is to be sensible of an uneasiness. The pain and pleasure, therefore, being the primary causes of vice and virtue, must also be the causes of all their effects, and consequently of pride and humility, which are the unavoidable attendants of that distinction.

But supposing this hypothesis of moral philosophy should be allowed to be false, it is still evident that pain and pleasure, if not the causes of vice and virtue, are at least inseparable from them. A generous and noble character affords a satisfaction even in the survey, and when presented to us, though only in a poem or fable, never fails to charm and delight us. On the other hand cruelty and treachery displease from their very nature, nor is it possible ever to reconcile us to these qualities, either in ourselves or others. Thus one hypothesis of morality is an undeniable proof of the foregoing system, and the other at worst agrees with it.

But pride and humility arise not from these qualities alone of the mind which, according to the vulgar systems of ethics, have been comprehended as parts of moral duty, but from any other that has a connection with pleasure and uneasiness. Nothing flatters our vanity more than the talent of pleasing by our wit, good humor, or any other accomplishment, and nothing gives us a more sensible mortification than a disappointment in any attempt of that nature. No one has ever been able to tell what *wit* is, and to show why such a system of thought must be received under that denomination and such another rejected. It is only by taste we can decide concerning it, nor are we possessed of any other standard upon which we can form a judgment of this kind. Now what is this *taste*, from which true and false wit in a manner receive their being and without which no thought can have a title to either of these denominations? It is plainly nothing but a sensation of pleasure from true wit and of uneasiness from false, without our being able to tell the reasons of that pleasure or uneasiness. The power of bestowing these opposite sensations is, therefore, the very essence of true and false wit, and consequently the cause of that pride or humility which arises from them.

There may, perhaps, be some who, being accustomed to the style of the schools and pulpit and having never considered human nature in any other light than that in which *they* place it, may here be surprised to hear me talk of virtue as exciting pride, which they look upon as a vice, and of vice as producing humility, which they have been taught to consider as a virtue. But not to dispute about words, I observe that by *pride* I understand that agreeable impression which arises in the mind when the view either of our virtue, beauty, riches, or power makes us satisfied with ourselves, and that by *humility* I mean the opposite impression. It is evident the former impression is not always vicious, nor the latter virtuous. The most rigid morality allows us to receive a pleasure from reflecting on a generous action, and it is by none esteemed a virtue to feel any fruitless remorses upon the thoughts of past villainy and baseness. Let us, therefore, examine these impressions considered in themselves, and inquire into their causes, whether placed on the mind or body, without troubling ourselves at present with that merit or blame which may attend them.

Section VIII.

OF BEAUTY AND DEFORMITY

Whether we consider the body as a part of ourselves, or assent to those philosophers who regard it as something external, it must still be allowed to be near enough connected with us to form one of these double relations which I have asserted to be necessary to the causes of pride and humility. Wherever, therefore, we can find the other relation of impressions to join to this of ideas, we may expect with assurance either of these passions, according as the impression is pleasant or uneasy. But *beauty* of all kinds gives us a peculiar delight and satisfaction, as *deformity* produces pain, upon whatever subject it may be placed and whether surveyed in an animate or inanimate object. If the beauty or deformity, therefore, be placed upon our own bodies, this pleasure or uneasiness must be converted into pride or humility, as having in this case all the circumstances requisite to produce a perfect transition of impressions and ideas. These opposite sensations are related to the opposite passions. The beauty or deformity is closely related to self, the object of both these passions. No wonder, then, our own beauty becomes an object of pride, and deformity of humility.

But this effect of personal and bodily qualities is not only a proof of the present system by showing that the passions arise not in this case without all the circumstances I have required, but may be employed as a stronger and more convincing argument. If we consider all the hypotheses which have been formed, either by philosophy or common reason, to explain the difference between beauty and deformity, we shall find that all of them resolve into this, that beauty is such an order and construction of parts as either by the *primary constitution* of our nature, by *custom*, or by *caprice*, is fitted to give a pleasure and satisfaction to the soul. This is the distinguishing character of beauty and forms all the difference between it and deformity, whose natural tendency is to produce uneasiness. Pleasure and pain, therefore, are not only necessary attendants of beauty and deformity but constitute their very essence. And indeed, if we consider that a great part of the beauty which we admire either in animals or in other objects is derived from the idea of convenience and utility, we shall make no scruple to assent to this opinion. That shape which produces strength is beautiful in one animal, and that which is a sign of agility in another. The order and convenience of a palace are no less essential to its beauty than its mere figure and appearance. In like manner the rules of architecture require that the top of a pillar should be more slender than its base, and that because such a figure conveys to us the idea of security, which is pleasant, whereas the contrary form gives us the apprehension of danger, which is uneasy. From innumerable instances of this kind, as well as from considering that beauty, like wit, cannot be defined but is discerned only by a taste or sensation, we may conclude that beauty is nothing but a form which produces pleasure, as deformity is a structure of parts which conveys pain; and since the power of producing pain and pleasure make in this manner the essence of beauty and deformity, all the effects of these qualities must be derived from the sensation, and among the rest pride and humility, which of all their effects are the most common and remarkable.

. . . . .

Section XI.

OF THE LOVE OF FAME

But beside these original causes of pride and humility,[1] there is a secondary one in the opinions of others which has an equal influence on the affections. Our reputation, our character, our name are considerations of vast weight and importance, and even the other causes of pride, virtue, beauty, and riches, have little influence when not seconded by the opinions and sentiments of others. In order to account for this phenomenon it will be necessary to take some compass, and first explain the nature of *sympathy*.

No quality of human nature is more remarkable, both in itself and in its consequences, than that propensity we have to sympathize with others, and to receive by communication their inclinations and sentiments, however different from or even contrary to our own. This is not only conspicuous in children, who implicitly embrace every opinion proposed to them, but also in men of the greatest judgment and understanding, who find it very difficult to follow their own reason or inclination in opposition to that of their friends and daily companions. To this principle we ought to ascribe the great uniformity we may observe in the humors and turn of thinking of those of the same nation; and it is much more probable that this resemblance arises from sympathy than from any influence of the soil and climate, which, though they continue invariably the same, are not able to preserve the character of a nation the same for a century together. A good-natured man finds himself in an instant of the same humor with his company, and even the proudest and most surly take a tincture from their countrymen and acquaintances. A cheer-

[1] [The causes referred to are discussed by Hume in the four sections immediately preceding this one, the last two of which have been omitted from this edition. Besides "vice and virtue" and "beauty and deformity," these causes include "external advantages and disadvantages" and "property and riches."—Ed.]

ful countenance infuses a sensible complacency and serenity into my mind, as an angry or sorrowful one throws a sudden damp upon me. Hatred, resentment, esteem, love, courage, mirth, and melancholy; all these passions I feel more from communication than from my own natural temper and disposition. So remarkable a phenomenon merits our attention, and must be traced up to its first principles.

When any affection is infused by sympathy, it is at first known only by its effects, and by those external signs in the countenance and conversation which convey an idea of it. This idea is presently converted into an impression, and acquires such a degree of force and vivacity as to become the very passion itself, and produce an equal emotion as any original affection. However instantaneous this change of the idea into an impression may be, it proceeds from certain views and reflections which will not escape the strict scrutiny of a philosopher, though they may the person himself who makes them.

It is evident that the idea or rather impression of ourselves is always intimately present with us, and that our consciousness gives us so lively a conception of our own person that it is not possible to imagine that anything can in this particular go beyond it. Whatever object, therefore, is related to ourselves must be conceived with a like vivacity of conception, according to the foregoing principles, and though this relation should not be so strong as that of causation, it must still have a considerable influence. Resemblance and contiguity are relations not to be neglected, especially when by an inference from cause and effect, and by the observation of external signs, we are informed of the real existence of the object which is resembling or contiguous.

Now it is obvious that nature has preserved a great resemblance among all human creatures, and that we never remark any passion or principle in others of which, in some degree or other, we may not find a parallel in ourselves. The case is the same with the fabric of the mind as with that of the body. However the parts may differ in shape or size, their structure and composition are in general the same. There is a very remarkable resemblance which preserves itself amidst all their variety, and this resemblance must very much contribute to make us enter into the sentiments of others, and embrace them with facility and pleasure. Accordingly we find that where, beside the general resemblance of our natures, there is any peculiar similarity in our manners or character or country or language, it facilitates the sympathy. The stronger the relation is between ourselves and any object the more easily does the imagination make the transition and convey to the related idea the vivacity of conception with which we always form the idea of our own person.

Nor is resemblance the only relation which has this effect, but receives new force from other relations that may accompany it. The sentiments of others have little influence when far removed from us, and require the relation of contiguity to make them communicate themselves entirely. The relations of blood, being a species of causation, may sometimes contribute to the same effect, as also acquaintance, which operates in the same manner with education and custom, as we shall see more fully afterward.[1] All these relations, when united together, convey the impression or consciousness of our own person to the idea of the sentiments or passions of others, and makes us conceive them in the strongest and most lively manner.

It has been remarked in the beginning of this treatise that all ideas are borrowed from impressions, and that these two kinds of perceptions differ only in the degrees of force and vivacity with which they strike upon the soul. The component parts of ideas and impressions are precisely alike. The manner and order of their appearance may be the same. The different degrees of their force and vivacity are, therefore, the only particulars that distinguish them, and as this difference may be removed, in some measure, by a relation between the impressions and ideas, it is no wonder an idea of a sentiment or passion may by this means be so enlivened as to become the very sentiment or passion. The lively idea of any object always approaches its impression, and it is certain we may feel sickness and pain from the mere force of imagination, and make a malady real by often thinking of it. But this is most remarkable in the opinions and affections, and it is there principally that a lively idea is converted into an im-

[1] Part II, Section IV.

pression. Our affections depend more upon ourselves and the internal operations of the mind than any other impressions, for which reason they arise more naturally from the imagination and from every lively idea we form of them. This is the nature and cause of sympathy, and it is after this manner we enter so deep into the opinions and affections of others whenever we discover them.

What is principally remarkable in this whole affair is the strong confirmation these phenomena give to the foregoing system concerning the understanding, and consequently to the present one concerning the passions, since these are analogous to each other. It is indeed evident that when we sympathize with the passions and sentiments of others, these movements appear at first in *our* mind as mere ideas, and are conceived to belong to another person as we conceive any other matter of fact. It is also evident that the ideas of the affections of others are converted into the very impressions they represent, and that the passions arise in conformity to the images we form of them. All this is an object of the plainest experience, and depends not on any hypothesis of philosophy. That science can only be admitted to explain the phenomena, though at the same time it must be confessed they are so clear of themselves that there is but little occasion to employ it. For besides the relation of cause and effect by which we are convinced of the reality of the passion with which we sympathize; besides this, I say, we must be assisted by the relations of resemblance and contiguity in order to feel the sympathy in its full perfection. And since these relations can entirely convert an idea into an impression and convey the vivacity of the latter into the former so perfectly as to lose nothing of it in the transition, we may easily conceive how the relation of cause and effect alone may serve to strengthen and enliven an idea. In sympathy there is an evident conversion of an idea into an impression. This conversion arises from the relation of objects to ourself. Ourself is always intimately present to us. Let us compare all these circumstances and we shall find that sympathy is exactly correspondent to the operations of our understanding, and even contains something more surprising and extraordinary.

It is now time to turn our view from the general consideration of sympathy to its influence on pride and humility when these passions arise from praise and blame, from reputation and infamy. We may observe that no person is ever praised by another for any quality which would not, if real, produce of itself a pride in the person possessed of it. The elogiums either turn upon his power or riches or family or virtue, all of which are subjects of vanity that we have already explained and accounted for. It is certain, then, that if a person considered himself in the same light in which he appears to his admirer, he would first receive a separate pleasure and afterwards a pride or self-satisfaction, according to the hypothesis above-explained. Now nothing is more natural than for us to embrace the opinions of others in this particular, both from *sympathy*, which renders all their sentiments intimately present to us, and from *reasoning*, which makes us regard their judgment as a kind of argument for what they affirm. These two principles of authority and sympathy influence almost all our opinions, but must have a peculiar influence when we judge of our own worth and character. Such judgments are always attended with passion,[1] and nothing tends more to disturb our understanding and precipitate us into any opinions, however unreasonable, than their connection with passion, which diffuses itself over the imagination and gives an additional force to every related idea. To which we may add that being conscious of great partiality in our own favor, we are peculiarly pleased with anything that confirms the good opinion we have of ourselves, and are easily shocked with whatever opposes it.

. . . . .

[1] Book I, Part III, Section X.

Part II.
OF LOVE AND HATRED

———•◦•———

Section I.

OF THE OBJECTS AND CAUSES OF
LOVE AND HATRED

IT IS ALTOGETHER impossible to give any definition of the passions of *love* and *hatred*, and that because they produce merely a simple impression, without any mixture or composition. It would be as unnecessary to attempt any description of them drawn from their nature, origin, causes and objects, and that both because these are the subjects of our present inquiry and because these passions of themselves are sufficiently known from our common feeling and experience. This we have already observed concerning pride and humility, and here repeat it concerning love and hatred; and indeed there is so great a resemblance between these two sets of passions that we shall be obliged to begin with a kind of abridgment of our reasonings concerning the former, in order to explain the latter.

As the immediate *object* of pride and humility is self or that identical person of whose thoughts, actions, and sensations we are intimately conscious, so the *object* of love and hatred is some other person of whose thoughts, actions, and sensations we are not conscious. This is sufficiently evident from experience. Our love and hatred are always directed to some sensible being external to us, and when we talk of *self-love*, it is not in a proper sense, nor has the sensation it produces anything in common with that tender emotion which is excited by a friend or mistress. It is the same case with hatred. We may be mortified by our own faults and follies, but never feel any anger or hatred except from the injuries of others.

But though the object of love and hatred be always some other person, it is plain that the object is not, properly speaking, the *cause* of these passions, or alone sufficient to excite them. For since love and hatred are directly contrary in their sensation and have the same object in common, if that object were also their cause, it would produce these opposite passions in an equal degree; and as they must, from the very first moment, destroy each other, none of them would ever be able to make its appearance. There must, therefore, be some cause different from the object.

If we consider the causes of love and hatred, we shall find they are very much diversified, and have not many things in common. The virtue, knowledge, wit, good sense, good humor of any person produce love and esteem, as the opposite qualities, hatred and contempt. The same passions arise from bodily accomplishments, such as beauty, force, swiftness, dexterity, and from their contraries, as likewise from the external advantages and disadvantages of family, possessions, clothes, nation, and climate. There is not one of these objects but what by its different qualities may produce love and esteem, or hatred and contempt.

From the view of these causes we may derive a new distinction between the *quality* that operates and the *subject* on which it is placed. A prince that is possessed of a stately palace commands the esteem of the people upon that account, and that *first* by the beauty of the palace, and *secondly* by the relation of property which connects it with him. The removal of either of these destroys the passion, which evidently proves that the cause is a compounded one.

It would be tedious to trace the passions of love and hatred through all the observations which we have formed concerning pride and humility, and which are equally applicable to both sets of passions. It will be sufficient to *remark* in general that the object of love and hatred is evidently some thinking person, and that the sensation of the former passion is always agreeable and of the latter uneasy. We may also *suppose* with some show of probability *that the cause of both these passions is always related to a thinking being,* and *that the cause of the former produces a separate pleasure and of the latter a separate uneasiness.*

One of these suppositions, *viz.*, that the cause of love and hatred must be related to a person or thinking being in order to produce these passions, is not only probable but too evident to be contested. Virtue and vice, when considered in the abstract, beauty and deformity, when placed on inanimate objects, poverty and riches, when belonging to a third person, excite no degree of love or hatred, esteem or contempt towards those who have no relation to them. A person looking out at a window sees me in the street, and beyond me a beautiful palace with which I have no concern; I believe none will pretend that this person will pay me the same respect as if I were owner of the palace.

It is not so evident at first sight that a relation of impressions is requisite to these passions, and that because in the transition the one impression is so much confounded with the other that they become in a manner undistinguishable. But as in pride and humility we have easily been able to make the separation and to prove that every cause of these passions produces a separate pain or pleasure, I might here observe the same method with the same success in examining particularly the several causes of love and hatred. But as I hasten to a full and decisive proof of these systems, I delay this examination for a moment, and in the meantime shall endeavor to convert to my present purpose all my reasonings concerning pride and humility by an argument that is founded on unquestionable experience.

There are few persons that are satisfied with their own character or genius or fortune who are not desirous of showing themselves to the world, and of acquiring the love and approbation of mankind. Now it is evident that the very same qualities and circumstances which are the causes of pride or self-esteem are also the causes of vanity or the desire of reputation, and that we always put to view those particulars with which in ourselves we are best satisfied. But if love and esteem were not produced by the same qualities as pride, according as these qualities are related to ourselves or others, this method of proceeding would be very absurd, nor could men expect a correspondence in the sentiments of every other person with those [they] themselves have entertained. It is true, few can form exact systems of the passions or make reflections on their general nature and resemblances. But without such a progress in philosophy, we are not subject to many mistakes in this particular, but are sufficiently guided by common experience as well as by a kind of *presentation,* which tells us what will operate on others by what we feel immediately in ourselves. Since then the same qualities that produce pride or humility cause love or hatred, all the arguments that have been employed to prove that the causes of the former passions excite a pain or pleasure independent of the passion will be applicable with equal evidence to the causes of the latter.

Section VI.

OF BENEVOLENCE AND ANGER

Ideas may be compared to the extension and solidity of matter, and impressions, especially reflective ones, to colors, tastes, smells, and other sensible qualities. Ideas never admit of a total union, but are endowed with a kind of impenetrability, by which they exclude each other, and are capable of forming a compound by their conjunction, not by their mixture. On the other hand, impressions and passions are susceptible of an entire union and, like colors, may be blended so perfectly together that each of them may lose itself, and contribute only to vary that uniform impression which arises from the whole. Some of the most curious phenomena of the human mind are derived from this property of the passions.

In examining those ingredients which are capable of uniting with love and hatred, I begin to be sensible, in some measure, of a misfortune that has attended every system of philosophy with which the world has been yet acquainted. It is commonly found that in accounting for the operations of nature by any particular hypothesis, among a number of experiments that quadrate exactly with the principles we would endeavor to establish, there is always some phenomenon which is more stubborn, and will not so easily bend to our purpose. We need not be surprised that this should happen in natural philosophy. The essence and composition of external bodies are so obscure that we must necessarily, in our reasonings or rather conjectures concerning them, involve ourselves in contradictions and absurdities. But as the perceptions of the mind are perfectly known, and I have used all imaginable caution in forming conclusions concerning them, I have always hoped to keep clear of those contradictions which have attended every other system. Accordingly, the difficulty which I have at present in my eye is nowise contrary to my system, but only departs a little from that simplicity which has been hitherto its principal force and beauty.

The passions of love and hatred are always followed by, or rather conjoined with, benevolence and anger. It is this conjunction which chiefly distinguishes these affections from pride and humility. For pride and humility are pure emotions in the soul, unattended with any desire, and not immediately exciting us to action. But love and hatred are not completed within themselves, nor rest in that emotion which they produce, but carry the mind to something further. Love is always followed by a desire of the happiness of the person beloved and an aversion to his misery, as hatred produces a desire of the misery and an aversion to the happiness of the person hated. So remarkable a difference between these two sets of passions of pride and humility, love and hatred, which in so many other particulars correspond to each other, merits our attention.

The conjunction of this desire and aversion with love and hatred may be accounted for by two different hypotheses. The first is that love and hatred have not only a *cause* which excites them, *viz.*, pleasure and pain, and an *object* to which they are directed, *viz.*, a person or thinking being, but likewise an *end* which they endeavor to attain, *viz.*, the happiness or misery of the person beloved or hated, all which views, mixing together, make only one passion. According to this system, love is nothing but the desire of happiness to another person, and hatred that of misery. The desire and aversion constitute the very nature of love and hatred. They are not only inseparable but the same.

But this is evidently contrary to experience. For though it is certain we never love any person without desiring his happiness, nor hate any without wishing his misery, yet these desires arise only upon the ideas of the happiness or misery of our friend or enemy being presented by the imagination, and are not absolutely essential to love and hatred. They are the most obvious and natural sentiments of these affections but not the only ones. The passions may express themselves in a hundred ways and may subsist a considerable time without our reflecting on the happiness or misery of their objects, which clearly proves that these desires are not the same with love and hatred, nor make any essential part of them.

We may, therefore, infer that benevolence and anger are passions different from love and hatred and only conjoined with them by the original constitution of the mind. As nature has given to the body certain appetites and inclinations which she increases, diminishes, or changes according to the situation of the fluids or solids, she has proceeded in the same manner with the mind. According as we are possessed with love or hatred, the correspondent desire of the happiness or misery of the person who is the object of these passions arises in the mind, and varies with each variation of these opposite passions. This order of things, abstractedly considered, is not necessary. Love and hatred might have been unattended with any such desires, or their particular connection might have been entirely reversed. If nature had so pleased, love might have had the same effect as hatred, and hatred as love. I see no contradiction in supposing a desire of producing misery annexed to love, and of happiness to hatred. If the sensation of the passion and desire be opposite, nature could have altered the sensation without altering the tendency of the desire, and by that means made them compatible with each other.

224

Part III.

OF THE WILL
AND DIRECT PASSIONS

Section I.

OF LIBERTY AND NECESSITY

WE COME NOW to explain the *direct* passions, or the impressions which arise immediately from good or evil, from pain or pleasure. Of this kind are *desire and aversion, grief and joy, hope and fear*.

Of all the immediate effects of pain and pleasure, there is none more remarkable than the WILL, and though, properly speaking, it be not comprehended among the passions, yet as the full understanding of its nature and properties is necessary to the explanation of them, we shall here make it the subject of our inquiry. I desire it may be observed that by the *will* I mean nothing but *the internal impression we feel and are conscious of when we knowingly give rise to any new motion of our body or new perception of our mind*. This impression, like the preceding ones of pride and humility, love and hatred, it is impossible to define and needless to describe any further, for which reason we shall cut off all those definitions and distinctions with which philosophers are wont to perplex rather than clear up this question, and entering at first upon the subject shall examine that long disputed question concerning *liberty and necessity* which occurs so naturally in treating of the will.[1]

. . . . .

[1] [The discussion which follows is closely paralleled by Hume's later discussion of liberty and necessity in Section VIII of the *Inquiry concerning Human Understanding*. Since this later discussion is the clearer and more detailed of the two, it has been included (pp. 338 ff. below) and the one here omitted in this edition.—Ed.]

Section III

OF THE INFLUENCING MOTIVES OF THE WILL

Nothing is more usual in philosophy, and even in common life, than to talk of the combat of passion and reason, to give the preference to reason, and to assert that men are only so far virtuous as they conform themselves to its dictates. Every rational creature, it is said, is obliged to regulate his actions by reason, and if any other motive or principle challenge the direction of his conduct he ought to oppose it, till it be entirely subdued, or at least brought to a conformity with that superior principle. On this method of thinking the greatest part of moral philosophy, ancient and modern, seems to be founded; nor is there an ampler field, as well for metaphysical arguments as popular declamations, than this supposed preeminence of reason above passion. The eternity, invariableness, and divine origin of the former have been displayed to the best advantage; the blindness, inconstancy, and deceitfulness of the latter have been as strongly insisted on. In order to show the fallacy of all this philosophy, I shall endeavor to prove *first* that reason alone can never be a motive to any action of the will, and *secondly* that it can never oppose passion in the direction of the will.

The understanding exerts itself after two different ways, as it judges from demonstration or probability, as it regards the abstract relations of our ideas, or those relations of objects of which experience only gives us information. I believe it scarce will be asserted that the first species of reasoning alone is ever the cause of any action. As its proper province is the world of ideas, and as the will always places us in that of realities, demonstration and volition seem, upon that account, to be totally removed from each other. Mathematics, indeed, are useful in all mechanical operations, and arithmetic in almost every art and profession, but it is not of themselves they have any influence. Mechanics are the art of regulating the motions of bodies *to some designed end or purpose,* and the reason why we employ arithmetic in fixing the proportions of numbers is only that we may discover the proportions of their influence and operation. A merchant is desirous of knowing the sum total of his accounts with any person, why, but that he may learn what sum will have the same *effects* in paying his debt and going to market as all the particular articles taken together. Abstract or demonstrative reasoning, therefore, never influences any of our actions but only as it directs our judgment concerning causes and effects, which leads us to the second operation of the understanding.

It is obvious that when we have the prospect of pain or pleasure from any object, we feel a consequent emotion of aversion or propensity, and are carried to avoid or embrace what will give us this uneasiness or satisfaction. It is also obvious that this emotion rests not here, but making us cast our view on every side, comprehends whatever objects are connected with its original one by the relation of cause and effect. Here then reasoning takes place to discover this relation, and according as our reasoning varies our actions receive a subsequent variation. But it is evident in this case that the impulse arises not from reason, but is only directed by it. It is from the prospect of pain or pleasure that the aversion or propensity arises towards any object, and these emotions extend themselves to the causes and effects of that object as they are pointed out to us by reason and experience. It can never in the least concern us to know that such objects are causes and such others effects if both the causes and effects be indifferent to us. Where the objects themselves do not affect us, their connection can never give them any influence, and it is plain that as reason is nothing but the discovery of this connection, it cannot be by its means that the objects are able to affect us.

Since reason alone can never produce any action or give rise to volition, I infer that the same faculty is as incapable of preventing volition, or of disputing the preference with any passion or emotion. This consequence is necessary. It is impossible reason could have the latter effect of preventing volition but by giving an impulse in a contrary direction to our passion, and that impulse, had it operated alone, would have been able to produce volition. Nothing can oppose or retard the impulse of passion but a contrary impulse, and if this contrary impulse ever arises from reason, that latter faculty must have an original influence on the will, and must be able to cause as well as hinder any act of volition. But if reason has no original influence, it is impossible it can withstand any principle which has such an efficacy, or ever keep the mind in suspense a moment. Thus it appears that the principle which opposes our passion cannot be the same with reason, and is only called so in an improper sense. We speak not strictly and philosophically when we talk of the combat of passion and of reason. Reason is and ought only to be the slave of the passions, and can never pretend to any other office than to serve and obey them. As this opinion may appear somewhat extraordinary, it may not be improper to confirm it by some other considerations.

A passion is an original existence, or, if you will, modification of existence, and contains not any representative quality which renders it a copy of any other existence or modification. When I am angry, I am actually possessed with the passion, and in that emotion have no more a reference to any other object than when I am thirsty or sick or more than five feet high. It is impossible, therefore, that this passion can be opposed by or be contradictory to truth and reason, since this contradiction consists in the disagreement of ideas, considered as copies, with those objects which they represent.

What may at first occur on this head is that as nothing can be contrary to truth or reason except what has a reference to it, and as the judgments of our understanding only have this reference, it must follow that passions can be contrary to reason only so far as they are *accompanied* with some judgment or opinion. According to this principle, which is so obvious and natural, it is only in two senses that any affection can be called unreasonable. First, when a passion such as hope or fear, grief or joy, despair or security is founded on the supposition of the existence of objects which really do not exist. Secondly, when in exerting any passion in action we choose means insufficient for the designed end and deceive ourselves in our judgment of causes and effects. Where a passion is neither founded on false suppositions nor chooses means insufficient for the end, the understanding can neither justify nor condemn it. It is not contrary to reason to prefer the destruction of the whole world to the scratching of my finger. It is not contrary to reason for me to choose my total ruin to prevent the least uneasiness of an *Indian* or person wholly unknown to me. It is as little contrary to reason to prefer even my own acknowledged lesser good to my greater, and have a more ardent affection for the former than the latter. A trivial good may, from certain circumstances, produce a desire superior to what arises from the greatest and most valuable enjoyment, nor is there anything more extraordinary in this than in mechanics to see one pound weight raise up a hundred by the advantage of its situation. In short, a passion must be accompanied with some false judgment in order to its being unreasonable, and even then it is not the passion, properly speaking, which is unreasonable, but the judgment.

The consequences are evident. Since a passion can never, in any sense, be called unreasonable but when founded on a false supposition or when it chooses means insufficient for the designed end, it is impossible that reason and passion can ever oppose each other or dispute for the government of the will and actions. The moment we perceive the falsehood of any supposition or the insufficiency of any means our passions yield to our reason without any opposition. I may desire any fruit as of an excellent relish, but whenever you convince me of my mistake my longing ceases. I may will the performance of certain actions as means of obtaining any desired good, but as my willing of these actions is only secondary and founded on the supposition that they are causes of the proposed effect, as soon as I discover the falsehood of that supposition they must become indifferent to me.

It is natural for one that does not examine objects with a strict philosophic eye to imagine that those actions of the mind are entirely the same which produce not a different sensation and are not immediately distinguishable to the feeling and perception. Reason, for instance, exerts itself without producing any sensible emotion, and except in the more sublime disquisitions of philosophy, or in the frivolous subtleties of the schools, scarce ever conveys any pleasure or uneasiness. Hence it proceeds that every action of the mind which operates with the same calmness and tranquillity is confounded with

22

reason by all those who judge of things from the first view and appearance. Now it is certain there are certain calm desires and tendencies which, though they be real passions, produce little emotion in the mind, and are more known by their effects than by the immediate feeling or sensation. These desires are of two kinds, either certain instincts originally implanted in our natures, such as benevolence and resentment, the love of life, and kindness to children, or the general appetite to good and aversion to evil, considered merely as such. When any of these passions are calm and cause no disorder in the soul, they are very readily taken for the determinations of reason, and are supposed to proceed from the same faculty with that which judges of truth and falsehood. Their nature and principles have been supposed the same because their sensations are not evidently different.

Beside these calm passions, which often determine the will, there are certain violent emotions of the same kind, which have likewise a great influence on that faculty. When I receive any injury from another, I often feel a violent passion of resentment which makes me desire his evil and punishment independent of all considerations of pleasure and advantage to myself. When I am immediately threatened with any grievous ill, my fears, apprehensions, and aversions rise to a great height and produce a sensible emotion.

The common error of metaphysicians has lain in ascribing the direction of the will entirely to one of these principles, and supposing the other to have no influence. Men often act knowingly against their interest, for which reason the view of the greatest possible good does not always influence them. Men often counteract a violent passion in prosecution of their interests and designs; it is not therefore the present uneasiness alone which determines them. In general we may observe that both these principles operate on the will, and where they are contrary that either of them prevails according to the *general* character or *present* disposition of the person. What we call strength of mind implies the prevalence of the calm passions above the violent, though we may easily observe there is no man so constantly possessed of this virtue as never on any occasion to yield to the solicitations of passion and desire. From these variations of temper proceeds the great difficulty of deciding concerning the actions and resolutions of men where there is any contrariety of motives and passions.

Section IV.

OF THE CAUSES OF THE VIOLENT PASSIONS

There is not in philosophy a subject of more nice speculation than this of the different *causes* and *effects* of the calm and violent passions. It is evident passions influence not the will in proportion to their violence or the disorder they occasion in the temper, but on the contrary that when a passion has once become a settled principle of action and is the predominant inclination of the soul, it commonly produces no longer any sensible agitation. As repeated custom and its own force have made everything yield to it, it directs the actions and conduct without that opposition and emotion which so naturally attend every momentary gust of passion. We must, therefore, distinguish between a calm and a weak passion, between a violent and a strong one. But notwithstanding this, it is certain that when we would govern a man and push him to any action, it will commonly be better policy to work upon the violent than the calm passions, and rather take him by his inclination than what is vulgarly called his *reason*. We ought to place the object in such particular situations as are proper to increase the violence of the passion. For we may observe that all depends upon the situation of the object, and that a variation in this particular will be able to change the calm and the violent passions into each other. Both these kinds of passions pursue good and avoid evil, and both of them are increased or diminished by the increase or diminution of the good or evil. But herein lies the difference between them: the same good, when near, will cause a violent passion, which, when remote, produces only a calm one. . . .

Section VIII.

THE SAME SUBJECT CONTINUED

. . . . . .

It may not be improper, before we leave this subject of the will, to resume, in a few words, all that has been said concerning it, in order to set the whole more distinctly before the eyes of the reader. What we commonly understand by *passion* is a violent and sensible emotion of mind when any good or evil is presented, or any object which, by the original formation of our faculties, is fitted to excite an appetite. By *reason* we mean affections of the very same kind with the former, but such as operate more calmly and cause no disorder in the temper, which tranquillity leads us into a mistake concerning them, and causes us to regard them as conclusions only of our intellectual faculties. Both the *causes* and *effects* of these violent and calm passions are pretty variable and depend in a great measure on the peculiar temper and disposition of every individual. Generally speaking, the violent passions have a more powerful influence on the will, though it is often found that the calm ones, when corroborated by reflection and seconded by resolution, are able to control them in their most furious movements. What makes this whole affair more uncertain is that a calm passion may easily be changed into a violent one, either by a change of temper or of the circumstances and situation of the object, as by the borrowing of force from any attendant passion, by custom, or by exciting the imagination. Upon the whole, this struggle of passion and of reason, as it is called, diversifies human life, and makes men so different not only from each other, but also from themselves in different times. Philosophy can only account for a few of the greater and more sensible events of this war, but must leave all the smaller and more delicate revolutions, as dependent on principles too fine and minute for her comprehension.

Section IX.

OF THE DIRECT PASSIONS

It is easy to observe that the passions, both direct and indirect, are founded on pain and pleasure, and that in order to produce an affection of any kind it is only requisite to present some good or evil. Upon the removal of pain and pleasure there immediately follows a removal of love and hatred, pride and humility, desire and aversion, and of most of our reflective or secondary impressions.

The impressions which arise from good and evil most naturally and with the least preparation are the *direct* passions of desire and aversion, grief and joy, hope and fear, along with volition. The mind by an *original* instinct tends to unite itself with the good and to avoid the evil, though they be conceived merely in idea, and be considered as to exist in any future period of time.

But supposing that there is an immediate impression of pain or pleasure, and *that* arising from an object related to ourselves or others, this does not prevent the propensity or aversion, with the consequent emotions, but, by concurring with certain dormant principles of the human mind, excites the new impressions of pride or humility, love or hatred. That propensity which unites us to the object or separates us from it still continues to operate, but in conjunction with the *indirect* passions, which arise from a double relation of impressions and ideas.

These indirect passions, being always agreeable or uneasy, give in their turn additional force to the direct passions, and increase our desire and aversion to the object. Thus a suit of fine clothes produces pleasure from their beauty, and this pleasure produces the direct passions, or the impressions of volition and desire. Again, when these clothes are considered as belonging to ourself, the double relation conveys to us the sentiment of pride, which is an indirect passion, and the pleasure which attends that passion returns back to the direct affections, and gives new force to our desire or volition, joy or hope.

When good is certain or probable it produces JOY. When evil is in the same situation there arises GRIEF or SORROW.

When either good or evil is uncertain, it gives rise to FEAR or HOPE, according to the degrees of uncertainty on the one side or the other.

DESIRE arises from good considered simply, and AVERSION is derived from evil. The WILL exerts itself when either the good or the absence of the evil may be attained by any action of the mind or body.

Beside good and evil, or in other words, pain and pleasure, the direct passions frequently arise from a natural impulse or instinct which is perfectly unaccountable. Of this kind is the desire of punishment to our enemies and of happiness to our friends, hunger, lust, and a few other bodily appetites. These passions, properly speaking, produce good and evil, and proceed not from them, like the other affections.

* * * * *

BOOK III.

OF MORALS

Part I.

OF VIRTUE AND VICE IN GENERAL

Section I.

MORAL DISTINCTIONS NOT DERIVED
FROM REASON

THERE IS AN inconvenience which attends all abstruse reasoning, that it may silence without convincing an antagonist, and requires the same intense study to make us sensible of its force that was at first requisite for its invention. When we leave our closet and engage in the common affairs of life, its conclusions seem to vanish, like the phantoms of the night on the appearance of the morning, and it is difficult for us to retain even that conviction which we had attained with difficulty. This is still more conspicuous in a long chain of reasoning, where we must preserve to the end the evidence of the first propositions, and where we often lose sight of all the most received maxims, either of philosophy or common life. I am not, however, without hopes that the present system of philosophy will acquire new force as it advances, and that our reasonings concerning *morals* will corroborate whatever has been said concerning the *understanding* and the *passions*. Morality is a subject that interests us above all others. We fancy the peace of society to be at stake in every decision concerning it, and it is evident that this concern must make our speculations appear more real and solid than where the subject is, in a great measure, indifferent to us. What affects us we conclude can never be a chimera, and as our passion is engaged on the one side or the other, we naturally think that the question lies within human comprehension, which in other cases of this nature we are apt to entertain some doubt of. Without this advantage I never should have ventured upon a third volume of such abstruse philosophy in an age wherein the greatest part of men seem agreed to convert reading into an amusement, and to reject everything that requires any considerable degree of attention to be comprehended.

It has been observed that nothing is ever present to the mind but its perceptions, and that all the actions of seeing, hearing, judging, loving, hating, and thinking fall under this denomination. The mind can never exert itself in any action which we may not comprehend under the term of *perception*, and consequently that term is no less applicable to those judgments by which we distinguish moral good and evil than to every other operation of the mind. To approve of one character, to condemn another, are only so many different perceptions.

Now as perceptions resolve themselves into two kinds, *viz.*, *impressions* and *ideas*, this distinction gives rise to a question with which we shall open up our present inquiry concerning morals, *whether it is by means of our* ideas *or* impressions *we distinguish between vice and virtue and pronounce an action blamable or praiseworthy*. This will immediately cut off all loose discourses and declamations, and reduce us to something precise and exact on the present subject.

Those who affirm that virtue is nothing but a conformity to reason, that there are eternal fitnesses and unfitnesses of things which are the same to every rational being that considers them, that the immutable measures of right and wrong impose an obligation not only on human creatures but also on the deity himself; all these systems concur in the opinion that morality, like truth, is discerned merely by ideas, and by their juxtaposition and comparison. In order, therefore, to judge of these systems, we need only consider whether it be possible, from reason alone, to distinguish between moral good and evil, or whether there must concur some other principles to enable us to make that distinction.

If morality had naturally no influence on human passions and actions, it were in vain to take such pains to inculcate it, and nothing would be more fruitless than that multitude of rules and precepts with which all moralists abound. Philosophy is commonly divided into *speculative* and *practical,* and as morality is always comprehended under the latter division, it is supposed to influence our passions and actions and to go beyond the calm and indolent judgments of the understanding. And this is confirmed by common experience, which informs us that men are often governed by their duties and are deterred from some actions by the opinion of injustice and impelled to others by that of obligation.

Since morals, therefore, have an influence on the actions and affections, it follows that they cannot be derived from reason, and that because reason alone, as we have already proved, can never have any such influence. Morals excite passions and produce or prevent actions. Reason of itself is utterly impotent in this particular. The rules of morality, therefore, are not conclusions of our reason.

No one, I believe, will deny the justness of this inference, nor is there any other means of evading it than by denying that principle on which it is founded. As long as it is allowed that reason has no influence on our passions and actions, it is in vain to pretend that morality is discovered only by a deduction of reason. An active principle can never be founded on an inactive, and if reason be inactive in itself, it must remain so in all its shapes and appearances, whether it exerts itself in natural or moral subjects, whether it considers the powers of external bodies or the actions of rational beings.

It would be tedious to repeat all the arguments by which

I have proved [1] that reason is perfectly inert, and can never either prevent or produce any action or affection. It will be easy to recollect what has been said upon that subject. I shall only recall on this occasion one of these arguments, which I shall endeavor to render still more conclusive and more applicable to the present subject.

Reason is the discovery of truth or falsehood. Truth or falsehood consists in an agreement or disagreement either to the *real* relations of ideas, or to *real* existence and matter of fact. Whatever, therefore, is not susceptible of this agreement or disagreement is incapable of being true or false, and can never be an object of our reason. Now it is evident our passions, volitions, and actions are not susceptible of any such agreement or disagreement, being original facts and realities, complete in themselves, and implying no reference to other passions, volitions, and actions. It is impossible, therefore, they can be pronounced either true or false, and be either contrary or conformable to reason.

This argument is of double advantage to our present purpose. For it proves *directly* that actions do not derive their merit from a conformity to reason nor their blame from a contrariety to it; and it proves the same truth more *indirectly* by showing us that as reason can never immediately prevent or produce any action by contradicting or approving of it, it cannot be the source of moral good and evil, which are found to have that influence. Actions may be laudable or blamable, but they cannot be reasonable or unreasonable. Laudable or blamable, therefore, are not the same with reasonable or unreasonable. The merit and demerit of actions frequently contradict and sometimes control our natural propensities. But reason has no such influence. Moral distinctions, therefore, are not the offspring of reason. Reason is wholly inactive, and can never be the source of so active a principle as conscience, or a sense of morals.

But perhaps it may be said that though no will or action can be immediately contradictory to reason, yet we may find such a contradiction in some of the attendants of the action,

[1] Book II, Part III, Section III.

that is, in its causes or effects. The action may cause a judgment or may be *obliquely* caused by one when the judgment
concurs with a passion, and by an abusive way of speaking,
which philosophy will scarce allow of, the same contrariety
may, upon that account, be ascribed to the action. How far
this truth or falsehood may be the source of morals it will
now be proper to consider.

It has been observed that reason, in a strict and philosophical sense, can have an influence on our conduct only after
two ways, either when it excites a passion by informing us of
the existence of something which is a proper object of it, or
when it discovers the connection of causes and effects, so as to
afford us means of exerting any passion. These are the only
kinds of judgment which can accompany our actions or can
be said to produce them in any manner, and it must be allowed that these judgments may often be false and erroneous.
A person may be affected with passion by supposing a pain
or pleasure to lie in an object which has no tendency to produce either of these sensations, or which produces the contrary to what is imagined. A person may also take false measures for attaining his end, and may retard, by his foolish
conduct, instead of forwarding the execution of any project.
These false judgments may be thought to affect the passions
and actions which are connected with them, and may be said
to render them unreasonable, in a figurative and improper
way of speaking. But though this be acknowledged, it is easy
to observe that these errors are so far from being the source
of all immorality that they are commonly very innocent, and
draw no manner of guilt upon the person who is so unfortunate as to fall into them. They extend not beyond a mistake
of *fact*, which moralists have not generally supposed criminal, as being perfectly involuntary. I am more to be lamented
than blamed if I am mistaken with regard to the influence of
objects in producing pain or pleasure, or if I know not the
proper means of satisfying my desires. No one can ever regard
such errors as a defect in my moral character. A fruit, for
instance, that is really disagreeable appears to me at a distance, and through mistake I fancy it to be pleasant and delicious. Here is one error. I choose certain means of reaching
this fruit which are not proper for my end. Here is a second

error, nor is there any third one which can ever possibly enter into our reasonings concerning actions. I ask, therefore, if a man in this situation and guilty of these two errors is to be regarded as vicious and criminal, however unavoidable they might have been? Or if it be possible to imagine that such errors are the sources of all immorality?

And here it may be proper to observe that if moral distinctions be derived from the truth or falsehood of those judgments, they must take place wherever we form the judgments, nor will there be any difference whether the question be concerning an apple or a kingdom, or whether the error be avoidable or unavoidable. For as the very essence of morality is supposed to consist in an agreement or disagreement to reason, the other circumstances are entirely arbitrary, and can never either bestow on any action the character of virtuous or vicious or deprive it of that character. To which we may add that this agreement or disagreement not admitting of degrees, all virtues and vices would of course be equal.

Should it be pretended that though a mistake of *fact* be not criminal, yet a mistake of *right* often is, and that this may be the source of immorality, I would answer that it is impossible such a mistake can ever be the original source of immorality, since it supposes a real right and wrong, that is, a real distinction in morals, independent of these judgments. A mistake, therefore, of right may become a species of immorality, but it is only a secondary one, and is founded on some other antecedent to it.

As to those judgments which are the *effects* of our actions and which, when false, give occasion to pronounce the actions contrary to truth and reason, we may observe that our actions never cause any judgment, either true or false, in ourselves, and that it is only on others they have such an influence. It is certain that an action on many occasions may give rise to false conclusions in others, and that a person who through a window sees any lewd behavior of mine with my neighbor's wife may be so simple as to imagine she is certainly my own. In this respect my action resembles somewhat a lie or falsehood, only with this difference, which is material, that I perform not the action with any intention of giving rise to a false judgment in another, but merely to satisfy my lust and passion. It causes, however, a mistake and false judgment by accident, and the falsehood of its effects may be ascribed, by some odd figurative way of speaking, to the action itself. But still I can see no pretext of reason for asserting that the tendency to cause such an error is the first spring or original source of all immorality.[1]

---

[1] One might think it were entirely superfluous to prove this if a late author, who has had the good fortune to obtain some reputation, had not seriously affirmed that such a falsehood is the foundation of all guilt and moral deformity. That we may discover the fallacy of his hypothesis we need only consider that a false conclusion is drawn from an action only by means of an obscurity of natural principles, which makes a cause be secretly interrupted in its operation by contrary causes, and renders the connection between two objects uncertain and variable. Now, as a like uncertainty and variety of causes take place even in natural objects and produce a like error in our judgment, if that tendency to produce error were the very essence of vice and immorality, it should follow that even inanimate objects might be vicious and immoral.

It is in vain to urge that inanimate objects act without liberty and choice. For as liberty and choice are not necessary to make an action produce in us an erroneous conclusion, they can be in no respect essential to morality; and I do not readily perceive, upon this system, how they can ever come to be regarded by it. If the tendency to cause error be the origin of immorality, that tendency and immorality would in every case be inseparable.

Add to this that if I had used the precaution of shutting the windows while I indulged myself in those liberties with my neighbor's wife, I should have been guilty of no immorality, and that because my action, being perfectly concealed, would have had no tendency to produce any false conclusion.

For the same reason, a thief who steals in by a ladder at a window and takes all imaginable care to cause no disturbance is in no respect criminal. For either he will not be perceived, or if he be, it is impossible he can produce any error, nor will anyone, from these circumstances, take him to be other than what he really is.

It is well known that those who are squint-sighted do very readily cause mistakes in others, and that we imagine they salute or are talking to one person while they address themselves to another. Are they therefore, upon that account, immoral?

Besides, we may easily observe that in all those arguments there is an evident reasoning in a circle. A person who takes possession of *another's* goods and uses them as his *own* in a manner declares them to be his own, and this falsehood is the source of the im-

Thus upon the whole, it is impossible that the distinction between moral good and evil can be made by reason, since that distinction has an influence upon our actions of which reason alone is incapable. Reason and judgment may, indeed, be the mediate cause of an action by prompting or by directing a passion. But it is not pretended that a judgment of this kind, either in its truth or falsehood, is attended with virtue or vice. And as to the judgments which are caused by our judgments, they can still less bestow those moral qualities on the actions which are their causes.

But to be more particular, and to show that those eternal immutable fitnesses and unfitnesses of things cannot be defended by sound philosophy, we may weigh the following considerations.

If the thought and understanding were alone capable of fixing the boundaries of right and wrong, the character of virtuous and vicious either must lie in some relations of objects

---

morality of injustice. But is property or right or obligation intelligible without an antecedent morality?

A man that is ungrateful to his benefactor in a manner affirms that he never received any favors from him. But in what manner? Is it because it is his duty to be grateful? But this supposes that there is some antecedent rule of duty and morals. Is it because human nature is generally grateful, and makes us conclude that a man who does any harm never received any favor from the person he harmed? But human nature is not so generally grateful as to justify such a conclusion. Or if it were, is an exception to a general rule in every case criminal, for no other reason than because it is an exception?

But what may suffice entirely to destroy this whimsical system is that it leaves us under the same difficulty to give a reason why truth is virtuous and falsehood vicious as to account for the merit or turpitude of any other action. I shall allow, if you please, that all immorality is derived from this supposed falsehood in action, provided you can give me any plausible reason why such a falsehood is immoral. If you consider rightly of the matter, you will find yourself in the same difficulty as at the beginning.

This last argument is very conclusive, because if there be not an evident merit or turpitude annexed to this species of truth or falsehood, it can never have any influence upon our actions. For whoever thought of forbearing any action because others might possibly draw false conclusions from it? Or who ever performed any that he might give rise to true conclusions?

or must be a matter of fact which is discovered by our reasoning. This consequence is evident. As the operations of human understanding divide themselves into two kinds, the comparing of ideas and the inferring of matter of fact, were virtue discovered by the understanding it must be an object of one of these operations, nor is there any third operation of the understanding which can discover it. There has been an opinion very industriously propagated by certain philosophers that morality is susceptible of demonstration, and though no one has ever been able to advance a single step in those demonstrations, yet it is taken for granted that this science may be brought to an equal certainty with geometry or algebra. Upon this supposition, vice and virtue must consist in some relations, since it is allowed on all hands that no matter of fact is capable of being demonstrated. Let us, therefore, begin with examining this hypothesis and endeavor, if possible, to fix those moral qualities which have been so long the objects of our fruitless researches. Point out distinctly the relations which constitute morality or obligation that we may know wherein they consist, and after what manner we must judge of them.

If you assert that vice and virtue consist in relations susceptible of certainty and demonstration, you must confine yourself to those *four* relations which alone admit of that degree of evidence, and in that case you run into absurdities from which you will never be able to extricate yourself. For as you make the very essence of morality to lie in the relations, and as there is no one of these relations but what is applicable not only to an irrational but also to an inanimate object, it follows that even such objects must be susceptible of merit or demerit. *Resemblance, contrariety, degrees in quality*, and *proportions in quantity and number:* all these relations belong as properly to matter as to our actions, passions, and volitions. It is unquestionable, therefore, that morality lies not in any of these relations, nor the sense of it in their discovery.[1]

---

[1] As a proof how confused our way of thinking on this subject commonly is, we may observe that those who assert that morality is demonstrable do not say that morality lies in the relations and that the relations are distinguishable by reason. They only say that

Should it be asserted that the sense of morality consists in the discovery of some relation distinct from these, and that our enumeration was not complete when we comprehended all demonstrable relations under four general heads, to this I know not what to reply till some one be so good as to point out to me this new relation. It is impossible to refute a system which has never yet been explained. In such a manner of fighting in the dark, a man loses his blows in the air, and often places them where the enemy is not present.

I must, therefore, on this occasion rest contented with requiring the two following conditions of anyone that would undertake to clear up this system. *First,* as moral good and evil belong only to the actions of the mind and are derived from our situation with regard to external objects, the relations from which these moral distinctions arise must lie only between internal actions and external objects, and must not be applicable either to internal actions compared among themselves or to external objects when placed in opposition to other external objects. For as morality is supposed to attend certain relations, if these relations could belong to internal actions considered singly, it would follow that we might be guilty of crimes in ourselves and independent of our situation with respect to the universe. And in like manner, if these moral relations could be applied to external objects, it would follow that even inanimate beings would be susceptible of moral beauty and deformity. Now it seems difficult to imagine that any relation can be discovered between our passions, volitions, and actions, compared to external objects, which

---

reason can discover such an action in such relations to be virtuous, and such another vicious. It seems they thought it sufficient if they could bring the word *relation* into the proposition without troubling themselves whether it was to the purpose or not. But here, I think, is plain argument. Demonstrative reason discovers only relations. But that reason, according to this hypothesis, discovers also vice and virtue. These moral qualities, therefore, must be relations. When we blame any action in any situation the whole complicated object of action and situation must form certain relations wherein the essence of vice consists. This hypothesis is not otherwise intelligible. For what does reason discover when it pronounces any action vicious? Does it discover a relation or a matter of fact? These questions are decisive, and must not be eluded.

relation might not belong either to these passions and volitions or to these external objects compared among *themselves*.

But it will be still more difficult to fulfill the *second* condition requisite to justify this system. According to the principles of those who maintain an abstract rational difference between moral good and evil and a natural fitness and unfitness of things, it is not only supposed that these relations, being eternal and immutable, are the same when considered by every rational creature, but their *effects* are also supposed to be necessarily the same, and it is concluded they have no less, or rather a greater, influence in directing the will of the deity than in governing the rational and virtuous of our own species. These two particulars are evidently distinct. It is one thing to know virtue and another to conform the will to it. In order, therefore, to prove that the measures of right and wrong are eternal laws, *obligatory* on every rational mind, it is not sufficient to show the relations upon which they are founded. We must also point out the connection between the relation and the will, and must prove that this connection is so necessary that in every well-disposed mind it must take place and have its influence, though the difference between these minds be in other respects immense and infinite. Now besides what I have already proved, that even in human nature no relation can ever alone produce any action; besides this, I say, it has been shown in treating of the understanding that there is no connection of cause and effect, such as this is supposed to be, which is discoverable otherwise than by experience, and of which we can pretend to have any security by the simple consideration of the objects. All beings in the universe, considered in themselves, appear entirely loose and independent of each other. It is only by experience we learn their influence and connection, and this influence we ought never to extend beyond experience.

Thus it will be impossible to fulfill the *first* condition required to the system of eternal rational measures of right and wrong, because it is impossible to show those relations upon which such a distinction may be founded. And it is as impossible to fulfill the *second* condition, because we cannot prove *a priori* that these relations, if they really existed and were perceived, would be universally forcible and obligatory.

But to make these general reflections more clear and convincing, we may illustrate them by some particular instances wherein this character of moral good or evil is the most universally acknowledged. Of all crimes that human creatures are capable of committing, the most horrid and unnatural is ingratitude, especially when it is committed against parents and appears in the more flagrant instances of wounds and death. This is acknowledged by all mankind, philosophers as well as the people; the question only arises among philosophers whether the guilt or moral deformity of this action be discovered by demonstrative reasoning or be felt by an internal sense and by means of some sentiment which the reflecting on such an action naturally occasions. This question will soon be decided against the former opinion if we can show the same relations in other objects without the notion of any guilt or iniquity attending them. Reason or science is nothing but the comparing of ideas and the discovery of their relations, and if the same relations have different characters it must evidently follow that those characters are not discovered merely by reason. To put the affair, therefore, to this trial, let us choose any inanimate object, such as an oak or elm, and let us suppose that by the dropping of its seed it produces a sapling below it, which springing up by degrees at last overtops and destroys the parent tree. I ask if in this instance there be wanting any relation which is discoverable in parricide or ingratitude? Is not the one tree the cause of the other's existence and the latter the cause of the destruction of the former, in the same manner as when a child murders his parent? It is not sufficient to reply that a choice or will is wanting. For in the case of parricide, a will does not give rise to any *different* relations, but is only the cause from which the action is derived, and consequently produces the *same* relations that in the oak or elm arise from some other principles. It is a will or choice that determines a man to kill his parent, and they are the laws of matter and motion that determine a sapling to destroy the oak from which it sprung. Here then the same relations have different causes, but still the relations are the same. And as their discovery is not in both cases attended with a notion of immorality, it follows that that notion does not arise from such a discovery.

But to choose an instance still more resembling, I would fain ask anyone why incest in the human species is criminal, and why the very same action and the same relations in animals have not the smallest moral turpitude and deformity? If it be answered that this action is innocent in animals because they have not reason sufficient to discover its turpitude, but that man, being endowed with that faculty which *ought* to restrain him to his duty, the same action instantly becomes criminal to him; should this be said, I would reply that this is evidently arguing in a circle. For before reason can perceive this turpitude, the turpitude must exist, and consequently is independent of the decisions of our reason, and is their object more properly than their effect. According to this system, then, every animal that has sense and appetite and will, that is, every animal, must be susceptible of all the same virtues and vices for which we ascribe praise and blame to human creatures. All the difference is that our superior reason may serve to discover the vice or virtue and by that means may augment the blame or praise. But still this discovery supposes a separate being in these moral distinctions, and a being which depends only on the will and appetite and which, both in thought and reality, may be distinguished from the reason. Animals are susceptible of the same relations with respect to each other as the human species, and therefore would also be susceptible of the same morality if the essence of morality consisted in these relations. Their want of a sufficient degree of reason may hinder them from perceiving the duties and obligations of morality, but can never hinder these duties from existing, since they must antecedently exist in order to their being perceived. Reason must find them and can never produce them. This argument deserves to be weighed, as being, in my opinion, entirely decisive.

Nor does this reasoning only prove that morality consists not in any relations that are the objects of science, but if examined will prove with equal certainty that it consists not in any *matter of fact* which can be discovered by the understanding. This is the *second* part of our argument, and if it can be made evident we may conclude that morality is not an object of reason. But can there be any difficulty in proving that vice and virtue are not matters of fact whose existence we can infer by reason? Take any action allowed to be vicious, willful murder, for instance. Examine it in all lights and see if you can find that matter of fact or real existence which you call *vice*. In whichever way you take it, you find only certain passions, motives, volitions, and thoughts. There is no other matter of fact in the case. The vice entirely escapes you as long as you consider the object. You never can find it till you turn your reflection into your own breast, and find a sentiment of disapprobation which arises in you towards this action. Here is a matter of fact, but it is the object of feeling, not of reason. It lies in yourself, not in the object. So that when you pronounce any action or character to be vicious, you mean nothing but that from the constitution of your nature you have a feeling or sentiment of blame from the contemplation of it. Vice and virtue, therefore, may be compared to sounds, colors, heat, and cold, which, according to modern philosophy, are not qualities in objects but perceptions in the mind; and this discovery in morals, like that other in physics, is to be regarded as a considerable advancement of the speculative sciences, though like that too it has little or no influence on practice. Nothing can be more real or concern us more than our own sentiments of pleasure and uneasiness, and if these be favorable to virtue and unfavorable to vice, no more can be requisite to the regulation of our conduct and behavior.

I cannot forbear adding to these reasonings an observation which may, perhaps, be found of some importance. In every system of morality which I have hitherto met with, I have always remarked that the author proceeds for some time in the ordinary way of reasoning and establishes the being of a God or makes observations concerning human affairs, when of a sudden I am surprised to find that instead of the usual copulations of propositions, *is* and *is not,* I meet with no proposition that is not connected with an *ought* or an *ought not.* This change is imperceptible, but is, however, of the last consequence. For as this *ought* or *ought not* expresses some new relation or affirmation, it is necessary that it should be observed and explained, and at the same time that a reason should be given for what seems altogether inconceivable, how this new relation can be a deduction from others which are entirely different from it. But as authors do not commonly use this precaution, I shall presume to recommend it to the readers, and am persuaded that this small attention would subvert all the vulgar systems of morality and let us see that the distinction of vice and virtue is not founded merely on the relations of objects, nor is perceived by reason.

Section II.

MORAL DISTINCTIONS DERIVED FROM
A MORAL SENSE

Thus the course of the argument leads us to conclude that since vice and virtue are not discoverable merely by reason or the comparison of ideas, it must be by means of some impression or sentiment they occasion that we are able to mark the difference between them. Our decisions concerning moral rectitude and depravity are evidently perceptions, and as all perceptions are either impressions or ideas, the exclusion of the one is a convincing argument for the other. Morality, therefore, is more properly felt than judged of, though this feeling or sentiment is commonly so soft and gentle that we are apt to confound it with an idea, according to our common custom of taking all things for the same which have any near resemblance to each other.

The next question is, OF what nature are these impressions and after what manner do they operate upon us? Here we cannot remain long in suspense, but must pronounce the impression arising from virtue to be agreeable, and that proceeding from vice to be uneasy. Every moment's experience must convince us of this. There is no spectacle so fair and beautiful as a noble and generous action, nor any which gives us more abhorrence than one that is cruel and treacherous. No enjoyment equals the satisfaction we receive from the company of those we love and esteem, as the greatest of all punishments is to be obliged to pass our lives with those we hate or condemn. A very play or romance may afford us instances of this pleasure which virtue conveys to us, and pain which arises from vice.

Now since the distinguishing impressions by which moral good or evil is known are nothing but *particular* pains or pleasures, it follows that in all inquiries concerning these moral distinctions it will be sufficient to show the principles which make us feel a satisfaction or uneasiness from the survey of any character in order to satisfy us why the character is laudable or blamable. An action or sentiment or character is virtuous or vicious. Why? Because its view causes a pleasure or uneasiness of a particular kind. In giving a reason, there-fore, for the pleasure or uneasiness, we sufficiently explain the vice or virtue. To have the sense of virtue is nothing but to *feel* a satisfaction of a particular kind from the contempla-tion of a character. The very *feeling* constitutes our praise or admiration. We go no further, nor do we inquire into the cause of the satisfaction. We do not infer a character to be virtuous because it pleases, but in feeling that it pleases after such a particular manner we in effect feel that it is virtuous. The case is the same as in our judgments concerning all kinds of beauty and tastes and sensations. Our approbation is im-plied in the immediate pleasure they convey to us.

I have objected to the system which establishes eternal ra-tional measures of right and wrong, that it is impossible to show, in the actions of reasonable creatures, any relations which are not found in external objects, and therefore, if morality always attended these relations, it were possible for inanimate matter to become virtuous or vicious. Now it may, in like manner, be objected to the present system, that if vir-tue and vice be determined by pleasure and pain, these quali-ties must in every case arise from the sensations, and conse-quently any object, whether animate or inanimate, rational or irrational, might become morally good or evil, provided it can excite a satisfaction or uneasiness. But though this objec-tion seems to be the very same, it has by no means the same force in the one case as in the other. For *first,* it is evident that under the term *pleasure* we comprehend sensations which are very different from each other, and which have only such a distant resemblance as is requisite to make them be expressed by the same abstract term. A good composition of music and a bottle of good wine equally produce pleasure, and what is more, their goodness is determined merely by the pleasure. But shall we say upon that account that the wine is harmonious, or the music of a good flavor? In like manner an inanimate object and the character or sentiments of any person may, both of them, give satisfaction, but as the satisfaction is different, this keeps our sentiments concerning them from being confounded, and makes us ascribe virtue to the one and not to the other. Nor is every sentiment of pleasure or pain which arises from characters and actions of that *peculiar* kind which makes us praise or condemn. The good qualities of an enemy are hurtful to us, but may still command our esteem and respect. It is only when a character is considered in general, without reference to our particular interest, that it causes such a feeling or sentiment as denominates it morally good or evil. It is true, those sentiments from interest and morals are apt to be confounded and naturally run into one another. It seldom happens that we do not think an enemy vicious, and can distinguish between his opposition to our interest and real villainy or baseness. But this hinders not but that the sentiments are, in themselves, distinct, and a man of temper and judgment may preserve himself from these illusions. In like manner, though it is certain a musical voice is nothing but one that naturally gives a *particular* kind of pleasure, yet it is difficult for a man to be sensible that the voice of an enemy is agreeable, or to allow it to be musical. But a person of a fine ear who has the command of himself can separate these feelings, and give praise to what deserves it.

Secondly, we may call to remembrance the preceding system of the passions in order to remark a still more considerable difference among our pains and pleasures. Pride and humility, love and hatred are excited when there is anything presented to us that both bears a relation to the object of the passion and produces a separate sensation related to the sensation of the passion. Now virtue and vice are attended with these circumstances. They must necessarily be placed either in ourselves or others and excite either pleasure or uneasiness, and therefore must give rise to one of these four passions, which clearly distinguishes them from the pleasure and pain arising from inanimate objects that often bear no relation to us. And this is, perhaps, the most considerable effect that virtue and vice have upon the human mind.

It may now be asked *in general* concerning this pain or pleasure that distinguishes moral good and evil, *From what principles is it derived and whence does it arise in the human mind?* To this I reply, *first,* that it is absurd to imagine that in every particular instance these sentiments are produced by an *original* quality and *primary* constitution. For as the number of our duties is, in a manner, infinite, it is impossible that our original instincts should extend to each of them, and from our very first infancy impress on the human mind all that multitude of precepts which are contained in the completest system of ethics. Such a method of proceeding is not conformable to the usual maxims by which nature is conducted, where a few principles produce all that variety we observe in the universe, and everything is carried on in the easiest and most simple manner. It is necessary, therefore, to abridge these primary impulses, and find some more general principles upon which all our notions of morals are founded.

But in the *second* place, should it be asked whether we ought to search for these principles in *nature* or whether we must look for them in some other origin, I would reply that our answer to this question depends upon the definition of the word *nature,* than which there is none more ambiguous and equivocal. If *nature* be opposed to miracles, not only the distinction between vice and virtue is natural but also every event which has ever happened in the world, *excepting those miracles on which our religion is founded.* In saying, then, that the sentiments of vice and virtue are natural in this sense, we make no very extraordinary discovery.

But *nature* may also be opposed to rare and unusual, and in this sense of the word, which is the common one, there may often arise disputes concerning what is natural or unnatural, and one may in general affirm that we are not possessed of any very precise standard by which these disputes can be decided. Frequent and rare depend upon the number of examples we have observed, and as this number may gradually increase or diminish, it will be impossible to fix any exact boundaries between them. We may only affirm on this head that if ever there was anything which could be called natural in this sense, the sentiments of morality certainly may, since there never was any nation of the world nor any single person in any nation who was utterly deprived of them and who never, in any instance, showed the least approbation or dislike of manners. These sentiments are so rooted in our constitution and temper that, without entirely confounding the human mind by disease or madness, it is impossible to extirpate and destroy them.

But *nature* may also be opposed to artifice as well as to what is rare and unusual, and in this sense it may be disputed whether the notions of virtue be natural or not. We readily forget that the designs and projects and views of men are principles as necessary in their operation as heat and cold, moist and dry; but taking them to be free and entirely our own, it is usual for us to set them in opposition to the other principles of nature. Should it, therefore, be demanded whether the sense of virtue be natural or artificial, I am of opinion that it is impossible for me at present to give any precise answer to this question. Perhaps it will appear afterwards that our sense of some virtues is artificial and that of others natural. The discussion of this question will be more proper when we enter upon an exact detail of each particular vice and virtue.[1]

Meanwhile it may not be amiss to observe from these definitions of *natural* and *unnatural* that nothing can be more unphilosophical than those systems which assert that virtue is the same with what is natural, and vice with what is unnatural. For in the first sense of the word *nature*, as opposed to miracles, both vice and virtue are equally natural; and in the second sense, as opposed to what is unusual, perhaps virtue will be found to be the most unnatural. At least it must be owned that heroic virtue, being as unusual, is as little natural as the most brutal barbarity. As to the third sense of the word, it is certain that both vice and virtue are equally artificial, and out of nature. For however it may be disputed whether

[1] In the following discourse *natural* is also opposed sometimes to *civil*, sometimes to *moral*. The opposition will always discover the sense in which it is taken.

the notion of a merit or demerit in certain actions be natural or artificial, it is evident that the actions themselves are artificial, and are performed with a certain design and intention; otherwise they could never be ranked under any of these denominations. It is impossible, therefore, that the character of natural and unnatural can ever, in any sense, mark the boundaries of vice and virtue.

Thus we are still brought back to our first position, that virtue is distinguished by the pleasure and vice by the pain that any action, sentiment, or character gives us by the mere view and contemplation. This decision is very commodious, because it reduces us to this simple question, *why any action or sentiment upon the general view or survey gives a certain satisfaction or uneasiness,* in order to show the origin of its moral rectitude or depravity, without looking for any incomprehensible relations and qualities which never did exist in nature, nor even in our imagination, by any clear and distinct conception. I flatter myself I have executed a great part of my present design by a statement of the question which appears to me so free from ambiguity and obscurity.

Part II.
OF JUSTICE AND INJUSTICE

Section I.

JUSTICE, WHETHER A NATURAL OR ARTIFICIAL VIRTUE

I HAVE already hinted that our sense of every kind of virtue is not natural, but that there are some virtues that produce pleasure and approbation by means of an artifice or contrivance which arises from the circumstances and necessity of mankind. Of this kind I assert *justice* to be, and shall endeavor to defend this opinion by a short and, I hope, convincing argument before I examine the nature of the artifice from which the sense of that virtue is derived.

It is evident that when we praise any actions, we regard only the motives that produced them, and consider the actions as signs or indications of certain principles in the mind and temper. The external performance has no merit. We must look within to find the moral quality. This we cannot do directly, and therefore fix our attention on actions, as on external signs. But these actions are still considered as signs, and the ultimate object of our praise and approbation is the motive that produced them.

After the same manner, when we require any action or blame a person for not performing it, we always suppose that one in that situation should be influenced by the proper motive of that action, and we esteem it vicious in him to be regardless of it. If we find, upon inquiry, that the virtuous motive was still powerful over his breast, though checked in its operation by some circumstances unknown to us, we retract our blame, and have the same esteem for him as if he had actually performed the action which we require of him.

It appears, therefore, that all virtuous actions derive their merit only from virtuous motives, and are considered merely as signs of those motives. From this principle I conclude that the first virtuous motive which bestows a merit on any action can never be a regard to the virtue of that action, but must be some other natural motive or principle. To suppose that the mere regard to the virtue of the action may be the first motive which produced the action and rendered it virtuous is to reason in a circle. Before we can have such a regard the action must be really virtuous, and this virtue must be derived from some virtuous motive, and consequently the virtuous motive must be different from the regard to the virtue of the action. A virtuous motive is requisite to render an action virtuous. An action must be virtuous before we can have a regard to its virtue. Some virtuous motive, therefore, must be antecedent to that regard.

Nor is this merely a metaphysical subtlety, but enters into all our reasonings in common life, though perhaps we may not be able to place it in such distinct philosophical terms.

We blame a father for neglecting his child. Why? Because it shows a want of natural affection, which is the duty of every parent. Were not natural affection a duty, the care of children could not be a duty, and it were impossible we could have the duty in our eye in the attention we give to our offspring. In this case, therefore, all men suppose a motive to the action distinct from a sense of duty.

Here is a man that does many benevolent actions, relieves the distressed, comforts the afflicted, and extends his bounty even to the greatest strangers. No character can be more amiable and virtuous. We regard these actions as proofs of the greatest humanity. This humanity bestows a merit on the actions. A regard to this merit is, therefore, a secondary consideration, and derived from the antecedent principle of humanity, which is meritorious and laudable.

In short, it may be established as an undoubted maxim, *that no action can be virtuous, or morally good, unless there be in human nature some motive to produce it, distinct from the sense of its morality.*

But may not the sense of morality or duty produce an action, without any other motive? I answer, it may, but this is no objection to the present doctrine. When any virtuous motive or principle is common in human nature, a person who feels his heart devoid of that motive may hate himself upon that account, and may perform the action without the motive, from a certain sense of duty, in order to acquire by practice that virtuous principle, or at least to disguise to himself as much as possible his want of it. A man that really feels no gratitude in his temper is still pleased to perform grateful actions, and thinks he has, by that means, fulfilled his duty. Actions are at first only considered as signs of motives, but it is usual, in this case as in all others, to fix our attention on the signs and neglect, in some measure, the thing signified. But though on some occasions a person may perform an action merely out of regard to its moral obligation, yet still this supposes in human nature some distinct principles which are capable of producing the action, and whose moral beauty renders the action meritorious.

Now to apply all this to the present case, I suppose a person to have lent me a sum of money, on condition that it be restored in a few days, and also suppose that after the expiration of the term agreed on he demands the sum. I ask, *What reason or motive have I to restore the money?* It will, perhaps, be said that my regard to justice and abhorrence of villainy and knavery are sufficient reasons for me, if I have the least grain of honesty or sense of duty and obligation. And this answer, no doubt, is just and satisfactory to man in his civilized state, and when trained up according to a certain discipline and education. But in his rude and more *natural* condition, if you are pleased to call such a condition natural, this answer would be rejected as perfectly unintelligible and sophistical. For one in that situation would immediately ask you, *Wherein consists this honesty and justice which you find in restoring a loan and abstaining from the property of others?* It does not surely lie in the external action. It must, therefore, be placed in the motive from which the external action is derived. This motive can never be a regard to the honesty of the action. For it is a plain fallacy to say that a virtuous motive is requisite to render an action honest, and at the same time that a regard to the honesty is the motive of the action. We can never have a regard to the virtue of an action unless the action be antecedently virtuous. No action can be virtuous but so far as it proceeds from a virtuous motive. A virtuous motive, therefore, must precede the regard to the virtue, and it is impossible that the virtuous motive and the regard to the virtue can be the same.

It is requisite, then, to find some motive to acts of justice and honesty distinct from our regard to the honesty, and in this lies the great difficulty. For should we say that a concern for our private interest or reputation is the legitimate motive to all honest actions, it would follow that wherever that concern ceases, honesty can no longer have place. But it is certain that self-love, when it acts at its liberty, instead of engaging us to honest actions, is the source of all injustice and violence, nor can a man ever correct those vices without correcting and restraining the *natural* movements of that appetite.

But should it be affirmed that the reason or motive of such actions is the *regard to public interest*, to which nothing is more contrary than examples of injustice and dishonesty;

should this be said, I would propose the three following considerations as worthy of our attention. *First,* public interest is not naturally attached to the observation of the rules of justice, but is only connected with it after an artificial convention for the establishment of these rules, as shall be shown more at large hereafter. *Secondly,* if we suppose that the loan was secret and that it is necessary for the interest of the person that the money be restored in the same manner (as when the lender would conceal his riches), in that case the example ceases, and the public is no longer interested in the actions of the borrower, though I suppose there is no moralist who will affirm that the duty and obligation ceases. *Thirdly,* experience sufficiently proves that men, in the ordinary conduct of life, look not so far as the public interest when they pay their creditors, perform their promises, and abstain from theft and robbery and injustice of every kind. That is a motive too remote and too sublime to affect the generality of mankind and operate with any force in actions so contrary to private interest as are frequently those of justice and common honesty.

In general, it may be affirmed that there is no such passion in human minds as the love of mankind, merely as such, independent of personal qualities, of services, or of relation to ourself. It is true, there is no human and indeed no sensible creature whose happiness or misery does not, in some measure, affect us when brought near to us and represented in lively colors. But this proceeds merely from sympathy, and is no proof of such a universal affection to mankind, since this concern extends itself beyond our own species. An affection between the sexes is a passion evidently implanted in human nature, and this passion not only appears in its peculiar symptoms but also in enflaming every other principle of affection, and raising a stronger love from beauty, wit, kindness than what would otherwise flow from them. Were there a universal love among all human creatures, it would appear after the same manner. Any degree of a good quality would cause a stronger affection than the same degree of a bad quality would cause hatred, contrary to what we find by experience. Men's tempers are different, and some have a propensity to the tender and others to the rougher affections. But in the main we may affirm that man in general, or human nature, is nothing but the object both of love and hatred, and requires some other cause which by a double relation of impressions and ideas may excite these passions. In vain would we endeavor to elude this hypothesis. There are no phenomena that point out any such kind affection to men, independent of their merit and every other circumstance. We love company in general, but it is as we love any other amusement. An *Englishman* in *Italy* is a friend; a *European* in *China;* and perhaps a man would be beloved as such were we to meet him in the moon. But this proceeds only from the relation to ourselves, which in these cases gathers force by being confined to a few persons.

If public benevolence, therefore, or a regard to the interests of mankind, cannot be the original motive to justice, much less can *private benevolence,* or a *regard to the interests of the party concerned,* be this motive. For what if he be my enemy and has given me just cause to hate him? What if he be a vicious man and deserves the hatred of all mankind? What if he be a miser and can make no use of what I would deprive him of? What if he be a profligate debauchee and would rather receive harm than benefit from large possessions? What if I be in necessity and have urgent motives to acquire something to my family? In all these cases, the original motive to justice would fail, and consequently the justice itself, and along with it all property, right, and obligation.

A rich man lies under a moral obligation to communicate to those in necessity a share of his superfluities. Were private benevolence the original motive to justice, a man would not be obliged to leave others in the possession of more than he is obliged to give them. At least the difference would be very inconsiderable. Men generally fix their affections more on what they are possessed of than on what they never enjoyed; for this reason it would be greater cruelty to dispossess a man of anything than not to give it him. But who will assert that this is the only foundation of justice?

Besides, we must consider that the chief reason why men attach themselves so much to their possessions is that they consider them as their property and as secured to them inviolably by the laws of society. But this is a secondary consideration and dependent on the preceding notions of justice and property.

A man's property is supposed to be fenced against every mortal in every possible case. But private benevolence is, and ought to be, weaker in some persons than in others, and in many or indeed in most persons must absolutely fail. Private benevolence, therefore, is not the original motive of justice.

From all this it follows that we have no real or universal motive for observing the laws of equity but the very equity and merit of that observance; and as no action can be equitable or meritorious where it cannot arise from some separate motive, there is here an evident sophistry and reasoning in a circle. Unless, therefore, we will allow that nature has established a sophistry and rendered it necessary and unavoidable, we must allow that the sense of justice and injustice is not derived from nature, but arises artificially, though necessarily, from education and human conventions.

I shall add as a corollary to this reasoning that since no action can be laudable or blamable without some motives or impelling passions distinct from the sense of morals, these distinct passions must have a great influence on that sense. It is according to their general force in human nature that we blame or praise. In judging of the beauty of animal bodies we always carry in our eye the economy of a certain species, and where the limbs and features observe that proportion which is common to the species we pronounce them handsome and beautiful. In like manner we always consider the *natural* and *usual* force of the passions when we determine concerning vice and virtue, and if the passions depart very much from the common measures on either side, they are always disapproved as vicious. A man naturally loves his children better than his nephews, his nephews better than his cousins, his cousins better than strangers, where everything else is equal. Hence arise our common measures of duty in preferring the one to the other. Our sense of duty always follows the common and natural course of our passions.

To avoid giving offense, I must here observe that when I deny justice to be a natural virtue, I make use of the word *natural* only as opposed to *artificial*. In another sense of the word, as no principle of the human mind is more natural than a sense of virtue, so no virtue is more natural than justice. Mankind is an inventive species, and where an invention is obvious and absolutely necessary, it may as properly be said to be natural as anything that proceeds immediately from original principles without the intervention of thought or reflection. Though the rules of justice be *artificial* they are not *arbitrary*. Nor is the expression improper to call them *laws of nature*, if by natural we understand what is common to any species, or even if we confine it to mean what is inseparable from the species.

Section II.

OF THE ORIGIN OF JUSTICE AND PROPERTY

We now proceed to examine two questions, *viz.*, concerning *the manner in which the rules of justice are established by the artifice of men,* and *concerning the reasons which determine us to attribute to the observance or neglect of these rules a moral beauty and deformity.* These questions will appear afterwards to be distinct. We shall begin with the former.

Of all the animals with which this globe is peopled, there is none towards whom nature seems, at first sight, to have exercised more cruelty than towards man, in the numberless wants and necessities with which she has loaded him, and in the slender means which she affords to the relieving these necessities. In other creatures these two particulars generally compensate each other. If we consider the lion as a voracious and carnivorous animal, we shall easily discover him to be very necessitous; but if we turn our eye to his make and temper, his agility, his courage, his arms, and his force, we shall find that his advantages hold proportion with his wants. The sheep and ox are deprived of all these advantages, but their appetites are moderate and their food is of easy purchase. In man alone this unnatural conjunction of infirmity and of necessity may be observed in its greatest perfection. Not only the food which is required for his sustenance flies his search and approach, or at least requires his labor to be produced, but he must be possessed of clothes and lodging to defend him against the injuries of the weather; though to consider him only in himself, he is provided neither with arms nor force nor other natural abilities which are in any degree answerable to so many necessities.

It is by society alone he is able to supply his defects and raise himself up to an equality with his fellow-creatures, and even acquire a superiority above them. By society all his infirmities are compensated, and though in that situation his wants multiply every moment upon him, yet his abilities are still more augmented, and leave him in every respect more satisfied and happy than it is possible for him in his savage and solitary condition ever to become. When every individual person labors apart and only for himself, his force is too small to execute any considerable work; his labor being employed in supplying all his different necessities, he never attains a perfection in any particular art, and as his force and success are not at all times equal, the least failure in either of these particulars must be attended with inevitable ruin and misery. Society provides a remedy for these *three* inconveniences. By the conjunction of forces our power is augmented; by the partition of employments our ability increases; and by mutual succor we are less exposed to fortune and accidents. It is by this additional *force, ability,* and *security* that society becomes advantageous.

But in order to form society it is requisite not only that it be advantageous but also that men be sensible of these advantages, and it is impossible, in their wild uncultivated state, that by study and reflection alone they should ever be able to attain this knowledge. Most fortunately, therefore, there is conjoined to those necessities whose remedies are remote and obscure another necessity, which, having a present and more obvious remedy, may justly be regarded as the first and original principle of human society. This necessity is no other than that natural appetite between the sexes, which unites them together and preserves their union till a new tie takes place in their concern for their common offspring. This new concern becomes also a principle of union between the parents and offspring and forms a more numerous society, where the parents govern by the advantage of their superior strength and wisdom and at the same time are restrained in the exercise of their authority by that natural affection which they bear their children. In a little time, custom and habit operating on the tender minds of the children makes them sensible of the advantages which they may reap from society, as well as fashions them by degrees for it by rubbing off those rough corners and untoward affections which prevent their coalition.

For it must be confessed that however the circumstances of human nature may render a union necessary and however those passions of lust and natural affection may seem to render it unavoidable, yet there are other particulars in our *natural temper* and in our *outward circumstances* which are very incommodious, and are even contrary to the requisite conjunction. Among the former, we may justly esteem our *selfishness* to be the most considerable. I am sensible that, generally speaking, the representations of this quality have been carried much too far, and that the descriptions which certain philosophers delight so much to form of mankind in this particular are as wide of nature as any accounts of monsters which we meet with in fables and romances. So far from thinking that men have no affection for anything beyond themselves, I am of opinion that though it be rare to meet with one who loves any single person better than himself, yet it is as rare to meet with one in whom all the kind affections, taken together, do not overbalance all the selfish. Consult common experience; do you not see that though the whole expense of the family be generally under the direction of the master of it, yet there are few that do not bestow the largest part of their fortunes on the pleasures of their wives and the education of their children, reserving the smallest portion for their own proper use and entertainment? This is what we may observe concerning such as have those endearing ties, and may presume that the case would be the same with others, were they placed in a like situation.

But though this generosity must be acknowledged to the honor of human nature, we may at the same time remark that so noble an affection, instead of fitting men for large societies, is almost as contrary to them as the most narrow selfishness. For while each person loves himself better than any other single person and in his love to others bears the greatest affection to his relations and acquaintances, this must necessarily produce an opposition of passions, and a consequent opposition of actions, which cannot but be dangerous to the new-established union.

It is, however, worthwhile to remark that this contrariety of passions would be attended with but small danger did it not concur with a peculiarity in our *outward circumstances*, which affords it an opportunity of exerting itself. There are three different species of goods which we are possessed of, the internal satisfaction of our minds, the external advantages of our body, and the enjoyment of such possessions as we have acquired by our industry and good fortune. We are perfectly secure in the enjoyment of the first. The second may be ravished from us, but can be of no advantage to him who deprives us of them. The last only are both exposed to the violence of others, and may be transferred without suffering any loss or alteration, while at the same time there is not a sufficient quantity of them to supply everyone's desires and necessities. As the improvement, therefore, of these goods is the chief advantage of society, so the *instability* of their possession, along with their *scarcity*, is the chief impediment.

In vain should we expect to find, in *uncultivated nature*, a remedy to this inconvenience, or hope for any inartificial principle of the human mind which might control those partial affections and make us overcome the temptations arising from our circumstances. The idea of justice can never serve to this purpose, or be taken for a natural principle, capable of inspiring men with an equitable conduct towards each other. That virtue, as it is now understood, would never have been dreamed of among rude and savage men. For the notion of injury or injustice implies an immorality or vice committed against some other person, and as every immorality is derived from some defect or unsoundness of the passions, and as this defect must be judged of, in a great measure, from the ordinary course of nature in the constitution of the mind, it will be easy to know whether we be guilty of any immorality with regard to others by considering the natural and usual force of those several affections which are directed towards them.

Now it appears that in the original frame of our mind, our strongest attention is confined to ourselves; our next is extended to our relations and acquaintance; and it is only the weakest which reaches to strangers and indifferent persons. This partiality, then, and unequal affection must not only have an influence on our behavior and conduct in society but even on our ideas of vice and virtue, so as to make us regard any remarkable transgression of such a degree of partiality, either by too great an enlargement or contraction of the affections, as vicious and immoral. This we may observe in our common judgments concerning actions, where we blame a person who either centers all his affections in his family or is so regardless of them as, in any opposition of interest, to give the preference to a stranger or mere chance acquaintance. From all which it follows that our natural uncultivated ideas of morality, instead of providing a remedy for the partiality of our affections, do rather conform themselves to that partiality, and give it an additional force and influence.

The remedy, then, is not derived from nature but from *artifice*, or more properly speaking, nature provides a remedy in the judgment and understanding for what is irregular and incommodious in the affections. For when men, from their early education in society, have become sensible of the infinite advantages that result from it and have besides acquired a new affection to company and conversation, and when they have observed that the principal disturbance in society arises from those goods which we call external and from their looseness and easy transition from one person to another, they must seek for a remedy by putting these goods, as far as possible, on the same footing with the fixed and constant advantages of the mind and body. This can be done after no other manner than by a convention entered into by all the members of the society to bestow stability on the possession of those external goods, and leave everyone in the peaceable enjoyment of what he may acquire by his fortune and industry. By this means, everyone knows what he may safely possess, and the passions are restrained in their partial and contradictory motions. Nor is such a restraint contrary to these passions, for if so, it could never be entered into nor maintained, but it is only contrary to their heedless and impetuous movement.

Instead of departing from our own interest or from that of our nearest friends by abstaining from the possessions of others, we cannot better consult both these interests than by such a convention, because it is by that means we maintain society, which is so necessary to their well-being and subsistence as well as to our own.

This convention is not of the nature of a *promise*, for even promises themselves, as we shall see afterwards, arise from human conventions. It is only a general sense of common interest, which sense all the members of the society express to one another, and which induces them to regulate their conduct by certain rules. I observe that it will be for my interest to leave another in the possession of his goods, *provided* he will act in the same manner with regard to me. He is sensible of a like interest in the regulation of his conduct. When this common sense of interest is mutually expressed and is known to both, it produces a suitable resolution and behavior. And this may properly enough be called a convention or agreement between us, though without the interposition of a promise, since the actions of each of us have a reference to those of the other, and are performed upon the supposition that something is to be performed on the other part. Two men who pull the oars of a boat do it by an agreement or convention, though they have never given promises to each other. Nor is the rule concerning the stability of possession the less derived from human conventions that it arises gradually, and acquires force by a slow progression and by our repeated experience of the inconveniences of transgressing it. On the contrary, this experience assures us still more that the sense of interest has become common to all our fellows, and gives us a confidence of the future regularity of their conduct, and it is only on the expectation of this that our moderation and abstinence are founded. In like manner are languages gradually established by human conventions without any promise. In like manner do gold and silver become the common measures of exchange, and are esteemed sufficient payment for what is of a hundred times their value.

After this convention concerning abstinence from the possessions of others is entered into and everyone has acquired a stability in his possessions, there immediately arise the ideas of justice and injustice, as also those of *property, right,* and *obligation.* The latter are altogether unintelligible without first understanding the former. Our property is nothing but those goods whose constant possession is established by the laws of society, that is, by the laws of justice. Those, therefore, who make use of the words *property,* or *right,* or *obligation,* before they have explained the origin of justice, or even make use of them in that explication, are guilty of a very gross fallacy, and can never reason upon any solid foundation. A man's property is some object related to him. This relation is not natural, but moral, and founded on justice. It is very preposterous, therefore, to imagine that we can have any idea of property without fully comprehending the nature of justice, and showing its origin in the artifice and contrivance of men. The origin of justice explains that of property. The same artifice gives rise to both. As our first and most natural sentiment of morals is founded on the nature of our passions, and gives the preference to ourselves and friends above strangers, it is impossible there can be naturally any such thing as a fixed right or property while the opposite passions of men impel them in contrary directions, and are not restrained by any convention or agreement.

No one can doubt that the convention for the distinction of property and for the stability of possessions is of all circumstances the most necessary to the establishment of human society, and that after the agreement for the fixing and observing of this rule, there remains little or nothing to be done towards settling a perfect harmony and concord. All the other passions beside this of interest are either easily restrained, or are not of such pernicious consequence when indulged. *Vanity* is rather to be esteemed a social passion, and a bond of union among men. *Pity* and *love* are to be considered in the same light. And as to *envy* and *revenge,* though pernicious, they operate only by intervals, and are directed against particular persons whom we consider as our superiors or enemies. This avidity alone of acquiring goods and possessions for ourselves and our nearest friends is insatiable, perpetual, universal, and directly destructive of society. There scarce is anyone who is not actuated by it, and there is no one who has not reason to fear from it when it acts without any restraint and gives way to its first and most natural movements. So that upon the whole, we are to esteem the difficulties in the establishment of society to be greater or less according to those we encounter in regulating and restraining this passion.

It is certain that no affection of the human mind has both a sufficient force and a proper direction to counterbalance the love of gain and render men fit members of society by making them abstain from the possessions of others. Benevolence to strangers is too weak for this purpose, and as to the other passions, they rather inflame this avidity when we observe that the larger our possessions are the more ability we have of gratifying all our appetites. There is no passion, therefore, capable of controlling the interested affection but the very affection itself, by an alteration of its direction. Now this alteration must necessarily take place upon the least reflection, since it is evident that the passion is much better satisfied by its restraint than by its liberty, and that in preserving society we make much greater advances in the acquiring possessions than in the solitary and forlorn condition which must follow upon violence and a universal license. The question, therefore, concerning the wickedness or goodness of human nature enters not in the least into that other question concerning the origin of society, nor is there anything to be considered but the degrees of men's sagacity or folly. For whether the passion of self-interest be esteemed vicious or virtuous, it is all a case, since itself alone restrains it. So that if it be virtuous, men become social by their virtue; if vicious, their vice has the same effect.

Now as it is by establishing the rule for the stability of possession that this passion restrains itself, if that rule be very abstruse and of difficult invention, society must be esteemed, in a manner, accidental, and the effect of many ages. But if it be found that nothing can be more simple and obvious than that rule, that every parent, in order to preserve peace among his children, must establish it, and that these first rudiments of justice must every day be improved as the society enlarges; if all this appear evident, as it certainly must, we may conclude that it is utterly impossible for men to remain any considerable time in that savage condition which precedes society, but that his very first state and situation may justly be esteemed social. This, however, hinders not but that philosophers may, if they please, extend their reasoning to the supposed *state of nature*, provided they allow it to be a mere philosophical fiction which never had and never could have any reality. Human nature being composed of two principal parts which are requisite in all its actions, the affections and understanding, it is certain that the blind motions of the former, without the direction of the latter, incapacitate men for society, and it may be allowed us to consider separately the effects that result from the separate operations of these two component parts of the mind. The same liberty may be permitted to moral which is allowed to natural philosophers, and it is very usual with the latter to consider any motion as compounded and consisting of two parts separate from each other, though at the same time they acknowledge it to be in itself uncompounded and inseparable.

This *state of nature*, therefore, is to be regarded as a mere fiction, not unlike that of the *golden age* which poets have invented, only with this difference, that the former is described as full of war, violence, and injustice, whereas the latter is painted out to us as the most charming and most peaceable condition that can possibly be imagined. The seasons in that first age of nature were so temperate, if we may believe the poets, that there was no necessity for men to provide themselves with clothes and houses as a security against the violence of heat and cold. The rivers flowed with wine and milk; the oaks yielded honey, and nature spontaneously produced her greatest delicacies. Nor were these the chief advantages of that happy age. The storms and tempests were not alone removed from nature, but those more furious tempests were unknown to human breasts which now cause such uproar and engender such confusion. Avarice, ambition, cruelty, selfishness were never heard of; cordial affection, compassion, sympathy were the only movements with which the human mind was yet acquainted. Even the distinction of *mine* and *thine* was banished from that happy race of mortals, and carried with them the very notions of property and obligation, justice and injustice.

This, no doubt, is to be regarded as an idle fiction, but yet deserves our attention, because nothing can more evidently show the origin of those virtues which are the subjects of our present inquiry. I have already observed that justice takes its rise from human conventions, and that these are intended as a remedy to some inconveniences which proceed from the concurrence of certain *qualities* of the human mind with the *situation* of external objects. The qualities of the mind are *selfishness* and *limited generosity*, and the situation of external objects is their *easy change*, joined to their *scarcity* in comparison of the wants and desires of men. But however philosophers may have been bewildered in those speculations, poets have been guided more infallibly by a certain taste or common instinct, which in most kinds of reasoning goes further than any of that art and philosophy with which we have been yet acquainted. They easily perceived if every man had a tender regard for another, or if nature supplied abundantly all our wants and desires, that the jealousy of interest which justice supposes could no longer have place, nor would there be any occasion for those distinctions and limits of property and possession which at present are in use among mankind. Increase to a sufficient degree the benevolence of men or the bounty of nature, and you render justice useless by supplying its place with much nobler virtues and more valuable blessings. The selfishness of men is animated by the few possessions we have in proportion to our wants, and it is to restrain this selfishness that men have been obliged to separate themselves from the community, and to distinguish between their own goods and those of others.

Nor need we have recourse to the fictions of poets to learn this, but beside the reason of the thing may discover the same truth by common experience and observation. It is easy to remark that a cordial affection renders all things common among friends, and that married people in particular mutually lose their property, and are unacquainted with the *mine* and *thine* which are so necessary and yet cause such disturbance in human society. The same effect arises from any alteration in the circumstances of mankind, as when there is such a plenty of anything as satisfies all the desires of men, in which case the distinction of property is entirely lost and everything remains in common. This we may observe with regard to air and water, though the most valuable of all external objects, and may easily conclude that if men were supplied with everything in the same abundance or if *everyone* had the same affection and tender regard for *everyone* as for himself, justice and injustice would be equally unknown among mankind.

Here then is a proposition which, I think, may be regarded as certain, *that it is only from the selfishness and confined generosity of men, along with the scanty provision nature has made for his wants, that justice derives its origin.* . . .

. . . . .

We come now to the *second* question we proposed, *viz., why we annex the idea of virtue to justice and of vice to injustice.* This question will not detain us long after the principles which we have already established. All we can say of it at present will be dispatched in a few words, and for further satisfaction the reader must wait till we come to the *third* part of this book. The *natural* obligation to justice, *viz.,* interest, has been fully explained, but as to the *moral* obligation or the sentiment of right and wrong, it will first be requisite to examine the natural virtues before we can give a full and satisfactory account of it.

After men have found by experience that their selfishness and confined generosity, acting at their liberty, totally incapacitate them for society, and at the same time have observed that society is necessary to the satisfaction of those very passions, they are naturally induced to lay themselves under the restraint of such rules as may render their commerce more safe and commodious. To the imposition, then, and observance of these rules, both in general and in every particular instance, they are at first induced only by a regard to interest, and this motive, on the first formation of society, is sufficiently strong and forcible. But when society has become numerous and has increased to a tribe or nation, this interest is more remote, nor do men so readily perceive that disorder and confusion follow upon every breach of these rules as in a more narrow and contracted society. But though in our own actions we may frequently lose sight of that interest which we have in maintaining order and may follow a lesser and more present interest, we never fail to observe the prejudice we receive, either mediately or immediately, from the injustice of others, as not being in that case either blinded by passion or biased by any contrary temptation. Nay when the injustice is so distant from us as no way to affect our interest, it still displeases us, because we consider it as prejudicial to human society and pernicious to everyone that approaches the person guilty of it. We partake of their uneasiness by *sympathy;* and as everything which gives uneasiness in human actions upon the general survey is called vice, and whatever produces satisfaction in the same manner is denominated virtue, this is the reason why the sense of moral good and evil follows upon justice and injustice. And though this sense, in the present case, be derived only from contemplating the actions of others, yet we fail not to extend it even to our own actions. The *general rule* reaches beyond those instances from which it arose, while at the same time we naturally *sympathize* with others in the sentiments they entertain of us. *Thus self-interest is the original motive to the* establishment *of justice, but a* sympathy *with public interest is the source of the* moral approbation *which attends that virtue.*

Though this progress of the sentiments be *natural* and even necessary, it is certain that it is here forwarded by the artifice of politicians, who, in order to govern men more easily and preserve peace in human society, have endeavored to produce an esteem for justice and an abhorrence of injustice. This, no doubt, must have its effect, but nothing can be more evident than that the matter has been carried too far by certain writers on morals, who seem to have employed their utmost efforts to extirpate all sense of virtue from among mankind. Any artifice of politicians may assist nature in the producing of those sentiments which she suggests to us, and may even on some occasions produce alone an approbation or esteem for any particular action, but it is impossible it should be the sole cause of the distinction we make between vice and virtue. For if nature did not aid us in this particular, it would be in vain for politicians to talk of *honorable* or *dishonorable, praiseworthy* or *blamable.* These words would be perfectly unintelligible and would no more have any idea annexed to them than if they were of a tongue perfectly unknown to us. The utmost politicians can perform is to extend the natural sentiments beyond their original bounds, but still nature must

furnish the materials and give us some notion of moral distinctions.

As public praise and blame increase our esteem for justice,
so private education and instruction contribute to the same
effect. For as parents easily observe that a man is the more
useful, both to himself and others, the greater degree of
probity and honor he is endowed with, and that those principles have greater force when custom and education assist
interest and reflection, for these reasons they are induced to
inculcate on their children from their earliest infancy the principles of probity, and teach them to regard the observance of
those rules by which society is maintained as worthy and
honorable, and their violation as base and infamous. By this
means the sentiments of honor may take root in their tender
minds, and acquire such firmness and solidity that they may
fall little short of those principles which are the most essential
to our natures, and the most deeply radicated in our internal
constitution.

What further contributes to increase their solidity is the
interest of our reputation, after the opinion *that a merit or demerit attends justice or injustice* is once firmly established
among mankind. There is nothing which touches us more
nearly than our reputation, and nothing on which our reputation more depends than our conduct with relation to the
property of others. For this reason, everyone who has any
regard to his character or who intends to live on good terms
with mankind, must fix an inviolable law to himself never, by
any temptation, to be induced to violate those principles which
are essential to a man of probity and honor.

I shall make only one observation before I leave this subject, *viz.,* that though I assert that in the *state of nature,* or
that imaginary state which preceded society, there be neither
justice nor injustice, yet I assert not that it was allowable in
such a state to violate the property of others. I only maintain
that there was no such thing as property, and consequently
could be no such thing as justice or injustice. I shall have occasion to make a similar reflection with regard to *promises*
when I come to treat of them, and I hope this reflection,
when duly weighed, will suffice or remove all odium from
the foregoing opinions with regard to justice and injustice.

Section V.

OF THE OBLIGATION OF PROMISES

That the rule of morality which enjoins the performance of promises is not *natural* will sufficiently appear from these two propositions which I proceed to prove, *viz., that a promise would not be intelligible before human conventions had established it,* and *that even if it were intelligible it would not be attended with any moral obligation.*

I say, *first,* that a promise is not intelligible naturally nor antecedent to human conventions, and that a man unacquainted with society could never enter into any engagements with another, even though they could perceive each other's thoughts by intuition. If promises be natural and intelligible, there must be some act of the mind attending these words, *I promise,* and on this act of the mind must the obligation depend. Let us, therefore, run over all the faculties of the soul and see which of them is exerted in our promises.

The act of the mind expressed by a promise is not a *resolution* to perform anything, for that alone never imposes any obligation. Nor is it a *desire* of such a performance, for we may bind ourselves without such a desire, or even with an aversion, declared and avowed. Neither is it the *willing* of that action which we promise to perform, for a promise always regards some future time, and the will has an influence only on present actions. It follows, therefore, that since the act of the mind which enters into a promise and produces its obligation is neither the resolving, desiring, nor willing any particular performance, it must necessarily be the *willing* of that *obligation* which arises from the promise. Nor is this only a conclusion of philosophy, but is entirely conformable to our common ways of thinking and of expressing ourselves, when we say that we are bound by our own consent and that the obligation arises from our mere will and pleasure. The only question, then, is whether there be not a manifest absurdity in supposing this act of the mind, and such an ab-

surdity as no man could fall into whose ideas are not confounded with prejudice and the fallacious use of language.

All morality depends upon our sentiments, and when any
action or quality of the mind pleases us *after a certain manner*, we say it is virtuous, and when the neglect or nonper-
formance of it displeases us *after a like manner* we say that
we lie under an obligation to perform it. A change of the obligation supposes a change of the sentiment, and a creation of a
new obligation supposes some new sentiment to arise. But it is
certain we can naturally no more change our own sentiments
than the motions of the heavens, nor by a single act of our
will, that is, by a promise, render any action agreeable or disagreeable, moral or immoral, which, without that act, would
have produced contrary impressions or have been endowed
with different qualities. It would be absurd, therefore, to will
any new obligation, that is, any new sentiment of pain or
pleasure, nor is it possible that men could naturally fall into
so gross an absurdity. A promise, therefore, is *naturally* something altogether unintelligible, nor is there any act of the
mind belonging to it.[1]

[1] Were morality discoverable by reason and not by sentiment, it
would be still more evident that promises could make no alteration
upon it. Morality is supposed to consist in relation. Every new imposition of morality, therefore, must arise from some new relation
of objects, and consequently the will could not produce *immediately* any change in morals but could have that effect only by
producing a change upon the objects. But as the moral obligation
of a promise is the pure effect of the will without the least change
in any part of the universe, it follows that promises have no *natural*
obligation.

Should it be said that this act of the will, being in effect a
new object, produces new relations and new duties, I would answer
that this is a pure sophism, which may be detected by a very
moderate share of accuracy and exactness. To will a new obligation
is to will a new relation of objects; and therefore if this new relation of objects were formed by the volition itself, we should in
effect will the volition, which is plainly absurd and impossible. The
will has here no object to which it could tend, but must return
upon itself *in infinitum*. The new obligation depends upon new
relations. The new relations depend upon a new volition. The new
volition has for object a new obligation, and consequently new
relations, and consequently a new volition, which volition again
has in view a new obligation, relation, and volition, without any

But, *secondly*, if there was any act of the mind belonging to it, it could not *naturally* produce any obligation. This appears evidently from the foregoing reasoning. A promise creates a new obligation. A new obligation supposes new sentiments to arise. The will never creates new sentiments. There could not naturally, therefore, arise any obligation from a promise, even supposing the mind could fall into the absurdity of willing that obligation.

The same truth may be proved still more evidently by that reasoning which proved justice in general to be an artificial virtue. No action can be required of us as our duty unless there be implanted in human nature some actuating passion or motive capable of producing the action. This motive cannot be the sense of duty. A sense of duty supposes an antecedent obligation, and where an action is not required by any natural passion it cannot be required by any natural obligation, since it may be omitted without proving any defect or imperfection in the mind and temper, and consequently without any vice. Now it is evident we have no motive leading us to the performance of promises, distinct from a sense of duty. If we thought that promises had no moral obligation, we never should feel any inclination to observe them. This is not the case with the natural virtues. Though there was no obligation to relieve the miserable, our humanity would lead us to it, and when we omit that duty, the immorality of the omission arises from its being a proof that we want the natural sentiments of humanity. A father knows it to be his duty to take care of his children, but he has also a natural inclination to it. And if no human creature had that inclination, no one could lie under any such obligation. But as there is naturally no inclination to observe promises distinct from a sense of their obligation, it follows that fidelity is no natural virtue, and that promises have no force antecedent to human conventions.

If anyone dissent from this, he must give a regular proof of

---

termination. It is impossible, therefore, we could ever will a new obligation, and consequently it is impossible the will could ever accompany a promise or produce a new obligation of morality.

these two propositions, *viz., that there is a peculiar act of the mind annexed to promises,* and *that consequent to this act of the mind there arises an inclination to perform, distinct from a sense of duty.* I presume that it is impossible to prove either of these two points, and therefore I venture to conclude that promises are human inventions, founded on the necessities and interests of society.

In order to discover these necessities and interests, we must consider the same qualities of human nature which we have already found to give rise to the preceding laws of society. Men being naturally selfish or endowed only with a confined generosity, they are not easily induced to perform any action for the interest of strangers except with a view to some reciprocal advantage which they had no hope of obtaining but by such a performance. Now as it frequently happens that these mutual performances cannot be finished at the same instant, it is necessary that one party be contented to remain in uncertainty and depend upon the gratitude of the other for a return of kindness. But so much corruption is there among men that, generally speaking, this becomes but a slender security, and as the benefactor is here supposed to bestow his favors with a view to self-interest, this both takes off from the obligation and sets an example of selfishness, which is the true mother of ingratitude. Were we, therefore, to follow the natural course of our passions and inclinations, we should perform but few actions for the advantage of others from disinterested views, because we are naturally very limited in our kindness and affection. And we should perform as few of that kind out of a regard to interest, because we cannot depend upon their gratitude. Here then is the mutual commerce of good offices in a manner lost among mankind, and everyone reduced to his own skill and industry for his well-being and subsistence. The invention of the law of nature concerning the *stability* of possession has already rendered men tolerable to each other; that of the *transference* of property and possession by consent has begun to render them mutually advantageous. But still these laws of nature, however strictly observed, are not sufficient to render them so serviceable to each other as by nature they are fitted to become. Though possession be *stable,* men may often reap but small advantage from it, while they are possessed of a greater quantity of any species of goods than they have occasion for and at the same time suffer by the want of others. The *transference* of property, which is the proper remedy for this inconvenience, cannot remedy it entirely, because it can only take place with regard to such objects as are *present* and *individual,* but not to such as are *absent* or *general.* One cannot transfer the property of a particular house twenty leagues distant, because the consent cannot be attended with delivery, which is a requisite circumstance. Neither can one transfer the property of ten bushels of corn or five hogsheads of wine by the mere expression and consent, because these are only general terms and have no direct relation to any particular heap of corn or barrels of wine. Besides, the commerce of mankind is not confined to the barter of commodities, but may extend to services and actions which we may exchange to our mutual interest and advantage. Your corn is ripe today; mine will be so tomorrow. It is profitable for us both that I should labor with you today and that you should aid me tomorrow. I have no kindness for you and know you have as little for me. I will not, therefore, take any pains upon your account, and should I labor with you upon my own account, in expectation of a return, I know I should be disappointed, and that I should in vain depend upon your gratitude. Here then I leave you to labor alone; you treat me in the same manner. The seasons change, and both of us lose our harvests for want of mutual confidence and security.

All this is the effect of the natural and inherent principles and passions of human nature; and as these passions and principles are unalterable, it may be thought that our conduct which depends on them must be so too, and that it would be in vain, either for moralists or politicians, to tamper with us or attempt to change the usual course of our actions with a view to public interest. And indeed, did the success of their designs depend upon their success in correcting the selfishness and ingratitude of men, they would never make any progress unless aided by omnipotence, which is alone able to new-mold the human mind and change its character in such fundamental articles. All they can pretend to is to give a new direction to those natural passions, and teach us that we can better satisfy our appetites in an oblique and artificial manner than by their headlong and impetuous motion. Hence I learn to do a service to another without bearing him any real kindness, because I foresee that he will return my service in expectation of another of the same kind, and in order to maintain the same correspondence of good offices with me or with others. And accordingly, after I have served him and he is in possession of the advantage arising from my action, he is induced to perform his part, as foreseeing the consequences of his refusal.

But though this self-interested commerce of men begins to take place and to predominate in society, it does not entirely abolish the more generous and noble intercourse of friendship and good offices. I may still do services to such persons as I love and am more particularly acquainted with without any prospect of advantage, and they may make me a return in the same manner without any view but that of recompensing my past services. In order, therefore, to distinguish those two different sorts of commerce, the interested and the disinterested, there is a *certain form of words* invented for the former, by which we bind ourselves to the performance of any action. This form of words constitutes what we call a *promise*, which is the sanction of the interested commerce of mankind. When a man says *he promises anything*, he in effect expresses a *resolution* of performing it, and along with that, by making use of this *form of words*, subjects himself to the penalty of never being trusted again in case of failure. A resolution is the natural act of the mind which promises express, but were there no more than a resolution in the case, promises would only declare our former motives and would not create any new motive or obligation. They are the conventions of men which create a new motive, when experience has taught us that human affairs would be conducted much more for mutual advantage were there certain *symbols* or *signs* instituted by which we might give each other security of our conduct in any particular incident. After these signs are instituted, whoever uses them is immediately bound by his interest to execute his engagements, and must never expect to be trusted any more if he refuse to perform what he promised.

Nor is that knowledge which is requisite to make mankind sensible of this interest in the *institution* and *observance* of promises to be esteemed superior to the capacity of human nature, however savage and uncultivated. There needs but a very little practice of the world to make us perceive all these consequences and advantages. The shortest experience of society discovers them to every mortal, and when each individual perceives the same sense of interest in all his fellows, he immediately performs his part of any contract, as being assured that they will not be wanting in theirs. All of them, by concert, enter into a scheme of actions calculated for common benefit, and agree to be true to their word, nor is there anything requisite to form this concert or convention but that everyone have a sense of interest in the faithful fulfilling of engagements, and express that sense to other members of the society. This immediately causes that interest to operate upon them, and interest is the *first* obligation to the performance of promises.

Afterwards a sentiment of morals concurs with interest and becomes a new obligation upon mankind. This sentiment of morality in the performance of promises arises from the same principles as that in the abstinence from the property of others. *Public interest, education,* and *the artifices of politicians* have the same effect in both cases. The difficulties that occur to us in supposing a moral obligation to attend promises, we either surmount or elude. For instance, the expression of a resolution is not commonly supposed to be obligatory, and we cannot readily conceive how the making use of a certain form of words should be able to cause any material difference. Here, therefore, we *feign* a new act of the mind which we call the *willing* an obligation, and on this we suppose the morality to depend. But we have proved already that there is no such act of the mind, and consequently that promises impose no natural obligation.

To confirm this, we may subjoin some other reflections concerning that will which is supposed to enter into a promise and to cause its obligation. It is evident that the will alone is never supposed to cause the obligation, but must be expressed by words or signs in order to impose a tie upon any man. The expression, being once brought in as subservient to the will, soon becomes the principal part of the promise, nor will a man be less bound by his word, though he secretly give a different direction to his intention and withhold himself both from a resolution and from willing an obligation. But though the expression makes on most occasions the whole of the promise, yet it does not always so, and one who should make use of any expression of which he knows not the meaning and which he uses without any intention of binding himself would not certainly be bound by it. Nay, though he knows its meaning, yet if he uses it in jest only and with such signs as show evidently he has no serious intention of binding himself, he would not lie under any obligation of performance; but it is necessary that the words be a perfect expression of the will, without any contrary signs. Nay, even this we must not carry so far as to imagine that one whom, by our quickness of understanding, we conjecture, from certain signs, to have an intention of deceiving us is not bound by his expression or verbal promise if we accept of it, but must limit this conclusion to those cases where the signs are of a different kind from those of deceit. All these contradictions are easily accounted for if the obligation of promises be merely a human invention for the convenience of society, but will never be explained if it be something *real* and *natural,* arising from any action of the mind or body.

. . . . .

Part III.
OF THE OTHER VIRTUES AND VICES

——— • ◆ • ———

Section I.

OF THE ORIGIN OF THE NATURAL
VIRTUES AND VICES

WE COME NOW to the examination of such virtues and vices as are entirely natural, and have no dependence on the artifice and contrivance of men. The examination of these will conclude this system of morals.

The chief spring or actuating principle of the human mind is pleasure or pain, and when these sensations are removed both from our thought and feeling we are, in a great measure, incapable of passion or action, of desire or volition. The most immediate effects of pleasure and pain are the propense and averse motions of the mind, which are diversified into volition, into desire and aversion, grief and joy, hope and fear, according as the pleasure or pain changes its situation and becomes probable or improbable, certain or uncertain, or is considered as out of our power for the present moment. But when along with this the objects that cause pleasure or pain acquire a relation to ourselves or others, they still continue to excite desire and aversion, grief and joy, but cause at the same time the indirect passions of pride or humility, love or hatred, which in this case have a double relation of impressions and ideas to the pain or pleasure.

We have already observed that moral distinctions depend entirely on certain peculiar sentiments of pain and pleasure, and that whatever mental quality in ourselves or others gives us a satisfaction by the survey or reflection is of course virtuous, as everything of this nature that gives uneasiness is vicious. Now since every quality in ourselves or others which gives pleasure always causes pride or love, as every one that produces uneasiness excites humility or hatred, it follows that these two particulars are to be considered as equivalent with regard to our mental qualities, *virtue* and the power of producing love or pride, *vice* and the power of producing humility or hatred. In every case, therefore, we must judge of the one by the other, and may pronounce any *quality* of the mind virtuous which causes love or pride, and any one vicious which causes hatred or humility.

If any *action* be either virtuous or vicious, it is only as a sign of some quality or character. It must depend upon durable principles of the mind which extend over the whole conduct and enter into the personal character. Actions themselves, not proceeding from any constant principle, have no influence on love or hatred, pride or humility, and consequently are never considered in morality.

This reflection is self-evident and deserves to be attended to, as being of the utmost importance in the present subject. We are never to consider any single action in our inquiries concerning the origin of morals, but only the quality or character from which the action proceeded. These alone are *durable* enough to affect our sentiments concerning the person. Actions are, indeed, better indications of a character than words, or even wishes and sentiments, but it is only so far as they are such indications that they are attended with love or hatred, praise or blame.

To discover the true origin of morals and of that love or hatred which arises from mental qualities, we must take the matter pretty deep, and compare some principles which have been already examined and explained.

We may begin with considering anew the nature and force of *sympathy*. The minds of all men are similar in their feelings and operations, nor can anyone be actuated by an affection of which all others are not, in some degree, susceptible. As in strings equally wound up, the motion of one communicates itself to the rest, so all the affections readily pass from one person to another, and beget correspondent movements in every human creature. When I see the *effects* of passion in the voice and gesture of any person, my mind immediately passes from these effects to their causes, and forms such a lively idea of the passion as is presently converted into the passion itself. In like manner, when I perceive the *causes* of any emotion, my mind is conveyed to the effects, and is actuated with a like emotion. Were I present at any of the more terrible operations of surgery, it is certain that even before it began, the preparation of the instruments, the laying of the bandages in order, the heating of the irons, with all the signs of anxiety and concern in the patients and assistants, would have a great effect upon my mind, and excite the strongest sentiments of pity and terror. No passion of another discovers itself immediately to the mind. We are only sensible of its causes or effects. From *these* we infer the passion, and consequently *these* give rise to our sympathy.

Our sense of beauty depends very much on this principle; and where any object has a tendency to produce pleasure in its possessor, it is always regarded as beautiful, as every object that has a tendency to produce pain is disagreeable and deformed. Thus the convenience of a house, the fertility of a field, the strength of a horse, the capacity, security, and swift-sailing of a vessel, form the principal beauty of these several objects. Here the object which is denominated beautiful pleases only by its tendency to produce a certain effect. That effect is the pleasure or advantage of some other person. Now the pleasure of a stranger for whom we have no friendship pleases us only by sympathy. To this principle, therefore, is owing the beauty which we find in everything that is useful. How considerable a part this is of beauty will easily appear upon reflection. Wherever an object has a tendency to produce pleasure in the possessor, or in other words is the proper *cause* of pleasure, it is sure to please the spectator by a delicate sympathy with the possessor. Most of the works of art are esteemed beautiful in proportion to their fitness for the use of man, and even many of the productions of nature derive their beauty from that source. Handsome and beautiful, on most occasions, is not an absolute but a relative quality, and pleases us by nothing but its tendency to produce an end that is agreeable.[1]

The same principle produces, in many instances, our senti-

[1] [Hume's note to this passage, a quotation from Quintilian's *Institutione Oratoria*, Bk. viii, has been omitted from this edition.—Ed.]

ments of morals, as well as those of beauty. No virtue is more esteemed than justice, and no vice more detested than injustice; nor are there any qualities which go further towards fixing the character either as amiable or odious. Now justice is a moral virtue merely because it has that tendency to the good of mankind, and indeed is nothing but an artificial invention to that purpose. The same may be said of allegiance, of the laws of nations, of modesty, and of good manners. All these are mere human contrivances for the interest of society. And since there is a very strong sentiment of morals which in all nations and all ages has attended them, we must allow that the reflecting on the tendency of characters and mental qualities is sufficient to give us the sentiments of approbation and blame. Now as the means to an end can only be agreeable where the end is agreeable, and as the good of society, where our own interest is not concerned or that of our friends, pleases only by sympathy, it follows that sympathy is the source of the esteem which we pay to all the artificial virtues.

Thus it appears *that* sympathy is a very powerful principle in human nature, *that* it has a great influence on our taste of beauty, and *that* it produces our sentiment of morals in all the artificial virtues. From thence we may presume that it also gives rise to many of the other virtues, and that qualities acquire our approbation because of their tendency to the good of mankind. This presumption must become a certainty when we find that most of those qualities which we *naturally* approve of have actually that tendency and render a man a proper member of society, while the qualities which we *naturally* disapprove of have a contrary tendency and render any intercourse with the person dangerous or disagreeable. For having found that such tendencies have force enough to produce the strongest sentiment of morals, we can never reasonably, in these cases, look for any other cause of approbation or blame, it being an inviolable maxim in philosophy that where any particular cause is sufficient for an effect we ought to rest satisfied with it, and ought not to multiply causes without necessity. We have happily attained experiments in the artificial virtues, where the tendency of qualities to the good of society is the *sole* cause of our approbation, without any suspicion of the concurrence of another principle. From thence we learn the force of that principle. And where that principle may take place and the quality approved of is really beneficial to society, a true philosopher will never require any other principle to account for the strongest approbation and esteem.

That many of the natural virtues have this tendency to the good of society no one can doubt of. Meekness, beneficence, charity, generosity, clemency, moderation, equity bear the greatest figure among the moral qualities, and are commonly denominated the *social* virtues to mark their tendency to the good of society. This goes so far that some philosophers have represented all moral distinctions as the effect of artifice and education, when skillful politicians endeavored to restrain the turbulent passions of men and make them operate to the public good by the notions of honor and shame. This system, however, is not consistent with experience. For, *first*, there are other virtues and vices beside those which have this tendency to the public advantage and loss. *Secondly*, had not men a natural sentiment of approbation and blame it could never be excited by politicians, nor would the words *laudable* and *praiseworthy*, *blamable* and *odious*, be any more intelligible than if they were a language perfectly unknown to us, as we have already observed. But though this system be erroneous, it may teach us that moral distinctions arise, in a great measure, from the tendency of qualities and characters to the interests of society, and that it is our concern for that interest which makes us approve or disapprove of them. Now we have no such extensive concern for society but from sympathy, and consequently it is that principle which takes us so far out of ourselves as to give us the same pleasure or uneasiness in the characters of others as if they had a tendency to our own advantage or loss.

The only difference between the natural virtues and justice lies in this, that the good which results from the former arises from every single act and is the object of some natural passion, whereas a single act of justice, considered in itself, may often be contrary to the public good, and it is only the concurrence of mankind in a general scheme or system of action which is advantageous. When I relieve persons in distress, my natural humanity is my motive; and so far as my succor extends, so far have I promoted the happiness of my fellow-creatures. But if we examine all the questions that come before any tribunal of justice we shall find that, considering each case apart, it would as often be an instance of humanity to decide contrary to the laws of justice as conformable to them. Judges take from a poor man to give to a rich; they bestow on the dissolute the labor of the industrious, and put into the hands of the vicious the means of harming both themselves and others. The whole scheme, however, of law and justice is advantageous to the society, and it was with a view to this advantage that men, by their voluntary conventions, established it. After it is once established by these conventions, it is *naturally* attended with a strong sentiment of morals, which can proceed from nothing but our sympathy with the interests of society. We need no other explication of that esteem which attends such of the natural virtues as have a tendency to the public good.

I must further add that there are several circumstances which render this hypothesis much more probable with regard to the natural than the artificial virtues. It is certain that the imagination is more affected by what is particular than by what is general, and that the sentiments are always moved with difficulty where their objects are, in any degree, loose and undetermined. Now every particular act of justice is not beneficial to society, but the whole scheme or system; and it may not, perhaps, be any individual person for whom we are concerned who receives benefit from justice, but the whole society alike. On the contrary, every particular act of generosity, or relief of the industrious and indigent, is beneficial, and is beneficial to a particular person who is not undeserving of it. It is more natural, therefore, to think that the tendencies of the latter virtue will affect our sentiments and command our approbation than those of the former; and therefore, since we find that the approbation of the former arises from their tendencies, we may ascribe, with better reason, the same cause to the approbation of the latter. In any number of similar effects, if a cause can be discovered for one, we ought to extend that cause to all the other effects which can be accounted for by it; but much more if these other effects be attended with peculiar circumstances which facilitate the operation of that cause.

Before I proceed further, I must observe two remarkable circumstances in this affair which may seem objections to the present system. The first may be thus explained. When any quality or character has a tendency to the good of mankind, we are pleased with it and approve of it, because it presents the lively idea of pleasure, which idea affects us by sympathy and is itself a kind of pleasure. But as this sympathy is very variable, it may be thought that our sentiments of morals must admit of all the same variations. We sympathize more with persons contiguous to us than with persons remote from us, with our acquaintances than with strangers, with our countrymen than with foreigners. But notwithstanding this variation of our sympathy, we give the same approbation to the same moral qualities in *China* as in *England*. They appear equally virtuous and recommend themselves equally to the esteem of a judicious spectator. The sympathy varies without a variation in our esteem. Our esteem, therefore, proceeds not from sympathy.

To this I answer: the approbation of moral qualities most certainly is not derived from reason or any comparison of ideas, but proceeds entirely from a moral taste and from certain sentiments of pleasure or disgust which arise upon the contemplation and view of particular qualities or characters. Now it is evident that those sentiments, whence-ever they are derived, must vary according to the distance or contiguity of the objects, nor can I feel the same lively pleasure from the virtues of a person who lived in *Greece* two thousand years ago that I feel from the virtues of a familiar friend and acquaintance. Yet I do not say that I esteem the one more than the other; and therefore, if the variation of the sentiment without a variation of the esteem be an objection, it must have equal force against every other system as against that of sympathy. But to consider the matter aright, it has no force at all, and it is the easiest matter in the world to account for it. Our situation with regard both to persons and things is in continual fluctuation, and a man that lies at a distance from us may, in a little time, become a familiar ac-

288 THE PHILOSOPHY OF DAVID HUME

quaintance. Besides, every particular man has a peculiar position with regard to others, and it is impossible we could ever converse together on any reasonable terms were each of us to consider characters and persons only as they appear from his peculiar point of view. In order, therefore, to prevent those continual *contradictions* and arrive at a more *stable* judgment of things, we fix on some *steady* and *general* points of view, and always, in our thoughts, place ourselves in them, whatever may be our present situation. In like manner, external beauty is determined merely by pleasure, and it is evident a beautiful countenance cannot give so much pleasure when seen at the distance of twenty paces as when it is brought nearer us. We say not, however, that it appears to us less beautiful, because we know what effect it will have in such a position, and by that reflection we correct its momentary appearance.

In general, all sentiments of blame or praise are variable, according to our situation of nearness or remoteness with regard to the person blamed or praised, and according to the present disposition of our mind. But these variations we regard not in our general decisions, but still apply the terms expressive of our liking or dislike in the same manner as if we remained in one point of view. Experience soon teaches us this method of correcting our sentiments, or at least of correcting our language, where the sentiments are more stubborn and inalterable. Our servant, if diligent and faithful, may excite stronger sentiments of love and kindness than *Marcus Brutus*, as represented in history, but we say not upon that account that the former character is more laudable than the latter. We know that were we to approach equally near to that renowned patriot he would command a much higher degree of affection and admiration. Such corrections are common with regard to all the senses, and indeed it were impossible we could ever make use of language or communicate our sentiments to one another did we not correct the momentary appearances of things and overlook our present situation.

It is therefore from the influence of characters and qualities upon those who have an intercourse with any person that we blame or praise him. We consider not whether the persons affected by the qualities be our acquaintances or strangers, countrymen or foreigners. Nay, we overlook our own interest in those general judgments, and blame not a man for opposing us in any of our pretensions when his own interest is particularly concerned. We make allowance for a certain degree of selfishness in men, because we know it to be inseparable from human nature and inherent in our frame and constitution. By this reflection we correct those sentiments of blame which so naturally arise upon any opposition.

But however the general principle of our blame or praise may be corrected by those other principles, it is certain they are not altogether efficacious, nor do our passions often correspond entirely to the present theory. It is seldom men heartily love what lies at a distance from them and what no way redounds to their particular benefit, as it is no less rare to meet with persons who can pardon another any opposition he makes to their interest, however justifiable that opposition may be by the general rules of morality. Here we are contented with saying that reason requires such an impartial conduct, but that it is seldom we can bring ourselves to it, and that our passions do not readily follow the determination of our judgment. This language will be easily understood if we consider what we formerly said concerning that *reason* which is able to oppose our passion, and which we have found to be nothing but a general calm determination of the passions founded on some distant view or reflection. When we form our judgments of persons merely from the tendency of their characters to our own benefit or to that of our friends, we find so many contradictions to our sentiments in society and conversation and such an uncertainty from the incessant changes of our situation that we seek some other standard of merit and demerit, which may not admit of so great variation. Being thus loosened from our first station, we cannot afterwards fix ourselves so commodiously by any means as by a sympathy with those who have any commerce with the person we consider. This is far from being as lively as when our own interest is concerned or that of our particular friends, nor has it such an influence on our love and hatred. But being equally conformable to our calm and general principles, it is said to have an equal authority over our reason and to command our judgment and opinion. We blame equally a bad action which we read of in history with one performed in our neighborhood the other day, the meaning of which is that we know from reflection that the former action would excite as strong sentiments of disapprobation as the latter, were it placed in the same position.

I now proceed to the *second* remarkable circumstance which I proposed to take notice of. Where a person is possessed of a character that in its natural tendency is beneficial to society, we esteem him virtuous and are delighted with the view of his character, even though particular accidents prevent its operation and incapacitate him from being serviceable to his friends and country. Virtue in rags is still virtue, and the love which it procures attends a man into a dungeon or desert, where the virtue can no longer be exerted in action and is lost to all the world. Now this may be esteemed an objection to the present system. Sympathy interests us in the good of mankind, and if sympathy were the source of our esteem for virtue, that sentiment of approbation could only take place where the virtue actually attained its end and was beneficial to mankind. Where it fails of its end, it is only an imperfect means, and therefore can never acquire any merit from that end. The goodness of an end can bestow a merit on such means alone as are complete and actually produce the end.

To this we may reply that where any object, in all its parts, is fitted to attain any agreeable end, it naturally gives us pleasure and is esteemed beautiful even though some external circumstances be wanting to render it altogether effectual. It is sufficient if everything be complete in the object itself. A house that is contrived with great judgment for all the commodities of life pleases us upon that account, though perhaps we are sensible that no one will ever dwell in it. A fertile soil and a happy climate delight us by a reflection on the happiness which they would afford the inhabitants, though at present the country be desert and uninhabited. A man whose limbs and shape promise strength and activity is esteemed handsome, though condemned to perpetual imprisonment. The imagination has a set of passions belonging to it upon which our sentiments of beauty much depend. These passions are moved by degrees of liveliness and strength which are inferior to *belief,* and independent of the real existence of their objects. Where a character is in every respect fitted to be beneficial to society, the imagination passes easily from the cause to the effect, without considering that there are still some circumstances wanting to render the cause a complete one. *General rules* create a species of probability which sometimes influences the judgment, and always the imagination.

It is true, when the cause is complete and a good disposition is attended with good fortune, which renders it really beneficial to society, it gives a stronger pleasure to the spectator and is attended with a more lively sympathy. We are more affected by it, and yet we do not say that it is more virtuous or that we esteem it more. We know that an alteration of fortune may render the benevolent disposition entirely impotent and therefore we separate, as much as possible, the fortune from the disposition. The case is the same as when we correct the different sentiments of virtue which proceed from its different distances from ourselves. The passions do not always follow our corrections, but these corrections serve sufficiently to regulate our abstract notions, and are alone regarded when we pronounce in general concerning the degrees of vice and virtue.

It is observed by critics that all words or sentences which are difficult to the pronunciation are disagreeable to the ear. There is no difference whether a man hear them pronounced or read them silently to himself. When I run over a book with my eye, I imagine I hear it all, and also, by the force of imagination, enter into the uneasiness which the delivery of it would give the speaker. The uneasiness is not real, but as such a composition of words has a natural tendency to produce it, this is sufficient to affect the mind with a painful sentiment and render the discourse harsh and disagreeable. It is a similar case where any real quality is, by accidental circumstances, rendered impotent, and is deprived of its natural influence on society.

Upon these principles we may easily remove any contradiction which may appear to be between the *extensive sympathy* on which our sentiments of virtue depend, and that *limited generosity* which I have frequently observed to be natural to men, and which justice and property suppose, according to the precedent reasoning. My sympathy with another may give me the sentiment of pain and disapprobation when any object is presented that has a tendency to give him uneasiness, though I may not be willing to sacrifice anything of my own interest or cross any of my passions for his satisfaction. A house may displease me by being ill-contrived for the convenience of the owner, and yet I may refuse to give a shilling towards the rebuilding of it. Sentiments must touch the heart to make them control our passions, but they need not extend beyond the imagination to make them influence our taste. When a building seems clumsy and tottering to the eye it is ugly and disagreeable, though we be fully assured of the solidity of the workmanship. It is a kind of fear which causes this sentiment of disapprobation, but the passion is not the same with that which we feel when obliged to stand under a wall that we really think tottering and insecure. The *seeming tendencies* of objects affect the mind, and the emotions they excite are of a like species with those which proceed from the *real consequences* of objects, but their feeling is different. Nay, these emotions are so different in their feeling that they may often be contrary without destroying each other, as when the fortifications of a city belonging to an enemy are esteemed beautiful upon account of their strength, though we could wish that they were entirely destroyed. The imagination adheres to the *general* views of things and distinguishes the feelings they produce from those which arise from our particular and momentary situation.

If we examine the panegyrics that are commonly made of great men, we shall find that most of the qualities which are attributed to them may be divided into two kinds, *viz.*, such as make them perform their part in society, and such as render them serviceable to themselves and enable them to promote their own interest. Their *prudence, temperance, frugality, industry, assiduity, enterprise, dexterity* are celebrated, as well as their *generosity* and *humanity*. If we ever give an indulgence to any quality that disables a man from making a figure in life, it is to that of *indolence*, which is not supposed to deprive one of his parts and capacity but only suspends their exercise, and that without any inconvenience to the person himself, since it is, in some measure, from his own choice. Yet indolence is always allowed to be a fault, and a very great one, if extreme; nor do a man's friends ever acknowledge him to be subject to it but in order to save his character in more material articles. He could make a figure, say they, if he pleased to give application. His understanding is sound, his conception quick, and his memory tenacious; but he hates business, and is indifferent about his fortune. And this a man sometimes may make even a subject of vanity, though with the air of confessing a fault, because he may think that this incapacity for business implies much more noble qualities, such as a philosophical spirit, a fine taste, a delicate wit, or a relish for pleasure and society. But take any other case; suppose a quality that, without being an indication of any other good qualities, incapacitates a man *always* for business and is destructive to his interest, such as a blundering understanding and a wrong judgment of everything in life, inconstancy and irresolution, or a want of address in the management of men and business. These are all allowed to be imperfections in a character, and many men would rather acknowledge the greatest crimes than have it suspected that they are, in any degree, subject to them.

It is very happy, in our philosophical researches, when we find the same phenomenon diversified by a variety of circumstances, and by discovering what is common among them can the better assure ourselves of the truth of any hypothesis we may make use of to explain it. Were nothing esteemed virtue but what were beneficial to society, I am persuaded that the foregoing explication of the moral sense ought still to be received, and that upon sufficient evidence. But this evidence must grow upon us when we find other kinds of virtue which will not admit of any explication except from that hypothesis. Here is a man who is not remarkably defective in his social qualities; but what principally recommends him is his dexterity in business, by which he has extricated himself from the greatest difficulties and conducted the most delicate affairs with a singular address and prudence. I find an esteem for him immediately to arise in me; his company is a satisfaction

to me, and before I have any further acquaintance with him,
I would rather do him a service than another whose character is in every other respect equal but is deficient in that
particular. In this case, the qualities that please me are all
considered as useful to the person and as having a tendency
to promote his interest and satisfaction. They are only regarded as means to an end, and please me in proportion to
their fitness for that end. The end, therefore, must be agreeable to me. But what makes the end agreeable? The person
is a stranger; I am no way interested in him, nor lie under
any obligation to him; his happiness concerns not me further
than the happiness of every human and indeed of every sensible creature: that is, it affects me only by sympathy. From
that principle, whenever I discover his happiness and good,
whether in its causes or effects, I enter so deeply into it that
it gives me a sensible emotion. The appearance of qualities
that have a *tendency* to promote it have an agreeable effect
upon my imagination, and command my love and esteem.

This theory may serve to explain why the same qualities,
in all cases, produce both pride and love, humility and hatred, and the same man is always virtuous or vicious, accomplished or despicable to others, who is so to himself. A person
in whom we discover any passion or habit which originally is
only incommodious to himself becomes always disagreeable
to us merely on its account, as on the other hand one whose
character is only dangerous and disagreeable to others can
never be satisfied with himself as long as he is sensible of
that disadvantage. Nor is this observable only with regard to
characters and manners, but may be remarked even in the
most minute circumstances. A violent cough in another gives
us uneasiness, though in itself it does not in the least affect
us. A man will be mortified if you tell him he has a stinking
breath, though it is evidently no annoyance to himself. Our
fancy easily changes its situation, and either surveying ourselves as we appear to others or considering others as they
feel themselves, we enter, by that means, into sentiments
which no way belong to us, and in which nothing but sympathy is able to interest us. And this sympathy we sometimes
carry so far as even to be displeased with a quality commodious to us merely because it displeases others and makes us

disagreeable in their eyes, though perhaps we never can have any interest in rendering ourselves agreeable to them.

There have been many systems of morality advanced by philosophers in all ages, but if they are strictly examined they may be reduced to two, which alone merit our attention. Moral good and evil are certainly distinguished by our *sentiments*, not by *reason*, but these sentiments may arise either from the mere species or appearance of characters and passions, or from reflections on their tendency to the happiness of mankind and of particular persons. My opinion is that both these causes are intermixed in our judgments of morals, after the same manner as they are in our decisions concerning most kinds of external beauty, though I am also of opinion that reflections on the tendencies of actions have by far the greatest influence and determine all the great lines of our duty. There are, however, instances, in cases of less moment, wherein this immediate taste or sentiment produces our approbation. Wit and a certain easy and disengaged behavior are qualities *immediately agreeable* to others, and command their love and esteem. Some of these qualities produce satisfaction in others by particular *original* principles of human nature which cannot be accounted for; others may be resolved into principles which are more general. This will best appear upon a particular inquiry.

As some qualities acquire their merit from their being *immediately agreeable* to others without any tendency to public interest, so some are denominated virtuous from their being *immediately agreeable* to the person himself who possesses them. Each of the passions and operations of the mind has a particular feeling, which must be either agreeable or disagreeable. The first is virtuous, the second vicious. This particular feeling constitutes the very nature of the passion, and therefore needs not be accounted for.

But however directly the distinction of vice and virtue may seem to flow from the immediate pleasure or uneasiness which particular qualities cause to ourselves or others, it is easy to observe that it has also a considerable dependence on the principle of *sympathy* so often insisted on. We approve of a person who is possessed of qualities *immediately agreeable* to those with whom he has any commerce, though perhaps we ourselves never reaped any pleasure from them. We also approve of one who is possessed of qualities that are *immediately agreeable* to himself, though they be of no service to any mortal. To account for this we must have recourse to the foregoing principles.

Thus, to take a general review of the present hypothesis, every quality of the mind is denominated virtuous which gives pleasure by the mere survey, as every quality which produces pain is called vicious. This pleasure and this pain may arise from four different sources. For we reap a pleasure from the view of a character which is naturally fitted to be useful to others, or to the person himself, or which is agreeable to others, or to the person himself. One may, perhaps, be surprised that amidst all these interests and pleasures we should forget our own, which touch us so nearly on every other occasion. But we shall easily satisfy ourselves on this head when we consider that, every particular person's pleasure and interest being different, it is impossible men could ever agree in their sentiments and judgments unless they chose some common point of view from which they might survey their object, and which might cause it to appear the same to all of them. Now, in judging of characters, the only interest or pleasure which appears the same to every spectator is that of the person himself whose character is examined, or that of persons who have a connection with him. And though such interests and pleasures touch us more faintly than our own, yet being more constant and universal, they counterbalance the latter even in practice, and are alone admitted in speculation as the standard of virtue and morality. They alone produce that particular feeling or sentiment on which moral distinctions depend.

As to the good or ill desert of virtue or vice, it is an evident consequence of the sentiments of pleasure or uneasiness. These sentiments produce love or hatred, and love or hatred, by the original constitution of human passion, is attended with benevolence or anger, that is, with a desire of making happy the person we love and miserable the person we hate. We have treated of this more fully on another occasion.

Section IV.

OF NATURAL ABILITIES

No distinction is more usual in all systems of ethics than that between *natural abilities* and *moral virtues,* where the former are placed on the same footing with bodily endowments and are supposed to have no merit or moral worth annexed to them. Whoever considers the matter accurately will find that a dispute upon this head would be merely a dispute of words, and that though these qualities are not altogether of the same kind, yet they agree in the most material circumstances. They are both of them equally mental qualities, and both of them equally produce pleasure and have of course an equal tendency to procure the love and esteem of mankind. There are few who are not as jealous of their character with regard to sense and knowledge as to honor and courage, and much more than with regard to temperance and sobriety. Men are even afraid of passing for good-natured lest *that* should be taken for want of understanding, and often boast of more debauches than they have been really engaged in to give themselves airs of fire and spirit. In short, the figure a man makes in the world, the reception he meets with in company, the esteem paid him by his acquaintances, all these advantages depend almost as much upon his good sense and judgment as upon any other part of his character. Let a man have the best intentions in the world and be the farthest from all injustice and violence, he will never be able to make himself be much regarded without a moderate share, at least, of parts and understanding. Since then natural abilities, though perhaps inferior, yet are on the same footing, both as to their causes and effects, with those qualities which we call moral virtues, why should we make any distinction between them?

Though we refuse to natural abilities the title of virtues, we must allow that they procure the love and esteem of mankind, that they give a new luster to the other virtues, and that a man possessed of them is much more entitled to our good will and services than one entirely void of them. It may, indeed, be pretended that the sentiment of approbation which those qualities produce, besides its being *inferior*, is also somewhat *different* from that which attends the other virtues. But this, in my opinion, is not a sufficient reason for excluding them from the catalogue of virtues. Each of the virtues, even benevolence, justice, gratitude, integrity, excites a different sentiment or feeling in the spectator. The characters of *Caesar* and *Cato*, as drawn by *Sallust*, are both of them virtuous in the strictest sense of the word, but in a different way; nor are the sentiments entirely the same which arise from them. The one produces love, the other esteem; the one is amiable, the other awful; we could wish to meet with the one character in a friend, the other character we would be ambitious of in ourselves. In like manner, the approbation which attends natural abilities may be somewhat different to the feeling from that which arises from the other virtues, without making them entirely of a different species. And indeed we may observe that the natural abilities, no more than the other virtues, produce not, all of them, the same kind of approbation. Good sense and genius beget esteem; wit and humor excite love.[1]

Those who represent the distinction between natural abilities and moral virtues as very material may say that the former are entirely involuntary, and have therefore no merit attending them, as having no dependence on liberty and free will. But to this I answer, *first*, that many of those qualities which all moralists, especially the ancients, comprehend under the title of moral virtues are equally involuntary and necessary with the qualities of the judgment and imagination. Of this nature are constancy, fortitude, magnanimity, and in short all the qualities which form the *great* man. I might say the same, in some degree, of the others, it being almost impossible for

[1] Love and esteem are at the bottom the same passions, and arise from like causes. The qualities that produce both are agreeable and give pleasure. But where this pleasure is severe and serious, or where its object is great and makes a strong impression, or where it produces any degree of humility and awe, in all these cases, the passion which arises from the pleasure is more properly denominated esteem than love. Benevolence attends both, but is connected with love in a more eminent degree.

the mind to change its character in any considerable article
or cure itself of a passionate or splenetic temper when they
are natural to it. The greater degree there is of these blamable qualities, the more vicious they become, and yet they
are the less voluntary. *Secondly,* I would have anyone give
me a reason why virtue and vice may not be involuntary, as
well as beauty and deformity. These moral distinctions arise
from the natural distinctions of pain and pleasure, and when
we receive those feelings from the general consideration of
any quality or character, we denominate it vicious or virtuous.
Now I believe no one will assert that a quality can never produce pleasure or pain to the person who considers it unless it
be perfectly voluntary in the person who possesses it. *Thirdly,*
as to free will, we have shown that it has no place with regard
to the actions, no more than the qualities of men. It is not a
just consequence that what is voluntary is free. Our actions
are more voluntary than our judgments, but we have not
more liberty in the one than in the other.

But though this distinction between voluntary and involuntary be not sufficient to justify the distinction between natural abilities and moral virtues, yet the former distinction will
afford us a plausible reason why moralists have invented the
latter. Men have observed that though natural abilities and
moral qualities be in the main on the same footing, there is,
however, this difference between them, that the former are
almost invariable by any art or industry, while the latter, or
at least the actions that proceed from them, may be changed
by the motives of rewards and punishments, praise and blame.
Hence legislators and divines and moralists have principally
applied themselves to the regulating of these voluntary actions, and have endeavored to produce additional motives for
being virtuous in that particular. They knew that to punish a
man for folly or exhort him to be prudent and sagacious would
have but little effect, though the same punishments and exhortations with regard to justice and injustice might have a
considerable influence. But as men in common life and conversation do not carry those ends in view, but naturally praise or
blame whatever pleases or displeases them, they do not seem
much to regard this distinction, but consider prudence under
the character of virtue as well as benevolence, and penetra-

tion as well as justice. Nay, we find that all moralists whose judgment is not perverted by a strict adherence to a system enter into the same way of thinking, and that the ancient moralists in particular made no scruple of placing prudence at the head of the cardinal virtues. There is a sentiment of esteem and approbation which may be excited in some degree by any faculty of the mind in its perfect state and condition, and to account for this sentiment is the business of *Philosophers*. It belongs to *Grammarians* to examine what qualities are entitled to the denomination of *virtue;* nor will they find, upon trial, that this is so easy a task as at first sight they may be apt to imagine.

. . . . .

Section VI.

CONCLUSION OF THIS BOOK

Thus upon the whole I am hopeful that nothing is wanting to an accurate proof of this system of ethics. We are certain that sympathy is a very powerful principle in human nature. We are also certain that it has a great influence on our sense of beauty when we regard external objects as well as when we judge of morals. We find that it has force sufficient to give us the strongest sentiments of approbation when it operates alone without the concurrence of any other principle, as in the cases of justice, allegiance, chastity, and good manners. We may observe that all the circumstances requisite for its operation are found in most of the virtues which have, for the most part, a tendency to the good of society, or to that of the person possessed of them. If we compare all these circumstances we shall not doubt that sympathy is the chief source of moral distinctions, especially when we reflect that no objection can be raised against this hypothesis in one case which will not extend to all cases. Justice is certainly approved of for no other reason than because it has a tendency to the public good, and the public good is indifferent to us except so far as

sympathy interests us in it. We may presume the like with regard to all the other virtues which have a like tendency to the
public good. They must derive all their merit from our sympathy with those who reap any advantage from them, as the
virtues which have a tendency to the good of the person possessed of them derive their merit from our sympathy with
him.

Most people will readily allow that the useful qualities of
the mind are virtuous because of their utility. This way of
thinking is so natural and occurs on so many occasions that
few will make any scruple of admitting it. Now this being
once admitted, the force of sympathy must necessarily be acknowledged. Virtue is considered as means to an end. Means
to an end are only valued so far as the end is valued. But
the happiness of strangers affects us by sympathy alone. To
that principle, therefore, we are to ascribe the sentiment of
approbation which arises from the survey of all those virtues
that are useful to society or to the person possessed of them.
These form the most considerable part of morality.

Were it proper in such a subject to bribe the reader's assent or employ anything but solid argument, we are here
abundantly supplied with topics to engage the affections. All
lovers of virtue (and such we all are in speculation, however
we may degenerate in practice) must certainly be pleased
to see moral distinctions derived from so noble a source,
which gives us a just notion both of the *generosity* and *capacity* of human nature. It requires but very little knowledge
of human affairs to perceive that a sense of morals is a principle inherent in the soul, and one of the most powerful that
enters into the composition. But this sense must certainly acquire new force when reflecting on itself it approves of those
principles from whence it is derived, and finds nothing but
what is great and good in its rise and origin. Those who resolve the sense of morals into original instincts of the human
mind may defend the cause of virtue with sufficient authority,
but want the advantage which those possess who account for
that sense by an extensive sympathy with mankind. According to their system, not only virtue must be approved of but

also the sense of virtue, and not only that sense but also the principles from whence it is derived. So that nothing is presented on any side but what is laudable and good.

This observation may be extended to justice and the other virtues of that kind. Though justice be artificial, the sense of its morality is natural. It is the combination of men in a system of conduct which renders any act of justice beneficial to society. But when once it has that tendency we *naturally* approve of it, and if we did not so, it is impossible any combination or convention could ever produce that sentiment.

Most of the inventions of men are subject to change. They depend upon humor and caprice. They have a vogue for a time, and then sink into oblivion. It may, perhaps, be apprehended that if justice were allowed to be a human invention, it must be placed on the same footing. But the cases are widely different. The interest on which justice is founded is the greatest imaginable, and extends to all times and places. It cannot possibly be served by any other invention. It is obvious and discovers itself on the very first formation of society. All these causes render the rules of justice steadfast and immutable, at least as immutable as human nature. And if they were founded on original instincts, could they have any greater stability?

The same system may help us to form a just notion of the *happiness* as well as of the *dignity* of virtue, and may interest every principle of our nature in the embracing and cherishing that noble quality. Who indeed does not feel an accession of alacrity in his pursuits of knowledge and ability of every kind when he considers that besides the advantages which immediately result from these acquisitions, they also give him a new luster in the eyes of mankind, and are universally attended with esteem and approbation? And who can think any advantages of fortune a sufficient compensation for the least breach of the *social* virtues, when he considers that not only his character with regard to others but also his peace and inward satisfaction entirely depend upon his strict observance of them, and that a mind will never be able to bear its own survey that has been wanting in its part to mankind and society? But I forbear insisting on this subject. Such reflections require a work apart, very different from the genius of the present. The anatomist ought never to emulate the painter, nor in his accurate dissections and portraitures of the smaller parts of the human body pretend to give his figures any graceful and engaging attitude or expression. There is even something hideous or at least minute in the views of things which he presents, and it is necessary the objects should be set more at a distance and be more covered up from sight to make them engaging to the eye and imagination. An anatomist, however, is admirably fitted to give advice to a painter, and it is even impracticable to excel in the latter art without the assistance of the former. We must have an exact knowledge of the parts, their situation and connection, before we can design with any elegance or correctness. And thus the most abstract speculations concerning human nature, however cold and unentertaining, become subservient to *practical morality,* and may render this latter science more correct in its precepts and more persuasive in its exhortations.

APPENDIX

THERE IS NOTHING I would more willingly lay hold of than an opportunity of confessing my errors, and should esteem such a return to truth and reason to be more honorable than the most unerring judgment. A man who is free from mistakes can pretend to no praises, except from the justness of his understanding, but a man who corrects his mistakes shows at once the justness of his understanding and the candor and ingenuity of his temper. I have not yet been so fortunate as to discover any very considerable mistakes in the reasonings delivered in the preceding volumes, except on one article. But I have found by experience that some of my expressions have not been so well chosen as to guard against all mistakes in the readers, and it is chiefly to remedy this defect I have subjoined the following appendix.

We can never be induced to believe any matter of fact except where its cause, or its effect, is present to us, but what the nature is of that belief which arises from the relation of cause and effect, few have had the curiosity to ask themselves. In my opinion this dilemma is inevitable. Either the belief is some new idea, such as that of *reality* or *existence,* which we join to the simple conception of an object, or it is merely a peculiar *feeling* or *sentiment.* That it is not a new idea annexed to the simple conception may be evinced from these two arguments. *First,* we have no abstract idea of existence, distinguishable and separable from the idea of particular objects. It is impossible, therefore, that this idea of existence can be annexed to the idea of any object, or form the difference between a simple conception and belief. *Secondly,* the mind has the command over all its ideas, and can separate, unite, mix, and vary them as it pleases, so that if belief consisted merely in a new idea, annexed to the conception, it would be in a man's power to believe what he pleased. We may, there-fore, conclude that belief consists merely in a certain feeling or sentiment, in something that depends not on the will, but must arise from certain determinate causes and principles of which we are not masters. When we are convinced of any matter of fact, we do nothing but conceive it, along with a certain feeling, different from what attends the mere *reveries* of the imagination. And when we express our incredulity con-cerning any fact, we mean that the arguments for the fact produce not that feeling. Did not the belief consist in a senti-ment different from our mere conception, whatever objects were presented by the wildest imagination would be on an equal footing with the most established truths founded on history and experience. There is nothing but the feeling or sentiment to distinguish the one from the other.

This, therefore, being regarded as an undoubted truth, *that belief is nothing but a peculiar feeling, different from the simple conception,* the next question that naturally occurs is *what is the nature of this feeling or sentiment, and whether it be analogous to any other sentiment of the human mind?* This question is important. For if it be not analogous to any other sentiment, we must despair of explaining its causes, and must consider it as an original principle of the human mind. If it be analogous, we may hope to explain its causes from analogy, and trace it up to more general principles. Now that there is a greater firmness and solidity in the conceptions which are the objects of conviction and assurance than in the loose and indolent reveries of a castle-builder, everyone will readily own. They strike upon us with more force; they are more present to us; the mind has a firmer hold of them, and is more actuated and moved by them. It acquiesces in them, and, in a manner, fixes and reposes itself on them. In short, they approach nearer to the impressions which are immedi-ately present to us, and are therefore analogous to many other operations of the mind.

There is not, in my opinion, any possibility of evading this conclusion but by asserting that belief, beside the simple conception, consists in some impression or feeling, distinguishable from the conception. It does not modify the conception and render it more present and intense; it is only annexed to it, after the same manner that *will* and *desire* are annexed to particular conceptions of good and pleasure. But the following considerations will, I hope, be sufficient to remove this hypothesis. *First,* it is directly contrary to experience and our immediate consciousness. All men have ever allowed reasoning to be merely an operation of our thoughts or ideas, and however those ideas may be varied to the feeling, there is nothing ever enters into our *conclusions* but ideas, or our fainter conceptions. For instance, I hear at present a person's voice, whom I am acquainted with, and this sound comes from the next room. This impression of my senses immediately conveys my thoughts to the person, along with all the surrounding objects. I point them out to myself as existent at present, with the same qualities and relations that I formerly knew them possessed of. These ideas take faster hold of my mind than the ideas of an enchanted castle. They are different to the feeling, but there is no distinct or separate impression attending them. It is the same case when I recollect the several incidents of a journey or the events of any history. Every particular fact is there the object of belief. Its idea is modified differently from the loose reveries of a castle-builder. But no distinct impression attends every distinct idea, or conception of matter of fact. This is the subject of plain experience. If ever this experience can be disputed on any occasion, it is when the mind has been agitated with doubts and difficulties, and afterwards, upon taking the object in a new point of view, or being presented with a new argument, fixes and reposes itself in one settled conclusion and belief. In this case there is a feeling distinct and separate from the conception. The passage from doubt and agitation to tranquillity and repose conveys a satisfaction and pleasure to the mind. But take any other case. Suppose I see the legs and thighs of a person in motion, while some interposed object conceals the rest of his body. Here it is certain the imagination spreads out the whole figure. I give him a head and shoulders and breast and neck. These members I conceive and believe him to be possessed of. Nothing can be more evident than that this whole operation is performed by the thought or imagination alone. The transition is immediate. The ideas presently strike us. Their customary connection with the present impression varies them and modifies them in a certain manner, but produces no act of the mind distinct from this peculiarity of conception. Let anyone examine his own mind and he will evidently find this to be the truth.

Secondly, whatever may be the case with regard to this distinct impression, it must be allowed that the mind has a firmer hold or more steady conception of what it takes to be matter of fact than of fictions. Why then look any further, or multiply suppositions without necessity?

Thirdly, we can explain the *causes* of the firm conception, but not those of any separate impression. And not only so, but the causes of the firm conception exhaust the whole subject, and nothing is left to produce any other effect. An inference concerning a matter of fact is nothing but the idea of an object that is frequently conjoined or is associated with a present impression. This is the whole of it. Every part is requisite to explain, from analogy, the more steady conception, and nothing remains capable of producing any distinct impression.

Fourthly, the *effects* of belief in influencing the passions and imagination can all be explained from the firm conception, and there is no occasion to have recourse to any other principle. These arguments, with many others enumerated in the foregoing volumes, sufficiently prove that belief only modifies the idea or conception, and renders it different to the feeling, without producing any distinct impression.

Thus upon a general view of the subject, there appear to be two questions of importance which we may venture to recommend to the consideration of philosophers, *whether there be anything to distinguish belief from the simple conception beside the feeling or sentiment,* and *whether this feeling be anything but a firmer conception, or a faster hold, that we take of the object?*

If, upon impartial inquiry, the same conclusion that I have formed be assented to by philosophers, the next business is to examine the analogy which there is between belief and other acts of the mind, and find the cause of the firmness and strength of conception; and this I do not esteem a difficult task. The transition from a present impression always enlivens and strengthens any idea. When any object is presented, the idea of its usual attendant immediately strikes us, as something real and solid. It is *felt*, rather than conceived, and approaches the impression from which it is derived in its force and influence. This I have proved at large. I cannot add any new arguments, though perhaps my reasoning on this whole question concerning cause and effect would have been more convincing had the following passages been inserted in the places which I have marked for them. I have added a few illustrations on other points where I thought it necessary.[1]

. . . . .

I had entertained some hopes that however deficient our theory of the intellectual world might be, it would be free from those contradictions and absurdities which seem to attend every explication that human reason can give of the material world. But upon a more strict review of the section concerning *personal identity*, I find myself involved in such a labyrinth that, I must confess, I neither know how to correct my former opinions nor how to render them consistent. If this be not a good *general* reason for skepticism, it is at least a sufficient one (if I were not already abundantly supplied) for me to entertain a diffidence and modesty in all my decisions. I shall propose the arguments on both sides, beginning with those that induced me to deny the strict and proper identity and simplicity of a self or thinking being.

When we talk of *self* or *substance*, we must have an idea annexed to these terms, otherwise they are altogether unintelligible. Every idea is derived from preceding impressions, and we have no impression of self or substance, as something simple and individual. We have, therefore, no idea of them in that sense.

Whatever is distinct is distinguishable, and whatever is distinguishable is separable by the thought or imagination.

---

[1] [There follow here four passages and one note to be inserted at various points in Part III of Book I. One of the passages is marked for insertion in a section that has been omitted from this edition and hence is itself omitted; the note also is omitted in this edition. The remaining three passages have been inserted at the proper places in the text of Book I, Part III.—Ed]

All perceptions are distinct. They are, therefore, distinguishable and separable, and may be conceived as separately existent, and may exist separately, without any contradiction or absurdity.

When I view this table and that chimney, nothing is present to me but particular perceptions, which are of a like nature with all the other perceptions. This is the doctrine of philosophers. But this table which is present to me and that chimney may and do exist separately. This is the doctrine of the vulgar, and implies no contradiction. There is no contradiction, therefore, in extending the same doctrine to all the perceptions.

In general, the following reasoning seems satisfactory. All ideas are borrowed from preceding perceptions. Our ideas of objects, therefore, are derived from that source. Consequently no proposition can be intelligible or consistent with regard to objects which is not so with regard to perceptions. But it is intelligible and consistent to say that objects exist distinct and independent, without any common *simple* substance or subject of inhesion. This proposition, therefore, can never be absurd with regard to perceptions.

When I turn my reflection on *myself*, I never can perceive this *self* without some one or more perceptions, nor can I ever perceive anything but the perceptions. It is the composition of these, therefore, which forms the self.

We can conceive a thinking being to have either many or few perceptions. Suppose the mind to be reduced even below the life of an oyster. Suppose it to have only one perception, as of thirst or hunger. Consider it in that situation. Do you conceive anything but merely that perception? Have you any notion of *self* or *substance*? If not, the addition of other perceptions can never give you that notion.

The annihilation which some people suppose to follow upon death and which entirely destroys this self is nothing but an extinction of all particular perceptions: love and hatred, pain and pleasure, thought and sensation. These therefore must be the same with self, since the one cannot survive the other.

Is *self* the same with *substance*? If it be, how can that question have a place concerning the subsistence of self under a change of substance? If they be distinct, what is the difference between them? For my part, I have a notion of neither, when conceived distinct from particular perceptions.

Philosophers begin to be reconciled to the principle *that we have no idea of external substance distinct from the ideas of particular qualities.* This must pave the way for a like principle with regard to the mind, *that we have no notion of it distinct from the particular perceptions.*

So far I seem to be attended with sufficient evidence. But having thus loosened all our particular perceptions, when[1] I proceed to explain the principle of connection which binds them together and makes us attribute to them a real simplicity and identity, I am sensible that my account is very defective, and that nothing but the seeming evidence of the precedent reasonings could have induced me to receive it. If perceptions are distinct existences, they form a whole only by being connected together. But no connections among distinct existences are ever discoverable by human understanding. We only *feel* a connection or determination of the thought to pass from one object to another. It follows, therefore, that the thought alone finds personal identity, when, reflecting on the train of past perceptions that compose a mind, the ideas of them are felt to be connected together, and naturally introduce each other. However extraordinary this conclusion may seem, it need not surprise us. Most philosophers seem inclined to think that personal identity *arises* from consciousness, and consciousness is nothing but a reflected thought or perception. The present philosophy, therefore, has so far a promising aspect. But all my hopes vanish when I come to explain the principles that unite our successive perceptions in our thought or consciousness. I cannot discover any theory which gives me satisfaction on this head.

In short there are two principles which I cannot render consistent, nor is it in my power to renounce either of them, *viz., that all our distinct perceptions are distinct existences,* and *that the mind never perceives any real connection among distinct existences.* Did our perceptions either inhere in something simple and individual, or did the mind perceive some

[1] Book I, p. 181.

real connection among them, there would be no difficulty in the case. For my part, I must plead the privilege of a skeptic, and confess that this difficulty is too hard for my understanding. I pretend not, however, to pronounce it absolutely insuperable. Others, perhaps, or myself, upon more mature reflections, may discover some hypothesis that will reconcile those contradictions.[1]

. . . . .

[1] [Here follow: (a) a paragraph in which Hume "confesses" two minor errors in Book I, (b) a paragraph noting two "errors of the press" in Book I, and (c) two passages and two notes to be inserted at various points in Parts I and II of Book I. One of Hume's confessions of error in (a) has been added as a footnote at the appropriate place in the text of Book I; the other has been omitted, since the error in question occurred in a section that has been omitted from this edition. The two errors in (b) have been corrected in the text. Of the passages and notes in (c), three are marked for insertion in sections of Part II of Book I that have been omitted from this edition and hence have themselves been omitted; the remaining one, a note, has been inserted at the appropriate place in the text of Book I, Part I.—Ed.]

AN INQUIRY

CONCERNING

HUMAN

UNDERSTANDING

CONTENTS

Section 1.

OF THE DIFFERENT SPECIES
OF PHILOSOPHY

MORAL PHILOSOPHY or the science of human nature may be treated after two different manners, each of which has its peculiar merit and may contribute to the entertainment, instruction, and reformation of mankind. The one considers man chiefly as born for action and as influenced in his measures by taste and sentiment, pursuing one object and avoiding another according to the value which these objects seem to possess, and according to the light in which they present themselves. As virtue, of all objects, is allowed to be the most valuable, this species of philosophers paint her in the most amiable colors, borrowing all helps from poetry and eloquence and treating their subject in an easy and obvious manner, and such as is best fitted to please the imagination and engage the affections. They select the most striking observations and instances from common life, place opposite characters in a proper contrast, and, alluring us into the paths of virtue by the views of glory and happiness, direct our steps in these paths by the soundest precepts and most illustrious examples. They make us *feel* the difference between vice and virtue; they excite and regulate our sentiments; and so they can but bend our hearts to the love of probity and true honor, they think that they have fully attained the end of all their labors.

The other species of philosophers consider man in the light of a reasonable rather than an active being, and endeavor to form his understanding more than cultivate his manners. They regard human nature as a subject of speculation, and with a narrow scrutiny examine it in order to find those principles which regulate our understanding, excite our sentiments, and make us approve or blame any particular object, action, or behavior. They think it a reproach to all literature that philosophy should not yet have fixed, beyond controversy, the foundation of morals, reasoning, and criticism, and should forever talk of truth and falsehood, vice and virtue, beauty and deformity, without being able to determine the source of these distinctions. While they attempt this arduous task, they are deterred by no difficulties, but proceeding from particular instances to general principles, they still push on their inquiries to principles more general, and rest not satisfied till they arrive at those original principles by which, in every science, all human curiosity must be bounded. Though their speculations seem abstract and even unintelligible to common readers, they aim at the approbation of the learned and the wise, and think themselves sufficiently compensated for the labor of their whole lives if they can discover some hidden truths which may contribute to the instruction of posterity.

It is certain that the easy and obvious philosophy will always, with the generality of mankind, have the preference above the accurate and abstruse, and by many will be recommended, not only as more agreeable, but more useful than the other. It enters more into common life, molds the heart and affections, and, by touching those principles which actuate men, reforms their conduct and brings them nearer to that model of perfection which it describes. On the contrary, the abstruse philosophy, being founded on a turn of mind which cannot enter into business and action, vanishes when the philosopher leaves the shade and comes into open day, nor can its principles easily retain any influence over our conduct and behavior. The feelings of our heart, the agitation of our passions, the vehemence of our affections dissipate all its conclusions, and reduce the profound philosopher to a mere plebeian.

This also must be confessed, that the most durable as well as justest fame has been acquired by the easy philosophy, and that abstract reasoners seem hitherto to have enjoyed

only a momentary reputation, from the caprice or ignorance
of their own age, but have not been able to support their
renown with more equitable posterity. It is easy for a profound philosopher to commit a mistake in his subtle reasonings, and one mistake is the necessary parent of another, while
he pushes on his consequences, and is not deterred from embracing any conclusion by its unusual appearance or its contradiction to popular opinion. But a philosopher who purposes only to represent the common sense of mankind in more
beautiful and more engaging colors, if by accident he falls
into error, goes no further, but renewing his appeal to common sense and the natural sentiments of the mind, returns
into the right path and secures himself from any dangerous
illusions. The fame of Cicero flourishes at present, but that of
Aristotle is utterly decayed. La Bruyère passes the seas and
still maintains his reputation, but the glory of Malebranche is
confined to his own nation and to his own age. And Addison,
perhaps, will be read with pleasure when Locke shall be
entirely forgotten.

The mere philosopher is a character which is commonly
but little acceptable in the world, as being supposed to contribute nothing either to the advantage or pleasure of society, while he lives remote from communication with mankind and is wrapped up in principles and notions equally
remote from their comprehension. On the other hand, the
mere ignorant is still more despised, nor is anything deemed
a surer sign of an illiberal genius in an age and nation where
the sciences flourish than to be entirely destitute of all relish
for those noble entertainments. The most perfect character is
supposed to lie between those extremes, retaining an equal
ability and taste for books, company, and business, preserving
in conversation that discernment and delicacy which arise
from polite letters, and in business that probity and accuracy
which are the natural result of a just philosophy. In order to
diffuse and cultivate so accomplished a character, nothing
can be more useful than compositions of the easy style and
manner which draw not too much from life, require no deep
application or retreat to be comprehended, and send back
the student among mankind full of noble sentiments and wise
precepts applicable to every exigency of human life. By means

of such compositions virtue becomes amiable, science agreeable, company instructive, and retirement entertaining.

Man is a reasonable being, and as such receives from science his proper food and nourishment. But so narrow are the
bonds of human understanding that little satisfaction can be
hoped for in this particular, either from the extent or security
of his acquisitions. Man is a sociable no less than a reasonable
being. But neither can he always enjoy company agreeable
and amusing, or preserve the proper relish for them. Man
is also an active being, and from that disposition as well as
from the various necessities of human life must submit to
business and occupation. But the mind requires some relaxation and cannot always support its bent to care and industry. It seems, then, that nature has pointed out a mixed
kind of life as most suitable to [the] human race, and secretly
admonished them to allow none of these biases to *draw* too
much, so as to incapacitate them for other occupations and
entertainments. Indulge your passion for science, says she, but
let your science be human and such as may have a direct
reference to action and society. Abstruse thought and profound researches I prohibit and will severely punish by the
pensive melancholy which they introduce, by the endless uncertainty in which they involve you, and by the cold reception your pretended discoveries shall meet with when communicated. Be a philosopher, but, amidst all your philosophy,
be still a man.

Were the generality of mankind contented to prefer the
easy philosophy to the abstract and profound, without throwing any blame or contempt on the latter, it might not be improper, perhaps, to comply with this general opinion and
allow every man to enjoy, without opposition, his own taste
and sentiment. But as the matter is often carried further, even
to the absolute rejecting of all profound reasonings or what is
commonly called *metaphysics*, we shall now proceed to consider what can reasonably be pleaded in their behalf.

We may begin with observing that one considerable advantage which results from the accurate and abstract philosophy
is its subservience to the easy and humane, which, without
the former, can never attain a sufficient degree of exactness in its sentiments, precepts, or reasonings. All polite letters

are nothing but pictures of human life in various attitudes and situations, and inspire us with different sentiments of praise or blame, admiration or ridicule, according to the qualities of the object which they set before us. An artist must be better qualified to succeed in this undertaking who, besides a delicate taste and a quick apprehension, possesses an accurate knowledge of the internal fabric, the operations of the understanding, the workings of the passions, and the various species of sentiment which discriminate vice and virtue. How painful soever this inward search or inquiry may appear, it becomes in some measure requisite to those who would describe with success the obvious and outward appearances of life and manners. The anatomist presents to the eye the most hideous and disagreeable objects, but his science is useful to the painter in delineating even a Venus or a Helen. While the latter employs all the richest colors of his art and gives his figures the most graceful and engaging airs, he must still carry his attention to the inward structure of the human body, the position of the muscles, the fabric of the bones, and the use and figure of every part or organ. Accuracy is, in every case, advantageous to beauty, and just reasoning to delicate sentiment. In vain would we exalt the one by depreciating the other.

Besides, we may observe in every art or profession, even those which most concern life or action, that a spirit of accuracy, however acquired, carries all of them nearer their perfection, and renders them more subservient to the interests of society. And though a philosopher may live remote from business, the genius of philosophy, if carefully cultivated by several, must gradually diffuse itself throughout the whole society and bestow a similar correctness on every art or calling. The politician will acquire greater foresight and subtlety in the subdividing and balancing of power, the lawyer more method and finer principles in his reasonings, and the general more regularity in his discipline and more caution in his plans and operations. The stability of modern governments above the ancient and the accuracy of modern philosophy have improved, and probably will still improve, by similar gradations.

Were there no advantage to be reaped from these studies

beyond the gratification of an innocent curiosity, yet ought not even this to be despised, as being one accession to those few safe and harmless pleasures which are bestowed on [the] human race. The sweetest and most inoffensive path of life leads through the avenues of science and learning, and whoever can either remove any obstructions in this way or open up any new prospect ought so far to be esteemed a benefactor to mankind. And though these researches may appear painful and fatiguing, it is with some minds as with some bodies, which being endowed with vigorous and florid health require severe exercise, and reap a pleasure from what, to the generality of mankind, may seem burdensome and laborious. Obscurity, indeed, is painful to the mind as well as to the eye, but to bring light from obscurity, by whatever labor, must needs be delightful and rejoicing.

But this obscurity in the profound and abstract philosophy is objected to, not only as painful and fatiguing, but as the inevitable source of uncertainty and error. Here indeed lies the justest and most plausible objection against a considerable part of metaphysics, that they are not properly a science, but arise either from the fruitless efforts of human vanity, which would penetrate into subjects utterly inaccessible to the understanding, or from the craft of popular superstitions, which, being unable to defend themselves on fair ground, raise these entangling brambles to cover and protect their weakness. Chased from the open country, these robbers fly into the forest, and lie in wait to break in upon every unguarded avenue of the mind and overwhelm it with religious fears and prejudices. The stoutest antagonist, if he remit his watch a moment, is oppressed. And many, through cowardice and folly, open the gates to the enemies, and willingly receive them with reverence and submission as their legal sovereigns.

But is this a sufficient reason why philosophers should desist from such researches and leave superstition still in possession of her retreat? Is it not proper to draw an opposite conclusion and perceive the necessity of carrying the war into the most secret recesses of the enemy? In vain do we hope that men, from frequent disappointment, will at last abandon such airy sciences and discover the proper province of human reason. For besides that many persons find too sensible an interest in perpetually recalling such topics, besides this, I say, the motive of blind despair can never reasonably have place in the sciences, since, however unsuccessful former attempts may have proved, there is still room to hope that the industry, good fortune, or improved sagacity of succeeding generations may reach discoveries unknown to former ages. Each adventurous genius will still leap at the arduous prize and find himself stimulated rather than discouraged by the failures of his predecessors, while he hopes that the glory of achieving so hard an adventure is reserved for him alone. The only method of freeing learning at once from these abstruse questions is to inquire seriously into the nature of human understanding and show, from an exact analysis of its powers and capacity, that it is by no means fitted for such remote and abstruse subjects. We must submit to this fatigue in order to live at ease ever after, and must cultivate true metaphysics with some care in order to destroy the false and adulterate. Indolence, which to some persons affords a safeguard against this deceitful philosophy, is, with others, overbalanced by curiosity, and despair, which at some moments prevails, may give place afterwards to sanguine hopes and expectations. Accurate and just reasoning is the only catholic remedy fitted for all persons and all dispositions, and is alone able to subvert that abstruse philosophy and metaphysical jargon which, being mixed up with popular superstition, renders it in a manner impenetrable to careless reasoners and gives it the air of science and wisdom.

Besides this advantage of rejecting, after deliberate inquiry, the most uncertain and disagreeable part of learning, there are many positive advantages which result from an accurate scrutiny into the powers and faculties of human nature. It is remarkable concerning the operations of the mind that, though most intimately present to us, yet, whenever they become the object of reflection, they seem involved in obscurity, nor can the eye readily find those lines and boundaries which discriminate and distinguish them. The objects are too fine to remain long in the same aspect or situation, and must be apprehended in an instant by a superior penetration, derived from nature and improved by habit and reflection. It becomes, therefore, no inconsiderable part of science barely to know the different operations of the mind, to separate them from each other, to class them under their proper heads, and to correct all that seeming disorder in which they lie involved when made the object of reflection and inquiry. This task of ordering and distinguishing, which has no merit when performed with regard to external bodies, the objects of our senses, rises in its value when directed toward the operations of the mind, in proportion to the difficulty and labor which we meet with in performing it. And if we can go no further than this mental geography, or delineation of the distinct parts and powers of the mind, it is at least a satisfaction to go so far, and the more obvious this science may appear (and it is by no means obvious) the more contemptible still must the ignorance of it be esteemed in all pretenders to learning and philosophy.

Nor can there remain any suspicion that this science is uncertain and chimerical, unless we should entertain such a skepticism as is entirely subversive of all speculation, and even action. It cannot be doubted that the mind is endowed with several powers and faculties, that these powers are distinct from each other, that what is really distinct to the immediate perception may be distinguished by reflection, and consequently that there is a truth and falsehood in all propositions on this subject, and a truth and falsehood which lie not beyond the compass of human understanding. There are many obvious distinctions of this kind, such as those between the will and understanding, the imagination and passions, which fall within the comprehension of every human creature, and the finer and more philosophical distinctions are no less real and certain, though more difficult to be comprehended. Some instances, especially late ones, of success in these inquiries may give us a juster notion of the certainty and solidity of this branch of learning. And shall we esteem it worthy [of] the labor of a philosopher to give us a true system of the planets and adjust the position and order of those remote bodies, while we affect to overlook those who, with so much success, delineate the parts of the mind, in which we are so intimately concerned?

But may we not hope that philosophy, if cultivated with care and encouraged by the attention of the public, may carry its researches still further and discover, at least in some degree, the secret springs and principles by which the human mind is actuated in its operation? Astronomers had long contented themselves with proving, from the phenomena, the true motions, order, and magnitude of the heavenly bodies, till a philosopher at last arose who seems, from the happiest reasoning, to have also determined the laws and forces by which the revolutions of the planets are governed and directed. The like has been performed with regard to other parts of nature. And there is no reason to despair of equal success in our inquiries concerning the mental powers and economy if prosecuted with equal capacity and caution. It is probable that one operation and principle of the mind depends on another, which again may be resolved into one more general and universal. And how far these researches may possibly be carried it will be difficult for us, before or even after a careful trial, exactly to determine. This is certain, that attempts of this kind are every day made even by those who philosophize the most negligently, and nothing can be more requisite than to enter upon the enterprise with thorough care and attention, that, if it lie within the compass of human understanding, it may at last be happily achieved; if not, it may, however, be rejected with some confidence and security. This last conclusion, surely, is not desirable, nor ought it to be embraced too rashly. For how much must we diminish from the beauty and value of this species of philosophy upon such a supposition? Moralists have hitherto been accustomed, when they considered the vast multitude and diversity of those actions that excite our approbation or dislike, to search for some common principle on which this variety of sentiments might depend. And though they have sometimes carried the matter too far, by their passion for some one general principle, it must, however, be confessed that they are excusable in expecting to find some general principles into which all the vices and virtues were justly to be resolved. The like has been the endeavor of critics, logicians, and even politicians; nor have their attempts been wholly unsuccessful, though perhaps longer time, greater accuracy, and more ardent application may bring these sciences still nearer their perfection. To throw up at once all pretensions of this kind may justly be deemed more rash, precipitate, and dogmatical than even the boldest and most affirmative philosophy that has ever attempted to impose its crude dictates and principles on mankind.

What though these reasonings concerning human nature seem abstract and of difficult comprehension? This affords no presumption of their falsehood. On the contrary, it seems impossible that what has hitherto escaped so many wise and profound philosophers can be very obvious and easy. And whatever pains these researches may cost us, we may think ourselves sufficiently rewarded, not only in point of profit but of pleasure, if, by that means, we can make any addition to our stock of knowledge in subjects of such unspeakable importance.

But as, after all, the abstractedness of these speculations is no recommendation, but rather a disadvantage to them, and as this difficulty may perhaps be surmounted by care and art and the avoiding of all unnecessary detail, we have, in the following inquiry, attempted to throw some light upon subjects from which uncertainty has hitherto deterred the wise, and obscurity the ignorant. Happy if we can unite the boundaries of the different species of philosophy by reconciling profound inquiry with clearness and truth with novelty! And still more happy if, reasoning in this easy manner, we can undermine the foundations of an abstruse philosophy which seems to have hitherto served only as a shelter to superstition and a cover to absurdity and error!

Section IV.

SKEPTICAL DOUBTS
CONCERNING THE OPERATIONS
OF THE UNDERSTANDING

———————

Part I.

ALL THE OBJECTS of human reason or inquiry may naturally be divided into two kinds, to wit, *Relations of Ideas* and *Matters of Fact*. Of the first kind are the sciences of Geometry, Algebra, and Arithmetic, and, in short, every affirmation which is either intuitively or demonstratively certain. *That the square of the hypotenuse is equal to the square of the two sides* is a proposition which expresses a relation between these figures. *That three times five is equal to the half of thirty* expresses a relation between these numbers. Propositions of this kind are discoverable by the mere operation of thought, without dependence on what is anywhere existent in the universe. Though there never were a circle or triangle in nature, the truths demonstrated by Euclid would forever retain their certainty and evidence.

Matters of fact, which are the second objects of human reason, are not ascertained in the same manner, nor is our evidence of their truth, however great, of a like nature with the foregoing. The contrary of every matter of fact is still possible, because it can never imply a contradiction and is conceived by the mind with the same facility and distinctness as if ever so conformable to reality. *That the sun will not rise tomorrow* is no less intelligible a proposition and implies no more contradiction than the affirmation *that it will rise*. We should in vain, therefore, attempt to demonstrate its falsehood. Were it demonstratively false, it would imply a contradiction, and could never be distinctly conceived by the mind.

It may, therefore, be a subject worthy of curiosity to inquire what is the nature of that evidence which assures us of any real existence and matter of fact beyond the present testimony of our senses or the records of our memory. This part of philosophy, it is observable, has been little cultivated either by the ancients or moderns; and, therefore, our doubts and errors in the prosecution of so important an inquiry may be the more excusable while we march through such difficult paths without any guide or direction. They may even prove useful by exciting curiosity and destroying that implicit faith and security which is the bane of all reasoning and free inquiry. The discovery of defects in the common philosophy, if any such there be, will not, I presume, be a discouragement, but rather an incitement, as is usual, to attempt something more full and satisfactory than has yet been proposed to the public.

All reasonings concerning matter of fact seem to be founded on the relation of *cause and effect*. By means of that relation alone we can go beyond the evidence of our memory and senses. If you were to ask a man why he believes any matter of fact which is absent, for instance, that his friend is in the country or in France, he would give you a reason, and this reason would be some other fact, as a letter received from him or the knowledge of his former resolutions and promises. A man finding a watch or any other machine in a desert island would conclude that there had once been men in that island. All our reasonings concerning fact are of the same nature. And here it is constantly supposed that there is a connection between the present fact and that which is inferred from it. Were there nothing to bind them together, the inference would be entirely precarious. The hearing of an articulate voice and rational discourse in the dark assures us of the presence of some person. Why? Because these are the effects of the human make and fabric, and closely connected with it. If we anatomize all the other reasonings of this nature, we shall find that they are founded on the relation of cause and effect, and that this relation is either near or remote, direct or collateral. Heat and light are collateral effects of fire, and the one effect may justly be inferred from the other.

If we would satisfy ourselves, therefore, concerning the nature of that evidence which assures us of matters of fact, we must inquire how we arrive at the knowledge of cause and effect.

I shall venture to affirm, as a general proposition which admits of no exception, that the knowledge of this relation is not, in any instance, attained by reasonings *a priori*, but arises entirely from experience, when we find that any particular objects are constantly conjoined with each other. Let an object be presented to a man of ever so strong natural reason and abilities, if that object be entirely new to him, he will not be able, by the most accurate examination of its sensible qualities, to discover any of its causes or effects. Adam, though his rational faculties be supposed, at the very first, entirely perfect, could not have inferred from the fluidity and transparency of water that it would suffocate him, or from the light and warmth of fire that it would consume him. No object ever discovers, by the qualities which appear to the senses, either the causes which produced it or the effects which will arise from it; nor can our reason, unassisted by experience, ever draw any inference concerning real existence and matter of fact.

This proposition, *that causes and effects are discoverable, not by reason, but by experience*, will readily be admitted with regard to such objects as we remember to have once been altogether unknown to us, since we must be conscious of the utter inability which we then lay under of foretelling what would arise from them. Present two smooth pieces of marble to a man who has no tincture of natural philosophy; he will never discover that they will adhere together in such a manner as to require great force to separate them in a direct line, while they make so small a resistance to a lateral pressure. Such events as bear little analogy to the common course of nature are also readily confessed to be known only by experience, nor does any man imagine that the explosion of gunpowder or the attraction of a loadstone could ever be discovered by arguments *a priori*. In like manner, when an effect is supposed to depend upon an intricate machinery or secret structure of parts, we make no difficulty in attributing all our knowledge of it to experience. Who will assert that he can give the ultimate reason why milk or bread is proper nourishment for a man, not for a lion or tiger?

But the same truth may not appear at first sight to have the same evidence with regard to events which have become familiar to us from our first appearance in the world, which bear a close analogy to the whole course of nature, and which are supposed to depend on the simple qualities of objects without any secret structure of parts. We are apt to imagine that we could discover these effects by the mere operation of our reason, without experience. We fancy that were we brought on a sudden into this world, we could at first have inferred that one billiard ball would communicate motion to another upon impulse, and that we needed not to have waited for the event in order to pronounce with certainty concerning it. Such is the influence of custom that where it is strongest it not only covers our natural ignorance but even conceals itself, and seems not to take place, merely because it is found in the highest degree.

But to convince us that all the laws of nature and all the operations of bodies without exception are known only by experience, the following reflections may perhaps suffice. Were any object presented to us, and were we required to pronounce concerning the effect which will result from it without consulting past observation, after what manner, I beseech you, must the mind proceed in this operation? It must invent or imagine some event which it ascribes to the object as its effect; and it is plain that this invention must be entirely arbitrary. The mind can never possibly find the effect in the supposed cause by the most accurate scrutiny and examination. For the effect is totally different from the cause, and consequently can never be discovered in it. Motion in the second billiard ball is a quite distinct event from motion in the first, nor is there anything in the one to suggest the smallest hint of the other. A stone or piece of metal raised into the air and left without any support immediately falls. But to consider the matter *a priori,* is there anything we discover in this situation which can beget the idea of a downward rather than an upward or any other motion in the stone or metal?

And as the first imagination or invention of a particular

effect in all natural operations is arbitrary where we consult not experience, so must we also esteem the supposed tie or connection between the cause and effect, which binds them together and renders it impossible that any other effect could result from the operation of that cause. When I see, for instance, a billiard ball moving in a straight line toward another, even suppose motion in the second ball should by accident be suggested to me as the result of their contact or impulse, may I not conceive that a hundred different events might as well follow from that cause? May not both these balls remain at absolute rest? May not the first ball return in a straight line or leap off from the second in any line or direction? All these suppositions are consistent and conceivable. Why then should we give the preference to one which is no more consistent or conceivable than the rest? All our reasonings *a priori* will never be able to show us any foundation for this preference.

In a word, then, every effect is a distinct event from its cause. It could not, therefore, be discovered in the cause, and the first invention or conception of it, *a priori*, must be entirely arbitrary. And even after it is suggested, the conjunction of it with the cause must appear equally arbitrary, since there are always many other effects which, to reason, must seem fully as consistent and natural. In vain, therefore, should we pretend to determine any single event or infer any cause or effect without the assistance of observation and experience.

Hence we may discover the reason why no philosopher who is rational and modest has ever pretended to assign the ultimate cause of any natural operation, or to show distinctly the action of that power which produces any single effect in the universe. It is confessed that the utmost effort of human reason is to reduce the principles productive of natural phenomena to a greater simplicity, and to resolve the many particular effects into a few general causes, by means of reasonings from analogy, experience, and observation. But as to the causes of these general causes, we should in vain attempt their discovery, nor shall we ever be able to satisfy ourselves by any particular explication of them. These ultimate springs and principles are totally shut up from human curiosity and inquiry. Elasticity, gravity, cohesion of parts, communication of motion by impulse, these are probably the ultimate causes and principles which we shall ever discover in nature; and we may esteem ourselves sufficiently happy if, by accurate inquiry and reasoning, we can trace up the particular phenomena to, or near to, these general principles. The most perfect philosophy of the natural kind only staves off our ignorance a little longer, as perhaps the most perfect philosophy of the moral or metaphysical kind serves only to discover larger portions of it. Thus the observation of human blindness and weakness is the result of all philosophy, and meets us at every turn in spite of our endeavors to elude or avoid it.

Nor is geometry, when taken into the assistance of natural philosophy, ever able to remedy this defect or lead us into the knowledge of ultimate causes by all that accuracy of reasoning for which it is so justly celebrated. Every part of mixed mathematics proceeds upon the supposition that certain laws are established by nature in her operations, and abstract reasonings are employed either to assist experience in the discovery of these laws or to determine their influence in particular instances where it depends upon any precise degree of distance and quantity. Thus it is a law of motion, discovered by experience, that the moment or force of any body in motion is in the compound ratio or proportion of its solid contents and its velocity, and consequently that a small force may remove the greatest obstacle or raise the greatest weight if, by any contrivance or machinery, we can increase the velocity of that force so as to make it an overmatch for its antagonist. Geometry assists us in the application of this law by giving us the just dimensions of all the parts and figures which can enter into any species of machine, but still the discovery of the law itself is owing merely to experience, and all the abstract reasonings in the world could never lead us one step toward the knowledge of it. When we reason *a priori* and consider merely any object or cause as it appears to the mind, independent of all observation, it never could suggest to us the notion of any distinct object, such as its effect, much less show us the inseparable and inviolable connection between them. A man must be very sagacious who could discover by reasoning that crystal is the effect of heat and ice of cold, without being previously acquainted with the operation of these qualities.

Part II.

But we have not yet attained any tolerable satisfaction with regard to the question first proposed. Each solution still gives rise to a new question as difficult as the foregoing and leads us on to further inquiries. When it is asked, *What is the nature of all our reasonings concerning matter of fact?* the proper answer seems to be that they are founded on the relation of cause and effect. When again it is asked, *What is the foundation of all our reasonings and conclusions concerning that relation?* it may be replied in one word, *experience*. But if we still carry on our sifting humor and ask, *What is the foundation of all conclusions from experience?* this implies a new question, which may be of more difficult solution and explication. Philosophers that give themselves airs of superior wisdom and sufficiency have a hard task when they encounter persons of inquisitive dispositions, who push them from every corner to which they retreat, and who are sure at last to bring them to some dangerous dilemma. The best expedient to prevent this confusion is to be modest in our pretensions, and even to discover the difficulty ourselves before it is objected to us. By this means we may make a kind of merit of our very ignorance.

I shall content myself in this section with an easy task and shall pretend only to give a negative answer to the question here proposed. I say then, that even after we have experience of the operations of cause and effect, our conclusions from that experience are *not* founded on reasoning or any process of the understanding. This answer we must endeavor both to explain and to defend.

It must certainly be allowed that nature has kept us at a great distance from all her secrets and has afforded us only the knowledge of a few superficial qualities of objects, while she conceals from us those powers and principles on which the influence of these objects entirely depends. Our senses inform us of the color, weight, and consistency of bread, but neither sense nor reason can ever inform us of those qualities which fit it for the nourishment and support of a human body. Sight or feeling conveys an idea of the actual motion of bodies, but as to that wonderful force or power which would carry on a moving body forever in a continued change of place, and which bodies never lose but by communicating it to others, of this we cannot form the most distant conception. But notwithstanding this ignorance of natural powers[1] and principles, we always presume, when we see like sensible qualities, that they have like secret powers, and expect that effects similar to those which we have experienced will follow from them. If a body of like color and consistency with that bread which we have formerly eaten be presented to us, we make no scruple of repeating the experiment and foresee with certainty like nourishment and support. Now this is a process of the mind or thought of which I would willingly know the foundation. It is allowed on all hands that there is no known connection between the sensible qualities and the secret powers, and consequently that the mind is not led to form such a conclusion concerning their constant and regular conjunction by anything which it knows of their nature. As to past *experience*, it can be allowed to give *direct* and *certain* information of those precise objects only, and that precise period of time, which fell under its cognizance; but why this experience should be extended to future times and to other objects which, for aught we know, may be only in appearance similar, this is the main question on which I would insist. The bread which I formerly ate nourished me; that is, a body of such sensible qualities was, at that time, endued with such secret powers. But does it follow that other bread must also nourish me at another time, and that like sensible qualities must always be attended with like secret powers? The consequence seems nowise necessary. At least it must be acknowledged that there is here a consequence drawn by the mind, that there is a certain step taken, a process of thought, and an inference which wants to be explained. These two propositions are far from being the same: *I have found that such an object has always been attended with such an effect,* and *I foresee*

[1] The word "power" is here used in a loose and popular sense. The more accurate explication of it would give additional evidence to this argument. See Section VII.

that other objects which are in appearance similar will be attended with similar effects. I shall allow, if you please, that the one proposition may justly be inferred from the other; I know, in fact, that it always is inferred. But if you insist that the inference is made by a chain of reasoning, I desire you to produce that reasoning. The connection between these propositions is not intuitive. There is required a medium which may enable the mind to draw such an inference, if indeed it be drawn by reasoning and argument. What that medium is I must confess passes my comprehension; and it is incumbent on those to produce it who assert that it really exists and is the origin of all our conclusions concerning matter of fact.

This negative argument must certainly, in process of time, become altogether convincing, if many penetrating and able philosophers shall turn their inquiries this way, and no one be ever able to discover any connecting proposition or intermediate step which supports the understanding in this conclusion. But as the question is yet new, every reader may not trust so far to his own penetration as to conclude, because an argument escapes his inquiry, that therefore it does not really exist. For this reason it may be requisite to venture upon a more difficult task, and enumerating all the branches of human knowledge, endeavor to show that none of them can afford such an argument.

All reasonings may be divided into two kinds, namely, demonstrative reasoning, or that concerning relations of ideas, and moral reasoning, or that concerning matter of fact and existence. That there are no demonstrative arguments in the case seems evident, since it implies no contradiction that the course of nature may change and that an object, seemingly like those which we have experienced, may be attended with different or contrary effects. May I not clearly and distinctly conceive that a body falling from the clouds and which in all other respects resembles snow has yet the taste of salt or feeling of fire? Is there any more intelligible proposition than to affirm that all the trees will flourish in December and January, and will decay in May and June? Now whatever is intelligible and can be distinctly conceived implies no contradiction, and can never be proved false by any demonstrative argument or abstract reasoning *a priori*.

If we be, therefore, engaged by arguments to put trust in past experience and make it the standard of our future judgment, these arguments must be probable only, or such as regard matter of fact and real existence, according to the division above-mentioned. But that there is no argument of this kind must appear if our explication of that species of reasoning be admitted as solid and satisfactory. We have said that all arguments concerning existence are founded on the relation of cause and effect, that our knowledge of that relation is derived entirely from experience, and that all our experimental conclusions proceed upon the supposition that the future will be conformable to the past. To endeavor, therefore, the proof of this last supposition by probable arguments, or arguments regarding existence, must be evidently going in a circle and taking that for granted which is the very point in question.

In reality, all arguments from experience are founded on the similarity which we discover among natural objects, and by which we are induced to expect effects similar to those which we have found to follow from such objects. And though none but a fool or madman will ever pretend to dispute the authority of experience or to reject that great guide of human life, it may surely be allowed a philosopher to have so much curiosity at least as to examine the principle of human nature which gives this mighty authority to experience and makes us draw advantage from that similarity which nature has placed among different objects. From causes which appear *similar,* we expect similar effects. This is the sum of all our experimental conclusions. Now it seems evident that if this conclusion were formed by reason, it would be as perfect at first and upon one instance as after ever so long a course of experience. But the case is far otherwise. Nothing is so like as eggs; yet no one, on account of this appearing similarity, expects the same taste and relish in all of them. It is only after a long course of uniform experiments in any kind that we attain a firm reliance and security with regard to a particular event. Now where is that process of reasoning which, from one instance, draws a conclusion so different from that which it infers from a hundred instances that are nowise different from that single one? This question I propose as much for the sake of information as with an intention of raising difficulties. I cannot find, I cannot imagine any such reasoning. But I keep my mind still open to instruction, if anyone will vouchsafe to bestow it on me.

Should it be said that, from a number of uniform experiments, we *infer* a connection between the sensible qualities and the secret powers, this, I must confess, seems the same difficulty couched in different terms. The question still recurs, on what process of argument this *inference* is founded? Where is the medium, the interposing ideas, which join propositions so very wide of each other? It is confessed that the color, consistency, and other sensible qualities of bread appear not of themselves to have any connection with the secret powers of nourishment and support. For otherwise we could infer these secret powers from the first appearance of these sensible qualities without the aid of experience, contrary to the sentiment of all philosophers and contrary to plain matter of fact. Here then is our natural state of ignorance with regard to the powers and influence of all objects. How is this remedied by experience? It only shows us a number of uniform effects resulting from certain objects, and teaches us that those particular objects at that particular time were endowed with such powers and forces. When a new object endowed with similar sensible qualities is produced, we expect similar powers and forces, and look for a like effect. From a body of like color and consistency with bread, we expect like nourishment and support. But this surely is a step or progress of the mind which wants to be explained. When a man says, *I have found, in all past instances, such sensible qualities conjoined with such secret powers,* and when he says, *similar sensible qualities will always be conjoined with similar secret powers,* he is not guilty of a tautology, nor are these propositions in any respect the same. You say that the one proposition is an inference from the other. But you must confess that the inference is not intuitive; neither is it demonstrative. Of what nature is it then? To say it is experimental is begging the question. For all inferences from experience suppose, as their foundation, that the future will resemble the past, and that similar powers will be conjoined with similar sensible qualities. If there be any suspicion that the course of nature may

change and that the past may be no rule for the future, all
experience becomes useless and can give rise to no inference
or conclusion. It is impossible, therefore, that any arguments
from experience can prove this resemblance of the past to the
future, since all these arguments are founded on the supposition of that resemblance. Let the course of things be
allowed hitherto ever so regular; that alone, without some
new argument or inference, proves not that for the future it
will continue so. In vain do you pretend to have learned the
nature of bodies from your past experience. Their secret
nature, and consequently all their effects and influence, may
change, without any change in their sensible qualities. This
happens sometimes, and with regard to some objects. Why
may it not happen always, and with regard to all objects?
What logic, what process of argument secures you against
this supposition? My practice, you say, refutes my doubts.
But you mistake the purport of my question. As an agent,
I am quite satisfied in the point; but as a philosopher who
has some share of curiosity, I will not say skepticism, I want
to learn the foundation of this inference. No reading, no
inquiry has yet been able to remove my difficulty or give me
satisfaction in a matter of such importance. Can I do better
than propose the difficulty to the public, even though, perhaps, I have small hopes of obtaining a solution? We shall
at least, by this means, be sensible of our ignorance, if we
do not augment our knowledge.

I must confess that a man is guilty of unpardonable arrogance who concludes, because an argument has escaped his
own investigation, that therefore it does not really exist. I
must also confess that, though all the learned, for several ages,
should have employed themselves in fruitless search upon
any subject, it may still, perhaps, be rash to conclude positively that the subject must therefore pass all human comprehension. Even though we examine all the sources of our
knowledge and conclude them unfit for such a subject, there
may still remain a suspicion that the enumeration is not
complete or the examination not accurate. But with regard
to the present subject, there are some considerations which
seem to remove all this accusation of arrogance or suspicion
of mistake.

It is certain that the most ignorant and stupid peasants, nay infants, nay even brute beasts, improve by experience, and learn the qualities of natural objects by observing the effects which result from them. When a child has felt the sensation of pain from touching the flame of a candle, he will be careful not to put his hand near any candle, but will expect a similar effect from a cause which is similar in its sensible qualities and appearance. If you assert, therefore, that the understanding of the child is led into this con- clusion by any process of argument or ratiocination, I may justly require you to produce that argument; nor have you any pretense to refuse so equitable a demand. You cannot say that the argument is abstruse and may possibly escape your inquiry, since you confess that it is obvious to the capacity of a mere infant. If you hesitate, therefore, a mo- ment, or if after reflection you produce an intricate or pro- found argument, you, in a manner, give up the question and confess that it is not reasoning which engages us to suppose the past resembling the future, and to expect similar effects from causes which are to appearance similar. This is the proposition which I intended to enforce in the present sec- tion. If I be right, I pretend not to have made any mighty discovery. And if I be wrong, I must acknowledge myself to be indeed a very backward scholar, since I cannot now dis- cover an argument which, it seems, was perfectly familiar to me long before I was out of my cradle.

Section VIII.

OF LIBERTY AND NECESSITY

Part I.

IT MIGHT REASONABLY be expected in questions which have been canvassed and disputed with great eagerness since the first origin of science and philosophy, that the meaning of all the terms, at least, should have been agreed upon among the disputants, and our inquiries, in the course of two thousand years, been able to pass from words to the true and real subject of the controversy. For how easy may it seem to give exact definitions of the terms employed in reasoning, and make these definitions, not the mere sound of words, the object of future scrutiny and examination? But if we consider the matter more narrowly, we shall be apt to draw a quite opposite conclusion. From this circumstance alone, that a controversy has been long kept on foot and remains still undecided, we may presume that there is some ambiguity in the expression, and that the disputants affix different ideas to the terms employed in the controversy. For as the faculties of the mind are supposed to be naturally alike in every individual—otherwise nothing could be more fruitless than to reason or dispute together—it were impossible, if men affix the same ideas to their terms, that they could so long form different opinions of the same subject, especially when they communicate their views, and each party turn themselves on all sides in search of arguments which may give them the victory over their antagonists. It is true, if men attempt the discussion of questions which lie entirely beyond the reach of human capacity, such as those concerning the origin of worlds or the economy of the intellectual system or region of spirits, they may long beat the air in their fruitless contests and never arrive at any determinate conclusion. But if the question regard any subject of common life and experience, nothing, one would think, could preserve the dispute so long undecided but some ambiguous expressions which keep the antagonists still at a distance and hinder them from grappling with each other.

This has been the case in the long disputed question concerning liberty and necessity, and to so remarkable a degree that, if I be not much mistaken, we shall find that all mankind, both learned and ignorant, have always been of the same opinion with regard to this subject, and that a few intelligible definitions would immediately have put an end to the whole controversy. I own that this dispute has been so much canvassed on all hands, and has led philosophers into such a labyrinth of obscure sophistry, that it is no wonder if a sensible reader indulge his ease so far as to turn a deaf ear to the proposal of such a question, from which he can expect neither instruction nor entertainment. But the state of the argument here proposed may, perhaps, serve to renew his attention, as it has more novelty, promises at least some decision of the controversy, and will not much disturb his ease by any intricate or obscure reasoning.

I hope, therefore, to make it appear that all men have ever agreed in the doctrine both of necessity and of liberty, according to any reasonable sense which can be put on these terms, and that the whole controversy has hitherto turned merely upon words. We shall begin with examining the doctrine of necessity.

It is universally allowed that matter, in all its operations, is actuated by a necessary force, and that every natural effect is so precisely determined by the energy of its cause that no other effect, in such particular circumstances, could possibly have resulted from it. The degree and direction of every motion is, by the laws of nature, prescribed with such exactness that a living creature may as soon arise from the shock of two bodies as motion in any other degree or direction than what is actually produced by it. Would we, therefore, form a just and precise idea of *necessity*, we must consider whence that idea arises when we apply it to the operation of bodies.

It seems evident that, if all the scenes of nature were continually shifted in such a manner that no two events bore any resemblance to each other, but every object was entirely new, without any similitude to whatever had been seen before, we should never, in that case, have attained the least idea of necessity or of a connection among these objects. We might say, upon such a supposition, that one object or event has followed another, not that one was produced by the other. The relation of cause and effect must be utterly unknown to mankind. Inference and reasoning concerning the operations of nature would, from that moment, be at an end, and the memory and senses remain the only canals by which the knowledge of any real existence could possibly have access to the mind. Our idea, therefore, of necessity and causation arises entirely from the uniformity observable in the operations of nature, where similar objects are constantly conjoined together, and the mind is determined by custom to infer the one from the appearance of the other. These two circumstances form the whole of that necessity which we ascribe to matter. Beyond the constant *conjunction* of similar objects, and the consequent *inference* from one to the other, we have no notion of any necessity or connection.

If it appear, therefore, that all mankind have ever allowed, without any doubt or hesitation, that these two circumstances take place in the voluntary actions of men and in the operations of mind, it must follow that all mankind have ever agreed in the doctrine of necessity, and that they have hitherto disputed merely for not understanding each other.

As to the first circumstance, the constant and regular conjunction of similar events, we may possibly satisfy ourselves by the following considerations. It is universally acknowledged that there is a great uniformity among the actions of men in all nations and ages, and that human nature remains still the same in its principles and operations. The same motives always produce the same actions; the same events follow from the same causes. Ambition, avarice, self-love, vanity, friendship, generosity, public spirit; these passions, mixed in various degrees and distributed through society, have been, from the beginning of the world, and still are the source of all the actions and enterprises which have ever been observed among mankind. Would you know the sentiments,

inclinations, and course of life of the Greeks and Romans?
Study well the temper and actions of the French and English:
you cannot be much mistaken in transferring to the former
most of the observations which you have made with regard
to the latter. Mankind are so much the same, in all times
and places, that history informs us of nothing new or strange
in this particular. Its chief use is only to discover the constant and universal principles of human nature by showing
men in all varieties of circumstances and situations, and
furnishing us with materials from which we may form our
observations and become acquainted with the regular springs
of human action and behavior. These records of wars, in-
trigues, factions, and revolutions are so many collections of
experiments by which the politician or moral philosopher
fixes the principles of his science, in the same manner as the
physician or natural philosopher becomes acquainted with
the nature of plants, minerals, and other external objects
by the experiments which he forms concerning them. Nor are
the earth, water, and other elements examined by Aristotle and
Hippocrates more like to those which at present lie under
our observation than the men described by Polybius and
Tacitus are to those who now govern the world.

Should a traveler returning from a far country bring us
an account of men wholly different from any with whom we
were ever acquainted, men who were entirely divested of
avarice, ambition, or revenge, who knew no pleasure but
friendship, generosity, and public spirit, we should immediately, from these circumstances, detect the falsehood and
prove him a liar with the same certainty as if he had stuffed
his narration with stories of centaurs and dragons, miracles
and prodigies. And if we would explode any forgery in history, we cannot make use of a more convincing argument
than to prove that the actions ascribed to any person are
directly contrary to the course of nature, and that no human
motives, in such circumstances, could ever induce him to such
a conduct. The veracity of Quintus Curtius is as much to be
suspected when he describes the supernatural courage of
Alexander, by which he was hurried on singly to attack
multitudes, as when he describes his supernatural force and

activity, by which he was able to resist them. So readily and universally do we acknowledge a uniformity in human motives and actions as well as in the operations of body.

Hence likewise the benefit of that experience acquired by long life and a variety of business and company, in order to instruct us in the principles of human nature and regulate our future conduct as well as speculation. By means of this guide we mount up to the knowledge of men's inclinations and motives from their actions, expressions, and even gestures, and again descend to the interpretation of their actions from our knowledge of their motives and inclinations. The general observations treasured up by a course of experience give us the clue of human nature and teach us to unravel all its intricacies. Pretexts and appearances no longer deceive us. Public declarations pass for the specious coloring of a cause. And though virtue and honor be allowed their proper weight and authority, that perfect disinterestedness so often pretended to is never expected in multitudes and parties, seldom in their leaders, and scarcely even in individuals of any rank or station. But were there no uniformity in human actions, and were every experiment which we could form of this kind irregular and anomalous, it were impossible to collect any general observations concerning mankind, and no experience, however accurately digested by reflection, would ever serve to any purpose. Why is the aged husbandman more skillful in his calling than the young beginner, but because there is a certain uniformity in the operation of the sun, rain, and earth toward the production of vegetables, and experience teaches the old practitioner the rules by which this operation is governed and directed?

We must not, however, expect that this uniformity of human actions should be carried to such a length as that all men, in the same circumstances, will always act precisely in the same manner, without making any allowance for the diversity of characters, prejudices, and opinions. Such a uniformity in every particular is found in no part of nature. On the contrary, from observing the variety of conduct in different men, we are enabled to form a greater variety of maxims, which still suppose a degree of uniformity and regularity.

Are the manners of men different in different ages and countries? We learn thence the great force of custom and education, which mold the human mind from its infancy and form it into a fixed and established character. Is the behavior and conduct of the one sex very unlike that of the other? It is thence we become acquainted with the different characters which nature has impressed upon the sexes, and which she preserves with constancy and regularity. Are the actions of the same person much diversified in the different periods of his life, from infancy to old age? This affords room for many general observations concerning the gradual change of our sentiments and inclinations, and the different maxims which prevail in the different ages of human creatures. Even the characters which are peculiar to each individual have a uniformity in their influence; otherwise our acquaintance with the persons and our observation of their conduct could never teach us their dispositions, or serve to direct our behavior with regard to them.

I grant it possible to find some actions which seem to have no regular connection with any known motives and are exceptions to all the measures of conduct which have ever been established for the government of men. But if we would willingly know what judgment should be formed of such irregular and extraordinary actions, we may consider the sentiments commonly entertained with regard to those irregular events which appear in the course of nature and the operations of external objects. All causes are not conjoined to their usual effects with like uniformity. An artificer who handles only dead matter may be disappointed of his aim, as well as the politician who directs the conduct of sensible and intelligent agents.

The vulgar, who take things according to their first appearance, attribute the uncertainty of events to such an uncertainty in the causes as makes the latter often fail of their usual influence, though they meet with no impediment in their operation. But philosophers, observing that almost in every part of nature there is contained a vast variety of springs and principles which are hid by reason of their minuteness or remoteness, find that it is at least possible the contrariety of events may not proceed from any contingency in the cause, but from the secret operation of contrary causes. This possibility is converted into certainty by further observation, when they remark that, upon an exact scrutiny, a contrariety of effects always betrays a contrariety of causes and proceeds from their mutual opposition. A peasant can give no better reason for the stopping of any clock or watch than to say that it does not commonly go right. But an artist easily perceives that the same force in the spring or pendulum has always the same influence on the wheels, but fails of its usual effect perhaps by reason of a grain of dust, which puts a stop to the whole movement. From the observation of several parallel instances, philosophers form a maxim, that the connection between all causes and effects is equally necessary, and that its seeming uncertainty in some instances proceeds from the secret opposition of contrary causes.

Thus for instance in the human body, when the usual symptoms of health or sickness disappoint our expectation, when medicines operate not with their wonted powers, when irregular events follow from any particular cause, the philosopher and physician are not surprised at the matter, nor are ever tempted to deny, in general, the necessity and uniformity of those principles by which the animal economy is conducted. They know that a human body is a mighty complicated machine, that many secret powers lurk in it which are altogether beyond our comprehension, that to us it must often appear very uncertain in its operations, and that therefore the irregular events which outwardly discover themselves can be no proof that the laws of nature are not observed with the greatest regularity in its internal operations and government.

The philosopher, if he be consistent, must apply the same reasonings to the actions and volitions of intelligent agents. The most irregular and unexpected resolutions of men may frequently be accounted for by those who know every particular circumstance of their character and situation. A person of an obliging disposition gives a peevish answer. But he has the toothache, or has not dined. A stupid fellow discovers an uncommon alacrity in his carriage. But he has met with a sudden piece of good fortune. Or even when an action, as sometimes happens, cannot be particularly accounted for, either by the person himself or by others, we know, in general, that the characters of men are to a certain degree inconstant and irregular. This is, in a manner, the constant character of human nature, though it be applicable in a more particular manner to some persons who have no fixed rule for their conduct, but proceed in a continual course of caprice and inconstancy. The internal principles and motives may operate in a uniform manner, notwithstanding these seeming irregularities, in the same manner as the winds, rains, clouds, and other variations of the weather are supposed to be governed by steady principles, though not easily discoverable by human sagacity and inquiry.

Thus it appears not only that the conjunction between motives and voluntary actions is as regular and uniform as that between the cause and effect in any part of nature, but also that this regular conjunction has been universally acknowledged among mankind and has never been the subject of dispute either in philosophy or common life. Now, as it is from past experience that we draw all inferences concerning the future, and as we conclude that objects will always be conjoined together which we find to have always been conjoined, it may seem superfluous to prove that this experienced uniformity in human actions is a source whence we draw *inferences* concerning them. But in order to throw the argument into a greater variety of lights, we shall also insist, though briefly, on this latter topic.

The mutual dependence of men is so great in all societies that scarce any human action is entirely complete in itself or is performed without some reference to the actions of others, which are requisite to make it answer fully the intention of the agent. The poorest artificer, who labors alone, expects at least the protection of the magistrate to insure him the enjoyment of the fruits of his labor. He also expects that when he carries his goods to market and offers them at a reasonable price he shall find purchasers, and shall be able, by the money he acquires, to engage others to supply him with those commodities which are requisite for his subsistence. In proportion as men extend their dealings and render their intercourse with others more complicated, they always comprehend in their schemes of life a greater variety of voluntary actions, which they expect, from the proper motives, to co-operate with their own. In all these conclusions they take their measures from past experience, in the same manner as in their reasonings concerning external objects, and firmly believe that men, as well as all the elements, are to continue in their operations the same that they have ever found them. A manufacturer reckons upon the labor of his servants for the execution of any work as much as upon the tools which he employs, and would be equally surprised were his expectations disappointed. In short, this experimental inference and reasoning concerning the actions of others enters so much into human life that no man, while awake, is ever a moment without employing it. Have we not reason, therefore, to affirm that all mankind have always agreed in the doctrine of necessity, according to the foregoing definition and explication of it?

Nor have philosophers ever entertained a different opinion from the people in this particular. For not to mention that almost every action of their life supposes that opinion, there are even few of the speculative parts of learning to which it is not essential. What would become of *history* had we not a dependence on the veracity of the historian, according to the experience which we have had of mankind? How could *politics* be a science if laws and forms of government had not a uniform influence upon society? Where would be the foundation of *morals* if particular characters had no certain or determinate power to produce particular sentiments, and if these sentiments had no constant operation on actions? And with what pretense could we employ our *criticism* upon any poet or polite author if we could not pronounce the conduct and sentiments of his actors either natural or unnatural to such characters and in such circumstances? It seems almost impossible, therefore, to engage either in science or action of any kind without acknowledging the doctrine of necessity, and this *inference* from motives to voluntary action, from characters to conduct.

And indeed when we consider how aptly *natural* and *moral* evidence link together and form only one chain of argument, we shall make no scruple to allow that they are of the same nature and derived from the same principles. A prisoner who has neither money nor interest discovers the impossibility of his escape as well when he considers the obstinacy of the jailer as the walls and bars with which he is surrounded, and in all attempts for his freedom chooses rather to work upon the stone and iron of the one than upon the inflexible nature of the other. The same prisoner, when conducted to the scaffold, foresees his death as certainly from the constancy and fidelity of his guards as from the operation of the ax or wheel. His mind runs along a certain train of ideas: the refusal of the soldiers to consent to his escape; the action of the executioner; the separation of the head and body; bleeding, convulsive motions, and death. Here is a connected chain of natural causes and voluntary actions, but the mind feels no difference between them in passing from one link to another, nor is less certain of the future event than if it were connected with the objects present to the memory or senses by a train of causes cemented together by what we are pleased to call a *physical* necessity. The same experienced union has the same effect on the mind, whether the united objects be motives, volition, and actions, or figure and motion. We may change the names of things, but their nature and their operation on the understanding never change.

Were a man whom I know to be honest and opulent, and with whom I live in intimate friendship, to come into my house, where I am surrounded with my servants, I rest assured that he is not to stab me before he leaves it in order to rob me of my silver standish; and I no more suspect this event than the falling of the house itself, which is new and solidly built and founded.—*But he may have been seized with a sudden and unknown frenzy.*—So may a sudden earthquake arise, and shake and tumble my house about my ears. I shall therefore change the suppositions. I shall say that I know with certainty that he is not to put his hand into the fire and hold it there till it be consumed. And this event I think I can foretell with the same assurance as that, if he throw himself out at the window and meet with no obstruction, he will not remain a moment suspended in the air. No suspicion of an unknown frenzy can give the least possibility to the former event, which is so contrary to all the known principles of human nature. A man who at noon leaves his purse full of gold on the pavement at Charing Cross may as well expect that it will fly away like a feather as that he will find it untouched an hour after. Above one-half of human reasonings contain inferences of a similar nature, attended with more or less degrees of certainty, proportioned to our experience of the usual conduct of mankind in such particular situations.

I have frequently considered what could possibly be the reason why all mankind, though they have ever, without hesitation, acknowledged the doctrine of necessity in their whole practice and reasoning, have yet discovered such a reluctance to acknowledge it in words, and have rather shown a propensity in all ages to profess the contrary opinion. The matter, I think, may be accounted for after the following manner. If we examine the operations of body and the production of effects from their causes, we shall find that all our faculties can never carry us further in our knowledge of this relation than barely to observe that particular objects are *constantly conjoined* together, and that the mind is carried by a *customary transition* from the appearance of one to the belief of the other. But though this conclusion concerning human ignorance be the result of the strictest scrutiny of this subject, men still entertain a strong propensity to believe that they penetrate further into the powers of nature and perceive something like a necessary connection between the cause and the effect. When again they turn their reflections toward the operations of their own minds and *feel* no such connection of the motive and the action, they are thence apt to suppose that there is a difference between the effects which result from material force and those which arise from thought and intelligence. But being once convinced that we know nothing further of causation of any kind than merely the *constant conjunction* of objects and the consequent *inference* of the mind from one to another, and finding that these two circumstances are universally allowed to have place in voluntary actions, we may be more easily led to own the same necessity common to all causes. And though this reasoning may contradict the systems of many philosophers in ascribing necessity to the determinations of the will, we shall find, upon reflection, that they dissent from it in words only, not in their real sentiment. Necessity, according to the sense in which it is here taken, has never yet been rejected, nor can ever, I think, be rejected by any philosopher. It may only, perhaps, be pretended that the mind can perceive in the operations of matter some further connection between the cause and effect, and a connection that has not place in the voluntary actions of intelligent beings. Now whether it be so or not can only appear upon examination, and it is incumbent on these philosophers to make good their assertion by defining or describing that necessity and pointing it out to us in the operations of material causes.

It would seem, indeed, that men begin at the wrong end of this question concerning liberty and necessity when they enter upon it by examining the faculties of the soul, the influence of the understanding, and the operations of the will. Let them first discuss a more simple question, namely, the operations of body and of brute unintelligent matter, and try whether they can there form any idea of causation and necessity, except that of a constant conjunction of objects and subsequent inference of the mind from one to another. If these circumstances form, in reality, the whole of that necessity which we conceive in matter, and if these circumstances be also universally acknowledged to take place in the operations of the mind, the dispute is at an end, [or] at least must be owned to be thenceforth merely verbal. But as long as we will rashly suppose that we have some further idea of necessity and causation in the operations of external objects, at the same time that we can find nothing further in the voluntary actions of the mind, there is no possibility of bringing the question to any determinate issue while we proceed upon so erroneous a supposition. The only method of undeceiving us is to mount up higher, to examine the narrow extent of science when applied to material causes, and to convince ourselves that all we know of them is the constant conjunction and inference above-mentioned. We may, perhaps, find that it is with difficulty we are induced to fix such narrow limits to human understanding. But we can afterwards find no difficulty when we come to apply this doctrine to the actions of the will. For as it is evident that these have a regular conjunction with motives and circumstances and character, and as we always draw inferences from one to the other, we must be obliged to acknowledge in words that necessity which we have already avowed in every deliberation of our lives and in every step of our conduct and behavior.[1]

But to proceed in this reconciling project with regard to the question of liberty and necessity—the most contentious question of metaphysics, the most contentious science—it will not require many words to prove that all mankind have ever agreed in the doctrine of liberty as well as in that of necessity, and that the whole dispute, in this respect also, has been hitherto merely verbal. For what is meant by liberty, when ap-

[1] The prevalence of the doctrine of liberty may be accounted for from another cause, viz., a false sensation or seeming experience which we have, or may have, of liberty or indifference in many of our actions. The necessity of any action, whether of matter or of mind, is not, properly speaking, a quality in the agent but in any thinking or intelligent being who may consider the action, and it consists chiefly in the determination of his thoughts to infer the existence of that action from some preceding objects; as liberty, when opposed to necessity, is nothing but the want of that determination, and a certain looseness or indifference which we feel in passing, or not passing, from the idea of one object to that of any succeeding one. Now we may observe that though, in *reflecting* on human actions, we seldom feel such a looseness or indifference, but are commonly able to infer them with considerable certainty from their motives and from the disposition of the agent, yet it frequently happens that in *performing* the actions themselves, we are sensible of something like it; and as all resembling objects are readily taken for each other, this has been employed as a demonstrative and even intuitive proof of human liberty. We feel that our actions are subject to our will on most occasions, and imagine we feel that the will itself is subject to nothing, because, when by a denial of it we are provoked to try, we feel that it moves easily every way, and produces an image of itself (or a *velleity*, as it is called in the schools), even on that side on which it did not settle. This image or faint motion, we persuade ourselves, could at that time have been completed into the thing itself, because, should that be denied, we find upon a second trial that at present it can. We consider not that the fantastical desire of showing liberty is here the motive of our actions. And it seems certain that however we may imagine we feel a liberty within ourselves, a spectator can commonly infer our actions from our motives and character, and even where he cannot, he concludes in general that he might, were he perfectly acquainted with every circumstance of our situation and temper, and the most secret springs of our complexion and disposition. Now this is the very essence of necessity, according to the foregoing doctrine.

plied to voluntary actions? We cannot surely mean that actions have so little connection with motives, inclinations, and circumstances that one does not follow with a certain degree of uniformity from the other, and that one affords no inference by which we can conclude the existence of the other. For these are plain and acknowledged matters of fact. By liberty, then, we can only mean *a power of acting or not acting, according to the determinations of the will;* that is, if we choose to remain at rest, we may; if we choose to move, we also may. Now this hypothetical liberty is universally allowed to belong to everyone who is not a prisoner and in chains. Here then is no subject of dispute.

Whatever definition we may give of liberty, we should be careful to observe two requisite circumstances: *first,* that it be consistent with plain matter of fact; *secondly,* that it be consistent with itself. If we observe these circumstances and render our definition intelligible, I am persuaded that all mankind will be found of one opinion with regard to it.

It is universally allowed that nothing exists without a cause of its existence, and that chance, when strictly examined, is a mere negative word and means not any real power which has anywhere a being in nature. But it is pretended that some causes are necessary, some not necessary. Here then is the advantage of definitions. Let anyone *define* a cause without comprehending, as a part of the definition, a *necessary connection* with its effect, and let him show distinctly the origin of the idea expressed by the definition, and I shall readily give up the whole controversy. But if the foregoing explication of the matter be received, this must be absolutely impracticable. Had not objects a regular conjunction with each other, we should never have entertained any notion of cause and effect; and this regular conjunction produces that inference of the understanding which is the only connection that we can have any comprehension of. Whoever attempts a definition of cause exclusive of these circumstances will be obliged either to employ unintelligible terms or such as are synonymous to the term which he endeavors to define.[1] And if the definition

[1] Thus if a cause be defined, *that which produces anything,* it is easy to observe that *producing* is synonymous to *causing.* In like manner, if a cause be defined, *that by which anything exists,* this

above-mentioned be admitted, liberty, when opposed to necessity, not to constraint, is the same thing with chance, which is universally allowed to have no existence.

Part II.

There is no method of reasoning more common, and yet none more blamable, than in philosophical disputes to endeavor the refutation of any hypothesis by a pretense of its dangerous consequences to religion and morality. When any opinion leads to absurdities it is certainly false, but it is not certain that an opinion is false because it is of dangerous consequence. Such topics, therefore, ought entirely to be forborne, as serving nothing to the discovery of truth, but only to make the person of an antagonist odious. This I observe in general, without pretending to draw any advantage from it. I frankly submit to an examination of this kind, and shall venture to affirm that the doctrines both of necessity and of liberty, as above explained, are not only consistent with morality, but are absolutely essential to its support.

Necessity may be defined two ways, conformably to the two definitions of *cause,* of which it makes an essential part. It consists either in the constant conjunction of like objects, or in the inference of the understanding from one object to another. Now necessity in both these senses (which, indeed, are at bottom the same) has universally, though tacitly, in the schools, in the pulpit, and in common life been allowed to belong to the will of man, and no one has ever pretended to deny that we can draw inferences concerning human actions, and that those inferences are founded on the experienced union of like actions with like motives, inclinations, and circumstances. The only particular in which anyone can differ is that either perhaps he will refuse to give the name of necessity to this property of human actions—but as long as the

---

is liable to the same objection. For what is meant by these words, *by which?* Had it been said that a cause is *that* after which *anything constantly exists,* we should have understood the terms. For this is, indeed, all we know of the matter. And this constancy forms the very essence of necessity, nor have we any other idea of it.

meaning is understood I hope the word can do no harm—or that he will maintain it possible to discover something further in the operations of matter. But this, it must be acknowledged, can be of no consequence to morality or religion, whatever it may be to natural philosophy or metaphysics. We may here be mistaken in asserting that there is no idea of any other necessity or connection in the actions of body, but surely we ascribe nothing to the actions of the mind but what everyone does and must readily allow of. We change no circumstance in the received orthodox system with regard to the will, but only in that with regard to material objects and causes. Nothing therefore can be more innocent at least than this doctrine.

All laws being founded on rewards and punishments, it is supposed as a fundamental principle that these motives have a regular and uniform influence on the mind, and both produce the good and prevent the evil actions. We may give to this influence what name we please, but as it is usually conjoined with the action, it must be esteemed a *cause* and be looked upon as an instance of that necessity which we would here establish.

The only proper object of hatred or vengeance is a person or creature endowed with thought and consciousness, and when any criminal or injurious actions excite that passion, it is only by their relation to the person, or connection with him. Actions are, by their very nature, temporary and perishing, and where they proceed not from some *cause* in the character and disposition of the person who performed them, they can neither redound to his honor if good, nor infamy if evil. The actions themselves may be blamable; they may be contrary to all the rules of morality and religion. But the person is not answerable for them, and as they proceeded from nothing in him that is durable and constant and leave nothing of that nature behind them, it is impossible he can, upon their account, become the object of punishment or vengeance. According to the principle, therefore, which denies necessity and consequently causes, a man is as pure and untainted after having committed the most horrid crime as at the first moment of his birth, nor is his character anywise concerned in his actions, since they are not derived from it, and the wickedness of the one can never be used as a proof of the depravity of the other.

Men are not blamed for such actions as they perform ignorantly and casually, whatever may be the consequences. Why but because the principles of these actions are only momentary and terminate in them alone? Men are less blamed for such actions as they perform hastily and unpremeditatedly than for such as proceed from deliberation. For what reason but because a hasty temper, though a constant cause or principle in the mind, operates only by intervals and infects not the whole character? Again, repentance wipes off every crime, if attended with a reformation of life and manners. How is this to be accounted for but by asserting that actions render a person criminal merely as they are proofs of criminal principles in the mind, and when, by an alteration of these principles, they cease to be just proofs, they likewise cease to be criminal? But except upon the doctrine of necessity, they never were just proofs, and consequently never were criminal.

It will be equally easy to prove, and from the same arguments, that *liberty*, according to that definition above-mentioned, in which all men agree, is also essential to morality, and that no human actions, where it is wanting, are susceptible of any moral qualities or can be the objects of approbation or dislike. For as actions are objects of our moral sentiment so far only as they are indications of the internal character, passions, and affections, it is impossible that they can give rise either to praise or blame where they proceed not from these principles, but are derived altogether from external violence.

I pretend not to have obviated or removed all objections to this theory with regard to necessity and liberty. I can foresee other objections derived from topics which have not here been treated of. It may be said, for instance, that if voluntary actions be subjected to the same laws of necessity with the operations of matter, there is a continued chain of necessary causes, preordained and predetermined, reaching from the original cause of all to every single volition of every human creature. No contingency anywhere in the universe, no indifference, no liberty. While we act, we are at the same time acted upon. The ultimate author of all our volitions is the Creator of the world, who first bestowed motion on this immense machine and placed all beings in that particular position whence every subsequent event, by an inevitable necessity, must result. Human actions, therefore, either can have no moral turpitude at all, as proceeding from so good a cause, or if they have any turpitude, they must involve our Creator in the same guilt, while he is acknowledged to be their ultimate cause and author. For as a man who fired a mine is answerable for all the consequences whether the train he employed be long or short, so wherever a continued chain of necessary causes is fixed, that being, either finite or infinite, who produces the first is likewise the author of all the rest, and must both bear the blame and acquire the praise which belong to them. Our clear and unalterable ideas of morality establish this rule upon unquestionable reasons when we examine the consequences of any human action, and these reasons must still have greater force when applied to the volitions and intentions of a being infinitely wise and powerful. Ignorance or impotence may be pleaded for so limited a creature as man, but those imperfections have no place in our Creator. He foresaw, he ordained, he intended all those actions of men which we so rashly pronounce criminal. And we must therefore conclude, either that they are not criminal, or that the Deity, not man, is accountable for them. But as either of these positions is absurd and impious, it follows that the doctrine from which they are deduced cannot possibly be true, as being liable to all the same objections. An absurd consequence, if necessary, proves the original doctrine to be absurd, in the same manner as criminal actions render criminal the original cause, if the connection between them be necessary and inevitable.

This objection consists of two parts, which we shall examine separately. *First*, that if human actions can be traced up, by a necessary chain, to the Deity, they can never be criminal, on account of the infinite perfection of that being from whom they are derived, and who can intend nothing but what is altogether good and laudable. Or, *secondly*, if they be criminal, we must retract the attribute of perfection which we ascribe to the Deity, and must acknowledge him to be the ultimate author of guilt and moral turpitude in all his creatures.

The answer to the first objection seems obvious and convincing. There are many philosophers who, after an exact scrutiny of the phenomena of nature, conclude that the WHOLE, considered as one system, is, in every period of its existence, ordered with perfect benevolence; and that the utmost possible happiness will, in the end, result to all created beings without any mixture of positive or absolute ill and misery. Every physical ill, say they, makes an essential part of this benevolent system, and could not possibly be removed even by the Deity himself, considered as a wise agent, without giving entrance to greater ill or excluding greater good which will result from it. From this theory some philosophers, and the ancient Stoics among the rest, derived a topic of consolation under all afflictions, while they taught their pupils that those ills under which they labored were in reality goods to the universe, and that to an enlarged view which could comprehend the whole system of nature every event became an object of joy and exultation. But though this topic be specious and sublime, it was soon found in practice weak and ineffectual. You would surely more irritate than appease a man lying under the racking pains of the gout by preaching up to him the rectitude of those general laws which produced the malignant humors in his body and led them through the proper canals to the sinews and nerves, where they now excite such acute torments. These enlarged views may, for a moment, please the imagination of a speculative man who is placed in ease and security, but neither can they dwell with constancy on his mind, even though undisturbed by the emotions of pain or passion, much less can they maintain their ground when attacked by such powerful antagonists. The affections take a narrower and more natural survey of their object, and by an economy more suitable to the infirmity of human minds, regard alone the beings around us, and are actuated by such events as appear good or ill to the private system.

The case is the same with *moral* as with *physical* ill. It cannot reasonably be supposed that those remote considerations which are found of so little efficacy with regard to one will have a more powerful influence with regard to the other. The mind of man is so formed by nature that, upon the appearance of certain characters, dispositions, and actions, it immediately feels the sentiment of approbation or blame; nor are there any emotions more essential to its frame and constitution. The characters which engage our approbation are chiefly such as contribute to the peace and security of human society, as the characters which excite blame are chiefly such as tend to public detriment and disturbance; whence it may reasonably be presumed that the moral sentiments arise, either mediately or immediately, from a reflection on these opposite interests. What though philosophical meditations establish a different opinion or conjecture, that everything is right with regard to the whole, and that the qualities which disturb society are, in the main, as beneficial, and are as suitable to the primary intention of nature, as those which more directly promote its happiness and welfare? Are such remote and uncertain speculations able to counterbalance the sentiments which arise from the natural and immediate view of the objects? A man who is robbed of a considerable sum, does he find his vexation for the loss anywise diminished by these sublime reflections? Why then should his moral resentment against the crime be supposed incompatible with them? Or why should not the acknowledgment of a real distinction between vice and virtue be reconcilable to all speculative systems of philosophy, as well as that of a real distinction between personal beauty and deformity? Both these distinctions are founded in the natural sentiments of the human mind, and these sentiments are not to be controlled or altered by any philosophical theory or speculation whatsoever.

The *second* objection admits not of so easy and satisfactory an answer, nor is it possible to explain distinctly how the Deity can be the immediate cause of all the actions of men without being the author of sin and moral turpitude. These are mysteries which mere natural and unassisted reason is very unfit to handle; and whatever system she embraces, she must find herself involved in inextricable difficulties and even contradictions at every step which she takes with regard to such subjects. To reconcile the indifference and contingency of human actions with prescience, or to defend absolute decrees and yet free the Deity from being the author of sin, has been found hitherto to exceed all the power of philosophy. Happy, if she be thence sensible of her temerity when she pries into these sublime mysteries, and leaving a scene so full of obscurities and perplexities, return with suitable modesty to her true and proper province, the examination of common life, where she will find difficulties enough to employ her inquiries, without launching into so boundless an ocean of doubt, uncertainty, and contradiction!

Section X.

OF MIRACLES

Part I.

THERE IS, in Dr. Tillotson's writings, an argument against the *real presence* which is as concise and elegant and strong as any argument can possibly be supposed against a doctrine so little worthy of a serious refutation. It is acknowledged on all hands, says that learned prelate, that the authority either of the Scripture or of tradition is founded merely on the testimony of the Apostles, who were eyewitnesses to those miracles of our Saviour by which He proved His divine mission. Our evidence, then, for the truth of the *Christian* religion is less than the evidence for the truth of our senses, because even in the first authors of our religion it was no greater, and it is evident it must diminish in passing from them to their disciples; nor can anyone rest such confidence in their testimony as in the immediate object of his senses. But a weaker evidence can never destroy a stronger; and therefore, were the doctrine of the real presence ever so clearly revealed in Scripture, it were directly contrary to the rules of just reasoning to give our assent to it. It contradicts sense, though both the Scripture and tradition, on which it is supposed to be built, carry not such evidence with them as sense when they are considered merely as external evidences, and are not brought home to everyone's breast by the immediate operation of the Holy Spirit.

Nothing is so convenient as a decisive argument of this kind, which must at least *silence* the most arrogant bigotry and superstition, and free us from their impertinent solicitations. I flatter myself that I have discovered an argument of a like nature which, if just, will, with the wise and learned, be an everlasting check to all kinds of superstitious delusion, and consequently will be useful as long as the world endures. For so long, I presume, will the accounts of miracles and prodigies be found in all history, sacred and profane.

Though experience be our only guide in reasoning concerning matters of fact, it must be acknowledged that this guide is not altogether infallible, but in some cases is apt to lead us into errors. One who in our climate should expect better weather in any week of June than in one of December would reason justly and conformably to experience, but it is certain that he may happen, in the event, to find himself mistaken. However, we may observe that in such a case he would have no cause to complain of experience, because it commonly informs us beforehand of the uncertainty by that contrariety of events which we may learn from a diligent observation. All effects follow not with like certainty from their supposed causes. Some events are found, in all countries and all ages, to have been constantly conjoined together; others are found to have been more variable, and sometimes to disappoint our expectations, so that in our reasonings concerning matter of fact there are all imaginable degrees of assurance, from the highest certainty to the lowest species of moral evidence.

A wise man, therefore, proportions his belief to the evidence. In such conclusions as are founded on an infallible experience, he expects the event with the last degree of assurance, and regards his past experience as a full *proof* of the future existence of that event. In other cases he proceeds with more caution: he weighs the opposite experiments; he considers which side is supported by the greater number of experiments; to that side he inclines, with doubt and hesitation; and when at last he fixes his judgment, the evidence exceeds not what we properly call *probability*. All probability, then, supposes an opposition of experiments and observations, where the one side is found to overbalance the other and to produce a degree of evidence proportioned to the superiority. A hundred instances or experiments on one side, and fifty on another, afford a doubtful expectation of any event, though a hundred uniform experiments, with only one that is contradictory, reasonably beget a pretty strong degree of assurance. In all cases we must balance the opposite experiments where they are opposite, and deduct the smaller number from the greater in order to know the exact force of the superior evidence.

To apply these principles to a particular instance, we may observe that there is no species of reasoning more common, more useful, and even necessary to human life than that which is derived from the testimony of men and the reports of eyewitnesses and spectators. This species of reasoning, perhaps, one may deny to be founded on the relation of cause and effect. I shall not dispute about a word. It will be sufficient to observe that our assurance in any argument of this kind is derived from no other principle than our observation of the veracity of human testimony and of the usual conformity of facts to the report of witnesses. It being a general maxim that no objects have any discoverable connection together, and that all the inferences which we can draw from one to another are founded merely on our experience of their constant and regular conjunction, it is evident that we ought not to make an exception to this maxim in favor of human testimony, whose connection with any event seems in itself as little necessary as any other. Were not the memory tenacious to a certain degree, had not men commonly an inclination to truth and a principle of probity, were they not sensible to shame when detected in a falsehood, were not these, I say, discovered by *experience* to be qualities inherent in human nature, we should never repose the least confidence in human testimony. A man delirious or noted for falsehood and villainy has no manner of authority with us.

And as the evidence derived from witnesses and human testimony is founded on past experience, so it varies with the experience and is regarded either as a *proof* or a *probability*, according as the conjunction between any particular kind of report and any kind of object has been found to be constant or variable. There are a number of circumstances to be taken into consideration in all judgments of this kind, and the ultimate standard by which we determine all disputes that may arise concerning them is always derived from experience and observation. Where this experience is not entirely uniform on any side, it is attended with an unavoidable contrariety in our judgments and with the same opposition and mutual destruction of argument as in every other kind of evidence. We frequently hesitate concerning the reports of others. We balance the opposite circumstances which cause any doubt or uncertainty; and when we discover a superiority on any side, we incline to it, but still with a diminution of assurance, in proportion to the force of its antagonist.

This contrariety of evidence, in the present case, may be derived from several different causes: from the opposition of contrary testimony, from the character or number of the witnesses, from the manner of their delivering their testimony, or from the union of all these circumstances. We entertain a suspicion concerning any matter of fact when the witnesses contradict each other, when they are but few or of a doubtful character, when they have an interest in what they affirm, when they deliver their testimony with hesitation, or on the contrary with too violent asseverations. There are many other particulars of the same kind which may diminish or destroy the force of any argument derived from human testimony.

Suppose, for instance, that the fact which the testimony endeavors to establish partakes of the extraordinary and the marvelous; in that case the evidence resulting from the testimony admits of a diminution, greater or less, in proportion as the fact is more or less unusual. The reason why we place any credit in witnesses and historians is not derived from any *connection* which we perceive *a priori* between testimony and reality, but because we are accustomed to find a conformity between them. But when the fact attested is such a one as has seldom fallen under our observation, here is a contest of two opposite experiences, of which the one destroys the other as far as its force goes, and the superior can only operate on the mind by the force which remains. The very same principle of experience which gives us a certain degree of assurance in the testimony of witnesses gives us also, in this case, another degree of assurance against the fact which they endeavor to establish; from which contradiction there necessarily arises a counterpoise and mutual destruction of belief and authority.

I should not believe such a story were it told me by Cato was a proverbial saying in Rome, even during the lifetime of that philosophical patriot.[1] The incredibility of a fact, it was allowed, might invalidate so great an authority.

The Indian prince who refused to believe the first relations concerning the effects of frost reasoned justly, and it naturally required very strong testimony to engage his assent to facts that arose from a state of nature with which he was unacquainted, and which bore so little analogy to those events of which he had had constant and uniform experience. Though they were not contrary to his experience, they were not conformable to it.[2]

But in order to increase the probability against the testimony of witnesses, let us suppose that the fact which they affirm, instead of being only marvelous, is really miraculous,

[1] Plutarch, in *vita Catonis*.

[2] No Indian, it is evident, could have experience that water did not freeze in cold climates. This is placing nature in a situation quite unknown to him, and it is impossible for him to tell *a priori* what will result from it. It is making a new experiment, the consequence of which is always uncertain. One may sometimes conjecture from analogy what will follow, but still this is but conjecture. And it must be confessed that, in the present case of freezing, the event follows contrary to the rules of analogy and is such as a rational Indian would not look for. The operations of cold upon water are not gradual, according to the degrees of cold, but whenever it comes to the freezing point, the water passes in a moment from the utmost liquidity to perfect hardness. Such an event, therefore, may be denominated *extraordinary* and requires a pretty strong testimony to render it credible to people in a warm climate. But still it is not *miraculous*, nor contrary to uniform experience of the course of nature in cases where all the circumstances are the same. The inhabitants of Sumatra have always seen water fluid in their own climate, and the freezing of their rivers ought to be deemed a prodigy. But they never saw water in Muscovy during the winter, and therefore they cannot reasonably be positive what would there be the consequence.

and suppose also that the testimony, considered apart and in itself, amounts to an entire proof; in that case there is proof against proof, of which the strongest must prevail, but still with a diminution of its force, in proportion to that of its antagonist.

A miracle is a violation of the laws of nature; and as a firm and unalterable experience has established these laws, the proof against a miracle, from the very nature of the fact, is as entire as any argument from experience can possibly be imagined. Why is it more than probable that all men must die, that lead cannot of itself remain suspended in the air, that fire consumes wood and is extinguished by water, unless it be that these events are found agreeable to the laws of nature, and there is required a violation of these laws, or in other words a miracle, to prevent them? Nothing is esteemed a miracle if it ever happen in the common course of nature. It is no miracle that a man, seemingly in good health, should die on a sudden, because such a kind of death, though more unusual than any other, has yet been frequently observed to happen. But it is a miracle that a dead man should come to life, because that has never been observed in any age or country. There must, therefore, be a uniform experience against every miraculous event, otherwise the event would not merit that appellation. And as a uniform experience amounts to a proof, there is here a direct and full *proof*, from the nature of the fact, against the existence of any miracle; nor can such a proof be destroyed or the miracle rendered credible but by an opposite proof which is superior.[1]

---

[1] Sometimes an event may not, *in itself, seem* to be contrary to the laws of nature, and yet if it were real it might, by reason of some circumstances, be denominated a miracle, because in *fact* it is contrary to these laws. Thus if a person claiming a divine authority should command a sick person to be well, a healthful man to fall down dead, the clouds to pour rain, the winds to blow, in short, should order many natural events, which immediately follow upon his command, these might justly be esteemed miracles, because they are really, in this case, contrary to the laws of nature. For if any suspicion remain that the event and command concurred by accident, there is no miracle and no transgression of the laws of nature. If this suspicion be removed, there is evidently a miracle and a transgression of these laws, because nothing can be more

The plain consequence is (and it is a general maxim worthy of our attention) that no testimony is sufficient to establish a miracle unless the testimony be of such a kind that its falsehood would be more miraculous than the fact which it endeavors to establish. And even in that case there is a mutual destruction of arguments, and the superior only gives us an assurance suitable to that degree of force which remains after deducting the inferior. When anyone tells me that he saw a dead man restored to life, I immediately consider with myself whether it be more probable that this person should either deceive or be deceived, or that the fact which he relates should really have happened. I weigh the one miracle against the other, and according to the superiority which I discover I pronounce my decision, and always reject the greater miracle. If the falsehood of his testimony would be more miraculous than the event which he relates, then, and not till then, can he pretend to command my belief or opinion.

Part II.

In the foregoing reasoning we have supposed that the testimony upon which a miracle is founded may possibly amount to an entire proof, and that the falsehood of that testimony would be a real prodigy. But it is easy to show that we have been a great deal too liberal in our concession, and that there never was a miraculous event established on so full an evidence.

For *first,* there is not to be found in all history any miracle attested by a sufficient number of men of such unquestioned good sense, education, and learning as to secure us against all

---

contrary to nature than that the voice or command of a man should have such an influence. A miracle may be accurately defined, *a transgression of a law of nature by a particular volition of the Deity, or by the interposition of some invisible agent.* A miracle may either be discoverable by men or not. This alters not its nature and essence. The raising of a house or ship into the air is a visible miracle. The raising of a feather, when the wind wants ever so little of a force requisite for that purpose, is as real a miracle, though not so sensible with regard to us.

delusion in themselves, of such undoubted integrity as to place them beyond all suspicion of any design to deceive others, of such credit and reputation in the eyes of mankind as to have a great deal to lose in case of their being detected in any falsehood, and at the same time attesting facts performed in such a public manner and in so celebrated a part of the world as to render the detection unavoidable; all which circumstances are requisite to give us a full assurance in the testimony of men.

Secondly, we may observe in human nature a principle which, if strictly examined, will be found to diminish extremely the assurance which we might, from human testimony, have in any kind of prodigy. The maxim by which we commonly conduct ourselves in our reasonings is that the objects of which we have no experience resemble those of which we have; that what we have found to be most usual is always most probable; and that where there is an opposition of arguments, we ought to give the preference to such as are founded on the greatest number of past observations. But though, in proceeding by this rule, we readily reject any fact which is unusual and incredible in an ordinary degree, yet in advancing further, the mind observes not always the same rule, but when anything is affirmed utterly absurd and miraculous, it rather the more readily admits of such a fact upon account of that very circumstance which ought to destroy all its authority. The passion of *surprise* and *wonder,* arising from miracles, being an agreeable emotion, gives a sensible tendency toward the belief of those events from which it is derived. And this goes so far that even those who cannot enjoy this pleasure immediately, nor can believe those miraculous events of which they are informed, yet love to partake of the satisfaction at second hand or by rebound, and place a pride and delight in exciting the admiration of others.

With what greediness are the miraculous accounts of travelers received, their descriptions of sea and land monsters, their relations of wonderful adventures, strange men, and uncouth manners? But if the spirit of religion join itself to the love of wonder, there is an end of common sense, and human testimony in these circumstances loses all pretensions to authority. A religionist may be an enthusiast and imagine he sees what has no reality. He may know his narrative to be false, and yet persevere in it with the best intentions in the world, for the sake of promoting so holy a cause. Or even where this delusion has not place, vanity, excited by so strong a temptation, operates on him more powerfully than on the rest of mankind in any other circumstances, and self-interest with equal force. His auditors may not have, and commonly have not, sufficient judgment to canvass his evidence. What judgment they have, they renounce by principle, in these sublime and mysterious subjects. Or if they were ever so willing to employ it, passion and a heated imagination disturb the regularity of its operations. Their credulity increases his impudence, and his impudence overpowers their credulity.

Eloquence, when at its highest pitch, leaves little room for reason or reflection, but addressing itself entirely to the fancy or the affections, captivates the willing hearers, and subdues their understanding. Happily, this pitch it seldom attains. But what a Tully or a Demosthenes could scarcely effect over a Roman or Athenian audience, very *Capuchin*, every itinerant or stationary teacher can perform over the generality of mankind, and in a higher degree, by touching such gross and vulgar passions.

The many instances of forged miracles and prophecies and supernatural events which, in all ages, have either been detected by contrary evidence or which detect themselves by their absurdity, prove sufficiently the strong propensity of mankind to the extraordinary and the marvelous, and ought reasonably to beget a suspicion against all relations of this kind. This is our natural way of thinking, even with regard to the most common and most credible events. For instance, there is no kind of report which arises so easily and spreads so quickly, especially in country places and provincial towns, as those concerning marriages, insomuch that two young persons of equal condition never see each other twice, but the whole neighborhood immediately join them together. The pleasure of telling a piece of news so interesting, of propagating it, and of being the first reporters of it spreads the intelligence. And this is so well known that no man of sense gives attention to these reports till he find them confirmed by some greater evidence. Do not the same passions, and others still stronger, incline the generality of mankind to believe and report, with the greatest vehemence and assurance, all religious miracles?

Thirdly, it forms a strong presumption against all supernatural and miraculous relations that they are observed chiefly to abound among ignorant and barbarous nations; or if a civilized people has ever given admission to any of them, that people will be found to have received them from ignorant and barbarous ancestors, who transmitted them with that inviolable sanction and authority which always attend received opinions. When we peruse the first histories of all nations, we are apt to imagine ourselves transported into some new world, where the whole frame of nature is disjointed and every element performs its operations in a different manner from what it does at present. Battles, revolutions, pestilence, famine, and death are never the effect of those natural causes which we experience. Prodigies, omens, oracles, judgments quite obscure the few natural events that are intermingled with them. But as the former grow thinner every page, in proportion as we advance nearer the enlightened ages, we soon learn that there is nothing mysterious or supernatural in the case, but that all proceeds from the usual propensity of mankind toward the marvelous, and that, though this inclination may at intervals receive a check from sense and learning, it can never be thoroughly extirpated from human nature.

It is strange, a judicious reader is apt to say upon the perusal of these wonderful historians, *that such prodigious events never happen in our days.* But it is nothing strange, I hope, that men should lie in all ages. You must surely have seen instances enough of that frailty. You have yourself heard many such marvelous relations started, which being treated with scorn by all the wise and judicious, have at last been abandoned even by the vulgar. Be assured that those renowned lies which have spread and flourished to such a monstrous height arose from like beginnings, but being sown in a more proper soil shot up at last into prodigies almost equal to those which they relate.

It was a wise policy in that false prophet Alexander, who, though now forgotten, was once so famous, to lay the first scene of his impostures in Paphlagonia, where, as Lucian tells us, the people were extremely ignorant and stupid, and ready to swallow even the grossest delusion. People at a distance, who are weak enough to think the matter at all worth inquiry, have no opportunity of receiving better information. The stories come magnified to them by a hundred circumstances. Fools are industrious in propagating the imposture, while the wise and learned are contented, in general, to deride its absurdity, without informing themselves of the particular facts by which it may be distinctly refuted. And thus the impostor above-mentioned was enabled to proceed from his ignorant Paphlagonians to the enlisting of votaries, even among the Grecian philosophers and men of the most eminent rank and distinction in Rome, nay, could engage the attention of that sage emperor Marcus Aurelius so far as to make him trust the success of a military expedition to his delusive prophecies.

The advantages are so great of starting an imposture among an ignorant people that, even though the delusion should be too gross to impose on the generality of them (*which, though seldom, is sometimes the case*), it has a much better chance for succeeding in remote countries than if the first scene had been laid in a city renowned for arts and knowledge. The most ignorant and barbarous of these barbarians carry the report abroad. None of their countrymen have a large correspondence, or sufficient credit and authority to contradict and beat down the delusion. Men's inclination to the marvelous has full opportunity to display itself. And thus a story which is universally exploded in the place where it was first started shall pass for certain at a thousand miles distance. But had Alexander fixed his residence at Athens, the philosophers at that renowned mart of learning had immediately spread throughout the whole Roman empire their sense of the matter, which, being supported by so great authority and displayed by all the force of reason and eloquence, had entirely opened the eyes of mankind. It is true, Lucian, passing by chance through Paphlagonia, had an opportunity of performing this good office. But, though much to be wished, it does not always happen that every Alexander meets with a Lucian, ready to expose and detect his impostures.

I may add as a *fourth* reason which diminishes the authority of prodigies, that there is no testimony for any, even those which have not been expressly detected, that is not opposed by an infinite number of witnesses, so that not only the miracle destroys the credit of testimony, but the testimony destroys itself. To make this the better understood, let us consider that in matters of religion whatever is different is contrary, and that it is impossible the religions of ancient Rome, of Turkey, of Siam, and of China should all of them be established on any solid foundation. Every miracle, therefore, pretended to have been wrought in any of these religions (and all of them abound in miracles), as its direct scope is to establish the particular system to which it is attributed, so has it the same force, though more indirectly, to overthrow every other system. In destroying a rival system, it likewise destroys the credit of those miracles on which that system was established, so that all the prodigies of different religions are to be regarded as contrary facts, and the evidences of these prodigies, whether weak or strong, as opposite to each other. According to this method of reasoning, when we believe any miracle of Mahomet or his successors, we have for our warrant the testimony of a few barbarous Arabians. And on the other hand, we are to regard the authority of Titus Livius, Plutarch, Tacitus, and, in short, of all the authors and witnesses, Grecian, Chinese, and Roman Catholic, who have related any miracle in their particular religion—I say, we are to regard their testimony in the same light as if they had mentioned the Mahometan miracle and had in express terms contradicted it with the same certainty as they have for the miracle they relate. This argument may appear oversubtle and refined, but is not in reality different from the reasoning of a judge who supposes that the credit of two witnesses maintaining a crime against anyone is destroyed by the testimony of two others who affirm him to have been two hundred leagues distant at the same instant when the crime is said to have been committed.

One of the best-attested miracles in all profane history is that which Tacitus reports of Vespasian, who cured a blind man in Alexandria by means of his spittle, and a lame man by the mere touch of his foot, in obedience to a vision of the god Serapis, who had enjoined them to have recourse to the Em-

peror for these miraculous cures. The story may be seen in
that fine historian[1] where every circumstance seems to add
weight to the testimony, and might be displayed at large with
all the force of argument and eloquence, if anyone were now
concerned to enforce the evidence of that exploded and idola-
trous superstition. The gravity, solidity, age, and probity of
so great an emperor, who, through the whole course of his life,
conversed in a familiar manner with his friends and courtiers,
and never affected those extraordinary airs of divinity assumed by Alexander and Demetrius. The historian, a contemporary writer noted for candor and veracity, and withal
the greatest and most penetrating genius perhaps of all antiquity, and so free from any tendency to credulity that he
even lies under the contrary imputation of atheism and profaneness. The persons from whose authority he related the
miracle, of established character for judgment and veracity,
as we may well presume; eyewitnesses of the fact, and confirming their testimony after the Flavian family was despoiled
of the empire and could no longer give any reward as the
price of a lie. *Utrumque qui interfuere nunc quoque memo-
rant, postquam nullum mendacio pretium.*[2] To which, if we
add the public nature of the facts, as related, it will appear
that no evidence can well be supposed stronger for so gross
and so palpable a falsehood.

There is also a memorable story related by Cardinal De
Retz, which may well deserve our consideration. When that
intriguing politician fled into Spain to avoid the persecution
of his enemies, he passed through Saragossa, the capital of
Aragon, where he was shown, in the cathedral, a man who
had served seven years as a doorkeeper and was well known
to everybody in town that had ever paid his devotions at that
church. He had been seen for so long a time wanting a leg,
but recovered that limb by the rubbing of holy oil upon the
stump, and the Cardinal assures us that he saw him with two
legs. This miracle was vouched by all the canons of the

---

[1] *Hist.*, lib. iv. cap. 81. Suetonius gives nearly the same account in
vita Vesp.
[2] [Both facts are told by eyewitnesses even now when falsehood
brings no reward.]

church, and the whole company in town were appealed to for a confirmation of the fact, whom the Cardinal found, by their zealous devotion, to be thorough believers of the miracle. Here the relater was also contemporary to the supposed prodigy, of an incredulous and libertine character as well as of great genius, the miracle of so *singular* a nature as could scarcely admit of a counterfeit, and the witnesses very numerous, and all of them in a manner spectators of the fact to which they gave their testimony. And what adds mightily to the force of the evidence and may double our surprise on this occasion is that the Cardinal himself, who relates the story, seems not to give any credit to it, and consequently cannot be suspected of any concurrence in the holy fraud. He considered justly that it was not requisite, in order to reject a fact of this nature, to be able accurately to disprove the testimony and to trace its falsehood through all the circumstances of knavery and credulity which produced it. He knew that, as this was commonly altogether impossible at any small distance of time and place, so was it extremely difficult, even where one was immediately present, by reason of the bigotry, ignorance, cunning, and roguery of a great part of mankind. He therefore concluded, like a just reasoner, that such an evidence carried falsehood upon the very face of it, and that a miracle supported by any human testimony was more properly a subject of derision than of argument.

There surely never was a greater number of miracles ascribed to one person than those which were lately said to have been wrought in France upon the tomb of Abbé Paris, the famous Jansenist, with whose sanctity the people were so long deluded. The curing of the sick, giving hearing to the deaf and sight to the blind, were everywhere talked of as the usual effects of that holy sepulcher. But what is more extraordinary, many of the miracles were immediately proved upon the spot, before judges of unquestioned integrity, attested by witnesses of credit and distinction, in a learned age, and on the most eminent theater that is now in the world. Nor is this all: a relation of them was published and dispersed everywhere, nor were the *Jesuits*, though a learned body supported by the civil magistrate, and determined enemies to those opinions in whose favor the miracles were said to have been wrought, ever able distinctly to refute or detect them.[1] Where shall we find such a number of circumstances agreeing to the corroboration of one fact? And what have we to oppose to such a cloud of witnesses but the absolute impossibility or miraculous nature of the events which they relate? And this surely, in the eyes of all reasonable people, will alone be regarded as a sufficient refutation.

Is the consequence just, because some human testimony has the utmost force and authority in some cases, when it relates the battles of Philippi or Pharsalia for instance, that therefore all kinds of testimony must in all cases have equal force and authority? Suppose that the Caesarean and Pompeian factions had, each of them, claimed the victory in these battles, and that the historians of each party had uniformly ascribed the advantage to their own side; how could mankind, at this distance, have been able to determine between them? The contrariety is equally strong between the miracles related by Herodotus or Plutarch, and those delivered by Mariana, Bede, or any monkish historian.

The wise lend a very academic faith to every report which favors the passion of the reported, whether it magnifies his country, his family, or himself, or in any other way strikes in with his natural inclinations and propensities. But what greater temptation than to appear a missionary, a prophet, an ambassador from heaven? Who would not encounter many dangers and difficulties in order to attain so sublime a character? Or if, by the help of vanity and a heated imagination, a man has first made a convert of himself and entered seriously into the delusion, who ever scruples to make use of pious frauds in support of so holy and meritorious a cause?

The smallest spark may here kindle into the greatest flame, because the materials are always prepared for it. The *avidum genus auricularum*,[2] the gazing populace, receive greedily, without examination, whatever soothes superstition and promotes wonder.

---

[1] This book was written by Mons. Montgeron, counsel or judge of the parliament of Paris, a man of figure and character, who was also a martyr to the cause, and is now said to be somewhere in a dungeon on account of his book.

[2] Lucretius.

How many stories of this nature have, in all ages, been detected and exploded in their infancy? How many more have been celebrated for a time, and have afterwards sunk into neglect and oblivion? Where such reports, therefore, fly about, the solution of the phenomenon is obvious, and we judge in conformity to regular experience and observation when we account for it by the known and natural principles of credulity and delusion. And shall we, rather than have recourse to so natural a solution, allow of a miraculous violation of the most established laws of nature?

I need not mention the difficulty of detecting a falsehood in any private or even public history at the place where it is said to happen, much more when the scene is removed to ever so small a distance. Even a court of judicature, with all the authority, accuracy, and judgment which they can employ, find themselves often at a loss to distinguish between truth and falsehood in the most recent actions. But the matter never comes to any issue if trusted to the common method of altercation and debate and flying rumors, especially when men's passions have taken part on either side.

In the infancy of new religions, the wise and learned commonly esteem the matter too inconsiderable to deserve their attention or regard. And when afterwards they would willingly detect the cheat, in order to undeceive the deluded multitude, the season is now past, and the records and witnesses which might clear up the matter have perished beyond recovery.

No means of detection remain but those which must be drawn from the very testimony itself of the reporters; and these, though always sufficient with the judicious and knowing, are commonly too fine to fall under the comprehension of the vulgar.

Upon the whole, then, it appears that no testimony for any kind of miracle has ever amounted to a probability, much less to a proof; and that, even supposing it amounted to a proof, it would be opposed by another proof derived from the very nature of the fact which it would endeavor to establish. It is experience only which gives authority to human testimony, and it is the same experience which assures us of the laws of nature. When, therefore, these two kinds of experience are contrary, we have nothing to do but subtract the one from the other and embrace an opinion either on one side or the other with that assurance which arises from the remainder. But according to the principle here explained, this subtraction, with regard to all popular religions, amounts to an entire annihilation; and therefore we may establish it as a maxim that no human testimony can have such force as to prove a miracle, and make it a just foundation for any such system of religion.

I beg the limitations here made may be remarked, when I say that a miracle can never be proved so as to be the foundation of a system of religion. For I own that otherwise there may possibly be miracles or violations of the usual course of nature, of such a kind as to admit of proof from human testimony, though perhaps it will be impossible to find any such in all the records of history. Thus suppose all authors in all languages agree that from the first of January, 1600, there was a total darkness over the whole earth for eight days; suppose that the tradition of this extraordinary event is still strong and lively among the people; that all travelers who return from foreign countries bring us accounts of the same tradition without the least variation or contradiction; it is evident that our present philosophers, instead of doubting the fact, ought to receive it as certain and ought to search for the causes whence it might be derived. The decay, corruption, and dissolution of nature is an event rendered probable by so many analogies that any phenomenon which seems to have a tendency toward that catastrophe comes within the reach of human testimony, if that testimony be very extensive and uniform.

But suppose that all the historians who treat of England should agree that on the first of January, 1600, Queen Elizabeth died; that both before and after her death she was seen by her physicians and the whole court, as is usual with persons of her rank; that her successor was acknowledged and proclaimed by the Parliament; and that, after being interred for a month, she again appeared, resumed the throne, and governed England for three years; I must confess that I should be surprised at the concurrence of so many odd circumstances, but should not have the least inclination to believe so miraculous an event. I should not doubt of her pretended death and of those other public circumstances that followed it; I should only assert it to have been pretended, and that it neither was, nor possibly could be, real. You would in vain object to me the difficulty and almost impossibility of deceiving the world in an affair of such consequence, the wisdom and solid judgment of that renowned Queen, with the little or no advantage which she could reap from so poor an artifice. All this might astonish me, but I would still reply that the knavery and folly of men are such common phenomena that I should rather believe the most extraordinary events to arise from their concurrence than admit of so signal a violation of the laws of nature.

But should this miracle be ascribed to any new system of religion, men in all ages have been so much imposed on by ridiculous stories of that kind that this very circumstance would be a full proof of a cheat, and sufficient, with all men of sense, not only to make them reject the fact but even reject it without further examination. Though the being to whom the miracle is ascribed be in this case almighty, it does not, upon that account, become a whit more probable, since it is impossible for us to know the attributes or actions of such a being otherwise than from the experience which we have of his productions in the usual course of nature. This still reduces us to past observation, and obliges us to compare the instances of the violation of truth in the testimony of men with those of the violation of the laws of nature by miracles, in order to judge which of them is most likely and probable. As the violations of truth are more common in the testimony concerning religious miracles than in that concerning any other matter of fact, this must diminish very much the authority of the former testimony and make us form a general resolution never to lend any attention to it, with whatever specious pretense it may be covered.

Lord Bacon seems to have embraced the same principles of reasoning.

We ought [says he] to make a collection or particular history of all monsters and prodigious births or productions, and in a word of everything new, rare, and extraordinary in nature. But this must be done with the most severe scrutiny, lest we depart from truth. Above all, every relation must be considered as suspicious which depends in any degree upon religion, as the prodigies of Livy. And no less so, everything that is to be found in the writers of natural magic or alchemy, or such authors who seem, all of them, to have an unconquerable appetite for falsehood and fable.[1]

I am the better pleased with the method of reasoning here delivered, as I think it may serve to confound those dangerous friends or disguised enemies to the *Christian religion* who have undertaken to defend it by the principles of human reason. Our most holy religion is founded on *faith*, not on reason, and it is a sure method of exposing it to put it to such a trial as it is by no means fitted to endure. To make this more evident, let us examine those miracles related in Scripture, and not to lose ourselves in too wide a field, let us confine ourselves to such as we find in the *Pentateuch*, which we shall examine according to the principles of these pretended Christians, not as the word or testimony of God himself, but as the production of a mere human writer and historian. Here then we are first to consider a book presented to us by a barbarous and ignorant people, written in an age when they were still more barbarous, and in all probability long after the facts which it relates, corroborated by no concurring testimony, and resembling those fabulous accounts which every nation gives of its origin. Upon reading this book we find it full of prodigies and miracles. It gives an account of a state of the world and of human nature entirely different from the present, of our fall from that state, of the age of man extended to near a thousand years, of the destruction of the world by a deluge, of the arbitrary choice of one people as the favorites of heaven, and that people the countrymen of the author, of their deliverance from bondage by prodigies the most astonishing imaginable. I desire anyone to lay his hand upon his heart and after a serious consideration declare whether he thinks that the falsehood of such a book, supported by such a testimony, would be more extraordinary and miraculous than all the miracles it relates, which is, however, necessary to

[1] *Nov. Org.*, lib. ii. aph. 29.

make it be received, according to the measures of probability above established.

What we have said of miracles may be applied, without any variation, to prophecies, and indeed all prophecies are real miracles and as such only can be admitted as proofs of any revelation. If it did not exceed the capacity of human nature to foretell future events, it would be absurd to employ any prophecy as an argument for a divine mission or authority from heaven. So that, upon the whole, we may conclude that the *Christian religion* not only was at first attended with miracles, but even at this day cannot be believed by any reasonable person without one. Mere reason is insufficient to convince us of its veracity. And whoever is moved by *faith* to assent to it is conscious of a continued miracle in his own person, which subverts all the principles of his understanding and gives him a determination to believe what is most contrary to custom and experience.

Section XII.

OF THE ACADEMICAL OR
SKEPTICAL PHILOSOPHY

———•—•———

Part I.

THERE IS NOT a greater number of philosophical reasonings displayed upon any subject than those which prove the existence of a Deity and refute the fallacies of *atheists;* and yet the most religious philosophers still dispute whether any man can be so blinded as to be a speculative atheist. How shall we reconcile these contradictions? The knights-errant who wandered about to clear the world of dragons and giants never entertained the least doubt with regard to the existence of these monsters.

The *skeptic* is another enemy of religion, who naturally provokes the indignation of all divines and graver philosophers, though it is certain that no man ever met with any such absurd creature, or conversed with a man who had no opinion or principle concerning any subject, either of action or speculation. This begets a very natural question. What is meant by a skeptic? And how far is it possible to push these philosophical principles of doubt and uncertainty?

There is a species of skepticism, *antecedent* to all study and philosophy, which is much inculcated by Descartes and others as a sovereign preservative against error and precipitate judgment. It recommends a universal doubt, not only of all our former opinions and principles, but also of our very faculties, of whose veracity, say they, we must assure ourselves by a chain of reasoning deduced from some original principle which cannot possibly be fallacious or deceitful. But neither is there any such original principle, which has a prerogative above others that are self-evident and convincing; or if there were, could we advance a step beyond it but by the use of those very faculties of which we are supposed to be already diffident. The Cartesian doubt, therefore, were it ever possible to be attained by any human creature (as it plainly is not), would be entirely incurable, and no reasoning could ever bring us to a state of assurance and conviction upon any subject.

It must, however, be confessed that this species of skepticism, when more moderate, may be understood in a very reasonable sense, and is a necessary preparative to the study of philosophy by preserving a proper impartiality in our judgments and weaning our mind from all those prejudices which we may have imbibed from education or rash opinion. To begin with clear and self-evident principles, to advance by timorous and sure steps, to review frequently our conclusions and examine accurately all their consequences—though by these means we shall make both a slow and a short progress in our systems—are the only methods by which we can ever hope to reach truth and attain a proper stability and certainty in our determinations.

There is another species of skepticism, *consequent* to science and inquiry, when men are supposed to have discovered either the absolute fallaciousness of their mental faculties or their unfitness to reach any fixed determination in all those curious subjects of speculation about which they are commonly employed. Even our very senses are brought into dispute by a certain species of philosophers, and the maxims of common life are subjected to the same doubt as the most profound principles or conclusions of metaphysics and theology. As these paradoxical tenets (if they may be called tenets) are to be met with in some philosophers, and the refutation of them in several, they naturally excite our curiosity and make us inquire into the arguments on which they may be founded.

I need not insist upon the more trite topics employed by the skeptics in all ages against the evidence of *sense*, such as those which are derived from the imperfection and fallaciousness of our organs on numberless occasions; the crooked appearance of an oar in water; the various aspects of objects according to their different distances; the double images which arise from the pressing one eye; with many other appearances of a like nature. These skeptical topics, indeed, are only sufficient to prove that the senses alone are not implicitly to be depended on, but that we must correct their evidence by reason and by considerations derived from the nature of the medium, the distance of the object, and the disposition of the organ, in order to render them, within their sphere, the proper *criteria* of truth and falsehood. There are other more profound arguments against the senses, which admit not of so easy a solution.

It seems evident that men are carried by a natural instinct or prepossession to repose faith in their senses, and that without any reasoning, or even almost before the use of reason, we always suppose an external universe, which depends not on our perception but would exist though we and every sensible creature were absent or annihilated. Even the animal creation are governed by a like opinion, and preserve this belief of external objects in all their thoughts, designs, and actions.

It seems also evident that when men follow this blind and powerful instinct of nature, they always suppose the very images presented by the senses to be the external objects, and never entertain any suspicion that the one are nothing but representations of the other. This very table which we see white, and which we feel hard, is believed to exist independent of our perception, and to be something external to our mind which perceives it. Our presence bestows not being on it; our absence does not annihilate it. It preserves its existence uniform and entire, independent of the situation of intelligent beings who perceive or contemplate it.

But this universal and primary opinion of all men is soon destroyed by the slightest philosophy, which teaches us that nothing can ever be present to the mind but an image or perception, and that the senses are only the inlets through which these images are conveyed, without being able to produce any immediate intercourse between the mind and the object. The table which we see seems to diminish as we remove farther from it. But the real table, which exists independent of us, suffers no alteration. It was, therefore, nothing but its image which was present to the mind. These are the obvious dictates of reason; and no man who reflects ever doubted that the existences which we consider when we say *this house* and *that tree* are nothing but perceptions in the mind, and fleeting copies or representations of other existences which remain uniform and independent.

So far, then, are we necessitated by reasoning to contradict or depart from the primary instincts of nature, and to embrace a new system with regard to the evidence of our senses. But here philosophy finds herself extremely embarrassed when she would justify this new system and obviate the cavils and objections of the skeptics. She can no longer plead the infallible and irresistible instinct of nature; for that led us to a quite different system, which is acknowledged fallible and even erroneous. And to justify this pretended philosophical system by a chain of clear and convincing argument, or even any appearance of argument, exceeds the power of all human capacity.

By what argument can it be proved that the perceptions of the mind must be caused by external objects, entirely different from them though resembling them (if that be possible), and could not arise either from the energy of the mind itself, or from the suggestion of some invisible and unknown spirit, or from some other cause still more unknown to us? It is acknowledged that in fact many of these perceptions arise not from anything external, as in dreams, madness, and other diseases. And nothing can be more inexplicable than the manner in which body should so operate upon mind as ever to convey an image of itself to a substance supposed of so different and even contrary a nature.

It is a question of fact whether the perceptions of the senses be produced by external objects resembling them. How shall this question be determined? By experience, surely, as all other questions of a like nature. But here experience is and must be entirely silent. The mind has never anything present to it but the perceptions, and cannot possibly reach any experience of their connection with objects. The supposition of such a connection is, therefore, without any foundation in reasoning.

To have recourse to the veracity of the Supreme Being in order to prove the veracity of our senses is surely making a very unexpected circuit. If his veracity were at all concerned in this matter, our senses would be entirely infallible, because it is not possible that he can ever deceive. Not to mention that, if the external world be once called in question, we shall be at a loss to find arguments by which we may prove the existence of that Being or any of his attributes.

This is a topic, therefore, in which the profounder and more philosophical skeptics will always triumph when they endeavor to introduce a universal doubt into all subjects of human knowledge and inquiry. Do you follow the instincts and propensities of nature, may they say, in assenting to the veracity of sense? But these lead you to believe that the very perception or sensible image is the external object. Do you disclaim this principle in order to embrace a more rational opinion, that the perceptions are only representations of something external? You here depart from your natural propensities and more obvious sentiments, and yet are not able to satisfy your reason, which can never find any convincing argument from experience to prove that the perceptions are connected with any external objects.

There is another skeptical topic of a like nature, derived from the most profound philosophy, which might merit our attention were it requisite to dive so deep in order to discover arguments and reasonings which can so little serve to any serious purpose. It is universally allowed by modern inquirers that all the sensible qualities of objects, such as hard, soft, hot, cold, white, black, etc., are merely secondary and exist not in the objects themselves, but are perceptions of the mind without any external archetype or model which they represent. If this be allowed with regard to secondary qualities, it must also follow with regard to the supposed primary qualities of extension and solidity, nor can the latter be any more entitled to that denomination than the former. The idea of extension is entirely acquired from the senses of sight and feeling; and if all the qualities perceived by the senses be in the mind, not in the object, the same conclusion must reach the idea of extension, which is wholly dependent on the sensible ideas or the ideas of secondary qualities. Nothing can save us from this conclusion but the asserting that the ideas of those primary qualities are attained by *abstraction*, an opinion which, if we examine it accurately, we shall find to be unintelligible and even absurd. An extension that is neither tangible nor visible cannot possibly be conceived; and a tangible or visible extension which is neither hard nor soft, black nor white, is equally beyond the reach of human conception. Let any man try to conceive a triangle in general which is neither *isosceles* nor *scalenum,* nor has any particular length or proportion of sides, and he will soon perceive the absurdity of all the scholastic notions with regard to abstraction and general ideas.[1]

Thus the first philosophical objection to the evidence of sense or to the opinion of external existence consists in this, that such an opinion, if rested on natural instinct, is contrary to reason and, if referred to reason, is contrary to natural instinct, and at the same time carries no rational evidence with

---

[1] This argument is drawn from Dr. Berkeley; and indeed most of the writings of that very ingenious author form the best lessons of skepticism which are to be found either among the ancient or modern philosophers, Bayle not excepted. He professes, however, in his title page (and undoubtedly with great truth) to have composed his book against the skeptics as well as against the atheists and freethinkers. But that all his arguments, though otherwise intended, are in reality merely skeptical appears from this, *that they admit of no answer and produce no conviction.* Their only effect is to cause that momentary amazement and irresolution and confusion which is the result of skepticism.

it to convince an impartial inquirer. The second objection goes further and represents this opinion as contrary to reason, at least if it be a principle of reason that all sensible qualities are in the mind, not in the object. Bereave matter of all its intelligible qualities, both primary and secondary, you in a manner annihilate it and leave only a certain unknown, inexplicable *something* as the cause of our perceptions, a notion so imperfect that no skeptic will think it worthwhile to contend against it.

Part II.

It may seem a very extravagant attempt of the skeptics to destroy *reason* by argument and ratiocination; yet is this the grand scope of all their inquiries and disputes. They endeavor to find objections both to our abstract reasonings and to those which regard matter of fact and existence.

The chief objection against all *abstract* reasonings is derived from the ideas of space and time, ideas which in common life and to a careless view are very clear and intelligible, but when they pass through the scrutiny of the profound sciences (and they are the chief object of these sciences) afford principles which seem full of absurdity and contradiction. No priestly *dogmas*, invented on purpose to tame and subdue the rebellious reason of mankind, ever shocked common sense more than the doctrine of the infinite divisibility of extension, with its consequences, as they are pompously displayed by all geometricians and metaphysicians with a kind of triumph and exultation. A real quantity, infinitely less than any finite quantity, containing quantities infinitely less than itself, and so on *in infinitum;* this is an edifice so bold and prodigious that it is too weighty for any pretended demonstration to support, because it shocks the clearest and most natural principles of human reason.[1] But what renders the matter more extraordi-

---

[1] Whatever disputes there may be about mathematical points, we must allow that there are physical points, that is, parts of extension which cannot be divided or lessened either by the eye or imagination. These images, then, which are present to the fancy or senses are absolutely indivisible, and consequently must be allowed by

nary is that these seemingly absurd opinions are supported by a chain of reasoning the clearest and most natural, nor is it possible for us to allow the premises without admitting the consequences. Nothing can be more convincing and satisfactory than all the conclusions concerning the properties of circles and triangles; and yet when these are once received, how can we deny that the angle of contact between a circle and its tangent is infinitely less than any rectilineal angle, that as you may increase the diameter of the circle *in infinitum,* this angle of contact becomes still less, even *in infinitum,* and that the angle of contact between other curves and their tangents may be infinitely less than those between any circle and its tangent, and so on, *in infinitum?* The demonstration of these principles seems as unexceptionable as that which proves the three angles of a triangle to be equal to two right ones, though the latter opinion be natural and easy, and the former big with contradiction and absurdity. Reason here seems to be thrown into a kind of amazement and suspense which, without the suggestions of any skeptic, gives her a diffidence of herself and of the ground on which she treads. She sees a full light which illuminates certain places, but that light borders upon the most profound darkness. And between these she is so dazzled and confounded that she scarcely can pronounce with certainty and assurance concerning any one object.

The absurdity of these bold determinations of the abstract sciences seems to become, if possible, still more palpable with regard to time than extension. An infinite number of real parts of time, passing in succession and exhausted one after another, appears so evident a contradiction that no man, one should think, whose judgment is not corrupted instead of being improved by the sciences, would ever be able to admit of it.

Yet still reason must remain restless and unquiet, even with regard to that skepticism to which she is driven by these seeming absurdities and contradictions. How any clear, distinct idea can contain circumstances contradictory to itself, or to

---

mathematicians to be infinitely less than any real part of extension; and yet nothing appears more certain to reason than that an infinite number of them composes an infinite extension. How much more an infinite number of those infinitely small parts of extension which are still supposed infinitely divisible?

any other clear, distinct idea, is absolutely incomprehensible, and is, perhaps, as absurd as any proposition which can be formed. So that nothing can be more skeptical or more full of doubt and hesitation than this skepticism itself, which arises from some of the paradoxical conclusions of geometry or the science of quantity.[1]

The skeptical objections to *moral* evidence, or to the reasonings concerning matter of fact, are either *popular* or *philosophical*. The popular objections are derived from the natural weakness of human understanding, the contradictory opinions which have been entertained in different ages and nations, the variations of our judgment in sickness and health, youth and old age, prosperity and adversity, the perpetual contradiction of each particular man's opinions and sentiments, with many other topics of that kind. It is needless to insist further on this head. These objections are but weak. For as, in common life, we reason every moment concerning fact and existence and cannot possibly subsist without continually employing this species of argument, any popular objections derived from thence must be insufficient to destroy that evidence. The great subverter of Pyrrhonism, or the excessive principles of skepticism, is action, and employment, and the occupations

[1] It seems to me not impossible to avoid these absurdities and contradictions if it be admitted that there is no such thing as abstract or general ideas, properly speaking, but that all general ideas are in reality particular ones attached to a general term which recalls, upon occasion, other particular ones that resemble in certain circumstances the idea present to the mind. Thus, when the term "horse" is pronounced, we immediately figure to ourselves the idea of a black or a white animal of a particular size or figure. But as that term is also usually applied to animals of other colors, figures, and sizes, these ideas, though not actually present to the imagination, are easily recalled, and our reasoning and conclusion proceed in the same way as if they were actually present. If this be admitted (as seems reasonable) it follows that all the ideas of quantity, upon which mathematicians reason, are nothing but particular, and such as are suggested by the senses and imagination, and consequently cannot be infinitely divisible. It is sufficient to have dropped this hint at present, without prosecuting it any further. It certainly concerns all lovers of science not to expose themselves to the ridicule and contempt of the ignorant by their conclusions, and this seems the readiest solution of these difficulties.

of common life. These principles may flourish and triumph in the schools, where it is indeed difficult, if not impossible, to refute them. But as soon as they leave the shade, and by the presence of the real objects which actuate our passions and sentiments are put in opposition to the more powerful principles of our nature, they vanish like smoke, and leave the most determined skeptic in the same condition as other mortals.

The skeptic, therefore, had better keep within his proper sphere and display those *philosophical* objections which arise from more profound researches. Here he seems to have ample matter of triumph, while he justly insists that all our evidence for any matter of fact which lies beyond the testimony of sense or memory is derived entirely from the relation of cause and effect; that we have no other idea of this relation than that of two objects which have been frequently *conjoined* together; that we have no argument to convince us that objects which have, in our experience, been frequently conjoined will likewise in other instances be conjoined in the same manner; and that nothing leads us to this inference but custom or a certain instinct of our nature, which it is indeed difficult to resist, but which, like other instincts, may be fallacious and deceitful. While the skeptic insists upon these topics, he shows his force, or rather, indeed, his own and our weakness, and seems, for the time at least, to destroy all assurance and conviction. These arguments might be displayed at greater length if any durable good or benefit to society could ever be expected to result from them.

For here is the chief and most confounding objection to *excessive* skepticism, that no durable good can ever result from it while it remains in its full force and vigor. We need only ask such a skeptic *what his meaning is, and what he proposes by all these curious researches*. He is immediately at a loss and knows not what to answer. A Copernican or Ptolemaic, who supports each his different system of astronomy, may hope to produce a conviction which will remain constant and durable with his audience. A Stoic or Epicurean displays principles which may not only be durable, but which have an effect on conduct and behavior. But a Pyrrhonian cannot expect that his philosophy will have any constant influence on

the mind, or if it had, that its influence would be beneficial
to society. On the contrary, he must acknowledge, if he will
acknowledge anything, that all human life must perish were
his principles universally and steadily to prevail. All discourse,
all action would immediately cease, and men remain in a
total lethargy till the necessities of nature, unsatisfied, put an
end to their miserable existence. It is true, so fatal an event is
very little to be dreaded. Nature is always too strong for principle. And though a Pyrrhonian may throw himself or others
into a momentary amazement and confusion by his profound
reasonings, the first and most trivial event in life will put to
flight all his doubts and scruples, and leave him the same in
every point of action and speculation with the philosophers of
every other sect, or with those who never concerned themselves in any philosophical researches. When he awakes from
his dream, he will be the first to join in the laugh against himself, and to confess that all his objections are mere amusement,
and can have no other tendency than to show the whimsical
condition of mankind, who must act and reason and believe,
though they are not able, by their most diligent inquiry, to
satisfy themselves concerning the foundation of these operations, or to remove the objections which may be raised
against them.

Part III.

There is, indeed, a more *mitigated* skepticism or *academi-
cal* philosophy which may be both durable and useful, and
which may, in part, be the result of this Pyrrhonism or *excessive* skepticism when its undistinguished doubts are, in some
measure, corrected by common sense and reflection. The
greater part of mankind are naturally apt to be affirmative
and dogmatical in their opinions, and while they see objects
only on one side and have no idea of any counterpoising argument, they throw themselves precipitately into the principles to which they are inclined, nor have they any indulgence
for those who entertain opposite sentiments. To hesitate or
balance perplexes their understanding, checks their passion,
and suspends their action. They are, therefore, impatient till

they escape from a state which to them is so uneasy, and they think that they can never remove themselves far enough from it by the violence of their affirmations and obstinacy of their belief. But could such dogmatical reasoners become sensible of the strange infirmities of human understanding, even in its most perfect state and when most accurate and cautious in its determinations, such a reflection would naturally inspire them with more modesty and reserve, and diminish their fond opinion of themselves and their prejudice against antagonists. The illiterate may reflect on the disposition of the learned, who, amidst all the advantages of study and reflection, are commonly still diffident in their determinations. And if any of the learned be inclined, from their natural temper, to haughtiness and obstinacy, a small tincture of Pyrrhonism might abate their pride by showing them that the few advantages which they may have attained over their fellows are but inconsiderable if compared with the universal perplexity and confusion which is inherent in human nature. In general, there is a degree of doubt and caution and modesty which, in all kinds of scrutiny and decision, ought forever to accompany a just reasoner.

Another species of *mitigated* skepticism which may be of advantage to mankind, and which may be the natural result of the Pyrrhonian doubts and scruples, is the limitation of our inquiries to such subjects as are best adapted to the narrow capacity of human understanding. The *imagination* of man is naturally sublime, delighted with whatever is remote and extraordinary, and running without control into the most distant parts of space and time in order to avoid the objects which custom has rendered too familiar to it. A correct *judgment* observes a contrary method and, avoiding all distant and high inquiries, confines itself to common life, and to such subjects as fall under daily practice and experience, leaving the more sublime topics to the embellishment of poets and orators, or to the arts of priests and politicians. To bring us to so salutary a determination, nothing can be more serviceable than to be once thoroughly convinced of the force of the Pyrrhonian doubt and of the impossibility that anything but the strong power of natural instinct could free us from it. Those who have a propensity to philosophy will still continue their researches, because they reflect that, besides the immediate pleasure attending such an occupation, philosophical decisions are nothing but the reflections of common life, methodized and corrected. But they will never be tempted to go beyond common life so long as they consider the imperfection of those faculties which they employ, their narrow reach, and their inaccurate operations. While we cannot give a satisfactory reason why we believe, after a thousand experiments, that a stone will fall or fire burn, can we ever satisfy ourselves concerning any determination which we may form with regard to the origin of worlds and the situation of nature from and to eternity?

This narrow limitation, indeed, of our inquiries is in every respect so reasonable that it suffices to make the slightest examination into the natural powers of the human mind, and to compare them with their objects, in order to recommend it to us. We shall then find what are the proper subjects of science and inquiry.

It seems to me that the only objects of the abstract sciences or of demonstration are quantity and number, and that all attempts to extend this more perfect species of knowledge beyond these bounds are mere sophistry and illusion. As the component parts of quantity and number are entirely similar, their relations become intricate and involved, and nothing can be more curious as well as useful than to trace, by a variety of mediums, their equality or inequality through their different appearances. But as all other ideas are clearly distinct and different from each other, we can never advance further, by our utmost scrutiny, than to observe this diversity and, by an obvious reflection, pronounce one thing not to be another. Or if there be any difficulty in these decisions, it proceeds entirely from the indeterminate meaning of words, which is corrected by juster definitions. That *the square of the hypotenuse is equal to the squares of the other two sides* cannot be known, let the terms be ever so exactly defined, without a train of reasoning and inquiry. But to convince us of this proposition, *that where there is no property there can be no injustice,* it is only necessary to define the terms and explain injustice to be a violation of property. This proposition is, indeed, nothing but a more imperfect definition. It is the same case with all those pretended syllogistical reasonings which may be found in every other branch of learning except the sciences of quantity and number; and these may safely, I think, be pronounced the only proper objects of knowledge and demonstration.

All other inquiries of men regard only matter of fact and existence, and these are evidently incapable of demonstration. Whatever *is* may *not be*. No negation of a fact can involve a contradiction. The nonexistence of any being, without exception, is as clear and distinct an idea as its existence. The proposition which affirms it not to be, however false, is no less conceivable and intelligible than that which affirms it to be. The case is different with the sciences, properly so called. Every proposition which is not true is there confused and unintelligible. That the cube root of 64 is equal to the half of 10 is a false proposition, and can never be distinctly conceived. But that Caesar, or the angel Gabriel, or any being never existed may be a false proposition, but still is perfectly conceivable and implies no contradiction.

The existence, therefore, of any being can only be proved by arguments from its cause or its effect, and these arguments are founded entirely on experience. If we reason *a priori*, anything may appear able to produce anything. The falling of a pebble may, for aught we know, extinguish the sun, or the wish of a man control the planets in their orbits. It is only experience which teaches us the nature and bounds of cause and effect, and enables us to infer the existence of one object from that of another.[1] Such is the foundation of moral reasoning, which forms the greater part of human knowledge, and is the source of all human action and behavior.

Moral reasonings are either concerning particular or general facts. All deliberations in life regard the former; as also all disquisitions in history, chronology, geography, and astronomy.

---

[1] That impious maxim of the ancient philosophy, *ex nihilo, nihil fit*, by which the creation of matter was excluded, ceases to be a maxim according to this philosophy. Not only the will of the Supreme Being may create matter, but, for aught we know *a priori*, the will of any other being might create it, or any other cause that the most whimsical imagination can assign.

The sciences which treat of general facts are politics, natural philosophy, physics, chemistry, etc., where the qualities, causes, and effects of a whole species of objects are inquired into.

Divinity or theology, as it proves the existence of a deity and the immortality of souls, is composed partly of reasonings concerning particular, partly concerning general facts. It has a foundation in *reason* so far as it is supported by experience. But its best and most solid foundation is *faith* and divine revelation.

Morals and criticism are not so properly objects of the understanding as of taste and sentiment. Beauty, whether moral or natural, is felt, more properly than perceived. Or if we reason concerning it and endeavor to fix its standard, we regard a new fact, to wit, the general taste of mankind, or some such fact, which may be the object of reasoning and inquiry.

When we run over libraries, persuaded of these principles, what havoc must we make? If we take in our hand any volume of divinity or school metaphysics, for instance, let us ask: *Does it contain any abstract reasoning concerning quantity or number?* No. *Does it contain any experimental reasoning concerning matter of fact and existence?* No. Commit it then to the flames, for it can contain nothing but sophistry and illusion.

AN INQUIRY

CONCERNING

THE PRINCIPLES

OF MORALS

CONTENTS

Section I.

OF THE GENERAL PRINCIPLES

OF MORALS

DISPUTES WITH MEN pertinaciously obstinate in their principles are, of all others, the most irksome, except perhaps those with persons entirely disingenuous, who really do not believe the opinions they defend, but engage in the controversy from affectation, from a spirit of opposition, or from a desire of showing wit and ingenuity superior to the rest of mankind. The same blind adherence to their own arguments is to be expected in both, the same contempt of their antagonists, and the same passionate vehemence in enforcing sophistry and falsehood. And as reasoning is not the source whence either disputant derives his tenets, it is in vain to expect that any logic which speaks not to the affections will ever engage him to embrace sounder principles.

Those who have denied the reality of moral distinctions may be ranked among the disingenuous disputants; nor is it conceivable that any human creature could ever seriously believe that all characters and actions were alike entitled to the affection and regard of everyone. The difference which nature has placed between one man and another is so wide, and this difference is still so much further widened by education, example, and habit that, where the opposite extremes come at once under our apprehension, there is no skepticism so scrupulous and scarce any assurance so determined as absolutely to deny all distinction between them. Let a man's insensibility be ever so great, he must often be touched with the images of *right* and *wrong*, and let his prejudices be ever so obstinate, he must observe that others are susceptible of like impressions. The only way, therefore, of converting an antagonist of this kind is to leave him to himself. For finding that nobody keeps up the controversy with him, it is probable he will at last of himself, from mere weariness, come over to the side of common sense and reason.

There has been a controversy started of late, much better worth examination, concerning the general foundation of *morals,* whether they be derived from *reason* or from *sentiment,* whether we attain the knowledge of them by a chain of argument and induction or by an immediate feeling and finer internal sense, whether, like all sound judgment of truth and falsehood, they should be the same to every rational intelligent being, or whether, like the perception of beauty and deformity, they be founded entirely on the particular fabric and constitution of the human species.

The ancient philosophers, though they often affirm that virtue is nothing but conformity to reason, yet in general seem to consider morals as deriving their existence from taste and sentiment. On the other hand, our modern inquirers, though they also talk much of the beauty of virtue and deformity of vice, yet have commonly endeavored to account for these distinctions by metaphysical reasonings and by deductions from the most abstract principles of the understanding. Such confusion reigned in these subjects that an opposition of the greatest consequence could prevail between one system and another, and even in the parts of almost each individual system, and yet nobody, till very lately, was ever sensible of it. The elegant Lord Shaftesbury, who first gave occasion to remark this distinction and who, in general, adhered to the principles of the ancients, is not himself entirely free from the same confusion.

It must be acknowledged that both sides of the question are susceptible of specious arguments. Moral distinctions, it may be said, are discernible by pure *reason.* Else whence the many disputes that reign in common life as well as in philosophy with regard to this subject, the long chain of proofs often produced on both sides, the examples cited, the authorities appealed to, the analogies employed, the fallacies detected, the inferences drawn, and the several conclusions adjusted to their proper principles. Truth is disputable, not taste. What exists in the nature of things is the standard of our judgment; what each man feels within himself is the standard of sentiment. Propositions in geometry may be proved, systems in physics may be controverted, but the harmony of verse, the tenderness of passion, the brilliancy of wit must give immediate pleasure. No man reasons concerning another's beauty, but frequently concerning the justice or injustice of his actions. In every criminal trial the first object of the prisoner is to disprove the facts alleged and deny the actions imputed to him, the second to prove that even if these actions were real they might be justified as innocent and lawful. It is confessedly by deductions of the understanding that the first point is ascertained; how can we suppose that a different faculty of the mind is employed in fixing the other?

On the other hand, those who would resolve all moral determinations into *sentiments* may endeavor to show that it is impossible for reason ever to draw conclusions of this nature. To virtue, say they, it belongs to be *amiable,* and vice *odious.* This forms their very nature or essence. But can reason or argumentation distribute these different epithets to any subjects, and pronounce beforehand that this must produce love and that hatred? Or what other reason can we ever assign for these affections but the original fabric and formation of the human mind, which is naturally adapted to receive them?

The end of all moral speculations is to teach us our duty, and by proper representations of the deformity of vice and beauty of virtue beget correspondent habits, and engage us to avoid the one and embrace the other. But is this ever to be expected from inferences and conclusions of the understanding, which of themselves have no hold of the affections or set in motion the active powers of men? They discover truths; but where the truths which they discover are indifferent and beget no desire or aversion, they can have no influence on conduct and behavior. What is honorable, what is fair, what is becoming, what is noble, what is generous takes possession of the heart and animates us to embrace and maintain it. What is intelligible, what is evident, what is probable, what is true procures only the cool assent of the understanding, and, gratifying a speculative curiosity, puts an end to our researches.

Extinguish all the warm feelings and prepossessions in favor of virtue and all disgust or aversion to vice, render men totally indifferent toward these distinctions, and morality is no longer a practical study, nor has any tendency to regulate our lives and actions.

These arguments on each side (and many more might be produced) are so plausible that I am apt to suspect they may, the one as well as the other, be solid and satisfactory, and that *reason* and *sentiment* concur in almost all moral determinations and conclusions. The final sentence, it is probable, which pronounces characters and actions amiable or odious, praiseworthy or blamable, that which stamps on them the mark of honor or infamy, approbation or censure, that which renders morality an active principle and constitutes virtue our happiness and vice our misery; it is probable, I say, that this final sentence depends on some internal sense or feeling which nature has made universal in the whole species. For what else can have an influence of this nature? But in order to pave the way for such a sentiment and give a proper discernment of its object, it is often necessary, we find, that much reasoning should precede, that nice distinctions be made, just conclusions drawn, distant comparisons formed, complicated relations examined, and general facts fixed and ascertained. Some species of beauty, especially the natural kinds, on their first appearance command our affection and approbation, and where they fail of this effect, it is impossible for any reasoning to redress their influence or adapt them better to our taste and sentiment. But in many orders of beauty, particularly those of the finer arts, it is requisite to employ much reasoning in order to feel the proper sentiment, and a false relish may frequently be corrected by argument and reflection. There are just grounds to conclude that moral beauty partakes much of this latter species and demands the assistance of our intellectual faculties in order to give it a suitable influence on the human mind.

But though this question concerning the general principles of morals be curious and important, it is needless for us at present to employ further care in our researches concerning it. For if we can be so happy, in the course of this inquiry, as to discover the true origin of morals, it will then easily appear how far either sentiment or reason enters into all determinations of this nature.[1] In order to attain this purpose, we shall endeavor to follow a very simple method. We shall analyze that complication of mental qualities which form what, in common life, we call *personal merit;* we shall consider every attribute of the mind which renders a man an object either of esteem and affection or of hatred and contempt, every habit or sentiment or faculty which, if ascribed to any person, implies either praise or blame and may enter into any panegyric or satire of his character and manners. The quick sensibility which, on this head, is so universal among mankind gives a philosopher sufficient assurance that he can never be considerably mistaken in framing the catalogue or incur any danger of misplacing the objects of his contemplation. He needs only enter into his own breast for a moment and consider whether or not he should desire to have this or that quality ascribed to him, and whether such or such an imputation would proceed from a friend or an enemy. The very nature of language guides us almost infallibly in forming a judgment of this nature, and as every tongue possesses one set of words which are taken in a good sense and another in the opposite, the least acquaintance with the idiom suffices, without any reasoning, to direct us in collecting and arranging the estimable or blamable qualities of men. The only object of reasoning is to discover the circumstances on both sides which are common to these qualities, to observe that particular in which the estimable qualities agree on the one hand and the blamable on the other, and thence to reach the foundation of ethics, and find those universal principles from which all censure or approbation is ultimately derived. As this is a question of fact, not of abstract science, we can only expect success by following the experimental method, and deducing general maxims from a comparison of particular instances. The other scientific method, where a general abstract principle is first established and is afterward

[1] See Appendix I.

branched out into a variety of inferences and conclusions, may be more perfect in itself, but suits less the imperfection of human nature, and is a common source of illusion and mistake in this as well as in other subjects. Men are now cured of their passion for hypotheses and systems in natural philosophy, and will hearken to no arguments but those which are derived from experience. It is full time they should attempt a like reformation in all moral disquisitions, and reject every system of ethics, however subtle or ingenious, which is not founded on fact and observation.

We shall begin our inquiry on this head by the consideration of the social virtues, benevolence and justice. The explication of them will probably give us an opening by which the others may be accounted for.

Section II.

OF BENEVOLENCE

Part I.

IT MAY BE ESTEEMED, perhaps, a superfluous task to prove that the benevolent or softer affections are *estimable* and, wherever they appear, engage the approbation and good will of mankind. The epithets, *sociable, good-natured, humane, merciful, grateful, friendly, generous, beneficent,* or their equivalents, are known in all languages, and universally express the highest merit which *human nature* is capable of attaining. Where these amiable qualities are attended with birth and power and eminent abilities, and display themselves in the good government or useful instruction of mankind, they seem even to raise the possessors of them above the rank of *human nature,* and make them approach in some measure to the divine. Exalted capacity, undaunted courage, prosperous success; these may only expose a hero or politician to the envy and ill will of the public. But as soon as the praises are added of humane and beneficent, when instances are displayed of lenity, tenderness, or friendship, envy itself is silent or joins the general voice of approbation and applause.

When Pericles, the great Athenian statesman and general, was on his deathbed, his surrounding friends, deeming him now insensible, began to indulge their sorrow for their expiring patron by enumerating his great qualities and successes, his conquests and victories, the unusual length of his administration, and his nine trophies erected over the enemies of the republic. *You forget,* cries the dying hero who had heard all, *you forget the most eminent of my praises, while you dwell so much on those vulgar advantages in which fortune had a principal share. You have not observed that no citizen has ever yet worn mourning on my account.*[1]

In men of more ordinary talents and capacity, the social virtues become, if possible, still more essentially requisite, there being nothing eminent, in that case, to compensate for the want of them, or preserve the person from our severest hatred as well as contempt. A high ambition, an elevated courage is apt, says Cicero, in less perfect characters, to degenerate into a turbulent ferocity. The more social and softer virtues are there chiefly to be regarded. These are always good and amiable.[2]

The principal advantage which Juvenal discovers in the extensive capacity of the human species is that it renders our benevolence also more extensive and gives us larger opportunities of spreading our kindly influence than what are indulged to the inferior creation.[3] It must, indeed, be confessed that by doing good only can a man truly enjoy the advantages of being eminent. His exalted station, of itself, but the more exposes him to danger and tempest. His sole prerogative is to afford shelter to inferiors who repose themselves under his cover and protection.

But I forget that it is not my present business to recommend generosity and benevolence, or to paint in their true colors all the genuine charms of the social virtues. These, in-

[1] Plutarch, in *Pericle.*
[2] Cicero, *de Officiis*, lib. i.
[3] *Sat.* xv. 139 et seq.

deed, sufficiently engage every heart on the first apprehension of them, and it is difficult to abstain from some sally of panegyric as often as they occur in discourse or reasoning. But our object here being more the speculative than the practical part of morals, it will suffice to remark (what will readily, I believe, be allowed) that no qualities are more entitled to the general good will and approbation of mankind than beneficence and humanity, friendship and gratitude, natural affection and public spirit, or whatever proceeds from a tender sympathy with others and a generous concern for our kind and species. These, wherever they appear, seem to transfuse themselves, in a manner, into each beholder, and to call forth, in their own behalf, the same favorable and affectionate sentiments which they exert on all around.

Part II.

We may observe that in displaying the praises of any humane, beneficent man there is one circumstance which never fails to be amply insisted on, namely, the happiness and satisfaction derived to society from his intercourse and good offices. To his parents, we are apt to say, he endears himself by his pious attachment and duteous care still more than by the connections of nature. His children never feel his authority but when employed for their advantage. With him the ties of love are consolidated by beneficence and friendship. The ties of friendship approach, in a fond observance of each obliging office, to those of love and inclination. His domestics and dependents have in him a sure resource, and no longer dread the power of fortune but so far as she exercises it over him. From him the hungry receive food, the naked clothing, the ignorant and slothful skill and industry. Like the sun, an inferior minister of providence, he cheers, invigorates, and sustains the surrounding world.

If confined to private life, the sphere of his activity is narrower, but his influence is all benign and gentle. If exalted into a higher station, mankind and posterity reap the fruit of his labors.

As these topics of praise never fail to be employed, and

with success, where we would inspire esteem for anyone, may it not thence be concluded that the *utility* resulting from the social virtues forms at least a *part* of their merit, and is one source of that approbation and regard so universally paid to them?

When we recommend even an animal or a plant as *useful* and *beneficial*, we give it an applause and recommendation suited to its nature. As, on the other hand, reflection on the baneful influence of any of these inferior beings always inspires us with the sentiment of aversion. The eye is pleased with the prospect of cornfields and loaded vineyards, horses grazing, and flocks pasturing, but flies the view of briars and brambles affording shelter to wolves and serpents.

A machine, a piece of furniture, a vestment, a house well contrived for use and convenience, is so far beautiful and is contemplated with pleasure and approbation. An experienced eye is here sensible to many excellences which escape persons ignorant and uninstructed.

Can anything stronger be said in praise of a profession such as merchandise or manufacture than to observe the advantages which it procures to society? And is not a monk and inquisitor enraged when we treat his order as useless or pernicious to mankind?

The historian exults in displaying the benefit arising from his labors. The writer of romance alleviates or denies the bad consequences ascribed to his manner of composition.

In general, what praise is implied in the simple epithet *useful!* What reproach in the contrary!

Your gods, says Cicero[1] in opposition to the Epicureans, cannot justly claim any worship or adoration, with whatever imaginary perfections you may suppose them endowed. They are totally useless and inactive. Even the Egyptians, whom you so much ridicule, never consecrated any animal but on account of its utility.

The skeptics assert,[2] though absurdly, that the origin of all religious worship was derived from the utility of inanimate objects, as the sun and moon to the support and well-being of

---

[1] *De nat. Deor.*, lib. i.
[2] Sextus *Empiricus, adversus Math.*, lib. ix.

mankind. This is also the common reason assigned by historians for the deification of eminent heroes and legislators.[1]

To plant a tree, to cultivate a field, to beget children; meritorious acts, according to the religion of Zoroaster.

In all determinations of morality, this circumstance of public utility is ever principally in view; and wherever disputes arise, either in philosophy or common life, concerning the bounds of duty, the question cannot, by any means, be decided with greater certainty than by ascertaining, on any side, the true interests of mankind. If any false opinion, embraced from appearances, has been found to prevail, as soon as further experience and sounder reasoning have given us juster notions of human affairs, we retract our first sentiment and adjust anew the boundaries of moral good and evil.

Giving alms to common beggars is naturally praised, because it seems to carry relief to the distressed and indigent. But when we observe the encouragement thence arising to idleness and debauchery, we regard that species of charity rather as a weakness than a virtue.

Tyrannicide, or the assassination of usurpers and oppressive princes, was highly extolled in ancient times, because it both freed mankind from many of these monsters and seemed to keep the others in awe whom the sword or poinard could not reach. But history and experience having since convinced us that this practice increases the jealousy and cruelty of princes, a Timoleon and a Brutus, though treated with indulgence on account of the prejudices of their times, are now considered as very improper models for imitation.

Liberality in princes is regarded as a mark of beneficence. But when it occurs that the homely bread of the honest and industrious is often thereby converted into delicious cates for the idle and the prodigal, we soon retract our heedless praises. The regrets of a prince for having lost a day were noble and generous. But had he intended to have spent it in acts of generosity to his greedy courtiers, it was better lost than misemployed after that manner.

Luxury, or a refinement on the pleasures and conveniences of life, had long been supposed the source of every corruption

[1] Diodorus Siculus, *passim*.

in government and the immediate cause of faction, sedition, civil wars, and the total loss of liberty. It was therefore universally regarded as a vice, and was an object of declamation to all satirists and severe moralists. Those who prove, or attempt to prove, that such refinements rather tend to the increase of industry, civility, and arts regulate anew our *moral* as well as *political* sentiments and represent as laudable or innocent what had formerly been regarded as pernicious and blamable.

Upon the whole, then, it seems undeniable *that* nothing can bestow more merit on any human creature than the sentiment of benevolence in an eminent degree, and *that* a *part* at least of its merit arises from its tendency to promote the interests of our species and bestow happiness on human society. We carry our view into the salutary consequences of such a character and disposition, and whatever has so benign an influence and forwards so desirable an end is beheld with complacency and pleasure. The social virtues are never regarded without their beneficial tendencies, nor viewed as barren and unfruitful. The happiness of mankind, the order of society, the harmony of families, the mutual support of friends are always considered as the result of their gentle dominion over the breasts of men.

How considerable a *part* of their merit we ought to ascribe to their utility will better appear from future disquisitions,[1] as well as the reason why this circumstance has such a command over our esteem and approbation.[2]

---

[1] Sections III and IV.
[2] Section V.

Section III.
OF JUSTICE

Part I.

THAT JUSTICE IS USEFUL to society and consequently that *part* of its merit, at least, must arise from that consideration, it would be a superfluous undertaking to prove. That public utility is the *sole* origin of justice and that reflections on the beneficial consequences of this virtue are the *sole* foundation of its merit; this proposition, being more curious and important, will better deserve our examination and inquiry.

Let us suppose that nature has bestowed on the human race such profuse *abundance* of all *external* conveniences that, without any uncertainty in the event, without any care or industry on our part, every individual finds himself fully provided with whatever his most voracious appetites can want or luxurious imagination wish or desire. His natural beauty, we shall suppose, surpasses all acquired ornaments, the perpetual clemency of the seasons renders useless all clothes or covering, the raw herbage affords him the most delicious fare, the clear fountain the richest beverage. No laborious occupation required, no tillage, no navigation. Music, poetry, and contemplation form his sole business; conversation, mirth, and friendship his sole amusement.

It seems evident that in such a happy state every other social virtue would flourish and receive tenfold increase, but the cautious, jealous virtue of justice would never once have been dreamed of. For what purpose make a partition of goods where everyone has already more than enough? Why give rise to property where there cannot possibly be any injury? Why call this object *mine* when, upon the seizing of it by another, I need but stretch out my hand to possess myself of what is equally valuable? Justice, in that case, being totally *useless*, would be an idle ceremonial and could never possibly have place in the catalogue of virtues.

We see, even in the present necessitous condition of mankind, that wherever any benefit is bestowed by nature in an unlimited abundance, we leave it always in common among the whole human race and make no subdivisions of right and property. Water and air, though the most necessary of all objects, are not challenged as the property of individuals, nor can any man commit injustice by the most lavish use and enjoyment of these blessings. In fertile, extensive countries with few inhabitants, land is regarded on the same footing. And no topic is so much insisted on by those who defend the liberty of the seas as the unexhausted use of them in navigation. Were the advantages procured by navigation as inexhaustible, these reasoners had never had any adversaries to refute, nor had any claims ever been advanced of a separate, exclusive dominion over the ocean.

It may happen in some countries at some periods that there be established a property in water, none in land,[1] if the latter be in greater abundance than can be used by the inhabitants, and the former be found with difficulty and in very small quantities.

Again, suppose that though the necessities of [the] human race continue the same as at present, yet the mind is so enlarged and so replete with friendship and generosity that every man has the utmost tenderness for every man, and feels no more concern for his own interest than for that of his fellows. It seems evident that the *use* of justice would, in this case, be suspended by such an extensive benevolence, nor would the divisions and barriers of property and obligation have ever been thought of. Why should I bind another by a deed or promise to do me any good office when I know that he is already prompted by the strongest inclination to seek my happiness and would of himself perform the desired service, except the hurt he thereby receives be greater than the benefit accruing to me; in which case he knows that, from my innate humanity and friendship, I should be the first to oppose my-

[1] *Genesis,* chap. xiii and xxi.

self to his imprudent generosity? Why raise landmarks between my neighbor's field and mine when my heart has made no division between our interests, but shares all his joys and sorrows with the same force and vivacity as if originally my own? Every man, upon this supposition, being a second self to another, would trust all his interests to the discretion of every man, without jealousy, without partition, without distinction. And the whole human race would form only one family, where all would lie in common and be used freely without regard to property, but cautiously too, with an entire regard to the necessities of each individual, as if our own interests were most intimately concerned.

In the present disposition of the human heart, it would perhaps be difficult to find complete instances of such enlarged affections; but still we may observe that the case of families approaches toward it, and the stronger the mutual benevolence is among the individuals the nearer it approaches, till all distinction of property be, in a great measure, lost and confounded among them. Between married persons the cement of friendship is by the laws supposed so strong as to abolish all division of possessions, and has often, in reality, the force ascribed to it. And it is observable that during the ardor of new enthusiasms, when every principle is inflamed into extravagance, the community of goods has frequently been attempted, and nothing but experience of its inconveniences, from the returning or disguised selfishness of men, could make the imprudent fanatics adopt anew the ideas of justice and of separate property. So true is it that this virtue derives its existence entirely from its necessary *use* to the intercourse and social state of mankind.

To make this truth more evident, let us reverse the foregoing suppositions and, carrying everything to the opposite extreme, consider what would be the effect of these new situations. Suppose a society to fall into such want of all common necessaries that the utmost frugality and industry cannot preserve the greater number from perishing, and the whole from extreme misery. It will readily, I believe, be admitted that the strict laws of justice are suspended in such a pressing emergency and give place to the stronger motives of necessity and self-preservation. Is it any crime, after a shipwreck, to seize whatever means or instrument of safety one can lay hold of, without regard to former limitations of property? Or if a city besieged were perishing with hunger, can we imagine that men will see any means of preservation before them and lose their lives from a scrupulous regard to what, in other situations, would be the rules of equity and justice? The *use* and *tendency* of that virtue is to procure happiness and security by preserving order in society. But where the society is ready to perish from extreme necessity, no greater evil can be dreaded from violence and injustice, and every man may now provide for himself by all the means which prudence can dictate or humanity permit. The public, even in less urgent necessities, opens granaries without the consent of proprietors, as justly supposing that the authority of magistracy may, consistent with equity, extend so far. But were any number of men to assemble without the tie of laws or civil jurisdiction, would an equal partition of bread in a famine, though effected by power and even violence, be regarded as criminal or injurious?

Suppose likewise that it should be a virtuous man's fate to fall into the society of ruffians, remote from the protection of laws and government; what conduct must he embrace in that melancholy situation? He sees such a desperate rapaciousness prevail, such a disregard to equity, such contempt of order, such stupid blindness to future consequences, as must immediately have the most tragical conclusion, and must terminate in destruction to the greater number and in a total dissolution of society to the rest. He, meanwhile, can have no other expedient than to arm himself, to whomever the sword he seizes, or the buckler, may belong, to make provision of all means of defense and security. And his particular regard to justice being no longer of *use* to his own safety or that of others, he must consult the dictates of self-preservation alone, without concern for those who no longer merit his care and attention.

When any man, even in political society, renders himself by his crimes obnoxious to the public, he is punished by the laws in his goods and person; that is, the ordinary rules of justice are, with regard to him, suspended for a moment, and it becomes equitable to inflict on him, for the *benefit* of society, what otherwise he could not suffer without wrong or injury.

The rage and violence of public war; what is it but a suspension of justice among the warring parties, who perceive that this virtue is now no longer of any *use* or advantage to them? The laws of war, which then succeed to those of equity and justice, are rules calculated for the *advantage* and *utility* of that particular state in which men are now placed. And were a civilized nation engaged with barbarians who observed no rules even of war, the former must also suspend their observance of them where they no longer serve to any purpose, and must render every action or rencounter as bloody and pernicious as possible to the first aggressors.

Thus the rules of equity or justice depend entirely on the particular state and condition in which men are placed, and owe their origin and existence to that *utility* which results to the public from their strict and regular observance. Reverse, in any considerable circumstance, the condition of men; produce extreme abundance or extreme necessity; implant in the human breast perfect moderation and humanity, or perfect rapaciousness and malice; by rendering justice totally *useless,* you thereby totally destroy its essence, and suspend its obligation upon mankind.

The common situation of society is a medium amidst all these extremes. We are naturally partial to ourselves and to our friends, but are capable of learning the advantage resulting from a more equitable conduct. Few enjoyments are given us from the open and liberal hand of nature, but by art, labor, and industry we can extract them in great abundance. Hence the ideas of property become necessary in all civil society; hence justice derives its usefulness to the public; and hence alone arises its merit and moral obligation.

These conclusions are so natural and obvious that they have not escaped even the poets in their descriptions of the felicity attending the golden age or the reign of Saturn. The seasons in that first period of nature were so temperate, if we credit these agreeable fictions, that there was no necessity for men to provide themselves with clothes and houses as a security against the violence of heat and cold. The rivers flowed with wine and milk, the oaks yielded honey, and nature spontaneously produced her greatest delicacies. Nor were these the chief advantages of that happy age. Tempests were not alone removed from nature, but those more furious tempests were unknown to human breasts, which now cause such uproar and engender such confusion. Avarice, ambition, cruelty, selfishness were never heard of; cordial affection, compassion, sympathy were the only movements with which the mind was yet acquainted. Even the punctilious distinction of *mine* and *thine* was banished from among that happy race of mortals, and carried with it the very notion of property and obligation, justice and injustice.

This *poetical* fiction of the *golden age* is, in some respects, of a piece with the *philosophical* fiction of the *state of nature*, only that the former is represented as the most charming and most peaceable condition which can possibly be imagined, whereas the latter is painted out as a state of mutual war and violence, attended with the most extreme necessity. On the first origin of mankind, we are told, their ignorance and savage nature were so prevalent that they could give no mutual trust, but must each depend upon himself and his own force or cunning for protection and security. No law was heard of, no rule of justice known, no distinction of property regarded. Power was the only measure of right, and a perpetual war of all against all was the result of men's untamed selfishness and barbarity.[1]

Whether such a condition of human nature could ever exist, or if it did could continue so long as to merit the appellation of a *state*, may justly be doubted. Men are necessarily born in a family society at least, and are trained up by their parents to some rule of conduct and behavior. But this must be admitted, that if such a state of mutual war and violence was ever real, the suspension of all laws of justice, from their absolute inutility, is a necessary and infallible consequence.

The more we vary our views of human life and the newer and more unusual the lights are in which we survey it, the

---

[1] This fiction of a state of nature as a state of war was not first started by Mr. Hobbes, as is commonly imagined. Plato endeavors to refute a hypothesis very like it in the 2d, 3d, and 4th books *de Republica*. Cicero, on the contrary, supposes it certain and universally acknowledged in the the following passage. [Hume here quotes a long passage from Cicero's *pro Sestio*, 1.42, which is omitted in this edition.—Ed.]

more shall we be convinced that the origin here assigned for the virtue of justice is real and satisfactory.

Were there a species of creatures intermingled with men, which, though rational, were possessed of such inferior strength, both of body and mind, that they were incapable of all resistance and could never, upon the highest provocation, make us feel the effects of their resentment, the necessary consequence, I think, is that we should be bound by the laws of humanity to give gentle usage to these creatures, but should not, properly speaking, lie under any restraint of justice with regard to them, nor could they possess any right or property exclusive of such arbitrary lords. Our intercourse with them could not be called society, which supposes a degree of equality, but absolute command on the one side and servile obedience on the other. Whatever we covet they must instantly resign. Our permission is the only tenure by which they hold their possessions, our compassion and kindness the only check by which they curb our lawless will. And as no inconvenience ever results from the exercise of a power so firmly established in nature, the restraints of justice and property, being totally *useless*, would never have place in so unequal a confederacy.

This is plainly the situation of men with regard to animals, and how far these may be said to possess reason I leave it to others to determine. The great superiority of civilized Europeans above barbarous Indians tempted us to imagine ourselves on the same footing with regard to them, and made us throw off all restraints of justice, and even of humanity, in our treatment of them. In many nations, the female sex are reduced to like slavery, and are rendered incapable of all property in opposition to their lordly masters. But though the males, when united, have in all countries bodily force sufficient to maintain this severe tyranny, yet such are the insinuation, address, and charms of their fair companions that women are commonly able to break the confederacy and share with the other sex in all the rights and privileges of society.

Were the human species so framed by nature as that each individual possessed within himself every faculty requisite both for his own preservation and for the propagation of his kind, were all society and intercourse cut off between man and man by the primary intention of the Supreme Creator, it seems evident that so solitary a being would be as much incapable of justice as of social discourse and conversation. Where mutual regards and forbearance serve to no manner of purpose, they would never direct the conduct of any reasonable man. The headlong course of the passions would be checked by no reflection on future consequences. And as each man is here supposed to love himself alone and to depend only on himself and his own activity for safety and happiness, he would on every occasion, to the utmost of his power, challenge the preference above every other being, to none of which he is bound by any ties, either of nature or of interest.

But suppose the conjunction of the sexes to be established in nature, a family immediately arises, and particular rules being found requisite for its subsistence, these are immediately embraced, though without comprehending the rest of mankind within their prescriptions. Suppose that several families unite together into one society which is totally disjoined from all others, the rules which preserve peace and order enlarge themselves to the utmost extent of that society, but becoming then entirely useless, lose their force when carried one step farther. But again suppose that several distinct societies maintain a kind of intercourse for mutual convenience and advantage, the boundaries of justice still grow larger, in proportion to the largeness of men's views and the force of their mutual connections. History, experience, reason sufficiently instruct us in this natural progress of human sentiments, and in the gradual enlargement of our regards to justice in proportion as we become acquainted with the extensive utility of that virtue.

Part II.

If we examine the *particular* laws by which justice is directed and property determined, we shall still be presented with the same conclusions. The good of mankind is the only object of all these laws and regulations. Not only is it requisite for the peace and interest of society that men's possessions should be separated, but the rules which we follow in making the separation are such as can best be contrived to serve further the interests of society.

We shall suppose that a creature possessed of reason but unacquainted with human nature deliberates with himself what *rules* of justice or property would best promote public interest and establish peace and security among mankind. His most obvious thought would be to assign the largest possessions to the most extensive virtue, and give everyone the power of doing good proportioned to his inclination. In a perfect theocracy, where a being infinitely intelligent governs by particular volitions, this rule would certainly have place and might serve to the wisest purposes. But were mankind to execute such a law, so great is the uncertainty of merit, both from its natural obscurity and from the self-conceit of each individual, that no determinate rule of conduct would ever result from it, and the total dissolution of society must be the immediate consequence. Fanatics may suppose *that dominion is founded on grace,* and *that saints alone inherit the earth,* but the civil magistrate very justly puts these sublime theorists on the same footing with common robbers, and teaches them by the severest discipline that a rule which in speculation may seem the most advantageous to society may yet be found in practice totally pernicious and destructive.

That there were *religious* fanatics of this kind in England during the civil wars we learn from history, though it is probable that the obvious *tendency* of these principles excited such horror in mankind as soon obliged the dangerous enthusiasts to renounce, or at least conceal, their tenets. Perhaps the *levelers,* who claimed an equal distribution of property, were a kind of *political* fanatics which arose from the religious species, and more openly avowed their pretensions, as carrying a more plausible appearance of being practicable in themselves as well as useful to human society.

It must, indeed, be confessed that nature is so liberal to mankind that, were all her presents equally divided among the species and improved by art and industry, every individual would enjoy all the necessaries and even most of the comforts of life, nor would ever be liable to any ills but such as might accidentally arise from the sickly frame and constitution of his body. It must also be confessed that wherever we depart from this equality we rob the poor of more satisfaction than we add to the rich, and that the slight gratification of a frivolous vanity in one individual frequently costs more than bread to many families and even provinces. It may appear withal that the rule of equality, as it would be highly *useful,* is not altogether *impracticable,* but has taken place, at least in an imperfect degree, in some republics, particularly that of Sparta, where it was attended, it is said, with the most beneficial consequences. Not to mention that the *agrarian* laws so frequently claimed in Rome and carried into execution in many Greek cities proceeded, all of them, from a general idea of the utility of this principle.

But historians and even common sense may inform us that however specious these ideas of *perfect* equality may seem, they are really at bottom *impracticable,* and were they not so, would be extremely *pernicious* to human society. Render possessions ever so equal, men's different degrees of art, care, and industry will immediately break that equality. Or if you check these virtues, you reduce society to the most extreme indigence, and instead of preventing want and beggary in a few, render it unavoidable to the whole community. The most rigorous inquisition too is requisite to watch every inequality on its first appearance, and the most severe jurisdiction to punish and redress it. But besides that so much authority must soon degenerate into tyranny and be exerted with great partialities, who can possibly be possessed of it in such a situation as is here supposed? Perfect equality of possessions, destroying all subordination, weakens extremely the authority of magistracy, and must reduce all power nearly to a level, as well as property.

We may conclude, therefore, that in order to establish laws for the regulation of property, we must be acquainted with the nature and situation of man, must reject appearances, which may be false, though specious, and must search for those rules which are, on the whole, most *useful* and *beneficial.* Vulgar sense and slight experience are sufficient for this purpose, where men give not way to too selfish avidity or too extensive enthusiasm.

Who sees not, for instance, that whatever is produced or improved by a man's art or industry ought forever to be secured to him, in order to give encouragement to such *useful* habits and accomplishments? That the property ought also to descend to children and relations, for the same *useful* purpose? That it may be alienated by consent, in order to beget that commerce and intercourse which is so *beneficial* to human society? And that all contracts and promises ought carefully to be fulfilled, in order to secure mutual trust and confidence, by which the general *interest* of mankind is so much promoted?

Examine the writers on the laws of nature and you will always find that whatever principles they set out with, they are sure to terminate here at last, and to assign, as the ultimate reason for every rule which they establish, the convenience and necessities of mankind. A concession thus extorted in opposition to systems has more authority than if it had been made in prosecution of them.

What other reason, indeed, could writers ever give why this must be *mine* and that *yours*, since uninstructed nature, surely, never made any such distinction? The objects which receive those appellations are of themselves foreign to us; they are totally disjoined and separated from us, and nothing but the general interests of society can form the connection.

Sometimes the interests of society may require a rule of justice in a particular case, but may not determine any particular rule among several which are all equally beneficial. In that case the slightest *analogies* are laid hold of, in order to prevent that indifference and ambiguity which would be the source of perpetual dissension. Thus possession alone, and first possession, is supposed to convey property where nobody else has any preceding claim and pretension. Many of the reasonings of lawyers are of this analogical nature, and depend on very slight connections of the imagination.

Does anyone scruple, in extraordinary cases, to violate all regard to the private property of individuals and sacrifice to public interest a distinction which had been established for the sake of that interest? The safety of the people is the supreme law. All other particular laws are subordinate to it and dependent on it. And if, in the *common* course of things, they be followed and regarded, it is only because the public safety and interest *commonly* demand so equal and impartial an administration.

Sometimes both *utility* and *analogy* fail and leave the laws of justice in total uncertainty. Thus it is highly requisite that prescription or long possession should convey property; but what number of days or months or years should be sufficient for that purpose it is impossible for reason alone to determine. *Civil laws* here supply the place of the natural *code* and assign different terms for prescription according to the different *utilities* proposed by the legislator. Bills of exchange and promissory notes, by the laws of most countries, prescribe sooner than bonds and mortgages and contracts of a more formal nature.

In general, we may observe that all questions of property are subordinate to the authority of civil laws, which extend, restrain, modify, and alter the rules of natural justice according to the particular *convenience* of each community. The laws have, or ought to have, a constant reference to the constitution of government, the manners, the climate, the religion, the commerce, the situation of each society. A late author of genius as well as learning has prosecuted this subject at large, and has established from these principles a system of political knowledge which abounds in ingenious and brilliant thoughts, and is not wanting in solidity.[1]

[1] The author of *L'esprit des loix*. This illustrious writer, however, sets out with a different theory, and supposes all right to be founded on certain *rapports* or relations, which is a system that, in my opinion, never will be reconciled with true philosophy. Father Malebranche, as far as I can learn, was the first that started this abstract theory of morals, which was afterwards adopted by Cudworth, Clarke, and others; and as it excludes all sentiment and pretends to found everything on reason, it has not wanted followers in this philosophic age. See Sect. I, Appendix I. With regard to justice, the virtue here treated of, the inference against this theory seems short and conclusive. Property is allowed to be dependent on civil laws; civil laws are allowed to have no other object but the interest of society. This therefore must be allowed to be the sole foundation of property and justice. Not to mention that our obligation itself to obey the magistrate and his laws is founded on nothing but the interests of society.

If the ideas of justice sometimes do not follow the dispositions

What is a man's property? Anything which it is lawful for him and for him alone to use. *But what rule have we by which we can distinguish these objects?* Here we must have recourse to statutes, customs, precedents, analogies, and a hundred other circumstances, some of which are constant and inflexible, some variable and arbitrary. But the ultimate point in which they all professedly terminate is the interest and happiness of human society. Where this enters not into consideration, nothing can appear more whimsical, unnatural, and even superstitious than all or most of the laws of justice and of property.

Those who ridicule vulgar superstitions and expose the folly of particular regards to meats, days, places, postures, apparel have an easy task, while they consider all the qualities and relations of the objects and discover no adequate cause for that affection or antipathy, veneration or horror, which have so mighty an influence over a considerable part of mankind. A Syrian would have starved rather than taste pigeon; an Egyptian would not have approached bacon; but if these species of food be examined by the senses of sight, smell, or taste, or scrutinized by the sciences of chemistry, medicine, or physics, no difference is ever found between them and any other species, nor can that precise circumstance be pitched on

---

of civil law, we shall find that these cases, instead of objections, are confirmations of the theory delivered above. Where a civil law is so perverse as to cross all the interests of society it loses all its authority, and men judge by the ideas of natural justice which are conformable to those interests. Sometimes also civil laws, for useful purposes, require a ceremony or form to any deed, and where that is wanting, their decrees run contrary to the usual tenor of justice; but one who takes advantage of such chicanes is not commonly regarded as an honest man. Thus the interests of society require that contracts be fulfilled, and there is not a more material article either of natural or civil justice. But the omission of a trifling circumstance will often, by law, invalidate a contract *in foro humano*, but not *in foro conscientiae*, as divines express themselves. In these cases, the magistrate is supposed only to withdraw his power of enforcing the right, not to have altered the right. Where his intention extends to the right and is conformable to the interests of society, it never fails to alter the right; a clear proof of the origin of justice and of property, as assigned above.

which may afford a just foundation for the religious passion. A fowl on Thursday is lawful food, on Friday abominable. Eggs, in this house and in this diocese, are permitted during Lent; a hundred paces farther, to eat them is a damnable sin. This earth or building yesterday was profane; today, by the muttering of certain words, it has become holy and sacred. Such reflections as these in the mouth of a philosopher, one may safely say, are too obvious to have any influence, because they must always, to every man, occur at first sight; and where they prevail not of themselves, they are surely obstructed by education, prejudice, and passion, not by ignorance or mistake.

It may appear to a careless view, or rather a too abstracted reflection, that there enters a like superstition into all the sentiments of justice, and that if a man expose its object, or what we call property, to the same scrutiny of sense and science, he will not, by the most accurate inquiry, find any foundation for the difference made by moral sentiment. I may lawfully nourish myself from this tree, but the fruit of another of the same species, ten paces off, it is criminal for me to touch. Had I worn this apparel an hour ago I had merited the severest punishment, but a man, by pronouncing a few magical syllables, has now rendered it fit for my use and service. Were this house placed in the neighboring territory it had been immoral for me to dwell in it, but being built on this side the river, it is subject to a different municipal law, and by its becoming mine I incur no blame or censure. The same species of reasoning, it may be thought, which so successfully exposes superstition is also applicable to justice; nor is it possible, in the one case more than in the other, to point out in the object that precise quality or circumstance which is the foundation of the sentiment.

But there is this material difference between *superstition* and *justice*, that the former is frivolous, useless, and burdensome, the latter is absolutely requisite to the well-being of mankind and existence of society. When we abstract from this circumstance (for it is too apparent ever to be overlooked) it must be confessed that all regards to right and property seem entirely without foundation, as much as the grossest and most vulgar superstition. Were the interests of society nowise concerned, it is as unintelligible why another's articulating certain sounds implying consent should change the nature of my actions with regard to a particular object as why the reciting of a liturgy by a priest, in a certain habit and posture, should dedicate a heap of brick and timber and render it thenceforth and forever sacred.[1]

[1] It is evident that the will or consent alone never transfers property, nor causes the obligation of a promise (for the same reasoning extends to both), but the will must be expressed by words or signs in order to impose a tie upon any man. The expression, being once brought in as subservient to the will, soon becomes the principal part of the promise; nor will a man be less bound by his word, though he secretly give a different direction to his intention and withhold the assent of his mind. But though the expression makes, on most occasions, the whole of the promise, yet it does not always so, and one who should make use of any expression of which he knows not the meaning, and which he uses without any sense of the consequences, would not certainly be bound by it. Nay, though he know its meaning, yet if he use it in jest only, and with such signs as evidently show that he has no serious intention of binding himself, he would not lie under any obligation of performance; but it is necessary that the words be a perfect expression of the will, without any contrary signs. Nay, even this we must not carry so far as to imagine that one whom, by our quickness of understanding we conjecture, from certain signs, to have an intention of deceiving us, is not bound by his expression or verbal promise if we accept of it, but must limit this conclusion to those cases where the signs are of a different nature from those of deceit. All these contradictions are easily accounted for if justice arise entirely from its usefulness to society, but will never be explained on any other hypothesis.

It is remarkable that the moral decisions of the *Jesuits* and other relaxed casuists were commonly formed in prosecution of some such subtleties of reasoning as are here pointed out, and proceed as much from the habit of scholastic refinement as from any corruption of the heart, if we may follow the authority of Mons. Bayle. See his Dictionary, article *Loyola*. And why has the indignation of mankind risen so high against these casuists, but because everyone perceived that human society could not subsist were such practices authorized, and that morals must always be handled with a view to public interest more than philosophical regularity? If the secret direction of the intention, said every man of sense, could invalidate a contract, where is our security? And yet a metaphysical schoolman might think that where an intention was sup-

These reflections are far from weakening the obligations of justice or diminishing anything from the most sacred attention to property. On the contrary, such sentiments must acquire new force from the present reasoning. For what stronger foundation can be desired or conceived for any duty than to observe that human society or even human nature could not subsist without the establishment of it, and will still arrive at greater degrees of happiness and perfection the more inviolable the regard is which is paid to that duty?

The dilemma seems obvious. As justice evidently tends to promote public utility and to support civil society, the sentiment of justice is either derived from our reflecting on that tendency, or like hunger, thirst, and other appetites, resentment, love of life, attachment to offspring, and other passions, arises from a simple original instinct in the human breast which nature has implanted for like salutary purposes. If the latter be the case, it follows that property, which is the object of justice, is also distinguished by a simple original instinct, and is not ascertained by any argument or reflection. But who is there that ever heard of such an instinct? Or is this a subject

---

posed to be requisite, if that intention really had no place, no consequence ought to follow and no obligation be imposed. The casuistical subtleties may not be greater than the subtleties of lawyers, hinted at above, but as the former are *pernicious* and the latter *innocent* and even *necessary*, this is the reason of the very different reception they meet with from the world.

It is a doctrine of the church of *Rome* that the priest, by a secret direction of his intention, can invalidate any sacrament. This position is derived from a strict and regular prosecution of the obvious truth that empty words alone, without any meaning or intention in the speaker, can never be attended with any effect. If the same conclusion be not admitted in reasonings concerning civil contracts, where the affair is allowed to be of so much less consequence than the eternal salvation of thousands, it proceeds entirely from men's sense of the danger and inconvenience of the doctrine in the former case. And we may thence observe that however positive, arrogant, and dogmatical any superstition may appear, it never can convey any thorough persuasion of the reality of its objects, or put them in any degree on a balance with the common incidents of life, which we learn from daily observation and experimental reasoning.

in which new discoveries can be made? We may as well expect to discover in the body new senses which had before escaped the observation of all mankind.

But further, though it seems a very simple proposition to say that nature, by an instinctive sentiment, distinguishes property, yet in reality we shall find that there are required for that purpose ten thousand different instincts, and these employed about objects of the greatest intricacy and nicest discernment. For when a definition of *property* is required, that relation is found to resolve itself into any possession acquired by occupation, by industry, by prescription, by inheritance, by contract, etc. Can we think that nature by an original instinct instructs us in all these methods of acquisition?

These words too, inheritance and contract, stand for ideas infinitely complicated, and to define them exactly a hundred volumes of laws and a thousand volumes of commentators have not been found sufficient. Does nature, whose instincts in men are all simple, embrace such complicated and artificial objects, and create a rational creature without trusting anything to the operation of his reason?

But even though all this were admitted, it would not be satisfactory. Positive laws can certainly transfer property. Is it by another original instinct that we recognize the authority of kings and senates and mark all the boundaries of their jurisdiction? Judges too, even though their sentence be erroneous and illegal, must be allowed, for the sake of peace and order, to have decisive authority and ultimately to determine property. Have we original, innate ideas of praetors and chancellors and juries? Who sees not that all these institutions arise merely from the necessities of human society?

All birds of the same species in every age and country build their nests alike; in this we see the force of instinct. Men in different times and places frame their houses differently; here we perceive the influence of reason and custom. A like inference may be drawn from comparing the instinct of generation and the institution of property.

How great soever the variety of municipal laws, it must be confessed that their chief outlines pretty regularly concur, because the purposes to which they tend are everywhere exactly similar. In like manner, all houses have a roof and walls, windows and chimneys, though diversified in their shape, figure, and materials. The purposes of the latter, directed to the conveniences of human life, discover not more plainly their origin from reason and reflection than do those of the former, which point all to a like end.

I need not mention the variations which all the rules of property receive from the finer turns and connections of the imagination, and from the subtleties and abstractions of law topics and reasonings. There is no possibility of reconciling this observation to the notion of original instincts.

What alone will beget a doubt concerning the theory on which I insist is the influence of education and acquired habits, by which we are so accustomed to blame injustice that we are not, in every instance, conscious of any immediate reflection on the pernicious consequences of it. The views the most familiar to us are apt, for that very reason, to escape us, and what we have very frequently performed from certain motives we are apt likewise to continue mechanically, without recalling on every occasion the reflections which first determined us. The convenience, or rather necessity, which leads to justice is so universal and everywhere points so much to the same rules that the habit takes place in all societies, and it is not without some scrutiny that we are able to ascertain its true origin. The matter, however, is not so obscure but that even in common life we have every moment recourse to the principle of public utility, and ask, *What must become of the world if such practices prevail? How could society subsist under such disorders?* Were the distinction or separation of possessions entirely useless, can anyone conceive that it ever should have obtained in society?

Thus we seem, upon the whole, to have attained a knowledge of the force of that principle here insisted on, and can determine what degree of esteem or moral approbation may result from reflections on public interest and utility. The necessity of justice to the support of society is the *sole* foundation of that virtue; and since no moral excellence is more highly esteemed, we may conclude that this circumstance of usefulness has, in general, the strongest energy and most entire command over our sentiments. It must therefore be the source of a considerable part of the merit ascribed to humanity, benevolence, friendship, public spirit, and other social virtues of that stamp, as it is the *sole* source of the moral approbation paid to fidelity, justice, veracity, integrity, and those other estimable and useful qualities and principles. It is entirely agreeable to the rules of philosophy and even of common reason, where any principle has been found to have a great force and energy in one instance, to ascribe to it a like energy in all similar instances. This indeed is Newton's chief rule of philosophizing.[1]

Section V.

WHY UTILITY PLEASES

Part I.

IT SEEMS SO NATURAL a thought to ascribe to their utility the praise which we bestow on the social virtues that one would expect to meet with this principle everywhere in moral writers as the chief foundation of their reasoning and inquiry. In common life we may observe that the circumstance of utility is always appealed to, nor is it supposed that a greater eulogy can be given to any man than to display his usefulness to the public and enumerate the services which he has performed to mankind and society. What praise, even of an inanimate form, if the regularity and elegance of its parts destroy not its fitness for any useful purpose! And how satisfactory an apology for any disproportion or seeming deformity if we can show the necessity of that particular construction for the use intended! A ship appears more beautiful to an artist or one moderately skilled in navigation where its prow is wide and swelling beyond its poop than if it were framed with a precise geomet-

[1] *Principia*, lib. iii.

rical regularity, in contradiction to all the laws of mechanics. A building whose doors and windows were exact squares would hurt the eye by that very proportion, as ill-adapted to the figure of a human creature, for whose service the fabric was intended. What wonder then that a man whose habits and conduct are hurtful to society and dangerous or pernicious to everyone who has an intercourse with him should, on that account, be an object of disapprobation, and communicate to every spectator the strongest sentiment of disgust and hatred? [1]

But perhaps the difficulty of accounting for these effects of usefulness, or its contrary, has kept philosophers from admitting them into their systems of ethics, and has induced them rather to employ any other principle in explaining the origin of moral good and evil. But it is no just reason for rejecting any principle confirmed by experience that we cannot give a satisfactory account of its origin, nor are able to resolve it into other more general principles. And if we would employ a little thought on the present subject, we need be at no loss to ac-

---

[1] We ought not to imagine, because an inanimate object may be useful as well as a man, that therefore it ought also, according to this system, to merit the appellation of *virtuous*. The sentiments excited by utility are, in the two cases, very different, and the one is mixed with affection, esteem, approbation, etc., and not the other. In like manner, an inanimate object may have good color and proportions as well as a human figure. But can we ever be in love with the former? There are a numerous set of passions and sentiments of which thinking rational beings are, by the original constitution of nature, the only proper objects; and though the very same qualities be transferred to an insensible, inanimate being, they will not excite the same sentiments. The beneficial qualities of herbs and minerals are, indeed, sometimes called their *virtues*, but this is an effect of the caprice of language which ought not to be regarded in reasoning. For though there be a species of approbation attending even inanimate objects when beneficial, yet this sentiment is so weak and so different from that which is directed to beneficent magistrates or statesmen that they ought not to be ranked under the same class or appellation.

A very small variation of the object, even where the same qualities are preserved, will destroy a sentiment. Thus the same beauty, transferred to a different sex, excites no amorous passion, where nature is not extremely perverted.

count for the influence of utility, and to deduce it from principles the most known and avowed in human nature.

From the apparent usefulness of the social virtues it has readily been inferred by skeptics, both ancient and modern, that all moral distinctions arise from education, and were at first invented and afterwards encouraged by the art of politicians, in order to render men tractable and subdue their natural ferocity and selfishness, which incapacitated them for society. This principle, indeed, of precept and education must so far be owned to have a powerful influence that it may frequently increase or diminish, beyond their natural standard, the sentiments of approbation or dislike, and may even in particular instances create, without any natural principle, a new sentiment of this kind, as is evident in all superstitious practices and observances. But that *all* moral affection or dislike arises from this origin will never surely be allowed by any judicious inquirer. Had nature made no such distinction, founded on the original constitution of the mind, the words *honorable* and *shameful, lovely* and *odious, noble* and *despicable* had never had place in any language; nor could politicians, had they invented these terms, ever have been able to render them intelligible or make them convey any idea to the audience. So that nothing can be more superficial than this paradox of the skeptics; and it were well if, in the abstruser studies of logic and metaphysics, we could as easily obviate the cavils of that sect as in the practical and more intelligible sciences of politics and morals.

The social virtues must, therefore, be allowed to have a natural beauty and amiableness which at first, antecedent to all precept or education, recommends them to the esteem of uninstructed mankind and engages their affections. And as the public utility of these virtues is the chief circumstance whence they derive their merit, it follows that the end which they have a tendency to promote must be some way agreeable to us and take hold of some natural affection. It must please either from considerations of self-interest or from more generous motives and regards.

It has often been asserted that as every man has a strong connection with society and perceives the impossibility of his solitary subsistence, he becomes, on that account, favorable to all those habits or principles which promote order in society and insure to him the quiet possession of so inestimable a blessing. As much as we value our own happiness and welfare, as much must we applaud the practice of justice and humanity, by which alone the social confederacy can be maintained and every man reap the fruits of mutual protection and assistance.

This deduction of morals from self-love, or a regard to private interest, is an obvious thought, and has not arisen wholly from the wanton sallies and sportive assaults of the skeptics. To mention no others, Polybius, one of the gravest and most judicious as well as most moral writers of antiquity, has assigned this selfish origin to all our sentiments of virtue.[1] But though the solid, practical sense of that author and his aversion to all vain subtleties render his authority on the present subject very considerable, yet is not this an affair to be decided by authority, and the voice of nature and experience seems plainly to oppose the selfish theory.

We frequently bestow praise on virtuous actions performed in very distant ages and remote countries, where the utmost subtlety of imagination would not discover any appearance of self-interest or find any connection of our present happiness and security with events so widely separated from us.

A generous, a brave, a noble deed performed by an adversary commands our approbation, while in its consequences it may be acknowledged prejudicial to our particular interest.

Where private advantage concurs with general affection for virtue, we readily perceive and avow the mixture of these distinct sentiments, which have a very different feeling and influence on the mind. We praise, perhaps, with more alacrity where the generous, humane action contributes to our particular interest. But the topics of praise which we insist on are very wide of this circumstance. And we may attempt to bring over others to our sentiments without endeavoring to convince them that they reap any advantage from the actions which we recommend to their approbation and applause.

Frame the model of a praiseworthy character, consisting of

[1] [Hume quotes two passages from Polybius' History, Bk. vi, chap. 4, in a footnote to this sentence; this footnote is omitted in this edition.—Ed.]

all the most amiable moral virtues. Give instances in which these display themselves after an eminent and extraordinary manner. You readily engage the esteem and approbation of all your audience, who never so much as inquire in what age and country the person lived who possessed these noble qualities, a circumstance, however, of all others the most material to self-love or a concern for our own individual happiness.

Once on a time a statesman, in the shock and contest of parties, prevailed so far as to procure by his eloquence the banishment of an able adversary, whom he secretly followed, offering him money for his support during his exile and soothing him with topics of consolation in his misfortunes. *Alas!* cries the banished statesman, *with what regret must I leave my friends in this city, where even enemies are so generous!* Virtue, though in an enemy, here pleased him. And we also give it the just tribute of praise and approbation; nor do we retract these sentiments when we hear that the action passed at Athens about two thousand years ago, and that the persons' names were Aeschines and Demosthenes.

What is that to me? There are few occasions when this question is not pertinent; and had it that universal, infallible influence supposed, it would turn into ridicule every composition and almost every conversation which contain any praise or censure of men and manners.

It is but a weak subterfuge, when pressed by these facts and arguments, to say that we transport ourselves by the force of imagination into distant ages and countries, and consider the advantage which we should have reaped from these characters had we been contemporaries and had any commerce with the persons. It is not conceivable how a *real* sentiment or passion can ever arise from a known *imaginary* interest, especially when our *real* interest is still kept in view, and is often acknowledged to be entirely distinct from the imaginary, and even sometimes opposite to it.

A man brought to the brink of a precipice cannot look down without trembling, and the sentiment of *imaginary* danger actuates him in opposition to the opinion and belief of *real* safety. But the imagination is here assisted by the presence of a striking object, and yet prevails not, except it be also aided by novelty and the unusual appearance of the object.

Custom soon reconciles us to heights and precipices, and wears off these false and delusive terrors. The reverse is observable in the estimates which we form of characters and manners, and the more we habituate ourselves to an accurate scrutiny of morals, the more delicate feeling do we acquire of the most minute distinctions between vice and virtue. Such frequent occasion, indeed, have we in common life to pronounce all kinds of moral determinations that no object of this kind can be new or unusual to us, nor could any *false* views or prepossessions maintain their ground against an experience so common and familiar. Experience being chiefly what forms the associations of ideas, it is impossible that any association could establish and support itself in direct opposition to that principle.

Usefulness is agreeable and engages our approbation. This is a matter of fact confirmed by daily observation. But *useful?* For what? For somebody's interest surely. Whose interest then? Not our own only, for our approbation frequently extends further. It must therefore be the interest of those who are served by the character or action approved of, and these we may conclude, however remote, are not totally indifferent to us. By opening up this principle we shall discover one great source of moral distinctions.

Part II.

Self-love is a principle in human nature of such extensive energy, and the interest of each individual is in general so closely connected with that of the community, that those philosophers were excusable who fancied that all our concern for the public might be resolved into a concern for our own happiness and preservation. They saw every moment instances of approbation or blame, satisfaction or displeasure toward characters and actions; they denominated the objects of these sentiments *virtues* or *vices;* they observed that the former had a tendency to increase the happiness and the latter the misery of mankind; they asked whether it were possible that we could have any general concern for society or any disinterested resentment of the welfare or injury of others; they found it simpler to consider all these sentiments as modifications of self-love; and they discovered a pretense at least for this unity of principle in that close union of interest which is so observable between the public and each individual.

But notwithstanding this frequent confusion of interests, it is easy to attain what natural philosophers, after Lord Bacon, have affected to call the *experimentum crucis,* or that experiment which points out the right way in any doubt or ambiguity. We have found instances in which private interest was separate from public, in which it was even contrary, and yet we observed the moral sentiment to continue, notwithstanding this disjunction of interests. And wherever these distinct interests sensibly concurred, we always found a sensible increase of the sentiment, and a more warm affection to virtue and detestation of vice, or what we properly call gratitude and revenge. Compelled by these instances we must renounce the theory which accounts for every moral sentiment by the principle of self-love. We must adopt a more public affection and allow that the interests of society are not, even on their own account, entirely indifferent to us. Usefulness is only a tendency to a certain end, and it is a contradiction in terms that anything pleases as means to an end where the end itself nowise affects us. If usefulness, therefore, be a source of moral sentiment, and if this usefulness be not always considered with a reference to self, it follows that everything which contributes to the happiness of society recommends itself directly to our approbation and good will. Here is a principle which accounts, in great part, for the origin of morality. And what need we seek for abstruse and remote systems when there occurs one so obvious and natural? [1]

[1] It is needless to push our researches so far as to ask why we have humanity or a fellow-feeling with others. It is sufficient that this is experienced to be a principle in human nature. We must stop somewhere in our examination of causes, and there are in every science some general principles beyond which we cannot hope to find any principle more general. No man is absolutely indifferent to the happiness and misery of others. The first has a natural tendency to give pleasure, the second pain. This everyone may find in himself. It is not probable that these principles can be resolved into principles more simple and universal, whatever attempts may have been made to that purpose. But if it were possible, it belongs

Have we any difficulty to comprehend the force of humanity and benevolence? Or to conceive that the very aspect of happiness, joy, prosperity gives pleasure, that of pain, suffering, sorrow communicates uneasiness? The human countenance, says Horace,[1] borrows smiles or tears from the human countenance. Reduce a person to solitude and he loses all enjoyment, except either of the sensual or speculative kind, and that because the movements of his heart are not forwarded by correspondent movements in his fellow creatures. The signs of sorrow and mourning, though arbitrary, affect us with melancholy, but the natural symptoms, tears and cries and groans, never fail to infuse compassion and uneasiness. And if the effects of misery touch us in so lively a manner, can we be supposed altogether insensible or indifferent toward its causes, when a malicious or treacherous character and behavior are presented to us?

. . . .

If any man, from a cold insensibility or narrow selfishness of temper, is unaffected with the images of human happiness or misery, he must be equally indifferent to the images of vice and virtue; as, on the other hand, it is always found that a warm concern for the interests of our species is attended with a delicate feeling of all moral distinctions, a strong resentment of injury done to men, a lively approbation of their welfare. In this particular, though great superiority is observable of one man above another, yet none are so entirely indifferent to the interests of their fellow creatures as to perceive no distinctions of moral good and evil, in consequence of the different tendencies of actions and principles. How, indeed, can we suppose it possible in anyone who wears a human heart, that if there be subjected to his censure one character or system of conduct which is beneficial, and another which is pernicious to his species or community, he will not so much as give a cool preference to the former or ascribe to it the smallest merit or regard? Let us suppose such a person ever so selfish, let pri-

_____

not to the present subject, and we may here safely consider these principles as original. Happy if we can render all the consequences sufficiently plain and perspicuous!

[1] *Ut ridentibus arrident, ita flentibus adsunt humani voltus.* Horace.

vate interest have engrossed ever so much his attention, yet in instances where that is not concerned he must unavoidably feel *some* propensity to the good of mankind and make it an object of choice, if everything else be equal. Would any man who is walking along tread as willingly on another's gouty toes, whom he has no quarrel with, as on the hard flint and pavement? There is here surely a difference in the case. We surely take into consideration the happiness and misery of others in weighing the several motives of action, and incline to the former where no private regards draw us to seek our own promotion or advantage by the injury of our fellow creatures. And if the principles of humanity are capable in many instances of influencing our actions, they must at all times have *some* authority over our sentiments, and give us a general approbation of what is useful to society and blame of what is dangerous or pernicious. The degrees of these sentiments may be the subject of controversy, but the reality of their existence, one should think, must be admitted in every theory or system.

A creature absolutely malicious and spiteful, were there any such in nature, must be worse than indifferent to the images of vice and virtue. All his sentiments must be inverted, and directly opposite to those which prevail in the human species. Whatever contributes to the good of mankind, as it crosses the constant bent of his wishes and desires, must produce uneasiness and disapprobation; and on the contrary, whatever is the source of disorder and misery in society must, for the same reason, be regarded with pleasure and complacency. Timon, who, probably from his affected spleen more than any inveterate malice, was denominated the man-hater, embraced Alcibiades with great fondness. *Go on, my boy!* cried he. *Acquire the confidence of the people. You will one day, I foresee, be the cause of great calamities to them.*[1] Could we admit the two principles of the Manichaeans, it is an infallible consequence that their sentiments of human actions, as well as of everything else, must be totally opposite, and that every instance of justice and humanity, from its necessary tendency, must please the one deity and displease the other.

[1] Plutarch, in *vita Alc.*

All mankind so far resemble the good principle that, where interest or revenge or envy perverts not our disposition, we are always inclined, from our natural philanthropy, to give the preference to the happiness of society and consequently to virtue above its opposite. Absolute, unprovoked, disinterested malice has never, perhaps, place in any human breast, or if it had, must there pervert all the sentiments of morals as well as the feelings of humanity. If the cruelty of Nero be allowed entirely voluntary, and not rather the effect of constant fear and resentment, it is evident that Tigellinus, preferably to Seneca or Burrhus, must have possessed his steady and uniform approbation.

A statesman or patriot who serves our own country in our own time has always a more passionate regard paid to him than one whose beneficial influence operated on distant ages or remote nations, where the good resulting from his generous humanity, being less connected with us, seems more obscure and affects us with a less lively sympathy. We may own the merit to be equally great, though our sentiments are not raised to an equal height in both cases. The judgment here corrects the inequalities of our internal emotions and perceptions, in like manner as it preserves us from error in the several variations of images presented to our external senses. The same object, at a double distance, really throws on the eye a picture of but half the bulk; yet we imagine that it appears of the same size in both situations, because we know that on our approach to it its image would expand on the eye, and that the difference consists not in the object itself but in our position with regard to it. And indeed, without such a correction of appearances, both in internal and external sentiment, men could never think or talk steadily on any subject, while their fluctuating situations produce a continual variation on objects and throw them into such different and contrary lights and positions.[1]

[1] For a like reason, the tendencies of actions and characters, not their real accidental consequences, are alone regarded in our moral determinations or general judgments, though in our real feeling or sentiment we cannot help paying greater regard to one whose station, joined to virtue, renders him really useful to society than to one who exerts the social virtues only in good intentions

The more we converse with mankind and the greater social intercourse we maintain, the more shall we be familiarized to these general preferences and distinctions, without which our conversation and discourse could scarcely be rendered intelligible to each other. Every man's interest is peculiar to himself, and the aversions and desires which result from it cannot be supposed to affect others in a like degree. General language, therefore, being formed for general use, must be molded on some more general views and must affix the epithets of praise or blame in conformity to sentiments which arise from the general interests of the community. And if these sentiments, in most men, be not so strong as those which have a reference to private good, yet still they must make some distinction, even in persons the most depraved and selfish, and must attach the notion of good to a beneficent conduct, and of evil to the contrary. Sympathy, we shall allow, is much fainter than our concern for ourselves, and sympathy with persons remote from us much fainter than that with persons near and contiguous; but for this very reason it is necessary for us, in our calm judgments and discourse concerning the characters of men, to neglect all these differences and render our sentiments more public and social. Besides that we ourselves often change our situation in this particular, we every day meet with persons who are in a situation different from us, and who could never converse with us were we to remain constantly in that position and point of view which is peculiar to ourselves. The intercourse of sentiments, therefore, in society and conversation makes us form some general unalterable standard by which we may approve or disapprove of characters and

---

and benevolent affections. Separating the character from the fortune by an easy and necessary effort of thought, we pronounce these persons alike, and give them the same general praise. The judgment corrects or endeavors to correct the appearance, but is not able entirely to prevail over sentiment.

Why is this peach tree said to be better than that other, but because it produces more or better fruit? And would not the same praise be given it, though snails or vermin had destroyed the peaches before they came to full maturity? In morals too, is not *the tree known by the fruit?* And cannot we easily distinguish between nature and accident, in the one case as well as in the other?

manners. And though the heart takes not part entirely with those general notions, nor regulates all its love and hatred by the universal, abstract differences of vice and virtue, without regard to self or the persons with whom we are more intimately connected, yet have these moral differences a considerable influence, and being sufficient at least for discourse, serve all our purposes in company, in the pulpit, on the theater, and in the schools.[1]

Thus in whatever light we take this subject, the merit ascribed to the social virtues appears still uniform and arises chiefly from that regard which the natural sentiment of benevolence engages us to pay to the interests of mankind and society. If we consider the principles of the human make, such as they appear to daily experience and observation, we must, *a priori*, conclude it impossible for such a creature as man to be totally indifferent to the well or ill-being of his fellow creatures, and not readily, of himself, to pronounce, where nothing gives him any particular bias, that what promotes their happiness is good, what tends to their misery is evil, without any further regard or consideration. Here then are the faint rudiments at least, or outlines, of a *general* distinction between actions; and in proportion as the humanity of the person is supposed to increase, his connection with those who are injured or benefited, and his lively conception of their misery or happiness, his consequent censure or approbation acquires proportionable vigor. There is no necessity that a generous action barely mentioned in an old history or remote gazette should communicate any strong feelings of applause and admiration. Virtue placed at such a distance is like a fixed star, which, though to the eye of reason it may appear as luminous as the sun in his meridian, is so infinitely removed as to affect

[1] It is wisely ordained by nature that private connections should commonly prevail over universal views and considerations; otherwise our affections and actions would be dissipated and lost, for want of a proper limited object. Thus a small benefit done to ourselves or our near friends excites more lively sentiments of love and approbation than a great benefit done to a distant commonwealth. But still we know here, as in all the senses, to correct these inequalities by reflection, and retain a general standard of vice and virtue, founded chiefly on general usefulness.

the senses neither with light nor heat. Bring this virtue nearer by our acquaintance or connection with the persons, or even by an eloquent recital of the case, our hearts are immediately caught, our sympathy enlivened, and our cool approbation converted into the warmest sentiments of friendship and regard. These seem necessary and infallible consequences of the general principles of human nature, as discovered in common life and practice.

Again, reverse these views and reasonings. Consider the matter *a posteriori*, and weighing the consequences inquire if the merit of social virtue be not, in a great measure, derived from the feelings of humanity with which it affects the spectators. It appears to be matter of fact that the circumstance of *utility*, in all subjects, is a source of praise and approbation; that it is constantly appealed to in all moral decisions concerning the merit and demerit of actions; that it is the *sole* source of that high regard paid to justice, fidelity, honor, allegiance, and chastity; that it is inseparable from all the other social virtues, humanity, generosity, charity, affability, lenity, mercy, and moderation; and, in a word, that it is a foundation of the chief part of morals, which has a reference to mankind and our fellow creatures.

It appears also that in our general approbation of characters and manners the useful tendency of the social virtues moves us not by any regards to self-interest, but has an influence much more universal and extensive. It appears that a tendency to public good and to the promoting of peace, harmony, and order in society does always, by affecting the benevolent principles of our frame, engage us on the side of the social virtues. And it appears, as an additional confirmation, that these principles of humanity and sympathy enter so deeply into all our sentiments and have so powerful an influence as may enable them to excite the strongest censure and applause. The present theory is the simple result of all these inferences, each of which seems founded on uniform experience and observation.

Were it doubtful whether there were any such principle in our nature as humanity or a concern for others, yet when we see, in numberless instances, that whatever has a tendency to promote the interests of society is so highly approved of, we ought thence to learn the force of the benevolent principle, since it is impossible for anything to please as means to an end where the end is totally indifferent. On the other hand, were it doubtful whether there were implanted in our nature any general principle of moral blame and approbation, yet when we see, in numberless instances, the influence of humanity, we ought thence to conclude that it is impossible but that everything which promotes the interest of society must communicate pleasure, and what is pernicious give uneasiness. But when these different reflections and observations concur in establishing the same conclusion, must they not bestow an undisputed evidence upon it?

It is however hoped that the progress of this argument will bring a further confirmation of the present theory, by showing the rise of other sentiments of esteem and regard from the same or like principles.

Section VI.

OF QUALITIES USEFUL TO OURSELVES

Part I.

IT SEEMS EVIDENT that where a quality or habit is subjected to our examination, if it appear in any respect prejudicial to the person possessed of it, or such as incapacitates him for business and action, it is instantly blamed and ranked among his faults and imperfections. Indolence, negligence, want of order and method, obstinacy, fickleness, rashness, credulity; these qualities were never esteemed by anyone indifferent to a character, much less extolled as accomplishments or virtues. The prejudice resulting from them immediately strikes our eye and gives us the sentiment of pain and disapprobation.

No quality, it is allowed, is absolutely either blamable or praiseworthy. It is all according to its degree. A due medium, say the Peripatetics, is the characteristic of virtue. But this medium is chiefly determined by utility. A proper celerity, for instance, and dispatch in business, is commendable. When defective, no progress is ever made in the execution of any purpose; when excessive, it engages us in precipitate and ill-concerted measures and enterprises. By such reasonings we fix the proper and commendable mediocrity in all moral and prudential disquisitions, and never lose view of the advantages which result from any character or habit.

Now as these advantages are enjoyed by the person possessed of the character, it can never be *self-love* which renders the prospect of them agreeable to us, the spectators, and prompts our esteem and approbation. No force of imagination can convert us into another person, and make us fancy that we, being that person, reap benefit from those valuable qualities which belong to him. Or if it did, no celerity of imagination could immediately transport us back into ourselves and make us love and esteem the person as different from us. Views and sentiments so opposite to known truth and to each other could never have place, at the same time, in the same person. All suspicion, therefore, of selfish regards is here totally excluded. It is a quite different principle which actuates our bosom, and interests us in the felicity of the person whom we contemplate. Where his natural talents and acquired abilities give us the prospect of elevation, advancement, a figure in life, prosperous success, a steady command over fortune, and the execution of great or advantageous undertakings, we are struck with such agreeable images and feel a complacency and regard immediately arise toward him. The ideas of happiness, joy, triumph, prosperity are connected with every circumstance of his character, and diffuse over our minds a pleasing sentiment of sympathy and humanity.[1]

[1] One may venture to affirm that there is no human creature to whom the appearance of happiness (where envy or revenge has no place) does not give pleasure; that of misery, uneasiness. This seems inseparable from our make and constitution. But they are only the more generous minds that are thence prompted to seek zealously the good of others, and to have a real passion for their welfare. With men of narrow and ungenerous spirits, this sym-

Let us suppose a person originally framed so as to have no manner of concern for his fellow creatures, but to regard the happiness and misery of all sensible beings with greater indifference than even two contiguous shades of the same color. Let us suppose, if the prosperity of nations were laid on the one hand and their ruin on the other, and he were desired to choose, that he would stand like the schoolman's ass, irresolute and undetermined between equal motives, or rather like the same ass between two pieces of wood or marble, without any inclination or propensity to either side. The consequence, I believe, must be allowed just, that such a person, being absolutely unconcerned either for the public good of a community or the private utility of others, would look on every quality, however pernicious or however beneficial to society or to its possessor, with the same indifference as on the most common and uninteresting object.

But if instead of this fancied monster we suppose a *man* to form a judgment or determination in the case, there is to him a plain foundation of preference, where everything else is equal; and however cool his choice may be, if his heart be selfish or if the persons interested be remote from him, there must still be a choice or distinction between what is useful and what is pernicious. Now this distinction is the same in all its parts with the *moral distinction* whose foundation has been so often, and so much in vain, inquired after. The same endowments of the mind, in every circumstance, are agreeable to the sentiment of morals and to that of humanity; the same temper is susceptible of high degrees of the one sentiment and of the other; and the same alteration in the objects, by their nearer approach or by connections, enlivens the one and the

---

pathy goes not beyond a slight feeling of the imagination, which serves only to excite sentiments of complacency or censure, and makes them apply to the object either honorable or dishonorable appellations. A griping miser, for instance, praises extremely *industry* and *frugality* even in others, and sets them in his estimation above all the other virtues. He knows the good that results from them, and feels that species of happiness with a more lively sympathy than any other you could represent to him, though perhaps he would not part with a shilling to make the fortune of the industrious man whom he praises so highly.

other. By all the rules of philosophy, therefore, we must conclude that these sentiments are originally the same, since in each particular, even the most minute, they are governed by the same laws and are moved by the same objects.

Why do philosophers infer with the greatest certainty that the moon is kept in its orbit by the same force of gravity that makes bodies fall near the surface of the earth, but because these effects are, upon computation, found similar and equal? And must not this argument bring as strong conviction in moral as in natural disquisitions?

To prove, by any long detail, that all the qualities useful to the possessor are approved of, and the contrary censured, would be superfluous. The least reflection on what is every day experienced in life will be sufficient. . . .

. . . . .

In this kingdom such continued ostentation, of late years, has prevailed among men in *active* life with regard to *public spirit,* and among those in *speculative* with regard to *benevolence,* and so many false pretensions to each have been no doubt detected, that men of the world are apt, without any bad intention, to discover a sullen incredulity on the head of those moral endowments, and even sometimes absolutely to deny their existence and reality. In like manner I find that of old the perpetual cant of the Stoics and Cynics concerning *virtue,* their magnificent professions and slender performances, bred a disgust in mankind; and Lucian, who though licentious with regard to pleasure is yet in other respects a very moral writer, cannot sometimes talk of virtue, so much boasted, without betraying symptoms of spleen and irony.[1] But surely this peevish delicacy, whenever it arises, can never be carried so far as to make us deny the existence of every species of merit and all distinction of manners and behavior. Besides *discretion, caution, enterprise, industry, assiduity, frugality, economy, good sense, prudence, discernment;* besides these endowments, I say, whose very names force an avowal of their merit, there are many others to which

[1] [Hume quotes three passages from as many works of Lucian— *viz., Timon, Icaromenippus,* and *Deorum concilium*—in a footnote to this sentence. This footnote is omitted in this edition.—Ed.]

the most determined skepticism cannot for a moment refuse the tribute of praise and approbation. *Temperance, sobriety, patience, constancy, perseverance, forethought, considerateness, secrecy, order, insinuation, address, presence of mind, quickness of conception, facility of expression;* these, and a thousand more of the same kind, no man will ever deny to be excellences and perfections. As their merit consists in their tendency to serve the person possessed of them, without any magnificent claim to public and social desert, we are the less jealous of their pretensions, and readily admit them into the catalogue of laudable qualities. We are not sensible that by this concession we have paved the way for all the other moral excellences, and cannot consistently hesitate any longer with regard to disinterested benevolence, patriotism, and humanity.

It seems, indeed, certain that first appearances are here, as usual, extremely deceitful, and that it is more difficult, in a speculative way, to resolve into self-love the merit which we ascribe to the selfish virtues above mentioned than that even of the social virtues, justice and beneficence. For this latter purpose we need but say that whatever conduct promotes the good of the community is loved, praised, and esteemed by the community, on account of that utility and interest of which everyone partakes; and though this affection and regard be, in reality, gratitude, not self-love, yet a distinction even of this obvious nature may not readily be made by superficial reasoners, and there is room at least to support the cavil and dispute for a moment. But as qualities which tend only to the utility of their possessor, without any reference to us or to the community, are yet esteemed and valued, by what theory or system can we account for this sentiment from self-love, or deduce it from that favorite origin? There seems here a necessity for confessing that the happiness and misery of others are not spectacles entirely indifferent to us, but that the view of the former, whether in its causes or effects, like sunshine or the prospect of well-cultivated plains (to carry our pretensions no higher), communicates a secret joy and satisfaction; the appearance of the latter, like a lowering cloud or barren landscape, throws a melancholy damp over the imagination. And this concession being once made, the difficulty is over, and a natural unforced interpretation of the phenomena of human life will afterward, we may hope, prevail among all speculative inquirers.[1]

. . . .

Section VII.

OF QUALITIES IMMEDIATELY AGREEABLE TO OURSELVES

WHOEVER HAS passed an evening with serious melancholy people and has observed how suddenly the conversation was animated and what sprightliness diffused itself over the countenance, discourse, and behavior of everyone on the accession of a good-humored, lively companion, such a one will easily allow that *cheerfulness* carries great merit with it and naturally conciliates the good will of mankind. No quality, indeed, more readily communicates itself to all around, because no one has a greater propensity to display itself in jovial talk and pleasant entertainment. The flame spreads through the whole circle, and the most sullen and morose are often caught by it. That the melancholy hate the merry, even though Horace says it, I have some difficulty to allow, because I have always observed that where the jollity is moderate and decent, serious people are so much the more delighted, as it dissipates the gloom with which they are commonly oppressed and gives them an unusual enjoyment.

From this influence of cheerfulness, both to communicate itself and to engage approbation, we may perceive that there is another set of mental qualities which, without any utility or any tendency to further good, either of the community or of the possessor, diffuse a satisfaction on the beholders and procure friendship and regard. Their immediate sensation to the person possessed of them is agreeable. Others enter into the

[1] [This is the end of Part I of this Section; the whole of Part II is omitted in this edition.—Ed.]

same humor and catch the sentiment by a contagion or natural sympathy; and as we cannot forbear loving whatever pleases, a kindly emotion arises toward the person who communicates so much satisfaction. He is a more animating spectacle. His presence diffuses over us more serene complacency and enjoyment. Our imagination, entering into his feelings and disposition, is affected in a more agreeable manner than if a melancholy, dejected, sullen, anxious temper were presented to us. Hence the affection and approbation which attend the former, the aversion and disgust with which we regard the latter.[1]

. . . . . .

We never excuse the absolute want of spirit and dignity of character, or a proper sense of what is due to one's self in society and the common intercourse of life. This vice constitutes what we properly call *meanness,* when a man can submit to the basest slavery in order to gain his ends, fawn upon those who abuse him, and degrade himself by intimacies and familiarities with undeserving inferiors. A certain degree of generous pride or self-value is so requisite that the absence of it in the mind displeases, after the same manner as the want of a nose, eye, or any of the most material features of the face or members of the body.[2]

[1] There is no man who, on particular occasions, is not affected with all the disagreeable passions, fear, anger, dejection, grief, melancholy, anxiety, etc. But these, so far as they are natural and universal, make no difference between one man and another, and can never be the object of blame. It is only when the disposition gives a *propensity* to any of these disagreeable passions that they disfigure the character, and by giving uneasiness convey the sentiment of disapprobation to the spectator.

[2] The absence of virtue may often be a vice, and that of the highest kind, as in the instance of ingratitude, as well as meanness. Where we expect a beauty, the disappointment gives an uneasy sensation and produces a real deformity. An abjectness of character, likewise, is disgustful and contemptible in another view. Where a man has no sense of value in himself, we are not likely to have any higher esteem of him. And if the same person who crouches to his superiors is insolent to his inferiors (as often happens), this contrariety of behavior, instead of correcting the former vice, aggravates it extremely by the addition of a vice still more odious. See Section VIII.

The utility of *courage*, both to the public and to the person possessed of it, is an obvious foundation of merit. But to anyone who duly considers of the matter it will appear that this quality has a peculiar luster, which it derives wholly from itself and from that noble elevation inseparable from it. Its figure, drawn by painters and by poets, displays in each feature a sublimity and daring confidence which catches the eye, engages the affections, and diffuses, by sympathy, a like sublimity of sentiment over every spectator.

. . . . .

Of the same class of virtues with courage is that undisturbed philosophical *tranquillity*, superior to pain, sorrow, anxiety, and each assault of adverse fortune. Conscious of his own virtue, say the philosophers, the sage elevates himself above every accident of life, and securely placed in the temple of wisdom, looks down on inferior mortals engaged in pursuit of honors, riches, reputation, and every frivolous enjoyment. These pretensions, no doubt, when stretched to the utmost, are by far too magnificent for human nature. They carry, however, a grandeur with them, which seizes the spectator and strikes him with admiration. And the nearer we can approach in practice to this sublime tranquillity and indifference (for we must distinguish it from a stupid insensibility), the more secure enjoyment shall we attain within ourselves, and the more greatness of mind shall we discover to the world. The philosophical tranquillity may indeed be considered only as a branch of magnanimity.

Who admires not Socrates, his perpetual serenity and contentment amidst the greatest poverty and domestic vexations, his resolute contempt of riches, and his magnanimous care of preserving liberty, while he refused all assistance from his friends and disciples, and avoided even the dependence of an obligation? Epictetus had not so much as a door to his little house or hovel, and therefore soon lost his iron lamp, the only furniture which he had worth taking. But resolving to disappoint all robbers for the future, he supplied its place with an earthen lamp, of which he very peaceably kept possession ever after.

Among the ancients, the heroes in philosophy, as well as

those in war and patriotism, have a grandeur and force of sentiment which astonishes our narrow souls, and is rashly rejected as extravagant and supernatural. They, in their turn, I allow, would have had equal reason to consider as romantic and incredible the degree of humanity, clemency, order, tranquillity, and other social virtues to which, in the administration of government, we have attained in modern times, had anyone been then able to have made a fair representation of them. Such is the compensation which nature, or rather education, has made in the distribution of excellences and virtues in those different ages.

The merit of *benevolence*, arising from its utility and its tendency to promote the good of mankind, has been already explained, and is, no doubt, the source of a *considerable* part of that esteem which is so universally paid to it. But it will also be allowed that the very softness and tenderness of the sentiment, its engaging endearments, its fond expressions, its delicate attentions, and all that flow of mutual confidence and regard which enters into a warm attachment of love and friendship; it will be allowed, I say, that these feelings, being delightful in themselves, are necessarily communicated to the spectators and melt them into the same fondness and delicacy. The tear naturally starts in our eye on the apprehension of a warm sentiment of this nature; our breast heaves, our heart is agitated, and every humane tender principle of our frame is set in motion and gives us the purest and most satisfactory enjoyment.

When poets form descriptions of Elysian fields, where the blessed inhabitants stand in no need of each other's assistance, they yet represent them as maintaining a constant intercourse of love and friendship, and soothe our fancy with the pleasing image of these soft and gentle passions. The idea of tender tranquillity in a pastoral Arcadia is agreeable from a like principle, as has been observed above.[1]

Who would live amidst perpetual wrangling and scolding and mutual reproaches? The roughness and harshness of these emotions disturb and displease us. We suffer by contagion

[1] Section V, Part II.

and sympathy, nor can we remain indifferent spectators, even though certain that no pernicious consequences would ever follow from such angry passions.

As a certain proof that the whole merit of benevolence is not derived from its usefulness, we may observe that, in a kind way of blame, we say a person is *too good*, when he exceeds his part in society and carries his attention for others beyond the proper bounds. In like manner, we say a man is *too high-spirited, too intrepid, too indifferent about fortune,* reproaches which really, at bottom, imply more esteem than many panegyrics. Being accustomed to rate the merit and demerit of characters chiefly by their useful or pernicious tendencies, we cannot forbear applying the epithet of blame when we discover a sentiment which rises to a degree that is hurtful. But it may happen, at the same time, that its noble elevation or its engaging tenderness so seizes the heart as rather to increase our friendship and concern for the person.[1]

. . . . . .

These are some instances of the several species of merit that are valued for the immediate pleasure which they communicate to the person possessed of them. No views of utility or of future beneficial consequences enter into this sentiment of approbation, yet is it of a kind similar to that other sentiment, which arises from views of a public or private utility. The same social sympathy, we may observe, or fellow feeling with human happiness or misery, gives rise to both; and this analogy, in all the parts of the present theory, may justly be regarded as a confirmation of it.

[1] Cheerfulness could scarce admit of blame from its excess, were it not that dissolute mirth, without a proper cause or subject, is a sure symptom and characteristic of folly, and on that account disgustful.

Section VIII.

OF QUALITIES IMMEDIATELY
AGREEABLE TO OTHERS [1]

AS THE MUTUAL SHOCKS in *society*, and the oppositions of interest and self-love, have constrained mankind to establish the laws of *justice* in order to preserve the advantages of mutual assistance and protection, in like manner the eternal contrarieties in *company* of men's pride and self-conceit have introduced the rules of *good manners* or *politeness* in order to facilitate the intercourse of minds and an undisturbed commerce and conversation. Among well-bred people a mutual deference is affected, contempt of others disguised, authority concealed, attention given to each in his turn, and an easy stream of conversation maintained, without vehemence, without interruption, without eagerness for victory, and without any airs of superiority. These attentions and regards are immediately *agreeable* to others, abstracted from any consideration of utility or beneficial tendencies. They conciliate affection, promote esteem, and extremely enhance the merit of the person who regulates his behavior by them.

Many of the forms of breeding are arbitrary and casual, but the thing expressed by them is still the same. A Spaniard goes out of his own house before his guest, to signify that he leaves him master of all. In other countries the landlord walks out last, as a common mark of deference and regard.

But in order to render a man perfect *good company*, he must have *wit* and *ingenuity* as well as good manners. What wit is it may not be easy to define, but it is easy surely to determine that it is a quality immediately *agreeable* to others,

[1] It is the nature and indeed the definition of virtue that it is *a quality of the mind agreeable to or approved of by everyone who considers or contemplates it*. But some qualities produce pleasure because they are useful to society or useful or agreeable to the person himself; others produce it more immediately, which is the case with the class of virtues here considered.

and communicating on its first appearance a lively joy and satisfaction to everyone who has any comprehension of it. The most profound metaphysics, indeed, might be employed in explaining the various kinds and species of wit, and many classes of it which are now received on the sole testimony of taste and sentiment might perhaps be resolved into more general principles. But this is sufficient for our present purpose, that it does affect taste and sentiment, and bestowing an immediate enjoyment, is a sure source of approbation and affection.

In countries where men pass most of their time in conversation and visits and assemblies, these *companionable* qualities, so to speak, are of high estimation and form a chief part of personal merit. In countries where men live a more domestic life, and either are employed in business or amuse themselves in a narrower circle of acquaintance, the more solid qualities are chiefly regarded. Thus I have often observed that among the French the first questions with regard to a stranger are, *Is he polite? Has he wit?* In our own country, the chief praise bestowed is always that of a *good-natured, sensible fellow.*

. . . . . .

But besides all the *agreeable* qualities the origin of whose beauty we can in some degree explain and account for, there still remains something mysterious and inexplicable which conveys an immediate satisfaction to the spectator, but how, or why, or for what reason, he cannot pretend to determine. There is a *manner,* a grace, an ease, a genteelness, an I-know-not-what, which some men possess above others, which is very different from external beauty and comeliness, and which, however, catches our affection almost as suddenly and powerfully. And though this *manner* be chiefly talked of in the passion between the sexes, where the concealed magic is easily explained, yet surely much of it prevails in all our estimation of characters, and forms no inconsiderable part of personal merit. This class of accomplishments, therefore, must be trusted entirely to the blind but sure testimony of taste and sentiment, and must be considered as a part of ethics left by nature to baffle all the pride of philosophy, and make her sensible of her narrow boundaries and slender acquisitions.

We approve of another because of his wit, politeness, modesty, decency, or any agreeable quality which he possesses, although he be not of our acquaintance nor has ever given us any entertainment by means of these accomplishments. The idea which we form of their effect on his acquaintance has an agreeable influence on our imagination and gives us the sentiment of approbation. This principle enters into all the judgments which we form concerning manners and characters.

Section IX.

CONCLUSION

Part I.

IT MAY JUSTLY APPEAR surprising that any man in so late an age should find it requisite to prove by elaborate reasoning that *personal merit* consists altogether in the possession of mental qualities *useful* or *agreeable* to the *person himself* or to *others*. It might be expected that this principle would have occurred even to the first rude, unpracticed inquirers concerning morals, and been received from its own evidence without any argument or disputation. Whatever is valuable in any kind so naturally classes itself under the division of *useful* or *agreeable*, the *utile* or the *dulce*, that it is not easy to imagine why we should ever seek further, or consider the question as a matter of nice research or inquiry. And as everything useful or agreeable must possess these qualities with regard either to the *person himself* or to *others*, the complete delineation or description of merit seems to be performed as naturally as a shadow is cast by the sun, or an image is reflected upon water. If the ground on which the shadow is cast be not broken and uneven, nor the surface from which the image is reflected disturbed and confused, a just figure is immediately presented, without any art or attention. And it seems a reasonable presumption that systems and hypotheses have perverted our natural understanding when a theory so simple and obvious could so long have escaped the most elaborate examination.

But however the case may have fared with philosophy, in common life these principles are still implicitly maintained, nor is any other topic of praise or blame ever recurred to when we employ any panegyric or satire, any applause or censure of human action and behavior. If we observe men in every intercourse of business or pleasure, in every discourse and conversation, we shall find them nowhere, except in the schools, at any loss upon this subject. What so natural, for instance, as the following dialogue? You are very happy, we shall suppose one to say, addressing himself to another, that you have given your daughter to Cleanthes. He is a man of honor and humanity. Everyone who has any intercourse with him is sure of *fair* and *kind* treatment.[1] I congratulate you too, says another, on the promising expectations of this son-in-law, whose assiduous application to the study of the laws, whose quick penetration and early knowledge both of men and business, prognosticate the greatest honors and advancement.[2] You surprise me, replies a third, when you talk of Cleanthes as a man of business and application. I met him lately in a circle of the gayest company, and he was the very life and soul of our conversation. So much wit with good manners, so much gallantry without affectation, so much ingenious knowledge so genteelly delivered, I have never before observed in anyone.[3] You would admire him still more, says a fourth, if you knew him more familiarly. That cheerfulness which you might remark in him is not a sudden flash struck out by company; it runs through the whole tenor of his life, and preserves a perpetual serenity on his countenance and tranquillity in his soul. He has met with severe trials, misfortunes as well as dangers, and by his greatness of mind was still superior to all of them.[4] The image, gentlemen, which you have here delineated of Cleanthes, cried I, is that of accomplished merit. Each of you has given a stroke of the pencil to his figure, and you have unawares exceeded all the pic-

[1] Qualities useful to others.
[2] Qualities useful to the person himself.
[3] Qualities immediately agreeable to others.
[4] Qualities immediately agreeable to the person himself.

tures drawn by Gratian or Castiglione. A philosopher might select this character as a model of perfect virtue.

And as every quality which is useful or agreeable to ourselves or others is, in common life, allowed to be a part of personal merit, so no other will ever be received, where men judge of things by their natural, unprejudiced reason, without the delusive glosses of superstition and false religion. Celibacy, fasting, penance, mortification, self-denial, humility, silence, solitude, and the whole train of monkish virtues; for what reason are they everywhere rejected by men of sense but because they serve to no manner of purpose, neither advance a man's fortune in the world nor render him a more valuable member of society, neither qualify him for the entertainment of company nor increase his power of self-enjoyment? We observe, on the contrary, that they cross all these desirable ends, stupefy the understanding and harden the heart, obscure the fancy and sour the temper. We justly, therefore, transfer them to the opposite column, and place them in the catalogue of vices, nor has any superstition force sufficient among men of the world to pervert entirely these natural sentiments. A gloomy, hair-brained enthusiast, after his death, may have a place in the calendar, but will scarcely ever be admitted, when alive, into intimacy and society, except by those who are as delirious and dismal as himself.

It seems a happiness in the present theory that it enters not into that vulgar dispute concerning the *degrees* of benevolence or self-love which prevail in human nature, a dispute which is never likely to have any issue, both because men who have taken part are not easily convinced and because the phenomena which can be produced on either side are so dispersed, so uncertain, and subject to so many interpretations that it is scarcely possible accurately to compare them or draw from them any determinate inference or conclusion. It is sufficient for our present purpose if it be allowed, what surely without the greatest absurdity cannot be disputed, that there is some benevolence, however small, infused into our bosom, some spark of friendship for human kind, some particle of the dove kneaded into our frame, along with the elements of the wolf and serpent. Let these generous sentiments be supposed ever so weak, let them be insufficient to move even a hand or finger of our body, they must still direct the determinations of our mind and where everything else is equal produce a cool preference of what is useful and serviceable to mankind above what is pernicious and dangerous. A *moral distinction*, therefore, immediately arises, a general sentiment of blame and approbation, a tendency, however faint, to the objects of the one and a proportionable aversion to those of the other. Nor will those reasoners who so earnestly maintain the predominant selfishness of human kind be anywise scandalized at hearing of the weak sentiments of virtue implanted in our nature. On the contrary, they are found as ready to maintain the one tenet as the other, and their spirit of satire (for such it appears, rather than of corruption) naturally gives rise to both opinions, which have, indeed, a great and almost an indissoluble connection together.

Avarice, ambition, vanity, and all passions vulgarly though improperly comprised under the denomination of *self-love* are here excluded from our theory concerning the origin of morals, not because they are too weak, but because they have not a proper direction for that purpose. The notion of morals implies some sentiment common to all mankind which recommends the same object to general approbation, and makes every man, or most men, agree in the same opinion or decision concerning it. It also implies some sentiment so universal and comprehensive as to extend to all mankind, and render the actions and conduct even of the persons the most remote an object of applause or censure, according as they agree or disagree with that rule of right which is established. These two requisite circumstances belong alone to the sentiment of humanity here insisted on. The other passions produce, in every breast, many strong sentiments of desire and aversion, affection and hatred, but these neither are felt so much in common nor are so comprehensive as to be the foundation of any general system and established theory of blame or approbation.

When a man denominates another his *enemy*, his *rival*, his *antagonist*, his *adversary*, he is understood to speak the language of self-love and to express sentiments peculiar to himself and arising from his particular circumstances and situation. But when he bestows on any man the epithets of *vicious* or *odious* or *depraved,* he then speaks another language and expresses sentiments in which he expects all his audience are to concur with him. He must here, therefore, depart from his private and particular situation and must choose a point of view common to him with others. He must move some universal principle of the human frame and touch a string to which all mankind have an accord and symphony. If he mean, therefore, to express that this man possesses qualities whose tendency is pernicious to society, he has chosen this common point of view and has touched the principle of humanity in which every man, in some degree, concurs. While the human heart is compounded of the same elements as at present, it will never be wholly indifferent to public good, nor entirely unaffected with the tendency of characters and manners. And though this affection of humanity may not generally be esteemed so strong as vanity or ambition, yet being common to all men, it can alone be the foundation of morals or of any general system of blame or praise. One man's ambition is not another's ambition, nor will the same event or object satisfy both. But the humanity of one man is the humanity of everyone, and the same object touches this passion in all human creatures.

But the sentiments which arise from humanity are not only the same in all human creatures and produce the same approbation or censure, but they also comprehend all human creatures; nor is there anyone whose conduct or character is not, by their means, an object to everyone of censure or approbation. On the contrary, those other passions, commonly denominated selfish, both produce different sentiments in each individual, according to his particular situation, and also contemplate the greater part of mankind with the utmost indifference and unconcern. Whoever has a high regard and esteem for me flatters my vanity; whoever expresses contempt mortifies and displeases me. But as my name is known but to a small part of mankind, there are few who come within the sphere of this passion, or excite on its account either my affection or disgust. But if you represent a tyrannical, insolent, or barbarous behavior, in any country or in any age of the world, I soon carry my eye to the pernicious tendency of such a conduct and feel the sentiment of repugnance and displeasure toward it. No character can be so remote as to be, in this light, wholly indifferent to me. What is beneficial to society or to the person himself must still be preferred. And every quality or action of every human being must by this means be ranked under some class or denomination expressive of general censure or applause.

What more, therefore, can we ask to distinguish the sentiments dependent on humanity from those connected with any other passion, or to satisfy us why the former are the origin of morals, not the latter? Whatever conduct gains my approbation by touching my humanity procures also the applause of all mankind by affecting the same principle in them. But what serves my avarice or ambition pleases these passions in me alone, and affects not the avarice and ambition of the rest of mankind. There is no circumstance of conduct in any man, provided it have a beneficial tendency, that is not agreeable to my humanity, however remote the person. But every man so far removed as neither to cross nor serve my avarice and ambition is regarded as wholly indifferent by those passions. The distinction, therefore, between these species of sentiment being so great and evident, language must soon be molded upon it and must invent a peculiar set of terms in order to express those universal sentiments of censure or approbation which arise from humanity, or from views of general usefulness and its contrary. *Virtue* and *vice* become then known; morals are recognized; certain general ideas are framed of human conduct and behavior; such measures are expected from men in such situations; this action is determined to be conformable to our abstract rule, that other contrary. And by such universal principles are the particular sentiments of self-love frequently controlled and limited.[1]

---

[1] It seems certain, both from reason and experience, that a rude, untaught savage regulates chiefly his love and hatred by the ideas of private utility and injury, and has but faint conceptions of a general rule or system of behavior. The man who stands opposite to him in battle he hates heartily, not only for the present moment, which is almost unavoidable, but forever after; nor is he satisfied without the most extreme punishment and vengeance. But we, accustomed to society and to more enlarged reflections, consider that this man is serving his own country and community, that any man in the same situation would do the same, that we ourselves

From instances of popular tumults, seditions, factions, panics, and of all passions which are shared with a multitude, we may learn the influence of society in exciting and supporting any emotion, while the most ungovernable disorders are raised, we find, by that means, from the slightest and most frivolous occasions. Solon was no very cruel, though perhaps an unjust, legislator, who punished neuters in civil wars; and few, I believe, would in such cases incur the penalty were their affection and discourse allowed sufficient to absolve them. No selfishness and scarce any philosophy have there force sufficient to support a total coolness and indifference, and he must be more or less than man who kindles not in the common blaze. What wonder, then, that moral sentiments are found of such influence in life, though springing from principles which may appear at first sight somewhat small and delicate? But these principles, we must remark, are social and universal. They form, in a manner, the *party* of human kind against vice or disorder, its common enemy. And as the benevolent concern for others is diffused in a greater or less degree over all men, and is the same in all, it occurs more frequently in discourse, is cherished by society and conversation, and the blame and approbation consequent on it are thereby roused from that lethargy into which they are probably lulled in solitary and uncultivated nature. Other passions, though perhaps originally stronger, yet being selfish and private, are often overpowered by its force, and yield the dominion of our breast to those social and public principles.

Another spring of our constitution that brings a great addi-

---

in like circumstances observe a like conduct, that in general human society is best supported on such maxims; and by these suppositions and views we correct, in some measure, our ruder and narrower passions. And though much of our friendship and enmity be still regulated by private considerations of benefit and harm, we pay at least this homage to general rules, which we are accustomed to respect, that we commonly pervert our adversary's conduct by imputing malice or injustice to him, in order to give vent to those passions which arise from self-love and private interest. When the heart is full of rage, it never wants pretenses of this nature, though sometimes as frivolous as those from which Horace, being almost crushed by the fall of a tree, affects to accuse of parricide the first planter of it.

tion of force to moral sentiment is the love of fame, which rules with such uncontrolled authority in all generous minds, and is often the grand object of all their designs and undertakings. By our continual and earnest pursuit of a character, a name, a reputation in the world, we bring our own deportment and conduct frequently in review and consider how they appear in the eyes of those who approach and regard us. This constant habit of surveying ourselves, as it were, in reflection keeps alive all the sentiments of right and wrong, and begets in noble natures a certain reverence for themselves as well as others, which is the surest guardian of every virtue. The animal conveniences and pleasures sink gradually in their value, while every inward beauty and moral grace is studiously acquired and the mind is accomplished in every perfection which can adorn or embellish a rational creature.

Here is the most perfect morality with which we are acquainted. Here is displayed the force of many sympathies. Our moral sentiment is itself a feeling chiefly of that nature. And our regard to a character with others seems to arise only from a care of preserving a character with ourselves; and in order to attain this end we find it necessary to prop our tottering judgment on the correspondent approbation of mankind.

But that we may accommodate matters and remove, if possible, every difficulty, let us allow all these reasonings to be false. Let us allow that when we resolve the pleasure which arises from views of utility into the sentiments of humanity and sympathy we have embraced a wrong hypothesis. Let us confess it necessary to find some other explication of that applause which is paid to objects, whether inanimate, animate, or rational, if they have a tendency to promote the welfare and advantage of mankind. However difficult it be to conceive that an object is approved of on account of its tendency to a certain end, while the end itself is totally indifferent, let us swallow this absurdity and consider what are the consequences. The preceding delineation or definition of *personal merit* must still retain its evidence and authority. It must still be allowed that every quality of the mind which is *useful* or *agreeable* to the *person himself* or to *others* communicates a pleasure to the spectator, engages his esteem, and is admitted under the honorable denomination of virtue or merit. Are not justice, fidelity, honor, veracity, allegiance, chastity esteemed solely on account of their tendency to promote the good of society? Is not that tendency inseparable from humanity, benevolence, lenity, generosity, gratitude, moderation, tenderness, friendship, and all the other social virtues? Can it possibly be doubted that industry, discretion, frugality, secrecy, order, perseverance, forethought, judgment, and this whole class of virtues and accomplishments, of which many pages would not contain the catalogue; can it be doubted, I say, that the tendency of these qualities to promote the interest and happiness of their possessor is the sole foundation of their merit? Who can dispute that a mind which supports a perpetual serenity and cheerfulness, a noble dignity and undaunted spirit, a tender affection and good will to all around, as it has more enjoyment within itself, is also a more animating and rejoicing spectacle than if dejected with melancholy, tormented with anxiety, irritated with rage, or sunk into the most abject baseness and degeneracy? And as to the qualities immediately *agreeable to others,* they speak sufficiently for themselves; and he must be unhappy indeed, either in his own temper or in his situation and company, who has never perceived the charms of a facetious wit or flowing affability, of a delicate modesty or decent genteelness of address and manner.

I am sensible that nothing can be more unphilosophical than to be positive or dogmatical on any subject, and that even if *excessive* skepticism could be maintained, it would not be more destructive to all just reasoning and inquiry. I am convinced that where men are the most sure and arrogant, they are commonly the most mistaken, and have there given reins to passion without that proper deliberation and suspense, which can alone secure them from the grossest absurdities. Yet I must confess that this enumeration puts the matter in so strong a light that I cannot, *at present,* be more assured of any truth which I learn from reasoning and argument than that personal merit consists entirely in the usefulness or agreeableness of qualities to the person himself possessed of them, or to others who have any intercourse with him. But when I reflect that though the bulk and figure of the earth have been measured and delineated, though the motions of the tides have been accounted for, the order and economy of the heavenly bodies subjected to their proper laws, and *infinite* itself reduced to calculation, yet men still dispute concerning the foundation of their moral duties; when I reflect on this, I say, I fall back into diffidence and skepticism, and suspect that an hypothesis so obvious, had it been a true one, would long ere now have been received by the unanimous suffrage and consent of mankind.

Part II.

Having explained the moral *approbation* attending merit or virtue, there remains nothing but briefly to consider our interested *obligation* to it, and to inquire whether every man who has any regard to his own happiness and welfare will not best find his account in the practice of every moral duty. If this can be clearly ascertained from the foregoing theory, we shall have the satisfaction to reflect that we have advanced principles which not only, it is hoped, will stand the test of reasoning and inquiry, but may contribute to the amendment of men's lives and their improvement in morality and social virtue. And though the philosophical truth of any proposition by no means depends on its tendency to promote the interests of society, yet a man has but a bad grace who delivers a theory, however true, which he must confess leads to a practice dangerous and pernicious. Why rake into those corners of nature which spread a nuisance all around? Why dig up the pestilence from the pit in which it is buried? The ingenuity of your researches may be admired, but your systems will be detested, and mankind will agree, if they cannot refute them, to sink them at least in eternal silence and oblivion. Truths which are *pernicious* to society, if any such there be, will yield to errors which are salutary and *advantageous*.

But what philosophical truths can be more advantageous to society than those here delivered, which represent virtue in all her genuine and most engaging charms and make us approach her with ease, familiarity, and affection? The dismal dress falls off with which many divines and some philosophers have covered her, and nothing appears but gentleness, humanity, beneficence, affability, nay even, at proper intervals, play, frolic, and gaiety. She talks not of useless austerities and rigors, suffering and self-denial. She declares that her sole purpose is to make her votaries and all mankind, during every instant of their existence, if possible, cheerful and happy; nor does she ever willingly part with any pleasure but in hopes of ample compensation in some other period of their lives. The sole trouble which she demands is that of just calculation and a steady preference of the greater happiness. And if any austere pretenders approach her, enemies to joy and pleasure, she either rejects them as hypocrites and deceivers, or if she admit them in her train, they are ranked, however, among the least favored of her votaries.

And, indeed, to drop all figurative expression, what hopes can we ever have of engaging mankind to a practice which we confess full of austerity and rigor? Or what theory of morals can ever serve any useful purpose unless it can show, by a particular detail, that all the duties which it recommends are also the true interest of each individual? The peculiar advantage of the foregoing system seems to be that it furnishes proper mediums for that purpose.

That the virtues which are immediately *useful* or *agreeable* to the person possessed of them are desirable in a view to self-interest it would surely be superfluous to prove. Moralists, indeed, may spare themselves all the pains which they often take in recommending these duties. To what purpose collect arguments to evince that temperance is advantageous and the excesses of pleasure hurtful? When it appears that these excesses are only denominated such because they are hurtful, and that if the unlimited use of strong liquors, for instance, no more impaired health or the faculties of mind and body than the use of air or water, it would not be a whit more vicious or blamable.

It seems equally superfluous to prove that the *companionable* virtues of good manners and wit, decency and genteelness are more desirable than the contrary qualities. Vanity alone, without any other consideration, is a sufficient motive to make us wish for the possession of these accomplishments. No man was ever willingly deficient in this particular. All our failures here proceed from bad education, want of capacity, or a perverse and unpliable disposition. Would you have your company coveted, admired, followed, rather than hated, despised, avoided? Can anyone seriously deliberate in the case? As no enjoyment is sincere without some reference to company and society, so no society can be agreeable, or even tolerable, where a man feels his presence unwelcome and discovers all around him symptoms of disgust and aversion.

But why, in the greater society or confederacy of mankind, should not the case be the same as in particular clubs and companies? Why is it more doubtful that the enlarged virtues of humanity, generosity, beneficence are desirable with a view to happiness and self-interest than the limited endowments of ingenuity and politeness? Are we apprehensive lest those social affections interfere, in a greater and more immediate degree than any other pursuits, with private utility, and cannot be gratified without some important sacrifice of honor and advantage? If so, we are but ill instructed in the nature of the human passions, and are more influenced by verbal distinctions than by real differences.

Whatever contradiction may vulgarly be supposed between the *selfish* and *social* sentiments or dispositions, they are really no more opposite than selfish and ambitious, selfish and revengeful, selfish and vain. It is requisite that there be an original propensity of some kind, in order to be a basis to self-love, by giving a relish to the objects of its pursuit, and none more fit for this purpose than benevolence or humanity. The goods of fortune are spent in one gratification or another. The miser who accumulates his annual income and lends it out at interest has really spent it in the gratification of his avarice. And it would be difficult to show why a man is more a loser by a generous action than by any other method of expense, since the utmost which he can attain by the most elaborate selfishness is the indulgence of some affection.

Now if life without passion must be altogether insipid and tiresome, let a man suppose that he has full power of modeling his own disposition, and let him deliberate what appetite or desire he would choose for the foundation of his happiness and enjoyment. Every affection, he would observe, when gratified by success, gives a satisfaction proportioned to its force and violence; but besides this advantage, common to all, the immediate feeling of benevolence and friendship, humanity and kindness, is sweet, smooth, tender, and agreeable, independent of all fortune and accidents. These virtues are besides attended with a pleasing consciousness or remembrance and keep us in humor with ourselves as well as others, while we retain the agreeable reflection of having done our part toward mankind and society. And though all men show a jealousy of our success in the pursuits of avarice and ambition, yet are we almost sure of their good will and good wishes so long as we persevere in the paths of virtue and employ ourselves in the execution of generous plans and purposes. What other passion is there where we shall find so many advantages united, an agreeable sentiment, a pleasing consciousness, a good reputation? But of these truths, we may observe, men are of themselves pretty much convinced; nor are they deficient in their duty to society because they would not wish to be generous, friendly, and humane, but because they do not feel themselves such.

Treating vice with the greatest candor and making it all possible concessions, we must acknowledge that there is not, in any instance, the smallest pretext for giving it the preference above virtue with a view to self-interest, except, perhaps, in the case of justice, where a man, taking things in a certain light, may often seem to be a loser by his integrity. And though it is allowed that without a regard to property no society could subsist, yet according to the imperfect way in which human affairs are conducted, a sensible knave, in particular incidents, may think that an act of iniquity or infidelity will make a considerable addition to his fortune, without causing any considerable breach in the social union and confederacy. That *honesty is the best policy* may be a good general rule, but is liable to many exceptions. And he, it may perhaps be thought, conducts himself with most wisdom who observes the general rule and takes advantage of all the exceptions.

I must confess that if a man think that this reasoning much requires an answer, it will be a little difficult to find any which will to him appear satisfactory and convincing. If his heart rebel not against such pernicious maxims, if he feel no reluctance to the thoughts of villainy or baseness, he has in-

462 THE PHILOSOPHY OF DAVID HUME

deed lost a considerable motive to virtue, and we may expect that his practice will be answerable to his speculation. But in all ingenuous natures the antipathy to treachery and roguery is too strong to be counterbalanced by any views of profit or pecuniary advantage. Inward peace of mind, consciousness of integrity, a satisfactory review of our own conduct, these are circumstances very requisite to happiness, and will be cherished and cultivated by every honest man who feels the importance of them.

Such a one has, besides, the frequent satisfaction of seeing knaves, with all their pretended cunning and abilities, betrayed by their own maxims, and while they purpose to cheat with moderation and secrecy, a tempting incident occurs, nature is frail, and they give in to the snare, whence they can never extricate themselves without a total loss of reputation and the forfeiture of all future trust and confidence with mankind.

But were they ever so secret and successful, the honest man, if he has any tincture of philosophy, or even common observation and reflection, will discover that they themselves are, in the end, the greatest dupes, and have sacrificed the invaluable enjoyment of a character, with themselves at least, for the acquisition of worthless toys and gewgaws. How little is requisite to supply the *necessities* of nature? And in a view to *pleasure*, what comparison between the unbought satisfaction of conversation, society, study, even health and the common beauties of nature, but above all the peaceful reflection on one's own conduct; what comparison, I say, between these and the feverish, empty amusements of luxury and expense? These natural pleasures, indeed, are really without price, both because they are below all price in their attainment and above it in their enjoyment.

Appendix I.

CONCERNING MORAL SENTIMENT

IF THE FOREGOING hypothesis be received, it will now be easy for us to determine the question first started,[1] concerning the general principles of morals; and though we postponed the decision of that question lest it should then involve us in intricate speculations which are unfit for moral discourses, we may resume it at present, and examine how far either *reason* or *sentiment* enters into all decisions of praise or censure.

One principal foundation of moral praise being supposed to lie in the usefulness of any quality or action, it is evident that *reason* must enter for a considerable share in all decisions of this kind, since nothing but that faculty can instruct us in the tendency of qualities and actions, and point out their beneficial consequences to society and to their possessor. In many cases, this is an affair liable to great controversy. Doubts may arise, opposite interests may occur, and a preference must be given to one side from very nice views and a small overbalance of utility. This is particularly remarkable in questions with regard to justice, as is, indeed, natural to suppose from that species of utility which attends this virtue.[2] Were every single instance of justice, like that of benevolence, useful to society, this would be a more simple state of the case and seldom liable to great controversy. But as single instances of justice are often pernicious in their first and immediate tendency, and as the advantage to society results only from the observance of the general rule and from the concurrence and combination of several persons in the same equitable conduct, the case here becomes more intricate and involved. The various circumstances of society, the various consequences of any practice, the various interests which may be proposed; these, on many occasions, are doubtful, and subject to great discussion and inquiry. The object of municipal laws is to

[1] Section II.
[2] See Appendix III.

fix all the questions with regard to justice; the debates of civil-
ians, the reflections of politicians, the precedents of history
and public records are all directed to the same purpose. And a
very accurate *reason* or *judgment* is often requisite to give the
true determination amidst such intricate doubts arising from
obscure or opposite utilities.

But though reason, when fully assisted and improved, be
sufficient to instruct us in the pernicious or useful tendency of
qualities and actions, it is not alone sufficient to produce any
moral blame or approbation. Utility is only a tendency to a
certain end, and were the end totally indifferent to us, we
should feel the same indifference toward the means. It is requisite a *sentiment* should here display itself, in order to give
a preference to the useful above the pernicious tendencies.
This sentiment can be no other than a feeling for the happiness of mankind and a resentment of their misery, since these
are the different ends which virtue and vice have a tendency
to promote. Here, therefore, *reason* instructs us in the several
tendencies of actions, and *humanity* makes a distinction in
favor of those which are useful and beneficial.

This partition between the faculties of understanding and
sentiment, in all moral decisions, seems clear from the preceding hypothesis. But I shall suppose that hypothesis false. It
will then be requisite to look out for some other theory that
may be satisfactory; and I dare venture to affirm that none
such will ever be found so long as we suppose reason to be
the sole source of morals. To prove this, it will be proper
to weigh the five following considerations.

I. It is easy for a false hypothesis to maintain some appearance of truth, while it keeps wholly in generals, makes use
of undefined terms, and employs comparisons instead of instances. This is particularly remarkable in that philosophy
which ascribes the discernment of all moral distinctions to reason alone, without the concurrence of sentiment. It is impossible that, in any particular instance, this hypothesis can so
much as be rendered intelligible, whatever specious figure it
may make in general declamations and discourses. Examine
the crime of *ingratitude,* for instance, which has place wherever we observe good will, expressed and known, together

with good offices performed, on the one side, and a return of ill will or indifference, with ill offices or neglect, on the other. Anatomize all these circumstances and examine, by your reason alone, in what consists the demerit or blame. You never will come to any issue or conclusion.

Reason judges either of *matter of fact* or of *relations.* Inquire then, *first,* where is that matter of fact which we here call *crime;* point it out, determine the time of its existence, describe its essence or nature, explain the sense or faculty to which it discovers itself. It resides in the mind of the person who is ungrateful. He must, therefore, feel it, and be conscious of it. But nothing is there except the passion of ill will or absolute indifference. You cannot say that these, of themselves, always and in all circumstances, are crimes. No; they are only crimes when directed toward persons who have before expressed and displayed good will toward us. Consequently, we may infer that the crime of ingratitude is not any particular individual *fact,* but arises from a complication of circumstances which, being presented to the spectator, excites the *sentiment* of blame, by the particular structure and fabric of his mind.

This representation, you say, is false. Crime, indeed, consists not in a particular *fact,* of whose reality we are assured by *reason,* but it consists in certain *moral relations* discovered by reason, in the same manner as we discover by reason the truths of geometry or algebra. But what are the relations, I ask, of which you here talk? In the case stated above I see first good will and good offices in one person, then ill will and ill offices in the other. Between these there is the relation of *contrariety.* Does the crime consist in that relation? But suppose a person bore me ill will or did me ill offices, and I, in return, were indifferent toward him, or did him good offices. Here is the same relation of *contrariety,* and yet my conduct is often highly laudable. Twist and turn this matter as much as you will, you can never rest the morality on relation, but must have recourse to the decisions of sentiment.

When it is affirmed that two and three are equal to the half of ten, this relation of equality I understand perfectly. I conceive that if ten be divided into two parts, of which one has as many units as the other, and if any of these parts be compared to two added to three, it will contain as many units as that compound number. But when you draw thence a comparison to moral relations, I own that I am altogether at a loss to understand you. A moral action, a crime such as ingratitude, is a complicated object. Does the morality consist in the relation of its parts to each other? How? After what manner? Specify the relation; be more particular and explicit in your propositions, and you will easily see their falsehood.

No, say you, the morality consists in the relation of actions to the rule of right, and they are denominated good or ill according as they agree or disagree with it. What then is this rule of right? In what does it consist? How is it determined? By reason, you say, which examines the moral relations of actions. So that moral relations are determined by the comparison of actions to a rule. And that rule is determined by considering the moral relations of objects. Is not this fine reasoning?

All this is metaphysics, you cry. That is enough; there needs nothing more to give a strong presumption of falsehood. Yes, reply I; here are metaphysics surely, but they are all on your side, who advance an abstruse hypothesis which can never be made intelligible, nor quadrate with any particular instance or illustration. The hypothesis which we embrace is plain. It maintains that morality is determined by sentiment. It defines virtue to be *whatever mental action or quality gives to a spectator the pleasing sentiment of approbation*, and vice the contrary. We then proceed to examine a plain matter of fact, to wit, what actions have this influence. We consider all the circumstances in which these actions agree, and thence endeavor to extract some general observations with regard to these sentiments. If you call this metaphysics and find anything abstruse here, you need only conclude that your turn of mind is not suited to the moral sciences.

II. When a man at any time deliberates concerning his own conduct (as whether he had better, in a particular emergency, assist a brother or a benefactor), he must consider these separate relations, with all the circumstances and situations of the persons, in order to determine the superior duty and obligation. And in order to determine the proportion of lines in any triangle, it is necessary to examine the nature of that figure, and the relations which its several parts bear to each other. But notwithstanding this appearing similarity in the two cases, there is at bottom an extreme difference between them. A speculative reasoner concerning triangles or circles considers the several known and given relations of the parts of these figures, and thence infers some unknown relation which is dependent on the former. But in moral deliberations we must be acquainted beforehand with all the objects and all their relations to each other, and from a comparison of the whole fix our choice or approbation. No new fact to be ascertained, no new relation to be discovered. All the circumstances of the case are supposed to be laid before us ere we can fix any sentence of blame or approbation. If any material circumstance be yet unknown or doubtful, we must first employ our inquiry or intellectual faculties to assure us of it, and must suspend for a time all moral decision or sentiment. While we are ignorant whether a man were aggressor or not, how can we determine whether the person who killed him be criminal or innocent? But after every circumstance, every relation is known, the understanding has no further room to operate, nor any object on which it could employ itself. The approbation or blame which then ensues cannot be the work of the judgment but of the heart, and is not a speculative proposition or affirmation, but an active feeling or sentiment. In the disquisitions of the understanding, from known circumstances and relations we infer some new and unknown. In moral decisions, all the circumstances and relations must be previously known, and the mind, from the contemplation of the whole, feels some new impression of affection or disgust, esteem or contempt, approbation or blame.

Hence the great difference between a mistake of *fact* and one of *right*, and hence the reason why the one is commonly criminal and not the other. When Oedipus killed Laius, he was ignorant of the relation, and from circumstances innocent and involuntary formed erroneous opinions concerning the action which he committed. But when Nero killed Agrippina, all the relations between himself and the person, and all the circumstances of the fact, were previously known to him, but the motive of revenge or fear or interest prevailed in his savage heart over the sentiments of duty and humanity. And when we express that detestation against him to which he himself in a little time became insensible, it is not that we see any relations of which he was ignorant, but that, from the rectitude of our disposition, we feel sentiments against which he was hardened, from flattery and a long perseverance in the most enormous crimes. In these sentiments then, not in a discovery of relations of any kind, do all moral determinations consist. Before we can pretend to form any decision of this kind, everything must be known and ascertained on the side of the object or action. Nothing remains but to feel, on our part, some sentiment of blame or approbation, whence we pronounce the action criminal or virtuous.

III. This doctrine will become still more evident if we compare moral beauty with natural, to which in many particulars it bears so near a resemblance. It is on the proportion, relation, and position of parts that all natural beauty depends, but it would be absurd thence to infer that the perception of beauty, like that of truth in geometrical problems, consists wholly in the perception of relations and was performed entirely by the understanding or intellectual faculties. In all the sciences our mind, from the known relations, investigates the unknown. But in all decisions of taste or external beauty, all the relations are beforehand obvious to the eye; and we thence proceed to feel a sentiment of complacency or disgust, according to the nature of the object and disposition of our organs.

Euclid has fully explained all the qualities of the circle, but has not, in any proposition, said a word of its beauty. The reason is evident. The beauty is not a quality of the circle. It lies not in any part of the line whose parts are equally distant from a common center. It is only the effect which that figure produces upon the mind, whose peculiar fabric or structure renders it susceptible of such sentiments. In vain would you look for it in the circle, or seek it, either by your senses or by mathematical reasonings, in all the properties of that figure.

Attend to Palladio and Perrault while they explain all the parts and proportions of a pillar. They talk of the cornice and frieze and base and entablature and shaft and architrave, and give the description and position of each of these members. But should you ask the description and position of its beauty, they would readily reply that the beauty is not in any of the parts or members of a pillar but results from the whole, when that complicated figure is presented to an intelligent mind, susceptible to those finer sensations. Till such a spectator appear, there is nothing but a figure of such particular dimensions and proportions; from his sentiments alone arise its elegance and beauty.

Again, attend to Cicero while he paints the crimes of a Verres or a Catiline; you must acknowledge that the moral turpitude results, in the same manner, from the contemplation of the whole, when presented to a being whose organs have such a particular structure and formation. The orator may paint rage, insolence, barbarity on the one side; meekness, suffering, sorrow, innocence on the other. But if you feel no indignation or compassion arise in you from this complication of circumstances, you would in vain ask him in what consists the crime or villainy which he so vehemently exclaims against, at what time or on what subject it first began to exist, and what has a few months afterwards become of it, when every disposition and thought of all the actors is totally altered or annihilated. No satisfactory answer can be given to any of these questions upon the abstract hypothesis of morals, and we must at last acknowledge that the crime or immorality is no particular fact or relation which can be the object of the understanding, but arises entirely from the sentiment of disapprobation which, by the structure of human nature, we unavoidably feel on the apprehension of barbarity or treachery.

IV. Inanimate objects may bear to each other all the same relations which we observe in moral agents, though the former can never be the object of love or hatred, nor are consequently susceptible of merit or iniquity. A young tree which overtops and destroys its parent stands in all the same relations with Nero when he murdered Agrippina, and if morality consisted merely in relations would, no doubt, be equally criminal.

V. It appears evident that the ultimate ends of human actions can never, in any case, be accounted for by *reason*, but recommend themselves entirely to the sentiments and affections of mankind, without any dependence on the intellectual faculties. Ask a man *why he uses exercises;* he will answer, *be-*

cause he desires to keep his health. If you then inquire *why he desires health,* he will readily reply, *because sickness is painful.* If you push your inquiries further and desire a reason *why he hates pain,* it is impossible he can ever give any. This is an ultimate end, and is never referred to any other object.

Perhaps to your second question, *why he desires health,* he may also reply that *it is necessary for the exercise of his calling.* If you ask *why he is anxious on that head,* he will answer, *because he desires to get money.* If you demand *why, it is the instrument of pleasure,* says he. And beyond this it is an absurdity to ask for a reason. It is impossible there can be a progress *in infinitum,* and that one thing can always be a reason why another is desired. Something must be desirable on its own account, and because of its immediate accord or agreement with human sentiment and affection.

Now as virtue is an end and is desirable on its own account, without fee or reward, merely for the immediate satisfaction which it conveys, it is requisite that there should be some sentiment which it touches, some internal taste or feeling, or whatever you please to call it, which distinguishes moral good and evil, and which embraces the one and rejects the other.

Thus the distinct boundaries and offices of *reason* and of *taste* are easily ascertained. The former conveys the knowledge of truth and falsehood; the latter gives the sentiment of beauty and deformity, vice and virtue. The one discovers objects as they really stand in nature, without addition or diminution; the other has a productive faculty, and gilding or staining all natural objects with the colors borrowed from internal sentiment raises, in a manner, a new creation. Reason, being cool and disengaged, is no motive to action, and directs only the impulse received from appetite or inclination, by showing us the means of attaining happiness or avoiding misery. Taste, as it gives pleasure or pain and thereby constitutes happiness or misery, becomes a motive to action, and is the first spring or impulse to desire and volition. From circumstances and relations, known or supposed, the former leads us to the discovery of the concealed and unknown. After all circumstances and relations are laid before us, the latter makes us feel from the whole a new sentiment of blame or approbation. The standard of the one, being founded on the nature of things, is eternal and inflexible, even by the will of the Supreme Being. The standard of the other, arising from the internal frame and constitution of animals, is ultimately derived from that Supreme Will which bestowed on each being its peculiar nature and arranged the several classes and orders of existence.

Appendix II.

OF SELF-LOVE

THERE IS A PRINCIPLE supposed to prevail among many, which is utterly incompatible with all virtue or moral sentiment; and as it can proceed from nothing but the most depraved disposition, so in its turn it tends still further to encourage that depravity. This principle is that all *benevolence* is mere hypocrisy, friendship a cheat, public spirit a farce, fidelity a snare to procure trust and confidence, and that while all of us, at bottom, pursue only our private interest, we wear these fair disguises in order to put others off their guard and expose them the more to our wiles and machinations. What heart one must be possessed of who professes such principles and who feels no internal sentiment that belies so pernicious a theory, it is easy to imagine, and also what degree of affection and benevolence he can bear to a species whom he represents under such odious colors and supposes so little susceptible of gratitude or any return of affection. Or if we should not ascribe these principles wholly to a corrupted heart, we must at least account for them from the most careless and precipitate examination. Superficial reasoners, indeed, observing many false pretenses among mankind and feeling, perhaps, no very strong restraint in their own disposition, might draw a general and a hasty conclusion, that all is equally corrupted, and that men, different from all other animals and indeed from all other species of existence, admit of no degrees of good or bad, but are, in every instance, the same creatures under different disguises and appearances.

There is another principle, somewhat resembling the former, which has been much insisted on by philosophers and has been the foundation of many a system, that whatever affection one may feel or imagine he feels for others, no passion is or can be disinterested, that the most generous friendship, however sincere, is a modification of self-love, and that even unknown to ourselves we seek only our own gratification, while we appear the most deeply engaged in schemes for the liberty and happiness of mankind. By a turn of imagination, by a refinement of reflection, by an enthusiasm of passion, we seem to take part in the interests of others, and imagine ourselves divested of all selfish considerations. But at bottom the most generous patriot and most niggardly miser, the bravest hero and most abject coward, have in every action an equal regard to their own happiness and welfare.

Whoever concludes from the seeming tendency of this opinion that those who make profession of it cannot possibly feel the true sentiments of benevolence or have any regard for genuine virtue, will often find himself, in practice, very much mistaken. Probity and honor were no strangers to Epicurus and his sect. Atticus and Horace seem to have enjoyed from nature and cultivated by reflection as generous and friendly dispositions as any disciple of the austerer schools. And among the modern, Hobbes and Locke, who maintained the selfish system of morals, lived irreproachable lives, though the former lay not under any restraint of religion which might supply the defects of his philosophy. An Epicurean or a Hobbist readily allows that there is such a thing as friendship in the world, without hypocrisy or disguise, though he may attempt, by a philosophical chemistry, to resolve the elements of this passion, if I may so speak, into those of another, and explain every affection to be self-love twisted and molded by a particular turn of imagination into a variety of appearances. But as the same turn of imagination prevails not in every man, nor gives the same direction to the original passion, this is sufficient, even according to the selfish system, to make the widest difference in human characters and denominate one man virtuous and humane, another vicious and meanly interested. I esteem the man whose self-love, by whatever means, is so directed as to give him a concern for others and render him serviceable to society, as I hate or despise him who has no regard to anything beyond his own gratifications and enjoyments. In vain would you suggest that these characters, though seemingly opposite, are at bottom the same, and that a very inconsiderable turn of thought forms the whole difference between them. Each character, notwithstanding these inconsiderable differences, appears to me, in practice, pretty durable and untransmutable. And I find not in this more than in other subjects that the natural sentiments arising from the general appearances of things are easily destroyed by subtle reflections concerning the minute origin of these appearances. Does not the lively, cheerful color of a countenance inspire me with complacency and pleasure, even though I learn from philosophy that all difference of complexion arises from the most minute differences of thickness in the most minute parts of the skin, by means of which a superficies is qualified to reflect one of the original colors of light and absorb the others?

But though the question concerning the universal or partial selfishness of man be not so material as is usually imagined to morality and practice, it is certainly of consequence in the speculative science of human nature, and is a proper object of curiosity and inquiry. It may not, therefore, be unsuitable in this place to bestow a few reflections upon it.[1]

The most obvious objection to the selfish hypothesis is that, as it is contrary to common feeling and our most unprejudiced notions, there is required the highest stretch of philosophy to establish so extraordinary a paradox. To the most careless observer there appear to be such dispositions as benevolence

---

[1] Benevolence naturally divides into two kinds, the *general* and the *particular*. The first is where we have no friendship or connection or esteem for the person, but feel only a general sympathy with him or a compassion for his pains and a congratulation with his pleasures. The other species of benevolence is founded on an opinion of virtue, on services done us, or on some particular connections. Both these sentiments must be allowed real in human nature, but whether they will resolve into some nice considerations of self-love is a question more curious than important. The former sentiment, to wit, that of general benevolence or humanity or sympathy, we shall have occasion frequently to treat of in the course of this inquiry, and I assume it as real from general experience, without any other proof.

and generosity, such affections as love, friendship, compassion, gratitude. These sentiments have their causes, effects, objects, and operations, marked by common language and observation, and plainly distinguished from those of the selfish passions. And as this is the obvious appearance of things, it must be admitted till some hypothesis be discovered which, by penetrating deeper into human nature, may prove the former affections to be nothing but modifications of the latter. All attempts of this kind have hitherto proved fruitless, and seem to have proceeded entirely from that love of *simplicity* which has been the source of much false reasoning in philosophy. I shall not here enter into any detail on the present subject. Many able philosophers have shown the insufficiency of these systems. And I shall take for granted what, I believe, the smallest reflection will make evident to every impartial inquirer.

But the nature of the subject furnishes the strongest presumption that no better system will ever, for the future, be invented in order to account for the origin of the benevolent from the selfish affections, and reduce all the various emotions of the human mind to a perfect simplicity. The case is not the same in this species of philosophy as in physics. Many a hypothesis in nature, contrary to first appearances, has been found on more accurate scrutiny solid and satisfactory. Instances of this kind are so frequent that a judicious as well as witty philosopher[1] has ventured to affirm, if there be more than one way in which any phenomenon may be produced, that there is a general presumption for its arising from the causes which are the least obvious and familiar. But the presumption always lies on the other side in all inquiries concerning the origin of our passions and of the internal operations of the human mind. The simplest and most obvious cause which can there be assigned for any phenomenon is probably the true one. When a philosopher, in the explication of his system, is obliged to have recourse to some very intricate and refined reflections and to suppose them essential to the production of any passion or emotion, we have reason to be extremely on our guard against so fallacious an hypothesis. The affections

[1] Mons. Fontenelle.

are not susceptible of any impression from the refinements of reason or imagination, and it is always found that a vigorous exertion of the latter faculties necessarily, from the narrow capacity of the human mind, destroys all activity in the former. Our predominant motive or intention is, indeed, frequently concealed from ourselves when it is mingled and confounded with other motives which the mind, from vanity or self-conceit, is desirous of supposing more prevalent. But there is no instance that a concealment of this nature has ever arisen from the abstruseness and intricacy of the motive. A man that has lost a friend and patron may flatter himself that all his grief arises from generous sentiments, without any mixture of narrow or interested considerations. But a man that grieves for a valuable friend who needed his patronage and protection, how can we suppose that his passionate tenderness arises from some metaphysical regards to a self-interest which has no foundation or reality? We may as well imagine that minute wheels and springs, like those of a watch, give motion to a loaded wagon, as account for the origin of passion from such abstruse reflections.

Animals are found susceptible of kindness, both to their own species and to ours; nor is there, in this case, the least suspicion of disguise or artifice. Shall we account for all *their* sentiments, too, from refined deductions of self-interest? Or if we admit a disinterested benevolence in the inferior species, by what rule of analogy can we refuse it in the superior?

Love between the sexes begets a complacency and good will very distinct from the gratification of an appetite. Tenderness to their offspring, in all sensible beings, is commonly able alone to counterbalance the strongest motives of self-love, and has no manner of dependence on that affection. What interest can a fond mother have in view who loses her health by assiduous attendance on her sick child, and afterwards languishes and dies of grief when freed, by its death, from the slavery of that attendance?

Is gratitude no affection of the human breast, or is that a word merely, without any meaning or reality? Have we no satisfaction in one man's company above another's, and no desire of the welfare of our friend, even though absence or death should prevent us from all participation in it? Or what is it commonly that gives us any participation in it, even while alive and present, but our affection and regard to him?

These and a thousand other instances are marks of a general benevolence in human nature, where no *real* interest binds us to the object. And how an *imaginary* interest, known and avowed for such, can be the origin of any passion or emotion seems difficult to explain. No satisfactory hypothesis of this kind has yet been discovered, nor is there the smallest probability that the future industry of men will ever be attended with more favorable success.

But further, if we consider rightly of the matter, we shall find that the hypothesis which allows of a disinterested benevolence, distinct from self-love, has really more *simplicity* in it and is more conformable to the analogy of nature than that which pretends to resolve all friendship and humanity into this latter principle. There are bodily wants or appetites, acknowledged by everyone, which necessarily precede all sensual enjoyment and carry us directly to seek possession of the object. Thus hunger and thirst have eating and drinking for their end, and from the gratification of these primary appetites arises a pleasure which may become the object of another species of desire or inclination that is secondary and interested. In the same manner, there are mental passions by which we are impelled immediately to seek particular objects, such as fame or power or vengeance, without any regard to interest, and when these objects are attained, a pleasing enjoyment ensues as the consequence of our indulged affections. Nature must, by the internal frame and constitution of the mind, give an original propensity to fame ere we can reap any pleasure from that acquisition, or pursue it from motives of self-love and a desire of happiness. If I have no vanity, I take no delight in praise; if I be void of ambition, power gives me no enjoyment; if I be not angry, the punishment of an adversary is totally indifferent to me. In all these cases there is a passion which points immediately to the object and constitutes it our good or happiness, as there are other secondary passions which afterwards arise and pursue it as a part of our happiness, when once it is constituted such by our original affections. Were there no appetite of any kind antecedent to self-love, that propensity could scarcely ever exert itself, because we should in that case have felt few and slender pains or pleasures, and have little misery or happiness to avoid or to pursue.

Now where is the difficulty in conceiving that this may likewise be the case with benevolence and friendship, and that, from the original frame of our temper, we may feel a desire of another's happiness or good, which, by means of that affection, becomes our own good, and is afterwards pursued from the combined motives of benevolence and self-enjoyment? Who sees not that vengeance, from the force alone of passion, may be so eagerly pursued as to make us knowingly neglect every consideration of ease, interest, or safety, and like some vindictive animals infuse our very souls into the wounds we give an enemy? [1] And what a malignant philosophy must it be that will not allow to humanity and friendship the same privileges which are indisputably granted to the darker passions of enmity and resentment? Such a philosophy is more like a satire than a true delineation or description of human nature, and may be a good foundation for paradoxical wit and raillery, but is a very bad one for any serious argument or reasoning.

[1] [Hume quotes passages from Vergil and from Seneca's *de Ira* in a footnote to this sentence; this footnote has been omitted in this edition.—Ed.]

OF THE
STANDARD
OF
TASTE

THE GREAT VARIETY of taste, as well as of opinion, which prevails in the world is too obvious not to have fallen under everyone's observation. Men of the most confined knowledge are able to remark a difference of taste in the narrow circle of their acquaintance, even where the persons have been educated under the same government, and have early imbibed the same prejudices. But those who can enlarge their view to contemplate distant nations and remote ages are still more surprised at the great inconsistency and contrariety. We are apt to call barbarous whatever departs widely from our own taste and apprehension, but soon find the epithet of reproach retorted on us. And the highest arrogance and self-conceit is at last startled on observing an equal assurance on all sides, and scruples, amidst such a contest of sentiment, to pronounce positively in its own favor.

As this variety of taste is obvious to the most careless inquirer, so will it be found, on examination, to be still greater in reality than in appearance. The sentiments of men often differ with regard to beauty and deformity of all kinds, even while their general discourse is the same. There are certain terms in every language which import blame, and others praise, and all men who use the same tongue must agree in their application of them. Every voice is united in applauding elegance, propriety, simplicity, spirit in writing, and in blaming fustian, affectation, coldness, and a false brilliancy. But when critics come to particulars this seeming unanimity vanishes, and it is found that they had affixed a very different meaning to their expressions. In all matters of opinion and science, the case is opposite. The difference among men is there oftener found to lie in generals than in particulars, and to be less in reality than in appearance. An explanation of the terms commonly ends the controversy, and the disputants are surprised to find that they had been quarrelling, while at bottom they agreed in their judgment.

Those who found morality on sentiment, more than on reason, are inclined to comprehend ethics under the former observation, and to maintain that in all questions which regard conduct and manners, the difference among men is really greater than at first sight it appears. It is indeed obvious that writers of all nations and all ages concur in applauding justice, humanity, magnanimity, prudence, veracity, and in blaming the opposite qualities. Even poets and other authors whose compositions are chiefly calculated to please the imagination are yet found, from Homer down to Fenelon, to inculcate the same moral precepts, and to bestow their applause and blame on the same virtues and vices. This great unanimity is usually ascribed to the influence of plain reason which, in all these cases, maintains similar sentiments in all men, and prevents those controversies to which the abstract sciences are so much exposed. So far as the unanimity is real, this account may be admitted as satisfactory; but we must also allow that some part of the seeming harmony in morals may be accounted for from the very nature of language. The word *virtue,* with its equivalent in every tongue, implies praise, as that of *vice* does blame; and no one, without the most obvious and grossest impropriety, could affix reproach to a term which in general acceptation is understood in a good sense, or bestow applause where the idiom requires disapprobation. Homer's general precepts, where he delivers any such, will never be controverted, but it is obvious that when he draws particular pictures of manners, and represents heroism in Achilles and prudence in Ulysses, he intermixes a much greater degree of ferocity in the former and of cunning and fraud in the latter than Fenelon would admit of. The sage Ulysses in the Greek poet seems to delight in lies and fictions, and often employs them without any necessity or even advantage; but his more scrupulous son, in the French epic writer, exposes himself to the most imminent perils rather than depart from the most exact line of truth and veracity.

The admirers and followers of the *Alcoran* insist on the

excellent moral precepts interspersed throughout that wild
and absurd performance. But it is to be supposed that the
Arabic words which correspond to the English *equity, justice,
temperance, meekness, charity,* were such as, from the constant use of that tongue, must always be taken in a good sense;
and it would have argued the greatest ignorance, not of
morals, but of language, to have mentioned them with any
epithets besides those of applause and approbation. But
would we know whether the pretended prophet had really
attained a just sentiment of morals? Let us attend to his narration and we shall soon find that he bestows praise on such
instances of treachery, inhumanity, cruelty, revenge, bigotry,
as are utterly incompatible with civilized society. No steady
rule of right seems there to be attended to, and every action
is blamed or praised so far only as it is beneficial or hurtful
to the true believers.

The merit of delivering true general precepts in ethics is
indeed very small. Whoever recommends any moral virtues
really does no more than is implied in the terms themselves.
That people who invented the word *charity* and used it in a
good sense inculcated more clearly and much more effica-
ciously the precept, *be charitable,* than any pretended legislator or prophet who should insert such a *maxim* in his writings. Of all expressions, those which, together with their other
meaning, imply a degree either of blame or approbation are
the least liable to be perverted or mistaken.

It is natural for us to seek a *standard of taste,* a rule by
which the various sentiments of men may be reconciled, [or]
at least a decision afforded, confirming one sentiment and condemning another.

There is a species of philosophy which cuts off all hopes of
success in such an attempt, and represents the impossibility of
ever attaining any standard of taste. The difference, it is said,
is very wide between judgment and sentiment. All sentiment
is right, because sentiment has a reference to nothing beyond
itself, and is always real, wherever a man is conscious of it.
But all determinations of the understanding are not right, because they have a reference to something beyond themselves, to wit, real matter of fact, and are not always conformable to that standard. Among a thousand different opinions

which different men may entertain of the same subject, there is one, and but one, that is just and true, and the only difficulty is to fix and ascertain it. On the contrary, a thousand different sentiments excited by the same object are all right, because no sentiment represents what is really in the object. It only marks a certain conformity of relation between the object and the organs or faculties of the mind, and if that conformity did not really exist, the sentiment could never possibly have being. Beauty is no quality in things themselves; it exists merely in the mind which contemplates them, and each mind perceives a different beauty. One person may even perceive deformity where another is sensible of beauty, and every individual ought to acquiesce in his own sentiment without pretending to regulate those of others. To seek the real beauty or real deformity is as fruitless an inquiry as to pretend to ascertain the real sweet or real bitter. According to the disposition of the organs, the same object may be both sweet and bitter, and the proverb has justly determined it to be fruitless to dispute concerning tastes. It is very natural, and even quite necessary, to extend this axiom to mental as well as bodily taste; and thus common sense, which is so often at variance with philosophy, especially with the skeptical kind, is found, in one instance at least, to agree in pronouncing the same decision.

But though this axiom, by passing into a proverb, seems to have attained the sanction of common sense, there is certainly a species of common sense which opposes it, [or] at least serves to modify and restrain it. Whoever would assert an equality of genius and elegance between Ogilby and Milton, or Bunyan and Addison, would be thought to defend no less an extravagance than if he had maintained a molehill to be as high as Teneriffe, or a pond as extensive as the ocean. Though there may be found persons who give the preference to the former authors, no one pays attention to such a taste, and we pronounce without scruple the sentiment of these pretended critics to be absurd and ridiculous. The principle of the natural equality of tastes is then totally forgotten, and while we admit it on some occasions, where the objects seem near an equality, it appears an extravagant paradox, or rather a palpable absurdity, where objects so disproportionate are compared together.

It is evident that none of the rules of composition are fixed by reasonings *a priori*, or can be esteemed abstract conclusions of the understanding from comparing those habitudes and relations of ideas which are eternal and immutable. Their foundation is the same with that of all the practical sciences, experience; nor are they anything but general observations concerning what has been universally found to please in all countries and in all ages. Many of the beauties of poetry and even of eloquence are founded on falsehood and fiction, on hyperboles, metaphors, and an abuse or perversion of terms from their natural meaning. To check the sallies of the imagination and to reduce every expression to geometrical truth and exactness would be the most contrary to the laws of criticism, because it would produce a work which, by universal experience, has been found the most insipid and disagreeable. But though poetry can never submit to exact truth, it must be confined by rules of art, discovered to the author either by genius or observation. If some negligent or irregular writers have pleased, they have not pleased by their transgressions of rule or order, but in spite of these transgressions; they have possessed other beauties, which were conformable to just criticism, and the force of these beauties has been able to overpower censure, and give the mind a satisfaction superior to the disgust arising from the blemishes. Ariosto pleases, but not by his monstrous and improbable fictions, by his bizarre mixture of the serious and comic styles, by the want of coherence in his stories, or by the continual interruptions of his narration. He charms by the force and clearness of his expression, by the readiness and variety of his inventions, and by his natural pictures of the passions, especially those of the gay and amorous kind; and however his faults may diminish our satisfaction, they are not able entirely to destroy it. Did our pleasure really arise from those parts of his poem which we denominate faults, this would be no objection to criticism in general; it would only be an objection to those particular rules of criticism which would establish such circumstances to be faults and would represent them as universally blamable. If they are found to please they cannot be faults, let the pleasure which they produce be ever so unexpected and unaccountable.

But though all the general rules of art are founded only on experience and on the observation of the common sentiments of human nature, we must not imagine that, on every occasion, the feelings of men will be conformable to these rules. Those finer emotions of the mind are of a very tender and delicate nature, and require the concurrence of many favorable circumstances to make them play with facility and exactness, according to their general and established principles. The least exterior hindrance to such small springs, or the least internal disorder, disturbs their motion, and confounds the operation of the whole machine. When we would make an experiment of this nature, and would try the force of any beauty or deformity, we must choose with care a proper time and place, and bring the fancy to a suitable situation and disposition. A perfect serenity of mind, a recollection of thought, a due attention to the object; if any of these circumstances be wanting, our experiment will be fallacious, and we shall be unable to judge of the catholic and universal beauty. The relation which nature has placed between the form and the sentiment will at least be more obscure, and it will require greater accuracy to trace and discern it. We shall be able to ascertain its influence, not so much from the operation of each particular beauty, as from the durable admiration which attends those works that have survived all the caprices of mode and fashion, all the mistakes of ignorance and envy.

The same Homer who pleased at Athens and Rome two thousand years ago is still admired at Paris and at London. All the changes of climate, government, religion, and language have not been able to obscure his glory. Authority or prejudice may give a temporary vogue to a bad poet or orator, but his reputation will never be durable or general. When his compositions are examined by posterity or by foreigners the enchantment is dissipated, and his faults appear in their true colors. On the contrary, a real genius, the longer his works endure and the more wide they are spread, the more sincere is the admiration which he meets with. Envy and jealousy have too much place in a narrow circle, and even familiar acquaintance with his person may diminish the applause due to his performances. But when these obstructions are removed the beauties which are naturally fitted to excite agreeable sentiments immediately display their energy, and while the world endures they maintain their authority over the minds of men.

It appears then that amidst all the variety and caprice of taste there are certain general principles of approbation or blame, whose influence a careful eye may trace in all operations of the mind. Some particular forms or qualities, from the original structure of the internal fabric, are calculated to please, and others to displease; and if they fail of their effect in any particular instance, it is from some apparent defect or imperfection in the organ. A man in a fever would not insist on his palate as able to decide concerning flavors; nor would one affected with the jaundice pretend to give a verdict with regard to colors. In each creature there is a sound and a defective state, and the former alone can be supposed to afford us a true standard of taste and sentiment. If in the sound state of the organ there be an entire or a considerable uniformity of sentiment among men, we may thence derive an idea of the perfect beauty; in like manner as the appearance of objects in daylight, to the eye of a man in health, is denominated their true and real color, even while color is allowed to be merely a phantasm of the senses.

Many and frequent are the defects in the internal organs which prevent or weaken the influence of those general principles on which depends our sentiment of beauty or deformity. Though some objects, by the structure of the mind, be naturally calculated to give pleasure, it is not to be expected that in every individual the pleasure will be equally felt. Particular incidents and situations occur which either throw a false light on the objects, or hinder the true from conveying to the imagination the proper sentiment and perception.

One obvious cause why many feel not the proper sentiment of beauty is the want of that *delicacy* of imagination which is requisite to convey a sensibility of those finer emotions. This delicacy everyone pretends to; everyone talks of it, and would reduce every kind of taste or sentiment to its standard. But as our intention in this essay is to mingle some light of the understanding with the feelings of sentiment, it will be proper to give a more accurate definition of delicacy than has hitherto been attempted. And not to draw our philosophy from too profound a source, we shall have recourse to a noted story in *Don Quixote.*

It is with good reason, says Sancho to the squire with the great nose, that I pretend to have a judgment in wine: this is a quality hereditary in our family. Two of my kinsmen were once called to give their opinion of a hogshead which was supposed to be excellent, being old and of a good vintage. One of them tastes it, considers it, and, after mature reflection, pronounces the wine to be good, were it not for a small taste of leather which he perceived in it. The other, after using the same precautions, gives also his verdict in favor of the wine, but with the reserve of a taste of iron, which he could easily distinguish. You cannot imagine how much they were both ridiculed for their judgment. But who laughed in the end? On emptying the hogshead, there was found at the bottom an old key with a leathern thong tied to it.

The great resemblance between mental and bodily taste will easily teach us to apply this story. Though it be certain that beauty and deformity, [no] more than sweet and bitter, are not qualities in objects, but belong entirely to the sentiment, internal or external, it must be allowed that there are certain qualities in objects which are fitted by nature to produce those particular feelings. Now as these qualities may be found in a small degree, or may be mixed and confounded with each other, it often happens that the taste is not affected with such minute qualities, or is not able to distinguish all the particular flavors, amidst the disorder in which they are presented. Where the organs are so fine as to allow nothing to escape them, and at the same time so exact as to perceive every ingredient in the composition, this we call delicacy of taste, whether we employ these terms in the literal or metaphorical sense. Here then the general rules of beauty are of use, being drawn from established models, and from the observation of what pleases or displeases when presented singly and in a high degree. And if the same qualities, in a continued composition and in a smaller degree, affect not the organs with a sensible delight or uneasiness, we exclude the person from all pretensions to this delicacy. To produce these

general rules or avowed patterns of composition is like finding the key with the leathern thong which justified the verdict of Sancho's kinsmen and confounded those pretended
judges who had condemned them. Though the hogshead
had never been emptied, the taste of the one was still equally
delicate, and that of the other equally dull and languid, but
it would have been more difficult to have proved the superiority of the former to the conviction of every bystander. In like
manner, though the beauties of writing had never been methodized or reduced to general principles, though no excellent
models had ever been acknowledged, the different degrees of
taste would still have subsisted, and the judgment of one man
been preferable to that of another; but it would not have been
so easy to silence the bad critic, who might always insist upon
his particular sentiment, and refuse to submit to his antagonist. But when we show him an avowed principle of art, when
we illustrate this principle by examples whose operation,
from his own particular taste, he acknowledges to be conformable to the principle, when we prove that the same principle may be applied to the present case, where he did not
perceive or feel its influence, he must conclude, upon the
whole, that the fault lies in himself, and that he wants the
delicacy which is requisite to make him sensible of every
beauty and every blemish in any composition or discourse.

It is acknowledged to be the perfection of every sense or
faculty to perceive with exactness its most minute objects, and
allow nothing to escape its notice and observation. The
smaller the objects are which become sensible to the eye, the
finer is that organ, and the more elaborate its make and composition. A good palate is not tried by strong flavors but by a
mixture of small ingredients, where we are still sensible of
each part, notwithstanding its minuteness and its confusion
with the rest. In like manner, a quick and acute perception of
beauty and deformity must be the perfection of our mental
taste; nor can a man be satisfied with himself while he sus-
pects that any excellence or blemish in a discourse has
passed him unobserved. In this case, the perfection of the man
and the perfection of the sense or feeling are found to be
united. A very delicate palate, on many occasions, may be a
great inconvenience both to a man himself and to his friends,

but a delicate taste of wit or beauty must always be a desirable quality, because it is the source of all the finest and most innocent enjoyments of which human nature is susceptible. In this decision the sentiments of all mankind are agreed. Wherever you can ascertain a delicacy of taste it is sure to meet with approbation, and the best way of ascertaining it is to appeal to those models and principles which have been established by the uniform consent and experience of nations and ages.

But though there be naturally a wide difference in point of delicacy between one person and another, nothing tends further to increase and improve this talent than *practice* in a particular art and the frequent survey or contemplation of a particular species of beauty. When objects of any kind are first presented to the eye or imagination the sentiment which attends them is obscure and confused, and the mind is, in a great measure, incapable of pronouncing concerning their merits or defects. The taste cannot perceive the several excellencies of the performance, much less distinguish the particular character of each excellency, and ascertain its quality and degree. If it pronounces the whole in general to be beautiful or deformed, it is the utmost that can be expected, and even this judgment a person so unpracticed will be apt to deliver with great hesitation and reserve. But allow him to acquire experience in those objects, his feeling becomes more exact and nice; he not only perceives the beauties and defects of each part, but marks the distinguishing species of each quality, and assigns it suitable praise or blame. A clear and distinct sentiment attends him through the whole survey of the objects, and he discerns that very degree and kind of approbation or displeasure which each part is naturally fitted to produce. The mist dissipates which seemed formerly to hang over the object; the organ acquires greater perfection in its operations and can pronounce, without danger of mistake, concerning the merits of every performance. In a word, the same address and dexterity which practice gives to the execution of any work is also acquired by the same means in the judging of it.

So advantageous is practice to the discernment of beauty that, before we can give judgment on any work of importance, it will even be requisite that that very individual performance be more than once perused by us and be surveyed in different lights with attention and deliberation. There is a flutter or hurry of thought which attends the first perusal of any piece, and which confounds the genuine sentiment of beauty. The relation of the parts is not discerned; the true characters of style are little distinguished; the several perfections and defects seem wrapped up in a species of confusion, and present themselves indistinctly to the imagination. Not to mention that there is a species of beauty which, as it is florid and superficial, pleases at first, but being found incompatible with a just expression either of reason or passion soon palls upon the taste, and is then rejected with disdain, [or] at least rated at a much lower value.

It is impossible to continue in the practice of contemplating any order of beauty without being frequently obliged to form *comparisons* between the several species and degrees of excellence, and estimating their proportion to each other. A man who has had no opportunity of comparing the different kinds of beauty is indeed totally unqualified to pronounce an opinion with regard to any object presented him. By comparison alone we fix the epithets of praise or blame and learn how to assign the due degree of each. The coarsest daubing contains a certain luster of colors and exactness of imitation, which are so far beauties and would affect the mind of a peasant or Indian with the highest admiration. The most vulgar ballads are not entirely destitute of harmony or nature, and none but a person familiarized to superior beauties would pronounce their numbers harsh or narration uninteresting. A great inferiority of beauty gives pain to a person conversant in the highest excellence of the kind and is for that reason pronounced a deformity, as the most finished object with which we are acquainted is naturally supposed to have reached the pinnacle of perfection and to be entitled to the highest applause. One accustomed to see and examine and weigh the several performances admired in different ages and nations can alone rate the merits of a work exhibited to his view and assign its proper rank among the productions of genius.

But to enable a critic the more fully to execute this undertaking, he must preserve his mind free from all *prejudice,* and allow nothing to enter into his consideration but the very object which is submitted to his examination. We may observe that every work of art, in order to produce its due effect on the mind, must be surveyed in a certain point of view, and cannot be fully relished by persons whose situation, real or imaginary, is not conformable to that which is required by the performance. An orator addresses himself to a particular audience, and must have a regard to their particular genius, interests, opinions, passions, and prejudices; otherwise he hopes in vain to govern their resolutions and inflame their affections. Should they even have entertained some prepossessions against him, however unreasonable, he must not overlook this disadvantage but, before he enters upon the subject, must endeavor to conciliate their affection, and acquire their good graces. A critic of a different age or nation who should peruse this discourse must have all these circumstances in his eye, and must place himself in the same situation as the audience in order to form a true judgment of the oration. In like manner, when any work is addressed to the public, though I should have a friendship or enmity with the author, I must depart from this situation, and considering myself as a man in general forget, if possible, my individual being and my peculiar circumstances. A person influenced by prejudice complies not with this condition, but obstinately maintains his natural position without placing himself in that point of view which the performance supposes. If the work be addressed to persons of a different age or nation, he makes no allowance for their peculiar views and prejudices, but, full of the manners of his own age and country, rashly condemns what seemed admirable in the eyes of those for whom alone the discourse was calculated. If the work be executed for the public, he never sufficiently enlarges his comprehension or forgets his interest as a friend or enemy, as a rival or commentator. By this means, his sentiments are perverted; nor have the same beauties and blemishes the same influence upon him as if he had imposed a proper violence on his imagination and had forgotten himself for a moment. So far his taste evidently departs from the true standard, and of consequence loses all credit and authority.

It is well known that in all questions submitted to the understanding, prejudice is destructive of sound judgment, and perverts all operations of the intellectual faculties. It is no less contrary to good taste, nor has it less influence to corrupt our sentiment of beauty. It belongs to *good sense* to check its influence in both cases, and in this respect, as well as in many others, reason, if not an essential part of taste, is at least requisite to the operations of this latter faculty. In all the nobler productions of genius, there is a mutual relation and correspondence of parts; nor can either the beauties or blemishes be perceived by him whose thought is not capacious enough to comprehend all those parts and compare them with each other in order to perceive the consistency and uniformity of the whole. Every work of art has also a certain end or purpose for which it is calculated, and is to be deemed more or less perfect as it is more or less fitted to attain this end. The object of eloquence is to persuade, of history to instruct, of poetry to please by means of the passions and the imagination. These ends we must carry constantly in our view when we peruse any performance, and we must be able to judge how far the means employed are adapted to their respective purposes. Besides, every kind of composition, even the most poetical, is nothing but a chain of propositions and reasonings; not always, indeed, the justest and most exact, but still plausible and specious, however disguised by the coloring of the imagination. The persons introduced in tragedy and epic poetry must be represented as reasoning and thinking and concluding and acting suitably to their character and circumstances, and without judgment, as well as taste and invention, a poet can never hope to succeed in so delicate an undertaking. Not to mention that the same excellence of faculties which contributes to the improvement of reason, the same clearness of conception, the same exactness of distinction, the same vivacity of apprehension, are essential to the operations of true taste, and are its infallible concomitants. It seldom or never happens that a man of sense who has experience in any art cannot judge of its beauty, and it is no less rare to meet with a man who has a just taste without a sound understanding.

Thus, though the principles of taste be universal and nearly, if not entirely, the same in all men, yet few are qualified to give judgment on any work of art or establish their own sentiment as the standard of beauty. The organs of internal sensation are seldom so perfect as to allow the general principles their full play and produce a feeling correspondent to those principles. They either labor under some defect or are vitiated by some disorder, and by that means excite a sentiment which may be pronounced erroneous. When the critic has no delicacy he judges without any distinction, and is only affected by the grosser and more palpable qualities of the object; the finer touches pass unnoticed and disregarded. Where he is not aided by practice his verdict is attended with confusion and hesitation. Where no comparison has been employed the most frivolous beauties, such as rather merit the name of defects, are the object of his admiration. Where he lies under the influence of prejudice all his natural sentiments are perverted. Where good sense is wanting he is not qualified to discern the beauties of design and reasoning, which are the highest and most excellent. Under some or other of these imperfections the generality of men labor, and hence a true judge in the finer arts is observed, even during the most polished ages, to be so rare a character. Strong sense, united to delicate sentiment, improved by practice, perfected by comparison, and cleared of all prejudice, can alone entitle critics to this valuable character, and the joint verdict of such, wherever they are to be found, is the true standard of taste and of beauty.

But where are such critics to be found? By what marks are they to be known? How distinguish them from pretenders? These questions are embarrassing, and seem to throw us back into the same uncertainty from which, during the course of this essay, we have endeavored to extricate ourselves.

But if we consider the matter aright, these are questions of fact, not of sentiment. Whether any particular person be endowed with good sense and a delicate imagination, free from prejudice, may often be the subject of dispute and be liable to great discussion and inquiry, but that such a character is valuable and estimable will be agreed in by all mankind. Where these doubts occur, men can do no more than in other disputable questions which are submitted to the understanding: they must produce the best arguments that their invention suggests to them; they must acknowledge a true and decisive standard to exist somewhere, to wit, real existence and matter of fact; and they must have indulgence to such as differ from them in their appeals to this standard. It is sufficient for our present purpose if we have proved that the taste of all individuals is not upon an equal footing, and that some men in general, however difficult to be particularly pitched upon, will be acknowledged by universal sentiment to have a preference above others.

But in reality, the difficulty of finding, even in particulars, the standard of taste is not so great as it is represented. Though in speculation we may readily avow a certain criterion in science and deny it in sentiment, the matter is found in practice to be much more hard to ascertain in the former case than in the latter. Theories of abstract philosophy, systems of profound theology, have prevailed during one age; in a successive period, these have been universally exploded, their absurdity has been detected, other theories and systems have supplied their place, which again gave place to their successors, and nothing has been experienced more liable to the revolutions of chance and fashion than these pretended decisions of science. The case is not the same with the beauties of eloquence and poetry. Just expressions of passion and nature are sure, after a little time, to gain public applause, which they maintain forever. Aristotle and Plato and Epicurus and Descartes may successively yield to each other, but Terence and Vergil maintain a universal, undisputed empire over the minds of men. The abstract philosophy of Cicero has lost its credit; the vehemence of his oratory is still the object of our admiration.

Though men of delicate taste be rare, they are easily to be distinguished in society by the soundness of their understanding and the superiority of their faculties above the rest of mankind. The ascendant which they acquire gives a prevalence to that lively approbation with which they receive any productions of genius and renders it generally predominant. Many men, when left to themselves, have but a faint and dubious perception of beauty, who yet are capable of relishing any fine stroke which is pointed out to them. Every convert to the admiration of the real poet or orator is the cause of some new conversion. And though prejudices may prevail for a time, they never unite in celebrating any rival to the true genius, but yield at last to the force of nature and just sentiment. Thus, though a civilized nation may easily be mistaken in the choice of their admired philosopher, they never have been found long to err in their affection for a favorite epic or tragic author.

But notwithstanding all our endeavors to fix a standard of taste and reconcile the discordant apprehensions of men, there still remain two sources of variation, which are not sufficient indeed to confound all the boundaries of beauty and deformity, but will often serve to produce a difference in the degrees of our approbation or blame. The one is the different humors of particular men; the other, the particular manners and opinions of our age and country. The general principles of taste are uniform in human nature; where men vary in their judgments, some defect or perversion in the faculties may commonly be remarked, proceeding either from prejudice, from want of practice, or from want of delicacy, and there is just reason for approving one taste and condemning another. But where there is such a diversity in the internal frame or external situation as is entirely blameless on both sides and leaves no room to give one the preference above the other, in that case a certain degree of diversity in judgment is unavoidable, and we seek in vain for a standard by which we can reconcile the contrary sentiments.

A young man whose passions are warm will be more sensibly touched with amorous and tender images than a man more advanced in years who takes pleasure in wise, philosophical reflections concerning the conduct of life and moderation of the passions. At twenty, Ovid may be the favorite author, Horace at forty, and perhaps Tacitus at fifty. Vainly would we, in such cases, endeavor to enter into the sentiments of others and divest ourselves of those propensities which are natural to us. We choose our favorite author as we do our friend, from a conformity of humor and disposition. Mirth or passion, sentiment or reflection; whichever of these most predominates in our temper, it gives us a peculiar sympathy with the writer who resembles us.

One person is more pleased with the sublime, another with the tender, a third with raillery. One has a strong sensibility to blemishes and is extremely studious of correctness; another has a more lively feeling of beauties and pardons twenty absurdities and defects for one elevated or pathetic stroke. The ear of this man is entirely turned toward conciseness and energy; that man is delighted with a copious, rich, and harmonious expression. Simplicity is affected by one, ornament by another. Comedy, tragedy, satire, odes, have each its partisans, who prefer that particular species of writing to all others. It is plainly an error in a critic to confine his approbation to one species or style of writing and condemn all the rest. But it is almost impossible not to feel a predilection for that which suits our particular turn and disposition. Such preferences are innocent and unavoidable, and can never reasonably be the object of dispute, because there is no standard by which they can be decided.

For a like reason, we are more pleased, in the course of our reading, with pictures and characters that resemble objects which are found in our own age or country than with those which describe a different set of customs. It is not without some effort that we renconcile ourselves to the simplicity of ancient manners, and behold princesses carrying water from the spring and kings and heroes dressing their own victuals. We may allow in general that the representation of such manners is no fault in the author nor deformity in the piece, but we are not so sensibly touched with them. For this reason, comedy is not easily transferred from one age or nation to another. A Frenchman or Englishman is not pleased with the *Andria* of Terence, or *Clitia* of Machiavelli, where the fine lady upon whom all the play turns never once appears to the spectators, but is always kept behind the scenes, suitably to the reserved humor of the ancient Greeks and modern Italians. A man of learning and reflection can make allowance for these peculiarities of manners, but a common audience can never divest themselves so far of their usual ideas and sentiments as to relish pictures which nowise resemble them.

But here there occurs a reflection which may, perhaps, be useful in examining the celebrated controversy concerning ancient and modern learning, where we often find the one side excusing any seeming absurdity in the ancients from the manners of the age, and the other refusing to admit this excuse, or at least admitting it only as an apology for the author, not for the performance. In my opinion, the proper boundaries in this subject have seldom been fixed between the contending parties. Where any innocent peculiarities of manners are represented, such as those above-mentioned, they ought certainly to be admitted, and a man who is shocked with them gives an evident proof of false delicacy and refinement. The poet's *monument more durable than brass* must fall to the ground like common brick or clay were men to make no allowance for the continual revolutions of manners and customs, and would admit of nothing but what was suitable to the prevailing fashion. Must we throw aside the pictures of our ancestors because of their ruffs and fardingales? But where the ideas of morality and decency alter from one age to another and where vicious manners are described without being marked with the proper characters of blame and disapprobation, this must be allowed to disfigure the poem, and to be a real deformity. I cannot, nor is it proper I should, enter into such sentiments, and however I may excuse the poet on account of the manners of his age I never can relish the composition. The want of humanity and of decency so conspicuous in the characters drawn by several of the ancient poets, even sometimes by Homer and the Greek tragedians, diminishes considerably the merit of their noble performances, and gives modern authors an advantage over them. We are not interested in the fortunes and sentiments of such rough heroes; we are displeased to find the limits of vice and virtue so much confounded; and whatever indulgence we may give to the writer on account of his prejudices, we cannot prevail on ourselves to enter into his sentiments, or bear an affection to characters which we plainly discover to be blamable.

The case is not the same with moral principles as with speculative opinions of any kind. These are in continual flux and revolution. The son embraces a different system from the father. Nay, there scarcely is any man who can boast of great constancy and uniformity in this particular. Whatever speculative errors may be found in the polite writings of any age or country, they detract but little from the value of those compositions. There needs but a certain turn of thought or imagination to make us enter into all the opinions which then prevailed and relish the sentiments or conclusions derived from them. But a very violent effort is requisite to change our judgment of manners, and excite sentiments of approbation or blame, love or hatred, different from those to which the mind from long custom has been familiarized. And where a man is confident of the rectitude of that moral standard by which he judges, he is justly jealous of it, and will not pervert the sentiments of his heart for a moment in complaisance to any writer whatsoever.

Of all speculative errors, those which regard religion are the most excusable in compositions of genius; nor is it ever permitted to judge of the civility or wisdom of any people, or even of single persons, by the grossness or refinement of their theological principles. The same good sense that directs men in the ordinary occurrences of life is not hearkened to in religious matters, which are supposed to be placed altogether above the cognizance of human reason. On this account, all the absurdities of the pagan system of theology must be overlooked by every critic who would pretend to form a just notion of ancient poetry, and our posterity, in their turn, must have the same indulgence to their forefathers. No religious principles can ever be imputed as a fault to any poet while they remain merely principles, and take not such strong possession of his heart, as to lay him under the imputation of *bigotry* and *superstition*. Where that happens, they confound the sentiments of morality and alter the natural boundaries of vice and virtue. They are therefore eternal blemishes, according to the principle above mentioned; nor are the prejudices and false opinions of the age sufficient to justify them.

It is essential to the Roman Catholic religion to inspire a violent hatred of every other worship, and to represent all pagans, mahometans, and heretics as the objects of divine wrath and vengeance. Such sentiments, though they are in reality very blamable, are considered as virtues by the zealots of that communion, and are represented in their tragedies and epic poems as a kind of divine heroism. This bigotry has disfigured two very fine tragedies of the French theater, *Polieucte* and *Athalia*, where an intemperate zeal for particular modes of worship is set off with all the pomp imaginable, and forms the predominant character of the heroes. "What is this?" says the sublime Joad to Josabet, finding her in discourse with Mathan the priest of Baal. "Does the daughter of David speak to this traitor? Are you not afraid lest the earth should open and pour forth flames to devour you both? Or lest these holy walls should fall and crush you together? What is his purpose? Why comes that enemy of God hither to poison the air which we breathe with his horrid presence?" Such sentiments are received with great applause on the theater of Paris, but at London the spectators would be full as much pleased to hear Achilles tell Agamemnon that he was a dog in his forehead and a deer in his heart, or Jupiter threaten Juno with a sound drubbing if she will not be quiet.

Religious principles are also a blemish in any polite composition when they rise up to superstition, and intrude themselves into every sentiment, however remote from any connection with religion. It is no excuse for the poet that the customs of his country had burdened life with so many religious ceremonies and observances that no part of it was exempt from that yoke. It must forever be ridiculous in Petrarch to compare his mistress Laura to Jesus Christ. Nor is it less ridiculous in that agreeable libertine, Boccace, very seriously to give thanks to God Almighty and the ladies for their assistance in defending him against his enemies.

DIALOGUES

CONCERNING

NATURAL

RELIGION

PREFACE - "PAMPHILUS TO HERMIPPUS"
Discusses reasons why Natural Religio
is suitable for dialogue form.

Name   Position

Demea ≡ dogmatic theology
Philo ≡ skepticism
Cleanthes ≡ philosophy & science

PAMPHILUS TO HERMIPPUS

IT HAS BEEN remarked, my Hermippus, that though the ancient philosophers conveyed most of their instruction in the form of dialogue, this method of composition has been little practised in later ages, and has seldom succeeded in the hands of those who have attempted it. Accurate and regular argument, indeed, such as is now expected of philosophical inquirers, naturally throws a man into the methodical and didactic manner where he can immediately, without preparation, explain the point at which he aims, and thence proceed, without interruption, to deduce the proofs on which it is established. To deliver a *system* in conversation scarcely appears natural; and while the dialogue-writer desires, by departing from the direct style of composition, to give a freer air to his performance and avoid the appearance of *author* and *reader*, he is apt to run into a worse inconvenience and convey the image of *pedagogue* and *pupil*. Or if he carries on the dispute in the natural spirit of good company by throwing in a variety of topics and preserving a proper balance among the speakers, he often loses so much time in preparations and transitions that the reader will scarcely think himself compensated, by all the graces of dialogue, for the order, brevity, and precision which are sacrificed to them.

There are some subjects, however, to which dialogue-writing is peculiarly adapted, and where it is still preferable to the direct and simple method of composition.

Any point of doctrine which is so *obvious* that it scarcely admits of dispute, but at the same time so *important* that it cannot be too often inculcated, seems to require some such method of handling it; where the novelty of the manner may compensate the triteness of the subject; where the vivacity of conversation may enforce the precept; and where the variety of lights, presented by various personages and characters, may appear neither tedious nor redundant.

Any question of philosophy, on the other hand, which is so *obscure* and *uncertain* that human reason can reach no fixed determination with regard to it, if it should be treated at all, seems to lead us naturally into the style of dialogue and conversation. Reasonable men may be allowed to differ where no one can reasonably be positive. Opposite sentiments, even without any decision, afford an agreeable amusement; and if the subject be curious and interesting, the book carries us, in a manner, into company and unites the two greatest and purest pleasures of human life, study and society.

Happily, these circumstances are all to be found in the subject of *natural religion*. What truth so obvious, so certain, as the being of a God, which the most ignorant ages have acknowledged, for which the most refined geniuses have ambitiously striven to produce new proofs and arguments? What truth so important as this, which is the ground of all our hopes, the surest foundation of morality, the firmest support of society, and the only principle which ought never to be a moment absent from our thoughts and meditations? But in treating of this obvious and important truth, what obscure questions occur concerning the nature of that Divine Being, his attributes, his decrees, his plan of providence? These have been always subjected to the disputations of men; concerning these human reason has not reached any certain determination; but these are topics so interesting that we cannot restrain our restless inquiry with regard to them, though nothing but doubt, uncertainty, and contradiction have as yet been the result of our most accurate researches.

This I had lately occasion to observe, while I passed, as usual, part of the summer season with Cleanthes, and was present at those conversations of his with Philo and Demea of which I gave you lately some imperfect account. Your curiosity, you then told me, was so excited that I must, of necessity, enter into a more exact detail of their reasonings, and display those various systems which they advanced with regard to so delicate a subject as that of natural religion. The remarkable contrast in their characters still further raised your expectations, while you opposed the accurate philosophical turn of Cleanthes to the careless skepticism of Philo, or compared either of their dispositions with the rigid inflexible orthodoxy of Demea. My youth rendered me a mere auditor of their disputes; and that curiosity natural to the early season of life has so deeply imprinted in my memory the whole chain and connection of their arguments that, I hope, I shall not omit or confound any considerable part of them in the recital.

Part I. [OF 12]

AFTER I JOINED the company, whom I found sitting in Cleanthes' library, DEMEA paid Cleanthes some compliments on the great care which he took of my education, and on his unwearied perseverance and constancy in all his friendships. The father of Pamphilus, said he, was your intimate friend; the son is your pupil, and may indeed be regarded as your adopted son, were we to judge by the pains which you bestow in conveying to him every useful branch of literature and science. You are no more wanting, I am persuaded, in prudence than in industry. I shall, therefore, communicate to you a maxim which I have observed with regard to my own children, that I may learn how far it agrees with your practice. The method I follow in their education is founded on the saying of an ancient, "that students of philosophy ought first to learn logics, then ethics, next physics, last of all the nature of the gods." [1] This science of natural theology, according to him, being the most profound and abstruse of any, required the maturest judgment in its students; and none but a mind enriched with all the other sciences can safely be entrusted with it.

Are you so late, says PHILO, in teaching your children the principles of religion? Is there no danger of their neglecting or rejecting altogether those opinions of which they have heard so little during the whole course of their education? It

[1] Chrysippus *apud* Plutarch, *de repug. Stoicorum.*

is only as a science, replied DEMEA, subjected to human reasoning and disputation, that I postpone the study of natural theology. To season their minds with early piety is my chief care; and by continual precept and instruction, and I hope too by example, I imprint deeply on their tender minds an habitual reverence for all the principles of religion. While they pass through every other science, I still remark the uncertainty of each part, the eternal disputations of men, the obscurity of all philosophy, and the strange, ridiculous conclusions which some of the greatest geniuses have derived from the principles of mere human reason. Having thus tamed their mind to a proper submission and self-diffidence, I have no longer any scruple of opening to them the greatest mysteries of religion, nor apprehend any danger from that assuming arrogance of philosophy, which may lead them to reject the most established doctrines and opinions.

Your precaution, says PHILO, of seasoning your children's minds early with piety is certainly very reasonable, and no more than is requisite in this profane and irreligious age. But what I chiefly admire in your plan of education is your method of drawing advantage from the very principles of philosophy and learning which, by inspiring pride and self-sufficiency, have commonly, in all ages, been found so destructive to the principles of religion. The vulgar, indeed, we may remark, who are unacquainted with science and profound inquiry, observing the endless disputes of the learned, have commonly a thorough contempt for philosophy, and rivet themselves the faster, by that means, in the great points of theology which have been taught them. Those who enter a little into study and inquiry, finding many appearances of evidence in doctrines the newest and most extraordinary, think nothing too difficult for human reason and, presumptuously breaking through all fences, profane the inmost sanctuaries of the temple. But Cleanthes will, I hope, agree with me that after we have abandoned ignorance, the surest remedy, there is still one expedient left to prevent this profane liberty. Let Demea's principles be improved and cultivated; let us become thoroughly sensible of the weakness, blindness, and narrow limits of human reason; let us duly consider its uncertainty and endless contrarieties, even in subjects of common life and practice; let the errors and deceits of our very senses be set before us, the insuperable difficulties which attend first principles in all systems, the contradictions which adhere to the very ideas of matter, cause and effect, extension, space, time, motion, and, in a word, quantity of all kinds, the object of the only science that can fairly pretend to any certainty or evidence. When these topics are displayed in their full light, as they are by some philosophers and almost all divines, who can retain such confidence in this frail faculty of reason as to pay any regard to its determinations in points so sublime, so abstruse, so remote from common life and experience? When the coherence of the parts of a stone, or even that composition of parts which renders it extended; when these familiar objects, I say, are so inexplicable, and contain circumstances so repugnant and contradictory, with what assurance can we decide concerning the origin of worlds or trace their history from eternity to eternity?

While Philo pronounced these words, I could observe a smile in the countenance both of Demea and Cleanthes. That of Demea seemed to imply an unreserved satisfaction in the doctrines delivered, but in Cleanthes' features I could distinguish an air of finesse, as if he perceived some raillery or artificial malice in the reasonings of Philo.

You propose then, Philo, said CLEANTHES, to erect religious faith on philosophical skepticism, and you think that, if certainty or evidence be expelled from every other subject of inquiry, it will all retire to these theological doctrines, and there acquire a superior force and authority. Whether your skepticism be as absolute and sincere as you pretend, we shall learn by and by, when the company breaks up; we shall then see whether you go out at the door or the window, and whether you really doubt if your body has gravity or can be injured by its fall, according to popular opinion, derived from our fallacious senses and more fallacious experience. And this consideration, Demea, may, I think, fairly serve to abate our ill-will to this humorous sect of the skeptics. If they be thoroughly in earnest, they will not long trouble the world with their doubts, cavils, and disputes; if they be only in jest, they are, perhaps, bad railers, but can never be very dangerous, either to the state, to philosophy, or to religion.

In reality, Philo, continued he, it seems certain that though a man in a flush of humor, after intense reflection on the many contradictions and imperfections of human reason, may entirely renounce all belief and opinion, it it impossible for him to persevere in this total skepticism or make it appear in his conduct for a few hours. External objects press in upon him; passions solicit him; his philosophical melancholy dissipates; and even the utmost violence upon his own temper will not be able, during any time, to preserve the poor appearance of skepticism. And for what reason impose on himself such a violence? This is a point in which it will be impossible for him ever to satisfy himself, consistently with his skeptical principles. So that upon the whole, nothing could be more ridiculous than the principles of the ancient Pyrrhonians if in reality they endeavored, as is pretended, to extend throughout the same skepticism which they had learned from the declamations of their schools, and which they ought to have confined to them.

In this view, there appears a great resemblance between the sects of the Stoics and Pyrrhonians, though perpetual antagonists; and both of them seem founded on this erroneous maxim, that what a man can perform sometimes and in some dispositions, he can perform always and in every disposition. When the mind, by Stoical reflections, is elevated into a sublime enthusiasm of virtue and strongly smit with any *species* of honor or public good, the utmost bodily pain and suffering will not prevail over such a high sense of duty; and it is possible, perhaps, by its means, even to smile and exult in the midst of tortures. If this sometimes may be the case in fact and reality, much more may a philosopher, in his school or even in his closet, work himself up to such an enthusiasm, and support in imagination the acutest pain or most calamitous event which he can possibly conceive. But how shall he support this enthusiasm itself? The bent of his mind relaxes and cannot be recalled at pleasure; avocations lead him astray; misfortunes attack him unawares; and the *philosopher* sinks by degrees into the *plebeian*.

I allow of your comparison between the Stoics and Skeptics, replied PHILO. But you may observe, at the same time, that though the mind cannot, in Stoicism, support the highest flights of philosophy, yet, even when it sinks lower, it still retains somewhat of its former disposition; and the effects of the Stoic's reasoning will appear in his conduct in common life, and through the whole tenor of his actions. The ancient schools, particularly that of Zeno, produced examples of virtue and constancy which seem astonishing to present times.

> Vain Wisdom all and false Philosophy.
> Yet with a pleasing sorcery could charm
> Pain, for a while, or anguish; and excite
> Fallacious Hope, or arm the obdurate breast
> With stubborn Patience, as with triple steel.[1]

In like manner, if a man has accustomed himself to skeptical considerations on the uncertainty and narrow limits of reason, he will not entirely forget them when he turns his reflection on other subjects; but in all his philosophical principles and reasoning, I dare not say in his common conduct, he will be found different from those who either never formed any opinions in the case or have entertained sentiments more favorable to human reason.

To whatever length anyone may push his speculative principles of skepticism, he must act, I own, and live and converse like other men; and for this conduct he is not obliged to give any other reason than the absolute necessity he lies under of so doing. If he ever carries his speculations further than this necessity constrains him, and philosophizes either on natural or moral subjects, he is allured by a certain pleasure and satisfaction which he finds in employing himself after that manner. He considers, besides, that everyone, even in common life, is constrained to have more or less of this philosophy; that from our earliest infancy we make continual advances in forming more general principles of conduct and reasoning; that the larger experience we acquire, and the stronger reason we are endued with, we always render our principles the more general and comprehensive; and that what we call *philosophy* is nothing but a more regular and methodical operation of the same kind. To philosophize on such subjects is nothing

[1] [Milton, *Paradise Lost*, Bk. ii.]

essentially different from reasoning on common life, and we may only expect greater stability, if not greater truth, from our philosophy on account of its exacter and more scrupulous method of proceeding.

But when we look beyond human affairs and the properties of the surrounding bodies, when we carry our speculations into the two eternities, before and after the present state of things, into the creation and formation of the universe, the existence and properties of spirits, the powers and operations of one universal Spirit, existing without beginning and without end, omnipotent, omniscient, immutable, infinite, and incomprehensible, we must be far removed from the smallest tendency to skepticism not to be apprehensive that we have here got quite beyond the reach of our faculties. So long as we confine our speculations to trade or morals or politics or criticism, we make appeals, every moment, to common sense and experience, which strengthen our philosophical conclusions and remove, at least in part, the suspicion which we so justly entertain with regard to every reasoning that is very subtle and refined. But in theological reasonings we have not this advantage, while at the same time we are employed upon objects which, we must be sensible, are too large for our grasp and, of all others, require most to be familiarized to our apprehension. We are like foreigners in a strange country, to whom everything must seem suspicious, and who are in danger every moment of transgressing against the laws and customs of the people with whom they live and converse. We know not how far we ought to trust our vulgar methods of reasoning in such a subject, since even in common life and in that province which is peculiarly appropriated to them we cannot account for them and are entirely guided by a kind of instinct or necessity in employing them.

All skeptics pretend that if reason be considered in an abstract view, it furnishes invincible arguments against itself, and that we could never retain any conviction or assurance on any subject were not the skeptical reasonings so refined and subtle that they are not able to counterpoise the more solid and more natural arguments derived from the senses and experience. But it is evident, whenever our arguments lose this advantage and run wide of common life, that the most refined skepticism comes to be upon a footing with them, and is able to oppose and counterbalance them. The one has no more weight than the other. The mind must remain in suspense between them, and it is that very suspense or balance which is the triumph of skepticism.

But I observe, says CLEANTHES, with regard to you, Philo, and all speculative skeptics, that your doctrine and practice are as much at variance in the most abstruse points of theory as in the conduct of common life. Wherever evidence discovers itself, you adhere to it, notwithstanding your pretended skepticism; and I can observe, too, some of your sect to be as decisive as those who make greater professions of certainty and assurance. In reality, would not a man be ridiculous who pretended to reject Newton's explication of the wonderful phenomenon of the rainbow because that explication gives a minute anatomy of the rays of light, a subject, forsooth, too refined for human comprehension? And what would you say to one who, having nothing particular to object to the arguments of Copernicus and Galileo for the motion of the earth, should withhold his assent on that general principle that these subjects were too magnificent and remote to be explained by the narrow and fallacious reason of mankind?

There is indeed a kind of brutish and ignorant skepticism, as you well observed, which gives the vulgar a general prejudice against what they do not easily understand, and makes them reject every principle which requires elaborate reasoning to prove and establish it. This species of skepticism is fatal to knowledge, not to religion, since we find that those who make greatest profession of it give often their assent, not only to the great truths of theism and natural theology, but even to the most absurd tenets which a traditional superstition has recommended to them. They firmly believe in witches, though they will not believe nor attend to the most simple proposition of Euclid. But the refined and philosophical skeptics fall into an inconsistency of an opposite nature. They push their researches into the most abstruse corners of science, and their assent attends them in every step, proportioned to the evidence which they meet with. They are even obliged to acknowledge that the most abstruse and remote objects are those which are best explained by philosophy. Light is in reality anatomized; the true system of the heavenly bodies is discovered and ascertained. But the nourishment of bodies by food is still an inexplicable mystery; the cohesion of the parts of matter is still incomprehensible. These skeptics, therefore, are obliged, in every question, to consider each particular evidence apart, and proportion their assent to the precise degree of evidence which occurs. This is their practice in all natural, mathematical, moral, and political science. And why not the same, I ask, in the theological and religious? Why must conclusions of this nature be alone rejected on the general presumption of the insufficiency of human reason, without any particular discussion of the evidence? Is not such an unequal conduct a plain proof of prejudice and passion?

Our senses, you say, are fallacious, our understanding erroneous, our ideas, even of the most familiar objects, extension, duration, motion, full of absurdities and contradictions. You defy me to solve the difficulties or reconcile the repugnancies which you discover in them. I have not capacity for so great an undertaking; I have not leisure for it; I perceive it to be superfluous. Your own conduct, in every circumstance, refutes your principles, and shows the firmest reliance on all the received maxims of science, morals, prudence, and behavior.

I shall never assent to so harsh an opinion as that of a celebrated writer,[1] who says that the skeptics are not a sect of philosophers, they are only a sect of liars. I may, however, affirm (I hope without offense) that they are a sect of jesters or railers. But for my part, whenever I find myself disposed to mirth and amusement, I shall certainly choose my entertainment of a less perplexing and abstruse nature. A comedy, a novel, or at most a history seems a more natural recreation than such metaphysical subtleties and abstractions.

In vain would the skeptic make a distinction between science and common life, or between one science and another. The arguments employed in all, if just, are of a similar nature, and contain the same force and evidence. Or if there be any difference among them, the advantage lies entirely on the side of theology and natural religion. Many principles of mechan-

---

[1] *L'art de penser.*

ics are founded on very abstruse reasoning, yet no man who has any pretensions to science, even no speculative skeptic, pretends to entertain the least doubt with regard to them. The Copernican system contains the most surprising paradox, and the most contrary to our natural conceptions, to appearances, and to our very senses, yet even monks and inquisitors are now constrained to withdraw their opposition to it. And shall Philo, a man of so liberal a genius and extensive knowledge, entertain any general undistinguished scruples with regard to the religious hypothesis, which is founded on the simplest and most obvious arguments and, unless it meets with artificial obstacles, has such easy access and admission into the mind of man?

And here we may observe, continued he, turning himself towards Demea, a pretty curious circumstance in the history of the sciences. After the union of philosophy with the popular religion, upon the first establishment of Christianity, nothing was more usual among all religious teachers than declamations against reason, against the senses, against every principle derived merely from human research and inquiry. All the topics of the ancient Academics were adopted by the Fathers, and thence propagated for several ages in every school and pulpit throughout Christendom. The Reformers embraced the same principles of reasoning, or rather declamation, and all panegyrics on the excellence of faith were sure to be interlarded with some severe strokes of satire against natural reason. A celebrated prelate, too,[1] of the Romish communion, a man of the most extensive learning, who wrote a demonstration of Christianity, has also composed a treatise which contains all the cavils of the boldest and most determined Pyrrhonism. Locke seems to have been the first Christian who ventured openly to assert that *faith* was nothing but a species of *reason,* that religion was only a branch of philosophy, and that a chain of arguments, similar to that which established any truth in morals, politics, or physics, was always employed in discovering all the principles of theology, natural and revealed. The ill use which Bayle and other libertines made of the philosophical skepticism of the Fathers and first

[1] Mons. Huet.

Reformers still further propagated the judicious sentiment of Mr. Locke. And it is now in a manner avowed, by all pretenders to reasoning and philosophy, that *atheist* and *skeptic* are almost synonymous. And as it is certain that no man is in earnest when he professes the latter principle, I would fain hope that there are as few who seriously maintain the former.

Don't you remember, said PHILO, the excellent saying of Lord Bacon on this head? That a little philosophy, replied CLEANTHES, makes a man an atheist; a great deal converts him to religion. That is a very judicious remark too, said PHILO. But what I have in my eye is another passage, where, having mentioned David's fool, who said in his heart there is no God, this great philosopher observes that the atheists nowadays have a double share of folly, for they are not contented to say in their hearts there is no God, but they also utter that impiety with their lips, and are thereby guilty of multiplied indiscretion and imprudence. Such people, though they were ever so much in earnest, cannot, methinks, be very formidable.

But though you should rank me in this class of fools, I cannot forbear communicating a remark that occurs to me, from the history of the religious and irreligious skepticism with which you have entertained us. It appears to me that there are strong symptoms of priestcraft in the whole progress of this affair. During ignorant ages, such as those which followed the dissolution of the ancient schools, the priests perceived that atheism, deism, or heresy of any kind could only proceed from the presumptuous questioning of received opinions, and from a belief that human reason was equal to everything. Education had then a mighty influence over the minds of men, and was almost equal in force to those suggestions of the senses and common understanding by which the most determined skeptic must allow himself to be governed. But at present, when the influence of education is much diminished and men, from a more open commerce of the world, have learned to compare the popular principles of different nations and ages, our sagacious divines have changed their whole system of philosophy and talk the language of Stoics, Platonists, and Peripatetics, not that of Pyrrhonians and Academics. If we distrust human reason we have now no other principle to lead us into religion. Thus, skeptics in one age, dogmatists in another; whichever system best suits the purpose of these reverend gentlemen in giving them as ascendant over mankind, they are sure to make it their favorite principle and established tenet.

It is very natural, said CLEANTHES, for men to embrace those principles by which they find they can best defend their doctrines, nor need we have any recourse to priestcraft to account for so reasonable an expedient. And surely nothing can afford a stronger presumption that any set of principles are true and ought to be embraced than to observe that they tend to the confirmation of true religion, and serve to confound the cavils of atheists, libertines, and free-thinkers of all denominations.

Part II.

I MUST OWN, Cleanthes, said DEMEA, that nothing can more surprise me than the light in which you have all along put this argument. By the whole tenor of your discourse, one would imagine that you were maintaining the being of a God against the cavils of atheists and infidels, and were necessitated to become a champion for that fundamental principle of all religion. But this, I hope, is not by any means a question among us. No man, no man at least of common sense, I am persuaded, ever entertained a serious doubt with regard to a truth so certain and self-evident. The question is not concerning the *being* but the *nature* of God. This I affirm, from the infirmities of human understanding, to be altogether incomprehensible and unknown to us. The essence of that Supreme Mind, his attributes, the manner of his existence, the very nature of his duration, these and every particular which regards so divine a Being are mysterious to men. Finite, weak, and blind creatures, we ought to humble ourselves in his august presence, and, conscious of our frailties, adore in silence his infinite perfections which eye hath not seen, ear hath not heard, neither hath it entered into the heart of man to conceive. They are covered in a deep cloud from human curiosity; it is profaneness to attempt penetrating through these

sacred obscurities, and next to the impiety of denying his existence is the temerity of prying into his nature and essence,
decrees and attributes.

But lest you should think that my *piety* has here got the
better of my *philosophy*, I shall support my opinion, if it
needs any support, by a very great authority. I might cite all
the divines, almost from the foundation of Christianity, who
have ever treated of this or any other theological subject, but
I shall confine myself, at present, to one equally celebrated
for piety and philosophy. It is Father Malebranche who, I
remember, thus expresses himself.[1] "One ought not so much,"
says he, "to call God a spirit in order to express positively
what he is, as in order to signify that he is not matter. He is a
Being infinitely perfect: of this we cannot doubt. But in the
same manner as we ought not to imagine, even supposing
him corporeal, that he is clothed with a human body as the
anthropomorphites asserted, under color that that figure was
the most perfect of any, so neither ought we to imagine that
the spirit of God has human ideas or bears any resemblance
to our spirit, under color that we know nothing more perfect
than a human mind. We ought rather to believe that as he
comprehends the perfections of matter without being material
. . . he comprehends also the perfections of created spirits
without being spirit, in the manner we conceive spirit; that
his true name is *He that is*, or, in other words, Being without
restriction, All Being, the Being infinite and universal."

After so great an authority, Demea, replied PHILO, as that
which you have produced, and a thousand more which you
might produce, it would appear ridiculous in me to add my
sentiment or express my approbation of your doctrine. But
surely, where reasonable men treat these subjects, the question can never be concerning the *being* but only the *nature* of
the Deity. The former truth, as you well observe, is unquestionable and self-evident. Nothing exists without a cause, and
the original cause of this universe (whatever it be) we call
God, and piously ascribe to him every species of perfection.
Whoever scruples this fundamental truth deserves every punishment which can be inflicted among philosophers, to wit,

[1] *Recherche de la vérité*, liv. 3. cap. 9.

the greatest ridicule, contempt, and disapprobation. But as all perfection is entirely relative, we ought never to imagine that we comprehend the attributes of this divine Being, or to suppose that his perfections have any analogy or likeness to the perfections of a human creature. Wisdom, thought, design, knowledge, these we justly ascribe to him because these words are honorable among men, and we have no other language or other conceptions by which we can express our adoration of him. But let us beware lest we think that our ideas anywise correspond to his perfections, or that his attributes have any resemblance to these qualities among men. He is infinitely superior to our limited view and comprehension, and is more the object of worship in the temple than of disputation in the schools.

In reality, Cleanthes, continued he, there is no need of having recourse to that affected skepticism so displeasing to you in order to come at this determination. Our ideas reach no farther than our experience. We have no experience of divine attributes and operations. I need not conclude my syllogism; you can draw the inference yourself. And it is a pleasure to me (and I hope to you, too) that just reasoning and sound piety here concur in the same conclusion, and both of them establish the adorably mysterious and incomprehensible nature of the Supreme Being.

Not to lose any time in circumlocutions, said CLEANTHES, addressing himself to Demea, much less in replying to the pious declamations of Philo, I shall briefly explain how I conceive this matter. Look round the world, contemplate the whole and every part of it: you will find it to be nothing but one great machine, subdivided into an infinite number of lesser machines, which again admit of subdivisions to a degree beyond what human senses and faculties can trace and explain. All these various machines, and even their most minute parts, are adjusted to each other with an accuracy which ravishes into admiration all men who have ever contemplated them. The curious adapting of means to ends throughout all nature resembles exactly, though it much exceeds, the productions of human contrivance, of human design, thought, wisdom, and intelligence. Since therefore the effects resemble each other, we are led to infer, by all the

MECHANISTIC VIEW

rules of analogy, that the causes also resemble, and that the Author of Nature is somewhat similar to the mind of man, though possessed of much larger faculties, proportioned to the grandeur of the work which he has executed. By this argument *a posteriori*, and by this argument alone, do we prove at once the existence of a Deity and his similarity to human mind and intelligence.

I shall be so free, Cleanthes, said DEMEA, as to tell you that from the beginning I could not approve of your conclusion concerning the similarity of the Deity to men; still less can I approve of the mediums by which you endeavor to establish it. What! No demonstration of the being of God! No abstract arguments! No proofs *a priori!* Are these which have hitherto been so much insisted on by philosophers all fallacy, all sophism? Can we reach no farther in this subject than experience and probability? I will not say that this is betraying the cause of a Deity; but surely, by this affected candor, you give advantages to atheists which they never could obtain by the mere dint of argument and reasoning.

What I chiefly scruple in this subject, said PHILO, is not so much that all religious arguments are by Cleanthes reduced to experience, as that they appear not to be even the most certain and irrefragable of that inferior kind. That a stone will fall, that fire will burn, that the earth has solidity, we have observed a thousand and a thousand times; and when any new instance of this nature is presented, we draw without hesitation the accustomed inference. The exact similarity of the cases gives us a perfect assurance of a similar event, and a stronger evidence is never desired nor sought after. But wherever you depart in the least from the similarity of the cases, you diminish proportionably the evidence, and may at last bring it to a very weak *analogy*, which is confessedly liable to error and uncertainty. After having experienced the circulation of the blood in human creatures, we make no doubt that it takes place in Titius and Maevius; but from its circulation in frogs and fishes it is only a presumption, though a strong one, from analogy, that it takes place in men and other animals. The analogical reasoning is much weaker when we infer the circulation of the sap in vegetables from our experience that the blood circulates in animals; and those who hastily followed that imperfect analogy are found, by more accurate experiments, to have been mistaken.

If we see a house, Cleanthes, we conclude with the greatest certainty that it had an architect or builder, because this is precisely that species of effect which we have experienced to proceed from that species of cause. But surely you will not affirm that the universe bears such a resemblance to a house that we can with the same certainty infer a similar cause, or that the analogy is here entire and perfect. The dissimilitude is so striking that the utmost you can here pretend to is a guess, a conjecture, a presumption concerning a similar cause; and how that pretension will be received in the world, I leave you to consider.

It would surely be very ill received, replied CLEANTHES, and I should be deservedly blamed and detested did I allow that the proofs of a Deity amounted to no more than a guess or conjecture. But is the whole adjustment of means to ends in a house and in the universe so slight a resemblance? The economy of final causes? The order, proportion, and arrangement of every part? Steps of a stair are plainly contrived that human legs may use them in mounting; and this inference is certain and infallible. Human legs are also contrived for walking and mounting; and this inference, I allow, is not altogether so certain because of the dissimilarity which you remark; but does it, therefore, deserve the name only of presumption or conjecture?

Good God! cried DEMEA, interrupting him. Where are we? Zealous defenders of religion allow that the proofs of a Deity fall short of perfect evidence! And you, Philo, on whose assistance I depended in proving the adorable mysteriousness of the Divine Nature, do you assent to all these extravagant opinions of Cleanthes? For what other name can I give them? Or why spare my censure when such principles are advanced, supported by such an authority, before so young a man as Pamphilus?

You seem not to apprehend, replied PHILO, that I argue with Cleanthes in his own way, and by showing him the dangerous consequences of his tenets hope at last to reduce him to our opinion. But what sticks most with you, I observe, is the representation which Cleanthes has made of the argument *a posteriori;* and finding that that argument is likely to escape your hold and vanish into air, you think it so disguised that you can scarcely believe it to be set in its true light. Now however much I may dissent in other respects from the dangerous principle of Cleanthes, I must allow that he has fairly represented that argument, and I shall endeavor so to state the matter to you that you will entertain no further scruples with regard to it.

Were a man to abstract from everything which he knows or has seen, he would be altogether incapable, merely from his own ideas, to determine what kind of scene the universe must be, or to give the preference to one state or situation of things above another. For as nothing which he clearly conceives could be esteemed impossible or implying a contradiction, every chimera of his fancy would be upon an equal footing; nor could he assign any just reason why he adheres to one idea or system and rejects the others which are equally possible.

Again, after he opens his eyes and contemplates the world as it really is, it would be impossible for him at first to assign the cause of any one event, much less of the whole of things, or of the universe. He might set his fancy a-rambling, and she might bring him in an infinite variety of reports and representations. These would all be possible, but being all equally possible, he would never of himself give a satisfactory account for his preferring one of them to the rest. Experience alone can point out to him the true cause of any phenomenon.

Now according to this method of reasoning, Demea, it follows (and is, indeed, tacitly allowed by Cleanthes himself) that order, arrangement, or the adjustment of final causes, is not of itself any proof of design, but only so far as it has been experienced to proceed from that principle. For aught we can know *a priori,* matter may contain the source or spring of order originally, within itself, as well as mind does; and there is no more difficulty in conceiving that the several elements, from an internal, unknown cause, may fall into the most exquisite arrangement, than to conceive that their ideas, in the great universal mind, from a like internal, unknown cause, fall into that arrangement. The equal possibility of both these suppositions is allowed. But by experience we find (according to Cleanthes) that there is a difference between them. Throw several pieces of steel together without shape or form; they will never arrange themselves so as to compose a watch. Stone and mortar and wood, without an architect, never erect a house. But the ideas in a human mind, we see, by an unknown, inexplicable economy, arrange themselves so as to form the plan of a watch or house. Experience, therefore, proves that there is an original principle of order in mind, not in matter. From similar effects we infer similar causes. The adjustment of means to ends is alike in the universe, as in a machine of human contrivance. The causes, therefore, must be resembling.

I was from the beginning scandalized, I must own, with this resemblance which is asserted between the Deity and human creatures, and must conceive it to imply such a degradation of the Supreme Being as no sound theist could endure. With your assistance, therefore, Demea, I shall endeavor to defend what you justly call the adorable mysteriousness of the Divine Nature, and shall refute this reasoning of Cleanthes, provided he allows that I have made a fair representation of it.

When Cleanthes had assented, PHILO, after a short pause, proceeded in the following manner.

That all inferences, Cleanthes, concerning fact are founded on experience, and that all experimental reasonings are founded on the supposition that similar causes prove similar effects, and similar effects similar causes, I shall not at present much dispute with you. But observe, I entreat you, with what extreme caution all just reasoners proceed in the transferring of experiments to similar cases. Unless the cases be exactly similar, they repose no perfect confidence in applying their past observation to any particular phenomenon. Every alteration of circumstances occasions a doubt concerning the event, and it requires new experiments to prove certainly that the new circumstances are of no moment or importance. A change in bulk, situation, arrangement, age, disposition of the air, or surrounding bodies, any of these particulars may be attended with the most unexpected consequences. And unless the objects be quite familiar to us, it is the highest temerity to expect with assurance, after any of these changes, an event similar to that which before fell under our observation. The slow and deliberate steps of philosophers here, if anywhere, are distinguished from the precipitate march of the vulgar, who, hurried on by the smallest similitude, are incapable of all discernment or consideration.

But can you think, Cleanthes, that your usual phlegm and philosophy have been preserved in so wide a step as you have taken when you compared to the universe, houses, ships, furniture, machines, and from their similarity in some circumstances inferred a similarity in their causes? Thought, design, intelligence, such as we discover in men and other animals, is no more than one of the springs and principles of the universe, as well as heat or cold, attraction or repulsion, and a hundred others which fall under daily observation. It is an active cause by which some particular parts of nature, we find, produce alterations on other parts. But can a conclusion, with any propriety, be transferred from parts to the whole? Does not the great disproportion bar all comparison and inference? From observing the growth of a hair, can we learn anything concerning the generation of a man? Would the manner of a leaf's blowing, even though perfectly known, afford us any instruction concerning the vegetation of a tree?

But allowing that we were to take the *operations* of one part of nature upon another for the foundation of our judgment concerning the *origin* of the whole (which never can be admitted), yet why select so minute, so weak, so bounded a principle as the reason and design of animals is found to be upon this planet? What peculiar privilege has this little agitation of the brain which we call *thought,* that we must thus make it the model of the whole universe? Our partiality in our own favor does indeed present it on all occasions, but sound philosophy ought carefully to guard against so natural an illusion.

So far from admitting, continued PHILO, that the operations of a part can afford us any just conclusion concerning the origin of the whole, I will not allow any one part to form a rule for another part if the latter be very remote from the former. Is there any reasonable ground to conclude that the inhabitants of other planets possess thought, intelligence, reason, or anything similar to these faculties in men? When nature has so extremely diversified her manner of operation in this small globe, can we imagine that she incessantly copies herself throughout so immense a universe? And if thought, as we may well suppose, be confined merely to this narrow corner and has even there so limited a sphere of action, with what propriety can we assign it for the original cause of all things? The narrow views of a peasant who makes his domestic economy the rule for the government of kingdoms is in comparison a pardonable sophism.

But were we ever so much assured that a thought and reason resembling the human were to be found throughout the whole universe, and were its activity elsewhere vastly greater and more commanding than it appears in this globe, yet I cannot see why the operations of a world constituted, arranged, adjusted, can with any propriety be extended to a world which is in its embryo state, and is advancing toward that constitution and arrangement. By observation we know somewhat of the economy, action, and nourishment of a finished animal, but we must transfer with great caution that observation to the growth of a fetus in the womb, and still more to the formation of an animalcule in the loins of its male parent. Nature, we find, even from our limited experience, possesses an infinite number of springs and principles which incessantly discover themselves on every change of her position and situation. And what new and unknown principles would actuate her in so new and unknown a situation as that of the formation of a universe, we cannot, without the utmost temerity, pretend to determine.

A very small part of this great system, during a very short time, is very imperfectly discovered to us; and do we thence pronounce decisively concerning the origin of the whole?

Admirable conclusion! Stone, wood, brick, iron, brass, have not, at this time, in this minute globe of earth, an order or arrangement without human art and contrivance; therefore, the universe could not originally attain its order and arrangement without something similar to human art. But is a part of nature a rule for another part very wide of the former? Is it a rule for the whole? Is a very small part a rule for the universe? Is nature in one situation a certain rule for nature in another situation vastly different from the former?

And can you blame me, Cleanthes, if I here imitate the prudent reserve of Simonides, who, according to the noted story, being asked by Hiero, *what God was,* desired a day to think of it, and then two days more, and after that manner continually prolonged the term, without ever bringing in his definition or description? Could you even blame me if I had answered at first, *that I did not know,* and was sensible that this subject lay vastly beyond the reach of my faculties? You might cry out skeptic and rallier as much as you pleased; but having found in so many other subjects much more familiar the imperfections and even contradictions of human reason, I never should expect any success from its feeble conjectures in a subject so sublime and so remote from the sphere of our observation. When two *species* of objects have always been observed to be conjoined together, I can *infer,* by custom, the existence of one wherever I *see* the existence of the other; and this I call an argument from experience. But how this argument can have place where the objects, as in the present case, are single, individual, without parallel or specific resemblance, may be difficult to explain. And will any man tell me with a serious countenance that an orderly universe must arise from some thought and art like the human because we have experience of it? To ascertain this reasoning it were requisite that we had experience of the origin of worlds; and it is not sufficient, surely, that we have seen ships and cities arise from human art and contrivance.

Philo was proceeding in this vehement manner, somewhat between jest and earnest, as it appeared to me, when he observed some signs of impatience in Cleanthes, and then immediately stopped short. What I had to suggest, said CLEANTHES is only that you would not abuse terms, or make use of popular expressions to subvert philosophical reasonings. You know that the vulgar often distinguish reason from experience even where the question relates only to matter of fact and existence, though it is found, where that *reason* is properly analyzed, that it is nothing but a species of experience. To prove by experience the origin of the universe from mind is not more contrary to common speech than to prove the motion of the earth from the same principle. And a caviller might raise all the same objections to the Copernican system which you have urged against my reasonings. Have you other earths, might he say, which you have seen to move? Have . . . ?

Yes! cried PHILO, interrupting him. We have other earths. Is not the moon another earth, which we see to turn round its center? Is not Venus another earth, where we observe the same phenomenon? Are not the revolutions of the sun also a confirmation, from analogy, of the same theory? All the planets, are they not earths which revolve about the sun? Are not the satellites moons which move round Jupiter and Saturn, and along with these primary planets round the sun? These analogies and resemblances, with others which I have not mentioned, are the sole proofs of the Copernican system; and to you it belongs to consider whether you have any analogies of the same kind to support your theory.

In reality, Cleanthes, continued he, the modern system of astronomy is now so much received by all inquirers and has become so essential a part even of our earliest education that we are not commonly very scrupulous in examining the reasons upon which it is founded. It is now become a matter of mere curiosity to study the first writers on that subject who had the full force of prejudice to encounter, and were obliged to turn their arguments on every side in order to render them popular and convincing. But if we peruse Galileo's famous *Dialogues* concerning the system of the world, we shall find that that great genius, one of the sublimest that ever existed, first bent all his endeavors to prove that there was no foundation for the distinction commonly made between elementary and celestial substances. The schools, proceeding from the illusions of sense, had carried this distinction very far, and had established the latter substances to be ingenerable, incorruptible, unalterable, impassible, and had assigned all the opposite qualities to the former. But Galileo, beginning with the moon, proved its similarity in every particular to the earth: its convex figure, its natural darkness when not illuminated, its density, its distinction into solid and liquid, the variations of its phases, the mutual illuminations of the earth and moon, their mutual eclipses, the inequalities of the lunar surface, etc. After many instances of this kind, with regard to all the planets, men plainly saw that these bodies became proper objects of experience, and that the similarity of their nature enabled us to extend the same arguments and phenomena from one to the other.

In this cautious proceeding of the astronomers you may read your own condemnation, Cleanthes, or rather may see that the subject in which you are engaged exceeds all human reason and inquiry. Can you pretend to show any such similarity between the fabric of a house and the generation of a universe? Have you ever seen nature in any such situation as resembles the first arrangement of the elements? Have worlds ever been formed under your eye, and have you had leisure to observe the whole progress of the phenomenon, from the first appearance of order to its final consummation? If you have, then cite your experience and deliver your theory.

Part III.

HOW THE MOST absurd argument, replied CLEANTHES, in the hands of a man of ingenuity and invention, may acquire an air of probability! Are you not aware, Philo, that it became necessary for Copernicus and his first disciples to prove the similarity of the terrestrial and celestial matter because several philosophers, blinded by old systems and supported by some sensible appearances, had denied this similarity? But that it is by no means necessary that theists should prove the similarity of the works of nature to those of art because this similarity is self-evident and undeniable? The same matter, a like form; what more is requisite to show an analogy between their causes and to ascertain the origin of all things from a divine purpose and intention? Your objections, I must freely tell you, are no better than the abstruse cavils of those philosophers who denied motion, and ought to be refuted in the same manner, by illustrations, examples, and instances rather than by serious argument and philosophy.

Suppose, therefore, that an articulate voice were heard in the clouds, much louder and more melodious than any which human art could ever reach; suppose that this voice were extended in the same instant over all nations and spoke to each nation in its own language and dialect; suppose that the words delivered not only contain a just sense and meaning, but convey some instruction altogether worthy of a benevolent Being superior to mankind. Could you possibly hesitate a moment concerning the cause of this voice, and must you not instantly ascribe it to some design or purpose? Yet I cannot see but all the same objections (if they merit that appellation) which lie against the system of theism may also be produced against this inference.

Might you not say that all conclusions concerning fact were founded on experience; that when we hear an articulate voice in the dark and thence infer a man, it is only the resemblance of the effects which leads us to conclude that there is a like resemblance in the cause; but that this extraordinary voice, by its loudness, extent, and flexibility to all languages, bears so little analogy to any human voice that we have no reason to suppose any analogy in their causes; and consequently that a rational, wise, coherent speech proceeded, you knew not whence, from some accidental whistling of the winds, not from any divine reason or intelligence? You see clearly your own objections in these cavils, and I hope too you see clearly that they cannot possibly have more force in the one case than in the other.

But to bring the case still nearer the present one of the universe, I shall make two suppositions which imply not any absurdity or impossibility. Suppose that there is a natural, universal, invariable language, common to every individual of human race, and that books are natural productions which perpetuate themselves in the same manner with animals and vegetables, by descent and propagation. Several expressions of our passions contain a universal language: all brute animals have a natural speech, which, however limited, is very intelligible to their own species. And as there are infinitely fewer parts and less contrivance in the finest composition of eloquence than in the coarsest organized body, the propagation of an *Iliad* or *Aeneid* is an easier supposition than that of any plant or animal.

Suppose, therefore, that you enter into your library thus peopled by natural volumes containing the most refined reason and most exquisite beauty; could you possibly open one of them and doubt that its original cause bore the strongest analogy to mind and intelligence? When it reasons and dis-

courses; when it expostulates, argues, and enforces its views
and topics; when it applies sometimes to the pure intellect,
sometimes to the affections; when it collects, disposes, and
adorns every consideration suited to the subject; could you
persist in asserting that all this, at the bottom, had really no
meaning, and that the first formation of this volume in the
loins of its original parent proceeded not from thought and
design? Your obstinacy, I know, reaches not that degree of
firmness; even your skeptical play and wantonness would be
abashed at so glaring an absurdity.

But if there be any difference, Philo, between this supposed
case and the real one of the universe, it is all to the advantage of the latter. The anatomy of an animal affords many
stronger instances of design then the perusal of Livy or
Tacitus; and any objection which you start in the former case,
by carrying me back to so unusual and extraordinary a scene
as the first formation of worlds, the same objection has place
on the supposition of our vegetating library. Choose then
your party, Philo, without ambiguity or evasion; assert either
that a rational volume is no proof of a rational cause or admit
of a similar cause to all the works of nature.

Let me here observe too, continued CLEANTHES, that this
religious argument, instead of being weakened by that skepticism so much affected by you, rather acquires force from it
and becomes more firm and undisputed. To exclude all
argument or reasoning of every kind is either affectation or
madness. The declared profession of every reasonable skeptic
is only to reject abstruse, remote, and refined arguments, to
adhere to common sense and the plain instincts of nature, and
to assent wherever any reasons strike him with so full a force
that he cannot, without the greatest violence, prevent it. Now
the arguments for natural religion are plainly of this kind,
and nothing but the most perverse, obstinate metaphysics
can reject them. Consider, anatomize the eye, survey its
structure and contrivance, and tell me, from your own feeling,
if the idea of a contriver does not immediately flow in upon
you with a force like that of sensation. The most obvious
conclusion, surely, is in favor [of] design, and it requires
time, reflection, and study to summon up those frivolous

though abstruse objections which can support infidelity. Who can behold the male and female of each species, the correspondence of their parts and instincts, their passions and whole course of life before and after generation, but must be sensible that the propagation of the species is intended by nature? Millions and millions of such instances present themselves through every part of the universe, and no language can convey a more intelligible, irresistible meaning than the curious adjustment of final causes. To what degree, therefore, of blind dogmatism must one have attained to reject such natural and such convincing arguments?

Some beauties in writing we may meet with which seem contrary to rules, and which gain the affections and animate the imagination in opposition to all the precepts of criticism and to the authority of the established masters of art. And if the argument for theism be, as you pretend, contradictory to the principles of logic, its universal, its irresistible influence proves clearly that there may be arguments of a like irregular nature. Whatever cavils may be urged, an orderly world, as well as a coherent, articulate speech, will still be received as an incontestable proof of design and intention.

It sometimes happens, I own, that the religious arguments have not their due influence on an ignorant savage and barbarian, not because they are obscure and difficult, but because he never asks himself any question with regard to them. Whence arises the curious structure of an animal? From the copulation of its parents. And these whence? From *their* parents? A few removes set the objects at such a distance that to him they are lost in darkness and confusion; nor is he actuated by any curiosity to trace them further. But this is neither dogmatism nor skepticism, but stupidity, a state of mind very different from your sifting, inquisitive disposition, my ingenious friend. You can trace causes from effects; you can compare the most distant and remote objects; and your greatest errors proceed not from barrenness of thought and invention but from too luxuriant a fertility, which suppresses your natural good sense by a profusion of unnecessary scruples and objections.

Here I could observe, Hermippus, that Philo was a little

embarrassed and confounded; but while he hesitated in de-livering an answer, luckily for him, DEMEA broke in upon the discourse and saved his countenance.

Your instance, Cleanthes, said he, drawn from books and language, being familiar, has, I confess, so much more force on that account; but is there not some danger too in this very circumstance, and may it not render us presumptuous by making us imagine we comprehend the Deity and have some adequate idea of his nature and attributes? When I read a volume, I enter into the mind and intention of the author; I become him, in a manner, for the instant, and have an im-mediate feeling and conception of those ideas which revolved in his imagination while employed in that composition. But so near an approach we never surely can make to the Deity. His ways are not our ways. His attributes are perfect but in-comprehensible. And this volume of nature contains a great and inexplicable riddle, more than any intelligible discourse or reasoning.

The ancient Platonists, you know, were the most religious and devout of all the pagan philosophers, yet many of them, particularly Plotinus, expressly declare that intellect or under-standing is not to be ascribed to the Deity, and that our most perfect worship of him consists, not in acts of veneration, reverence, gratitude, or love, but in a certain mysterious self-annihilation or total extinction of all our faculties. These ideas are, perhaps, too far stretched, but still it must be acknowl-edged that, by representing the Deity as so intelligible and comprehensible and so similar to a human mind, we are guilty of the grossest and most narrow partiality, and make ourselves the model of the whole universe.

All the *sentiments* of the human mind—gratitude, resent-ment, love, friendship, approbation, blame, pity, emulation, envy—have a plain reference to the state and situation of man, and are calculated for preserving the existence and promoting the activity of such a being in such circumstances. It seems therefore unreasonable to transfer such sentiments to a supreme existence or to suppose him actuated by them; and the phenomena, besides, of the universe will not support us in such a theory. All our *ideas* derived from the senses are confessedly false and illusive, and cannot therefore be supposed to have place in a supreme intelligence. And as the ideas of internal sentiment, added to those of the external senses, compose the whole furniture of human understanding, we may conclude that none of the *materials* of thought are in any respect similar in the human and in the divine intelligence. Now as to the *manner* of thinking, how can we make any comparison between them or suppose them anywise resembling? Our thought is fluctuating, uncertain, fleeting, successive, and compounded; and were we to remove these circumstances we absolutely annihilate its essence, and it would in such a case be an abuse of terms to apply to it the name of thought or reason. At least, if it appear more pious and respectful (as it really is) still to retain these terms when we mention the Supreme Being, we ought to acknowledge that their meaning, in that case, is totally incomprehensible, and that the infirmities of our nature do not permit us to reach any ideas which in the least correspond to the ineffable sublimity of the divine attributes.

Part IV.

IT SEEMS STRANGE to me, said CLEANTHES, that you, Demea, who are so sincere in the cause of religion, should still maintain the mysterious, incomprehensible nature of the Deity, and should insist so strenuously that he has no manner of likeness or resemblance to human creatures. The Deity, I can readily allow, possesses many powers and attributes of which we can have no comprehension. But if our ideas, so far as they go, be not just and adequate and correspondent to his real nature, I know not what there is in this subject worth insisting on. Is the name, without any meaning, of such mighty importance? Or how do you mystics, who maintain the absolute incomprehensibility of the Deity, differ from skeptics or atheists, who assert that the first cause of all is unknown and unintelligible? Their temerity must be very great if, after rejecting the production by a mind—I mean a mind resembling the human (for I know of no other)—they pretend to assign, with certainty, any other specific intelligible cause; and their conscience must be very scrupulous indeed if they refuse to call the universal unknown cause a God or Deity, and to bestow on him as many sublime eulogies and unmeaning epithets as you shall please to require of them.

Who could imagine, replied DEMEA, that Cleanthes, the calm, philosophical Cleanthes, would attempt to refute his antagonists by affixing a nickname to them, and, like the common bigots and inquisitors of the age, have recourse to invective and declamation instead of reasoning? Or does he not perceive that these topics are easily retorted, and that *anthropomorphite* is an appellation as invidious and implies as dangerous consequences as the epithet of *mystic* with which he has honored us? In reality, Cleanthes, consider what it is you assert when you represent the Deity as similar to a human mind and understanding. What is the soul of man? A composition of various faculties, passions, sentiments, ideas, united, indeed, into one self or person, but still distinct from each other. When it reasons, the ideas which are the parts of its discourse arrange themselves in a certain form or order which is not preserved entire for a moment, but immediately gives place to another arrangement. New opinions, new passions, new affections, new feelings arise which continually diversify the mental scene and produce in it the greatest variety and most rapid succession imaginable. How is this compatible with that perfect immutability and simplicity which all true theists ascribe to the Deity? By the same act, say they, he sees past, present, and future; his love and hatred, his mercy and justice, are one individual operation; he is entire in every point of space and complete in every instant of duration. No succession, no change, no acquisition, no diminution. What he is implies not in it any shadow of distinction or diversity. And what he is this moment he ever has been and ever will be, without any new judgment, sentiment, or operation. He stands fixed in one simple, perfect state; nor can you ever say, with any propriety, that this act of his is different from that other, or that this judgment or idea has been lately formed and will give place, by succession, to any different judgment or idea.

I can readily allow, said CLEANTHES, that those who maintain the perfect simplicity of the Supreme Being, to the extent in which you have explained it, are complete mystics, and

chargeable with all the consequences which I have drawn
from their opinion. They are, in a word, atheists, without
knowing it. For though it be allowed that the Deity possesses
attributes of which we have no comprehension, yet ought we
never to ascribe to him any attributes which are absolutely
incompatible with that intelligent nature essential to him. A
mind whose acts and sentiments and ideas are not distinct
and successive, one that is wholly simple and totally immutable, is a mind which has no thought, no reason, no will,
no sentiment, no love, no hatred, or, in a word, is no mind
at all. It is an abuse of terms to give it that appellation, and
we may as well speak of limited extension without figure, or
of number without composition.

Pray consider, said PHILO, whom you are at present in-
veighing against. You are honoring with the appellation of
atheist all the sound, orthodox divines, almost, who have
treated of this subject; and you will at last be yourself found,
according to your reckoning, the only sound theist in the
world. But if idolaters be atheists, as I think may justly be
asserted, and Christian theologians the same, what becomes
of the argument, so much celebrated, derived from the universal consent of mankind?

But because I know you are not much swayed by names
and authorities, I shall endeavor to show you a little more
distinctly the inconveniences of that anthropomorphism which
you have embraced, and shall prove that there is no ground
to suppose a plan of the world to be formed in the divine
mind, consisting of distinct ideas differently arranged, in the
same manner as an architect forms in his head the plan of a
house which he intends to execute.

It is not easy, I own, to see what is gained by this
supposition, whether we judge of the matter by *reason* or by
experience. We are still obliged to mount higher in order to
find the cause of this cause which you had assigned as
satisfactory and conclusive.

If *reason* (I mean abstract reason, derived from inquiries
a priori) be not alike mute with regard to all questions concerning cause and effect, this sentence at least it will venture
to pronounce: that a mental world or universe of ideas requires a cause as much as does a material world or universe

of objects, and, if similar in its arrangement, must require a similar cause. For what is there in this subject which should occasion a different conclusion or inference? In an abstract view they are entirely alike, and no difficulty attends the one supposition which is not common to both of them.

Again, when we will needs force *experience* to pronounce some sentence, even on these subjects which lie beyond her sphere, neither can she perceive any material difference in this particular between these two kinds of worlds, but finds them to be governed by similar principles, and to depend upon an equal variety of causes in their operations. We have specimens in miniature of both of them. Our own mind resembles the one, a vegetable or animal body the other. Let experience, therefore, judge from these samples. Nothing seems more delicate, with regard to its causes, than thought; and as these causes never operate in two persons after the same manner, so we never find two persons who think exactly alike. Nor indeed does the same person think exactly alike at any two different periods of time. A difference of age, of the disposition of his body, of weather, of food, of company, of books, of passions, any of these particulars, or others more minute, are sufficient to alter the curious machinery of thought and communicate to it very different movements and operations. As far as we can judge, vegetables and animal bodies are not more delicate in their motions, nor depend upon a greater variety or more curious adjustment of springs and principles.

How therefore shall we satisfy ourselves concerning the cause of that Being whom you suppose the Author of Nature, or, according to your system of anthropomorphism, the ideal world into which you trace the material? Have we not the same reason to trace that ideal world into another ideal world or new intelligent principle? But if we stop and go no further, why go so far? Why not stop at the material world? How can we satisfy ourselves without going on *in infinitum?* And after all, what satisfaction is there in that infinite progression? Let us remember the story of the Indian philosopher and his elephant. It was never more applicable than to the present subject. If the material world rests upon a similar ideal world, this ideal world must rest upon some other, and so on without end. It were better, therefore, never to look beyond the present material world. By supposing it to contain the principle of its order within itself, we really assert it to be God, and the sooner we arrive at that divine Being, so much the better. When you go one step beyond the mundane system, you only excite an inquisitive humor which it is impossible ever to satisfy.

To say that the different ideas which compose the reason of the Supreme Being fall into order of themselves and by their own nature is really to talk without any precise meaning. If it has a meaning, I would fain know why it is not as good sense to say that the parts of the material world fall into order of themselves and by their own nature. Can the one opinion be intelligible, while the other is not so?

We have, indeed, experience of ideas which fall into order of themselves and without any *known* cause. But I am sure we have a much larger experience of matter which does the same, as in all instances of generation and vegetation where the accurate analysis of the cause exceeds all human comprehension. We have also experience of particular systems of thought and of matter which have no order, of the first in madness, of the second in corruption. Why then should we think that order is more essential to one than the other? And if it requires a cause in both, what do we gain by your system in tracing the universe of objects into a similar universe of ideas? The first step which we make leads us on forever. It were therefore wise in us to limit all our inquiries to the present world, without looking further. No satisfaction can ever be attained by these speculations which so far exceed the narrow bounds of human understanding.

It was usual with the Peripatetics, you know, Cleanthes, when the cause of any phenomenon was demanded, to have recourse to their *faculties* or *occult qualities* and to say, for instance, that bread nourished by its nutritive faculty, and senna purged by its purgative. But it has been discovered that this subterfuge was nothing but the disguise of ignorance, and that these philosophers, though less ingenuous, really said the same thing with the skeptics or the vulgar who fairly confessed that they knew not the cause of these phenomena. In like manner, when it is asked what cause produces order in the ideas of the Supreme Being, can any other reason be assigned by you anthropomorphites than that it is a *rational* faculty, and that such is the nature of the Deity? But why a similar answer will not be equally satisfactory in accounting for the order of the world, without having recourse to any such intelligent creator as you insist on, may be difficult to determine. It is only to say that *such* is the nature of material objects, and that they are all originally possessed of a faculty of order and proportion. These are only more learned and elaborate ways of confessing our ignorance; nor has the one hypothesis any real advantage above the other, except in its greater conformity to vulgar prejudices.

You have displayed this argument with great emphasis, replied CLEANTHES. You seem not sensible how easy it is to answer it. Even in common life, if I assign a cause for any event, is it any objection, Philo, that I cannot assign the cause of that cause, and answer every new question which may incessantly be started? And what philosophers could possibly submit to so rigid a rule, philosophers who confess ultimate causes to be totally unknown, and are sensible that the most refined principles into which they trace the phenomena are still to them as inexplicable as these phenomena themselves are to the vulgar? The order and arrangement of nature, the curious adjustment of final causes, the plain use and intention of every part and organ, all these bespeak in the clearest language an intelligent cause or author. The heavens and the earth join in the same testimony; the whole chorus of nature raises one hymn to the praises of its Creator. You alone, or almost alone, disturb this general harmony. You start abstruse doubts, cavils, and objections; you ask me what is the cause of this cause? I know not, I care not, that concerns not me. I have found a Deity, and here I stop my inquiry. Let those go further who are wiser or more enterprising.

I pretend to be neither, replied PHILO; and for that very reason I should never, perhaps, have attempted to go so far, especially when I am sensible that I must at last be contented to sit down with the same answer which, without further trouble, might have satisfied me from the beginning. If I am still to remain in utter ignorance of causes and can absolutely give an explication of nothing, I shall never esteem it any advantage to shove off for a moment a difficulty which you acknowledge must immediately, in its full force, recur upon me. Naturalists indeed very justly explain particular effects by more general causes though these general causes themselves should remain in the end totally inexplicable, but they never surely thought it satisfactory to explain a particular effect by a particular cause which was no more to be accounted for than the effect itself. An ideal system, arranged of itself, without a precedent design, is not a whit more explicable than a material one which attains its order in a like manner; nor is there any more difficulty in the latter supposition than in the former.

Part V.

BUT TO SHOW you still more inconveniences, continued PHILO, in your anthropomorphism, please to take a new survey of your principles. *Like effects prove like causes.* This is the experimental argument; and this, you say too, is the sole theological argument. Now it is certain that the liker the effects are which are seen and the liker the causes which are inferred, the stronger is the argument. Every departure on either side diminishes the probability and renders the experiment less conclusive. You cannot doubt of the principle; neither ought you to reject its consequences.

All the new discoveries in astronomy which prove the immense grandeur and magnificence of the works of nature are so many additional arguments for a Deity, according to the true system of theism; but according to your hypothesis of experimental theism, they become so many objections, by removing the effects still further from all resemblance to the effects of human art and contrivance. For if Lucretius,[1] even following the old system of the world, could exclaim:

[1] Lib. ii. 1095. [Who can rule the sum, who hold in his hand with controlling force the strong reins, of the immeasurable deep? Who can at once make all the different heavens to roll and warm with ethereal fires all the fruitful earths, or be present in all places at all times? (H.A.J. Munro's translation)]

quis regere immensi summam, quis habere profundi
indu manu validas potis est moderanter habenas,
quis pariter caelos omnis convertere et omnis
ignibus aetheriis terras suffire feracis,
omnibus inve locis esse omni tempore praesto?

If Tully[1] esteemed this reasoning so natural as to put it into
the mouth of his Epicurean:

Quibus enim oculis animi intueri potuit vester Plato fabri-
cam illam tanti operis, qua construi a deo atque aedificari
mundum facit? quae molitio, quae ferramenta, qui vectes,
quae machinae, qui ministri tanti muneris fuerunt? quem
ad modum autem oboedire et parere voluntati architecti
aër ignis aqua terra potuerunt?

If this argument, I say, had any force in former ages, how
much greater must it have at present when the bounds of
nature are so infinitely enlarged and such a magnificent scene
is opened to us? It is still more unreasonable to form our idea
of so unlimited a cause from our experience of the narrow
productions of human design and invention.

The discoveries by microscopes, as they open a new
universe in miniature, are still objections according to you,
arguments according to me. The further we push our researches of this kind, we are still led to infer the universal
cause of all to be vastly different from mankind, or from any
object of human experience and observation.

And what say you to the discoveries in anatomy, chemistry,
botany? . . . These surely are no objections, replied
CLEANTHES; they only discover new instances of art and contrivance. It is still the image of mind reflected on us from
innumerable objects. Add a mind *like the human,* said PHILO.

[1] *De nat. Deor.,* lib. i. [For with what eyes of the mind was your
Plato able to see that workhouse of such stupendous toil, in which
he makes the world to be modeled and built by God? What
materials, what tools, what bars, what machines, what servants
were employed in so vast a work? How could the air, fire, water,
and earth pay obedience and submit to the will of the architect?
(C.D. Yonge's translation)]

I know of no other, replied CLEANTHES. And the liker the better, insisted PHILO. To be sure, said CLEANTHES.

Now, Cleanthes, said PHILO, with an air of alacrity and triumph, mark the consequences. *First*, by this method of reasoning you renounce all claim to infinity in any of the attributes of the Deity. For as the cause ought only to be proportioned to the effect, and the effect, so far as it falls under our cognizance, is not infinite, what pretensions have we, upon your suppositions, to ascribe that attribute to the divine Being? You will still insist that, by removing him so much from all similarity to human creatures, we give in to the most arbitrary hypothesis, and at the same time weaken all proofs of his existence.

Secondly, you have no reason, on your theory, for ascribing perfection to the Deity, even in his finite capacity, or for supposing him free from every error, mistake, or incoherence in his undertakings. There are many inexplicable difficulties in the works of nature which, if we allow a perfect author to be proved *a priori*, are easily solved, and become only seeming difficulties from the narrow capacity of man, who cannot trace infinite relations. But according to your method of reasoning, these difficulties become all real, and perhaps will be insisted on as new instances of likeness to human art and contrivance. At least you must acknowledge that it is impossible for us to tell, from our limited views, whether this system contains any great faults or deserves any considerable praise if compared to other possible and even real systems. Could a peasant, if the *Aeneid* were read to him, pronounce that poem to be absolutely faultless, or even assign to it its proper rank among the productions of human wit, he who had never seen any other production?

But were this world ever so perfect a production, it must still remain uncertain whether all the excellences of the work can justly be ascribed to the workman. If we survey a ship, what an exalted idea must we form of the ingenuity of the carpenter who framed so complicated, useful, and beautiful a machine? And what surprise must we feel when we find him a stupid mechanic who imitated others, and copied an art which, through a long succession of ages, after multiplied trials, mistakes, corrections, deliberations, and controversies, had been gradually improving? Many worlds might have been botched and bungled, throughout an eternity, ere this system was struck out; much labor lost, many fruitless trials made, and a slow but continued improvement carried on during infinite ages in the art of world-making. In such subjects, who can determine where the truth, nay, who can conjecture where the probability lies, amidst a great number of hypotheses which may be proposed, and a still greater which may be imagined?

And what shadow of an argument, continued PHILO, can you produce from your hypothesis to prove the unity of the Deity? A great number of men join in building a house or ship, in rearing a city, in framing a commonwealth; why may not several deities combine in contriving and framing a world? This is only so much greater similarity to human affairs. By sharing the work among several, we may so much further limit the attributes of each, and get rid of that extensive power and knowledge which must be supposed in one deity and which, according to you, can only serve to weaken the proof of his existence. And if such foolish, such vicious creatures as man can yet often unite in framing and executing one plan, how much more those deities or demons, whom we may suppose several degrees more perfect?

To multiply causes without necessity is indeed contrary to true philosophy, but this principle applies not to the present case. Were one deity antecedently proved by your theory, who were possessed of every attribute requisite to the production of the universe, it would be needless, I own (though not absurd), to suppose any other deity existent. But while it is still a question whether all these attributes are united in one subject or dispersed among several independent beings, by what phenomena in nature can we pretend to decide the controversy? Where we see a body raised in a scale, we are sure that there is in the opposite scale, however concealed from sight, some counterpoising weight equal to it; but it is still allowed to doubt whether that weight be an aggregate of several distinct bodies or one uniform united mass. And if the weight requisite very much exceeds anything which we have ever seen conjoined in any single body, the former supposition becomes still more probable and natural. An intelligent being of such vast power and capacity as is necessary to produce the universe, or, to speak in the language of ancient philosophy, so prodigious an animal, exceeds all analogy and even comprehension.

But further, Cleanthes, men are mortal, and renew their species by generation, and this is common to all living creatures. The two great sexes of male and female, says Milton, animate the world. Why must this circumstance, so universal, so essential, be excluded from those numerous and limited deities? Behold, then, the theogeny of ancient times brought back upon us.

And why not become a perfect anthropomorphite? Why not assert the deity or deities to be corporeal, and to have eyes, a nose, mouth, ears, etc.? Epicurus maintained that no man had ever seen reason but in a human figure, therefore the gods must have a human figure. And this argument, which is deservedly so much ridiculed by Cicero, becomes, according to you, solid and philosophical.

In a word, Cleanthes, a man who follows your hypothesis is able, perhaps, to assert or conjecture that the universe sometime arose from something like design, but beyond that position he cannot ascertain one single circumstance, and is left afterwards to fix every point of his theology by the utmost license of fancy and hypothesis. This world, for aught he knows, is very faulty and imperfect, compared to a superior standard, and was only the first rude essay of some infant deity who afterwards abandoned it, ashamed of his lame performance. It is the work only of some dependent, inferior deity, and is the object of derision to his superiors. It is the production of old age and dotage in some superannuated deity, and ever since his death has run on at adventures, from the first impulse and active force which it received from him. You justly give signs of horror, Demea, at these strange suppositions, but these, and a thousand more of the same kind, are Cleanthes' suppositions, not mine. From the moment the attributes of the Deity are supposed finite, all these have place. And I cannot, for my part, think that so wild and unsettled a system of theology is, in any respect, preferable to none at all.

These suppositions I absolutely disown, cried CLEANTHES;

they strike me, however, with no horror, especially when proposed in that rambling way in which they drop from you. On the contrary, they give me pleasure when I see that, by the utmost indulgence of your imagination, you never get rid of the hypothesis of design in the universe, but are obliged at every turn to have recourse to it. To this concession I adhere steadily, and this I regard as a sufficient foundation for religion.

Part VI.

IT MUST BE a slight fabric indeed, said DEMEA, which can be erected on so tottering a foundation. While we are uncertain whether there is one deity or many, whether the deity or deities to whom we owe our existence be perfect or imperfect, subordinate or supreme, dead or alive, what trust or confidence can we repose in them? What devotion or worship address to them? What veneration or obedience pay them? To all the purposes of life the theory of religion becomes altogether useless, and even with regard to speculative consequences its uncertainty, according to you, must render it totally precarious and unsatisfactory.

To render it still more unsatisfactory, said PHILO, there occurs to me another hypothesis which must acquire an air of probability from the method of reasoning so much insisted on by Cleanthes. That like effects arise from like causes: this principle he supposes the foundation of all religion. But there is another principle of the same kind, no less certain and derived from the same source of experience, that where several known circumstances are observed to be similar, the unknown will also be found similar. Thus, if we see the limbs of a human body, we conclude that it is also attended with a human head, though hid from us. Thus, if we see, through a chink in a wall, a small part of the sun, we conclude that were the wall removed we should see the whole body. In short, this method of reasoning is so obvious and familiar that no scruple can ever be made with regard to its solidity.

Now if we survey the universe, so far as it falls under our knowledge, it bears a great resemblance to an animal or organized body, and seems actuated with a like principle of life and motion. A continual circulation of matter in it produces no disorder, a continual waste in every part is incessantly repaired, the closest sympathy is perceived throughout the entire system, and each part or member, in performing its proper offices, operates both to its own preservation and to that of the whole. The world therefore, I infer, is an animal, and the Deity is the *soul* of the world, actuating it, and actuated by it.

You have too much learning, Cleanthes, to be at all surprised at this opinion, which, you know, was maintained by almost all the theists of antiquity, and chiefly prevails in their discourses and reasonings. For though sometimes the ancient philosophers reason from final causes, as if they thought the world the workmanship of God, yet it appears rather their favorite notion to consider it as his body, whose organization renders it subservient to him. And it must be confessed that, as the universe resembles more a human body than it does the works of human art and contrivance, if our limited analogy could ever, with any propriety, be extended to the whole of nature, the inference seems juster in favor of the ancient than the modern theory.

There are many other advantages, too, in the former theory which recommended it to the ancient theologians. Nothing more repugnant to all their notions, because nothing more repugnant to common experience, than mind without body, a mere spiritual substance which fell not under their senses nor comprehension, and of which they had not observed one single instance throughout all nature. Mind and body they knew because they felt both; an order, arrangement, organization, or internal machinery in both they likewise knew, after the same manner, and it could not but seem reasonable to transfer this experience to the universe, and to suppose the divine mind and body to be also coeval and to have, both of them, order and arrangement naturally inherent in them and inseparable from them.

Here, therefore, is a new species of *anthropomorphism,* Cleanthes, on which you may deliberate, and a theory which seems not liable to any considerable difficulties. You are too much superior, surely, to *systematical prejudices* to find any more difficulty in supposing an animal body to be, originally, of itself or from unknown causes, possessed of order and organization, than in supposing a similar order to belong to mind. But the *vulgar prejudice* that body and mind ought always to accompany each other ought not, one should think, to be entirely neglected, since it is founded on *vulgar experience*, the only guide which you profess to follow in all these theological inquiries. And if you assert that our limited experience is an unequal standard by which to judge of the unlimited extent of nature, you entirely abandon your own hypothesis, and must thenceforward adopt our mysticism, as you call it, and admit of the absolute incomprehensibility of the Divine Nature.

This theory, I own, replied CLEANTHES, has never before occurred to me, though a pretty natural one; and I cannot readily, upon so short an examination and reflection, deliver any opinion with regard to it. You are very scrupulous indeed, said PHILO; were I to examine any system of yours, I should not have acted with half that caution and reserve in starting objections and difficulties to it. However, if anything occur to you, you will oblige us by proposing it.

Why then, replied CLEANTHES, it seems to me that though the world does, in many circumstances, resemble an animal body, yet is the analogy also defective in many circumstances the most material: no organs of sense, no seat of thought or reason, no one precise origin of motion and action. In short, it seems to bear a stronger resemblance to a vegetable than to an animal, and your inference would be so far inconclusive in favor of the soul of the world.

But in the next place, your theory seems to imply the eternity of the world, and that is a principle which, I think, can be refuted by the strongest reasons and probabilities. I shall suggest an argument to this purpose which, I believe, has not been insisted on by any writer. Those who reason from the late origin of arts and sciences, though their inference wants not force, may perhaps be refuted by considerations derived from the nature of human society, which is in continual revolution between ignorance and knowledge, liberty and slavery, riches and poverty; so that it is impossible for us, from our limited experience, to foretell with assurance what events may or may not be expected. Ancient learning and history seem to have been in great danger of entirely perishing after the inundation of the barbarous nations, and had these convulsions continued a little longer or been a little more violent, we should not probably have now known what passed in the world a few centuries before us. Nay, were it not for the superstition of the Popes, who preserved a little jargon of Latin in order to support the appearance of an ancient and universal church, that tongue must have been utterly lost; in which case the Western world, being totally barbarous, would not have been in a fit disposition for receiving the Greek language and learning, which was conveyed to them after the sacking of Constantinople. When learning and books had been extinguished, even the mechanical arts would have fallen considerably to decay, and it is easily imagined that fable or tradition might ascribe to them a much later origin than the true one. This vulgar argument, therefore, against the eternity of the world seems a little precarious.

But here appears to be the foundation of a better argument. Lucullus was the first that brought cherry trees from Asia to Europe, though that tree thrives so well in many European climates that it grows in the woods without any culture. Is it possible that, throughout a whole eternity, no European had ever passed into Asia and thought of transplanting so delicious a fruit into his own country? Or if the tree was once transplanted and propagated, how could it ever afterwards perish? Empires may rise and fall, liberty and slavery succeed alternately, ignorance and knowledge give place to each other, but the cherry tree will still remain in the woods of Greece, Spain, and Italy, and will never be affected by the revolutions of human society.

It is not two thousand years since vines were transplanted into France, though there is no climate in the world more favorable to them. It is not three centuries since horses, cows, sheep, swine, dogs, corn, were known in America. Is it possible that during the revolutions of a whole eternity there never arose a Columbus who might open the communication between Europe and that continent? We may as well imagine that all men would wear stockings for ten thousand years and never have the sense to think of garters to tie them. All these seem convincing proofs of the youth or rather infancy of the world, as being founded on the operation of principles more constant and steady than those by which human society is governed and directed. Nothing less than a total convulsion of the elements will ever destroy all the European animals and vegetables which are now to be found in the Western world.

And what argument have you against such convulsions, replied PHILO? Strong and almost incontestable proofs may be traced over the whole earth that every part of this globe has continued for many ages entirely covered with water. And though order were supposed inseparable from matter and inherent in it, yet may matter be susceptible of many and great revolutions, through the endless periods of eternal duration. The incessant changes to which every part of it is subject seem to intimate some such general transformations; though at the same time it is observable that all the changes and corruptions of which we have ever had experience are but passages from one state of order to another; nor can matter ever rest in total deformity and confusion. What we see in the parts, we may infer in the whole; at least that is the method of reasoning on which you rest your whole theory. And were I obliged to defend any particular system of this nature (which I never willingly should do), I esteem none more plausible than that which ascribes an eternal inherent principle of order to the world, though attended with great and continual revolutions and alterations. This at once solves all difficulties; and if the solution, by being so general, is not entirely complete and satisfactory, it is at least a theory that we must sooner or later have recourse to, whatever system we embrace. How could things have been as they are, were there not an original inherent principle of order somewhere, in thought or in matter? And it is very indifferent to which of these we give the preference. Chance has no place on any hypothesis, skeptical or religious. Everything is surely governed by steady, inviolable laws. And were the inmost essence of things laid open to us, we should then discover a scene of which, at present, we can have no idea. Instead of admiring the order of natural beings, we should clearly see that it was absolutely impossible for them, in the smallest article, ever to admit of any other disposition.

Were anyone inclined to revive the ancient pagan theology which maintained, as we learn from Hesiod, that this globe was governed by 30,000 deities, who arose from the unknown powers of nature, you would naturally object, Cleanthes, that nothing is gained by this hypothesis, and that it is as easy to suppose all men and animals, beings more numerous but less perfect, to have sprung immediately from a like origin. Push the same inference a step further and you will find a numerous society of deities as explicable as one universal deity who possesses within himself the powers and perfections of the whole society. All these systems, then, of skepticism, polytheism, and theism you must allow, on your principles, to be on a like footing, and that no one of them has any advantage over the others. You may thence learn the fallacy of your principles.

Part VII.

BUT HERE, continued PHILO, in examining the ancient system of the soul of the world, there strikes me, all on a sudden, a new idea which, if just, must go near to subvert all your reasoning, and destroy even your first inferences on which you repose such confidence. If the universe bears a greater likeness to animal bodies and to vegetables than to the works of human art, it is more probable that its cause resembles the cause of the former than that of the latter, and its origin ought rather to be ascribed to generation or vegetation than to reason or design. Your conclusion, even according to your own principles, is therefore lame and defective.

Pray open up this argument a little further, said DEMEA, for I do not rightly apprehend it in that concise manner in which you have expressed it.

Our friend Cleanthes, replied PHILO, as you have heard, asserts that since no question of fact can be proved otherwise than by experience, the existence of a Deity admits not of proof from any other medium. The world, says he, resembles the works of human contrivance; therefore its cause must also resemble that of the other. Here we may remark that the operation of one very small part of nature, to wit, man, upon another very small part, to wit, that inanimate matter lying within his reach, is the rule by which Cleanthes judges of the origin of the whole; and he measures objects, so widely disproportioned by the same individual standard. But to waive all objections drawn from this topic, I affirm that there are other parts of the universe (besides the machines of human invention) which bear still a greater resemblance to the fabric of the world, and which therefore afford a better conjecture concerning the universal origin of this system. These parts are animals and vegetables. The world plainly resembles more an animal or a vegetable than it does a watch or a knitting-loom. Its cause, therefore, it is more probable, resembles the cause of the former. The cause of the former is generation or vegetation. The cause, therefore, of the world we may infer to be something similar or analogous to generation or vegetation.

But how is it conceivable, said DEMEA, that the world can arise from anything similar to vegetation or generation?

Very easily, replied PHILO. In like manner as a tree sheds its seed into the neighboring fields and produces other trees, so the great vegetable, the world, or this planetary system, produces within itself certain seeds which, being scattered into the surrounding chaos, vegetate into new worlds. A comet, for instance, is the seed of a world, and after it has been fully ripened by passing from sun to sun and star to star, it is at last tossed into the unformed elements which everywhere surround this universe, and immediately sprouts up into a new system.

Or if, for the sake of variety (for I see no other advantage), we should suppose this world to be an animal, a comet is the egg of this animal, and in like manner as an ostrich lays its egg in the sand, which, without any further care, hatches the egg and produces a new animal, so . . . I understand you, says DEMEA. But what wild, arbitrary suppositions are these? What *data* have you for such extraordinary conclusions? And is the slight, imaginary resemblance of the world to a vegetable or an animal sufficient to establish the same inference with regard to both? Objects which are in general so widely different—ought they to be a standard for each other?

Right, cries PHILO. This is the topic on which I have all

along insisted. I have still asserted that we have no *data* to establish any system of cosmogony. Our experience, so imperfect in itself and so limited both in extent and duration, can afford us no probable conjecture concerning the whole of things. But if we must needs fix on some hypothesis, by what rule, pray, ought we to determine our choice? Is there any other rule that the greater similarity of the objects compared? And does not a plant or an animal, which springs from vegetation or generation, bear a stronger resemblance to the world than does any artificial machine, which arises from reason and design?

But what is this vegetation and generation of which you talk, said DEMEA? Can you explain their operations, and anatomize that fine internal structure on which they depend?

As much, at least, replied PHILO, as Cleanthes can explain the operations of reason, or anatomize that internal structure on which *it* depends. But without any such elaborate disquisitions, when I see an animal, I infer that it sprang from generation; and that with as great certainty as you conclude a house to have been reared by design. These words, *generation, reason,* mark only certain powers and energies in nature whose effects are known, but whose essence is incomprehensible; and one of these principles, more than the other, has no privilege for being made a standard to the whole of nature.

In reality, Demea, it may reasonably be expected that the larger the views are which we take of things, the better will they conduct us in our conclusions concerning such extraordinary and such magnificent subjects. In this little corner of the world alone, there are four principles, *reason, instinct, generation, vegetation,* which are similar to each other and are the causes of similar effects. What a number of other principles may we naturally suppose in the immense extent and variety of the universe, could we travel from planet to planet and from system to system, in order to examine each part of this mighty fabric? Any one of these four principles above mentioned (and a hundred others which lie open to our conjecture) may afford us a theory by which to judge of the origin of the world; and it is a palpable and egregious partiality to confine our view entirely to that principle by which our own minds operate. Were this principle more intelligible on that account, such a partiality might be somewhat excusable. But reason, in its internal fabric and structure, is really as little known to us as instinct or vegetation; and perhaps even that vague, undeterminate word *nature*, to which the vulgar refer everything, is not at the bottom more inexplicable. The effects of these principles are all known to us from experience, but the principles themselves and their manner of operation are totally unknown; nor is it less intelligible or less conformable to experience to say that the world arose by vegetation from a seed shed by another world, than to say that it arose from a divine reason or contrivance, according to the sense in which Cleanthes understands it.

But methinks, said DEMEA, if the world had a vegetative quality and could sow the seeds of new worlds into the infinite chaos, this power would be still an additional argument for design in its author. For whence could arise so wonderful a faculty but from design? Or how can order spring from anything which perceives not that order which it bestows?

You need only look around you, replied PHILO, to satisfy yourself with regard to this question. A tree bestows order and organization on that tree which springs from it, without knowing the order; an animal in the same manner on its offspring; a bird on its nest; and instances of this kind are even more frequent in the world than those of order which arise from reason and contrivance. To say that all this order in animals and vegetables proceeds ultimately from design is begging the question; nor can that great point be ascertained otherwise than by proving, *a priori*, both that order is, from its nature, inseparably attached to thought, and that it can never of itself or from original unknown principles belong to matter.

But further, Demea, this objection which you urge can never be made use of by Cleanthes, without renouncing a defense which he has already made against one of my objections. When I inquired concerning the cause of that supreme reason and intelligence into which he resolves everything, he told me that the impossibility of satisfying such inquiries could never be admitted as an objection in any species of philosophy. *We must stop somewhere*, says he, *nor is it ever within the reach of human capacity to explain ultimate causes or*

*show the last connections of any objects. It is sufficient if the
steps, so far as we go, are supported by experience and observation.* Now that vegetation and generation, as well as
reason, are experienced to be principles of order in nature is
undeniable. If I rest my system of cosmogony on the former,
preferably to the latter, it is at my choice. The matter seems
entirely arbitrary. And when Cleanthes asks me what is the
cause of my great vegetative or generative faculty, I am
equally entitled to ask him the cause of his great reasoning
principle. These questions we have agreed to forbear on both
sides; and it is chiefly his interest on the present occasion to
stick to this agreement. Judging by our limited and imperfect
experience, generation has some privileges above reason. For
we see every day the latter arise from the former, never the
former from the latter.

Compare, I beseech you, the consequences on both sides.
The world, say I, resembles an animal; therefore it is an
animal; therefore it arose from generation. The steps, I confess, are wide, yet there is some small appearance of analogy
in each step. The world, says Cleanthes, resembles a machine;
therefore it is a machine; therefore it arose from design. The
steps here are equally wide, and the analogy less striking.
And if he pretends to carry on *my* hypothesis a step further,
and to infer design or reason from the great principle of
generation on which I insist, I may, with better authority,
use the same freedom to push further *his* hypothesis, and
infer a divine generation or theogony from his principle of
reason. I have at least some faint shadow of experience,
which is the utmost that can ever be attained in the present
subject. Reason, in innumerable instances, is observed to arise
from the principle of generation, and never to arise from any
other principle.

Hesiod and all the ancient mythologists were so struck with
this analogy that they universally explained the origin of
nature from an animal birth, and copulation. Plato too, so far
as he is intelligible, seems to have adopted some such notion
in his *Timaeus*.

The Brahmins assert that the world arose from an infinite
spider, who spun this whole complicated mass from his
bowels, and annihilates afterwards the whole or any part of

it, by absorbing it again and resolving it into his own essence. Here is a species of cosmogony which appears to us ridiculous because a spider is a little contemptible animal whose operations we are never likely to take for a model of the whole universe. But still, here is a new species of analogy, even in our globe. And were there a planet wholly inhabited by spiders (which is very possible), this inference would there appear as natural and irrefragable as that which in our planet ascribes the origin of all things to design and intelligence, as explained by Cleanthes. Why an orderly system may not be spun from the belly as well as from the brain, it will be difficult for him to give a satisfactory reason.

I must confess, Philo, replied CLEANTHES, that of all men living, the task which you have undertaken, of raising doubts and objections, suits you best, and seems, in a manner, natural and unavoidable to you. So great is your fertility of invention that I am not ashamed to acknowledge myself unable, on a sudden, to solve regularly such out-of-the-way difficulties as you incessantly start upon me, though I clearly see, in general, their fallacy and error. And I question not but you are yourself, at present, in the same case, and have not the solution so ready as the objection, while you must be sensible that common sense and reason are entirely against you, and that such whimsies as you have delivered may puzzle but never can convince us.

Part VIII.

WHAT YOU ASCRIBE to the fertilty of my invention, replied PHILO, is entirely owing to the nature of the subject. In subjects adapted to the narrow compass of human reason there is commonly but one determination which carries probability or conviction with it; and to a man of sound judgment all other suppositions but that one appear entirely absurd and chimerical. But in such questions as the present, a hundred contradictory views may preserve a kind of imperfect analogy, and invention has here full scope to exert itself. Without any great effort of thought, I believe that I could, in an instant, propose other systems of cosmogony which would have some faint appearance of truth, though it is a thousand, a million to one if either yours or any one of mine be the true system.

For instance, what if I should revive the old Epicurean hypothesis? This is commonly, and I believe justly, esteemed the most absurd system that has yet been proposed; yet I know not whether, with a few alterations, it might not be brought to bear a faint appearance of probability. Instead of supposing matter infinite, as Epicurus did, let us suppose it finite. A finite number of particles is only susceptible of finite transposition; and it must happen, in an eternal duration, that every possible order or position must be tried an infinite number of times. This world, therefore, with all its events, even the most minute, has before been produced and destroyed, and will again be produced and destroyed, without any bounds and limitations. No one who has a conception of the powers of infinite, in comparison of finite, will ever scruple this determination.

But this supposes, said DEMEA, that matter can acquire motion without any voluntary agent or first mover.

And where is the difficulty, replied PHILO, of that supposition? Every event, before experience, is equally difficult and incomprehensible, and every event, after experience, is equally easy and intelligible. Motion in many instances, from gravity, from elasticity, from electricity, begins in matter, without any known voluntary agent; and to suppose always, in these cases, an unknown voluntary agent is mere hypothesis, and hypothesis attended with no advantages. The beginning of motion in matter itself is as conceivable *a priori* as its communication from mind and intelligence.

Besides, why may not motion have been propagated by impulse through all eternity, and the same stock of it, or nearly the same, be still upheld in the universe? As much as is lost by the composition of motion, as much is gained by its resolution. And whatever the causes are, the fact is certain that matter is and always has been in continual agitation, as far as human experience or tradition reaches. There is not probably, at present, in the whole universe, one particle of matter at absolute rest.

And this very consideration too, continued PHILO, which we have stumbled on in the course of the argument, suggests a new hypothesis of cosmogony that is not absolutely absurd and improbable. Is there a system, an order, an economy of things, by which matter can preserve that perpetual agitation which seems essential to it, and yet maintain a constancy in the forms which it produces? There certainly is such an economy, for this is actually the case with the present world. The continual motion of matter, therefore, in less than infinite transpositions, must produce this economy or order, and by its very nature that order, when once established, supports itself for many ages, if not to eternity. But wherever matter is so poised, arranged, and adjusted as to continue in perpetual motion, and yet preserve a constancy in the forms, its situation must, of necessity, have all the same appearance of art and contrivance which we observe at present. All the parts of each form must have a relation to each other and to the whole; and the whole itself must have a relation to the other parts of the universe, to the element in which the form subsists, to the materials with which it repairs its waste and decay, and to every other form which is hostile or friendly. A defect in any of these particulars destroys the form, and the matter of which it is composed is again set loose, and is thrown into irregular motions and fermentations till it unite itself to some other regular form. If no such form be prepared to receive it, and if there be a great quantity of this corrupted matter in the universe, the universe itself is entirely disordered, whether it be the feeble embryo of a world in its first beginnings that is thus destroyed or the rotten carcase of one languishing in old age and infirmity. In either case, a chaos ensues, till finite though innumerable revolutions produce at last some forms whose parts and organs are so adjusted as to support the forms amidst a continued succession of matter.

Suppose (for we shall endeavor to vary the expression) that matter were thrown into any position by a blind, unguided force; it is evident that this first position must in all probability be the most confused and most disorderly imaginable, without any resemblance to those works of human contrivance which, along with a symmetry of parts, discover an adjustment of means to ends and a tendency to self-preservation. If the actuating force cease after this operation, matter must remain forever in disorder and continue an immense chaos, without any proportion or activity. But suppose that the actuating force, whatever it be, still continues in matter, this first position will immediately give place to a second, which will likewise in all probability be as disorderly as the first, and so on through many successions of changes and revolutions. No particular order or position ever continues a moment unaltered. The original force, still remaining in activity, gives a perpetual restlessness to matter. Every possible situation is produced, and instantly destroyed. If a glimpse or dawn of order appears for a moment, it is instantly hurried away and confounded by that never-ceasing force which actuates every part of matter.

Thus the universe goes on for many ages in a continued succession of chaos and disorder. But is it not possible that it may settle at last, so as not to lose its motion and active force (for that we have supposed inherent in it), yet so as to preserve a uniformity of appearance amidst the continual motion and fluctuation of its parts? This we find to be the case with the universe at present. Every individual is perpetually changing, and every part of every individual; and yet the whole remains, in appearance, the same. May we not hope for such a position, or rather be assured of it from the eternal revolutions of unguided matter; and may not this account for all the appearing wisdom and contrivance which is in the universe? Let us contemplate the subject a little, and we shall find that this adjustment, if attained by matter, of a seeming stability in the forms, with a real and perpetual revolution or motion of parts, affords a plausible, if not a true solution of the difficulty.

It is in vain, therefore, to insist upon the uses of the parts in animals or vegetables, and their curious adjustment to each other. I would fain know how an animal could subsist unless its parts were so adjusted? Do we not find that it immediately perishes whenever this adjustment ceases, and that its matter corrupting tries some new form? It happens, indeed, that the parts of the world are so well adjusted that some regular form immediately lays claim to this corrupted matter, and if it were not so, could the world subsist? Must it not dissolve as well as the animal, and pass through new positions and situations, till in a great but finite succession it fall at last into the present or some such order?

It is well, replied CLEANTHES, you told us that this hypothesis was suggested on a sudden, in the course of the argument. Had you had leisure to examine it, you would soon have perceived the insuperable objections to which it is exposed. No form, you say, can subsist unless it possess those powers and organs requisite for its subsistence; some new order or economy must be tried, and so on, without intermission, till at last some order which can support and maintain itself is fallen upon. But according to this hypothesis, whence arise the many conveniences and advantages which men and all animals possess? Two eyes, two ears, are not absolutely necessary for the subsistence of the species. [The] human race might have been propagated and preserved without horses, dogs, cows, sheep, and those innumerable fruits and products which serve to our satisfaction and enjoyment. If no camels had been created for the use of man in the sandy deserts of Africa and Arabia, would the world have been dissolved? If no loadstone had been framed to give that wonderful and useful direction to the needle, would human society and the human kind have been immediately extinguished? Though the maxims of nature be in general very frugal, yet instances of this kind are far from being rare, and any one of them is a sufficient proof of design, and of a benevolent design, which gave rise to the order and arrangement of the universe.

At least, you may safely infer, said PHILO, that the foregoing hypothesis is so far incomplete and imperfect, which I shall not scruple to allow. But can we ever reasonably expect greater success in any attempts of this nature? Or can we ever hope to erect a system of cosmogony that will be liable to no exceptions, and will contain no circumstance repugnant to our limited and imperfect experience of the analogy of nature? Your theory itself cannot surely pretend to any such advantage, even though you have run into *anthropomorphism*, the better to preserve a conformity to common experience. Let us once more put it to trial. In all instances which we have ever seen, ideas are copied from real objects, and are ectypal, not archetypal, to express myself in learned terms.

You reverse this order and give thought the precedence. In all instances which we have ever seen, thought has no influence upon matter, except where that matter is so conjoined with it as to have an equal reciprocal influence upon it. No animal can move immediately anything but the members of its own body, and indeed the equality of action and reaction seems to be a universal law of nature. But your theory implies a contradiction to this experience. These instances, with many more which it were easy to collect (particularly the supposition of a mind or system of thought that is eternal or, in other words, an animal ingenerable and immortal); these instances, I say, may teach all of us sobriety in condemning each other, and let us see that as no system of this kind ought ever to be received from a slight analogy, so neither ought any to be rejected on account of a small incongruity. For that is an inconvenience from which we can justly pronounce no one to be exempted.

All religious systems, it is confessed, are subject to great and insuperable difficulties. Each disputant triumphs in his turn, while he carries on an offensive war and exposes the absurdities, barbarities, and pernicious tenets of his antagonist. But all of them, on the whole, prepare a complete triumph for the *skeptic,* who tells them that no system ought ever to be embraced with regard to such subjects, for this plain reason, that no absurdity ought ever to be assented to with regard to any subject. A total suspense of judgment is here our only reasonable resource. And if every attack, as is commonly observed, and no defense, among theologians, is successful, how complete must be *his* victory who remains always, with all mankind, on the offensive, and has himself no fixed station or abiding city which he is ever, on any occasion, obliged to defend?

Part IX.

BUT IF SO MANY difficulties attend the argument *a posteriori,* said DEMEA, had we not better adhere to that simple and sublime argument *a priori* which, by offering to us infallible demonstration, cuts off at once all doubt and difficulty? By this argument, too, we may prove the *infinity* of the divine attributes, which, I am afraid, can never be ascertained with certainty from any other topic. For how can an effect which either is finite or, for aught we know, may be so, how can such an effect, I say, prove an infinite cause? The unity too of the Divine Nature it is very difficult if not absolutely impossible to deduce merely from contemplating the works of nature; nor will the uniformity alone of the plan, even were it allowed, give us any assurance of that attribute. Whereas the argument *a priori* . . .

You seem to reason, Demea, interposed CLEANTHES, as if those advantages and conveniences in the abstract argument were full proofs of its solidity. But it is first proper, in my opinion, to determine what argument of this nature you choose to insist on; and we shall afterwards, from itself better than from its *useful* consequences, endeavor to determine what value we ought to put upon it.

The argument, replied DEMEA, which I would insist on is the common one. Whatever exists must have a cause or reason of its existence, it being absolutely impossible for anything to produce itself or be the cause of its own existence. In mounting up, therefore, from effects to causes, we must either go on in tracing an infinite succession without any ultimate cause at all, or must at last have recourse to some ultimate cause that is *necessarily* existent. Now that the first supposition is absurd may be thus proved. In the infinite chain or succession of causes and effects, each single effect is determined to exist by the power and efficacy of that cause which immediately preceded; but the whole eternal chain or succession, taken together, is not determined or caused by anything; and yet it is evident that it requires a cause or reason, as much as any particular object which begins to exist in time. The question is still reasonable, why this particular succession of causes existed from eternity, and not any other succession or no succession at all. If there be no necessarily existent being, any supposition which can be formed is equally possible; nor is there any more absurdity in nothing's having existed from eternity than there is in that succession of causes which constitutes the universe. What was it, then, which determined something to exist rather than nothing, and bestowed being on a particular possibility, exclusive of the rest? *External causes* there are supposed to be none. *Chance* is a word without a meaning. Was it *nothing?* But that can never produce anything. We must, therefore, have recourse to a necessarily existent Being, who carries the *reason* of his existence in himself, and who cannot be supposed not to exist without an express contradiction. There is consequently such a Being; that is, there is a Deity.

I shall not leave it to Philo, said CLEANTHES (though I know that starting objections is his chief delight), to point out the weakness of this metaphysical reasoning. It seems to me so obviously ill-grounded, and at the same time of so little consequence to the cause of true piety and religion, that I shall myself venture to show the fallacy of it.

I shall begin with observing that there is an evident absurdity in pretending to demonstrate a matter of fact, or to prove it by any arguments *a priori*. Nothing is demonstrable unless the contrary implies a contradiction. Nothing that is distinctly conceivable implies a contradiction. Whatever we conceive as existent, we can also conceive as nonexistent. There is no being, therefore, whose nonexistence implies a contradiction. Consequently there is no being whose existence is demonstrable. I propose this argument as entirely decisive, and am willing to rest the whole controversy upon it.

It is pretended that the Deity is a necessarily existent being; and this necessity of his existence is attempted to be explained by asserting that if we knew his whole essence or nature we should perceive it to be as impossible for him not to exist as for twice two not to be four. But it is evident that this can never happen, while our faculties remain the same as at present. It will still be possible for us, at any time, to conceive the nonexistence of what we formerly conceived to exist; nor can the mind ever lie under a necessity of supposing any object to remain always in being, in the same manner as we lie under a necessity of always conceiving twice two to be four. The words, therefore, *necessary existence,* have no meaning, or, which is the same thing, none that is consistent.

But further, why may not the material universe be the necessarily existent Being, according to this pretended explication of necessity? We dare not affirm that we know all the qualities of matter; and for aught we can determine, it may contain some qualities which, were they known, would make its nonexistence appear as great a contradiction as that twice two is five. I find only one argument employed to prove that the material world is not the necessarily existent Being; and this argument is derived from the contingency both of the matter and the form of the world. "Any particle of matter," it is said,[1] "may be *conceived* to be annihilated, and any form may be *conceived* to be altered. Such an annihilation or alteration, therefore, is not impossible." But it seems a great partiality not to perceive that the same argument extends equally to the Deity, so far as we have any conception of him, and that the mind can at least imagine him to be nonexistent or his attributes to be altered. It must be some unknown, inconceivable qualities which can make his nonexistence appear impossible or his attributes unalterable; and no reason can be assigned why these qualities may not belong to matter. As they are altogether unknown and inconceivable, they can never be proved incompatible with it.

Add to this that in tracing an eternal succession of objects it seems absurd to inquire for a general cause or first author. How can anything that exists from eternity have a cause, since that relation implies a priority in time and a beginning of existence?

In such a chain too, or succession of objects, each part is caused by that which preceded it, and causes that which succeeds it. Where then is the difficulty? But the *whole*, you say, wants a cause. I answer that the uniting of these parts into a whole, like the uniting of several distinct counties into one kingdom, or several distinct members into one body, is performed merely by an arbitrary act of the mind, and has no influence on the nature of things. Did I show you the particular causes of each individual in a collection of twenty particles of matter, I should think it very unreasonable should you afterwards ask me what was the cause of the whole twenty. This is sufficiently explained in explaining the cause of the parts.

[1] Dr. Clarke.

Though the reasonings which you have urged, Cleanthes, may well excuse me, said PHILO, from starting any further difficulties, yet I cannot forbear insisting still upon another topic. It is observed by arithmeticians that the products of 9 compose always either 9 or some lesser product of 9 if you add together all the characters of which any of the former products is composed. Thus, of 18, 27, 36, which are products of 9, you make 9 by adding 1 to 8, 2 to 7, 3 to 6. Thus, 369 is a product also of 9; and if you add 3, 6, and 9, you make 18, a lesser product of 9.[1] To a superficial observer so wonderful a regularity may be admired as the effect either of chance or design; but a skillful algebraist immediately concludes it to be the work of necessity, and demonstrates that it must forever result from the nature of these numbers. Is it not probable, I ask, that the whole economy of the universe is conducted by a like necessity, though no human algebra can furnish a key which solves the difficulty? And instead of admiring the order of natural beings, may it not happen that, could we penetrate into the intimate nature of bodies, we should clearly see why it was absolutely impossible they could ever admit of any other disposition? So dangerous is it to introduce this idea of necessity into the present question! And so naturally does it afford an inference directly opposite to the religious hypothesis!

But dropping all these abstractions, continued PHILO, and confining ourselves to more familiar topics, I shall venture to add an observation, that the argument *a priori* has seldom been found very convincing, except to people of a metaphysical head who have accustomed themselves to abstract reasoning, and who, finding from mathematics that the understanding frequently leads to truth through obscurity and contrary to first appearances, have transferred the same habit of thinking to subjects where it ought not to have place. Other people, even of good sense and the best inclined to religion, feel always some deficiency in such arguments, though they are not perhaps able to explain distinctly where it lies. A certain proof that men ever did and ever will derive their religion from other sources than from this species of reasoning.

[1] *Republique des Lettres*, Aug. 1685.

Part X.

IT IS MY OPINION, I own, replied DEMEA, that each man feels, in a manner, the truth of religion within his own breast, and from a consciousness of his imbecility and misery, rather than from any reasoning, is led to seek protection from that Being on whom he and all nature is dependent. So anxious or so tedious are even the best scenes of life that futurity is still the object of all our hopes and fears. We incessantly look forward and endeavor by prayers, adoration, and sacrifice to appease those unknown powers whom we find, by experience, so able to afflict and oppress us. Wretched creatures that we are! What resource for us amidst the innumerable ills of life, did not religion suggest some methods of atonement and appease those terrors with which we are incessantly agitated and tormented?

I am indeed persuaded, said PHILO, that the best and indeed the only method of bringing everyone to a due sense of religion is by just representations of the misery and wickedness of men. And for that purpose a talent of eloquence and strong imagery is more requisite than that of reasoning and argument. For is it necessary to prove what everyone feels within himself? It is only necessary to make us feel it, if possible, more intimately and sensibly.

The people, indeed, replied DEMEA, are sufficiently convinced of this great and melancholy truth. The miseries of life, the unhappiness of man, the general corruptions of our nature, the unsatisfactory enjoyment of pleasures, riches, honors, these phrases have become almost proverbial in all languages. And who can doubt of what all men declare from their own immediate feeling and experience?

In this point, said PHILO, the learned are perfectly agreed with the vulgar; and in all letters, *sacred* and *profane*, the topic of human misery has been insisted on with the most pathetic eloquence that sorrow and melancholy could inspire. The poets, who speak from sentiment, without a system, and whose testimony has therefore the more authority, abound in images of this nature. From Homer down to Dr. Young, the whole inspired tribe have ever been sensible that no other representation of things would suit the feeling and observation of each individual.

As to authorities, replied DEMEA, you need not seek them. Look round this library of Cleanthes. I shall venture to affirm that, except authors of particular sciences such as chemistry or botany, who have no occasion to treat of human life, there is scarce one of those innumerable writers from whom the sense of human misery has not, in some passage or other, extorted a complaint and confession of it. At least the chance is entirely on that side, and no one author has ever, so far as I can recollect, been so extravagant as to deny it.

There you must excuse me, said PHILO. Leibniz has denied it, and is perhaps the first[1] who ventured upon so bold and paradoxical an opinion, at least the first who made it essential to his philosophical system.

And by being the first, replied DEMEA, might he not have been sensible of his error? For is this a subject in which philosophers can propose to make discoveries, especially in so late an age? And can any man hope by a simple denial (for the subject scarcely admits of reasoning) to bear down the united testimony of mankind, founded on sense and consciousness?

And why should man, added he, pretend to an exemption from the lot of all other animals? The whole earth, believe me, Philo, is cursed and polluted. A perpetual war is kindled amongst all living creatures. Necessity, hunger, want stimulate the strong and courageous; fear, anxiety, terror agitate the weak and infirm. The first entrance into life gives anguish to the new-born infant and to its wretched parent; weakness, impotence, distress attend each stage of that life, and it is at last finished in agony and horror.

Observe too, says PHILO, the curious artifices of nature in order to embitter the life of every living being. The stronger prey upon the weaker and keep them in perpetual terror and anxiety. The weaker too, in their turn, often prey upon the stronger, and vex and molest them without relaxation. Con-

[1] That sentiment had been maintained by Dr. King and some few others before Leibniz, though by none of so great fame as that German philosopher.

sider that innumerable race of insects, which either are bred on the body of each animal or, flying about, infix their stings in him. These insects have others still less than themselves which torment them. And thus on each hand, before and behind, above and below, every animal is surrounded with enemies which incessantly seek his misery and destruction.

Man alone, said DEMEA, seems to be, in part, an exception to this rule. For by combination in society he can easily master lions, tigers, and bears, whose greater strength and agility naturally enable them to prey upon him.

On the contrary, it is here chiefly, cried PHILO, that the uniform and equal maxims of nature are most apparent. Man, it is true, can, by combination, surmount all his *real* enemies and become master of the whole animal creation; but does he not immediately raise up to himself *imaginary* enemies, the demons of his fancy, who haunt him with superstitious terrors and blast every enjoyment of life? His pleasure, as he imagines, becomes in their eyes a crime; his food and repose give them umbrage and offense; his very sleep and dreams furnish new materials to anxious fear; and even death, his refuge from every other ill, presents only the dread of endless and innumerable woes. Nor does the wolf molest more the timid flock than superstition does the anxious breast of wretched mortals.

Besides, consider, Demea. This very society by which we surmount those wild beasts, our natural enemies, what new enemies does it not raise to us? What woe and misery does it not occasion? Man is the greatest enemy of man. Oppression, injustice, contempt, contumely, violence, sedition, war, calumny, treachery, fraud, by these they mutually torment each other, and they would soon dissolve that society which they had formed were it not for the dread of still greater ills which must attend their separation.

But though these external insults, said DEMEA, from animals, from men, from all the elements, which assault us form a frightful catalogue of woes, they are nothing in comparison of those which arise within ourselves, from the distempered condition of our mind and body. How many lie under the lingering torment of diseases? Hear the pathetic enumeration of the great poet.

Intestine stone and ulcer, colic-pangs,
Demoniac frenzy, moping melancholy,
And moon-struck madness, pining atrophy,
Marasmus, and wide-wasting pestilence.
Dire was the tossing, deep the groans: *Despair*
Tended the sick, busiest from couch to couch.
And over them triumphant *Death* his dart
Shook: but delay'd to strike, though oft invok'd
With vows, as their chief good and final hope.[1]

The disorders of the mind, continued DEMEA, though more secret, are not perhaps less dismal and vexatious. Remorse, shame, anguish, rage, disappointment, anxiety, fear, dejection, despair, who has ever passed through life without cruel inroads from these tormentors? How many have scarcely ever felt any better sensations? Labor and poverty, so abhorred by everyone, are the certain lot of the far greater number, and those few privileged persons who enjoy ease and opulence never reach contentment or true felicity. All the goods of life united would not make a very happy man, but all the ills united would make a wretch indeed; and any one of them almost (and who can be free from every one?), nay often the absence of one good (and who can possess all?) is sufficient to render life ineligible.

Were a stranger to drop on a sudden into this world, I would show him, as a specimen of its ills, a hospital full of diseases, a prison crowded with malefactors and debtors, a field of battle strewed with carcases, a fleet foundering in the ocean, a nation languishing under tyranny, famine, or pestilence. To turn the gay side of life to him and give him a notion of its pleasures, whither should I conduct him? To a ball, to an opera, to court? He might justly think that I was only showing him a diversity of distress and sorrow.

There is no evading such striking instances, said PHILO, but by apologies which still further aggravate the charge. Why have all men, I ask, in all ages, complained incessantly of the miseries of life? . . . They have no just reason, says one; these complaints proceed only from their discontented, re-

[1] [Milton, *Paradise Lost*, Bk. xi.]

pining, anxious disposition. . . . And can there possibly, I reply, be a more certain foundation of misery than such a wretched temper?

But if they were really as unhappy as they pretend, says my antagonist, why do they remain in life? . . .

Not satisfied with life, afraid of death.

This is the secret chain, say I, that holds us. We are terrified, not bribed to the continuance of our existence.

It is only a false delicacy, he may insist, which a few refined spirits indulge, and which has spread these complaints among the whole race of mankind. . . . And what is this delicacy, I ask, which you blame? Is it anything but a greater sensibility to all the pleasures and pains of life? And if the man of a delicate, refined temper, by being so much more alive than the rest of the world, is only so much more unhappy, what judgment must we form in general of human life?

Let men remain at rest, says our adversary, and they will be easy. They are willing artificers of their own misery. . . . No! reply I; an anxious languor follows their repose, disappointment, vexation, trouble, their activity and ambition.

I can observe something like what you mention in some others, replied CLEANTHES, but I confess I feel little or nothing of it in myself, and hope that it is not so common as you represent it.

If you feel not human misery yourself, cried DEMEA, I congratulate you on so happy a singularity. Others, seemingly the most prosperous, have not been ashamed to vent their complaints in the most melancholy strains. Let us attend to the great, the fortunate emperor, Charles V, when, tired with human grandeur, he resigned all his extensive dominions into the hands of his son. In the last harangue which he made on that memorable occasion, he publicly avowed *that the greatest prosperities which he had ever enjoyed had been mixed with so many adversities that he might truly say he had never enjoyed any satisfaction or contentment.* But did the retired life in which he sought for shelter afford him any greater happiness? If we may credit his son's account, his repentance commenced the very day of his resignation.

Cicero's fortune, from small beginnings, rose to the greatest luster and renown; yet what pathetic complaints of the ills of life do his familiar letters, as well as philosophical discourses, contain? And suitably to his own experience, he introduces Cato, the great, the fortunate Cato, protesting in his old age that had he a new life in his offer he would reject the present.

Ask yourself, ask any of your acquaintance, whether they would live over again the last ten or twenty years of their life. No! but the next twenty, they say, will be better:

> And from the dregs of life, hope to receive
> What the first sprightly running could not give.[1]

Thus at last they find (such is the greatness of human misery, it reconciles even contradictions) that they complain at once of the shortness of life and of its vanity and sorrow.

And is it possible, Cleanthes, said PHILO, that after all these reflections, and infinitely more which might be suggested, you can still persevere in your anthropomorphism, and assert the moral attributes of the Deity, his justice, benevolence, mercy, and rectitude, to be of the same nature with these virtues in human creatures? His power, we allow, is infinite; whatever he wills is executed; but neither man nor any other animal is happy; therefore he does not will their happiness. His wisdom is infinite; he is never mistaken in choosing the means to any end; but the course of nature tends not to human or animal felicity; therefore it is not established for that purpose. Through the whole compass of human knowledge there are no inferences more certain and infallible than these. In what respect, then, do his benevolence and mercy resemble the benevolence and mercy of men?

Epicurus' old questions are yet unanswered.

Is he willing to prevent evil, but not able? Then is he impotent. Is he able, but not willing? Then is he malevolent. Is he both able and willing? Whence then is evil?

[1] [Dryden, *Aureng-Zebe*, Act iv.]

You ascribe, Cleanthes (and I believe justly), a purpose and intention to nature. But what, I beseech you, is the object of that curious artifice and machinery which she has displayed in all animals? The preservation alone of individuals, and propagation of the species. It seems enough for her purpose if such a rank be barely upheld in the universe, without any care or concern for the happiness of the members that compose it. No resource for this purpose; no machinery in order merely to give pleasure or ease; no fund of pure joy and contentment; no indulgence without some want or necessity accompanying it. At least, the few phenomena of this nature are overbalanced by opposite phenomena of still greater importance.

Our sense of music, harmony, and indeed beauty of all kinds gives satisfaction, without being absolutely necessary to the preservation and propagation of the species. But what racking pains, on the other hand, arise from gouts, gravels, megrims, toothaches, rheumatisms, where the injury to the animal machinery is either small or incurable? Mirth, laughter, play, frolic seem gratuitous satisfactions which have no further tendency; spleen, melancholy, discontent, superstition are pains of the same nature. How then does the divine benevolence display itself, in the sense of you anthropomorphites? None but we mystics, as you were pleased to call us, can account for this strange mixture of phenomena, by deriving it from attributes infinitely perfect but incomprehensible.

And have you at last, said CLEANTHES smiling, betrayed your intentions, Philo? Your long agreement with Demea did indeed a little surprise me, but I find you were all the while erecting a concealed battery against me. And I must confess that you have now fallen upon a subject worthy of your noble spirit of opposition and controversy. If you can make out the present point, and prove mankind to be unhappy or corrupted, there is an end at once of all religion. For to what purpose establish the natural attributes of the Deity, while the moral are still doubtful and uncertain?

You take umbrage very easily, replied DEMEA, at opinions the most innocent and the most generally received, even amongst the religious and devout themselves; and nothing can be more surprising than to find a topic like this, concerning the wickedness and misery of man, charged with no less than atheism and profaneness. Have not all pious divines and preachers who have indulged their rhetoric on so fertile a subject, have they not easily, I say, given a solution of any difficulties which may attend it? This world is but a point in comparison of the universe; this life but a moment in comparison of eternity. The present evil phenomena, therefore, are rectified in other regions, and in some future period of existence. And the eyes of men, being then opened to larger views of things, see the whole connection of general laws, and trace, with adoration, the benevolence and rectitude of the Deity through all the mazes and intricacies of his providence.

No! replied CLEANTHES, no! These arbitrary suppositions can never be admitted, contrary to matter of fact, visible and uncontroverted. Whence can any cause be known but from its known effects? Whence can any hypothesis be proved but from the apparent phenomena? To establish one hypothesis upon another is building entirely in the air, and the utmost we ever attain by these conjectures and fictions is to ascertain the bare possibility of our opinion; but never can we, upon such terms, establish its reality.

The only method of supporting divine benevolence (and it is what I willingly embrace) is to deny absolutely the misery and wickedness of man. Your representations are exaggerated; your melancholy views mostly fictitious; your inferences contrary to fact and experience. Health is more common than sickness, pleasure than pain, happiness than misery. And for one vexation which we meet with, we attain, upon computation, a hundred enjoyments.

Admitting your position, replied PHILO, which yet is extremely doubtful, you must at the same time allow that, if pain be less frequent than pleasure, it is infinitely more violent and durable. One hour of it is often able to outweigh a day, a week, a month of our common insipid enjoyments; and how many days, weeks, and months are passed by several in the most acute torments? Pleasure, scarcely in one instance, is ever able to reach ecstasy and rapture; and in no one instance can it continue for any time at its highest pitch and altitude. The spirits evaporate, the nerves relax, the fabric is disordered, and the enjoyment quickly degenerates into fatigue and uneasiness. But pain often—good God, how often!—rises to torture and agony; and the longer it continues, it becomes still more genuine agony and torture. Patience is exhausted, courage languishes, melancholy seizes us, and nothing terminates our misery but the removal of its cause, or another event, which is the sole cure of all evil, but which, from our natural folly, we regard with still greater horror and consternation.

But not to insist upon these topics, continued PHILO, though most obvious, certain, and important, I must use the freedom to admonish you, Cleanthes, that you have put the controversy upon a most dangerous issue, and are unawares introducing a total skepticism into the most essential articles of natural and revealed theology. What! no method of fixing a just foundation for religion unless we allow the happiness of human life, and maintain a continued existence even in this world, with all our present pains, infirmities, vexations, and follies, to be eligible and desirable! But this is contrary to everyone's feeling and experience. It is contrary to an authority so established as nothing can subvert. No decisive proofs can ever be produced against this authority; nor is it possible for you to compute, estimate, and compare all the pains and all the pleasures in the lives of all men and of all animals. And thus by your resting the whole system of religion on a point which, from its very nature, must forever be uncertain, you tacitly confess that that system is equally uncertain.

But allowing you what never will be believed, at least, what you never possibly can prove, that animal or at least human happiness in this life exceeds its misery, you have yet done nothing. For this is not, by any means, what we expect from infinite power, infinite wisdom, and infinite goodness. Why is there any misery at all in the world? Not by chance, surely. From some cause then. Is it from the intention of the Deity? But he is perfectly benevolent. Is it contrary to his intention? But he is almighty. Nothing can shake the solidity of this reasoning, so short, so clear, so decisive, except we assert that these subjects exceed all human capacity, and that our common measures of truth and falsehood are not applicable to them, a topic which I have all along insisted on, but which you have from the beginning rejected with scorn and indignation.

But I will be contented to retire still from this entrenchment, for I deny that you can ever force me in it. I will allow that pain or misery in man is *compatible* with infinite power and goodness in the Deity, even in your sense of these attributes. What are you advanced by all these concessions? A mere possible compatibility is not sufficient. You must *prove* these pure, unmixed, and uncontrollable attributes from the present mixed and confused phenomena, and from these alone. A hopeful undertaking! Were the phenomena ever so pure and unmixed, yet, being finite, they would be insufficient for that purpose. How much more, where they are also so jarring and discordant?

Here, Cleanthes, I find myself at ease in my argument. Here I triumph. Formerly, when we argued concerning the natural attributes of intelligence and design, I needed all my skeptical and metaphysical subtlety to elude your grasp. In many views of the universe and of its parts, particularly the latter, the beauty and fitness of final causes strike us with such irresistible force that all objections appear (what I believe they really are) mere cavils and sophisms; nor can we then imagine how it was ever possible for us to repose any weight on them. But there is no view of human life or of the condition of mankind from which, without the greatest violence, we can infer the moral attributes or learn that infinite benevolence, conjoined with infinite power and infinite wisdom, which we must discover by the eyes of faith alone. It is your turn now to tug the laboring oar, and to support your philosophical subtleties against the dictates of plain reason and experience.

Part XI.

I SCRUPLE not to allow, said CLEANTHES, that I have been apt to suspect the frequent repetition of the word *infinite*, which we meet with in all theological writers, to savor more of panegyric than of philosophy, and that any purposes of reasoning, and even of religion, would be better served were we to rest contented with more accurate and more moderate expressions. The terms *admirable, excellent, superlatively great, wise,* and *holy,* these sufficiently fill the imaginations of men; and anything beyond, besides that it leads into absurdities, has no influence on the affections or sentiments. Thus, in the present subject, if we abandon all human analogy, as seems your intention, Demea, I am afraid we abandon all religion and retain no conception of the great object of our adoration. If we preserve human analogy, we must forever find it impossible to reconcile any mixture of evil in the universe with infinite attributes; much less can we ever prove the latter from the former. But supposing the Author of Nature to be finitely perfect, though far exceeding mankind, a satisfactory account may then be given of natural and moral evil, and every untoward phenomenon be explained and adjusted. A less evil may then be chosen in order to avoid a greater; inconveniences be submitted to in order to reach a desirable end; and in a word benevolence, regulated by wisdom and limited by necessity, may produce just such a world as the present. You, Philo, who are so prompt at starting views and reflections and analogies, I would gladly hear at length, without interruption, your opinion of this new theory; and if it deserve our attention, we may afterwards, at more leisure, reduce it into form.

My sentiments, replied PHILO, are not worth being made a mystery of, and therefore, without any ceremony, I shall deliver what occurs to me with regard to the present subject. It must, I think, be allowed that, if a very limited intelligence, whom we shall suppose utterly unacquainted with the universe, were assured that it were the production of a very good, wise, and powerful Being, however finite, he would, from his conjectures, form *beforehand* a different notion of it from what we find it to be by experience; nor would he ever imagine, merely from these attributes of the cause of which he is informed, that the effect could be so full of vice and misery and disorder as it appears in this life. Supposing now that this person were brought into the world, still assured that it was the workmanship of such a sublime and benevolent Being, he might, perhaps, be surprised at the disappointment, but would never retract his former belief, if founded on any very solid argument, since such a limited intelligence must be sensible of his own blindness and ignorance, and must allow that there may be many solutions of those phenomena which will forever escape his comprehension. But supposing, which is the real case with regard to man, that this creature is not antecedently convinced of a supreme intelligence, benevolent and powerful, but is left to gather such a belief from the appearances of things; this entirely alters the case, nor will he ever find any reason for such a conclusion. He may be fully convinced of the narrow limits of his understanding, but this will not help him in forming an inference concerning the goodness of superior powers, since he must form that inference from what he knows, not from what he is ignorant of. The more you exaggerate his weakness and ignorance, the more diffident you render him, and give him the greater suspicion that such subjects are beyond the reach of his faculties. You are obliged, therefore, to reason with him merely from the known phenomena, and to drop every arbitrary supposition or conjecture.

Did I show you a house or palace where there was not one apartment convenient or agreeable, where the windows, doors, fires, passages, stairs, and the whole economy of the building were the source of noise, confusion, fatigue, darkness, and the extremes of heat and cold, you would certainly blame the contrivance without any further examination. The architect would in vain display his subtlety, and prove to you that, if this door or that window were altered, greater ills would ensue. What he says may be strictly true; the alteration of one particular, while the other parts of the building remain, may only augment the inconveniences. But still you would assert in general that, if the architect had had skill and good intentions, he might have formed such a plan of the whole, and might have adjusted the parts in such a manner as would have remedied all or most of these inconveniences. His ignorance, or even your own ignorance of such a plan, will never convince you of the impossibility of it. If you find any inconveniences and deformities in the building, you will always, without entering into any detail, condemn the architect.

In short, I repeat the question. Is the world, considered in general and as it appears to us in this life, different from what a man or such a limited being would, *beforehand*, expect from a very powerful, wise, and benevolent Deity? It must be strange prejudice to assert the contrary. And from thence I conclude that, however consistent the world may be, allowing certain suppositions and conjectures, with the idea of such a Deity, it can never afford us an inference concerning his existence. The consistency is not absolutely denied, only the inference. Conjectures, especially where infinity is excluded from the divine attributes, may perhaps be sufficient to prove a consistency, but can never be foundations for any inference.

There seem to be *four* circumstances on which depend all or the greatest part of the ills that molest sensible creatures; and it is not impossible but all these circumstances may be necessary and unavoidable. We know so little beyond common life, or even of common life, that, with regard to the economy of a universe, there is no conjecture, however wild, which may not be just, nor any one, however plausible, which may not be erroneous. All that belongs to human understanding, in this deep ignorance and obscurity, is to be skeptical or at least cautious, and not to admit of any hypothesis whatever, much less of any which is supported by no appearance of probability. Now this I assert to be the case with regard to all the causes of evil and the circumstances on which it depends. None of them appear to human reason in the least degree necessary or unavoidable, nor can we suppose them such, without the utmost license of imagination.

The *first* circumstance which introduces evil is that contrivance or economy of the animal creation by which pains, as well as pleasures, are employed to excite all creatures to action, and make them vigilant in the great work of self-preservation. Now pleasure alone, in its various degrees, seems to human understanding sufficient for this purpose. All animals might be constantly in a state of enjoyment; but when urged by any of the necessities of nature, such as thirst, hunger, weariness, instead of pain, they might feel a diminution of pleasure, by which they might be prompted to seek that object which is necessary to their subsistence. Men pursue pleasure as eagerly as they avoid pain; at least [they] might have been so constituted. It seems, therefore, plainly possible to carry on the business of life without any pain. Why then is any animal ever rendered susceptible of such a sensation? If animals can be free from it an hour, they might enjoy a perpetual exemption from it, and it required as particular a contrivance of their organs to produce that feeling as to endow them with sight, hearing, or any of the senses. Shall we conjecture that such a contrivance was necessary, without any appearance of reason? And shall we build on that conjecture as on the most certain truth?

But a capacity of pain would not alone produce pain were it not for the *second* circumstance, *viz.*, the conducting of the world by general laws; and this seems nowise necessary to a very perfect Being. It is true, if everything were conducted by particular volitions, the course of nature would be perpetually broken, and no man could employ his reason in the conduct of life. But might not other particular volitions remedy this inconvenience? In short, might not the Deity exterminate all ill, wherever it were to be found, and produce all good, without any preparation or long progress of causes and effects?

Besides, we must consider that, according to the present economy of the world, the course of nature, though supposed exactly regular, yet to us appears not so, and many events are uncertain, and many disappoint our expectations. Health and sickness, calm and tempest, with an infinite number of other accidents whose causes are unknown and variable, have a great influence both on the fortunes of particular persons and on the prosperity of public societies; and indeed all human life, in a manner, depends on such accidents. A being, therefore, who knows the secret springs of the universe might easily, by particular volitions, turn all these accidents to the good of mankind and render the whole world happy, without discovering himself in any operation. A fleet whose purposes were salutary to society might always meet with a fair wind; good princes enjoy sound health and long life; persons born to power and authority be framed with good tempers and virtuous dispositions. A few such events as these, regularly and wisely conducted, would change the face of the world, and yet would no more seem to disturb the course of nature or confound human conduct than the present economy of things, where the causes are secret and variable and compounded. Some small touches given to Caligula's brain in his infancy might have converted him into a Trajan. One wave, a little higher than the rest, by burying Caesar and his fortune in the bottom of the ocean, might have restored liberty to a considerable part of mankind. There may, for aught we know, be good reasons why Providence interposes not in this manner, but they are unknown to us; and though the mere supposition that such reasons exist may be sufficient to *save* the conclusion concerning the divine attributes, yet surely it can never be sufficient to *establish* that conclusion.

If everything in the universe be conducted by general laws, and if animals be rendered susceptible of pain, it scarcely seems possible but some ill must arise in the various shocks of matter and the various concurrence and opposition of general laws. But this ill would be very rare were it not for the *third* circumstance which I proposed to mention, *viz.*, the great frugality with which all powers and faculties are distributed to every particular being. So well adjusted are the organs and capacities of all animals, and so well fitted to their preservation, that, as far as history or tradition reaches, there appears not to be any single species which has yet been extinguished in the universe. Every animal has the requisite endowments, but these endowments are bestowed with so scrupulous an economy that any considerable diminution must entirely destroy the creature. Wherever one power is increased, there is a proportional abatement in the others. Animals which excel in swiftness are commonly defective in force. Those which possess both are either imperfect in some of their senses or are oppressed with the most craving wants. The human species, whose chief excellence is reason and sagacity, is of all others the most necessitous and the most deficient in bodily advantages, without clothes, without arms, without food, without lodging, without any convenience of life, except what they owe to their own skill and industry. In short, nature seems to have formed an exact calculation of the necessities of her creatures, and, like a *rigid master,* has afforded them little more powers or endowments than what are strictly sufficient to supply those necessities. An *indulgent parent* would have bestowed a large stock in order to guard against accidents, and secure the happiness and welfare of the creature in the most unfortunate concurrence of circumstances. Every course of life would not have been so surrounded with precipices that the least departure from the true path, by mistake or necessity, must involve us in misery and ruin. Some reserve, some fund, would have been provided to ensure happiness, nor would the powers and the necessities have been adjusted with so rigid an economy. The Author of Nature is inconceivably powerful; his force is supposed great, if not altogether inexhaustible; nor is there any reason, as far as we can judge, to make him observe this strict frugality in his dealings with his creatures. It would have been better, were his power extremely limited, to have created fewer animals, and to have endowed these with more faculties for their happiness and preservation. A builder is never esteemed prudent who undertakes a plan beyond what his stock will enable him to finish.

In order to cure most of the ills of human life, I require not that man should have the wings of the eagle, the swiftness of the stag, the force of the ox, the arms of the lion, the scales of the crocodile or rhinoceros; much less do I demand the sagacity of an angel or cherubim. I am contented to take an increase in one single power or faculty of his soul. Let him be endowed with a greater propensity to industry and labor, a more vigorous spring and activity of mind, a more constant bent to business and application. Let the whole species possess naturally an equal diligence with that which many individuals are able to attain by habit and reflection, and the most beneficial consequences, without any allay of ill, is the immediate and necessary result of this endowment. Almost all the moral as well as natural evils of human life arise from idleness; and were our species, by the original constitution of their frame, exempt from this vice or infirmity, the perfect cultivation of land, the improvement of arts and manufactures, the exact execution of every office and duty, immediately follow; and men at once may fully reach that state of society which is so imperfectly attained by the best regulated government. But as industry is a power, and the most valu-

able of any, nature seems determined, suitably to her usual
maxims, to bestow it on men with a very sparing hand, and
rather to punish him severely for his deficiency in it than to
reward him for his attainments. She has so contrived his
frame that nothing but the most violent necessity can oblige
him to labor; and she employs all his other wants to overcome, at least in part, the want of diligence, and to endow
him with some share of a faculty of which she has thought
fit naturally to bereave him. Here our demands may be allowed very humble, and therefore the more reasonable. If we
required the endowments of superior penetration and judgment, of a more delicate taste of beauty, of a nicer sensibility
to benevolence and friendship, we might be told that we im-
piously pretend to break the order of nature, that we want to
exalt ourselves into a higher rank of being, that the presents
which we require, not being suitable to our state and condition, would only be pernicious to us. But it is hard, I dare to
repeat it, it is hard that, being placed in a world so full of
wants and necessities, where almost every being and element
is either our foe or refuses its assistance, we should also have
our own temper to struggle with, and should be deprived of
that faculty which can alone fence against these multiplied
evils.

The *fourth* circumstance whence arises the misery and ill
of the universe is the inaccurate workmanship of all the
springs and principles of the great machine of nature. It must
be acknowledged that there are few parts of the universe
which seem not to serve some purpose, and whose removal
would not produce a visible defect and disorder in the whole.
The parts hang all together, nor can one be touched without
affecting the rest, in a greater or less degree. But at the same
time, it must be observed that none of these parts or principles, however useful, are so accurately adjusted as to keep
precisely within those bounds in which their utility consists;
but they are, all of them, apt, on every occasion, to run into
the one extreme or the other. One would imagine that this
grand production had not received the last hand of the maker,
so little finished is every part, and so coarse are the strokes
with which it is executed. Thus the winds are requisite to
convey the vapors along the surface of the globe, and to assist

men in navigation; but how often, rising up to tempests and hurricanes, do they become pernicious? Rains are necessary to nourish all the plants and animals of the earth; but how often are they defective, how often excessive? Heat is requisite to all life and vegetation, but is not always found in the due proportion. On the mixture and secretion of the humors and juices of the body depend the health and prosperity of the animal, but the parts perform not regularly their proper function. What more useful than all the passions of the mind, ambition, vanity, love, anger? But how often do they break their bounds and cause the greatest convulsions in society? There is nothing so advantageous in the universe but what frequently becomes pernicious, by its excess or defect; nor has nature guarded, with the requisite accuracy, against all disorder or confusion. The irregularity is never perhaps so great as to destroy any species, but is often sufficient to involve the individuals in ruin and misery.

On the concurrence, then, of these *four* circumstances does all or the greatest part of natural evil depend. Were all living creatures incapable of pain, or were the world administered by particular volitions, evil never could have found access into the universe; and were animals endowed with a large stock of powers and faculties, beyond what strict necessity requires, or were the several springs and principles of the universe so accurately framed as to preserve always the just temperament and medium, there must have been very little ill in comparison of what we feel at present. What then shall we pronounce on this occasion? Shall we say that these circumstances are not necessary, and that they might easily have been altered in the contrivance of the universe? This decision seems too presumptuous for creatures so blind and ignorant. Let us be more modest in our conclusions. Let us allow that, if the goodness of the Deity (I mean a goodness like the human) could be established on any tolerable reasons *a priori*, these phenomena, however untoward, would not be sufficient to subvert that principle, but might easily, in some unknown manner, be reconcilable to it. But let us still assert that, as this goodness is not antecedently established but must be inferred from the phenomena, there can be no grounds for such an inference while there are so many ills in the universe, and while these ills might so easily have been remedied, as far as human understanding can be allowed to judge on such a subject. I am skeptic enough to allow that the bad appearances, notwithstanding all my reasonings, may be compatible with such attributes as you suppose. But surely they can never prove these attributes. Such a conclusion cannot result from skepticism, but must arise from the phenomena, and from our confidence in the reasonings which we deduce from these phenomena.

Look round this universe. What an immense profusion of beings, animated and organized, sensible and active! You admire this prodigious variety and fecundity. But inspect a little more narrowly these living existences, the only beings worth regarding. How hostile and destructive to each other! How insufficient all of them for their own happiness! How contemptible or odious to the spectator! The whole presents nothing but the idea of a blind nature, impregnated by a great vivifying principle, and pouring forth from her lap, without discernment or parental care, her maimed and abortive children!

Here the Manichaean system occurs as a proper hypothesis to solve the difficulty; and no doubt in some respects it is very specious, and has more probability than the common hypothesis, by giving a plausible account of the strange mixture of good and ill which appears in life. But if we consider, on the other hand, the perfect uniformity and agreement of the parts of the universe, we shall not discover in it any marks of the combat of a malevolent with a benevolent being. There is indeed an opposition of pains and pleasures in the feelings of sensible creatures, but are not all the operations of nature carried on by an opposition of principles, of hot and cold, moist and dry, light and heavy? The true conclusion is that the original source of all things is entirely indifferent to all these principles, and has no more regard to good above ill than to heat above cold, or to drought above moisture, or to light above heavy.

There may *four* hypotheses be framed concerning the first causes of the universe: *that* they are endowed with perfect goodness; *that* they have perfect malice; *that* they are opposite and have both goodness and malice; *that* they have neither goodness nor malice. Mixed phenomena can never prove the two former unmixed principles. And the uniformity and steadiness of general laws seem to oppose the third. The fourth, therefore, seems by far the most probable.

What I have said concerning natural evil will apply to moral with little or no variation, and we have no more reason to infer that the rectitude of the Supreme Being resembles human rectitude than that his benevolence resembles the human. Nay, it will be thought that we have still greater cause to exclude from him moral sentiments, such as we feel them, since moral evil, in the opinion of many, is much more predominant above moral good than natural evil above natural good.

But even though this should not be allowed, and though the virtue which is in mankind should be acknowledged much superior to the vice, yet so long as there is any vice at all in the universe, it will very much puzzle you anthropomorphites how to account for it. You must assign a cause for it without having recourse to the first cause. But as every effect must have a cause, and that cause another, you must either carry on the progression *in infinitum* or rest on that original principle, who is the ultimate cause of all things. . . .

Hold! hold! cried DEMEA. Whither does your imagination hurry you? I joined in alliance with you in order to prove the incomprehensible nature of the Divine Being and refute the principles of Cleanthes, who would measure everything by a human rule and standard. But I now find you running into all the topics of the greatest libertines and infidels, and betraying that holy cause which you seemingly espoused. Are you secretly, then, a more dangerous enemy than Cleanthes himself?

And are you so late in perceiving it, replied CLEANTHES? Believe me, Demea, your friend Philo, from the beginning, has been amusing himself at both our expense; and it must be confessed that the injudicious reasoning of our vulgar theology has given him but too just a handle of ridicule. The total infirmity of human reason, the absolute incomprehensibility of the Divine Nature, the great and universal misery and still greater wickedness of men; these are strange topics, surely, to be so fondly cherished by orthodox divines and doctors. In

ages of stupidity and ignorance, indeed, these principles may
safely be espoused; and perhaps no views of things are more
proper to promote superstition than such as encourage the
blind amazement, the diffidence, and melancholy of mankind.
But at present . . .

Blame not so much, interposed PHILO, the ignorance of
these reverend gentlemen. They know how to change their
style with the times. Formerly it was a most popular theological topic to maintain that human life was vanity and misery,
and to exaggerate all the ills and pains which are incident to
men. But of late years divines, we find, begin to retract this
position and maintain, though still with some hesitation, that
there are more goods than evils, more pleasures than pains,
even in this life. When religion stood entirely upon temper
and education, it was thought proper to encourage melancholy, as indeed mankind never have recourse to superior
powers so readily as in that disposition. But as men have now
learned to form principles and to draw consequences, it is necessary to change the batteries, and to make use of such arguments as will endure at least some scrutiny and examination.
This variation is the same (and from the same causes) with
that which I formerly remarked with regard to skepticism.

Thus Philo continued to the last his spirit of opposition,
and his censure of established opinions. But I could observe
that Demea did not at all relish the latter part of the discourse, and he took occasion soon after, on some pretense or
other, to leave the company.

Part XII.

AFTER Demea's departure, Cleanthes and Philo continued the
conversation in the following manner. Our friend, I am afraid,
said CLEANTHES, will have little inclination to revive this topic
of discourse while you are in company; and to tell the truth,
Philo, I should rather wish to reason with either of you apart
on a subject so sublime and interesting. Your spirit of controversy, joined to your abhorence of vulgar superstition, carries
you strange lengths when engaged in an argument; and there

is nothing so sacred and venerable, even in your own eyes, which you spare on that occasion.

I must confess, replied PHILO, that I am less cautious on the subject of natural religion than on any other, both because I know that I can never, on that head, corrupt the principles of any man of common sense, and because no one, I am confident, in whose eyes I appear a man of common sense will ever mistake my intentions. You in particular, Cleanthes, with whom I live in unreserved intimacy, you are sensible that, notwithstanding the freedom of my conversation and my love of singular arguments, no one has a deeper sense of religion impressed on his mind, or pays more profound adoration to the Divine Being, as he discovers himself to reason in the inexplicable contrivance and artifice of nature. A purpose, an intention, a design strikes everywhere the most careless, the most stupid thinker; and no man can be so hardened in absurd systems as at all times to reject it. *That nature does nothing in vain* is a maxim established in all the schools merely from the contemplation of the works of nature, without any religious purpose; and, from a firm conviction of its truth, an anatomist who had observed a new organ or canal would never be satisfied till he had also discovered its use and intention. One great foundation of the Copernican system is the maxim *that nature acts by the simplest methods, and chooses the most proper means to any end;* and astronomers often, without thinking of it, lay this strong foundation of piety and religion. The same thing is observable in other parts of philosophy. And thus all the sciences almost lead us insensibly to acknowledge a first intelligent Author; and their authority is often so much the greater as they do not directly profess that intention.

It is with pleasure I hear Galen reason concerning the structure of the human body. The anatomy of a man, says he,[1] discovers above 600 different muscles; and whoever duly considers these will find that in each of them nature must have adjusted at least ten different circumstances in order to attain the end which she proposed: proper figure, just magnitude,

[1] *De formatione fœtus.*

right disposition of the several ends, upper and lower position of the whole, the due insertion of the several nerves, veins, and arteries; so that, in the muscles alone, above 6000 several views and intentions must have been formed and executed. The bones he calculates to be 284; the distinct purposes aimed at in the structure of each, above forty. What a prodigious display of artifice, even in these simple and homogeneous parts! But if we consider the skin, ligaments, vessels, glandules, humors, the several limbs and members of the body, how must our astonishment rise upon us, in proportion to the number and intricacy of the parts so artificially adjusted! The further we advance in these researches, we discover new scenes of art and wisdom, but descry still, at a distance, further scenes beyond our reach: in the fine internal structure of the parts, in the economy of the brain, in the fabric of the seminal vessels. All these artifices are repeated in every different species of animal, with wonderful variety, and with exact propriety, suited to the different intentions of nature in framing each species. And if the infidelity of Galen, even when these natural sciences were still imperfect, could not withstand such striking appearances, to what pitch of pertinacious obstinacy must a philosopher in this age have attained who can now doubt of a Supreme Intelligence!

Could I meet with one of this species (who, I thank God, are very rare) I would ask him: supposing there were a God who did not discover himself immediately to our senses, were it possible for him to give stronger proofs of his existence than what appear on the whole face of nature? What indeed could such a Divine Being do but copy the present economy of things, render many of his artifices so plain that no stupidity could mistake them, afford glimpses of still greater artifices which demonstrate his prodigious superiority above our narrow apprehensions, and conceal altogether a great many from such imperfect creatures? Now according to all rules of just reasoning, every fact must pass for undisputed when it is supported by all the arguments which its nature admits of, even though these arguments be not, in themselves, very numerous or forcible. How much more in the present case where no human imagination can compute their number, and no understanding estimate their cogency!

I shall further add, said CLEANTHES, to what you have so well urged, that one great advantage of the principle of theism is that it is the only system of cosmogony which can be rendered intelligible and complete, and yet can throughout preserve a strong analogy to what we every day see and experience in the world. The comparison of the universe to a machine of human contrivance is so obvious and natural, and is justified by so many instances of order and design in nature, that it must immediately strike all unprejudiced apprehensions and procure universal approbation. Whoever attempts to weaken this theory cannot pretend to succeed by establishing in its place any other that is precise and determinate. It is sufficient for him if he start doubts and difficulties, and by remote and abstract views of things reach that suspense of judgment which is here the utmost boundary of his wishes. But besides that this state of mind is in itself unsatisfactory, it can never be steadily maintained against such striking appearances as continually engage us into the religious hypothesis. A false, absurd system, human nature, from the force of prejudice, is capable of adhering to with obstinacy and perseverance. But no system at all, in opposition to a theory supported by strong and obvious reason, by natural propensity, and by early education, I think it absolutely impossible to maintain or defend.

So little, replied PHILO, do I esteem this suspense of judgment in the present case to be possible that I am apt to suspect there enters somewhat of a dispute of words into this controversy, more than is usually imagined. That the works of nature bear a great analogy to the productions of art is evident; and according to all the rules of good reasoning we ought to infer, if we argue at all concerning them, that their causes have a proportional analogy. But as there are also considerable differences, we have reason to suppose a proportional difference in the causes, and in particular ought to attribute a much higher degree of power and energy to the supreme cause than any we have ever observed in mankind. Here then the existence of a *Deity* is plainly ascertained by reason; and if we make it a question whether, on account of these analogies, we can properly call him a *mind* or *intelligence*, notwithstanding the vast difference which may reasonably be supposed between him and human minds, what is this but a mere verbal controversy? No man can deny the analogies between the effects; to restrain ourselves from inquiring concerning the causes is scarcely possible. From this inquiry the legitimate conclusion is that the causes have also an analogy; and if we are not contented with calling the first and supreme cause a *God* or *Deity*, but desire to vary the expression, what can we call him but *Mind* or *Thought*, to which he is justly supposed to bear a considerable resemblance?

All men of sound reason are disgusted with verbal disputes, which abound so much in philosophical and theological inquiries; and it is found that the only remedy for this abuse must arise from clear definitions, from the precision of those ideas which enter into any argument, and from the strict and uniform use of those terms which are employed. But there is a species of controversy which, from the very nature of language and of human ideas, is involved in perpetual ambiguity and can never, by any precaution or any definitions, be able to reach a reasonable certainty or precision. These are the controversies concerning the degrees of any quality or circumstance. Men may argue to all eternity whether Hannibal be a great, or a very great, or a superlatively great man, what degree of beauty Cleopatra possessed, what epithet of praise Livy or Thucydides is entitled to, without bringing the controversy to any determination. The disputants may here agree in their sense and differ in the terms, or *vice versa*, yet never be able to define their terms so as to enter into each other's meaning, because the degrees of these qualities are not, like quantity or number, susceptible of any exact mensuration, which may be the standard in the controversy. That the dispute concerning theism is of this nature, and consequently is merely verbal, or perhaps, if possible, still more incurably ambiguous, will appear upon the slightest inquiry. I ask the theist if he does not allow that there is a great and immeasurable, because incomprehensible, difference between the *human* and the *divine* mind. The more pious he is, the more readily will he assent to the affirmative, and the more will he be disposed to magnify the difference. He will even assert that the difference is of a nature which cannot be too much magnified. I next turn to the atheist, who, I assert, is only nominally so and can never possibly be in earnest, and I ask him whether, from the coherence and apparent sympathy in all the parts of this world, there be not a certain degree of analogy among all the operations of nature, in every situation and in every age; whether the rotting of a turnip, the generation of an animal, and the structure of human thought be not energies that probably bear some remote analogy to each other. It is impossible he can deny it; he will readily acknowledge it. Having obtained this concession, I push him still further in his retreat, and I ask him if it be not probable that the principle which first arranged and still maintains order in this universe bears not also some remote inconceivable analogy to the other operations of nature, and among the rest to the economy of human mind and thought. However reluctant, he must give his assent. Where then, cry I to both these antagonists, is the subject of your dispute? The theist allows that the original intelligence is very different from human reason; the atheist allows that the original principle of order bears some remote analogy to it. Will you quarrel, gentlemen, about the degrees, and enter into a controversy which admits not of any precise meaning, nor consequently of any determination? If you should be so obstinate, I should not be surprised to find you insensibly change sides; while the theist, on the one hand, exaggerates the dissimilarity between the Supreme Being and frail, imperfect, variable, fleeting, and mortal creatures; and the atheist, on the other, magnifies the analogy among all the operations of nature, in every period, every situation, and every position. Consider then where the real point of controversy lies; and if you cannot lay aside your disputes, endeavor, at least, to cure yourselves of your animosity.

And here I must also acknowledge, Cleanthes, that, as the works of nature have a much greater analogy to the effects of *our* art and contrivance than to those of *our* benevolence and justice, we have reason to infer that the natural attributes of the Deity have a greater resemblance to those of men than his moral have to human virtues. But what is the consequence? Nothing but this, that the moral qualities of man are more defective in their kind than his natural abilities. For as the

Supreme Being is allowed to be absolutely and entirely perfect, whatever differs most from him departs the farthest from the supreme standard of rectitude and perfection.[1]

These, Cleanthes, are my unfeigned sentiments on this subject; and these sentiments, you know, I have ever cherished and maintained. But in proportion to my veneration for true religion is my abhorrence of vulgar superstitions; and I indulge a peculiar pleasure, I confess, in pushing such principles, sometimes into absurdity, sometimes into impiety. And you are sensible that all bigots, notwithstanding their great aversion to the latter above the former, are commonly equally guilty of both.

My inclination, replied CLEANTHES, lies, I own, a contrary way. Religion, however corrupted, is still better than no religion at all. The doctrine of a future state is so strong and necessary a security to morals that we never ought to abandon or neglect it. For if finite and temporary rewards and punishments have so great an effect, as we daily find, how much greater must be expected from such as are infinite and eternal?

How happens it then, said PHILO, if vulgar superstition be so salutary to society, that all history abounds so much with accounts of its pernicious consequences on public affairs? Factions, civil wars, persecutions, subversions of government, oppression, slavery, these are the dismal consequences which always attend its prevalance over the minds of men. If the

---

[1] It seems evident that the dispute between the skeptics and dogmatists is entirely verbal, or at least regards only the degrees of doubt and assurance which we ought to indulge with regard to all reasoning; and such disputes are commonly, at the bottom, verbal and admit not of any precise determination. No philosophical dogmatist denies that there are difficulties both with regard to the senses and to all science, and that these difficulties are, in a regular, logical method, absolutely insoluable. No skeptic denies that we lie under an absolute necessity, notwithstanding these difficulties, of thinking and believing and reasoning with regard to all kinds of subjects, and even of frequently assenting with confidence and security. The only difference, then, between these sects, if they merit that name, is that the skeptic, from habit, caprice, or inclination, insists most on the difficulties, the dogmatist, for like reasons, on the necessity.

religious spirit be ever mentioned in any historical narration, we are sure to meet afterwards with a detail of the miseries which attend it. And no period of time can be happier or more prosperous than those in which it is never regarded or heard of.

The reason of this observation, replied CLEANTHES, is obvious. The proper office of religion is to regulate the heart of men, humanize their conduct, infuse the spirit of temperance, order, and obedience; and as its operation is silent and only enforces the motives of morality and justice, it is in danger of being overlooked and confounded with these other motives. When it distinguishes itself and acts as a separate principle over men, it has departed from its proper sphere and has become only a cover to faction and ambition.

And so will all religion, said PHILO, except the philosophical and rational kind. Your reasonings are more easily eluded than my facts. The inference is not just, because finite and temporary rewards and punishments have so great influence that therefore such as are infinite and eternal must have so much greater. Consider, I beseech you, the attachment which we have to present things, and the little concern which we discover for objects so remote and uncertain. When divines are declaiming against the common behavior and conduct of the world, they always represent this principle as the strongest imaginable (which indeed it is), and describe almost all human kind as lying under the influence of it, and sunk into the deepest lethargy and unconcern about their religious interests. Yet these same divines, when they refute their speculative antagonists, suppose the motives of religion to be so powerful that, without them, it were impossible for civil society to subsist; nor are they ashamed of so palpable a contradiction. It is certain, from experience, that the smallest grain of natural honesty and benevolence has more effect on men's conduct than the most pompous views suggested by theological theories and systems. A man's natural inclination works incessantly upon him; it is forever present to the mind, and mingles itself with every view and consideration; whereas religious motives, where they act at all, operate only by starts and bounds, and it is scarcely possible for them to become altogether habitual to the mind. The force of the greatest gravity, say the philosophers, is infinitely small in comparison of that of the least impulse, yet it is certain that the smallest gravity will, in the end, prevail above a great impulse, because no strokes or blows can be repeated with such constancy as attraction and gravitation.

Another advantage of inclination: it engages on its side all the wit and ingenuity of the mind, and when set in opposition to religious principles seeks every method and art of eluding them; in which it is almost always successful. Who can explain the heart of man, or account for those strange salvos and excuses with which people satisfy themselves when they follow their inclinations in opposition to their religious duty? This is well understood in the world; and none but fools ever repose less trust in a man because they hear that, from study and philosophy, he has entertained some speculative doubts with regard to theological subjects. And when we have to do with a man who makes a great profession of religion and devotion, has this any other effect upon several who pass for prudent than to put them on their guard, lest they be cheated and deceived by him?

We must further consider that philosophers, who cultivate reason and reflection, stand less in need of such motives to keep them under the restraint of morals, and that the vulgar, who alone may need them, are utterly incapable of so pure a religion as represents the Deity to be pleased with nothing but virtue in human behavior. The recommendations to the Divinity are generally supposed to be either frivolous observances or rapturous ecstasies or a bigoted credulity. We need not run back into antiquity or wander into remote regions to find instances of this degeneracy. Amongst ourselves, some have been guilty of that atrociousness, unknown to the Egyptian and Grecian superstitions, of declaiming, in express terms, against morality, and representing it as a sure forfeiture of the divine favor if the least trust or reliance be laid upon it.

But even though superstition or enthusiasm should not put itself in direct opposition to morality, the very diverting of the attention, the raising up a new and frivolous species of merit, the preposterous distribution which it makes of praise and blame, must have the most pernicious consequences, and weaken extremely men's attachment to the natural motives of justice and humanity.

Such a principle of action likewise, not being any of the familiar motives of human conduct, acts only by intervals on the temper, and must be roused by continual efforts in order to render the pious zealot satisfied with his own conduct and make him fulfil his devotional task. Many religious exercises are entered into with seeming fervor where the heart, at the time, feels cold and languid. A habit of dissimulation is by degrees contracted, and fraud and falsehood become the predominant principle. Hence the reason of that vulgar observation that the highest zeal in religion and the deepest hypocrisy, so far from being inconsistent, are often or commonly united in the same individual character.

The bad effects of such habits, even in common life, are easily imagined; but where the interests of religion are concerned, no morality can be forcible enough to bind the enthusiastic zealot. The sacredness of the cause sanctifies every measure which can be made use of to promote it.

The steady attention alone to so important an interest as that of eternal salvation is apt to extinguish the benevolent affections, and beget a narrow, contracted selfishness. And when such a temper is encouraged, it easily eludes all the general precepts of charity and benevolence.

Thus the motives of vulgar superstition have no great influence on general conduct, nor is their operation favorable to morality, in the instances where they predominate.

Is there any maxim in politics more certain and infallible than that both the number and authority of priests should be confined within very narrow limits, and that the civil magistrate ought, forever, to keep his *fasces* and *axes* from such dangerous hands? But if the spirit of popular religion were so salutary to society, a contrary maxim ought to prevail. The greater number of priests and their greater authority and riches will always augment the religious spirit. And though the priests have the guidance of this spirit, why may we not expect a superior sanctity of life and greater benevolence and moderation from persons who are set apart for religion, who are continually inculcating it upon others, and who must themselves imbibe a greater share of it? Whence comes it then, that in fact the utmost a wise magistrate can propose with regard to popular religions is, as far as possible, to make a saving game of it, and to prevent their pernicious consequences with regard to society? Every expedient which he tries for so humble a purpose is surrounded with inconveniences. If he admits only one religion among his subjects, he must sacrifice, to an uncertain prospect of tranquillity, every consideration of public liberty, science, reason, industry, and even his own independence. If he gives indulgence to several sects, which is the wiser maxim, he must preserve a very philosophical indifference to all of them, and carefully restrain the pretensions of the prevailing sect; otherwise he can expect nothing but endless disputes, quarrels, factions, persecutions, and civil commotions.

True religion, I allow, has no such pernicious consequences, but we must treat of religion as it has commonly been found in the world; nor have I anything to do with that speculative tenet of theism which, as it is a species of philosophy, must partake of the beneficial influence of that principle, and at the same time must lie under a like inconvenience of being always confined to very few persons.

Oaths are requisite in all courts of judicature, but it is a question whether their authority arises from any popular religion. It is the solemnity and importance of the occasion, the regard to reputation, and the reflecting on the general interests of society, which are the chief restraints upon mankind. Custom house oaths and political oaths are but little regarded even by some who pretend to principles of honesty and religion; and a Quaker's asseveration is with us justly put upon the same footing with the oath of any other person. I know that Polybius[1] ascribes the infamy of Greek faith to the prevalence of the Epicurean philosophy; but I know also that Punic faith had as bad a reputation in ancient times as Irish evidence has in modern, though we cannot account for these vulgar observations by the same reason. Not to mention that Greek faith was infamous before the rise of the Epicurean philosophy; and Euripides,[2] in a passage which I shall point

[1] Lib. vi. cap. 54.
[2] *Iphigenia in Tauride.*

out to you, has glanced a remarkable stroke of satire against his nation, with regard to this circumstance.

Take care, Philo, replied CLEANTHES, take care; push not matters too far; allow not your zeal against false religion to undermine your veneration for the true. Forfeit not this principle, the chief, the only great comfort in life and our principal support amidst all the attacks of adverse fortune. The most agreeable reflection which it is possible for human imagination to suggest is that of genuine theism, which represents us as the workmanship of a Being perfectly good, wise, and powerful; who created us for happiness; and who, having implanted in us immeasurable desires of good, will prolong our existence to all eternity, and will transfer us into an infinite variety of scenes, in order to satisfy those desires and render our felicity complete and durable. Next to such a Being himself (if the comparison be allowed), the happiest lot which we can imagine is that of being under his guardianship and protection.

These appearances, said PHILO, are most engaging and alluring, and with regard to the true philosopher, they are more than appearances. But it happens here, as in the former case, that with regard to the greater part of mankind, the appearances are deceitful, and that the terrors of religion commonly prevail above its comforts.

It is allowed that men never have recourse to devotion so readily as when dejected with grief or depressed with sickness. Is not this a proof that the religious spirit is not so nearly allied to joy as to sorrow?

But men, when afflicted, find consolation in religion, replied CLEANTHES. Sometimes, said PHILO; but it is natural to imagine that they will form a notion of those unknown beings, suitable to the present gloom and melancholy of their temper, when they betake themselves to the contemplation of them. Accordingly, we find the tremendous images to predominate in all religions; and we ourselves, after having employed the most exalted expression in our descriptions of the Deity, fall into the flattest contradiction in affirming that the damned are infinitely superior in number to the elect.

I shall venture to affirm that there never was a popular religion which represented the state of departed souls in such a light as would render it eligible for human kind that there should be such a state. These fine models of religion are the mere product of philosophy. For as death lies between the eye and the prospect of futurity, that event is so shocking to nature that it must throw a gloom on all the regions which lie beyond it, and suggest to the generality of mankind the idea of Cerberus and Furies, devils, and torrents of fire and brimstone.

It is true, both fear and hope enter into religion, because both these passions, at different times, agitate the human mind, and each of them forms a species of divinity suitable to itself. But when a man is in a cheerful disposition, he is fit for business, or company, or entertainment of any kind; and he naturally applies himself to these and thinks not of religion. When melancholy and dejected, he has nothing to do but brood upon the terrors of the invisible world, and to plunge himself still deeper in affliction. It may indeed happen that, after he has, in this manner, engraved the religious opinions deep into his thought and imagination, there may arrive a change of health or circumstances which may restore his good humor and, raising cheerful prospects of futurity, make him run into the other extreme of joy and triumph. But still it must be acknowledged that, as terror is the primary principle of religion, it is the passion which always predominates in it, and admits but of short intervals of pleasure.

Not to mention that these fits of excessive, enthusiastic joy, by exhausting the spirits, always prepare the way for equal fits of superstitious terror and dejection; nor is there any state of mind so happy as the calm and equable. But this state it is impossible to support where a man thinks that he lies in such profound darkness and uncertainty, between an eternity of happiness and an eternity of misery. No wonder that such an opinion disjoints the ordinary frame of the mind and throws it into the utmost confusion. And though that opinion is seldom so steady in its operation as to influence all the actions, yet it is apt to make a considerable breach in the temper, and to produce that gloom and melancholy so remarkable in all devout people.

It is contrary to common sense to entertain apprehensions or terrors upon account of any opinion whatsoever, or to imagine that we run any risk hereafter, by the freest use of our reason. Such a sentiment implies both an *absurdity* and an *inconsistency*. It is an absurdity to believe that the Deity has human passions, and one of the lowest of human passions, a restless appetite for applause. It is an inconsistency to believe that, since the Deity has this human passion, he has not others also, and in particular a disregard to the opinions of creatures so much inferior.

To know God, says Seneca, *is to worship him.* All other worship is indeed absurd, superstitious, and even impious. It degrades him to the low condition of mankind, who are delighted with entreaty, solicitation, presents, and flattery. Yet is this impiety the smallest of which superstition is guilty. Commonly, it depresses the Deity far below the condition of mankind, and represents him as a capricious demon who exercises his power without reason and without humanity! And were that Divine Being disposed to be offended at the vices and follies of silly mortals, who are his own workmanship, ill would it surely fare with the votaries of most popular superstitions. Nor would any of the human race merit his *favor* but a very few, the philosophical theists, who entertain, or rather indeed endeavor to entertain, suitable notions of his divine perfections. As the only persons entitled to his *compassion* and *indulgence* would be the philosophical skeptics, a sect almost equally rare, who, from a natural diffidence of their own capacity, suspend or endeavor to suspend all judgment with regard to such sublime and such extraordinary subjects.

If the whole of natural theology, as some people seem to maintain, resolves itself into one simple, though somewhat ambiguous, at least undefined proposition, *that the cause or causes of order in the universe probably bear some remote analogy to human intelligence;* if this proposition be not capable of extension, variation, or more particular explication; if it affords no inference that affects human life, or can be the source of any action or forbearance; and if the analogy, imperfect as it is, can be carried no further than to the human intelligence and cannot be transferred, with any appearance of probability, to the other qualities of the mind; if this really be the case, what can the most inquisitive, contemplative, and religious man do more than give a plain, philosophical assent to the proposition, as often as it occurs, and believe that the arguments on which it is established exceed the objections which lie against it? Some astonishment, indeed, will naturally arise from the greatness of the object, some melancholy from its obscurity, some contempt of human reason that it can give no solution more satisfactory with regard to so extraordinary and magnificent a question. But believe me, Cleanthes, the most natural sentiment which a well-disposed mind will feel on this occasion is a longing desire and expectation that heaven would be pleased to dissipate, at least alleviate, this profound ignorance, by affording some more particular revelation to mankind, and making discoveries of the nature, attributes, and operations of the divine object of our faith. A person, seasoned with a just sense of the imperfections of natural reason, will fly to revealed truth with the greatest avidity, while the haughty dogmatist, persuaded that he can erect a complete system of theology by the mere help of philosophy, disdains any further aid and rejects this adventitious instructor. To be a philosophical skeptic is, in a man of letters, the first and most essential step toward being a sound, believing Christian, a proposition which I would willingly recommend to the attention of Pamphilus; and I hope Cleanthes will forgive me for interposing so far in the education and instruction of his pupil.

Cleanthes and Philo pursued not this conversation much further; and as nothing ever made greater impression on me than all the reasonings of that day, so I confess that, upon a serious review of the whole, I cannot but think that Philo's principles are more probable than Demea's, but that those of Cleanthes approach still nearer to the truth.

MODERN LIBRARY GIANTS

A series of sturdily bound and handsomely printed, full-sized library editions of books formerly available only in expensive sets. These volumes contain from 600 to 1,400 pages each.

THE MODERN LIBRARY GIANTS REPRESENT A
SELECTION OF THE WORLD'S GREATEST BOOKS